VICTORIAN POETRY

VICTORIAN POETRY

Poetry, poetics and politics

Isobel Armstrong

London and New York

First published 1993
by Routledge
11 New Fetter Lane, London EC4P 4EE

Simultaneously published in the USA and Canada
by Routledge
29 West 35th Street, New York, NY 10001

Paperback first published 1996

Routledge is an International Thomson Publishing company

© 1993 Isobel Armstrong

Typeset by Intype, London
Printed and bound in Great Britain by
TJ Press (Padstow) Ltd, Cornwall

British Library Cataloguing in Publication Data
A catalogue record for this book is available from the British Library

Library of Congress Cataloguing in Publication Data
A catalogue record for this book is available from the Library of Congress

ISBN 0-415-03016-1 (hbk)
ISBN 0-415-14425-6 (pbk)

IN MEMORIAM (1988)

Arthur Humphreys
Allon White

CONTENTS

Part III Another Culture? Another Poetics?

PREFACE

The poetry and poetics of the Victorian period were intertwined, often in arresting ways, with theology, science, philosophy, theories of language and politics. As cultural and intellectual change became progressively more apparent, two traditions of poetry developed, one exploring various strategies for democratic, radical writing, the other developing, in different forms, a conservative poetry. I have taken John Stuart Mill's description of these two movements, 'two systems of concentric circles', as the title of my first chapter, though I do not think these circles met and merged quite as he would have liked them to, particularly if one remembers the working-class and women poets who often worked outside these spheres. However, a study of these two great interacting circles discloses the immense sophistication and subtlety of Victorian poetry. It is a poetry, whether it belongs to democratic or conservative formations, which asks more demanding and radical questions of its culture than other genres of the period, experimenting with forms and poetic language commensurate with this complexity. The novel, with its need to gain the consent of a wide readership, could not afford such experiments. In reading the poets in this way I have excluded much material. But it seemed that this exploration would best reveal how the prolific creativity of these writers belongs recognisably to our own cultural situation and, conversely, exists in sharp separation from it. Victorian culture is our precursor culture, but, like the duck/rabbit, with its mutually exclusive configurations, we find in it important affinities – and differences which are just as important. Victorian poetry was written, for instance, in a society which was not a democracy. On the other hand, that was what Arnold called one of its 'modern problems', and one of the excitements of reading the poetry of this period is to understand the imaginative energy invested in such 'modern problems'. My study begins, of course, before Victoria came to the throne in 1837, because Tennyson and Browning identified 'modern problems' in their early work of the 1830s.

Beyond the horizon of one book, like Pope's mountain peaks, another usually appears, a prospect both pleasurable and daunting. While this book was being completed my work opened up possibilities for further research. Women's poetry and working-class poetry by both men and women are capable of very much more extensive discussion. Anglophone poetry written in Britain's colonial territories during the nineteenth century is technically 'Victorian' poetry, but it seemed appropriate that such work should be studied by scholars familiar with the history and culture of those regions.

Victorian texts are now being re-edited to the high standards of modern textual scholarship. Where I could not use such modern editions I have cited generally available texts. I was not able to take advantage of the Longman Annotated Texts edition of Browning by John Woolford and Daniel Karlin. Like many, however, I owe an enormous debt to Christopher Ricks's great edition of Tennyson's poetry in the Longman series, which has enabled scholars and critics to explore Tennyson with a depth and richness quite impossible before its appearance. I have benefited from the abundance of criticism of Victorian poetry which has appeared in the last decade. Lack of space has prevented me from referring to it in detail. But the importance of the pioneering work of Martha Vicinus on working-class poetry and W. David Shaw's explorations of Victorian epistemology should not go unmentioned.

ACKNOWLEDGEMENTS

I am grateful to Professor R. A. Foakes for asking me to write a critical history of Victorian poetry, and for his patience and encouragement while it was being written. The greater part of this book was completed while I held a Chair of English at the University of Southampton. I should like to thank Derek Attridge, Frank Stack, Maud Ellmann, Robert Young, Jonathon Sawday, John Peacock, Laura Marcus, Tony Crowley, Peter Middleton and Ken Hirschkop for creating an academic environment in which it was a pleasure to write. Tony Crowley spared time to read and check parts of the manuscript and I benefited from his suggestions and comment. I am grateful in particular to Maud Ellmann for the warmth of her intellectual generosity. Graduate students now themselves teaching in universities were an inspiring and challenging presence. I owe special thanks to Steve Bamlett, Steve Barfield, Joseph Bristow, Andy Cooper, Tom Furniss, Josephine McDonagh, Carl Plasa, Lindsay Smith, Andrew Thacker and Steve Vine. George Levine and Elaine Showalter both discussed the early stages of this book with me and offered valuable comment. I thank the University of Southampton for providing me with funds for research assistance. Dr Catherine Sharrock's energy and enthusiasm were as helpful as her meticulousness. Any shortcomings in the book are my own. Alison Hamlin's patience in preparing the manuscript was as enduring as her cheerfulness. Laurel Brake, Tom Healy, Michael Slater, Andrew Sanders, Carol Watts and Helen Carr provided helpful support during the completion of the book after I moved to Birkbeck College, University of London. Above all I thank P. A. W. Collins for years of inspiration and support.

Parts of this book have appeared in *News from Nowhere*, vol. 5, 1988, 38–63, *Dickens and Other Victorians*, ed. Joanne Shattock, Macmillan, 1989 and *Tennyson: Seven Essays*, ed. P. A. W. Collins, Macmillan, 1992.

INTRODUCTION

REREADING VICTORIAN POETRY

WHAT KIND OF HISTORY?

Critical history generally divides literature into blocks, corresponding with literary periods. I begin with the difficulty of thinking about history in this way.

The habit of thinking of literary periods as segments creates the same kind of history that produces it. The Victorian period has always been regarded as isolated between two periods, Romanticism and modernism. Thus Victorian poetry is seen in terms of transition. It is on the way somewhere. It is either on the way from Romantic poetry, or on the way to modernism. It is situated between two kinds of excitement, in which it appears not to participate. What has been called the 'genetic' history of continuous development through phases and periods, a form of history which the Victorians themselves both helped to create and to question, sees Victorian poetry as a gap in that development.[1] Modernism, in spite of its desire to see itself in terms of a break with history, actually endorses that continuity, for a radical break must break with something. And correspondingly it endorses the gap which Victorian poetry is seen to inhabit. The anxieties of modernism, trying to do without history, repress whatever relations the Victorians may seem to bear to twentieth-century writing. Thus Joyce's frivolous 'Lawn Tennyson, gentleman poet' appears dressed for tennis in *Ulysses*. Virginia Woolf dissociates herself from the Victorians in her unscrupulously brilliant impressionistic account of them in *Orlando*.[2] There ivy covers buildings and large families come into being with almost equally magical suddenness. She intuitively registers the drive to produce in Victorian society, whether it is children or industrial goods, and the need to muffle. The eroticisms and the euphemisms of bourgeois capitalism and its ideology, its inordinate excesses and concealments, are embodied in the voluptuous taxidermy of the stuffed sofa.

So the major critical and theoretical movements of the twentieth century have been virtually silent about Victorian poetry. As the stranded remnants of high bourgeois liberalism, the poets have been consigned to sepia. New

1

criticism, encouraged by T. S. Eliot, who said that Tennyson and Browning merely 'ruminated', considered Victorian poetry to lie outside its categories.[3] When Raymond Williams began to theorise the cultural criticism which has been so fruitful in *Culture and Society*, he concentrated on the nineteenth-century novel.[4] Feminism likewise made its claims through a critique primarily of the novel.[5] Deconstruction concentrated on Romantic poetry, blatantly periodising in a way which goes against its theoretical preconceptions.[6] No major European critic has seen Victorian poetry as relevant to his or her purpose. It is symbolism and imagism which have proved attractive when the novel was displaced as a centre of interest. Walter Benjamin wrote wonderfully on Baudelaire,[7] but Lukács or Bakhtin on Tennyson would be unthinkable. Oddly, biography in this area *has* flourished. The worse the poets seem to be, the more avidly their lives are recuperated. We 'covet' biography, as Browning once brilliantly said.[8] And biographers have dominated in literary scholarship of the Victorian period, even though Browning turns out to be a brash opportunist and Tennyson a surly and duplicitous snob.[9] An honourably uncovetous study is Lionel Trilling's classic biography of Matthew Arnold.[10]

What, then, can be the motive for writing about Victorian poetry? Is it worth it? The enterprise cannot be justified in terms of the genetic history which would simply fill in the gap, re-create continuity and restore the forgotten. Some principles must govern this reclaiming process beyond the notion of even continuity and positivist accounts of development. For if continuity exists at all, we create it ourselves. There is no unbroken continuity independent of us with its own external process. Foucault's suspicion of positivist history is based on a belief that it is precisely asymmetry, discontinuity and difference, which we also create ourselves, that are important.[11] Nor can this poetry simply be 'revalued', for since value is a function of the unstable movement of current adjustments of aesthetic worth, the likelihood is that a body of literature will be unquestioningly translated into the terms of whatever theory is deemed to be important at the moment. Unless some principles secure revaluation, it becomes simply a means of appropriating new literary territory. However transcendent it may seem, the notion of value is as relativistic and incoherent as positivist history. Too often to 'revalue' the Victorian poets is to claim that they were like us, but inadvertently.

A way of beginning to rediscover the importance of Victorian poetry is to consider the heavy silence surrounding it in the twentieth century as a striking cultural phenomenon in itself. We have to see that silence historically. T. S. Eliot's dismissive account of Tennyson deflects attention from the Tennysonian echoes in *The Waste Land* and *Four Quartets*. Yeats, virtually quoting Shelley in 'The Second Coming', silently appropriates Tennyson's 'The Kraken' as the governing motive of his poem.[12] We have learned to understand that to constitute something as a gap is a strategy for concealing anxiety. What kind of anxieties could the Victorians have created for the twentieth century and why are they still culturally significant? To clarify these anxieties it is necessary to see what the Victorian poets themselves were worried about.

They thought of themselves as modern. 'Modern', in spite of its long history, has a resurgence as a Victorian term – the 'modern' element in literature (Arnold), 'modern' love (Meredith), a 'modern' landlord (William Allingham).[13] To see yourself as modern is actually to define the contemporary self-consciously and this is simultaneously an act which historicises the modern. Victorian modernism sees itself as new but it does not, like twentieth-century modernism, conceive itself in terms of a radical break with a past. Victorian modernism, as it emerges in its poetics, describes itself as belonging to a condition of crisis which has emerged directly from economic and cultural change. In fact, Victorian poetics begins to conceptualise the idea of culture as a category and includes itself within the definition. To be modern was to be overwhelmingly secondary. Harold Bloom's term, 'belatedness', would be useful to describe this perception, except that his belatedness is far too restricted. It is narrowed to an essentially personalised oedipal struggle with the precursor poet – Browning and Shelley, Tennyson and Keats, Arnold and Wordsworth. If his term is adopted it must be used to designate a far wider and more consciously searching understanding of what it is to be secondary.[14] The Victorian poets *were* post-Romantic but to understand the political and aesthetic consequences of this it is necessary to see what being post-Romantic entailed. For to be 'new', or 'modern' or 'post-Romantic' was to confront and self-consciously to conceptualise *as* new elements that are still perceived as the constitutive forms of our own condition. Whether a poet was a subversive reactionary, as Tennyson was, or attempting to write a radical poetry, as Browning was, such a poet was 'modern' or secondary in a number of ways, all of which involved the reformation of the categories of knowledge. A belated poet was post-revolutionary, existing with the constant possibility of mass political upheaval and fundamental change in the structure of society, which meant that the nature of society had to be redefined. Belatedness was post-industrial and post-technological, existing with and theorising the changed relationships and new forms of alienated labour which capitalism was consolidating, and conscious of the predatory search for new areas of exploitation which was creating a new colonial 'outside' to British society. It was post-teleological and scientific, conceiving beliefs, including those of Christianity, anthropologically in terms of belief *systems* and representations through myth. Simply because of its awareness of teleological insecurity, Victorian poetry is arguably the last theological poetry to be written.

Lastly, the supreme condition of posthumousness, it was post-Kantian. This meant, in the first place, that the category of art (and for the

Victorians this was almost always poetry) was becoming 'pure'. Art occupied its own area, a self-sufficing aesthetic realm over and against practical experience. It was *outside* the economy of instrumental energies (for in Kant art and technology spring into being simultaneously as necessary opposites). And yet it was at once apart and central, for it had a mediating function, representing and interpreting life. These contradictions were compounded by post-Kantian accounts of representation, which adapted Kant to make both the status and the mode of art problematical by seeing representations as the constructs of consciousness which is always at a remove from what it represents. Thus the possibility of a process of endless redefinition and an ungrounded, unstable series of representations was opened out. So the Victorian poets were the first group of writers to feel that what they were doing was simply unnecessary and redundant. For the very category of art itself created this redundancy.

The writer who seized the interrelationship of these new conditions – the conditions of being post-revolutionary, post-industrial, post-teleological and post-Kantian – was Carlyle. Carlyle's pathology, which is itself a part of the conditions he describes, has often deflected attention from his understanding of a new historical situation, an understanding as bold as that of Marx, writing a decade after Carlyle in the 1840s. The reactionary and the radical critiques converge. In his essay, 'Signs of the times' (1829), Carlyle perceived that the new distribution of wealth generated in an industrial nation had transformed the structure of society and was 'strangely altering the old relations'. The relationship of labour to the products of labour, in a situation in which 'nothing is now done directly . . . old modes of exertion are discredited and thrown aside', radically changed the conceptualisation of work.[15] Mechanisation, compounding the effect of the division of labour, depersonalised the labourer and arbitrarily removed the products of labour from him, thus opening up a gap between work and its results. Self-creation through work was no longer possible because the *connection* between work and the world which labour supposedly transforms had been severed. The labourer had no control over his products and the visible cause-and-effect relationship in work and its results had been eliminated. Carlyle attributed this to mechanisation, Marx to the nature of capital, but they both describe alienated labour.[16]

Carlyle extended this alienation to political structures. Democracy was a form of alienation and mechanisation because in the same way that products were dissociated from workers and outside their control, political representation was actually a way of dissociating people from relationships by depending on a depersonalised proxy form, the vote, which was empty of content. It is in fact a mere empty 'sign' of the times. (We must remember that none of the poems discussed in this book was written in a full democracy.) The vote is another example of a situation where nothing is done 'directly'.[17] People leave a mark or sign on a voting paper, but

4

nothing else. The paradoxical conservative argument that democracy is the most abstract way of conceiving of people enables him to ask oddly radical questions: what does representation represent? What are signs signs of? In *Sartor Resartus* (1831) Carlyle connects the representational signs of mechanised printing with the nature of money. 'Movable types', he writes punningly, can demobilise armies and create revolutions of democratic reform.

He means, of course, that rapid mechanical reproduction and dissemination of language can influence as never before in history because the printed word can belong to everyone. But he also means that 'type' is movable because printing removes language and places it and its effects beyond the control of the writer. It is subject to arbitrary interpretation and because of this the fixed and universal 'Type', ultimately a theological notion, embodying permanent values, can no longer sustain itself and is the subject of arbitrary signification. Money works in the same way and the currency of money and print are connected. A piece of leather, marked with a sign and exchanged for goods, becomes a representation or substitute which, separated from the things it represents, can take on varying meaning in circulation and become the subject of arbitrary regulation. Carlyle was as aware as Marx of the capriciousness of money as a metaphorical system. Money and movable types work together as forms of arbitrary power.

> He who first shortened the labour of Copyists by device of *Movable Types* was disbanding hired Armies, and cashiering most Kings and Senates, and creating a whole new Democratic world: he had invented the Art of Printing. The first ground handful of Nitre, Sulphur, and Charcoal drove Monk Schwartz's pestle through the ceiling: what will the last do? Achieve the final undisputed prostration of Force under Thought, of Animal courage under Spiritual. A simple invention it was in the old world Grazier, – sick of lugging his slow Ox about the country till he got it bartered for corn or oil, – to take a piece of Leather, and thereon scratch or stamp the mere Figure of an Ox (or *Pecus*); put it in his pocket, and call it *Pecunia*, Money. Yet hereby did Barter grow Sale, the Leather Money is now Golden and Paper, and all miracles have been out-miracled: for there are Rothschilds and English National Debts; and who has sixpence is Sovereign (to the length of sixpence) over all men; commands Cooks to feed him, Philosophers to teach him, Kings to mount guard over him, – to the length of sixpence.[18]

The move which makes the produce of exploited and alienated labour in a free market structurally similar to alienated political representation, to the uncontrolled representations of language circulating through mechanical printing and to the arbitrary signification of money, brings work, politics, economics and language strikingly together under the problem of representation and the alienated sign. Carlyle himself is torn between conservative dread and celebration but he retrieved a Pyrrhic victory from his analysis by later conceiving the sign as mythos. The *mythos*, the Greek name for 'word', is society's representations, the imaginative symbol by which it lives. The mythos is continually open to new definition. Renewed representations are the means by which change occurs. The mythos, or a view of culture as a series of representations, is the idealist's version of ideology, the product of imaginative and not material conditions. Christianity, Carlyle thought, would be superseded.[19] The mythos creates as many problems as it solves, for if it unifies it also fragments, and if it secures a place for imaginative representation it simultaneously undermines it and makes it vulnerable by allowing it to be perpetually dissolved and recomposed. In fact, the essence of the mythos is its secondariness, its capacity for failing to relate to the circumstances of its production, to be always mismatched, because history is always superseding it. Indeed it contributes to its own supersession by undoing and remaking history. The mythos itself is alienated. It is secondary.

We could find this matrix of problems of which Victorian poetry is a part at many points in the nineteenth century, but Carlyle expresses them most incisively. They are familiar to anyone reading Romantic poetry, too. But this should not be surprising since, as Carlyle recognised, they belong to fundamental changes wrought at the end of the eighteenth century. It is the habit of marking off Victorian from Romantic which disguises the anxieties common to early and later nineteenth-century writers. But there is a difference, a difference in perception, for Victorian poets lived with these problems in an acute and morbid form because they intensified with continued economic and political change in the nineteenth century. With that change new forms of knowledge arose, knowledge of science in particular, which now demanded negotiation. And Victorian poets had to include, in their comprehension of these conditions, the Romantic experience of them as well. Hence the intensely historicised consciousness I have described. That historicised consciousness is also a deeply politicised consciousness, political in the sense that the displacement of the aesthetic realm into secondariness forces the poet to conceptualise him- or herself as external to and over and against what comes to be seen as life. A crisis of representation both engenders and is engendered by this act of division. There is a multiple fracture, as it were, for life itself, working in contrary motion to the alienation of art, is established as a condition of estrangement. Relations are indirect and mystified where 'nothing is now done directly', where the self separated from nature cannot be created through an economy of harmonious work on the world. Victorian poetry is obsessed with a series of displacements effected by these redefined relations, and helps to bring these redefinitions about. The problems of agency and consciousness, labour, language and representation become central. Teleology is displaced by epistemology and politics because *relationships* and their representation become the contested area, between self and society, self and labour, self and nature, self and language and above all between self and the lover. Gender becomes a primary focus of anxiety and investigation in Victorian poetry which is unparalleled in its preoccupation with sexuality and what it is to love. For the creativity of love epitomises the act of relationship itself and dramatises its vulnerability. Carlyle puts the failure of romantic love at the centre of *Sartor Resartus* and this motivates the politics of the book.[20] And since the terms of both self and other in all these acts of relationship are unstable, the poet constantly works to create their content anew and constantly revises representations of them, making the act of representation a focus of anxiety. It is for this that Tennyson's 'idle' tears are shed (for the tears of the lyric subject precisely do not 'work' but dissolve the world and the self), that Browning's 'infinite passion' is expended in excess of the finite object and for which Christina Rossetti's goblin fruit are exchanged. The effort to renegotiate a content to every relationship between self and the world is the Victorian poet's project. It is a simultaneously personal and cultural project and carries the poet into new genres and a new exploration of language. It entails renegotiating the terms of self and world themselves.

It is possible now to return to the modernists' silence about Victorian poetry. It is clear that the nature of the experiencing subject, the problems of representation, fiction and language, are just as much the heart of Victorian problems as they are the preoccupations of modernism. The difference is that the Victorians see them as problems, the modernists do not. Where the Victorians strive to give a content to these problems, political, sexual, epistemological, and to formulate a cultural critique, the moderns celebrate the elimination of content. Victorian problems become abstracted, formalised and aestheticised. The difference is ideological, as the stuffing of the Victorian sofa disappears and art becomes self-reflexive and self-referential. Eliot shores up the ruins of a culture with the fragments of art, Yeats strives to make the golden bird of aesthetics sing out of the frenzied images of creation. The modernist repression of the Victorians comes surely from an understanding that the Victorians had anticipated the self-reflexive condition and rejected it. The modernists are haunted by the Victorians because they are haunted by the plenitude of content which eludes them. For them the Victorians are lumpenly ethical or theological.[21] The task of a history of Victorian poetry is to restore the questions of politics, not least sexual politics, and the epistemology and language which belong to it. I have left the generalisations about modernism here flagrantly unsupported in the belief that a study of Victorian poetry will bear them out. It is interesting, though beyond the scope of this study, that postmodernist writers often attribute a teleology to modernism in just the same way that modernists denigrated the teleological Victorians.

I have answered the question of 'what kind of history?' by deciding to concentrate on those moments in Victorian poetry where its cultural project was defined, and to write a series of essays rather than a continuous history, in which the allocation of space to different poets is deliberately uneven. Thus the two fundamentally different intellectual formations, which defined themselves as avant-garde, and to which the early poetry of Browning and Tennyson respectively belonged, are given considerable attention because they engender two kinds of poetry. One depends on aestheticised politics and the other depends on politicised aesthetics, and these traditions evolve and interact later in the century.[22] The coded words 'Grotesque' and 'Type' often refer to a radical and conservative poetry respectively. The poets clustered round these formations and who have now vanished are discussed, not because they have vanished, for often they have vanished with good reason, but because they illuminate the projects of the two groups. In Part II chapters on Clough, Arnold and Morris pursue the debates of the earlier formations. These are followed by two essays on what happened to Tennyson and Browning in the 1850s and by a chapter on women's poetry, where I have chosen to put Christina Rossetti at the centre. This is partly because renewed contemporary feminist interest in Elizabeth Barrett Browning makes the task of writing at length about her poetry less urgent than it used to be. Space can thus be given to the poetry of Mrs Hemans, L. E. L., Dora Greenwell, Jean Ingelow and others in a long and powerful tradition of women's poetry. The experiments of Meredith, Hopkins, Swinburne and James Thomson occupy the last part of this book, experiments which we might call premodernist. The book ends with a Postscript on the last representatives of the Victorian conservative and radical poetic traditions, the early Yeats and Hardy's *The Dynasts*, where the vulnerable cohesions of the Victorian project disperse. The history of Victorian poetry is the gradual assent to self-reflexive art and the struggle against such an assent. I have not attempted a policy of inclusion, but have decided to write on what seems important to the reconsideration of Victorian poetry now. Therefore Matthew Arnold and Dante Gabriel Rossetti feature less strongly than the customary canon of Victorian poetry might insist. I have also assumed that much of what goes on in the 1890s is pre-empted by earlier poets. I have looked at some working-class writing. But, even accepting these principles of selection, I am well aware, as my Preface points out, how restricted my discussion is.

Though revaluation for its own sake does not seem to me appropriate it is obvious that I have made a number of value judgements in the cause of rereading Victorian poetry. In the depth and range of their projects and in the beauty and boldness of their experiments with language, Tennyson, Browning and Christina Rossetti stand pre-eminent. If it is incumbent upon the writer of a critical history to ask 'what kind of history?' it is also necessary to ask 'what kind of criticism?' in order to indicate why particular choices have been made.

WHAT KIND OF CRITICISM?

The most arresting discussions of Victorian poetry recently have come from Marxists, feminists and deconstruction. A critical history cannot be written from outside these debates with a false neutrality, for these are the contexts in which readers will read new discussions and the poets themselves.

Alan Sinfield's *Alfred Tennyson* is an impressive Marxist intervention which has quite properly shaken up accounts of Victorian poetry.[23] He reads Tennyson as a cultural materialist and inevitably sees him, as he was, as a conservative poet. Sinfield's hindsight enables him to argue that Tennyson's aesthetic solutions to political problems were either timid or straightforwardly reactionary. The poet's evasiveness leads to a perpetual emptying out of signification in which language resorts to a fetishistic preoccupation with its own surfaces rather than being deployed in the service of exploring meaning. Two difficulties emerge in the necessity to establish an unequivocally reactionary Tennyson. First, in order to pin Tennyson to political and religious positions, Sinfield has to eliminate the possibility of ambiguity in poetic language. Or when confronted with two contending meanings he has to opt for one as being 'really' the intended meaning. Similarly, in order to argue Tennyson's political bad faith he has to argue that Tennyson's 'real' interests as a sympathiser with the landed gentry and as a supporter of nationalism and imperialistic interests must give a poem a particular historical meaning even when it appears to be struggling against it. Thus he virtually makes Tennyson personally responsible for the colonialist ravaging of Tahiti as a result of 'The Lotos-Eaters'. He excludes the element of struggle with the element of ambiguity.

Eve Sedgwick's brilliant feminist reading of *The Princess* in *Between Men* adopts rather the same strategy.[24] She argues that far from being a para-feminist poem, as the stated project of *The Princess* insists, Tennyson's poem actually or 'really' deals with the patriarchal homosocial bonding which makes women an object of exchange between men. She makes an impressive analysis of the structure of the poem in order to demonstrate the case. However, rather like Sinfield, she makes her argument stick by first excluding ambiguity, or staying with those elements of ambiguity which corroborate the case. Secondly, the deconstruction of the poem has to take place by the introduction of a very narrow form of intentionality. Tennyson 'meant' to write a poem in celebration of women but the manifest intention of the text is subverted by its latent homosocial desires. This distinction between what is meant and what happens assumes that the text has a manifest and a latent content, a conscious and unconscious desire. The difficulty about this is that everything that is observed is all there in the text anyway, and it is a strangely arbitrary decision which makes some elements of the text manifest and some latent, some conscious and some unconscious, since all elements of the text are actually manifest. A process of selection has gone on, in which the critic has decided to select an intentional and an unintentional project. To simplify a text's projects and then to invoke the complexities of the text itself to undermine the simple project is an odd procedure. A text is not quite like a patient in analysis and actually anticipates these strategies of deconstruction by enabling them to take place.

The problem of deciding what is 'really' a poet's interests politically or what is 'really' intentional as against unconscious can be circumvented by a more generous understanding of the text as struggle. A text is endless struggle and contention, struggle with a changing project, struggle with the play of ambiguity and contradiction. This is a way of reading which gives equal weight to a text's stated project and the polysemic and possibly wayward meanings it generates. 'The Lotos-Eaters', for instance, can be read as a struggle with an impossible ideology of consciousness, labour and consumption which lays bare the poverty of accounts of social relationships underlying these conceptions in a language which libidinously orchestrates the deranged perceptions and desires of the subject, who is either consumed by work or destroyed by cessation from it. Rather than longing for retreat, the poem struggles with what constitutes the self as divided between labour and the cessation of labour. Its exploration is nearer to Marx's understanding of the estranged labour which converts all energy expended outside work into subhuman or animal experience than to an account of the text as a simple desire for escape and exploitation of resources. The desire for escape is involved, of course, in the struggle with the nature of work. But it is not the primary 'intentional' project of the poem.

To see the text as a complex entity defining and participating in an area of struggle and contention is to make intentionality a much wider and more complex affair and to include the contradictions and uncontrolled nature of language within the text's project. For the escape of language from univocal order becomes one of the text's areas of contention and not part of its latent unconscious. (And, as I have suggested in my discussion of Carlyle, the advantage of this strategy is that the Victorians themselves were aware of the 'escape' of language from control.) Perhaps this encounters the danger of accepting complexity to the extent that we can map deconstructive processes on to the text, and, as it were, leave the text alone with its intricacies and to its ludic activities. To do this, however, would be to attribute to the text a composure with its difficulties which few texts have. It would be precisely not to engage in that understanding of the unsettled nature of the text which deconstruction has elicited. And it ignores the ideological struggles of the text. Post-Derridean criticism, however, tends to ignore the aspect of active struggle in a text. Volosinov, taking up a different form of the Hegelian tradition than the one from which deconstruction stems, puts the struggle with language at the centre of a text, and such a concentration on language should help in the rereading of Victorian poetry.[25]

A clever critic of Browning, Herbert Tucker, has noticed the linguistic intricacy of Victorian poetry and used the strategies of deconstruction in *Browning's Beginnings* to elicit Browning's complexities, but he tends to stay with them rather than to probe what is problematical and conflicting.[26] To concentrate on the ludic energies of language rather than its conflicts is to miss the underlying element of struggle in poetry of this period, its engagement with a content, its political awareness. What is linguistically and formally complex in Victorian poetry seems to me to arise from stress. To understand what is stressful, and why, it is important to link linguistic and formal contradictions to the substantive issues at stake in the poems – issues of politics, gender and epistemology, the problem of relationship and the continual attempts to reinvest the content of self and other. An earlier generation of writers attempted to understand the form of Victorian poetry as the function of a complex of social and psychosocial problems. E. D. H. Johnson, in *The Alien Vision of Victorian Poetry*, explored the terms of Victorian poetry in relation to an increasingly severe lesion between the poet and society.[27] Robert Langbaum in *The Poetry of Experience* studied the dramatic monologue as an attempted solution to a cultural crisis in which the conceptualisation of the self and its relations acknowledged a split between insight and judgement, empathy and detachment.[28] Though Johnson tends to remain too narrowly with existential subjectivity and Langbaum's readings return a trifle rapidly to the ethical, these books are important in their attempts to read Victorian poetry in a sophisticated way in terms of a cultural analysis, attempts which, along with Morse Peckham's readings of Victorian poetry, seem to have terminated the valuable project they began.[29]

Perhaps what was lacking in these studies (and which may account for the subsequent lack of creative followers) was an account of the language of Victorian poetry in relation to both formal and cultural problems, an attempt to see these things as inseparable from one another. The link between cultural complexities and the complexities of language is indirect but can be perceived. We might start with the nature of language in Victorian poetry. For to read a Victorian poem is to be made acutely aware of the fact that it is made of language. Whether it is the strange, arcane artifice of Tennyson's early poems or the splutter of speech in Browning, the limpid economy of Christina Rossetti, Swinburne's swamping rhythms, Hopkins's muscle-bound syntax, the sheer verbalness of poetry is foregrounded. It is as if the poet's secondariness takes a stand

11

on the self-conscious assertion of the unique discourse of poetry. This is connected with the overdetermination of ambiguity. The open nerve of exposed feeling in Tennyson is registered in a language fraught with ambiguity. Christina Rossetti's distilled exactitude analyses into an equally precise ambiguity. Signification in Browning shifts and lurches almost vertiginously. The structural ambiguities of Romantic syntax have intensified to an extent that coalescing syntax and semantic openness is the norm. In an age of 'movable type' and mechanical reproduction in which signification moves beyond the immediate control of the writer it is as if the writer can only resort to an openness in advance of the reader, testing out the possibilities of systematic misprision. Such language draws attention to the nature of words as a medium of representation. In the same way poets resort to songs and speech, as if to foreground the act of reading a secondary text, for the song is not sung but read, and the speech is not spoken but written.

Hopkins saw the openness of his contemporaries as anarchy and flux and desperately tried to arrest it, reintroducing an agonised, sundered language of ambiguity in spite of himself.[30] Arnold saw it as the product of disorganised subjectivity, and in a brilliant phrase, summed up nineteenth-century poetry as 'the dialogue of the mind with itself', and attempted to freeze poetry back into classical form.[31] Neither, however, saw that this was a systematic and organised ambiguity. The doubleness of language is not local but structural. It must be read closely, not loosely. It is not the disorganised expression of subjectivity but a way of exploring and interrogating the grounds of its representation. What the Victorian poet achieved was often quite literally two concurrent poems in the same words.

Schopenhauer wrote of the lyric poet as uttering between two poles of feeling, between the pure undivided condition of unified selfhood and the needy, fracturing self-awareness of the interrogating consciousness.[32] The Victorian poet does not swing between these two forms of utterance but dramatises and objectifies their simultaneous existence. There is a kind of duplicity involved here, for the poet often invites the simple reading by presenting a poem as lyric expression as the perceiving subject speaks. Mariana's lament or Fra Lippo Lippi's apologetics are expressions, indeed, composed in an expressive form. But in a feat of recomposition and externalisation the poem turns its expressive utterance around so that it becomes the opposite of itself, not only the *subject's* utterance but the *object* of analysis and critique. It is, as it were, reclassified as drama in the act of being literal lyric expression. To re-order lyric expression as drama is to give it a new content and to introduce the possibility of interrogation and critique. Mariana's torture in isolation, for instance, is the utterance of a subjective psychological condition, but that psychological expression is reversed into being the object of analysis and restructured as a symptomatic form by the act of narration, which draws attention to the reiterated refrain of the poem as Mariana's speech, speech which attempts to arrest temporality while time moves on in the narrator's commentary. The poignant expression of exclusion to which Mariana's state gives rise, and which is reiterated in the marking of barriers – the moat itself, the gate with clinking latch, the curtained casement, the hinged doors – is simultaneously an analysis of the hypersensitive hysteria induced by the coercion of sexual taboo. These are hymenal taboos, which Mariana is induced, by a cultural consensus which is hidden from her, to experience as her own condition. Hidden from her, but not from the poem, the barriers are man-made, cunningly constructed through the material fabric of the house she inhabits, the enclosed spaces in which she is confined. It is the narrative voice which describes these spaces, not Mariana as speaker.

The dramatic nature of Victorian poetry was understood by its earliest critics, by W. J. Fox and Arthur Hallam in particular, but seems to have been lost to later readers.[33] Twentieth-century readers have been right to see the dramatic monologue as the primary Victorian genre, even though they have too often codified it in terms of technical features. Other devices, such as the framed narrative or the dream, dialogue or parody, are related to it. All enable double forms to emerge. Rather than to elicit its technical features, it is preferable to see what this dramatic form enabled the poet to explore. By seeing utterance both as subject and as object, it was possible for the poet to explore expressive psychological forms simultaneously as psychological conditions *and* as constructs, the phenomenology of a culture, projections which indicate the structure of relationships. I have called this objectification of consciousness a phenomenological form because phenomenology seeks to describe and analyse the manifestations of consciousness rather than its internal condition. Thus such a reading relates consciousness to the external forms of the culture in which it exists. The gap between subjective and objective readings often initiates a debate between a subject-centred or expressive and a phenomenological or analytical reading, but above all it draws attention to the act of representation, the act of relationship and the mediations of language, different in a psychological and in a phenomenological world.

The double poem is a deeply sceptical form. It draws attention to the epistemology which governs the construction of the self and its relationships and to the cultural conditions in which those relationships are made. It is an expressive model and an epistemological model simultaneously. Epistemological and hermeneutic problems are built into its very form, for interpretation, and what the act of interpretation involves, are questioned in the very existence of the double model. It must expose relationships of power, for the epistemological reading will explore things of which the expressive reading is unaware and go beyond the experience of the lyric speaker. It is inveterately political not only because it opens up an exploration of the unstable entities of self and world and the simultaneous

13

problems of representation and interpretation, but because it is founded on debate and contest. It has to give the entities of self and world a provisional content in order to dramatise the debate. The Victorian dramatic poem is not the dialogue of the mind with itself so much as the dialogue of the poem with itself, using the dialogue of the mind, the labour of the self on the world, as its lyric entry into the phenomenological world which is a labour on that labour. If the poet knows that the act of representation is fraught with problems, and if it is not clear to what misprisions the poem might be appropriated, then a structure which analyses precisely that uncertainty and which makes that uncertainty belong to struggle and debate, a structure which fills that uncertainty with content, is the surest way to establish poetic form. The surest way to answer uncertainty is creative agnosticism.

The dialogue created by the debates between expressive and phenomenological modes might seem to lead to a kind of poetry which can be described as 'dialogic' in Bakhtin's terms. Bakhtin denied poetry the dialogic form on the ground that it was irreducibly monologic, the product of a single, unified and non-conflictual poetic voice. It would be easy to educe examples of poetry, and particularly Victorian poems, which suggest otherwise, but there are difficulties in assimilating Victorian poetry to a dialogic model, although this is a step in the right direction.[34] The struggle between two kinds of reading is highly complex. It is not a question of a simple dialogue or dialectic form in which the opposition between two terms is fixed and settled. Such an opposition too often is what the dialogic has come to mean. But we have only to look at 'Mariana' to see that the cultural or phenomenological reading which changes the status of Mariana's utterance as lyric expression is subject to unsettling pressures in its turn. In the phenomenological reading, Mariana's anguish becomes no longer something for which she is psychologically responsible. When under the scrutiny of phenomenological critique the terrible privacy of her obsessional condition, her inability to gaze on the external world except at night, becomes the function of a death wish to which she has been induced without fully realising that she has been driven to it. On the other hand, this suicidal condition asks questions of the cultural reading. Is not the phenomenological reading too ready to concede that this is a situation 'without hope of change', too ready to metaphorise Mariana's emotions in terms of projection onto the external world ('blackest moss', 'blacken'd water'), which becomes an extension of her condition even though the landscape operates quite independently of her? The external world becomes both her psychic environment and an existence from which she is irretrievably estranged. The phenomenological reading seems uncertain of these relations. Is it not too ready to narrow the grounds of feminine sexuality as the passive object of experience (notice the 'wooing wind')? Thus it arrives at a self-fulfilling reading of estrangement in which Mariana *must* be alienated. And so the status of the phenomenological reading is changed. It cannot be metacommentary with clean hands entirely in charge of the grounds of debate. And this reflects back onto Mariana as subject. Her loathing of the day and the derangement of her perception is a rebellious act in this context, and questions have to be asked about her autonomy and the extent of her passivity. It might well be that the fragmented self she becomes is both cause and effect of a particular way of conceiving of feminine subjectivity. And it is difficult to say whether Mariana's condition is a violent protest or a passive response to such conceptions of the feminine. What is here is nothing so straightforward as a simple opposition but a dynamic text in which lyric description and analysis are repeatedly redefining the terms of a question and contending for its ground. To probe the status of one form of utterance is to call forth an analysis of the status of *that* interpretation, and so on. If this is a dialogue or a dialectical form it is so in all the antagonistic complexity of the Hegelian master–slave dialectic in which the mediations between different positions are so rapid and subtle, so continually changing places in the relationship of authority, that the play of difference can hardly be resolved. Bakhtin's dialogism is clearly derived from this, indeed, just as Volosinov's (preferable to me) linguistic model is, but it is worth going back to Hegel to restate the complexity of the case. For the status of the hermeneutic act is continually reinvestigated in the double poem at the same time as the terms of the struggle are invested with a new content.

To see the text as struggle continually investing terms with a new content is to see it as a responsive rather than as a symptomatic discourse. Both the Marxist and feminist readings to which I have referred consider the Victorian poem in different ways as a symptom of the political unconscious and thus irrevocably blind to its own meaning. No text can account for the way it is read in future cultures but it can establish the grounds of the struggle for meaning. There is a difference between what is blindfold and what is unpredictable. What I would call a new Hegelian reading avoids symptomatic interpretations, just as it avoids the endless ludic contradictions which sometimes emerge from deconstruction. A text which struggles with the logic of its own contradictions is in any case arguably nearer, though not identical with, Derridean principles, in which a text is threatened by collapse from internal oppositions, than to the systematic incoherence which deconstruction sometimes elicits.

True to its status as a transitional form Victorian poetry has either been used to confirm a general critical theory, as in the readings of Bloom, or been seen simply as an instance of a particular historical case, for which a particular critical reading is necessary, as in the readings of Johnson or Langbaum. What I have done is to develop the political implications of Johnson's work and the epistemological implications of Langbaum. Langbaum is also concerned with the double reading, though his way of seeing the judgemental reading as a *control* on the empathetic reading seems to me to state the problem too rigidly in moral rather than analytical terms. It is without that sense of a new content which evolves when the subjective reading reverses into critique and so back and forth between critique and expressive form. 'Mariana' is an exemplary case of this process.

When the full importance of Victorian poetry is recognised, however, it becomes apparent that it need not be discussed either as illustrative material for theory or as a particular case. It surely marks an extraordinarily self-conscious moment of awareness in history. A poetic form and a language were evolved which not only make possible a sophisticated exploration of new categories of knowledge in modern culture but also the philosophical criticism adequate to it. The sense of secondariness with which Victorian poetry comes into being produces the double poem, two poems in one. The double poem, with its systematically ambiguous language, out of which expressive and phenomenological readings emerge, is a structure commensurate with the 'movable type' which Carlyle saw as both the repercussion and the cause of shifts in nineteenth-century culture. The double poem belongs to a post-teleological, post-revolutionary, post-industrial and post-Kantian world and its interrelated manifestations. The double poem signifies a godless, non-teleological world because as soon as two readings become possible and necessary, the permanent and universal categories of the 'type' dissolve. For the 'type' is of course an ancient theological word, meaning those fixed categories of thought and language ordained by God which governed relationships, well before it becomes associated with print. The double reading inevitably dissolves such fixity, just as it means a shift from ontology to epistemology, a shift from investigating the grounds of being to a sceptical interrogation of the grounds of knowledge, which becomes phenomenology, not belief. In a post-revolutionary world in which power is supposedly vested in many rather than a privileged class, the double poem dramatises relationships of power. In the twofold reading, struggle is structurally necessary and becomes the organising principle, as critique successively challenges and redefines critique. Movable type, where technology mobilises the logos, makes the process of signification a political matter as it opens up a struggle for the meaning of words which is part of the relations of power explored through the structures of the poem. Hence the poet's systematic exploration of ambiguity. This reveals not only the confounding complexities of language and the anxieties this generates but boldly establishes that play of possibility in which meaning can be decided. It draws attention to the fact that meaning *is* decided by cultural consensus even while its ambiguity offers the possibility of challenging that consensus through the double reading. The poem of the post-industrial world recognises the displacement of relationships in its structure as well as in its language. The formal ploy in which the uttering subject becomes object and the poem reverses

16

relationships not once but many times indicates that epistemological uneasiness in which subject and object, self and world, are no longer in lucid relation with one another but have to be perpetually redefined. The structure of the double poem emerges from the condition in which self-creation in the world is no longer straightforward but indirect and problematical and in which, as Carlyle said, 'nothing is done directly'. Finally, the double structure inevitably draws attention to the act of interpretation, since one reading encounters another and moves to a new content in the process. Hermeneutic self-consciousness leads in its turn to concentration on the nature of representation, for if interpretation is in question as a construct, so also are the categories of thought it deals with. In a post-Kantian world the double poem becomes a representation of representation, not only secondary historically but a second-order activity in itself. Mariana's poignant utterance is framed as the solipsistic constructions of her world and this reflects back on the complexity of the framing process which presents that self-enclosed utterance. It too cannot be exempted from the second-order status. If one utterance is a representation, so is the other. Both are ideological and both confront one another.

It would not be too much to claim that the genesis of modern form and its *problems* arise in the double poem, just as the possibilities for a criticism which interrogates the nature of the speaking subject and deconstructs the contradictory assumptions of the text are generated out of the double reading. The philosophical premises for a criticism commensurate with this complexity arise in the twentieth century and not in the nineteenth century but they follow from nineteenth-century poetic experiment which, I suggest, is bolder and more self-conscious than most poetry subsequent to it. This is not to argue neatly that Victorian poetry should be studied because it 'produces' and confirms the deconstructive moment and that here we have the 'original' deconstructive form. Rather it should be recognised that the deconstructive moment *is* a historical moment, and that Victorian poetry anticipates its strategies and moves beyond it. For, committed to going through the process of 'movable type', the double poem confronts the scepticism of the deconstructive moment and challenges it. Victorian poems are sceptical and affirmative simultaneously for they compel a strenuous reading and assume an active reader who will participate in the struggle of the lyric voice, a reader with choices to make, choices which are created by the terms of the poem itself. The active reader is compelled to be internal to the poem's contradictions and recomposes the poem's processes in the act of comprehending them as ideological struggle. There is no end to struggle because there is no end to the creative constructs and the renewal of content which its energy brings forth.

Rereading Victorian poetry, then, involves a reconsideration of the way we conceptualise history and culture, and the way we see the politics of poetry. It also involves rethinking some of the major criticism of this

17

century, Marxist and feminist criticism and deconstruction, and considering how the language and form of Victorian poetry question the theories they have developed. Putting the stuffing back into the Victorian sofa then becomes a process of reconstruction which asks living questions.

Throughout this introduction I have used Tennyson's 'Mariana' as a running commentary on the arguments I have put forward about the double poem and its significance. As a tail-piece I include a brief discussion of Browning's 'Love among the Ruins' to indicate how the general principles discussed above might work.

The risk-taking, ambiguous forms of the double lyric are present in the first poem in *Men and Women*, 'Love among the Ruins'. Why was this poem, an ostensibly affirmative statement of subjective values, 'love is best', given primacy in the two volumes, and how is its title to be interpreted – *Love* among the Ruins, Love among the *Ruins*? Are these teleological as well as material ruins? Both present and past reject an ordered universe, one by depending on private subjectivity and the other by depending on violence. The different emphases on 'Love' and 'Ruins' enunciate contending terms, the certainties of private passion over and against a communal but now fragmented history and culture which has become simply archaeology. Perhaps Volney's *The Ruins of Empire* (1791) is behind the title of the poem.[35]

A lover anticipates a meeting with a girl on the site of an unnamed, obliterated city – Babylon, Rome, anywhere. The poem looks like a simple antithesis between the consummation of intense passion and the wasteful aggression, violence and cupidity of a vanished society – a primitive will to power through war and gold. It is arranged as a series of flowing lines which alternate with curt, abrupt, single anapaests and are punctuated by them like a drum beat. (Browning rearranged the stanzas after 1855 but this does not affect the essential form of the poem.) The short lines mockingly disrupt the easy, homogeneous flow of the long lines but – and a conviction of the strangeness of *this* poem grows – the long lines make perfect sense without them. The short lines can be repressed. Except for the fifth and the last stanza and for the completion of each stanza, they are inessential. It is as if another more critical language is refusing to be excluded and threatening private feeling with a mocking analysis of its limitations. This is movable type, or removable type, in action. There are two poems here. One is a simple celebration of private feeling, which attempts to exclude everything but the moment of union. The other is an assent to, or at least a recognition of, the subversive and dangerous energies of an alien culture, its aggression and power and its predominantly male hierarchy.

> Where the quiet-coloured end of evening smiles,
>> Miles and miles

On the solitary pastures where our sheep
  Half-asleep
Tinkle homeward thro' the twilight, stray or stop
  As they crop –
Was the site once of a city great and gay,
  (So they say). . . .

(i)

All the mountains topped with temples, all the glades'
  Colonnades,
All the causeys, bridges, aqueducts, – and then,
  All the men!
When I do come, she wil speak not, she wil stand. . . .

(vi)

In the first stanza the short lines impart a suspect tedium and torpor to the pastoral, a tedium which is absent without them. The plenitude of the city and above all its populace is repressed in the sixth stanza without the short lines to insist upon them. 'Where the quiet-coloured end of evening smiles,/On the solitary pastures where our sheep//Tinkle homeward thro' the twilight'. 'All the causeys, bridges, aqueducts, – and then,/When I do come, she wil speak not'. 'Shut them in', the lover says of the competitive violences of the past, but with inadvertent ambiguity. The long lines attempt to shut away the mocking pressure of the half-lines, but they are shut *into* the poem, for the lovers' privacy is defined against them. 'Love is best' is defensively defined against the ironies and energies the short lines represent. The relationship between the long and short lines, each a critique of the other, is what enables the poem to be both actor and spectator of itself. Browning knew about the hubris of lovers, and gives assent to passionate feeling, but subjective experience becomes its opposite, the object of investigation. It shuts out history, culture, here. The lovers exist in 'undistinguished grey' (v), extra-historical, extra-cultural, context-less, not redeeming, but perpetuating 'the Ruins' about them. In stanza v history converges on them as the violent figures of the past, 'breathless, dumb', are allowed to share the same syntax with the girl who is also, the structure allows, 'breathless, dumb'. The will to see passion as self-sufficing is as aggressive and exclusive as the desires of the dead society for triumph and empire. All history waits 'Till *I* come', one form of the syntax hubristic-ally proposes. Revelation in history is reserved for the puny lover. There is a struggle between two interpretations of the same syntax here and this culminates the series of reversals in which the priorities of the language of feeling and its values and the language of history change places as first one and then another achieves dominance. The pressures of power explored in the structure of the post-revolutionary double poem are apparent here.

  'Love among the Ruins', written the day after 'Childe Roland to the

Dark Tower came' and sharing with it the landscape of ruin and tower, initiates *Men and Women* because it enacts and subverts a contemporary mythos inherited from Romantic values, a myth about the all-sufficing energies of mutual passion and the setting up of private enclaves of feeling against the crude values of threatening culture. But the structure of the poem makes it clear that this myth is a construct and entails and depends upon another more seductive but equally vitiating myth. The values of private passion necessarily entail a structuring of social and cultural relationships in terms of fracture, the splitting off of individuals from an alien culture. The lesions and breakages which come into being in the arrangement of the long and short lines are inherent in the account of isolated human nature, the myth of estrangement, the fall from a unified culture.

> How different with us moderns! With us too the image of the human species is projected in magnified form into separate individuals – but as fragments, not in different combinations. . . . We see not merely individual, but whole classes of men, developing but one part of their potentialities. . . .
>
> It was civilisation itself which inflicted this wound upon modern man. Once the increase of empirical knowledge, and more exact modes of thought, made sharper divisions between the sciences inevitable, and once the increasingly complex machinery of State necessitated a more rigorous separation of ranks and operations, then the inner unity of human nature was severed too, and a disastrous conflict set its harmonious powers at variance.[36]

This is Schiller defining the fractures of modern scientific culture. 'Love among the Ruins', more savagely controlled and ironical, points to the fallaciousness of the account of original unity as well as analysing in its form the structure of estrangement. Browning is likely to have found this kind of cultural diagnosis in Carlyle as well as directly from the German writing which was frequently Carlyle's source. In *Sartor Resartus* Carlyle asked for a new *mythos* and new *symbols* to emerge from the ruins of the old. The 'Genius of Mechanism' smothers the soul, and the poet, a phoenix out of the fire (one is reminded of the fiery landscape at the end of 'Childe Roland'), 'Prometheus-like can shape new symbols', a Shelleyan task, 'and bring new Fire from Heaven to fix it there'. Symbols emerge out of silence, and 'Fantasy', the Promethean imagination, 'plays into the small prose domain of sense'.[37] 'Love among the Ruins' is about the exhaustion of symbol and the emergence of a new and impoverished mythos. However, the new symbol creates a silence in which the poet's Promethean task can, perhaps, begin again. The girl, 'breathless, dumb', 'will speak not'. Perhaps when she *does* speak, instead of being the addressee of a lover haunted by the male culture of the past, the present can be changed. After all, Elizabeth Barrett Browning was writing *Aurora Leigh* (1856) when this poem was being written. But the poem carries with it the possibility that the cry for mythos may itself be a symptom of exhaustion. The last cry of secondariness. It stands at the head of *Men and Women* because it implicitly interrogates the possibility of creating a Promethean symbol in a culture which defines itself as fragmented. It knows itself as a sceptical representation of the mythos and understands its second-order status. Lawrence intuitively and perhaps unconsciously grasped something of the meaning of 'Love among the Ruins' when he made Birkin quote it as he approaches London with Gerald in *Women In Love* (chapter 5). He quotes it just after he is wondering whether it is possible to have a total and all-sufficing relationship with a woman and just before he wonders if twentieth-century culture is not so exhausted that it should be destroyed: 'Humanity is a dead letter' because it can produce no new embodiment of 'the incomprehensible'. Thus he arrives at Carlyle's definition of symbol. Browning's poem is uncannily prescient: it sees just how long the myths about myth and cultural exhaustion and fragmentation might last. It is a step ahead of Lawrence, however, because it refuses the romantic account of the feminine with which Birkin struggles.

The regressing ironies of this poem mean that it refuses to privilege the statement 'love is best'. But this *is* a double poem, and sceptical and affirmative readings struggle actively with one another to gain the ascendent in a strenuous effort to reorder the processes of the poem's movable type. The deficiencies and impoverishment of the subjectivist confessional are declared through the critique mounted by the energy of past society. The violence of that society, however, establishes the need for love and negatively enables the statement 'love is best' to be given a new content. The reordering is always provisional, always dependent on the evolution of new possibilities from the particulars of the poem, but it is necessarily a continuous process of construction and reconstruction.

This post-Hegelian reading recognises the antagonistic struggle of dialectic rather than its resolutions or its free play. It assumes that an active ideological creativity is constitutively at work in the poem's structure and language and is thus necessarily a political and cultural way of reading. Such a criticism is particularly appropriate to Victorian poetry, perhaps, but it is relevant to all nineteenth- and twentieth-century poetry. Since Victorian poetry is the most sophisticated poetic form, and the most politically complex, to arise in the past two hundred years it is proper that Victorian poems should generate principles for reading the poetry of the past two hundred years.

Part I

CONSERVATIVE AND BENTHAMITE AESTHETICS OF THE AVANT-GARDE

Tennyson and Browning
in the 1830s

1

TWO SYSTEMS
OF CONCENTRIC CIRCLES

One fact, however, is sufficiently evident, that we are in a state of transition: that old things are passing away and giving place to new; and that society is in the very act, an act ever attended with convulsive throes and conflicting fears and hopes, of assuming a new form, – brighter and happier may it be than all the past! Whichever way we look we behold symptoms of change. The billows are tossing and tumbling, heaving, rolling and breaking, at every point of the compass. The public mind has outgrown public institutions, which must soon be shattered unless possessed of flexibility to admit of a proportionate expansion. Our forms, laws, establishments, whether for the purpose of education, commerce, politics, or religion, are become so insufficient to represent the intelligence, harmonize with the condition, satisfy the wants, and realize the desires of the community that they must evidently undergo extensive changes, – gradual and peaceful changes it is to be hoped. . . . The work has commenced, we are in the process of renovation; in some departments its rate may be more rapid than in others, but it extends to all. The conflict for reform in the Legislature is but the type and index of a wider, deeper, and mightier conflict between principles which began their struggle for mastery over man in the Garden of Eden, and shall continue till the Kingdoms of this world become the Kingdoms of our God and of his Christ. That struggle is like the elemental strife of the material world. It is like the storm that clears the heavens. It is the process by which Providence conducts mankind to higher and yet higher degrees of knowledge and happiness.

According to the law of progress, both individual and social, by which God governs the world, the transition is made from one gradation of order, harmony, and beauty to a higher gradation, by the intervention of a state of apparent confusion and conflict. . . .

The question of reform in the representation of the people could never have arisen into its present interest and importance but in connexion with a strong and general conviction of the necessity of a multitude of other changes which it is expected will be facilitated by the adoption of that measure. The Church cannot remain as it is; its temples have long ceased to be national, in any other respect save that of the taxation by which they are supported. . . . The Law cannot remain as it is . . . public opinion demands more than any man will be found bold enough to propose in an unreformed parliament . . . almost every man who has either had occasion to enforce the payment of a just debt, or to resist an unfair demand, is impatient of the needless delay, complication, and expense of the present system. Education cannot remain as it is. The poor must be educated, though it be at the public expense . . . nor will the word education continue to designate merely reading and writing for the offspring of poor parents, and Latin and Greek for that of the rich ones. Science, history, and morals, the elements of real knowledge, are ceasing to be excluded. . . . The means for disseminating information cannot remain as they are. The taxes on paper, books, newspapers etc., have been rightly described as taxes on knowledge. They intercept information in its passage to the people. . . . They suppress or restrict. . . . Above all, the relative condition of the working class cannot remain the same. A different principle in the distribution of wealth must gradually make its way into society, and speedily commence its operation. It cannot be necessary to civilized society, that the producers of its wealth should be kept on the very borders of starvation, and paupers succeed to paupers, world without end. It cannot be necessary that the interests of the lower classes, and of all above them, should be in a state of interminable and bitter hostility. . . . These evils have made themselves felt through the whole frame of society. The perception of them has generated the science of political economy.

(W. J. Fox, *Monthly Repository*)[1]

One duty I still feel I have to perform . . . it is my last but my greatest: when I think of it, I am full of hope, and to it all my thoughts and feelings turn: It is to lend my hand to do the great work of regenerating England, not by Political institutions! not by extrinsic and conventional forms! By a higher and a holier work, by breathing into her the vigorous feeling of a Poet, and a Religious man, by pouring out the dull and stagnant blood which circulates in her veins, to replenish them with a youthful stream, fresh from the heart . . . my hope is in ourselves [R. C. Trench, John Sterling, F. D. Maurice], and in that spirit of a higher feeling which the young men of this age universally possess. . . . Wordsworth has begun. . . . My plan of operation I will expound . . . thus much, that we must strike through Education, and first at the Universities. . . . We shall

do nothing until we get rid of AntiChrist, and he walks abroad boldly in a Doctor of Divinity's hood, and his thought and cry are 'Nego!'
(Letter from John Kemble to William Bodham Donne, from Germany, 1829)[2]

The country is in a more awful state than you can well conceive. . . . While I write Maddingley [sic], or some adjoining village, is in a state of conflagration, and the sky above is coloured flame-red. This is one of a thousand such actions committed daily through England. The laws are almost suspended; the money of foreign factions is at work with a population exasperated into reckless fury.
(Letter from Arthur Hallam to Richard Chenevix Trench, 1830)[3]

The passages which introduce this chapter have a characteristic rhetoric. William Johnson Fox, writing as editor of a radical Utilitarian and Unitarian journal at the beginning of 1832, the year of the great Reform Bill, argues passionately for fundamental structural change in the country's institutions, in religion, parliamentary representation, the law, education, a change which necessitates the redistribution of wealth. Nothing, he reiterates, can 'remain as it is'. It is a pre-eminently public debate, mounted through the polemic of the printed word in the cadences of political oratory. The second group of quotations is from the private letters of a university coterie, the opposite pole from public journalism, a group of friends who all belonged to an exclusive society, the Cambridge Apostles, in the 1830s. Written with the sophisticated élan of shared intimacy, the project under discussion is not political change but the 'regeneration' of society, not revolution, as Arthur Hallam's sickened fear of the rick-burners round Cambridge indicates, but a transformation of the mind of the country. They were as much against the 1832 Reform Bill as Fox was for it. Browning was associated with Fox and the *Monthly Repository* group, Tennyson belonged to the Apostles. These groups represent two quite different intellectual formations in the 1830s. Yet both conceived themselves as avant-garde, experimenting with the new in political, theological and aesthetic matters, defining new categories and defamiliarising the old. Avant-garde as a term for experimental minority groups had not been invented. But arguably these two formations were the first recognisably avant-garde groups to emerge in Britain. Both were in the process of defining what minority groups of intellectuals might mean in a culture, and since the very notion of a culture was new, and the idea of the minority intellectual, this entailed constructing the idea of culture and defining what in particular a literary culture was. While the *Monthly Repository* was dissenting and radical, and the Apostles were subversive conservatives nominally assenting to the Anglican establishment, they did have some things in common. Both groups belonged to a new middle-class intelligentsia who repudiated aristocratic privilege and wanted change. Both saw themselves as living in

27

a time of unprecedented crisis when poverty was endemic and violence ever possible. By virtue of dissent the radicals were excluded from power. Theoretically, the Apostles were not. However, both groups explored a theology which transgressed orthodoxy and both saw literature and politics as inseparable from one another. In fact, both groups are at the beginnings of the conceptualisation of literature and the 'literary' as a distinct category with a particularly important part to play in the education of a mass culture.

Later in the century these groups, or their formative ideas, interpenetrated and together developed the terms in which literature, and poetry in particular, was to be discussed. They were both part of the 'shock' spreading from what John Stuart Mill described in 1838 as 'two systems of concentric circles' created by Bentham, the 'Progressive', on the one hand, and Coleridge, the 'Conservative', on the other.[4] The way in which they 'meet and intersect' conditions the form of discussions of poetry and poetry itself. But in the early 1830s the experience of crisis and the radical intellectual and political events which Mill both describes and participated in were perceived differently by each group. To borrow from Walter Benjamin's distinction, the *Monthly Repository* group developed a politicised aesthetics while the Apostles developed an aestheticised politics. This chapter describes what this meant for the early work of Tennyson and Browning and the poets surrounding them. But since the way these groups conceptualised poetry and culture is fundamentally important to the nature of Victorian poetry up to the time of the early Yeats and Hardy, this chapter explores the formative moment of Victorian poetry at some length. For radicals and conservatives were both, as Mill put it, 'the greater questioner of things established'.[5] Both were writing at the limits of what has been called the conventional 'doxa'. One group developed Benthamite thought, the other the thought of the late Coleridge.[6] One wrote at the limit of the radical, one at the limit of the conservative doxa. So much so that there are no real equivalents for these formations in twentieth-century thought and one must be cautious about using terminology.

There is no simple reflective relationship between the poets and the intellectual positions of the groups to which they were connected, no straightforward co-relation between theory and praxis. Rather both Tennyson and Browning belonged to intellectual formations developing strenuous and often contradictory debates. Both poets are actively in dialogue with the ideas circulating in their groups. Nevertheless their intellectual provenance is recognisable. Tennyson is marked by the dazzling brilliance and insouciance of Arthur Hallam and Browning by the energetic polemic of William Johnson Fox, whom he called his literary godfather. Hallam reviewed Tennyson's early poems in 1831. Fox printed some of Browning's earlier poems in the *Monthly Repository* and reviewed *Pauline* in 1833. Indeed, since *Pauline* sold no copies it did not exist except in the pages of the *Monthly Repository*.

Before considering the early work of Tennyson and Browning it is important to look briefly at the debates being negotiated in each group to see what possibilities open up for two kinds of art. In both a highly self-conscious debate on the interconnected questions, literature and ideology, consciousness and knowledge, language and the nature of class, culture, race and gender, was being pursued on very different lines. Though these headings are not strictly separable they are convenient and will indicate the sophistication of the enterprise undertaken both by the *Monthly Repository* and the Apostles. Discussion of the individual poets later in the chapter will elaborate this preliminary account of two formations.

When W. J. Fox took over the *Monthly Repository* in the early 1830s (he became editor in 1828 and bought it in 1831) it is clear that its project changed. From being a sectarian and Unitarian organ with radical traditions it became a more overtly political journal with the aim of forging a Utilitarian, Benthamite aesthetic. Fox's aim was to deepen and enrich the Benthamite tradition by correcting misapprehensions of it and associating it above all with literature. His reading of Benthamism meant in the first place, the dissemination of *pleasure* in its widest sense, the democratisation of literature and the exploration of the links between literature and politics. These links were not simply between the *Zeitgeist* or a loosely defined 'spirit of the age' but involve the conceptualising of what we would now call an ideological relation between literature and the power structure of society.

It is typical of Fox that he welcomed album books, popular gatherings of contemporary writing for the middle classes, while Tennyson viewed them with contempt or professed contempt. Fox was excited by these as sociological phenomena indicating the wider dissemination of literature, and commented on the accessibility of the writing in contrast to the narrow and intimidating presentation of tales and poems in former times.[7] This political and sociological awareness is part of a *Monthly Repository* tradition: in 1820, Thomas Noon Talfourd had attacked Hazlitt's anti-levelling account of art, in which Hazlitt had described the 'literature of power' in hierarchical terms as an aristocracy of letters, distinguishing the aristocracy of taste from actual political democracy. Talfourd saw this celebration of arbitrary power and superstitious faith as an ideological manipulation for political purposes which went back to Burke, who 'made the cause of tyranny appear the cause of the imagination and the affections'.[8] Hazlitt's radical and Unitarian background must have made this resort to the reactionary a major betrayal. It does not seem to have occurred to Talfourd that Hazlitt was being ironical, so serious is his democratic feeling. Fox's constant attack on Scott and his politics of privilege are of a piece with such positions.[9] But he went much further than other writers to make 'the

29

imagination and the affections' belong to a radical analysis. Talfourd had argued that particular imaginative associations do not belong of necessity to evocations of power. They can be directed towards a range of phenomena, particularly the natural landscape which, he thought (perhaps naively), is innocent of class. Imaginative associations can be constructed through culture. Fox carried this analysis much further into cultural relativism. A proper democratic poetry should take modern subjects and scenes such as the French Revolution or the prisons as its materials. It should also become a poetry of the poor: and poetry *for* the poor or *about* the poor would be different from poetry *by* the poor because the history of the working class is formed in different circumstances. He did not seem to be aware that there already *was* a working-class poetry of broadside ballads and street songs for the barely literate which often took the workhouse and the factory as their theme, but instead he thought of this as a poetry of the future. Poetry will differ, and the interpretation of poetry will differ, according to the 'peculiar mental habits' of generations and classes.[10] In other words, it is historically specific. In 1832 the *Monthly Repository* published a series of surveys of Herder's work.[11] Fox has clearly read Herder as a cultural relativist – in contrast to the Apostles who read him as the theorist of historical continuity and racial and cultural cohesion. His view that poetry is 'incarnate' in different cultural forms at different points in history, that it depends on class and country, barbaric and civilised, oriental or northern environments, comes out of Herder, who developed the recognisably modern and intertwined ideas of race, nation and culture. What Fox added is that poetry will be different if it is written by a rich man or a poor man – and he might have also added that it would be different if it were written by a woman.

Fox never really solved the problem of creating a poetry which was genuinely popular any more than he resolved the problematical status of poems written by middle-class poets – something which Browning seems to have recognised – but he did attempt an ideological analysis of the difficulties of a working-class writing. He published the work of Ebenezer Elliott, the corn-law rhymer, throughout his editorship. He published directly political lampoons by R. H. Horne and others: Horne's 'Political Oratorio' has a chorus of mechanics demanding a share in the results of their labour. And he published poets who wrote (sometimes rather weakly and derivatively) in the style of Shelley, the poet of revolution, transformation and change.[12] Though he came near to presenting poetry as a form of social and psychological engineering, because the poet can 'influence the associations of unnumbered minds', he never ceased to believe that poetry participates in critique and creates ideological change.[13] For him Wordsworth and Coleridge had reneged on radical principles and he could only accept them by arguing that they were unintentionally radical and Benthamite. Thus 'Mr Coleridge is . . . a "greatest happiness" man'.[14]

Where Fox began with an analysis of power, cultural relativism and political change, the Apostles started from an idea of historical continuity and a unified culture. But – and this is what makes their propositions about literature and ideology complex and contradictory – they were fully aware that continuity and unity were constructs rather than a possible reality. There is an uncertainty of definition about their political readings. Arthur Hallam was instrumental in publishing Shelley's 'Adonais', Fox's revolutionary poet, though he seems to have admired Shelley as a mythic poet of what he called 'sensation' rather than for any revolutionary possibilities.[15] The Apostles were described as a 'Wordsworthian-Germano-Coleridgean' group, and this was the intellectual formation they developed. And yet R. C. Trench, renouncing 'despairing' and the reading of Shelley and his revolutionary views, clearly once possessed political sympathies with Shelley.[16] With John Kemble, Trench took a major part in attempting to restore the liberal pretender to the Spanish throne in 1830.[17] Hallam and Tennyson took a minor part in the enterprise. This anti-reactionary expedition, underplayed and minimised by their descendants and biographers alike, was a traumatic affair which ended in the execution of one of their friends. It is one of the unspoken repressed elements of Tennyson's early poetry. Robert Boyd was shot for treason on the beach at Malaga.

If the Apostles were not above becoming 'foreign factions', as Hallam put it, in Spain, they dreaded and probably fantasised about the work of such interlopers at home during the Captain Swing riots of the early 1830s. They wanted a transformation of the mind of the country, but not through direct political change. Like Carlyle, they thought of institutional reform as mechanistic, superficial and *abstract*. In his brilliant review of Tennyson's early poems Hallam analysed the cultural fracture and alienation of post-revolutionary Europe as the modern condition.[18] If it could be retrieved at all, and Hallam doubted that it could, a lost *organic* national unity could be, as it were, artificially re-created by the re-education of the whole social imagination through the deep powers of myth. It is a paradoxically demythologised belief in the revival of mythic structures, which are self-consciously historicised as the possession of the nation's past. Where Fox was a positivist demythologiser who hoped for a new working-class art, the Apostles looked self-consciously to a revival of the *peasant* imagination. This is another possible reading of Herder, who said that national myth represented the lost wholeness of intuition as experience and sensation. The poetry of sensation rather than thought advocated in Hallam's review is a covert acknowledgement of Herder and comes together with the references to the traditional ballads of Scott as a programme for a new poetry.

The Apostles read Herder, Schiller and indigenous British mythographers on Indo-European forms of myth, Faber, Bryant and Sir Henry Jones.[19] However, their conceptualisation of myth is both sophisticated and contradictory. Schiller had seen mythic writing as the province of the 'naive' poet. The modern, self-conscious reflective poet has moved beyond its simplicities. Hallam, however, deftly reintroduces the mythic poetry of sensation in his review by proposing that the knowing, modern 'sentimental' poet consciously writes a belated or latter-day 'naive' poetry of the senses which deliberately excludes reflection.[20] In this way the poet achieves a devious power in a split and fragmented culture. And yet such poetry seems to disrupt the unity it is claiming to create. The poetry of sensation, as Hallam called it, is a marginalised minority poetry, working from the outside, defamiliarising habitual forms of thought by exploring disruptive conditions of perception which will ultimately reconfigure consciousness but which act immediately as a kind of ideological solvent through the non-rational power of mythic experience. This is a subliminal critique, operating subversively and secretly, in contradistinction to Fox's conscious critique.

Thomas Keightley's *The Fairy Mythology* (1828) seems to have been a cult book among the Apostles and no work more demonstrates the irreconcilable elements of their theory. Keightley writes that myth is unifying, the expression of folk imagination imaginatively grasped by other classes. It works through intuition and sense as another form of knowledge prior to the division between subject and object. It is used by the powerful as the repressive weapon of the dominant class and thus frequently changes its meaning and its application. It is not *true*.[21] It is not clear to whom myth 'belongs' in Keightley's discussion, but it appears to behave like ideology because it is a representation and severs the correspondence between representation and fact.

The Apostles were stronger on the notion of representation than the Fox group, for whom poetry was not exactly 'truth' either. Instead, for these reconstructed Utilitarians, it was pure expressive *feeling* more often than a mediated representation. This created problems, as will later be seen. But the matter of representation leads to epistemological questions of consciousness and knowledge and is best discussed through them.

Just as Fox looked to a literature of change his philosophy of mind was concerned with the psychology of active agency which worked on the world. The Apostles, on the other hand, were more concerned with the 'pure' nature of identity. Interestingly, associationism, where experience was thought to be built up through the connections of data from the exterior world, was seen as the progressive theory of mind at that time and politicised by being connected with the radical ideas of Bentham. Coleridge has done his work too well by suggesting that associationism is a mechanistic, sterile and inchoate account of consciousness, and we now see it in these terms: associationism, however, was taken seriously as the democratic form precisely because it emphasised the influence of environment and the external world on the self rather than the innate and privileged independent power of mind. Associationism held out the possibility of transforming consciousness through training and education, culture and nurture. Moreover, the *tabula rasa* meant that everyone starts off with the same handicap. Fox sees associationist psychology as central to a new art. Poetry will be concerned with analysing 'modern' conditions of mind, dramatically projecting and exploring different associative processes as they are formed in different environments.[22] It is in this way that poetry is knowledge based on science, a science of mind. When one remembers that Unitarian theology came nearest of all forms of dissent to a humanistic religion in which God, if not to be identified with pure human mind, at least provides a model for it, it is clear that a humanist teleology is at work in Fox's aesthetic.

Fox's epistemology throws great emphasis on the energetic interpretative act of the perceiver or reader in two ways. First, in poetry, mental events are represented and externalised through a kind of dramatic projection which makes them publicly accessible. It is open to all readers to perceive and analyse the public significance of a dialectic of feeling. There were disagreements between *Monthly Repository* writers here, as will be seen when Browning's reworking of dramatic epistemology is discussed. Mill preferred to remain with the dialectic of feeling alone. But for Fox this elides to a theory of drama and is a belief in drama as the central art form. Drama is ideologically important because it objectifies self-projection and conflict, and explores the structure of relationships in their full complexity. It is an open form.[23] The intense concentration of the *Monthly Repository* on dramatic criticism and its political significance – there was a running debate on the politics of *Coriolanus*[24] – makes the adoption of drama as a form by writers such as Talfourd and Browning understandable. It is no accident that Browning's first play, *Strafford*, presaging later work, goes back to the civil war in England, the time when democratic principles were first at stake, or, to the early nineteenth century, seemed to be.

Drama throws emphasis on to the hermeneutic act and the status of the text in the psychology of reading. Advanced German biblical criticism, which found its earliest disseminations in the *Monthly Repository*, gave rise to a tradition of analysis in the journal. A discussion of Schleiermacher's study of St Luke's Gospel in 1827, for instance, takes the unstable text for granted. The narrative of the Gospel is transmitted through a chain of second-generation witnesses and thus its 'truth' must likewise be the construction of the reader. What constitutes a text is an active process of construction and reconstruction. Its only ground is the hermeneutic history of previous acts of construction.[25]

Hallam professed himself to be partially a Hartleyan associationist, but unlike Fox he saw associationist psychology as passive and fragmenting. The continuity of identity through time could only be guaranteed by a Kantian a priori act which assumed the coherence of identity. (The Apostles' passion for German thought is everywhere testified: Kemble in

33

Germany is described as immersed in 'metaphysics and meerschaums, smoking [probably opium] and Schelling'.[26]) However, the self is continually trembling back into a condition of sensation. The self is discontinuous, formed of 'fragments of being', the 'common character of a series of momentary beings'.[27] In his essay on Cicero Hallam defended Epicurean epistemology and insisted that emotion is the ground of consciousness and true knowledge: 'the agent acted from feeling, and *was* by feeling: thoughts were but the ligatures that held together the delicate materials of emotion'.[28] As we shall see, one of the problems here is a failure to describe what 'sensation' and 'feeling' really were. However, the mass of primal sensation which Herder thought to be constitutive of consciousness seems to Hallam a richer intuitional and imaginative experience than reflection and paradoxically nearer to the moral life because it has a *content*, whereas thought is abstract. It is not surprising to find that Hallam's God in 'Theodicaea Novissima', in contrast to the Unitarian God of mind, is a God of love, a God of libido and absolute unmediated sexuality, the model of which is sexual consummation itself. Hallam's God is a God of the body.[29]

As for Schiller, so for the Apostles; the true moral life consists in a free play emancipated from the demands of the practical. It is significant that the Apostles, in contrast to Fox's interest in technology and sociology, found the 'pure' sciences of particular importance to them, and were often informed of the more recent developments in astronomy, geology and philology well before scientific work was published. And, of course, poetry, too, must be pure of practical morality. It was misconceived and misdirected to attempt direct instrumental practical change. Not only does the regeneration of society come about through the transformation of imaginative life, but rather than creating change consciousness *is* change itself in a world of flux. Scientific theory endorsed this theory of flux. We know flux rather than essence. William Whewell, for instance, well known to the Apostles, considered the instability of the universe in his Bridgewater Treatise on astronomy. Scientific scepticism endorses a world in which all truth must be representation superseded by further representation.[30] In the essay on Cicero Hallam professed himself unalarmed by the propositions of either geology or the higher criticism on the grounds that changing representations are all we can know.[31] This affirmative deconstruction has something in common with the hermeneutic constructs of the Fox circle. Both, it is worth emphasising, were equally liberating intellectually. Both were seen in political terms. The difference is that where the *Monthly Repository* circle find a public context for theorising consciousness the Apostles do not. Consciousness is necessarily concerned with the politics of privacy.

If representation of the world and its constructed nature are at issue, it is to be expected that theories of language will be, as they are, critically important to both the Fox and Apostles formations. Again, the difference between them is congruent with differences in politics and epistemology. For the Fox formation language is made by culture, for the Apostles it is given. J. S. Mill and Fox were interested in different kinds of language theory, but again, a clear Benthamite tradition emerges which emphasises the capacity of language to reorder and restructure experience. Mill's essays on poetry in the *Monthly Repository* owe some of their propositions on language and culture to Dugald Stewart. Stewart argued that language was a thoroughly artificial, culturally created system. Stewart pays great attention to the reordering capacities of syntax, when the 'normal' successive order of a sentence is disrupted. It is too easy to anticipate the end of a linear sentence. Poetic ordering of language disrupts expectations and makes possible a new grasp of structural relationships through syntax, as if the language is restructuring successive associative chains in order to give them a new shape and relationship. Language is a play with succession and simultaneity which can retrain experience.[32]

It is to Bentham himself that this group owed their most interesting theory of language, which developed out of Bentham's examinations of legal fictions, a theory of which Fox certainly knew, and which Browning seems to have absorbed.[33] For Bentham language is at once the greatest conjuror of illusion and the greatest social invention. Language for Bentham is made rather than given, since it creates 'fictions', that is words, such as 'soul', for which there is no corresponding entity in reality.[34] The status of these constructs is logically puzzling. On the one hand we anchor them by treating them as if they represent what is 'real' and thus human invention genuinely impinges on and transforms social experience. On the other hand they are conceptual phantasms and constantly threaten to become the distortions of solipsism. Linguistic fictions can be used, as in law, for the purpose of exploitation and oppression.

The Apostles avoid the epistemological insecurity of language by viewing meaning as a given through the continuity of history. It is equally a construct, but history is the bearer of truth, truth as historical evolution, through the independent workings of etymology and philology. Above all precision of language is necessary because it must be obedient to the etymological truth of history. Language, like myth, is a possession of the totality of a culture and not that of individuals.

Herder said that each culture's physiognomy showed in its speech and it is to him that Hallam probably owes a physiological theory of language. In his essay on Tennyson he insisted that the pure aural sign could be in itself the bearer of meaning through the sensations rather than ideas it evoked. It is as if he is working towards a language of pure feeling which is exempt from conceptual reference. It reaches down to the primordial flood of sensation which is at the basis of language. Herder had suggested that language and consciousness are born simultaneously when the primal mass is abstracted into categories, but Hallam remains with the delicate and complex organic filaments of sensation prior to consciousness, adopting the sophisticated primitivism characteristic of the Apostles.[35] It is always to the deep continuities and structures that the Apostles are attracted. Hence Grimm and Bopp attracted Kemble: through them the Indo-European roots of the English language became apparent.

Where gender and sexuality are concerned, critical to both formations, the same pattern of conceptualisation emerges. The Fox group questions the immutability of social arrangements and the fixed nature of gender. The Apostles start from the fixity of gender. Gender was crucial to the Fox group because it exposed a fundamentally oppressed group and repressive and authoritarian institutions. The campaign for political liber-ation and suffrage was intense – Fox and his peers were probably the first organised *group* of British feminists. Mill called women slaves, toys and property in an article which sees the status of women as culturally deter-mined and anticipates his essay *On the Subjection of Women* by twenty-five years.[36] Women and divinity, women and education, women and politics, are central preoccupations.[37] Fox not only published women writers (such as Harriet Martineau) and actively encouraged them but made sure that his male writers were feminists. Horne, for instance, attacked Hazlitt in an aside – 'It would appear . . . that he had never met . . . with any woman of superior intellect.'[38] These views were outrageous in the early 1830s. There is indeed an element of outrage in the campaign. The Saint-Simonians were embraced, Milton's treatises on divorce were espoused – indeed Mill recommended polygamy rather than prostitution – and Fox and Mill carried out the repudiation of marriage in their personal lives. Browning's elopement later is of a piece with this behaviour.

The Apostles, of course, were quite different but in their own way as subversive. Hallam celebrates women not because they can be played with but because they can *play*. Women are liberated into a complex life of sensation and the affections and, because they are not doomed to abstrac-tion and rationality, like men, are closer to the rich productive life of emotion and imagination. Both Herder and Schiller had seen women as privileged because they are close to the life of the non-rational. It follows that women are closer to the transforming mythic imagination. Hallam praised women's special consciousness in poem after poem. They 'prisoner take/Th'enmarvailed *sense*' (my emphasis). They 'change our being's mode' and 'break/In twain the bonds of custom'.[39] Tennyson's *Arabian Nights* gives him the remembered sensation of sucking sherbert, and by sense Hallam means the corporal physicality of eye, ear and mouth, the world to which women belonged.[40] Women are like the poet of sensation, subvers-ively attacking entrenched, habitual opinion by dissolving and re-forming associative patterns. Thus they are the real agents of cultural transform-ation through the imagination. They are at work in the semiotic code, as

36

Kristeva puts it. The conceptualisation of gender is neither as patronising nor as unsubtle as it might seem. And clearly, by asking for a poetry of sensation, Hallam was putting the feminisation of poetry – and men – at the centre of his project. At least the male appropriation of the feminine suggests an admiration for it.

Subsequent sections of this chapter will explore the intense dialogue between Tennyson and the post-Coleridgean formation and between Browning and the post-Benthamite formation and will expand and clarify the general positions marked out here. In some ways, Tennyson with Hallam, and Browning with Fox, posthumously debated the questions explored in the 1830s for the rest of their poetic lives – though it has to be remembered that they anticipated questions which began to circulate more generally only in the 1850s. It should already be clear that, however different, both groups were formulating an aesthetics commensurate with a 'modern' situation, with a culture which was post-teleological, post-technological, post-revolutionary and post-Kantian. Mill was right not to polarise the Coleridgean and Benthamite traditions. He saw even in 1838 that the Victorian episteme would be the history of the interpenetration and realignment of these formations in many and complex ways.

The two groups shared an intensely self-conscious cultural awareness. They saw the connections between literature and power and acknowledged that poetry was a cultural construction. The mythic poetics of the Tennyson group and the dramatic poetics of the Browning group diverged, as one moved to the past rather than the present, and to a seemingly depoliticised, universalising mode of writing rather than direct class awareness and political intervention. But both saw that the definition of consciousness was the key to the problem of agency and the labour of the self upon the world which was threatened in a mechanistic society and made problematical by incipient political upheaval. Both saw that the teleological world was passing over into an epistemological order where questions of representation were critical because a world of symbolic constructions could no longer be grounded in universal, permanently valid truths. The consequential realisation that language and theories of language must be a contested area in an era of movable type and the unstable sign is common to both groups. Both saw that the question of gender is crucial to their aesthetics.

Both formations move towards the double poem in different ways. The theory of the Browning group enables the poem to be staged as an expressive fiction or psychological moment which becomes critique when its dramatic nature emerges in the structure of the poem. Though Hallam silently appropriates and endorses Fox's dramatic theory in his review of Tennyson in 1831, and conflates this quite permissibly with the poetry of sensation which projects feeling on to objects, he reaches the double poem by his awareness of the existence of two consciousnesses in writing. The unself-conscious, simple and unreflective feeling of the naive poet he discovered in Schiller is being contrived by the highly self-conscious reflective poet of a sophisticated modern culture. The poetry of sensation is being created by the poetry of reflection by a ruse which returns the poem to a dramatic status.

Mill characterised the Benthamite formation by the externalising empirical question, 'Is it true?' and the Coleridgean formation by the inwardness which asks, 'What is the meaning of it?' It is arguable that he neutralises and effaces Bentham's radicalism in the cause of making him acceptable as an empirical codifier, but the two kinds of question do suggest how the double poem can be reached as it were from opposite ends. The literal, psychologised moment of a Browning poem begins with the question 'Is it true?' and ends by asking about the meaning of the poem's configuration of language. The arcane, symbolic mythopoeic Tennyson poem persuades an inwardness of reading which can gain entry into the text by asking 'What is the meaning of it?' and only later proceeds to the problematical question of truth. It may be that the friction between the two kinds of question is what brings the double poem into being. Foucault thinks of the post-Enlightenment sense of crisis, from which emerges a re-formation of knowledge, as the origin of a two-way epistemological fracture. The double fracture is the result of the problematical relation between consciousness or self and the 'mode of being of objects' or the world.[41] Knowledge which fragments into positivist empirical analysis a posteriori puts aside the status of consciousness just as synthesis a priori puts aside the status of the empirical: and both have problems with the nature of representation because both postpone an essential element in the representative process. Mill's different questions, 'Is it true?' and 'What is the meaning of it?', seem to correspond to the analysis a posteriori and the synthesis a priori. In these terms one could see the double poem as a product of problematical understandings of representation and epistemological fracture, both questioning and reproducing its problems in innumerable ways.

Certainly just as Mill speaks of the concentric circles of 'shock' given by two forms of thought one can think of the 'shock' created by the early poetry of Tennyson and Browning as rippling outwards into the century. Though both were coterie poets until the 1840s, both dominated the century. Tennyson's hold on intellectuals loosened in the 1860s after the watershed of the Crimean war, though his general popularity grew. Browning's appeal was restricted to intellectuals until the 1890s and spread to a wider group subsequently. Even while Tennyson seemed an old-fashioned and tedious writer to young poets, particularly after the publication of Edward Fitzgerald's version of *The Rubaiyat of Omar Khayyam* in 1859, the aesthetics of the Hallam group was reappropriated and reinterpreted in different ways by other groups almost until the end of the century. In fact, the poetics of the aestheticised politics of the Hallam circle is recognisable even when its principles are used against Tennyson himself, while the radical politicised aesthetics of the Fox circle disappears or becomes oddly assimilated to later manifestations of Hallam's poetics. Clough and Arnold divide uneasily over the question of politics and aesthetics. A new kind of compromised liberalism emerges from their conflict. In Swinburne a radical politics modulates into a transgressive individualism based on sensation. Morris normalises the poetry of sensation in his later poetry by assimilating it to a therapeutic aesthetics in direct opposition to the pathologising of sensation which appears in the poetry of Dante Gabriel Rossetti and in his own earlier and much more radical work. But Morris's early poetry is revolutionary in content and form, as he fuses the poetry of sensation with a new radical aesthetic derived from Ruskin. It is harder to see what is going on among women poets because they do not work within male traditions.

Benjamin's terms, aestheticised politics, and its opposite, politicised aesthetics, are convenient, but have to be adopted with caution because they refer to a different historical situation, that between the great wars of the twentieth century. He was not thinking of the early nineteenth-century context when he developed his terminology. It is as difficult to account for the staying power of Hallam's poetics as it is to explain the slow disappearance of the radical tradition. The subversive conservatism of the Hallam group was not fascist in the sense that Benjamin understood it. It was a contradictory collection of ideas. It held to an idealised cultural unity at the same time as it explored private political subversion through the shock of sensation. It took the form of conservative anarchy, understanding all representation as trope, the constant change of an ungrounded flux of new representation, even while it held to the organic continuities of history and myth which could somehow hold new representations in check. Its strength was its understanding of the power of myth, the imaginative hold of myth and its permanent possibility of reinterpretation. This was the very thing the Fox group foundered on. It tended to literalise poetry as psychological experience. While it asked fundamental questions – what is a truly political and democratic poetry when it is not the simple replication of political principles? – with a seriousness unknown to the Apostles, it failed to address the question of representation as fully as the Apostles. Only Browning found a way, through Bentham, of engaging with the strenuous imaginative exercise of constructing ideological fictions. But fictions, though perhaps capable of a more radical critique than myth, are historically specific and possibly more vulnerable, requiring an immediate grasp of detail and reference not intrinsic to myth. Add to this the capacity of fictions to create an infinite regression of hermeneutic activity in which a sophisticated consciousness grasps poetic materials as constructions along with its own response to them, and it is possible to see why fictions lack the reproducible solidity and substance of myth. This may be one of the reasons why a great, radical experiment did not find successors. The concern of this chapter, however, is with the early formations in which neither the subsequent decadence of aestheticised politics nor the decline of politicised aesthetics was apparent. It is concerned with a phase of intense experiment and innovation. Chapters 2 and 3 consider Tennyson's early work and his dialogue with Hallam and other contemporary poets. Chapters 4 and 5 discuss Browning's early work and his dialogue with Fox and the poets round the *Monthly Repository*.

2

EXPERIMENTS OF 1830

Tennyson and the
formation of subversive,
conservative poetry

Tennyson, winner of the Chancellor's Gold Medal with the prize poem, 'Timbuctoo', at Cambridge in 1829, was already the contributor to a volume of poems before he arrived there, *Poems by Two Brothers* (1827) – actually written by three brothers, for Frederick Tennyson contributed to the volume as well as Charles and Alfred – and the writer of some precocious juvenilia. It is *Poems, Chiefly Lyrical* (1830), however, which startles with its experiments, coming out of an intellectual environment arresting for the boldness and intensity of its enquiries and insouciant originality.

Poems, Chiefly Lyrical, ends with a Heraclitean lyric to impermanence, 'Οἱ ῥέοντες', which is well aware of the Pyrrhic victory of scepticism: 'All truth is change'.

> All thoughts, all creeds, all dreams are true,
>   All visions wild and strange;
> Man is the measure of all truth
>   Unto himself. All truth is change:
>
> $$(1–4)^1$$

If we have faith in what we 'dream', and if 'all things are as they seem to all' (7), if all experience is representation, then there can be 'Nor good nor ill, nor light nor shade,/Nor essence nor eternal laws' (10–11). The paradoxically firm certainties and negations of this scepticism may owe something to Goethe's Faust's celebration of life as dream and representation at the end of *Faust*, but the consequences of the paradox are understood in the laconic footnote: 'this very opinion is only true relatively to the flowing philosophers'.[2] The relativist position is itself subject to the relativist principle. The 'true' sceptic must accept that his own position can be undermined by relativism itself. The poem's placing at the end of the volume throws the contents of the book retrospectively into flux and makes its explorations provisional. It makes each poem an experiment in those discontinuous moments of consciousness which, Hallam was to insist, were the self.

The 'flowing' philosophers were being redefined in terms of the new physics, astronomy and geology at Cambridge. William Whewell, Master of Trinity when Tennyson was at Cambridge, and whose speculations he would have known, was deeply involved in theorising astronomy in terms of flux. He opened up a world in which the stability of the universe could not be guaranteed. The poem is part of this new discourse. Whewell was to write later in volume III of the Bridgewater Treatises (*On Astronomy and General Physics*, 1833):

> The fact really is, that changes are taking place in the motions of the heavenly bodies, which have gone on progressively from the first dawn of science. . . . The moon has been moving quicker and quicker from the time of the first recorded eclipses, and is now in advance, by about four times her own breadth, of what her place would have been if it had not been affected by this acceleration. . . . Will these changes go on without limit or reaction?[3]

It is an odd position, because the Bridgewater Treatises were endowed to consolidate natural theology by bringing in the weight of new scientific discovery to endorse it. Whewell makes it clear that the nature of the physical world does not guarantee the positions of natural theology, which sees evidences of God in the natural world. He rests on revealed religion. The importance of this to Tennyson's early work is not simply that his poems constitute a rejection of natural theology or even that they assent to a permanently destabilised universe. First, the world is a strange, *un*natural, not 'natural' place, properly a place of 'visions wild and strange'. Secondly, a condition of change without limit makes all experience the materials of retrospection. In particular we are trapped into a series of questions about origins which are forever displacing one another. This produces, as Whewell realised, a continual state of backwards questions as the consciousness is forced to 'pursue this train of enquiries unremittingly'; necessarily every question becomes secondary and subject to instability by the nature of the 'acceleration' of change the moment they are being asked.[4] Experience must always be a series of backwards questions about one place *from another place*, an alternative place which is never the place where one 'would have been' because, like the moon, we are in motion. The strangeness of Tennyson's early poems, one's sense of their being written from another place or an alternative space, their quality of secondariness, comes from this experientially retrospective world. Such a world calls into question not only the coherence of consciousness but the possibility of what Whewell called 'free volition'.[5] How far is 'free volition' rather than material necessity a possibility in this universe? The question applies to both God and man.

Already the possibility of the double poem is available in this retrospective mode, where experience can only grasp experience by positing a prior consciousness which is under analysis by a subsequent state. It is only by turning this scepticism on its head and making it the condition of knowledge that one can return, though perilously, to an understanding of volition and continuity, the continuity of a history of reconstruction. That Tennyson can shift such philosophical weight with the agile movement of a light, graceful lyric is evidence of his confidence at this time. The poem exhibits the confidence of the Apostles. At the forefront of new thinking, it is a confidence which is always paradoxical, dismantling traditional positions whether on politics, theology or aesthetics with an exhilarating iconoclasm and yet endorsing those traditional positions with a new, iconoclastic traditionalism. The deftness of 'Οἱ ῥέοντες' goes some way to explaining why these early poems, so slight, perhaps, in comparison with *In Memoriam* or *Maud*, should have seemed remarkable in 1830, producing readings which struggle with one another. These poems, with their highly wrought artifice of simplicity, are like fragile-looking objects which weigh unexpectedly heavy in the hand. *Poems, Chiefly Lyrical* has to be seen as a maverick collection, as wayward and experimental as any avant-garde twentieth-century poetic experiment.

The innovative nature of the 1830 poems can best be grasped by seeing what kind of work was acceptable as poetry at the time as a preliminary to a discussion of *Poems, Chiefly Lyrical*. To do this I shall consider one of the popular album books which Tennyson professed to despise, though he wrote for them. My theme is Tennyson's gradual retreat from the daring of the earliest poems as he realised the implications of these texts in subsequent work published in 1832 and 1842. The decadence of the poetry of sensation manifested not only in his work but in that of his group posed serious problems for an aesthetic of subversive conservatism. The search for new solutions is apparent towards the end of what we think of as the first phase of Tennyson's work up to 1842. He was tempted towards the more reactionary strain of Tory poetry which was current when he began writing and this tradition is also discussed. But Tennyson never fully conceded to it.

'Three summers back . . . I swore an oath, that I would never again have to do with their vapid books', Tennyson wrote in 1836.[6] The 'vapid' books were the popular annual album collections of poetry and prose which represented themselves as anthologies of polite literature, appealing productions for a literary public anxious to be acquainted with current literature. Tennyson had contributed poems both to *The Gem* and to *Friendship's Offering*. A look at some of the contributions alongside his in

Friendship's Offering for 1832 immediately suggests why the poems of 1830 were so striking.

Actually, the individual poems reproduced in this anthology are less suspect than the indiscriminate and incoherent eclecticism of the collection, which is a mixture of poems and tales. It is a mélange of poems of every style, and, interestingly, by poets from widely differing social classes. It contains poems by John Clare ('The Thrush's Nest'), the rural poet thought of as a peasant writer, by the gentleman-poet Barry Cornwall ('For Music') and by Allan Cunningham, the stonemason poet from Dumfries, whose poem is a vigorous Burns-like Scots vernacular song, 'The Poets Love. A Song', whose last stanza ends, 'I'm drunk with her love'. Cornwall and Cunningham were recommended as models to Tennyson in 1832 by John Wilson ('Christopher North') in his banteringly hostile review of *Poems*, 1830.[7] The collection ranges from a Keatsian pastiche by Thomas Pringle, 'A Dream of Fairy Land', which transforms the Keatsian dream into an un-Keatsian moral allegory about the struggle between the 'deluded' 'Senses' and 'Spirit', to a lyric by the Hon. Mrs Norton, 'There is no Trace of Thee around'.[8] Turning strongly and violently on itself with 'I *know* thou hast been here:/I know thou hast, though nought remains', after beginning with a description of loss, simply generalised through landscape, Norton's lyric owes something to the formulaic quality of ballad writing:

> There is no trace of thee around,
> Beloved! in this abode;
> The winds sweep o'er the silent ground
> Where once thy footsteps trode.
> There is no shadow in the glen –
> No echo on the hill –
> The sun that sets, shall rise again
> And find them lonely still!

Yet this strong lyric is jostled by 'vapid' lyrics such as Cornwall's 'For Music', and James Montgomery's 'The Lily'. 'Come again! Come again!/ Sunshine cometh after rain', Cornwall's lyric begins, with its faintly literary diction ('Called by many a vernal strain') and ends, 'Come again! O, come again!/Like the sunshine after rain'. Montgomery's poem is in praise of female innocence and virginity.

> Flower of light! forget thy birth,
> Daughter of the sordid earth
> Lift the beauty of thine eye
> To the blue etheral sky.

The girl whose name is Lily will be rewarded for virginity by a life in heaven.

So may she whose name I write,
Be herself a Flower of Light,
Live a life of innocence,
Die, – to be transported hence
To that Garden in the skies,
Where the Lily never dies.[9]

The model for most of the poems is the simple song; demotic or literary, or the didactic lyric.

Since Tennyson's elaborate, self-conscious simplicity was described by Wilson as 'distinguished silliness' – 'Alfred cuts a foolish figure' – and since it is clear that his offence for Wilson is among other offences to have celebrated the erotic, and to be classified as effeminate, it is as well to have an example of what was offered as conventional simplicity in the annuals before looking at Tennyson's work.[10] Turning to some of the lyrics of 1830, what makes them look 'silly' is both a contrived, highly literary, self-conscious lyricism and their presentation of this *as if* it is innocent. For the poems have no built-in account of their meaning, no indication as to why they exist. Arthur Hallam, who also privately circulated a volume, *Poems*, in 1830, a month before *Poems, Chiefly Lyrical* appeared in June, writes far more explicitly than Tennyson of sexuality, of feverish social upheaval, of theories of mind, of a redefined God, of scientific ideas, of theories of art and myth. In Tennyson's poems these are concealed and coded. The description of the *Poems* as 'Chiefly Lyrical' allies them with Wordsworth's *Lyrical Ballads*, which Hallam mentions in his review, and the epithet points silently to a tradition of subversive experiment. But these are not quite the lyrical ballads of Wordsworth's collection any more than they are like the songs and ballads of the albums. Wordsworth's work was viewed equivocally by Hallam, as we shall see, and the ballad was reinterpreted in a sophisticated and highly literary way. As the word 'lyrical' suggests, meaning is to be derived from song-like, seemingly spontaneous utterance, through the configuration of expressive form and language and through the sequence of narrative. Meaning is not explicit, but emerges through the temporal movement of the poem and the changing psychological relationships it makes. It is a poetry which can only be understood through the process of change itself. This procedure, as will shortly be explained, is the result of the aesthetic and cultural theory of the Apostles group and its distrust of reflective verse. But this is only a part of the explanation.

One problem for Tennyson is the bewildering number of Romantic models before him – Coleridge, Wordsworth, Keats, Shelley, Byron. There are traces of all these poets in the early work but they are not 'influences'. Rather a self-conscious critique is made of them. The 'silliness', the contrived and strangely inaccessible naiveté, is partly a way of circumventing imitation of prior Romantic models, but it is also a way of making strange the nature of the poetic act itself and revealing it as artifice. This in its turn makes for the 'visions wild and strange' which the 'flowing philosophers' endorse. It enables the poem to be an experiment with the experience which comes from another place, an experiment in alternative worlds and consciousnesses. The poet, 'in advance', as Whewell would say, of what his place would have been had it not been displaced by the acceleration of change, experiments with the strange disjunctions between one form of life and another. That is why the early poems not only take their materials from myths and legends but are about constituting myths and legends and their mysterious alienation. The inaccessible naiveté is a prerequisite for rendering the closedness of the past which the retrospective poet addresses with his backwards questions. The poem is at once expressive artefact and deeply analytical structure as it opens up a space between the alternative experience being constructed and the processes of its construction.

The twin poems, 'The Merman' and 'The Mermaid', which aroused Wilson's anger and Fox's enthusiasm, are arresting examples of Tennyson's arcane simplicity and simultaneous analytical interrogation. They both begin with identical questions in two-stress lines which cunningly combine frailty and strength. 'Who would be/A merman bold,/Sitting alone' (1–3). 'Who would be/A mermaid fair,/Singing alone' (1–3). It is a reversal of the conventions, for, as in John Leyden's 'The Mermaid', which Tennyson read in Scott's *Minstrelsy of the Scottish Border*, it is usually mermaids who seduce human beings, not humans who consider becoming mermen. 'In her dwelling, and in her appearance, the mermaid of the northern nations resembles the Syren of the ancients', the preliminary note to 'The Mermaid' runs in Scott's collection.[11] So the poem constructs an alternative myth of the northern 'Syren' and questions what this means by an extraordinary act of elision. The first sections are ambiguously seductive invitations by mermen and mermaids, and at the same time they can be read as possibly human questions by gendered men and women. Who *would* be a merman or maid? In each case the questions have a different meaning. They are like two sides of a dialogue conducted simultaneously in the same words. Not only does the nature of volition, the meaning of 'would', change according to the human or non-human status of the speaker but if the questions are asked by mermen, they become the seductive invitations of another species who understand 'would' as unproblematical desire. If they are asked by human beings they are speculations on identity and difference, likeness and unlikeness, and 'would' carries the cautious self-interrogation of the subjunctive and speaks of volition and the will.

W. J. Fox is right when he sees the poems, acutely, as about 'the principle of thought injected by a strong volition', the impossibly self-conscious human will to imagine and be the life of another species.[12] John Wilson is equally right and acute when he complains of the flagrant sexuality of subaqueous life – 'Her mother ought to keep a sharp lookout upon her', for 'she is of an amorous temperament, and a strong Anti-Malthusian'.[13] Interestingly, when showing that the principles of deduction and perception will be different according to the place where the perceiver is, Lyell chooses to exemplify the completely coherent but completely provisional conclusions and categories of the perceiver by positing the perceptions of some 'dusky melancholy sprite', 'like Umbriel', a being 'entirely confined to the nether world', unable to 'emerge into the regions of water and of air; and if this being should busy himself in investigating the structure of the globe, he might frame theories the exact converse of those usually adopted by human philosophers'.[14] *The Principles of Geology* and Tennyson's mer-poems were published in the same year. Both fantastically propose an alternative world, in the order of science fiction, where 'theories' of life differ from those of the upper world, though Tennyson's beings have emerged into the ambiguous 'regions of water'. Both explore the implications of consciousness in another place.

Unlike Leyden's unwilling human lover who says, 'That heart, that riots wild and free,/Can hold no sympathy with mine',[15] if you 'would' be a merman in Tennyson's poem you would be given over to the sheer liberation of sexual frolic and pursuit, a pure principle of male 'power' – 'I would fill the sea-halls with a voice of power' (10). The freedom of the non-human Ariel in *The Tempest*, which echoes in the refrain 'Merrily, merrily' is a freedom defined through sexuality. There is a reminiscence of Shelley's *Prometheus Unbound* in 'The Mermaid', but both the paired poems invoke the landscape of freedom in Shelley's poem which can emerge when one kind of 'will', the will to tyranny, power and political despotism, has been abandoned.[16] 'Blue Proteus and his humid nymphs' will no longer track the path of human ships 'by blood and groans,/And desolation, and the mingled voice/Of slavery and command' (*Prometheus Unbound*, III. ii. 29–30). The poems are rather like the cosmological frolic of freedom in Act IV of *Prometheus* in their metrical virtuosity. The leaps and chases, the skirmishes with precious stones, 'Turkis and agate and almondine' (32) which are simply innocent ammunition here, not luxury articles, take place in a world free of any economy but the pleasure principle. Tennyson may have remembered the rather sinister story prefacing Leyden's 'The Mermaid' in which an explorer in a diving-bell unsuccessfully tries to seize the precious stones in a merman's palace.[17]

Interestingly, the mermaid's negotiations with sexuality are rather different from that of the merman. The mermaid is confronted with a sea snake who approaches and surrounds her hall, but she masters its phallic power with her song. The power of her song transforms events, extinguishing the immortality of the mermen who 'Die in their hearts for the love of me' (30). W. D. Paden, whose book on Tennyson's use of contemporary writings on mythology is one of the lasting works on Tennyson's poetry, points out that true human love extinguishes the immortality of a merman.[18] He is uncertain of the status of the serpent, but thinks of it elsewhere as an ambiguous principle of evil and good capable of perpetual self-renewal, as described in Faber's religious mythologising, which Tennyson knew. In Leyden's poem, the mermaids are exhorted to 'chain' a huge and evil sea monster, but here it seems that the mermaid's power can persuade the monster's ambiguous nature to metamorphose into love. So far, so Shelleyan, but, like the ambiguous serpent, this poem has a slippery double nature. In the mermaid's exultant subaqueous world subservient sexual roles are reversed as she cavorts among 'diamond-ledges', as she selects her lover-king, and as she attracts with her power the concentrated gaze of all the beings of the watery universe. Their united gaze seems to define her being as serpent and sea creatures are 'coiled' and curl peaceably round her: 'All things that are forkèd, and hornèd, and soft. . . ./All looking down for the love of me' (53, 55). The last lines are an erotic and blasphemous adaptation of the liturgy – 'All things . . . praise Him'. The adoration of the universe is deflected from God and His being to the mermaid. The mermaid's fierce predatory energies are no more relevant to the ethical or to the divine than Blake's proverbs of Hell in which 'Exuberance is Beauty'.[19] As such, her sexual energies are celebrated. But to see what the poem is doing beyond this one has to remember Fox's realisation that the mermen and maids are imagined by a human being. Just as the worthless sea diamonds would become negotiable, as riches in the human world, so the mermaid's powers would be transformed by being subject to human categories, among them, possibly, the moral. The poem is nothing like so simple as a plain opposition between the 'non-moral' sea world and the human world which is subject to moral categories. That the diamonds would be barter in the human world might suggest human corruption, even though human sexual morality would curb the arrant libido of the sea world. But 'economic' morality begins to make the curbing of sexual energy suspect. 'Human' categories are morally ambiguous and doubtful in comparison with the sea world's single principles of sensuous delight and power. The ambiguous nature of the sea serpent is an ever present threat to the human world. It can be quelled by the mermaid, but it does not seem possible for *human* beings to achieve this. In Leyden's poem the speaker depends upon the mermaids to defeat the sea serpent.

The 'reading' and foraging of mermaid/mermen stories seems to be a latecomer to the study of legend, a 'modern' early nineteenth-century phenomenon. Grimm's amorous water world, which Tennyson would have known from T. C. Croker's *Fairy Legends*, Leyden's latter-day ballad, these are readings of the strange-seeming, deceptively semi-human world of the mermaid by sophisticated minds aware of the secondariness of their myth-making.[20] The deceptive similarities between sea and human world put the categories of the human world in doubt at the same time as they open up a longing for an alternative 'human' paradigm. It is the 'half-ness' of the mermaid world which fascinates, its parallels and not-parallels with human categories. Tennyson's paired poems incorporate this self-consciousness. His 'readers' of the mermen and mermaids are post-Shelleyan, self-conscious 'modern' readers, latecomers to the world of legend. In a characteristically overt poem, 'Written on the Banks of the Tay', Hallam recognises this self-consciousness when he describes a child at play, and revises the Romantic acceptance of the immediacy of the child's feeling. Though 'childhood seems the only leech/For all the heart-aches of a rough world caught', nevertheless self-consciousness must be concurrent with delight in the naive. 'We wish to be a twofold thing,/And keep our present self to watch within!'[21] Modern, 'two-fold' poetry, Hallam said in his review of *Poems, Chiefly Lyrical*, can no longer deal with the '*usual*', simple sympathies and affections because it is no longer simple itself, and precisely disturbs the habitual associations of convention.[22] This is what these poems seem to be doing. To be jolted self-consciously into imagining the libido of a mermaid is to be jolted from a number of habitual associations. One of these is the nature of sexual relationships and gender itself. These poems are each (at one level) the imagining of a man and a woman and yet they are not in neat opposition. The mermaid pursued by the mermen in the first poem is precisely not the mermaid who speaks in the second, any more than the sea king she chooses is from among those mermen 'laughing' in sexual play in the first poem. Each poem is slightly misaligned with the other. The relationship of opposition between the genders is not quite the same in each poem, and this allows for a shift of play in the categories of male and female which in turn shifts accustomed concepts of opposition.

As the interacting sets of misprisions between the subaqueous world and the human world accumulate, the complexity and ambitiousness of Tennyson's project in the early poems becomes apparent. Put in the words of the last poem in his volume it was to construct and experiment with the myth of a universe where 'all things are as they seem to all', where good and ill and eternal laws are provisional. This, in the context of a society which seemed on the verge of revolution and lawlessness, is an urgent project. It is 'The Kraken' which illuminates the project most, but it can best be reached through 'Mariana' and the account of feminine sexuality being explored by Hallam.

Many of Arthur Hallam's poems are in praise of women, as are the poems which begin the sequence of *Poems* (1830) – 'Claribel', 'Lilian', 'Isabel' and later 'Mariana' and 'Adeline'. Hallam's praise is adventurous and belongs to a new attempt to redefine the importance of women in a culture. He celebrates women because they are nearer to the life of the affections and the senses, because, less amenable to the power of reflection than men, they can *play*. It is a back-handed kind of feminism to praise women, as did Schiller and Herder, because they are nearer to the primitive sources of feeling, but the rationale is nevertheless sophisticated. Play, Hallam writes, in 'A Farewell to the South', makes women strong.

Dante's Beatrice awakened transforming powers and transformed the life of a whole nation.[23] Play carries with it the emancipation from reason and the constraints of the law. Women can transcend the fixity and restriction not only of man-made laws but of the natural laws which bind possibility. It is a large claim. 'Nothing is law to thee', Hallam wrote, in an early sonnet, 'On the Madonna Del Gran Duca'. The Madonna is free because she sees 'right' through her capacity for 'intellectual beauty' (an allusion to Shelley) without being bound by external laws.[24]

Tennyson's 'Mariana' is not so straightforward as this. It portrays a woman cut off from sense and from the external world and precisely subject to the law, the sexual laws of men, even though her obsessive grief seems to confound the law of temporality by returning her continually to the same emotion. It is an exploration of damaged feminine sexuality restricted to the repetition of a single feeling. It is the reverse of a world where 'All truth is change' and perhaps the negation of change strangely converts the sceptic's principles into assurance. For where there is no change, madness is incipient because all things are the same.

> The sparrow's chirrup on the roof,
>   The slow clock ticking, and the sound
> Which to the wooing wind aloof
>   The poplar made, did all confound
> Her sense;
>
>   (73–7)

The meaning of '*confound*/Her sense' here is that the senses were both appalled and that they were *confused* one with another. As the clock ticks concurrently with the sparrow's chirrup and as the aloof poplar responds to wooing wind, the vowel sounds describing each object become 'confounded'. Experience is no longer distinct. The reference is to the Mariana of Shakespeare's *Measure for Measure*, who is deserted by Angelo, though ultimately married off to him. The epigraph hints at an ambiguous sexual reference, since Mariana is a sexual substitute for Isabella in a by no means morally straightforward situation. The reference hints at the violence of a condition in which women are used as mere substitutes. The reference is also to another much more ambiguous context, to the Mariana who is the actress–courtesan of Goethe's *Wilhelm Meister*. Behind the poem is a coded reference to a double standard of sexual mores. Pregnant, and deserted by Wilhelm as the result of a misunderstanding, Mariana writes a series of letters before she dies in childbirth to which the words of Tennyson's refrain run parallel.[25]

> She only said, 'My life is dreary,
>   He cometh not,' she said;
> She said, 'I am aweary, aweary,
>   I would that I were dead!'
>
> (69–72)

This parallel allies the poem with the obsessive 'O misery!' uttered by Wordsworth's Martha in 'The Thorn', another seemingly betrayed and isolated woman for whom repetition becomes a principle of existence. A fixed idea without evolution, repetition without progression; this is not the Wordsworthian repetition engendered by a condition of energy and intensity. It is as if the energy required to sustain the repetition of the death wish creates a disjunction between the speaker and what is observed. The refrain becomes more and more a non-sequitur, more and more cut off from a relation between things in the external world as it ceases to be a response to the external world and becomes a response to itself.

The disjunction replicates the way in which Mariana's circumstances have forced her into isolation. She falls victim to a habit-forming, addictive, self-perpetuating associative pattern. The social world becomes a phantasm, just as circumstances have withdrawn it from her. She is 'without hope of change' (29). However (stanza iii), time *is* changing the landscape. The latch clinks, bats flit, night fowl crow, the poplar's shadow moves across her bed. But these things are simply assimilated into the principle of grief. Everything is mismatched. The ultimate recognition of temporality and change brings the finality of despair. As the refrain changes from 'He cometh not' to 'He *will* not come . . ./O God, that I were dead!' (82, 84) (my emphasis), the present tense moves to the future tense with a finely punning certitude. 'Will' has the force of a prediction at the same time as indicating the difference between Mariana's lack of volition and the lover's freedom – for he can *choose* not to meet her.

In his review of the 1830 *Poems* Hallam claims Tennyson as a poet of sensation rather than of reflection, arguing that 'the energetic principle of love for the beautiful' controls and educates the perceptions into 'That delicate sense of fitness' which saves the life of the senses from corrupting into sensuality.[26] Here, in 'Mariana', the senses have been atrophied and the energetic principle stopped up as absence forces desire to produce itself over and over again. Does repetition remain the same, the poem seems to ask, or does it move experience on? Is the cyclical change from night to day another form of repetition, or is it change? Change and the nature of volition become critical questions when psychological conditions are elided with political concerns, and the problem of revolutionary change comes to the fore. What revolutionary change is, how it comes about and what its consequences are is one of the subliminal themes of the 1830 volume, as the poems consider the areas of experience outside the control of 'free volition', and whether or not it is subject to 'laws'.

Hallam, though it was he who seems to have adamantly theorised a radically non-reflective poetry, is a far more overtly reflective writer than Tennyson, and the Apostles' concerns, particularly about revolution, can be seen more overtly in his work. He writes, true to his theoretical principles, that his senses 'swim/In a keen madness of delight', but his own work is not the poetry of immediate sensation.[27] His 'Timbuctoo', submitted at the same time as Tennyson's prize poem, is packed with philosophical references to the nature of mind ('Palaces and pleasure domes', 'matter of strange thought'), to Shelley (in particular the veiled maid of *Alastor*), to Coleridge and to Wordsworth, and quotes 'Tintern Abbey', 'the affections gently lead us on'.[28] Indeed, the allusions to earlier Romantic poets are scarcely assimilated in this poem about the destruction of tyranny and the disappearance of slavery, which can be defeated by the powers of mind.

But Hallam was not always so optimistic. In a sonnet to Tennyson, which seems to have been written in May 1831, Hallam writes explicitly of the powers of love, which can be destroyed by political tyranny, social upheaval and revolution. Love, and 'love-born joy',

> Grows fevered in the world's unholy strife,
> And sinks destroyed by that it would destroy!
> Beloved, from the boisterous deeds that fill
> The measure up of this unquiet time,
> The dull monotonies of Faction's chime
> And irrepressible thoughts, foreboding ill,
> I turn to thee, as is a heaven apart.... [29]

This account of a 'fevered', 'unquiet time', is not a set of poetical tropes, any more, perhaps, than the model of Shakespeare's homosexual sonnets is unimportant. The previous summer, just after the publication of *Poems, Chiefly Lyrical*, Hallam and Tennyson had taken part in the disastrous attempt to make contact with the Spanish rebel, Ojeda, in which Trench, Kemble, Sterling and Sterling's cousin, Robert Boyd, were also involved. Boyd's death in Spain, and appalling troubles at home, are behind this sonnet. The letter quoted earlier, which Hallam wrote to Trench in December 1830, while Trench was still in Gibraltar, and deeply involved in the Spanish expedition, expresses his profound fear of revolution, as we have seen, as the Captain Swing riots reddened the skies over Cambridge. Revolution seemed imminent and inevitable in a country economically and socially disordered, part of a chain of revolutions in Europe. The Apostles helped to defend Cambridge against the rick-burning Captain Swing rioters. They were aware of the contradictions of a conservative position which they conceived of as revolutionary, but which was against revolution in fact and against legislation for change. This ideological paradox is well

expressed in the light verses written by Henry Lushington and George
Venables, 'Swing, at Cambridge', where the writers see themselves as both
conservative and radical.

> And, yet I know we did not scorn
> The hungry multitude;
> Or hate them, that their evil chance,
> Of want and woe and ignorance,
> Had made them fierce and rude.
>
> But doubtful in our dazzling prime,
> We watched the struggle of the time,
> The war of new and old;
> We loved the past with Tory love
> Yet more than Radicals we strove
> For coming years of gold.[30]

What non-revolutionary transformation meant to this group will be seen
later, but one poem in particular is concerned with change: Tennyson's
'The Kraken' makes no overt reference to 'feverish times', but it can be
read as a political poem which codes revolutionary references by assimilating them into myth. It discloses an uneasy, riven, political experience. The
Kraken rises like the return of the repressed in a cataclysmic death. But
it is not clear whether it belongs to the inert forces of reaction or the
mindless violence of revolutionary action. It is not clear whether it is a
poem of Shelleyan liberation, or Christian apocalypse, or pagan transformation, or the doomed violence of political upheaval. Some of these readings
are compatible, aligning themselves either with positive transformations or
with ultimate destruction, but the negative and positive readings are in
opposition. Here the double poem falls apart. And yet these oppositions
are subsumed by a further problem. The status and possibility of volition
in events is crucial to the poem, as the Kraken's mindless, inert existence
is swayed by the movement of its environment, the sea.

The Kraken

> Below the thunders of the upper deep;
> Far, far beneath in the abysmal sea,
> His ancient, dreamless, uninvaded sleep
> The Kraken sleepeth: faintest sunlights flee
> About his shadowy sides: above him swell
> Huge sponges of millenial growth and height;
> And far away into the sickly light,
> From many a wondrous grot and secret cell

53

Unnumbered and enormous polypi
Winnow with giant arms the slumbering green.
There hath he lain for ages and will lie
Battening upon huge seaworms in his sleep,
Until the latter fire shall heat the deep;
Then once by man and angels to be seen,
In roaring he shall rise and on the surface die.

Using, as in the mermen and mermaid poems, the undersea world as a curious misaligned analogue of the upper world, the poem reaches towards the post-revolutionary liberation of Shelley's *Prometheus Unbound*. 'Battening upon huge seaworms in his sleep' (12), the Kraken's environment resembles the haunts of the Genii whom Demogorgon awakes from 'Oblivion', from their dwelling in the zones of man's mind, in heaven and in inert matter – 'the dull weed some sea-worm battens on' (*Prometheus Unbound*, IV. 542). A Shelleyan reading would endorse the destruction of the Kraken if we assume that the mythical being is a principle of mindless repression. Instinctively feeding in its 'dreamless' (3) sleep, without the psychic experience even of the unconscious, the Kraken approaches almost to the condition of mindless, organic matter as it gluts itself on its prey in a relationship which confirms a biological hierarchy of predator and preyed upon. Its feeding makes it monstrously just post-foetal and yet it is an 'ancient' (3) and primal creature. It must be logically unaware of all action, including its own, and all vision. It is oblivious of the 'faintest sunlights', the refracted lights which 'flee' over its body (4). It is unaware of the swollen sponges and polypi which seem to be impeded in movement by their own hugeness in the retarding medium of the water, like moon-walkers. Indeed, the energy of these undersea things is vicarious, endowed by the movement of the sea. But the sea is itself 'slumbering' (10). It too is inert, at the mercy of other forces, as it enables the giant arms of the polypi to 'winnow' (10) it.

It is these interacting, but massively inert and unconscious forces which also contaminate the alternative and contradictory readings of the poem. 'The Kraken' is a pre-eminent example of Tennyson's way of setting up competing propositions within a single framework. It is in the tradition of Coleridge's early prophetic poetry such as 'Religious Musings' or 'The Destiny of Nations'. Like Coleridge, Tennyson, with his combined reading of Nordic legend and of Sir William Jones's account of the myths of the Orient (which were thought to be the legends of the earliest beginnings of civilisation), conflates and reconfigures legend to provide symbols of catastrophic change. But there are several mythic propositions in 'The Kraken'. One is the post-Christian Shelleyan reading. Allied with it is a reading which embodies the pagan structures of G. S. Faber's religious mythologising which are parallel with Christian myth but deviate from it.

W. D. Paden suggests that the sea snake is Faber's evil principle which belongs to the dissolutions incorporated in the *mystae* but which is a dissolution denoting transformation.[31] Another and opposite reading is apocalyptic and Christian, the cosmic theological discourse of Revelation, the purgative destruction of the world: 'a great mountain burning, with fire was cast into the sea. . . . And a third part of the creatures which were in the sea and had life, died'. Rather than being about transformation, the Christian reading is about *endings*. This is allied with another reading directly associated with the horror of political revolution rather than its liberation. The primitive folk mythology quoted in Scott's *Minstrelsy of the Scottish Border* associates the Kraken unequivocally with revolution.

> They, who, in works of navigation, on the coasts of Norway, employ themselves in fishing or merchandize, do all agree in this strange story, that there is a serpent there, which is of a vast magnitude, namely two hundred feet long, and moreover twenty feet thick . . . which will go alone from his holes, in a clear night in summer, and devours calves, lambs, and hogs, or else he goes into the sea to feed on polypus, locusts and all sorts of sea-crabs. This snake disquiets the skippers, and he puts up his head on high, like a pillar, and catcheth away men, and he devours them; '*and this hapneth not but it signifies some wonderful change of the Kingdom near at hand; namely, that the princes shall die, or be banished; or some tumultous wars shall presentlie follow*'.[32]

The presence of multiple and conflicting mythologies here makes the point that 'mythic' reading is by its nature multiple. This is recognised in 'Supposed Confessions of a Second-Rate Sensitive Mind', a poem which owes its title to a phrase from Goethe's *Wilhelm Meister*.[33] There the speaker talks of the multiple choice of creed that has been made available in modern society. He wonders whether he will 'compare/All creeds till we have found the one,/If one there be?' (175–6). Because mythic forms are reinterpreted afresh in different historical situations, no permanent reading is possible. New myths and new readings of myth are constantly evolved. The 'latter fire' presages the fires of Madingley which Hallam saw as the beginnings of revolution, but there are contradictory readings of the event in the poem. It cannot be read syncretically as the myths are *not* parallel. It is Promethean freedom, *or* it is Christian judgement, *or* it is evil capable of transformation, *or* it is the sheer sick horror of fatalistic legend which sees revolution deterministically. It can be each of these representations but it cannot be all at once. Just as the poem is not quite a sonnet, they do not match.

But Tennyson does not leave all these meanings in play with a ludic conservative-anarchistic reading of the horror of all political change. The poem insists on the inert, unconscious life of the Kraken, whichever of the readings may be preferable as available myths of revolution. It is the living example of oblivion because its actions occur without volition. According to which of the myths are activated, utopian or conservative, the Kraken is the principle of transformation, of mindless destruction, or evil, or the helpless victim of external forces. But in each case inertia which does not know it is inertia is the dangerous element. The massive inertia which can only resist movement and change is the Kraken's being. The upheaval of death can only be seen 'once' because the world is destroyed by it, and this must be the end of all myth. Kraken-like, myths carry meaning but do not know their own meanings until reinterpretation makes new meaning possible. This is why the connection of myth and politics is so close in the nineteenth century. For once the notion of reinterpretable myth is established, the concept of ideology becomes possible. Ideology carries the principle of oblivion and inertia with it because it cannot be 'seen' as representation unless it is destroyed. When it is seen *as* ideology, its power is weakened. Some impossible cataclysm as the agent of destruction or a traumatic defamiliarisation can destroy ideology. The poem seems to be pessimistically exploring the conditions under which myth and ideology are destroyed and remade. And so the poem is deeply concerned with exploring the sources of action. Whether the Kraken belongs to the inert forces of reaction or is the mindless violence of repressed energy are interpretations which must involve ideological choice. The full nature of an ideology, and its consequences can never be known, but the conditions of ideological conflict *can* be imagined, the millennial horror of the Kraken's death.

This peculiarly radical conservatism, which dreads change and sees its necessity, even the necessity of violence, makes these early poems both evasive and subversively bold. Each characteristic seems to be a condition of the other. The poems are not written out of conflict so much as a self-conscious, secondary knowledge of the nature of conflict. Ultimately the contradictory accounts of revolution are all representations and cannot be validated because, as the last poem in the volume has it, 'all dreams are true'. Nevertheless, all dreams struggle against one another because all assert different truths and it is possible to conceptualise and analyse conflict. This seems to be the work of the latter-day, secondary poet who is at least in possession of the capacity to ask the backwards questions envisaged by Whewell. The paired poems 'Nothing will die' and 'All things will die' can suitably end this discussion of the 1830 poems because they embody Tennyson's method of turning ontological statements, naive statements in the sense that they are expressed with unsceptical certitude, into conflicting myths. In these poems it is not the conflict so much as the analysis of the grounds of conflict which is at issue. Together they turn on the conceptualisation of what appears to human consciousness as one of the 'eternal laws', which are cast in doubt by '*Οἱ ῥέοντες*', death. But even what death is turns out to be problematic.

Like 'The Merman' and 'The Mermaid', these two poems depend on a mismatching of relationships. 'Nothing will die' begins by asking when the flow of life and the beating heart will cease. 'All things will die' begins by affirming the continuing life of river, wind and cloud. It seems that each poem ought to be asking the other's questions or making each other's statements.

> When will the stream be aweary of flowing
> > Under my eye?
> > > ('Nothing will die', 1–2)

> Clearly the blue river chimes in its flowing
> > Under my eye;
> > > ('All things will die', 1–2)

'Nothing will die' goes on to challenge a pessimistic account of the universe, but in doing so incorporates the new discourses of astronomy and geology which can only refute the case, for they envisage a godless universe.

> Nothing will die;
> All things will change
> Through eternity.
> 'Tis the world's winter;
> Autumn and summer
> Are gone long ago;
> Earth is dry to the centre,
> But spring, a new comer,
> A spring rich and strange,
> Shall make the winds blow
> Round and round, . . .
> > (14–24)

The simple, carefree, song is a versification of new geological theory. In a later letter Tennyson refers punningly to the great 'Geological winter' proposed by Charles Lyell in the first volume of his *Principles of Geology*. It seems that he knew of these speculations before Lyell's book appeared in 1830. There Lyell speculates on a series of hypotheses concerning climatic change which transforms the surface of the earth and annihilates species. He considers the climatic conditions 'which different combinations of geological circumstances may produce'. He will 'first consider the conditions necessary for bringing about the extreme of cold, or what may be called the winter of the "great year", or geological cycle, and afterwards, the conditions requisite for producing the maximum of heat, or the summer of the same year'.[34] These are the changes Tennyson expresses as 'the world's winter' which dries earth to the core, succeeded by the new geological spring. The world of transformation in *The Tempest* which is hinted in Ariel's song of sea change, and produced what is 'rich and strange', comes into being with the great geological cycle. The vast continuities of the geological world 'change, but it will not fade' (31), a further quotation from Ariel through Shelley.[35] But such optimism logically brings in its train a world in which neither of the conditions of life expressed in the creed are important. 'The world was never made. . . . Nothing was born'. For the creed the son was 'begotten' and the world 'made' or created by God. But not in this poem, as it carelessly tosses the vocabularies of Christian and scientific ontologies.

'All things will die' is not the opposite of 'nothing will die'. For 'death' becomes a question of representation. It is the conceptualisation of the word 'die' which is at issue. In the first poem inorganic matter cannot 'die' as it is already 'dead'. It cannot therefore conceptualise 'death' and it displaces human death. In the second poem organic and conscious life can die and conceptualise death – 'The jaw is falling,/The red cheek paling' (31–2). It is, however, a condition of human death that it both *can* and *cannot* conceptualise 'eternity' – 'For even and morn/Ye will never see/ Through eternity' (44–6). To think of death as the other, the not-self, is both the guarantee of identity, which is created out of this opposition, and an impossible labour. Here Tennyson is playing with dialectic, playing in the strong sense that Hallam believes women can play, in order to deal with the impossible. He is in fact playing with the nature of laws and the limits they impose on consciousness. But the laws appear to be constructed by the human mind, whether they are Christian or geological. It is an attempt, not to 'prove' anything about death but to show how the struggle to invest the idea of death with a different content comes about.

A new conservatism which deconstructs and preserves myth simultaneously, which is prepared to consider rival Christian and scientific ontologies as constructs, which enquires into utopian and reactionary myths of violence and repression, which explores the erotic impulse and the ambiguous nature of libido and the will in different environments, which is concerned with the social violence perpetrated on the energies of sexuality, which is prepared above all to turn these into something mysterious, 'rich and strange', by postulating them as experience from another 'place' – with all this the 1830 poems make a subversive critique of fixed positions, defamiliarising them with extraordinary confidence. Ariel's song haunts them, suggesting a confidence in transformation even when Tennyson subjects his own enquiries to critique. Though we should remember that *The Tempest* is an ambiguous reference at this time. It is available to both conservative and radical readings.[36]

It appears that the form of analysis whereby the sceptical latter-day poet constructs and analyses the naive experience is a discovery which

58

gave the poet an enormous sense of power. It is not radical poetry in the sense that Browning's early work is, but it is subversive. It was certainly thought of as subversive *and* radical by the enraged John Wilson in *Blackwood's Magazine*, whose traditional Tory views were deeply unsettled – as they were no doubt meant to be. His is a furious reaction to subversive experiment and his attack on Tennyson is straightforwardly ideological. He thought of him as a sceptical mystifier (the importance of the reactionary critique of Tennyson is that it has some substance), and mistakenly as a member of a radical coterie, and a revolutionary. 'One of the saddest misfortunes that can befall a young poet is to be the Pet of a Coterie'.[37] He got his coterie wrong, associating Tennyson with Keats and Leigh Hunt rather than the new conservatism of the Apostles, but he believed that Tennyson's poems were subversive, and grasps the political importance of the collection.

A 'deep-fermenting tempest' (Wilson intuitively picks up the reference to Shakespeare's play in Tennyson's volume) of social unrest was brewing. 'On the beautiful green grass of England . . . may there glisten in the sun but the pearly dew drops; may they be brushed away but by the footsteps of Labour issuing from his rustic lodge. But Europe, long ere bright heads are grey, will see blood poured out like water; and there will be the noise of many old establishments quaking to their foundations, or rent asunder, or overthrown'.[38] In this context, he claimed, Tennyson's work was disruptive, not consolidating. What we see here is the head-on clash between traditional Toryism and a new conservatism. For Wilson, his own antirevolutionary politics meant an inevitable aesthetic of *unifying* feeling and common sympathy:

> At present he has small power over the common feelings and thoughts of men. His feebleness is distressing at all times when he makes an appeal to their ordinary sympathies. And the reason is, that he fears to look such sympathies boldly in the face, – and will be – metaphysical. What all the human race see and feel, he seems to think cannot be poetical; he is not aware of the transcendent and eternal grandeur of common-place and all-time truths, which are the staple of all poetry.

Like Wordsworth, the great poets put common experience into language which 'rather records than reveals, spiritualising while it embodies'.[39] At a time of crisis it is the function of the poet to be socially cohesive, to produce patriotism. It is interesting that he sees 'Labour' issuing from a 'rustic lodge' and not from the industrial city. It is a reactionary reading of Wordsworth in terms of the commonplace (though a reading perfectly guaranteed by the work of the later Wordsworth), outraged by Hallam's disparaging dismissal of Wordsworth. But its fury arises from the way Hallam's review of Tennyson seemed a travesty of Wilson's own positions, as much as with Tennyson himself. It was fury at a critical and political position as well as with the poetry of Tennyson.

We shall see later what was meant by a patriotic and reactionary poetry of universals which 'records' faithfully in contrast to Tennyson's 'metaphysical' work. A look at Hallam's review clarifies the aesthetic to which Tennyson was closest. Its singularity lies in the fact that it comes from a conservative group who were theorising afresh the very Tory positions adopted by Wilson. When Wilson describes Tennyson as 'metaphysical' he is referring to the speculative philosophy and conceptualisation of culture which emanated from Germany. Like Wilson, the Apostles believed nostalgically in tradition, in traditional forms of literature, in a cultural unity forged by poetry and in a Christian society. But behind Hallam's review is a context of reading and exploration which reinterprets these things in a daring and self-conscious way, with access to the philology, science, philosophy, comparative religion and mythography, historiography and theology, which were being explored not only by Whewell, but by other Trinity teachers, Connop Thirlwell and Julius Hare. Since literature, religion and language were seen in terms of cultural relativism, all forms of thought became the imaginative and intellectual expression of the life of a people. Just as the Bible became a historical work, a set of sacred writings expressing the life of a nation at the time its books were written, and thus open to historical investigation by scientific methods, so, Hallam is quick to grasp, modern culture could be historicised. Neither science nor scientific theology were destructive of belief, for him at least. They were 'modern' forms of thought. In an urbane aside in his prize-winning essay on Cicero written in 1831, Hallam writes of 'the anxiety to promote the cause of morals' which raises 'a factious clamour against the discoveries of Geology, and any effectual application of criticism to the style and tenor of the Biblical writings'.[40] John Kemble, who later became a professional philologist, was in particular a German enthusiast. The Apostles' response to German thinking is evident here. Following Coleridge a generation earlier they were confident of the liberating power of German thought, confident that it clarified a whole set of intellectual and cultural problems. They differ from Coleridge by extending his Kantian reading into a kind of affirmative deconstruction rather than a transcendental aesthetic, though for both, post-Kantian thinking affirms a new understanding of belief. It is important to see that this confidence supports the brilliant effrontery of Hallam's review of the 1830 volume. It is an essay which clearly both deeply attracted and disturbed Tennyson. It is one of the high points of early Victorian criticism and its analyses resonate throughout the century. It is in direct opposition to Wilson's presuppositions. Modern poetry never can be popular – 'modern poetry, in proportion to its depth and truth, is likely to have little immediate authority over public opinion. Admirers it will have, sects consequently it will form', but true artists will be like 'isolated peaks' in a mountain landscape. A secondary group of writers will become popular cultural 'mediators'.[41] The explanation for this lies in the fragmented conditions of modern culture. Above all, 'the prevalence of social activity' withdraws energy from the 'subjective' experience which is the material of poetry in proportion to 'objective' amelioration.[42]

> Those different powers of poetic disposition, the energies of Sensitive [or 'Sensuous', the footnote says], of Reflective, of Passionate Emotion, which in former times were intermingled, and derived from mutual support an extensive empire over the feelings of men, were not restrained within separate spheres of agency. The whole system no longer worked harmoniously, and by intrinsic harmony acquired external freedom; but there arose a violent and unusual action in the several component functions, each for itself, all striving to reproduce the regular power which the whole had once enjoyed. Hence the melancholy, which so evidently characterises the spirit of modern poetry; hence that return of the mind upon itself, and the habit of seeking relief in idiosyncrasies rather than community of interest.[43]

This is such an important essay that it requires detailed discussion. It clearly influenced Tennyson, but just as clearly he was in debate with it throughout the 1830s and 1840s: it is of major significance as cultural analysis, but just as clearly the analysis is 'produced' by cultural conditions, particularly the position of the intellectual in a new mass culture.

Hallam sees modern culture as inflicting a violent wound on 'community of interest', implicitly because of the division of labour and economic competition – 'each for itself'. His historicising of modern culture depends directly on Schiller. Schiller had written of the same schismatic divisions which he saw immediately reflected in the political organisation of the modern state.

> It was civilisation itself which inflicted this wound upon modern man. Once the increase of empirical knowledge, and more exact modes of thought, made sharper divisions between the sciences inevitable, and once the increasingly complex machinery of State necessitated a more rigorous separation of ranks and occupations, then the inner unity of human nature was severed too, and a disastrous conflict set its harmonious powers at variance. The intuitive and the speculative understanding [for Hallam, 'sensation and reflection'] now withdrew in hostility to take up positions in their respective fields, whose frontiers they now began to guard with jealous mistrust. . . . While in the one a riotous imagination ravages the hard-won fruits of the intellect, in another the spirit of abstraction stifles the fire at which the heart should have warmed itself and the imagination been kindled.[44]

This, part of which has already been quoted in connection with Browning, is a locus classicus of the Romantic definition of consciousness and culture. In repeating it, Hallam appears to be taking it even further. We can never go back. 'Repentance is unlike innocence'. Just as in his poem on a child's sensibility, the self-conscious reflective faculty is always concurrent with pure sensuous delight. He seems to be proposing an arrant and politically damaging élitism, as the poet withdraws to minority coteries, something akin to Hazlitt's aristocracy of taste. However, though this is Wilson's reading of his position, it is only partially true and the situation is more complex than this. The poet is rescued from isolation, another possible reading goes, precisely by conceding to the division of faculties and the division of labour by writing a poem of 'sensation' rather than 'reflection'. 'It is not true', he writes, 'that the highest species of poetry is the reflective', as the 'false glosses' and 'narrow apprehensions' of the Wordsworthians would propose.[45] Interestingly, in order to sustain his position, Hallam relies on associationist psychological theory, rather than an account of mind as creative sui generis. Wilson begins his review with a strangely passionate anti-élitist burlesque of the 'creative' theories of mind which were revolutionary in his day and in which he makes clear he still believes. Hallam's repudiation of this belief with a 'materialist' theory infuriated him:

> Almost all men, women, and children, are poets, except those who write verses . . . every thing is poetry which is not mere sensation. We are poets at all times when our minds are makers . . . we create nine-tenths at least of what appears to exist externally. . . . Oysters are poets. Nobody will deny that, who ever in the neighbourhood of Prestonpans beheld them passionately gaping, on their native bed, for the flow of tide coming again to awaken all their energies from the wide Atlantic. Nor less so are snails.[46]

So Wilson wrote. But for Hallam, the poets privileging sensation, for him primarily Keats and Shelley, appear to grant the poet a privileged position partly because the poetry of sensation requires 'exertion' in a way that 'reflection' does not. But the principle of association enables Hallam to fight 'reflection' on its own ground as well. Reflection hardens into custom, convention and moral orthodoxies through the very principle of association and repetition. Thus it is *'morally* impossible', he says, for a reader to respond to new forms of thought in poetry. But, he says, it is not *'physically* impossible' to do so if the poet works through the sensuous principles of association rather than through the connections of thoughts.[47] It is through sensation that the rigid, atrophying grip of conventional morality can be dissolved. The poet has to be anti-socially marginalised and has to work through the subversive power of sensation because he or she is transforming consciousness with the aim of breaking up old configurations of thought and opening new. The 'forces of association' are only too ready to work in the direction of consolidating 'with little effort' 'the *usual* passions of the heart' which are often dealt with 'in a simple state', without applying the transforming powers of high imagination. 'Love, friendship, ambition, religion, etc., are matters of daily experience'.[48] It requires a different, sensuous principle of association to break up old patterns.

Hallam's point is that once the didactic and moral enters into art, once it deals with – and the list of the 'usual' passions includes all the 'common' ideologically cohesive feelings which for Wilson should be the matter of poetry – love, friendship, ambition, religion, atrophy sets in. Hence, 'whatever is mixed up with art, and appears under its semblance, is always more favourably regarded than art free and unalloyed'. Part of Hallam's strategy in avoiding an account of the mind as a 'maker' is that this account of mind often assumed the immediate intuition of a permanent moral instinct. Furthermore, if we assume the priority of reflection to sensation, the moral life becomes fixed and abstract. This was behind his perception of 'the sudden blank and deficiency' of Cicero's rational ethical system.[49] Morality does not rest on rational universals but is particular and constantly redefined by unique feeling. Although he condemns the 'evanescent' sensationalism of the Epicureans, 'there was this method in the Epicurean theory, that it laid the basis of morality in the right quarter. Sentiment, not thought, was declared the motive power'.[50] Since self is composed of 'fragments of being', and is 'the common character' of a series of 'momentary beings', the way to transform 'self' or consciousness was to attack through sensation the 'ligatures' of habitual thought which bind the self in a coherent chain of association. Hence Hallam is at pains to point out in the Tennyson review that the education of sensation is more precise, more morally subtle, than the power of reflection. 'That delicate sense of fitness', a phrase used in the Cicero essay as well, 'which grows with the growth of artist feelings, and strengthens with their strength, until it acquires a celerity and weight of decision hardly inferior to the correspondent judgments of conscience',[51] produces a trained sensitivity which is at least parallel to the ethical if not superior to it. So another form of morality comes in by the back door, but in order to do so the coherence of identity has to be dissolved.

Hallam's attack on conventional morality has enormous implications for the nature of identity and morality as well as for aesthetics because it reverses the customary account of the workings of the mind current in theological orthodoxy. Thomas Chalmers, consolidating the rational Christianity of natural theology in the first volume of the Bridgewater Treatises, argued in a section entitled 'The power and operation of habit', that thought *precedes* feeling in the law of association. Reflection thus 'forces' moral habits upon the mind and by repeated acts of moral decision, an ethical and virtuous character is sustained and strengthened. 'This order forces itself upon the mind with a strength proportional to the frequency of its repetition'. Thus virtue becomes a self-fulfilling prophecy through the act of recurrence. 'And this law of habit when enlisted on the side of righteousness, not only strengthens and makes sure our resistance to vice, but facilitates the most arduous performances of virtue'. Continual 'acts of virtue ripen into habits; and the goodly and permanent result is the formation or establishment of a virtuous character'.[52] Cicero, it is clear, is a kind of Roman version of the natural theologian for Hallam. This, Hallam says, is the current orthodoxy, and he thinks it damaging because it is a law of habit without content. It is deadening and mechanical and absolutely refuses the possibility of change. Behind the essay is the Apostles' hatred of Paley's *Evidences of Christianity*. 'Mariana' might almost have been written to prove the sterility of repeated thought which becomes a 'law of habit' emptied of content except the need to reproduce itself. The function of art is not only to dissolve 'habit' but to lay bare the structure of habit and its empty content. Thus art becomes an ideological solvent as 'sensation' constantly reorders relationships between consciousness and the external world, severing the ligatures of thought which stabilises the 'delicate materials of emotion'. Hallam self-consciously redefines the Romantic fusion of subject and object as a structure which is capable of the continual 'adjustment' of relationships through sense. Relationship and identity are thus always a provisional construct. External and internal worlds can be 'fused' by emotion and by the same token dissolved again. Such relationships 'seem' 'natural', but are in fact constantly open to change. Among the five 'distinctive excellencies' of Tennyson's poetry are:

> his power of embodying himself in ideal characters, or rather moods of character, with such extreme accuracy of adjustment, that the circumstances of the narration seem to have a natural correspondence with the predominant feeling, and, as it were, to be evolved from it by assimilative force . . . his vivid, picturesque delineation of objects, and the peculiar skill with which he holds all of them *fused*, to borrow a metaphor from science, in a medium of strong emption.[53]

The continually adjusted fusion and dissolution of relationship effect change by ultimately reconfiguring thought. This is how the poet operating from the outside produces 'under-currents' which will in time sensibly affect the principal stream. The poet is effective after all. It is fascinating to see Hallam, an Adorno before his time, struggling to articulate the idea of the avant-garde (he frequently uses military images) and its political effectiveness despite, or because of, its minority status. But we should never forget the two-edged nature of the avant-garde – its tendency to collapse into the aristocracy of taste and conservative anarchy. Kemble thought that the regeneration of the mind of the country should begin from above in the universities, those bastions of privilege. Just as a small band of young men tried to change the hegemony in Spain, so a minority élite was to transform a people.

Wilson was right to be threatened by Hallam's essay and understood exactly what was at issue. Before moving on to consider the 'Tory' poetry to which Tennyson's was opposed, and to the repercussions of Hallam's review in later work of the Tennyson coterie, one further aspect of the essay requires discussion, its account of poetic language. For it is here that poetry is unifying at a deep level. Poetry makes a frontal attack on preconceived values. Poems such as 'Supposed Confessions of a Second-Rate Sensitive Mind', exploring conflict in 'this epoch of social development' attack the defensive 'fortresses of opinion' which 'ordinary tempers' construct for themselves:[54] these 'fortresses' are dissolved in particular through language. The theory, like so much of Hallam's thought, is paradoxical. The language of poetry succeeds through distinctness of image, concise boldness, 'accuracy and elaborate splendour' and 'consummate art'.[55] Since the poetry of sensation is not bound with the 'ligaments' of thought, precision is essential for the representation of sensation, and the compensating elements of pattern, metre and sound are utilised for 'suggestive power'.[56] Quoting Coleridge from *Aids to Reflection* on the evils of 'confounding the distinct senses of words', Hallam makes it clear that to keep the 'distinct' unique meaning of words is to reflect the historical evolution of the language. The 'Saxon element' coexists with 'Latin and Roman derivatives' in a 'compound language' which embodies the history of a culture.[57] Such a language provides a profound, alternative cohesiveness to the moral cohesiveness required of conventional theories of poetry, and redresses the isolation of the poet by tapping the mythic continuities of a whole people. It is in deep linguistic structures that the spirit of a culture is consolidated, and not in the superficially 'patriotic' poetry which Wilson demanded. Language is the repository of the 'truth' of historical meaning and is almost independent of the poet. This Hallam would have learned from Herder and Schiller. Speaking of the 'modern' ballads of *Poems* (1830), Hallam writes that 'the art of one generation cannot *become* that of another', but the artist can make 'a new and legitimate combination' by transferring 'the spirit of the past' in a provisional 'temporary form' to his own consciousness.[58] The exploration of ballad (and by extension mythic form and legend) becomes a profound exploration of the continuity of history by the very fact of its being historicised in modern contexts. Its independent truth is reapplied, the same and yet transformed. 'Oriana' is like 'Fair Helen of Kirconnel' in Scott's *Minstrelsy* but is not the same, just as a line transferred from an ancient ballad at the end of Tennyson's poem – 'I hear the roaring of the sea' – resonates with its past and new, contemporary meaning. (And he might have added that the simple, primal conflict which leads to the death of Fair Helen is replaced by a more ambiguous tragedy of accident and deflected intention in 'Oriana'.)

Language is at once loaded with history and yet empty of content, structures of sheer sound which conveys meaning. Through sound the sign mediates the non-rational, the 'subtle' and 'rapid' sensations which do not leave 'signatures in language'.[59] The formal organization of musical pattern and tone becomes the 'sign' of feeling and sign and feeling reciprocally suggest one another, by-passing the semantic and conceptual aspects of signification. The comparative philologists, Grimm and Bopp, to which the Apostles had access through Kemble in particular, were beginning to think of language in terms of structure and form rather than content. Hallam dangerously combines two incompatible theories here. But they do share one assumption: in both theories meaning is not intrinsic to particular words. In one meaning is distinct, but it is culturally made, the result of the historical process. In the second, formal relationships and structural organisation are paramount and meaning secondary. Both allowed Hallam to construct a new language of the senses to disrupt the fixities of convention and 'sensibly affect the principal stream' of thought.[60] Just as the poetry of sensation dissolves continuous identity, so its language almost does without signification.

The sophisticated carelessness of this essay – we remember that Hallam was committed to the strengthening process of play – takes remarkable risks with dazzling equivocation. It was written at a time of political ferment but detaches itself from immediate concerns to analyse them covertly in true disinterested Kantian fashion as a form of cultural crisis – compare W. J. Fox at the same time, whose polemic begins this book. Hallam's essay is deliberately written out of and in terms of contradiction: the playful, feminised poet is disengaged from popular life and at the same time deeply involved with it because s/he is able to deconstruct entrenched positions: s/he is non-moral but returns to the moral through the senses which repudiate the ethical by enabling the work of sensation to mount a critique of a limited morality: s/he is possessed of a modern, fragmented consciousness yet in touch with the continuities of the past and of the self through this very fragmentation: s/he uses a language which is full of meaning and yet empty of content and returns to meaning by being representation without signification. In taking over, via Schiller, the Kantian aesthetic of disinterested free play and making an intransigent distinction between sensation and reflection Hallam never fully defined what he intended by these terms. Emotion, feeling, sensuous experience, sense data, intuition, are all rather different but all possible significations of 'sensation'. Unlike Kant, for whom 'reflection' might be glossed as epistemological ideas (in the third critique at least) and 'sensation' as the unique representations of the data of experience by consciousness, Hallam was not exact and left unquestioned a dichotomy between thought and sensation which was filtered through Schiller into categories which actually construct the division they describe. For Kant and for Schiller (who simplified Kant)

66

the aesthetic mediates ideas and immediate experience, but for Hallam
unique, unmediated sensation *is* the aesthetic. Its uniqueness, and thus its
resistance to appropriation and abstraction is what appealed to him. The
essay rescues itself from incoherence time and again by its paradoxical
conviction that to destabilise fixed positions is a reconstructive act. And
consciousness does avail itself of reflections by presenting the train of
associative sensation as a retrospective act, capable of reflexive analysis by
as it were historicising the consciousness and working upon it with the
analyst's understanding which comes from the acknowledgement of the
latter-day poet that all experience is comprehended in a series of backwards
questions.

Certainly in theorising the 'two-fold' consciousness of the poet of sensation, who is aware of his latter-day understanding of his experience as
sensation not quite concurrently with his experience itself, Hallam was
preparing the way for a peculiarly Tennysonian exploration of the double
poem. Tennyson seems to have worked with the grain of Hallam's assumptions in the 1830 poems and more and more against the grain of the essay
as he subsequently subjected it to a critique over the next decade. Hallam's
essay steers dangerously round cultural élitism, marginalisation, aestheticism, formalism and an anti-rational account of the function of sensation
as individualised, anarchic, ideological disruption. By virtue of its unique,
unrepeatable nature – for no sensation in time can ever be quite like another
– it refuses to enter an economy of communication even to the point of
negating some of the functions of language, and yet it revels in a fecund,
'anti-Malthusian' (as Fox put it) self-production which is an alternative
form of exchange and communication and grants itself the prerogative of
sporadic and covert attack on the fortress of enemy ideas, a kind of guerrilla
warfare. The positions of Hallam's essay are taken up, fractured, developed
and reappropriated by different formations in different and often contradictory ways throughout the century – by Arnold, the Pre-Raphaelites,
Hopkins, Pater, Swinburne and Yeats. The shock of the intervention made
by Tennyson's early poetry together with Hallam's essay can best be understood by looking at some forms of the Tory poetry which was the object of
their attack – John Wilson's own poetry; the poet he regarded as important,
John Keble, and the poet he hated, Robert Montgomery, who was also
disliked by Hallam. All three represent aspects of the reactionary tradition.
Tennyson's slow and tentative critique of Hallam can then be understood
as an attempt not to return to this kind of poetry but an attempt to work
his way out of a series of political and aesthetic problems.

TORY POETRY: THE STRENGTH OF REACTION

John Wilson Croker, a later and far cruder reviewer than John Wilson,
was to attack Tennyson's *Poems* (1832).[61] He had produced a patriotic epic

celebrating the defeat of the French in Spain by England, the first decisive blow to Napoleon's power, *The Battle of Talavera* (1812), which is a fair indication of the national poem advocated by Tory reviewers. It is a fast-moving martial poem, and though it deals movingly with the ruin of battle, there is no doubt of the writer's frank exultation when France retreats. There are bloodier and more violent celebrations of battle in poems to Wellington and Nelson, but this is a fair representation of Tory patriotism.

> With rapid step and humbled thought,
>   All night she holds her way:
> Leaving, to Britain's conquering sons,
> Standards rent and ponderous guns,
>   The trophies of the fray!
>
>   (xxxiii)[62]

'Woe to you tyrant! to his legion woe!' John Wilson also wrote, in 'The Magic Mirror', a poem which curiously anticipates 'The Lady of Shalott'. The poet sees scenes of national conflict and battles from the Scottish border ballads in a magic mirror and then turns to consolidate national spirit by an attack on France and the war in Spain. 'Ye savage slaves that shame the name of France!'[63] The need for patriotic epic and narrative, or songs and ballads celebrating the high moments of a national past, is one of the requisites of Tory poetry. And there is all the difference between this patriotic antiquarian understanding of ballad and the Apostles' consciously theorised view of myth and history, as an imaginative construct which holds a nation together. It is interesting that Bulwer Lytton, friend of Tennyson's hated grandfather and also reviewer of his poems, accomplished a change of poetic style with a change of allegiance from radical to conservative. He moved from society Byronism (taken to even greater lengths by his son, 'Owen Meredith') to the flat grandeur of a national epic, *King Arthur* (1846).

Scott is seen by Tory poets as the great precursor poet of the narrative of simple chivalry, romance, national event and above all, action. For the Apostles he was rather the poet of a lost culture. A struggle for the interpretation of history is going on between two kinds of conservatism. However, the national narrative poem takes a second place to the values of simplicity and plainness in what becomes a recognisable Tory aesthetic in Wilson's work. Simplicity and plainness, which 'records' and 'idealises', provides a direct, unmediated access to 'ordinary sympathies' and universal and self-evident moral truths apparent to common sense, things which unite us all. These are apparent in the work of Wordsworth above all. The struggle for the meaning of Wordsworth is as ideologically important as the interpretation of Scott. The Tory Wordsworth is the Wordsworth of *The Excursion*; the Apostles' Wordsworth is the poet of *Lyrical Ballads*. Wilson constructed a 'tradition' of national and Christian poetry which runs through Burns, Southey, Moore, Rogers, Scott and Wordsworth to John Keble.[64] How important the purity of this tradition is can be seen from Keble's own condemnation of the 'vicious' radical, 'Leigh Hunt and his miserable followers'.[65] For the Tory simple language conveys purity of moral feeling or is used for descriptive purposes to celebrate the universal Nature which corroborates moral feeling. Thus it is not only the content of Leigh Hunt's *Story of Rimini*, for instance, which distinguishes it as radical poetry. Its use of language distinguishes it, too. In this story of a tragically illicit love, interestingly consummated with blushes over a reading of the story of Lancelot and Guinevere, the language is used for psychological purposes. The florid, un-Malthusian abundance of diction represents the charged emotional condition of sexual desire. This is not the language which records and idealises, uniting us despite social difference. Hunt was deemed 'corrupt' because his language leads us away from common, shared moral experience. Here, reliefs in an exotic, 'lurking' pavilion surrounded with vines and orange trees, portray nymphs:

> Some by the water side on bowery shelves
> Leaning at will, – some in the water sporting
> With sides half swelling forth, and looks of courting, –
> Some in a flowery dell, hearing a swain
> Play on his pipe . . .

>   some sleeping
> Under the trees, with fauns and satyrs peeping, –
> Or, sidelong-eyed, pretending not to see
> The latter in the brakes come creepingly, . . .
>   (*The Story of Rimini*, canto III)[66]

But this excess is not Wilson's way. His poetry is interesting for its passionate reading of Wordsworth through Burke and for optimistic Enlightenment values in which the simple ties and common passions are consolidated by a rational Nature. His work is written in a language of slightly elevated plainness, a pure diction with a hint of sublimity. His major poem is written to conservatise Wordsworth's *Excursion* – a truly reactionary enterprise! Though he believed that *The Excursion* was flawed by its 'Religion' and its doctrinal vagueness, Wordsworth's poetry was paramount for its 'experiences of human life' and meditations on the 'moral government of this world'.[67] And he was the 'High Priest' of 'Nature'. But there is a theological problem: 'Was Margaret a Christian? . . . If she was – then the picture painted of her and her agonies, is a libel not only on her character, but on the character of all other poor Christian women in this Christian land'.[68] Wordsworth never shows her turning to God for comfort. His own narrative poem, *The Isle of Palms* (1812), on the other hand, is a demonstration of what a doctrinally 'correct' reading should be, so it is a Wordsworthian corrective to Wordsworth, an odd poem. Where the Margaret of Wordsworth's 'Ruined Cottage' in *The Excursion* despaired, the grieving mother of a shipwrecked son, alone in Wales, does not entirely break down. Though she wanders daily along the beach in agony, she is saved by a loving God, who reunites her with 'three Christian souls restored', as the shipwrecked son returns with wife and child.

The Isle of Palms (1812) has a contemporary setting in the war with France. 'Britannia rule the waves!' accompanies the arrival of ships of war in port. Mary and Fitzowen survive a shipwreck and life on a desert island, during which they 'marry' and, in spite of praying much of the time, conceive a child which is not born of a 'heavenly sire'. The piety of the poem is insistent, yet it is written to celebrate the intrinsic purity of spontaneous natural feeling. Mary and Fitzowen are not named until canto II but are described as generalised, heroic figures – the 'Figure', 'Youth', 'Orphean Maid' – in order to raise these lowly people to idealised proportions. Because they 'love/Each other and believe in God', they respond to the life of the island with pure Wordsworthian 'eye and ear'. Because they are bound by the ties of affection and memory they are blessed by Nature and can participate in the energies of natural life on the Indian isle.

> Where are they in the hours of day?
> – The birds are happy on the spray,
> The dolphins on the deep,
> Whether they wanton full of life,
> Or, wearied with their playful strife,
> Amid the sunshine sleep.[69]

It is a primitivism which simply endorses social ties, normalising the exotic and bringing the island into line with European moral values. The 'natural' and social ties of family which constitute the bonds of moral life spring from *innate* moral passion. Here Wilson manages to simplify Rousseau and Wordsworth at one blow.

> When dimly descending behind the sea
> From the Mountain Isle of Liberty,
> Oh! many a sigh pursued thy vanish'd sail;
> And oft an eager crowd will stand
> With straining gaze on the Indian strand,
> Thy wonted gleam to hail.
> For thou art laden with Beauty and Youth,
> With Honour bold, and spotless Truth,
> With fathers, who have left in a home of rest
> Their infants smiling at the breast,
> With children, who have bade their parents farewell,
> Or who go to the land where their parents dwell.[70]

The natural ties are consolidated through landscape in an oddly circular way. Here the mountain landscape of Snowdon with its 'calm majesty and pleasing dread', filtered through Burke and Wordsworth, is anthropomorphised as a giant gazing with love at the rising dawn. The end product is a thoroughly un-Wordsworthian personification as nature experiences 'natural' human sympathy writ large.

> Among the Cambrian hills we stand!
> By dear compulsion chain'd unto the strand
> Of a still Lake, yet sleeping in the mist,
> The thin blue mist that beautifies the morning:
> Old Snowdon's gloomy brow the sun hath kiss'd,
> Till, rising like a giant from his bed,
> High o'er the mountainous sea he lifts his head,
> The loneliness of Nature's reign adorning
> With a calm majesty and pleasing dread.
> A spirit is singing from the coves
> Yet dim and dark; that spirit loves
> To sing unto the Dawn,
> When first he sees the shadowy veil,
> As if by some slow-stealing gale,
> From her fair face withdrawn.
> How the Lake brightens while we gaze!
> Impatient for the flood of rays
> That soon will bathe its breast:
> Where rock, and hill, and cloud, and sky,
> Even like its peaceful self, will lie
> Ere long in perfect rest.[71]

It is a thoroughly Eurocentric poem. There is no sense of the otherness of the Indies (which are simply the tool of British trade), no attempt to grasp them in terms of myth or an alien culture. The Tory coherence of nationhood in universal feeling precludes this, just as the bonds of universal feeling make social change unnecessary.

   It is a matter for speculation as to when Wilson's serious respect for the cohesive turns into the exercise of coercion. He praised Keble's 'perfect sincerity' and consequently the simplicity which 'we cannot doubt' will 'find its way into many of the dwellings of humble life. Such descent, if descent it be, must be of all receptions the most delightful to the heart of a Christian poet'.[72] One can begin to see why popularity and why religion as a topic were suspect for Hallam when Keble's essay on 'Sacred Poetry' is put against Wilson's much more straightforward belief in the efficacy of the moral. Though this essay was praised by Julius Hare, whom Hallam respected, it is strangely devious. Keble respects power, the power evident in 'the whole of modern history', in 'the rapid increase of colonisation, *from Christian nations only'.*[73] This has made the dissemination of Christianity possible. He believes in the power of the simple expression 'of feelings' as the basis of sacred poetry. But it is inappropriate to *'indulge'* in 'violent emotion' and debasing 'rapture'.[74] Yet, if intense emotion is incompatible with the reserve required of devotional writing, it is nevertheless the case that devotional poetry must appeal to a wide range of readers. The sacred writer who exercises decorum must be content with a smaller number of readers, and 'few sacred poets are popular'.[75] But there is another way out. Such a writer 'must veil, as it were, the sacredness of the subject – not necessarily by allegory, for it may be done in a thousand other ways – and so deceive the world of taste into devotional reading'.[76] Such deceiving poetry Keble calls the 'indirect' mode as opposed to the 'direct' mode of Christian exposition or didactic verse. He prefers the 'indirect' mode because it enables the sacred poet to reach a wider audience – but in disguise.

How does this theory of duplicity, insinuation, subterfuge and subliminal manipulation relate to Hallam, whose theory it resembles? What Keble proposes is in fact a subtle theory of emotional displacement through symbolic representation. Truth is figured by what conceals it. A reader is persuaded by what is not said. This was to preoccupy Tennyson in the 1850s, but is in direct opposition to Hallam's belief that simplicity is ideologically suspect. For Keble a poem's limpid, seemingly unmediated surface is intended to 'deceive' and conceals the exercise of power. Keble's devotional poem is a double poem in disguise. Though two extremes meet here in the understanding that poetry 'insensibly' affects the main current, Hallam's robust materialist belief in unrepressed sensation refuses manipulation, because it establishes frank ties with 'the beautiful' and the concrete world. The withdrawal of the poet from popularity is a withdrawal from the overt exercise of power just as the production of polysemic myths is a way of deconstructing the privileged Christian myth. On the other hand, there is no doubt that the predispositions of conservative anarchy underlying Hallam's aesthetics make for a suspect convergence of the two theories, because both work by indirection. If we look at the poem Wilson admired in *The Christian Year*, a number of 'the thousand other ways' in which the poet can be 'indirect' can be seen.

Fifteenth Sunday after Trinity

Sweet nurslings of the vernal skies,
    Bathed in soft airs, and fed with dew,
What more than magic in you lies,
    To fill the heart's fond view?
In childhood's sports companions gay,

In sorrow, on Life's downward way,
How soothing! in our last decay
  Memorials prompt and true.

Relics ye are of Eden's bowers,
  As pure, as fragrant, and as fair,
As when ye crown'd the sunshine hours
  Of happy wanderers there.
Fall'n all beside – the world of life,
How is it stain'd with fear and strife!
In Reason's world what storms are rife,
  What passions rage and glare!

But cheerful and unchanged the while
  Your first and perfect form ye shew,
The same that won Eve's matron smile
  In the world's open glow.
The stars of Heaven a course are taught
Too high above our human thought; –
Ye may be found if ye are sought,
  And as we gaze we know.

Ye dwell beside our paths and homes,
  Our paths of sin, our homes of sorrow,
And guilty man, where'er he roams,
  Your innocent mirth may borrow.
The birds of air before us fleet,
They cannot brook our shame to meet –
But we may taste your solace sweet,
  And come again to-morrow.

Ye fearless in your nests abide –
  Nor may we scorn, too proudly wise,
Your silent lessons, undescried
  By all but lowly eyes;
For ye could draw th'admiring gaze
Of Him who worlds and hearts surveys:
Your order wild, your fragrant maze,
  He taught us how to prize.

Yet felt your Maker's smile that hour,
  As when he paused and own'd you good;
His blessing on earth's primal bower,
  Yet felt it all renew'd.
What care ye now, if winter's storm
Sweep ruthless o'er each silken form?

73

Christ's blessing at your heart is warm,
　　Ye fear no vexing mood.

Alas! of thousand bosoms kind,
　　That daily court you and caress,
How few the happy secret find
　　Of your calm loveliness!
'Live for to-day! to-morrow's light
To-morrow's cares shall bring to sight.
Go, sleep like closing flowers at night,
　　And Heaven thy morn will bless.'[77]

This poem is written to the text 'consider the lilies of the field how they grow: they toil not, neither do they spin'. The poem proceeds by circumlocutions and hints – of 'more than magic' significance which can be 'sought,/And as we gaze we know', of 'silent lessons', of the 'happy secret'. The lily is the lily of the Annunciation, signifying the coming of Christ the Redeemer as man and the perfect virginity which bore him – 'the happy secret'. The event is referred to indirectly through the Old Testament typology of Eve's 'matron smile' in Eden which is 'renew'd' in the Annunciation. The 'shame' in stanza 4 is fallen sexuality, which is why the lilies are memorials of death as well as life in the first stanza. The lily can withstand the 'ruthless' violation of its 'silken form' because it knows of the eventual redemption of 'Christ's blessing'. The lily's beauty, fragrance, innocence, loveliness and warmth are celebrated with direct simplicity, but all the time these are a 'veil' for an indirect theological commentary on sexuality. Keble's theory is a kind of back-to-front Wordsworthianism – the repression and deflection of feeling, not its immediate expressive overflow.

Robert Montgomery's *The Omnipresence of the Deity* (1828) is an offensive poem. Interestingly, both Wilson and Hallam were offended by it and these agreements between two men split on other aesthetic questions indicate the immense ideological variation in Tory and conservative poetry at the beginning of the century. The poem has to be given some attention, however, partly because its immense popularity is an index of what was generally acceptable as the poetry of Christian morality but also in order to understand how deeply Victorian aesthetics is involved with theology. Hallam refers contemptuously to the 'triumphant progress' of the 'omnipresence' at the start of his review of Tennyson, and Wilson devotes a whole essay to attacking it.[78] The poem propounds the optimistic, deistic natural theology which Hallam's essay is concerned to refute – 'The whole panorama of Nature is a silent attestation of the presence of its divine Architect'.[79] If you believe that the universe offers rational evidence of God's presence, then everything in the world, natural and human, must become rational illustrations of the goodness of God. The organisation of

74

society admits of no change, therefore, and is self-confirming, just as deistic belief itself is. And it follows that a morality of rational training and exemplary argument will be regarded as the most powerful defence against scepticism. The celebration of God as 'thy dread UBIQUITY' (Part I) is oddly inconsistent to the extent that Montgomery believed that 'our own isle' is 'preeminently favoured with the Presence of the Deity'.[80] Here is the cohesiveness of patriotism so desired by the Tory critic. Part I concerns the presence of the Deity in nature. Part II considers it as 'influencing the changeful scenes and affairs of Human Life' and Part III attacks atheism, the cause of the French Revolution – 'perverted Freedom', not 'Delightful Liberty' – and draws 'a moral from the nation's crimes'. It ends with two contrasting depictions of a sceptic's and a Christian's death. While the Christian is 'calm, as an infant to the mother's breast', the sceptic is somewhat restless.

> He gnash'd, and quail'd, and raised a hideous shriek,
> Rounded his eyes into a ghastly glare.

Wilson rightly found this contrast shockingly immoral, but the account of divine providence in Part II is almost equally so, from the 'cheering hopes' of the battlefield, to the drowning sailor saved by providence.[81] Exemplary pictures of virtue are offered to us. In this picture the assumption is that the rural worker can be resigned to his lot and enjoy 'Plenty' on the Sabbath in the form of familial affection rather than food. Written at a time when a starving populace could barely sustain themselves, this passage on Sunday in a rural worker's home is a piece of gross idealisation.

> Emblem of peace! – upon the village plain
> Thou dawn'st a blessing to the toil-worn swain;
> Soon as thy smiles athwart the upland play,
> His bosom gladdens with the brightening day;
> Humble and happy, to his lot resigned.
> He feels the inward Sabbath of the mind. . . .
> There shall kind Plenty wear her sweetest smiles;
> There shall his rosy children play their wiles;
> And there the meek-eyed mother muse and joy,
> And court with frequent kiss her infant boy.[82]

It seems that Wilson was able to approve of this passage, as he talks of the 'common joys and common griefs' experienced by those who worship God in a 'lowly building' or in a cathedral. Tory aesthetics here refuse to be convinced by the persuasion of 'Intellect' as Wilson calls it, but point instead to the common feeling of 'the heart' which for them transcends the boundaries of class. Subversive conservative aesthetics, on the other hand, refuses to be convinced either by the rational intellect or the common feelings of 'the heart' because both reinforce blind acceptance of optimistic providence, through habit.[83] This poem's providential morality continued to be sufficiently repugnant to Tennyson to be parodied in *In Memoriam*. There is a sardonic and sceptical reference to Montgomery's happy mariner, who drowns but to be providentially rescued, in section VI – 'O mother, praying God will save/Thy sailor, – while thy head is bowed,/His heavy-shotted hammock-shroud/Drops in his vast and wandering grave'.[84]

3

1832: CRITIQUE OF
THE POETRY OF SENSATION

Poems (1832) sustains the almost breathtaking originality of *Poems, Chiefly Lyrical*. But it also begins to offer a critique of Hallam's positions. Less than a year after it was published, Hallam died. Some of the exuberance disappears from this group, who were increasingly dispersed in the subsequent decade. However, letters indicate how Tennyson's aesthetic evolved. The poetry of a number of friends – R. Monckton Milnes, R. C. Trench and the more distant John Sterling, friend of F. D. Maurice – indicates the pressures to which he responded. The movement to *Poems* (1842) is a movement of slow modification and adaptation. Some of the poems most heavily revised from 1832 to 1842 suggest in what direction Tennyson's work was moving. The poems are increasingly concerned with labour, appropriation and power, and with the forms in which culture perpetrates violence. Where volition and change, the themes of 1830, come into play they are defined in a cultural context. The movement is from an analysis in terms of individual psychology in 1832 to a firmer cultural analysis in 1842, even though, sometimes, it takes a cruder moral form.

The poems of 1832 are enigmatic in the same way as those of 1830, not declaring their meaning, refusing immediate interpretation, requiring that 'exertion' which Hallam required to dissolve the 'fortresses of opinion'. 'The Palace of Art', 'The Lotos-Eaters' and 'The Lady of Shalott', were all much altered in 1842, and in particular 'The Palace of Art'. All these are double poems of a highly self-conscious kind, but they presage the destruction or decadence of the poetry of sensation and search both for another politics and a new aesthetic. It is proper to say that by 1842 subversive conservatism was in a quandary.

Written in answer to Trench's reproach, 'Tennyson, we cannot live in Art', 'The Palace of Art' is too easily read as the journey of the solipsist soul from the aesthetic to the moral life.[1] It is described as 'a sort of allegory' in the dedication to Trench, but remembering the deceptive, indirect allegory of Tractarian aesthetics, akin to the aesthetics of Hallam in some ways, as has been seen, it would be best not to assume that it is immediately explicable. The Soul, a female figure whose feminine status will be examined

77

shortly, 'shuts out Love', according to the dedicatory poem, and aestheticises both 'Knowledge' and 'Good'. The poem itself gives some content to these abstractions, exploring the way in which desire mutates into cold, libidinal power (more emphatic in 1842), just as it bodies out Tennyson's unhelpful comment – 'the Godlike life is with man and for man'.[2] Though that is certainly an unorthodox comment, one interpretation suggests that the 'Godlike' is a creation of the human imagination.

It is immediately apparent that the poem is not written in terms of the poetry of 'sensation', but in a more measured and abstract rhetorical, perhaps 'Ciceronian', manner. The Soul's 'pleasure-house' and its appurtenances at first sight resembles the 'pleasure-dome' of Coleridge's 'Kubla Khan', a poem much debated by the Apostles.[3] Yet even in 1832 'The Palace of Art' is not committed to the sensuous symbolism of that poem. It is colder, more ordered and distant, as the stanzaic form fragments the observations into discrete, objectified moments. The 'I' of the poem is a detached, self-conscious observer, always external to the allegorical 'Soul', granting it a long lease of the pleasure house constructed for it. The lack of 'sensation' may arise because not only isolation but stability is desired for the Soul. 'Reign thou apart, . . . Still as, while Saturn whirls' (14, 15): Saturn's ring, Whewell says, was regarded as evidence for the stability of the universe, emerging from vapour detached from the sun and cooled into permanent form.[4] In 1842 stanzas on the *fixity* of the Soul's narcissism became the second section of the poem (stanzas XXIX–XXXVI in 1832). Displaying the voluptuary Keatsian elements, there is a consummate conflation of the *powerful* fountain of 'Kubla Khan' in the 'Spouted fountain-floods' (28) of Tennyson's poem and the rainbow torrent of the Arve in Shelley's 'Mont Blanc'. The 'torrent-bow' (36) of the waterfall suggests the refracted light of the rainbow torrent of the Arve. Both things suggested the energy and creativity of mind to the earlier poets – the capacity to make new combinations, as in refracted light. The Soul, however, turns away from these and burns incense to herself in self-worship, while the excluded world responds to this mystification. In 1832 the excluded world is introduced directly – ''Twas wonderful to look upon' (41). In 1842 this was sharpened to an ironical understanding of the blinding nature of myth: 'who shall gaze . . . with unblinded eyes . . . ?' (41, 42).

The alienated Soul passes through a series of discrete, enclosed rooms which are a museum or, rather, mausoleum to the whole culture and knowledge of the civilised world, occidental and oriental. Her environment is at once fragmented and overdetermined – not one picture but many, not one religion, but many – so that no myth is privileged above another: 'every legend fair' (125). Christianity, the 'maid-mother by a crucifix' (93) (followed by Venus in 1832 (XV)), is condensed into the emblems of the incarnation and the passion in a brief phrase. Arthurian legend (Faber's interpretation of the Arthurian legend in terms of the rites of the *mystae* was, we have seen, known to Tennyson), the origins of Roman polity, India, home of Sanskrit (which the early mythographers, known to Tennyson, Sir William Jones and Herder, believed to have been the origin of the human race), and Greece, which Hallam thought of as a culture of the feelings in comparison with the rationality of Rome, all coexist.[5] These legends of the Caucasian or Indo-European mind are jumbled together, just as portraits of the great philosophers and poets are hung in no historical order – Milton, Shakespeare, Dante, Homer. All is contemporary, simultaneous, available, and thus all is estranged. A ludic experiment with estranged forms is one result of this simultaneous existence of all cultures and myths: they have also become pure aesthetic artefacts and thus 'pure' commodities, available for use as representations – for the art of the Palace consists of representations of representations – in an aesthetic economy which plunders indiscriminately in spite of its purity. Since each representation is simply the equivalent of another they exist in a self-enclosed system. Hallam's 'pure' art thus becomes drained of meaning and history, a 'pure' luxury commodity.

The brilliant stroke in this analysis of a historicised culture which must be fragmented is the induction of the Soul through landscape painting, which suggests that the poem addresses not only Hallam but also Wilson. Wilson had ended his review of the 1830 poems with the praise of landscape description as the proper subject of the poet:

> long withdrawing vales, where midway between the flowery foreground, and in the distance of blue mountain ranges, some great city lifts up its dim-seen spires through the misty smoke . . . the breast of old ocean . . . or as if an earthquake shook the pillars of the caverned depths, tumbling the foam of his breakers, mast-high, if mast be there, till the canvas ceases to be silent.[6]

There is a palimpsestic revision of the pictorial section from 1832 to 1842 and the elements of Wilson's description are restlessly reconfigured – fitting, perhaps, in a poem which is about a palimpsestic culture. In 1832 the city and the flowery foreground appears – 'Some showed far-off thick woods mounted with towers . . . long walks and lawns and beds and bowers', to be replaced in 1842 (69–72) with a seascape of 'bellowing caves' (71). The lonely, isolated figure in a surreal landscape is supplemented in 1842 with stanzas depicting human exploitation of the land in the grazing of cattle, and in reaping, in 'sultry toil' (77), a double exploitation of land and human labour. Human beings, and more so in 1842, are *not* in harmonious relationship with nature. There is an irony in the 1842 phrase, 'but every landscape fair,/As fit for every mood of mind' (89–90). At a stroke Wilson's programme for descriptive poetry, and the Romantic account of the unity of mind and world, subject and object (which includes Hallam's account of Tennyson as a poet capable of creating moods which seem to evolve a 'natural correspondence' in the external world), are exposed as a fallacy. If the world is 'fit' for every mood of mind, as it is 'fitted' in Wordsworth's *Excursion*, that is because the mind does violence to landscape by appropriating a correspondence which it makes itself.[7] It exploits landscape in imagination and literally by exploiting people's labour on it. The landscapes preface the poem in 1832 because they destroy the basis of Romantic epistemology and its confident assumptions about the unifying power of mind. This pre-eminently modern substitute for religion, a relation with a landscape, is undermined from the start.

In 1832 the element of hubristic possession and appropriation is empha-sised because the famous line 'I take possession of men's minds and deeds' was placed earlier.

> 'I take possession of men's minds and deeds.
> I live in all things great and small.
> I dwell apart, holding no forms of creeds,
> But contemplating all.'
>
> (Note to l. 128, 1842)

An indiscriminate self-projection to which consciousness always remains external leads, not to the 'complex' (19) states of being the Soul believes in but to repetition. She 'multiplied' (3) all that she saw, inhabiting discrepant mythologies – 'Madonna, Ganymede,/Or Asiatic dame' (7–8) – while remaining detached. The whole of history and consciousness is available as a means to power – 'Lord over Nature, Lord of the visible earth,/Lord of the senses five' (179–80). It is power out of control. In 1832 the Soul is not only a historian or rather a historicist but, as a footnote adding extra stanzas indicates, a chemist, physicist, astronomer and a sensuous Epicurean. Ricks notes some deleted manuscript stanzas which include philosophical thought 'from Plato to the German' (note to l. 186, 1842). Indeed, it looks as though Tennyson had trouble in controlling and selecting the forms of thought over which the Soul exercises its power; the fields of knowledge are arbitrary, very much as they become for the Soul of the poem. In 1842 it is the Soul's isolation and indifference to a suffering history which is emphasised in stanzas inserted into section V (141–64). She 'trod' (157) over 'cycles of the human tale' (146). 'I sit apart, holding no forms of creeds' (211) is strongly defined in relation to political and social irresponsibility in 1842. Slavery and revolution are alike irrelevant to the Soul.

> The people here, a beast of burden slow,
> Toiled onward, pricked with goads and stings;
> Here played, a tiger, rolling to and fro
> The heads and crowns of kings.
>
> (149–52)

The Soul's contempt for the people as 'swine' (199) was added even later in 1851 in a tasteless attempt to castigate her 'God-like isolation' (197) further. Tennyson's increasing emphasis on the Soul's isolation is in some ways a misprision of the earlier poem and suggests if nothing else how unstable and uneasy is the text we call 'The Palace of Art', just like Hallam's discontinuous phases of being. In 1832 the aesthetic principle appears to include within itself all human history and forms of thought, however helpless in its pluralism. In 1842, on the other hand, the aesthetic principle appears to have become a principle of exclusion set up in opposition to 'life' and society. Hence the passages on the Soul's unscrupulous empathies disappear, for empathy is at least an inclusive project, even though the Soul's empathies are misused in the pursuit of power. The move is from a 'Romantic' to a 'Victorian' conception of art. In 1832 everything is appropriated by a hubristic imagination. In 1842 the poem becomes an analysis of mistaken categories in which art is defined falsely as that which is not 'mixed up' (in Hallam's phrase) with life: but once the opposition has been established the attempt to heal it simply endorses the fracture. Hallam's political strategy, which enables the poet to dissolve orthodoxies, becomes acutely vulnerable.

Another mark of the 1842 revisions is the increasing helplessness of the feminine Soul. Hallam's essay 'On sympathy' conceives of the Soul as autonomous and feminine, just as in 'The Palace of Art'. The Soul is gendered as feminine because of Hallam's belief in the capacity of women to transgress fixed forms, though in Tennyson's poem it is sometimes androgynous, 'Lord' of the five senses. Hallam argues that the capacity for empathy is not a function of *narcissistic* power. Consciousness itself is not an undivided unity but a series of 'forms of self' and 'successive states', existing 'piece-meal, and in the continual flux of a stream'.[8] Thus the act of empathy, or sympathy, can never be an appropriation of the other by a total self, for the divided self will always recognise difference. 'Impetuous desire' to 'blend emotions and desires with those apparent in the kindred spirit' produces an identification of the 'perceived being with herself' which is conditioned by her understanding of it as other, a not-self.[9] The narcissistic rush of spirit and its *check* is the basis of morality and altruism. In 'The Palace of Art' of 1832, Tennyson explores a condition of narcissistic empathy in which the ego remains self-interested. It is a series of experimental, detached, power-seeking identifications for the sake of self-aggrandisement and thus the self is always 'outside' experience. It is a condition, as Tennyson says, without 'Love'. Hallam's God of love is a God of passion, libido and sexuality, derived from Plato, but peculiarly his own. The paradigm of divine love is the 'intense' experience of the erotic – 'I mean direct, immediate, absorbing affection for one object, on the ground of similarity perceived, and with a view to more complete [i.e. sexual] union'.[10] Moreover, such love cannot be complete unless it has

81

understood incompletion, 'collision with opposing principles', or evil.[11] This God has nothing to do with theories of moral training or innate ethical sense subscribed to by natural theologians.

Effectively in 1842 the Soul is denied the sexuality which is in fact, for Hallam, constitutive of identity and relationships. Because Tennyson deleted the passages concerning the Soul's capacity for empathy, which were there in 1832, the Soul's world becomes increasingly passionless, unsexual and abstract. In 1842 she can 'prate' of the 'moral instinct' (205), the natural theologian's innate virtue consolidated by habit. All knowledge becomes a 'form' (211) of creed without content. The atrophied passions convert knowledge into a form of power which fails to create living relationships. The trauma is the more violent when she understands this incompleteness. The feminised Soul is crushed under the weight of a fragmented culture and cannot reconstruct it. Her crisis is much more like the crisis of Dorothea in Rome in George Eliot's *Middlemarch* forty years later than the hubris attributed to Tennyson by Trench. That the Soul is imaged as feminine suggests that the collapse of feminised art is an index of the poet's understanding of the real condition of women in contemporary culture. Certainly the collapse of feminised art issues in madness. It cannot maintain itself in an abstract and instrumental world which is always assimilating art to its own model, always replicating in art the alienating conditions of its own culture. Feminised art cannot be invoked to supplement an arid society but will simply reproduce its pathology and derangement, as in the deranged landscapes contemplated by the Soul. In a poem of 1829, 'Lines written at Malvern', Hallam writes that all knowledge springs from 'Our senses five'.[12] The Soul's lordship over the five senses in Tennyson's poem is precisely to subordinate and crush their possibilities. In a beautiful poem addressed to Tennyson, Hallam writes of a mad girl seen in an asylum, 'the mansion of the mad'. The girl is locked into a palace of art and solipsist pleasure to which 'nought external seemed akin'.[13] Hence the dissociation and alienation of madness. But Hallam explicitly refuses a 'penal' judgement. It is a world without a strong sense of the other, a world of deranged libido where the disabled mind makes no correlations through the passions. At the end of 'The Palace of Art' the landscapes at the beginning of the poem reappear in fragments as a nightmarish psychological *paysage intérieur*. They must logically become these enclosed and reflexive mental representations because the Soul has found no principle of relationships with things external. Sensation turns in upon itself and represents itself. The ending of the poem has often been considered perfunctory as a description of new commitment and identification with that beyond self:

> 'Make me a cottage in the vale', she said,
> 'Where I may mourn and pray'.
>
> (290–1)

Another reading is that the poverty of the ending comes about because there is no solution to the complex condition of alienation in the poem, least of all a misguided, punitive course of Christian self-abnegation, which is simply to reverse lordship and repeat the abstract patterns of the Soul's experience of externality in another form.

'The Lady of Shalott' can be a useful transition from 'The Palace of Art', with its empty and pathologised culture, to 'The Lotos-Eaters', for it configures concerns which appear separately in the other poems – feminine sexuality, art and language, oppressed labour, race. It is almost always seen as a critique of the isolated artist, cut off from life, and elided with 'The Palace of Art'. The Lady is thought of as retreating into the aesthetic world of infinite regression designated by the weaving which reproduces the mirror reflections which reproduce the world. 'The Lady of Shalott' is also identified with the sensuous withdrawal of 'The Lotos-Eaters'. But such a regress is alien to both 'The Palace of Art' and 'The Lotos-Eaters', and the categories of art and life are inadequate to all the poems if only because they are precisely what is being questioned in them. Even the more sophisticated Lacanian version of traditional accounts of 'The Lady of Shalott', as the failure of the primal consciousness of the mirror phase to recognise the radical disjunction of the symbolic order which constitutes the social order of the law, simply expresses this rigid opposition in a different language. 'The Lady of Shalott', which has no source, and is in fact the conflation of a number of mythic structures, is a modern myth, sealed off from interpretation with all the mysteriousness and inaccessibility of myth as surely as the Lady is sealed in her tower. As in 'The Palace of Art', breakdown and trauma are at the centre of the poem as the 'fairy' Lady breaks the taboo on access to the human world when she sees Lancelot, and dies. Fusing the many myths of the weaving lady, from Arachne to Penelope, with the myths of reflection carried by Narcissus and Echo (in 1842 her song 'echoes cheerly'), this is a poem of longing for sexual love, change and transformation, which is denied change. The Lady is a doomed victim, and dies a sacrificial death, failing to come into sexuality and language.

As with so many of the early poems, two readings are simultaneously at work. In one the Lady is locked into rigid oppositions, between the rural and the urban, an older order of labour by hand and mercantilism and trade, an organic, integrated world and a fragmented commercial world, between isolation and community, between passivity and action and aggression, female and male, the aesthetic and the 'real'. Unable to mediate these oppositions she appears to be condemned to passivity and death. In 1832 these oppositions are consolidated through the Lady's final message, '*The charm is broken utterly*' (169), which in 1842 was replaced by the wondering gaze of the knights and Lancelot's uncomprehending speech. Despite the tragic poignance of the Lady's death, the condemnation of woman to passivity seems deeply repressive, just as the rigid oppositions are deterministically conservative in their fixity.

Read as an expressive poem in which an assent to the experiencing subject's affective understanding of its predicament is foremost, the poem avails itself of this oppositional reading. George Eliot, who liked the poem, reread it in exactly this way when, in *The Mill on the Floss*, she made Maggie's tragic predicament, an unsuccessful attempt to break out of restriction, echo that of the Lady. Read as analysis beyond what the perception of the experiencing subject can encompass, as critique which is precisely concerned with the limits of expressive representation and representation itself, a second poem emerges which dissolves and interrogates the fixed positions and oppositions of the first and redefines its aesthetics and politics. This second reading is present both in 1832 and 1842, but 1842 exposes the problematic nature of the Lady's position more emphatically.

It must be remembered that this consummately arcane and beautiful poem is the latter-day poet's reconstruction of mythic representation. As well as discovering in Keightley's *The Fairy Mythology* that myths are part of a primal, indigenous peasant culture where the imaginative life of a nation resides, an intuitive form of thought which possesses an organic wholeness prior to thought, and in particular to artificial society, Tennyson would also have read that myths are instruments of power and ideology, used by a ruling class to coerce the ruled, and frequently changing with a change of power. Keightley wrote that myths are a 'poetic fiction' and that 'all the ancient systems of heathen religion were devised by philosophers for the instruction of rude tribes'.[14] Changes of religious faith transform the meaning of myths. So they become the instrument of the 'artificial' world. What is the status of myth? What is the relation between myth and power? What are the conditions of change? These are central questions in the analytical poem, the second lyric within the lyric.

The Lady is subject to a coercive taboo whose source and meaning she does not understand. 'She has heard a whisper say,/A curse is on her if she stay/ . . . She knows not what the curse may be' (39–40, 42). One of the conditions of the threat of the curse is that she does not 'stay' or cease from labour. For all its magical aesthetic quality, the weaving of the web is ceaseless work without escape and without *pleasure*. In 1832 the Lady worked without extremes of feeling – 'She lives with little joy or fear' (46). The Lady works just as the agrarian reapers work (they were pluralised in 1842). This affinity is illuminated by Carlyle in *Sartor Resartus* when he brings women and workers together, relating weavers at 'Arkwright looms' and 'silent Arachne' weavers who are all, he says, subject to and subjects of different kinds of cultural myth.[15] It seems that Tennyson is manoeuvring together the constraints working on women and the compulsions working on other forms of labour. The reapers and the Cambridge rick-burners reacting to the corn laws, the starving handloom weavers who were being displaced by new industrial processes, these hover just outside the poem and become strangely aligned with the imprisoned Lady. The possibility of change is explored through her psyche, as she becomes a representation of alienation and work.

She is unaware of the constraints worked upon her and obedient to the mysterious power until the appearance of lovers in the mirror forces her to reconceptualise her world as phantasmal and secondary, mere representation. It has not seemed so to her until this point: 'I am half sick of shadows' (71). The appearance of Lancelot brings the shock of a radically changed perception. Indeed the poem works structurally as a series of shocks and disjunctions. The shock of Lancelot's appearance, the violent shattering of the mirror, the disintegration of the web, the Lady's death. A correlative of these physical shocks are the gaps and disjunctions of the narrative which have the same effect, creating discontinuity and unsettling interpretation, just as the brilliant colours of the poem dazzle and confound. (The poetry of sensation is brilliantly at work here.) The powerful sexuality of Lancelot, physically close – 'A bow-shot from her bower-eaves' (73) – but oddly distanced by the dazzling double reflection of him and his image in the water refracted in the mirror, brings the culminating sense of lack which forces the Lady into action. The curse, suggesting the biblical curse of labour and sexuality, is invoked. But there is a strange irony here: if this is the curse of labour and sexuality the Lady was already subject to these in her isolated life in the tower. What was lacking was the sense of lack which forces a *realisation* of estrangement and oppression. The curse is the myth of power, a representation, which kept the Lady subject. But the double irony is that the curse comes 'true' as the condition of her realisation, at the very moment when she redefines her life as a condition of lack. Thus myths do materially organise experience.

It seems that in the simultaneous second poem which is critique rather than expressive experience, Tennyson is exploring not so much the passivity of the suffering subject but the recognition of lack as the precondition of a changed perception of the world which precipitates action. It is the moment when myth is recognised *as* myth, or as ideology, which enables action, and the construction of a new myth. The repercussions for feminine sexuality and for oppressed labour are the same. They are not caught in a determined world of rigid opposition but can transform it. In the first, expressive poem, however, the revolutionary moment fails. In the second, analytical poem, its failure is contradictory and ambiguous. The second poem loosens and reconfigures the rigidity of the first. The structural oppositions set up do not fall into a symmetry of positive and negative attributes. Power operates in the world of Camelot as much as in the tower of Shalott. If the world of the Lady is affective and passive in contrast to the world of action, that world of action is an aggressive one.

The world of Camelot which the Lady sees in her mirror is hierarchical, aristocratic and organised by religious feeling. It is an archaic world of simple exchange and barter. It is strangely mismatched with the sophisticated culture of Camelot as it is presented at the end of the poem. The mirror itself, far from being a static reflecting entity changes from blue to crystal. Indeed it is not clear whether the pictures in the mirror are always reflections of externality or the figures woven in the fabric and returned to the mirror, and thus may be constructs of the Lady's mind. The mirror is contradictory, and breaks down the opposition between art and 'reality' and with it the two opposing worlds. The world outside the tower is equally a confusion of reflection, image and figure. The Lady takes on the function of the mirror with her 'glassy countenance' as she floats down the river to Camelot. It is not clear whether her new song is a song of triumph or defeat. In 1832 she is compared to the swan whose death in the pagan mysteries Tennyson read of would have been the beginnings of transformation.[16] The Lady moves from picture to writing, abstract signs which confirm absence because they are substitutive symbols. But whether this is a liberation into the representative freedom of the sign or the dissociation of a unified mode of figuring is an open question. One thing is clear: she does not name herself but places herself in a pregiven hierarchy when she writes that she is 'The Lady of Shalott'. The 1842 revisions increase the sense that she is struggling with the need to represent herself but constantly deprived of this capacity. Lancelot speaks *for* her at the end of the poem, just as she earlier mirrors not herself but him. In 1842 Tennyson swept away the descriptive material which decorated her in jewels and colours, replacing these with images of work and toil and making her blanker, more empty, the mysterious other who defeats signification. No one has seen her. She is metonymically the blank space of flowers figured in the second stanza of the poem which displaces her at the moment when she is expected to appear. The sexual politics of the poem suggest that the sensuous freedom of femininity which can break the bonds of custom is severely restricted, and has repercussions in the wider politics of oppression. Like 'The Lotos-Eaters' the poem ends with a revolutionary situation *without* revolution. Turning from 'The Lady of Shalott' to that poem, it becomes evident that in 1842, this was Tennyson's most intense critique of oppression – but this time in a male world which uncannily seems to contain only one gender.

It is arguable that in many cases the revisions of 1842 create two incompatible texts within the same poem. This is a perfectly reasonable assumption. The 1832 poems, however, work by positing contradictions. The 1842 revisions tend to shift these more emphatically in the direction of critique, consciously textualising and exposing them and forcing contradictions into the open. This can be seen particularly in 'The Lotos-Eaters' and its heavy, luxuriant passivity, where Tennyson returns to the life and language of sensation.

The poem rolls its orchestration of enervated, slumbrous cadences to end, in 1832, in delirium, and in 1842 in the careless retreat of Epicurean gods. It is at once the culminating expression of the poetry of sensation and its greatest critique. Its motive is from Homeric myth, the enchanted fruit of the Lotos given to Odysseus' sailors. As a modern myth it carries along in its waves of sound the great literary testimonies against sloth, reminiscences of Spenser's *Fairy Queen*, and virtual quotation from Thomson's *Castle of Indolence*, and subjects them to unsettling investigation. The 'sultry toil' of 'The Palace of Art' reappears as the mariners repudiate labour. The analogue of the Lotos-Eaters is, of course, the opium-eater, as the drugged, semi-conscious cadences and their paradoxical intensity suggest – 'And deep-asleep he seemed, yet all awake' (35). It is no accident that the mariners' need for the Lotos is to allay the horrors of labour, for opium was often taken by industrial workers for the same reason.[17] Characteristic of the double poem, 'The Lotos-Eaters' is both the *expression* of the addictive desire in which drug requires further drugging, and an *analysis* of the conditions under which the unhappy consciousness and the unhappy body come into being. The unhappy consciousness is forced to construe experience in terms of passivity and consumption, a consumption which becomes consuming. In one reading a passive consciousness is the *result* of eating the Lotos. In the second reading exhaustion *causes* the addictive need to forget, rather than being the result of consuming the magic fruit. Behind the second reading is the cruelty of work, brute, mindless labour. This reading considers the conditions which *constitute* consciousness, volition and labour in passive terms, the conditions which force the need for the Lotos upon the mariners, and which necessitate the exhausted, semi-conscious reverie of forgetting, the longing for mindless life.

Tennyson brilliantly makes strange the postulates underlying mechanised labour and exploitation by transposing them to a 'colonial' island strangely like John Wilson's Isle of Palms. In circular fashion these postulates bring the world of mechanised labour into being as well as being generated by these very things. The contradictory terms of exploitation, in which natives offer resources which the intruders interpret as the magical release from toil, but which turn out to belong to the very conditions of labour, are disclosed by the simple move of allowing them to occur in another 'place', Homer's Greece. The colonial dream of magical consumption is located exactly in the mythological landscape from which its fantasies of obliterating the connection between labour and consumption derive, the untouched exotic island waiting for sailors to arrive.

It is important to see that the poem is not concerned with the literal, physical conditions of labour, but (true to Hallam's propositions) with the physical and mental world of *sensations* which emerges from oppressed labour. Moreover, as the poem proceeds, the material sensations which are so amazingly lyricised are seen to be inseparable from an account of consciousness which is both cause and effect of the experience of crushing passivity and toil. In other words, Tennyson is writing of the postulates on which the world of mechanised labour is founded, and which have changed the material world, as well as portraying the psychological state which arises from it. The poem works with four interrelated postulates in order to construe a world of alienation in which labour must be *the* consuming and destructive force. These are disclosed in the Introduction to the Choric Song and are, first, a world without the a priori category of time, so that acts of mind are the discontinuous fragments of being which so interested Hallam. Secondly, a world without agency is posited (partly a consequence of the world without time), a passive reaction to external powers. Thirdly, the poem posits a world in which consciousness is the reproduction of internal genetic physical sensations which echo in the caverns of the ear – 'And *music* in his ears his beating heart did make' (36) – so that consciousness is a sound system produced from the pulses of the blood, from sensation itself. Lastly it posits a world without language. The voices of the mariners become thin and sink to whispers. As the organisation of the Choric Song suggests, it seems to be a language without reference except to itself. In 1842, in the added coda about the gods, language has reached the state of pure aural signifier, a 'tale of little meaning', though 'the words are strong'. Why do these conditions belong together?

As we have seen, the postulates about consciousness, labour and language are circular and cause and effect of one another. The structure of the Introduction predetermines that of the Choric Song even though the Choric Song supposedly follows the changed condition which succeeds to the eating of the Lotos. In fact the Introduction, with a strange backwards relationship to the song, is an intensification of it, and the song adumbrates the elements of its preface rather than allowing the preface to explain the song. It is a condition without sequence, of repetition without progression and disjunction without change. Repetition, a feature of the new form of labour, is the key to the postulates of the Introduction. It is produced out of mesmeric repetition as parallelism and pattern take precedence over reference: 'The Lotos *blooms below* the barren peak:/The Lotos *blows* by every winding creek' (145–6) (my emphasis). Repetition reconfigures the same sound elements and destroys sequence as the Lotos flowers and falls, blooms and blows, simultaneously. Opposite conditions coexist and turn out to be forms of one another. If this is 'A land where all things always seemed the same!' (24), temporal conditions are suspended and all experience exists simultaneously (and logically not at all) as afternoon, moon and sunset occur together. Perceptual contradictions arise from this: the stream is intermittently in motion and still, creating that heightened nervous tension and uncertainty by which the poetry of sensation dissolves habitual associations and dislocates the sign. Water like a 'downward smoke' (8) reverses attributes (for logically it could flow upwards if smoke can fall downwards) and is 'Slow-dropping' (11). The correlative of this is both a frightful intensity and a dulled half-awareness which is projected into the Choric Song in the 'half-dream' (101), the 'half-drop't eyelid' (135) and the continual repetition of falling water, breaking waves and echoing caves which echo and repeat so continuously that experience takes place as a world of secondary reverberation, a kind of aural disorder. A 'modern', internal, psychological language in which objects are projections or evolve in correspondence with a state of mind – 'languid air' (5), 'weary dream' (6), 'slumbrous sheet of foam' (13) – exists side by side with an external world expressed through formal, archaic and artificial diction – '*Up-clomb* the shadowy pine against the *woven* copse' (18) (my emphasis). The historical disjunctions effected by this linguistic misalignment make both internal and external exist in hallucinatory estrangement from one another. Though it flagrantly borrows, sometimes almost word for word, from Thomson's *Castle of Indolence* (1748) the poem dissipates Thomson's rational and moral order, just as it dissolves the highly organised Spenserian stanza.

> And up the hills, on either side, a wood
> Of blackening pines, ay waving to and fro,
> Sent forth a sleepy horror through the blood;
> And where this valley winded out, below,
> The murmuring main was heard, and scarcely heard, to flow.
>
> A pleasing land of drowsyness it was:
> Of dreams that wave before the half-shut eye;
> And of gay castles in the clouds that pass,
> Forever flushing round a summer sky:
> There eke the sweet delights that witchingly
> Instil a wanton sweetness through the breast,
> And the calm pleasures always hovered nigh;
> But whate'er smacked of noyance, or unrest,
> Was far far off expelled from this delicious nest.
>
> (*The Castle of Indolence*, v, vi)

Just as Tennyson's poem disorganises the syntax and perceptual order of Thomson's poem, so he disorganises the rationally paired moral opposition between indolence and industry and shows it to be incoherent. The dichotomy between withdrawal and toil is an antithesis produced by and producing the passive account of consciousness and labour which is the condition of the Lotos-eating existence. It is predicated on the erasing of the link between labour and the objects of consumption, which is why the magical lethargy of the Lotos-Eaters is as uncomfortable and alienating as mechanical labour itself. Like Thomson, Tennyson allows the Lotos-Eaters to believe that labour is the differentiating characteristic of consciousness in that unlike animals or plants it *knows* that it exists and labours.

> All things have rest: why should we toil alone,
> We only toil, who are the first of things,
> And make perpetual moan,
>
> (60–2)

But labour here is marked by neither self-creation nor exertion or agency. It is suffering rather than labour, because it is imposed on a passive recipient, which is defined and defines itself as passive. To labour on the sea is to be driven to labour by the rocking waves, inert external force – 'Is there any peace/In ever *climbing* up the *climbing* wave?' (94–5) (my emphasis): 'We have had enough of action, and of motion, we,/*Rolled* to starboard, *rolled* to larboard, when the surge was seething free' (150–1) (my emphasis). The surge is not 'free', any more than the sailors are, but this is a way of denoting the structural conditions of work which Carlyle was recognising at the same time. 'The sailor furls his sail, and lays down his oar', just as 'the shuttle drops from the fingers of the weaver'.[18] Work was passive and mechanical, Carlyle recognised, because the conditions of labour had structurally changed, as the *results* of work no longer returned to the labourer, the great differentiating feature of the new systems of the division of labour from earlier forms of work. Tennyson brilliantly renders, not the literal relation of worker and product, but the psychological state the new indirect relations create. For the Lotos-Eaters all experience is always emptying out, because identity itself is transformed, 'taken from us' (91), into an estranged past when consciousness has no direct access to what it makes: *production*, materially and psychologically, is a *subtraction* from identity; 'ah, why/Should life all labour be? . . . Let us alone. What is it that will last?/All things are taken from us, and become/Portions and parcels of the dreadful Past' (86–8, 90–2). Experience loses its immediacy and belongs to the phantasmal past, 'dreadful' because the past itself is a series of disintegrated 'portions' which have been 'taken from' the ever disappearing present.

A 'genetic history of what we see *in* the mind', Carlyle says, not an understanding of the nature of consciousness itself, is the consequence of a passive, materialist theory of mind; and a mechanical account of labour is a postulate of this epistemology; they bring each other into being.[19] 'And music in his ears his beating heart did make' (36), Tennyson writes of the Lotos-Eaters who have been reduced to creatures of the history of their own physical sensations. The associationist philosophers, according to Carlyle (Locke, Hume and Reid in particular), ignore the metaphysical questions of necessity, Free Will, Mind and Matter, and produce an incoherent epistemology in which the lethargic consciousness fragments into sensation. This is dangerously close to Hallam's 'fragments of self'. Tennyson is concerned with the incoherence of such a consciousness and with its symptoms. The reduction of experience to the genetically produced 'music' of sensation in the ear means that the physical basis of mind develops a longing for the 'pure' sensation, its own physical essence divorced from thought. For if labour manifests itself in the unhappy awareness of a depleted consciousness, pleasure can only be found in immediate physical experience. But 'pure' sensation is impossible except in a condition where one could not by definition be aware of it – hence the yellow leaf and the overmellow apple grow and drop to the ground without volition (iii). Or if the passive consciousness cannot consume itself in the narcotic of forgetting it is forced to posit the present as a continual act of memory. For if consciousness is divided into lost experience and awareness of that loss, it is continually ahead of (or, by the same token, behind) its 'real' essence or immediate life, which it is forced to reconstruct as the past to constitute identity. Even the future will be a future memory, as the subjunctive here suggests.

> How sweet it were, hearing the downward stream, . . .
> To muse and brood and live again in memory. . . .
> (99, 110)

Experience as memory is the correlative of a mechanistic order. Hence the language of non sequitur and, in fact, the disappearance of language – voices are 'thin' and speech is 'whispered' – because the music reproduced in the ear is not only secondary but turns back on itself to reproduce a past sound again. The 'dewy echoes calling/From cave to cave' (39–40) re-sound through hollow spaces, as in the ear, as ever receding simulacra of themselves. In this reading language always represents a prior representation in a regress which is further and further from the experience which generates it. That is why the sounds of the island are scarcely heard. The music of the island (Tennyson never ceased to work upon *The Tempest*) falls almost soundlessly upon the ear. Language finally becomes pure sound only representing itself. The descriptive strategy of the poem is to bring this condition into being by displacing one comparison with another, which thus recedes from its source in the world. Music is softer than falling rose petals and then as soundless as condensing dew on granite (46–9). The mutual regress of language and consciousness here reminds one of Hallam's analysis of the modern self which withdraws into consciousness, issuing in melancholy and the sense of loss. The subject becomes a representation which only it can read. The loss of reference runs parallel to the dissociation of consciousness from what it has made in the world.

Fatalism is the necessary condition of a subject without continuity and

91

volition, Carlyle believed. It is this which is emphasised in 1842 with the addition of a passage in which the mariners find the possibility of returning to make an intervention in the 'confusion' (128) of their island home unthinkable. By definition a return to the past is literally unthinkable, because it can only be a new representation. The Lotos-Eaters imagine themselves to be horrendously posthumous to their social world, already part of history and art, somebody else's fictions, as their 'great deeds' (123) are sung by minstrels. The 'long labour' (130) of return is impossible. The failure to participate in history becomes critical in 1842, when the question of the will as agent is introduced and with it a set of directly moral and social issues. Carlyle's reference to Hume and Reid is part of a debate which is theological in essence. It was begun in 1830 by Sir William Hamilton, who attempted to rehabilitate the thinking of Reid by differentiating him sharply from Hume.[20] J. F. Ferrier continued this discussion in 1838–9, in a series of essays in *Blackwood's Magazine*, 'An introduction to the philosophy of consciousness'.[21] For Ferrier consciousness is locked into relationship with the world, since the mind brings its own categories to objects in the world, and frames them with its perceptual constructions, which cannot be divorced from things. Agency is created by the will, which is the antagonistic principle intruding on the life of simple sensation. Its struggle to exist and control the immediacy of experience through a reflexive act constitutes freedom. Otherwise the self must exist as 'reverie' without action in a world which is essentially violent because, like a being in the sea, consciousness is at the mercy of what is external to it. Here Ferrier oddly reproduces the violence done to the Lotos-Eaters by passive toil, for in avoiding the violence of the external world of sensation the will resorts to an equally violent act of domination over the senses.

> Nature and her powers have now no constraining hold over him; he stands out of her jurisdiction. In this act he has taken himself out of her hands into his own; he has made himself his own master. In this act he has displaced his sensations, and his sensations no longer monopolise him; they have no longer the complete mastery over him. In this act he has thrust his passions from their place, and his passions have lost their supreme ascendancy.[22]

Ferrier's argument is subtle and transforms sceptical argument into affirmation. In another part of his discussion he writes of sceptical philosophy:

> What sort of picture have their researches presented to our observation? Not the picture of a man; but the representation of an automaton, that is what it cannot help being, – a phantom dreaming what it cannot but dream – an engine performing what it *must* perform [Cf. the violence done to the Lotos-Eater in passive toil] – an

incarnate reverie – a weathercock, shifting helplessly in the winds of sensibility – a wretched association-machine, through which ideas pass linked together by laws over which the machine itself has no control – anything, in short, except that free and self-sustained centre of underived, and therefore responsible activity, which we call *Man*.[23]

As 'dreaming phantoms' or 'incarnate reverie' the mariners have been made incapable of 'mastering' their world. And yet Ferrier's intervening 'will' is an oddly uneasy and external faculty. 'Underived' from genetic history and intruding sui generis upon it, it is an idealist will, brought in to redress a materialist psychology. The ending added to 'The Lotos-Eaters' in 1842 pulls the poem in this direction, as the irresponsible Epicurean gods refuse to intervene in history. It appears to support a hypothesis which assumes the critical necessity of will, yet exposes its actual externality and idealism among the slothful gods. In 1832 the Lotos-Eaters propose to 'abide in the golden vale/ . . . till the Lotos fail' (26–7) in delirious ecstasy. So, in the Malthusian dread of scarcity which is not the dialectical opposite but the complement of the fantasy of the exploitation of magical fecundity, nature's stocks can be exhausted. The drug is a commodity which will inevitably, and disastrously, run out, leaving the Lotos-Eaters to their suicidal frenzy. The shock of this ending is extraordinarily appropriate both to the fantasy of endlessly exploitable colonial resources in the South Pacific and to the despair which Carlyle saw as the terminal moment of scepticism. It is also appropriate to a poem which was to be revised in the hungry 1840s, the era of cholera, starvation and massive hardship for an overcrowded and impoverished populace. But Tennyson altered it. The Lotos-Eaters reverse their oppressed position by an imaginary act in which they become gods, 'careless of mankind' (155) and dissociated from human life, regarding the catastrophes they actually create as things which happen without their responsibility – 'and the bolts are *hurled*/Far below them' (156–7). Gods repudiating agency and power: these are the mirror images of the oppressed consciousness without power. The gods turn away from the damage they wreak upon men, seemingly unaware of the relationship of exploitation between deities and men, who supplicate and sacrifice to the gods to no avail. Men, victims of famine, plague, war and natural disaster, caught up in a deluded religion which constructs divinity as a power to be appeased, a power which will intervene if the 'praying hands' (161) of the suffering persist in sacrifice, are caught up in a mystified relationship to the powers above.

Suffering men and careless gods are predicated on one another. The 1842 ending is fiercely ideological as the passage from Lucretius which is the basis of this coda is transformed into a master–slave nightmare. The ending does, paradoxically, return the mariners to the divided 'confusion' of human society, but human society is made strange in the act of imagination which sees it from another place, from the heaven of the Epicurean gods. Aristocratic detachment and the refusal of action and agency, oppressed toil and exploitation, are here forms of one another. It is a fierce analysis of the structure of an existing political situation. The coda introduces a critique which goes far beyond 1832 as it envisages a universe which conceives the idealist will as external to it and irrelevant to its affairs, 'underived' from experience indeed. Neither art nor language have a place here. The gods may aestheticise the 'doleful song' (162) of suffering and lamentation, but it is 'Like a tale of little meaning, though the words are strong' (164). The lamentation is uninterpretable as sign and meaning split apart, a consequence of the mariners' alienated music of the beating heart, where sound only refers to itself, and the object of signification slips into oblivion, just as the result of their labour upon the world is 'taken from' them and passes over into the memory. The coda is a strange place in which to find Hallam's poetry of pure sound. The life of pure sensation, Ferrier said, is blind – and deaf.[24]

The slumbrous cadences of 'The Lotos-Eaters' betray a real anxiety, as they struggle to represent a materialism which actually makes consciousness more and more phantasmal and to change the opposition between escape and toil by giving it a new political content. It can quite rightly be read as an overwhelming threnody on the desire to escape into forgetting, but that very desire constitutes an analysis and critique of deep contradictions. The additions of 1842 consolidate the critique. They are an extraordinary response to the worsening social conditions of the 1840s and turn the poem of 1832 virtually into a new text as the brutalising suffering of the 1840s finds a place in it. Change without change, engagement simultaneous with detachment, the continuity of the past as against the rupture of the present, a poetry of sound where meaning is the history of that sound rather than new signification – the risky, paradoxical subversiveness of the Apostles seems to have become increasingly difficult to hold as political and aesthetic positions and breaks down under the pressure of the 1840s. What might replace that aesthetic is one of the preoccupations of 1842.

LOSS OF NERVE: THE DECADENCE OF THE POETRY OF SENSATION AND A NEW CONSERVATISM

There was a loss of nerve in the 1840s. Tennyson's capacity to lure the energies of the unconscious into language and set them at play, as the poem simultaneously works on critique, wavers and loses its confidence. The double poem collapses, to reappear in a different form in *In Memoriam* (1850). The paradoxically disruptive aesthetics of organicist conservatism fragments and is displaced by a new account of poetry. The union of interdependent theories of consciousness, ideology, language and sexuality which underlies the early poems disintegrates. Hallam's failure to give adequate definition to the terms of 'sensation' and 'reflection' proved fatal as poetry was theorised antithetically either in terms of the discourse of moral statement or as a much weaker picturesque poetry of empathy rather than 'sensation', an empathy Ruskin was later to term the pathetic fallacy. The poetry of empathy abandons that provisional, experimental projection of consciousness and volition on to the other which exposes the structural relationship between subject and object, self and world, and which opens up a space for the analysis of categories and the play of representation. The mythic forms of the historicised consciousness disappear. Empathy is the expressive poet's outwards flow of emotion which attaches to and elides with the solid external world. This world echoes the categories of subjectivity unproblematically and returns human experience back to the perceiver. Thus it is a poetry of confirmation, not analysis, and deals with all the 'usual' themes – love, friendship, religion – which Hallam rejected. It is a kind of humanised form of natural theology which finds evidence for the existence of stable human values in the external world. The elision of consciousness with the world provides no space for an account of the sign or language as constructing relationships. Rather, language is not intrinsic to the construction of meaning but is an after-effect. Experience has to be translated into words and objectified, just as the external world reproduces human experience. Detail proliferates in the effort to fix and picture. Signification becomes the effect of external detail. The pretty Tennyson, always latent, emerges. For the difference between the two accounts of poetry is so fine that the poetry of sensation is always in danger of collapsing into the poetry of domesticated external description. But the art of the pretty Tennyson is no longer the feminised art of the Apostles, making and breaking forms at will. The appropriative power of the expressive poet is masculinised as the product of strength, the capacity to confirm and stabilise, ultimately the capacity of the ego to control the world by making it return the subject's experience.

The death of Hallam, the dispersal of the Apostles and above all the steadily worsening and disruptive social conditions of the late 1830s and 1840s, are all responsible for this loss of nerve. That poetry should enfranchise a wider readership, reaching out to the excluded, was also a factor in this change. A less arcane and simpler poetry, a moralised aesthetics rather than an aestheticised politics seemed to be the conservative answer to the radicals' demand for a poetry of the people.

It is strange that Tennyson's nerve was undermined at the very point when he was demonstrating a magnificent control over his material in the confident and often devastatingly analytical revisions of earlier work in 1842. Nevertheless, he nervously protects himself with conventionalities in other poems and defensively includes much more direct topical reference – 'The Gardener's Daughter', 'Audley Court', 'Walking to the Mail'. The new poems of 1842 are both clearer and more confused, more discursive, more concerned with the clear line of narrative and idyll, and yet have a tendency to disintegrate into dispersed descriptive detail.[25] The ballads are more like imitations than recreations ('The May Queen', 'Lady Clare'), the narratives are more like exemplary verse novella concerned with class problems rather than culture and less like the symbolic myths of the earlier decade. The tone becomes aggressive. It is hard to believe that the appalling racism of 'Locksley Hall' and the statement that fifty years of Europe are preferable to a cycle of Cathay can be serious positions after the profound understanding of the importance of ancient cultures and myth in the earlier work, but the problem with this poem is precisely its uncertainty of tone. Nothing enables one to see how far it is a dramatic poem or whether the virulent bluster has a deconstructive moment. It is partly about the move from hopeful conservative organicism to rancid Toryism but it is not carefully discriminated. If it is a parody it is a bad parody and seems written in deference to pessimistic aristocratic Toryism rather than to the new audience which Tennyson's reviewers asked him to reach.[26] The same uncertainty can be seen in the struggle of 'The Two Voices', which ends with the sight of a Christian family. The speaker knows that such simplicity is not within reach of his complex consciousness, but the picture is all too like the optimistic deistic piety of Robert Montgomery, with the reservation that the bourgeois couple displaces the working-class family.

> One walked between his wife and child,
> With measured footfall firm and mild,
> And now and then he gravely smiled.
>
> The prudent partner of his blood
> Leaned on him, faithful, gentle, good,
> Wearing the rose of womanhood.
>
> And in their double love secure,
> The little maiden walked demure,
> Pacing with downward eyelids pure.
>
> (412–20)

Tennyson talked of 'the need of going forward' after Hallam's death, but actually writes of a continually dissolving horizon in 'Ulysses':

> Yet all experience is an arch wherethrough
> Gleams that untravelled world, whose margin fades
> For ever and for ever. . . .
>
> (19–21)

This uncertainty is a correlative of the dissolution of the early aesthetics. Towards the 1840s Tennyson's work was pulling in two directions. One took him towards the common-sense Wordsworthianism which assumed that simplicity of diction, permanent and universal moral truths which 'transcend' the immediately political and exemplary tales, are a way of gaining access to the sympathies of a wide audience. R. C. Trench and John Sterling (who reviewed the 1842 volume) exemplify such assumptions – in whose poetry in fact the ethics and aesthetics of traditional Tory poetry reappear in a redefined form. The other pull was towards lyric sensuousness such as is to be found in the work of Monckton Milnes. But Milnes's work represents the decadence of the poetry of sensation. It is not grounded on the epistemological daring of the earlier Apostles and demonstrates how vulnerable an untheorised, libidinal luxuriance could be. It was Sterling who assimilated the poetry of sensation back into a theory of moral empathy – and tamed it.[27] This domesticating process is the subject of this section, which concludes the discussion of the post-Coleridgean formation to which Tennyson's early poetry belongs.

In 1835 Edward Fitzgerald wrote anxiously to Tennyson asking him not to let well-meaning friends 'wean' him 'away from indulging in quaint and wonderful imaginations, and screw you up too tightly to moral purpose'.[28] Such 'screwing up' is clearly present in Tennyson's ambivalent response to Henry Taylor's anti-Romantic Preface to his long heroic drama, *Philip Van Artevelde*, published in 1834. In a letter to James Spedding, to whom he showed many of his new compositions, and who was himself far more interested in 'moral purpose' than Fitzgerald, Tennyson wrote, 'I think him a noble fellow. I close with him in most that he says of modern poetry though it may be that he does not take sufficiently into consideration the *peculiar* strength evolved by such writers as Byron and Shelley which however mistaken they may be did yet give the world another heart and new pulses – and so are we kept going. . . . But Philip . . . makes me shamed of my own faults'.[29] True, he was writing to Spedding, who had been flattered by Taylor's recognition of his own writing. But he had also written, in the same letter, as if he contemplated two very distinct kinds of poetry, one which was all 'Sweetness and conciseness and magnificence' and another which was concerned with 'Choice of words and precision in combining them'.[30] Taylor certainly condemned the element of 'sweetness' and 'magnificence' in Romantic poetry.

Taylor's Preface, dated May 1834, is in fact a sweeping reversal of all that Hallam had admired in the work of Keats and Shelley. The Preface attempts to restore the poetry of reflection, a 'higher, graver' and more responsible faculty than 'profusion of imagery' produced by irresponsible 'indulgence in the mere luxuries of poetry'.[31] Taylor's main target is Byron who had always been regarded critically by the Apostles. Sterling early wrote a critique of his work in the *Athenaeum*, which Tennyson knew.[32] But, nearer home, Shelley also comes in for attack. What must have been particularly unsettling, however, is Taylor's directly moral and rational attack on a poetry of sensation. Wilson had criticised Tennyson for ignoring common sympathies, for being obscure and for failing to understand the moral nature of simple meditative poetry. But he liked the richness and sweetness of Tennyson's poetry. And he thought it self-conscious and misguided, but not immoral. Taylor, however, is far more extreme. He saw such poetry as deeply anti-rational and immoral. The same complaints as Wilson made of Tennyson do reappear, but with a puritanical and ethical self-righteousness and rigidity. Where Wilson wanted poetry to 'record' and 'idealise', Taylor wanted it to inform and instruct. Not only did Romantic poetry refuse to walk upon the common earth or to breathe the common air, as Wilson remarked of Tennyson, but it turned away absolutely from life and from morality, from 'the mazes of life in all its classes and under all its circumstances'.[33]

The lack of subtlety in comparison with Hallam is plain to see. Where Hallam saw the poetry of sensation as the result of conscious choice, Taylor believes it to occur through deficiency, 'when a thought was not forthcoming'. Where Hallam sees the poetry of sensation in epistemological and psychological terms, Taylor sees 'profusion of imagery' and 'beauty of language' as 'external embellishments'. Where Hallam sees the alienated position of the artist in relation to the analysis of a cultural condition, Taylor converts this into a straight opposition between art and life. Where Hallam had been careful to insist that the poetry of sensation evolves through subtle psychological relationships with the world, Taylor makes an opposition between form and content, language and the world – 'They wanted . . . subject matter'. It is clear to him that an 'image' is irrelevant to 'subject matter' and has no content.[34]

> They [Romantic poets] exhibit, therefore, many of the most attractive graces and charms of poetry – its vital warmth not less than its external embellishments – and had not the admiration which they excited tended to produce an indifference to higher, graver, and more various endowments, no one would have said that it was, in any evil sense, excessive. . . .
>
> So keen was the sense of what the new poets possessed, that it never seemed to be felt that anything was deficient in them. Yet their deficiencies were not unimportant. They wanted, in the first place, subject-matter. A feeling came more easily to them than a reflection, and an image was always at hand when a thought was not forthcoming. Either they did not look upon mankind with observant eyes, or they did not feel it to be any part of their vocation to turn what they saw to account. It did not belong to poetry, in their apprehension, to thread the mazes of life in all its classes and under all its circumstances, common as well as romantic, and, seeing all things, to infer and to instruct: on the contrary, it was to stand aloof from

everything that is plain and true; to have little concern with what is rational or wise; it was to be, like music, a moving and enchanting art, acting upon the fancy, the affections, the passions, but scarcely connected with the exercise of the intellectual faculties. These writers had, indeed, adopted a tone of language which is hardly consistent with the state of mind in which a man makes much use of his understanding. The realities of nature, and the truths which they suggest, would have seemed cold and incongruous if suffered to mix with the strains of impassioned sentiment and glowing imagery in which they poured themselves forth. Spirit was not to be debased by any union with matter in their effusions, dwelling, as they did, in a region of poetical sentiment which did not permit them to walk upon the common earth or to breathe the common air.[35]

Because Taylor's distinction between form and content converts the poetry of sensation (which, for Hallam, *was* a content) into formalism he is quick to see that the language of such poetry aspires to music by releasing itself from reference. But for him this is an abstract, empty sensuousness which is politically dangerous. The conflation of an unmasculine sexual licence with political anarchy, always incipient in the traditional Tory attacks on Tennyson, but never so strongly expressed, is easily made. Byron's expenditure of 'uninformed energy' – 'he turned his genius loose' – combined with poverty of material, 'a want of material to work up', dissipates his work. The fear that a profligate expenditure of energy brings impotence with it underlies his hostility. Byron's heroes, 'in the eyes of a reader of masculine judgment', want 'strength'.[36]

But it is Shelley for whom the metaphors of sexuality and anarchy most strongly enter critical discourse as models of the imagination. What alarms Taylor about Shelley is the capacity of the poetic language to restructure relationships and unfix signification by creating new orders of reference for the sign. And Shelley destabilises the fixed constitution of relationships by undermining a dualistic epistemology. His aim was to 'unrealize' every object, 'presenting them under forms and combinations in which they are never to be seen through the mere medium of our eyesight'. Shelley 'decomposed' things and so abandons 'natural order and coherency'.[37] In other words, Shelley's representations question rational dualism and the assumption that there is an unmediated, 'natural' relationship between the seer and what is seen. The authority of reason and the natural order are usurped by the imagination as imposter and its rebellious, self-conferred authority. The imagination explicitly enters into the master–slave relationship. Taylor would halt this by returning words to things and refusing the open play of signification.

They would transfer the domicile of poetry to regions where reason, far from having any *supremacy* or *rule*, is all but unknown, an alien and an outcast; to seats of anarchy and abstraction, where imagination exercises the shadow of an authority, over a people of phantoms, in a land of dreams. [my emphasis][38]

Taylor at least recognised that Shelley's poetry is concerned with power. His own massive, anti-revolutionary dramatic poem, *Philip Van Artevelde*, written in a style of plain, stodgy high seriousness is predictably about a political usurper who is defeated by the contradictions of the attempt to rule rationally when his rule rests on initial subversion. However rational his reasons for revolt, insubordination sets off a chain of anarchy. It is actually an attack on trade unionism and combination. It is set in Flanders at the end of the fourteenth century, a time when the 'Commonality' were everywhere thought to be in danger of rising against 'the Feudal Lords and men of substance'.[39] The parallel with contemporary Europe is explicit. Having challenged traditional, corrupt aristocratic rule, Van Artevelde is faced with controlling the activities of the dangerous 'White-Hoods' who support his cause, combinations of labour analogous to modern trade unions. The extent of Taylor's reactionary hatred of 'anarchy' is disclosed here. It is in relation to the unions that Taylor quotes James Spedding's anonymous pamphlet against political unions because its arguments are relevant to his play. Flanders has 'something like the same forms and divisions' as England.[40] Covertly the play is about the Tolpuddle Martyrs, who were transported for combination. Spedding's liberal, Anglican, post-Coleridgean conservatism comes together with Taylor's more intransigent positions. Spedding, writing typically with a belief in the organic unity of a nation, argues that trade unions are divisive and have little to do with 'the real freedom of a nation' because they force men to act in 'multitudes' where the individual voice is drowned. Thus they are 'fraught with destruction'. Here is Carlyle's sense that organised labour and representation abstracts the identity and creates an estranging split between the self in its living immediacy and the sign which represents the authentic self. For Taylor the mistake is to believe that 'inauthenticated' merit can be given abstract political form at all. And if Artevelde's case is fundamentally flawed, the only solution is to remain within a hierarchy as the lesser of two evils. Repressive reason is preferable to anarchic reason. The problem is, however, that the democratic Artevelde too often makes convincing sense.

> But we are here no niggards of respect
> To merit's unauthenticated forms,
> And therefore do I answer you, and thus:–
> You speak of insurrections: bear in mind
> Against what rule my father and myself
> Have been insurgent: whom did we supplant?
> There was a time, so ancient records tell,

100

There were communities, scarce known by name
In these degenerate days, but once far-famed,
Where liberty and justice hand in hand
Ordered the common weal.[41]

Taylor's split between sensuous writing and moral writing is one which actually exists in the poetry of Tennyson's friends. It was a fracture to which the precarious subtlety of the earlier aesthetics exposed poetry. It is possible to see through the writings of these contemporaries how the decadence of the poetry of sensation calls forth its opposite, moral and reflective writing, and how these reconfigure in the new poetry of affective moral empathy. The writing of Monckton Milnes represents sensation-based, aesthetic or Keatsian poetry and its politics. Milnes was, of course, the first serious biographer of Keats and editor of his letters. It is interesting to see the fusion of Keats and Tennyson in his work, and to watch the simplifications and travesties of much more complex positions and more subtle language.

In his *Memorials of a Tour in Some Parts of Greece, Chiefly Poetical* (1834), about which he wrote to Tennyson, there are several direct thefts of Tennysonian vocabulary. His poem, 'Tempe', is a simplified version of 'The Lotos-Eaters' and filches its 'emerald-coloured water falling' (vii) in a poem which declares a need to escape into the 'delicious calm' of the past. The references are directly sexual and erotic, and the poem falls into the easy opposition between escape and duty which Tennyson's poem avoids and implicitly criticises.

Now this delicious calm *entices* us,
These platan shades, to let the dull world go.
A poet's *mistress* is a hallowed thing,
And all the beauties of his verse become
Her own; so be it with the poet's vale.
Listen those emerald waters murmuring.
Behold the cliffs, that wall the god's old home,
And float into the Past with softly swelling sail. [my emphasis][42]

If one compares the syntax in which Tennyson's emerald waters appear with these lines the difference between Milnes's poem, with its slack, inconsequential syntax, and Tennyson's strength, becomes clear. With extraordinary virtuosity Tennyson organises section VII of 'The Lotos-Eaters' with a main verb which falls only in the last line – 'Only to hear *were* sweet' (144) (my emphasis). Up to this point the whole section is held together with present participles and infinitives – 'to watch, . . . to hear . . . to watch . . . to hear'. These constructions cancel action and allow each discrete perception to act independently, even though it repeats almost exactly in meaning and grammatical structure what has preceded it.

Tennyson allows syntactical and grammatical structures to create meaning by creating a sequence of forms without causal dependence on one another – the fate of the passive consciousness. This stanza is an ostensive definition of what Hallam meant by the conveying of meaning through structure and sound and organically related grammatical forms. Tennyson's discontinuous syntax is not the voluptuary's escape, but registers the process of forgetting.

If Milnes simplifies, he does not always trivialise the Apostles' response to the immediacy and unifying agency of myth. But his work bifurcated as he continued to publish and splits into exactly the opposition between aesthetic form and moral experience which Tennyson's early poetry seeks to analyse and investigate. The poetry of sensation decays as it ceases to be a way of exploring experience from another place but occupies a marginalised position which slides easily from seeing itself as the solvent of custom to becoming fixed in a permanently transgressive mode. Such a fixity contradicts the fluent, exploratory drama of the poetry of sensation. It consolidates rather than heals the permanently split culture to which the Apostles believed themselves to be the heirs. In 'Greek Mythology', a poem in hexameters which contains another theft from 'The Lotos-Eaters', Milnes evokes the naive poet described by Schiller who works with what Tennyson called the 'new pulses' of transforming feeling. Here Milnes writes of the 'new senses' which are reflexively created by the interaction of mind and nature, man and the world.

> fresh in his boyhood,
> Out of his own exuberant life, man gave unto nature,
> And new senses awoke, through every nerve of creation![43]

The 'dream' and seeming construct reality. We can only accept the reflections of mind as truth, he writes. But here the poet's dream is not experience itself, constructing and reconstructing the universe, as it is for Tennyson, but is set in opposition to 'falsities that seem'. As Tennyson saw, theoretically there can be no 'falsities' if the sceptic's 'truth' holds, just as there can be no opposition between the truths of dream and waking. Milnes's version of the 'flowing' philosophy is different.

> Alas! we cannot quite awake, –
>   But when we feel we dream,
> That hour, our heart is strong to shake
>   The falsities that seem.
> For our bark is on the angle
>   Of a wide and bending stream,
> Whose bosky banks entangle
>   The eye's divergent beam; –
> The ridgy steeps hide in the way,

> Whither the stream is quest,
> As on a lake, the mirror'd day
> Repeats its waveless rest.[44]

The split in Milnes's work can be seen in the naive, smug social responsibility of *Poetry for the People* (1840) which attempts to provide 'specimens' of poetry for the masses.

> Heart of the People: Working men!
> Marrow and nerve of human powers;
> Who on your sturdy backs sustain
> Through Streaming Time this world of ours.
>   ('Labour')[45]

Milnes can only admire the resignation of the poor to suffering. However, the people are exhorted to remember that even the wealthy work – labour 'Is lord and master of us all' – and to remember that they can sustain themselves on the simple pleasures of the senses, books, family loyalty and children.[46] To compare this naive, quiescent account of labour with 'The Lotos-Eaters' and its analysis of the consciousness of oppressed labour is to see that Milnes has not addressed the problem. The conservative discourse of culture breaks down in an attempt to get to grips with class. In *Palm Leaves* (1844), a volume which, true to the Apostles' understanding of the deep unity of myth, tries to fuse Christian and oriental myth, Milnes endorses and simplifies the poet's commitment to 'beauty' in such a way as to suggest the anarchy described by Taylor. It is another example of the breakdown and failure of the poetry of sensation. The motive of 'The Thinker and the Poet' is interesting: the poet has no attachment to an exclusive system of thought, culture or ideology but moves from history to history, culture to culture, myth to myth. The use of the many wives of the harem to suggest the promiscuous embodiments of the poet is a deliberate attempt to indicate the poet's refusal of limit in aesthetic detachment, but it cannot but suggest a licentious and careless response to the imagination. It is vulgar Keatsianism, or vulgar Tennysonianism, and represents the commitment to sensuous energy condemned by Taylor in his reactionary backlash. The jingle metre does not help. It misses urbanity.

> Often Allah grants indulgent
> Pleasure that may guard from sin:
> Hence your wives may number four:
> Though he best consults his reason,
> Best secures his house from treason,
> Who takes one and wants no more. . . .
> But the heaven-enfranchised Poet
> Must have no exclusive home,
> He must feel, and freely show it, –

103

Phantasy is made to roam.
He must give his passions range.
He must serve no single duty,
But from Beauty pass to Beauty, . . .
With all races, of all ages,
He must people his Hareem. . . . .[47]

Milnes's work is always on the verge of a rather sticky luxuriance which has Leigh Hunt and Keats behind it as well as Tennyson. Two other writers suggest the contrary movement of Victorian poetry towards Wordsworth. Wordsworth's poetry could be assimilated and appropriated in an almost inexhaustible number of ways. The poetry of Trench and Sterling represents two ways of reading Wordsworth. It is part of the record of the Victorian reading of Wordsworth through Tennyson. Trench, the friend who drew forth 'The Palace of Art' by telling Tennyson that he could not live in art, developed a 'Wordsworthian' poetry of exemplary tale and moralised commentary. The poems carefully point their ethical meaning and always end with an elucidatory stanza about the significance of an event or situation. Trench represents one of the pressures pushing Tennyson in the direction of 'moral purpose'. What he does is to take the lyrical ballad of Wordsworth and demystify the action into straightforward moral or religious significance. In fact, situations are Christianised into religious texts for meditation. The language is plain, with a trace of elevated diction, and the rhyme and metre are carefully regular. This poem is clearly modelled on poems like 'Expostulation and reply' or 'We are seven', in which adults demonstrate a blank failure to comprehend the insights of children. Here a didactic lesson is drawn from a child's disobedience. Repressively, a father forbids his child to play among churchyard graves. But the child converts the father.

A Walk in a Churchyard

We walked within the churchyard bounds,
  My little boy and I –
He laughing, running happy rounds,
  I pacing mournfully.

'Nay, child! it is not well,' I said,
  'Among the graves to shout,
To laugh and play among the dead,
  And make this noisy rout.'

A moment to my side he clung,
  Leaving his merry play,
A moment stilled his joyous tongue,
  Almost as hushed as they:

Then, quite forgetting the command
  In life's exulting burst
Of early glee, let go my hand,
  Joyous as at the first.

And now I did not check him more,
  For, taught by Nature's face,
I had grown wiser than before
  Even in that moment's space:

She spread no funeral-pall above
  That patch of churchyard ground,
But the same azure vault of love
  As hung o'er all around.

And white clouds o'er that spot would pass,
  As freely as elsewhere;
The sunshine on no other grass
  A richer hue might wear.

And formed from out that very mould
  In which the dead did lie,
The daisy with its eye of gold
  Looked up into the sky.

The rook was wheeling overhead,
  Nor hastened to be gone –
The small bird did its glad notes shed,
  Perched on a gray head-stone.

And God, I said, would never give
  This light upon the earth,
Nor bid in childhood's heart to live
  These springs of gushing mirth –

If our one wisdom were to mourn,
  And linger with the dead,
To nurse, as wisest, thoughts forlorn
  Of worm and earthy bed.

Oh, no! the glory earth puts on,
  The child's unchecked delight,
Both witness to a triumph won,
  (If we but read aright) –

A triumph won o'er sin and death,
  From these the Savior saves;

> And, like a happy infant, Faith
> Can play among the graves.[48]

The first four verses describe the incident. Then follows the meditation which brings God and nature together, with a hint of 'the sunshine in the grass' of the 'Immortality' ode – 'The sunshine on no other grass/A richer hue might wear'. God, the poet remembers, created a joyous nature. Thus he proceeds to a conclusion and a final allegorical significance as Faith is personified as a happy infant. This poem has the Apostles' respect for pleasure as a principle of feeling, closed into a moral straitjacket. Trench's work always moves in the direction of the poetry of reflection. Consider the meditative octosyllabic couplets of 'The Descent of the Rhone': it begins with a section on the power of memory to invoke the grandeur of nature 'To the spirit's inward eye' – another half quotation from Wordsworth – and ends with the translation of the movement of travel down the Rhone into an expected symbol – life and eternity.

> That we are from childhood's morn
> On a mightier river borne,
> Which is rolling evermore
> To a sea without a shore:
> Life the river, and the sea
> That we seek – eternity.[49]

Imperturbably, Trench can turn the near truisms and hesitant unorthodox moral moments of Wordsworth's poems into real commonplaces. Unlike Keble's poems, Trench's morality is obvious because he thought Wordsworth's was. His Wordsworth guaranteed this, just as Wilson's Wordsworth guaranteed the purity of the commonplace. He can also transform the subtle conflict of 'The Palace of Art' and 'The Lady of Shalott' into a straightforward opposition. This is an account of the life of the 'Spirit' in 'The Story of Justin Martyr' who vows – 'to dwell alone,/My spirit on its lordly throne'. The Spirit dwells in isolation in a world of moral self-control and transcendent truths (in art, poetry and sculpture). Its aim is to be pure from all that is worldly and to escape 'the chain/Of custom', the rigid, associative principles which Hallam thought the artist should break, but which here, by implication, are chains we should wish to wear.

> And how before me from my youth
> A phantom ever on the wing,
> Appearing now, now vanishing,
> Had flitted, looking out from shrine,
> From painting, or from work divine
> Of poet's, or of sculptor's art;
> And how I feared it might depart,

That beauty which alone could shed
Light on my life – and then I said,
I would beneath its shadow dwell,
And would all lovely things compel,
All that was beautiful or fair
In art or nature, earth or air,
To be as ministers to me,
To keep me pure, to keep me free
From worldly service, from the chain
Of custom, and from earthly stain;[50]

The result is anxiety and depressive feeling, relieved only by a mysterious
Angel who suggests that presumptuous neglect of God is the cause of
despair. The simplifications and moralising of Tennyson's poem are
interesting. The psychological and epistemological subtleties disappear in
these loosely strung couplets, deriving their reflective plainness from
Wordsworth, their prolixity from Trench. It is fascinating to see the Victorian poet, whether through Wordsworth or Keats, writing and rewriting
the seminal early poems, 'The Palace of Art' and 'The Lotos-Eaters' in
particular.

Wilson's common-sense Wordsworth, Trench's moral Wordsworth; to
these one must add Sterling's decorative Wordsworth. Reviewing Tennyson's 1842 poems, Sterling asked for a poet who would be able to grasp
and transmute the spirit of the age. 'Our overwrought materialism fevered
by its own excess into spiritual dreams' required a poetry which would
return this intensity back to the world in 'crystalline clearness and lustre'.[51]
Wordsworth, though a fine poet of ethical meditation and 'stern speculation', has turned away from 'the present movements of life', or immediate
contemporary events, and 'has made it far less his aim to represent what
lies around him by means of self-transference into all its feelings'. Neither
has Tennyson any more than Wordsworth achieved 'the prophetic task' of
the poet. But there is one class of poems for which Sterling praises Tennyson highly because they introduce a new 'clearness, solidity, and certainty
of mind' into the volume. The poems he means are the idylls – 'Dora',
'The Gardener's Daughter', 'Walking to the Mail', 'Audley Court'. These
blank-verse poems are in 'a style almost unattempted in the earlier series'
and have a 'quiet completeness and depth, a sweetness arising from the
happy balance of thought, feeling, and expression'.[52] Sterling compares
these narrative poems with the great narratives of Wordsworth – 'Michael',
'The Brothers', the story of Margaret in *The Excursion*. Wordsworth's English idylls, however, have a certain remoteness and coldness (Sterling's
tone is apologetic and regretful here). They are too much under 'the
dominion of the moral idea'. They are 'grave', they are 'penitential'.[53]
These criticisms are followed by effusive praise, as if to compensate for

this derogation of respect for the master. It is clear that Tennyson's English idylls are preferable to Wordsworth's for their grace and feeling. Tennyson's idylls soften the Wordsworthian paradigm and *domesticate* it. The reasons offered for approval of such poems are fascinating. Both legendary and philosophical and moral poetry are 'subordinate' to the idyll. Simple, everyday narratives are paramount. In them the 'sweet and fervid impulse of the heart' is under careful intellectual control (perhaps because a story line requires this). But above all, the poet's capacity for empathy is freely given. Feeling identifies itself with 'the delightful affections' – love, joy, compassion, sadness, as far as we can tell from Sterling's descriptions of these idylls. Tennyson is 'the most genial poet of English rural life'.[54]

So all Hallam's excluded categories are reintroduced. In particular, the poet's empathy 'melts out as one long happy sigh into union with the visibly beautiful'. The passage is worth quoting at length so that the implication of its vocabulary can be grasped. Wordsworth's idylls are domesticated and made decorative. In the same way, the poetry of sensation is moralised. For, in addition, the poet's imagination is fused and lost in 'union' with the beautiful. Sterling does not mean the complex, provisional experimental projection of consciousness into the other which makes one newly aware of the relation of subject and object, described by Hallam a decade earlier. He means the projection of self into the beautiful things of the external world so that these *echo* human feelings, endorsing and confirming the emotional and moral certainties of experience. The heart, the solid core of the affective life, has replaced the fluid senses as the motive force of Sterling's new poetry. That certainties exist is what Sterling's appreciation of the idylls is built upon. The world reflects back the emotional and the moral, made beautiful to the perceiver, reassuring him or her of the centrality of the consciousness. It is a new conservatism, not the Tory rereading of Wordsworth one finds in Wilson a generation before. This is a peculiarly Victorian reading of moral empathy. It created a new poetic structure which was negotiated by Arnold, Clough and the Pre-Raphaelites and beyond for the rest of the century. It is present not only in Tennyson's idylls but in the work of Sterling himself. This is where the pretty Tennyson comes from, as the beauty of the external world is reproduced in detail as an equivalent of a psychological and moral condition rather than being a new form of representation which explores each new moment of the mind's understanding of the otherness of the world. Language is extrinsic to the poetry of moral empathy because it follows and registers an experience prior to language. It is intrinsic to the poetry of sensation because it constructs the process of experience and is indivisible from it. Sterling wrote,

In his work there has been art enough required and used to give

such clear and graceful roundness; but all skill of labour, all intellectual purpose, kept behind the sweet and fervid impulse of the heart.
Thus, all that we call affection, imagination, intellect, melts out as
one long happy sigh into union with the visibly beautiful, and with
every glowing breath of human life.[55]

Art, labour and intellect are 'kept behind' the impulse of the heart. They
are dominated by the affective – 'kept behind' suggests a firm repression
– and follow it like an echo. The materiality of language is subsidiary to
the prior 'impulse'. The attempt is to retrieve the idea of the beautiful in
Hallam's life of sensation but to displace it into the decoration of moral
and emotional experience. Tennyson's 'The Gardener's Daughter' records
a conversation on this very question of the reciprocal self-confirming union
of emotion and the world, which suggests that Tennyson was aware of a
new strategy.

> And Eustace turned, and smiling said to me,
> 'Hear how the bushes echo! by my life,
> These birds have joyful thoughts. Think you they sing
> Like poets, from the vanity of song?
> Or have they any sense of what they sing?
> And would they praise the heavens for what they have?'
> And I made answer, 'Were there nothing else
> For which to praise the heavens but only love,
> That only love were cause enough for praise.'
>
> (96–104)

The 'sense' of the poet is rational sense, not the poetry of sensation, which
seems now to be explicitly excluded from this new poetics. The poet
projects the emotion of love onto the birds, which makes sense of the
universe. Thus by 1842, the year of virtually the worst economic recession
of the century, the year of violent Chartist agitation, conservative poetics
attempts to unify through empathy and the harmonious moral universe.

Sterling's poem, more grudgingly named 'The Sexton's Daughter' in
Poems (1839) (perhaps he knew of Tennyson's idylls, as 'The Gardener's
Daughter' was written, though not published, in the early 1830s), is clearly
an attempt to soften the Wordsworthian idyll. The long, hard life of the
sexton's daughter, in which she becomes estranged from her father and
family and finally dies, the grieving father at her grave, is a narrative with
plenty of opportunity for suggesting the union of man and nature through
the pathetic fallacy. Human feelings are projected onto the world and
imaged and returned to the perceiver at important moments in the narrative. This is a typical passage from Sterling's poem.

> November days are dull and dark,
> And well they teach the heart to ponder,

109

Which sometimes needs must pause to mark
How fades from earth its garb of wonder.

We breathe at whiles so charmed an air,
By sound each leaf's light fall we learn,
No breeze disturbs the spider's snare,
That hangs with dew the stately fern.

Soon heaves within the boundless frame
A strong and sullen gust of life,
And rolling waves and woods proclaim
The untuned world's increasing strife.

Mid boom and clang and stormy swell,
And shadows dashed by blast and rain,
Leaves heaped, whirled, routed, sweep the dell,
And glimpses course the leaden main.

And yet, though inward drawn and still,
There beats a hidden heart of joy;
Beneath the old year's mantle chill
Sleeps, mute and numb, the unconscious boy.[56]

Tennyson was to transform this conventional poetry of ethico-affective anthropomorphic pathos only much later in *In Memoriam* (1850). (Indeed, the poems of calm and storm seem to draw on Sterling.) In Sterling's hands this mode possesses an uneasiness without the complexity of Tennyson's uneasiness, as the generalised quintessential Englishness of pastoral idyll is used to drain immediacy from suffering in a rural community. It is a style which becomes increasingly unconvincing in the scenes describing the emigrant community in North America to which the narrative moves in the last part of the poem, attempting to erase the discontinuity of colonial relationships by affirming continuity of style. For there both Englishness and universal anthropomorphic feeling are threatened. Nevertheless the poetic strategies are clear. The desired effect is to confirm and to console, as human emotion, transcending all difference of class and nation, comes to be shared by the natural world, suggesting a nature, and a God, which are there to support the human soul.

Such Victorian Wordsworthianism makes an easy step to simple anthropomorphism and the pathetic fallacy, domesticating both feeling and the world by making them forms of one another. This seems to belong to a desperate desire to produce a new account of communality which would transcend social division. It travesties more complex theories of mind and consciousness, such as are to be found in Wordsworth himself, in Hallam's theory, in early Tennyson, in Ferrier and in W. J. Fox, to whom this discussion will shortly move. It assumes not only that nature confirms human values, but that these values are already fixed and changeless. Hence the psychological theory of empathy tends to appear in conservative texts, as poetry demonstrates a reassuring experience. Hence Ruskin's attack in *Modern Painters*, for he believed that such a transference of feeling was sentimental and untruthful. There is no room for a theory of language in this poetics, as a simple, expressive account of projection as 'union' with the beautiful takes place. This model of male consummation is one which precedes the mediating function of language. Hence the image-making capacity of language collapses into description and discursive writing. Moral empathy is something into which sophisticated theories can too easily dissolve. It is appropriate, therefore, to consider the genesis of this quintessential Victorian form. Tennyson and Browning were both to grapple with the problem of empathy. The move from feminised sensation to masculine empathy and union, confirming the fixity of human values, which are reflected into and back from the world, makes it possible to return to the idea of the permanent Type so insistently emphasised in Keble's theological aesthetics. Indeed, the idea of the universal Type and the idea of moral empathy often merge in poetry at this time. This was to preoccupy Tennyson, one of the great questioners of his own conservatism, in *In Memoriam*. Before leaving Tennyson to consider Browning's response to the 1830s, however, it is worth remembering that neither, Tennyson in particular, did what was expected of them. Instead of a national epic or a bunch of domestic idylls *The Princess* (1848) was Tennyson's next major poem, a burlesque and a feminist tract.

4

EXPERIMENTS IN THE 1830s
Browning and the
Benthamite formation

It must have been unsettling to the Hallam group to discover that his favourable review of their coterie poet was pre-empted in the most unexpected quarter. W. J. Fox reviewed Tennyson's *Poems, Chiefly Lyrical* in the *Westminster Review*, which was avowedly anti-conservative and Utilitarian, in January 1831, about six months before Hallam's *Englishman's Magazine* article appeared. In the *Westminster Review* Tennyson was associated with social progress and improvement and annexed to a radical programme of change. Poetry was not mythological but contemporary. The French Revolution was a greater theme than the fall of Troy. Scientific change did not make the world strange but demythologised the poet's imagination by bringing it into the realm of literal, psychological knowledge – the 'science of mind', or the new positivist understanding of association which underpinned radical political principles and above all *philosophical* radicalism, upon which the *Monthly Repository* prided itself. When Fox wrote that the poet injects 'the principle of volition' into 'the pineal gland' of alien species he was thinking of the post-Cartesian theory which supposed the pineal gland to unify the mind and body. Thus the new poetry is a materialist, psychological poetry. It is allied with reason and thought and does not dissociate sensation and reflection. It is essentially a dramatic, sociological poetry because it depends on projection into the not-self and an analysis of different orders of experience. Its ideological importance is that it extends the range of knowledge into what is other to us and brings it into the area of rational and imaginative understanding and debate. It is decisively in the public arena, whereas Hallam's theories marginalise poetry. To Fox this provided an exhilarating, functional place for imaginative writing and made it essentially democratic.

Part of Hallam's purpose in his own discussion was to correct what he saw as fundamental misprisions of Tennyson's work by Fox, to whom he refers. The difference, as has been remarked, is between aestheticised politics and politicised aesthetics. The two theories are not structurally dissimilar and Fox had some brilliant things to say about Tennyson's experiments with alien states of volition and perception and in particular

112

paid sensitive attention to the poems about women. What differentiates Fox and Hallam is the political interpretation they put upon a similar theorising of consciousness. In addition, the materialist Fox has no theory of language or representation, believing that it is through powerful emotion that the poet directly transforms 'the associations of unnumbered minds', whereas for Hallam, nearer to idealist positions, the poet covertly dissolved the fortress of opinion by reconfiguring image and representation. Like later critics of Tennyson, Fox presents an expressive theory of empathy. What saved his theory from the narcissistic replication of unchanging categories is his understanding of difference in psychological conditions, difference created by class and history. But it is probable that Browning's poetry, constantly in dialogue with Fox, did not evolve confidently until it had evolved a theory of language.

Fox's account of Browning's *Pauline* (1833), the most serious and least perfunctory of any of the discussions of it, is unexpectedly tentative in comparison with his review of Tennyson.[1] For *Pauline* belongs to his politicised aesthetics and sexual politics in a supremely uncomfortable way. He was rightly cautious. It is an elusive, restless and equivocal work. It is part of the poem's project that it cannot immediately be assimilated into *Monthly Repository* middle-class radicalism. Though it begins with *Monthly Repository* premises it stands in agnostic and interrogative relation to them.

Fox ended his review of Tennyson with a warning which just as much applies to *Pauline*. He warns Tennyson against becoming an inward-looking sceptic, disporting himself amongst the 'flowing philosophers', thus sacrificing 'rapid and extensive popularity', and asks him to commit himself to the 'higher work' of ideological 'influence'.[2] The truly democratic poem can transform belief and disseminate political principles through its power over the associative process and the imagination. Poetry transforms psychological patterns through the power of emotion. Emotion can 'influence the associations of unnumbered minds' because it can 'command the sympathies of the heart'. Emotion can alter the patterns of a whole culture, exciting an understanding of abstract principles through feelings. Poets work openly, directly and powerfully on a huge populace. They can

> influence the associations of unnumbered minds; they can command the sympathies of unnumbered hearts; they disseminate principles; they can give those principles power over men's imaginations; they can excite in a good cause the sustained enthusiasm that is sure to conquer; they can blast the laurels of the tyrants, and hallow the memories of the martyrs of patriotism; they can act with a force, the extent of which it is difficult to estimate, upon national feelings and character, and consequently upon national happiness.[3]

'Command', 'power', 'conquer', 'blast', 'force': Fox's vocabulary suggests that he is thoroughly aware of the ideological importance of emotion. The

Shelleyan poet legislates through an open transaction of power. Because he assumes that the associative process is not passive and requires the active consent of imagination and 'enthusiasm', Fox avoids the authoritarian implications of his aesthetic – but only just. His belief in the essential goodness of emotion is naive, though he did believe that it is emotion which activates the reason and sees no disjunction between 'the reasoning and imaginative faculties'. Quoting the *Monthly Repository*'s idol, Milton, with a characteristically inflammatory reference to the 'Treatises on divorce', he claims that emotion, reason and radical politics go together.

> Produce who can the name of any first-rate poet who is not a sound reasoner. Not Milton; for his defence of the people of England, the worthy oration of a nation's advocate pleading for his country at the world's bar, and for the verdict of posterity, his 'Areopagitica', and his 'Treatises on Divorce', would have made his name great, though he had never dreamed that delicious dream of Paradise.[4]

Though he praised Browning's *Pauline* for 'the ties of association flowing hither and thither like the films of a spider's web', Fox did not find the poem he needed.[5] For in Browning's text a violently expressive poem negotiates indirectly with the discourse of power and apparently repudiates both the revolutionary and the sexual politics which were intrinsic to the *Repository* programme. As we shall see, by juxtaposing the poem with the *Repository* programme, Browning was struggling both to criticise and develop *Repository* politics. A disorganised and involuted narrative takes the immediate language of psychological process to extremes. As if the associative process is directly transferred to the page, the flow of consciousness is registered in an amorphous syntax which is both elliptical and impacted. At times it is virtually a sceptical parody of the *Repository* programme just as it becomes a parody of Shelley. And yet if Browning had written nothing else this would be an important poem. Investigating the formal and political possibilities of 'the science of mind', it evolves another kind of poem as it discovers the limits of the first. It makes a series of epistemological shifts which become structural elements in the text and crucial to Browning's later work. The expressive, psychological poem is turned against itself. As the text discovers the double poem in the act of understanding its own secondary status in history and culture, the text is reaffirmed, but this time as *commentary* and *drama* by committing outrage on conventional expectations of narrative signification. In the process it outrages convention, whether this takes the form of moral or aesthetic expectation. If Tennyson's very early poems are covertly scandalous, Browning's *Pauline* is directly so, and then transforms and displaces its propositions. It manifests the waywardness and elaborate circumventions which were to characterise his work. Nevertheless, Browning creates a new kind of radical poem in *Pauline*. It has to find a new form in order to be a poem about

the breaking of cultural forms. The discoveries made in *Pauline* are fundamentally important to Browning's poetry and to later Victorian poetry and
poetics. Thus it is essential to understand the new textual strategies
adopted in the poem. The discussion which follows considers the poem in
some detail.

Mill, in a commentary almost as frenetic as the morbid self-consciousness
of which he accused Browning, concentrates on *Pauline*'s sexual politics.
This is a useful point of entry into the poem because the sexual relationship
is part of the poem's dealings with power and ideology. No doubt Fox's
tentativeness arose from Mill's outrage. He returned his review copy to
Fox, which included notes which Browning later saw, thus initiating a
debate with Mill which resonates in Browning's later work. To Mill, *Pauline*
was simply a hysterical poem. Before discussing his critique of the poem,
a brief account of *Pauline* will be helpful. It is a long confessional monologue
addressed to an enigmatic figure, Pauline, who at one point annotates the
text. It describes a near psychotic breakdown which occurs in the attempt
to remake the self through sexuality, religion, politics. The impossibility
of being a Romantic poet is its theme. In the course of the poem, a new
account of subjectivity, politics, language and textuality emerges. This is
why it is an important if unsuccessful experiment.

'With considerable poetic powers, this writer seems to me possessed with
a more intense and morbid self-consciousness than I ever knew in any
sane human being'.[6] Mill's description of the hypersensitive confessional
mode and what he regarded as virtually insane psychology are, not surprisingly, the emphases which subsequent writers have noticed. In addition,
however, Mill was outraged by the sexual politics implied in the poem
and, indeed, the greater proportion of his commentary is taken up with
this.

> I should think it a *sincere confession*, though of a most unlovable state,
> if the 'Pauline' were not evidently a mere phantom. All about her is
> full of inconsistency – he neither loves her nor fancies he loves her
> yet insists upon *talking* love to her – if she *existed* and loved him, he
> treats her most ungenerously and unfeelingly. All his aspirations and
> yearnings and regrets point to other things, never to her – then, *he
> pays her off* towards the end by a piece of flummery, amounting to
> the modest request that she will love him and love with him and
> give herself up to him *without* his *loving her, moyennant quoi* [in return
> for which] he will think her and call her everything that is handsome
> and he promises her that she shall find it mighty pleasant. Then he
> leaves off by saying he knows he shall have changed his mind by
> tomorrow, and despise 'these intents which seem so fair', but that
> having been thus visited once no doubt he will again – and is
> therefore in perfect joy [–] bad luck to him! as the Irish say.[7]

Mill was an accurate reader, but he did not see the ironies of the poem. What he describes *is* exactly the emotional trajectory of the speaker in relation to Pauline and is as inconsistent and despicable as Mill perceives. The poem is virtually a parody of the conventional sexual relations which it was the avowed purpose of *Monthly Repository* policy to change. And it is interesting that Mill speaks in terms of an economy. A pay-off can only occur if sexuality and conventional propriety go together, as they do for the *Repository* writers, who saw the economic dependence of women on men as one of the problems of sexual politics. Both women and men, including Mill himself, nearly thirty years before he published *On the Subjection of Women*, wrote on the project of transforming the political and economic status of women, on the necessity of female education and on redefining assumptions about the inferiority of women. The emancipation of women was a central part of the journal's programme and, by the standards of the time, one of its more outrageous propositions. Mill's rage is understandable when one remembers that he had written in 1832 ('A political and social anomaly') that the legal condition of women as the property of their husbands made women 'toys to be sported with, slaves to be commanded, and in ignorant pride that they are so'.[8] In 1833, the year *Pauline* was published, William Bridges Adams wrote on the condition of women in society affirming that women were the moral equal of men.[9] He was later, in 1835, to write a Shelleyan poem on the nature of women, 'A Vision', which rejects notions of domination and dependence. This, like *Pauline*, but less deviously, owes something to Shelley's *Epipsychidion* (1821). Fox, who also believed in women's suffrage, was always attentive to women's poetry, as we have seen, and to the legal questions surrounding marriage. The tireless writing of Harriet Martineau, whose first article concerned women and divinity, and who wrote extensively for the *Monthly Repository* until 1832, was another forum for debate on women's issues.[10] Mary Leman Grimstone's remarks epitomise the aggression and feeling which was often brought to the debate. She argues that women who believe that it is not a woman's place to enter politics are not non-political but fundamentally conservative.

> Politics, it is said, are incompatible with gentleness, with softness, with general amiability – tush! . . . Politics are incompatible with inanity, with indifference, with the show, not the substance, of those principles of which real gentleness, real softness, real amiability, are the effect and effusion. . . . Unfortunately for this country, and in fact for all countries, women are mostly conservatives, and lie like manure at the root of many a political plant which breathes pestilence upon nations, keeping institutions in a vitality which they would not otherwise retain. God grant that every woman was a rational revolutionist.[11]

So *Pauline*, if we take the relationship between speaker and woman as psychologically literal, as Mill did, appears to violate the passionately held sexual politics of the *Repository* group. But Pauline has a devious relation to these principles. Her complex presence becomes a critique of romantic 'love' (the permanence of 'love' is behind Mill's commentary): she is there as a paradigm of the power relations of conventional sexual expectations; and those master–slave patterns become a proxy for other political and aesthetic relations in the poem, and particularly for the speaker's nego- tiations with Shelley's work and its implications. Pauline, muse, mistress, schoolmistress, mother, mentor, warder, therapist, stand-in for the Dorothy Wordsworth of 'Tintern Abbey' (to which references in the poem abound) and, above all, *editor* of the poem, is an extension of the poet's narcissism in one reading, such as is to be found in Shelley's *Epipsychidion*. But on another reading she is an extension who has got away, freed from the speaker's personality and her status as object. She is both the addressee and object, and an editor, of the same text, a writing subject and annotator who appears to be both in and outside the text's control. Her footnotes open up a space between text and commentary which displaces the inner expressive movement of the text, which always assumes an identity of its statements with the 'truth', and forces it into another position as an external, hermeneutic object, capable of analysis and investigation. In this sense the poem becomes a democratic work by opening itself to interrog- ation. This strategy of displacement is at work whether Browning is writing about sexual politics, about Shelley or about a programme of political reform. In *Pauline* he was already developing a number of sophisticated ways of enabling a poem to have two different kinds of content at once. Since the movement of his work is towards a state when it can do the same things without the footnotes and make them unspoken, it is important to consider what is going on in *Pauline*. In particular it is important to consider how this could be seen as a move to create a democratic poetry. For undoubtedly the poem is searching for the structural conditions of a democratic reading. Such a poem is rather different from the double poem developed by Tennyson. Ultimately *Pauline* fails, but its failure is the condition of further experiment.

Pauline's commentary does not simply open up an alternative reading, but the two readings come into play with one another. Included in the poem and yet including it, her commentary casts doubt on the credibility of the text and its expressive movement. For Pauline the annotator, the poem is 'dream and confusion', 'unintelligible': it ought to be burned.[12] She has rational power over the text, seeing it as a series of discontinuous impulses and not the utterance of a coherent subject. On the other hand, her commentary is simply part of the poem's discourse, an added footnote or variant reading of irrational feeling, and not a privileged overview. The crisis of the poem arises from the contradictory reversals and repositionings occasioned by this odd relationship of feminine 'rationality' and male 'irrationality'. In the event one side or the other does not become dominant, but the structure of domination does become clear. Relations of power in the poem become apparent as a series of frantic alternations of dependence and exploitation, withdrawal and return, which seem to be indefinitely repeated. Pauline is the poet's possession, his 'own', 'mine', in a mute and passive subservience which can 'smile', 'take' or facilitate the objectification of his feelings. She can receive 'All shapes, and shames, and veil without a fear/That form which music follows like a slave' (45–6). Music, or poetry, is subservient to the forms of the past which only Pauline can mask or veil: that is, feminine sexuality becomes a way of representing past trauma, concealing and revealing it. But if Pauline is a form of substitution as an extension of the poet's consciousness, her status as the occasion of symbolic meaning makes her also an enclosing and powerfully imprisoning watcher or even warder, as the pun on 'secured' as both protective and *binding* suggests here: 'Nor doubt that each [fear] would pass, ne'er to return/To one so watched, so loved, and so secured' (8–9). Her panting breast, loosened hair and arms 'Drawing me to thee', build 'up a screen/To shut me in with thee' (4–5). They are claustrophobic as well as erotic. To be shut in, however, in another reversal, is to be enabled to take imaginative release: 'unlock the sleepless brood/Of fancies from my soul' (6–7).

Enclosure and restriction are the occasion of expression, so the woman facilitates repression *and* creative freedom. The poem begins by recognising the deep, contradictory sexual origin of experience and signification, in which sexuality and power are bound up with one another. It also recognises that the speaker's relation to Pauline is not only caught in violent swings between domination and subservience but also that these swings are constantly repeated, caught in repetition.

If the neurotically repeated sexual pattern is an analogue for relations in other spheres, in art, and in politics, the task of the poem is to release itself from repetition and to find new forms of signification. Gender relations in the poem have a structural parallel to the mastery of the poet by Shelley, and the dominance of the ideology and the politics of the radical formation (it is interesting here that Browning described Fox as his literary godfather) which have to be thrown off or reshaped if the poet is to be free. The effort to change an oedipal pattern is made throughout the poem. The female principle is represented as a violently destructive harpy, because it is the source of disruptive knowledge, and has to become a 'bright slave', a 'chained thing', a 'power repressed' (620–34): or it is reversed as passive sufferer, helpless like the naked and vulnerable Andromeda chained to a rock and only 'secure' in God's love (650–76). But the reversal does not change the power-ridden structure of gender relations. The gazing eyes and loosened hair of the Andromeda passage simply reconfigures the account of Pauline at the start of the poem. The pattern

118

does not change even when the speaker transposes his gender and figures himself as a 'young witch' (122) or a female swan (102).

The poet is chained to repetition as surely as Andromeda is chained to her rock. The materials of myth as the subject of poetry are rejected because they compulsively rehearse a repeated oedipal scene of violence and insane killing. Yet in re-enacting the transmission of sexual revenge from one killing to another, of Ajax, of the murder of Agamemnon by Clytemnestra, of Clytemnestra by Orestes, the poem declares a flagrant oedipal relation to past culture in the act of loosening itself from it. The extraordinary lyric evocation of Aeschylus and Sophocles, themselves part of a chain of 'family' textual transmission, presents protagonists committing outrages and being outraged. It is as if the latter-day, secondary text has a violence done to it and does violence to its progenitors. Like Orestes, it is unable to liberate itself and tells the same story to the point of madness. Here the king is

> Treading the purple calmly to his death,
>   While round him, like the clouds of eve, all dusk,
> The giant shades of fate, silently flitting,
> Pile the dim outline of the coming doom;
>   And him sitting alone in blood, while friends
> Are hunting far in the sunshine, and the boy,
> With his white breast and brow and clustering curls
> Streaked with his mother's blood, and striving hard
> To tell his story ere his reason goes.
>
> (568–76)

Here melodrama, always parasitic on 'real' drama, becomes a staging device to make self-conscious repetition circumvent the domination of prior texts. This domination, as the poem's later critique of both Shelley and Wordsworth makes clear, is not an enslavement to individual figures, but to forms of thought and to the whole culture they represent. Shelley and Wordsworth are the poets, or cult figures, whom Mill called respectively the poets of nature and of culture in one of the two essays on poetry he published in the *Monthly Repository* in 1833, the year he read *Pauline*.[13] He saw them as enormously important cultural figures, but *Pauline* has a more difficult relation with them. As the creature of history, which includes his own sexuality, the speaker in *Pauline* cannot make himself anew ideologically or imaginatively until he has accomplished a traumatic break from the past.

The project of breaking cultural forms is allied with the attempt to escape from the repetition of structures of domination. As we have seen, sexuality becomes a model for other relationships of power. Sexual relations can be released from power, the narrator tells Pauline, if the repressions on which they are based are exposed: 'cast away restraint, lest a worse thing/Wait for us in the darkness' (41–2). But as usual, this locks the poem in one of its paradoxical checks. For, however liberating, free, expressive and confessional poetry seems to necessitate infinite repetition. It wards off darkness and the pathological return of the repressed by compulsively bringing it into the light. However, in a further paradox, escape from repetition is constituted by repetition itself. When self-conscious understanding of the act of repetition is integral to the poem, it achieves a distancing effect. Repetition becomes a form of alienation and another textual structure emerges out of the same words. For the recourse to repetition makes that repetition into a text, just as Pauline is made into a text, as well as being an editor, by virtue of her footnotes, which denote her intervention and textualise it. A daring and reckless poem emerges which exults in its mimicry – of Shelley, of Wordsworth, of Fox. The strategy of repetition becomes an act of detachment which enables the poet to make himself anew ideologically because it opens up a gap between the writer and his past. The possibility of critique emerges as the poem is staged as a scene of repetition in which secondariness effects an epistemological shift. That is why parody is at the heart of the poem. All the experience of the poem then becomes second-order statement. The poem is no longer history but historicising, no longer exposition, but hermeneutics and commentary, no longer beliefs but belief systems and ideology, no longer expression but expressionism, no longer discourse but symptomatic psychological states which can be demythologised as ideology. Representation in language is no longer a referential act but a fictive construct. All signification is a comment on itself. The epistemological risk exposes the power of one text over another, but also challenges the authenticity of the second text as well as that of the prior text which it repeats.

Such a double alienation is to be seen through the poet's response to Shelley, the master revolutionary. In a strangely painless act of betrayal which is at the heart of the poem, Shelleyan idealism and utopian beliefs are displaced as dream and representation. 'And suddenly without heartwreck I awoke/As from a dream: I said, "'twas beautiful,/Yet but a dream, and so adieu to it!" ' (448–51). The sceptic's moment of awakening, itself a parody of the familiar Romantic awakening to loss in Shelley's *Alastor*, carries with it the realisation of its own status as the history of transmission. If Shelley's idealism is a dream from which the poem awakes, the subsequent awakening is also a dream or fiction. Thus the poem is exhaustively concerned with the nature of transmission. And here Browning incorporates in the structure of his poem the techniques of the fractured text which were being learned from the new biblical criticism which the *Monthly Repository* was actively disseminating. The Bible was beginning to be seen as a discontinuous, edited narrative written at different times by different authors. Its meaning is problematical because events are not literal truths but constructions and reconstructions. *Pauline* is a discontinuous 'biblical' text reconstructed out of earlier thought and open to the hermeneutic process. A radical 'theological' poem emerges concurrently with a political attempt to free the text into a democratic reading by making it available as critique.

That the theological content of this subversive 'biblical' reading is, of course, Shelley's thought and politics, the work of a poet known as an atheist, is part of the scandalous project of breaking cultural forms. God, for this poem, is a blank space, a darkness without signifying power. The possibility of 'perfecting mankind' (458) associated with Shelley, a new humanistic 'theology', displaces old transcendence. But this, too, the poem's ironies see, is a repetition of the old transcendence in a new form, so that political passion is not only ideological construct but structure rather than belief. The epigraphs suggest the *Pauline* poet's strategy. His project overlaps with Shelley's, but in repeating it, becomes different. It must be grasped as history, not thought. Shelley's *Alastor* (1816) ends, 'Nature's vast frame, the web of human things,/Birth and the grave, that are not as they were' (719–20). *Pauline* begins with a statement attributed (mistakenly) to Marot: 'I am no longer what I was,/Nor would I ever know how to be that again'. With the use of the first-person pronoun *Alastor*'s terminal moment is transposed into a characteristic subjectivised form as the history of self displaces the history of culture and autobiography psychologises biography. The epigraph from Cornelius Agrippa warns of the poem's subversions, teaching 'forbidden things', propagating misprision by 'scattering the seeds of heresies'. The poem is a 'corrupt' text in two senses. It transmits Shelley, and Wordsworth as well as Shelley, through travesty and this travesty opens up subversive knowledge. The way not to repeat these poets' projects over again is precisely to repeat them in a form which exposes them. The 'forbidden knowledge' comes about through the recognition that the transmission itself is a fractured, discontinuous text without authority just as much as the inauthentic experience of the prior works.

The *Monthly Repository*'s understanding of German textual criticism indicates the difficulties created by the opening up of the problematical text. The rationalism of Unitarian Christianity assimilated (forty years ahead of its time) the problematical text with ease. Thus, 'The meaning of the Sacred writings is to be made out precisely in the same way as that of any other writers of equal antiquity'.[14] If a 'correct text' could not be established through grammatical and philological evidence, then 'recourse' must be made to historical speculation which not only relativises the text in a specific culture but derives its meaning and consistency from internal evidence which is then confirmed by the text itself. 'Recourse must be had to the context, to the object and design of the writer, to the habits of thinking, and the peculiar phraseology of his age and country. And finally, it is impossible to avoid taking into consideration the general principles of the writer and the doctrine he proposes to establish'.[15] A correct text is a speculative matter, because it is achieved on relativist principles.

In a study of Frederick Schleiermacher's *A Critical Essay on the Gospel of St Luke* in 1827, the writer accepts an account of this Gospel as an unstable text in which the author is displaced and for which meaning must be problematical. St Luke's Gospel is the stringing together of separate 'fragments', discontinuous narratives, almost certainly written at different times. The transmission of evidence and the 'literal' truth of events become a matter of construction and reconstruction, for those who were directly in touch with the teachings of Jesus would be less likely to write down his teaching than those who had not known the historical Jesus and who were *instructed* by those in touch with him. The deconstructive process is a positivist exercise here but opens up the whole theoretical problem of interpretation.

> The opinion of Schleiermacher, we think, will gain ground, as theologians accustom themselves to consider the question critically rather than dogmatically. At the lowest computation, half a century must have elapsed from the birth of Jesus to the publication of this history – a still longer period to the composition of the introductory chapters of Matthew, supposing them to have stood from the first in the Greek. Unless then we are to lay aside all ordinary rules of evidence in judging of the records of Christianity, (which is in other words to say, that the truth of Christianity cannot be historically proved at all,) we are justified in allowing only a limited credibility to accounts of events, some of which were known originally only to one or two individuals . . . and which bear in parts such strong internal marks of improbability.[16]

For the *Pauline* poet the displacement effected through repetition and transmission is both a triumph and a betrayal. Hence the poem's complexity. The poet of *Alastor* is already a posthumous poet, reading the ruins of Indo-European history like a text and constructing meaning through an act of imagination. 'He lingered, poring on memorials/Of the world's youth. . . . And gazed, till meaning on his vacant mind/Flashed like strong inspiration'.[17] The *Pauline* poet can disown Shelley and become posthumous in a different way by rereading him. The *Alastor* poet pursues the visionary dream and the veilèd maid who bestows it even though the dream may be self-projection – 'Her voice was like the voice of his own soul' (153). The *Pauline* poet repeats self-projection as self-pursuit, becoming the thing 'I fled' (97). Like the *Alastor* poet who awakes to 'the cold light of morning', the *Pauline* poet awakes, but to the cold recognition of the prior text's inauthenticity and to his own. The *Alastor* poet moves into the recesses of the mind's ever perpetuated landscapes. The *Pauline* poet, in a virtuoso description which is both creative rewriting and travesty, retreats to the

122

depth of consciousness through the tangled boughs of a woodland land-scape only to be caught in self-absorbed replications of the psyche, meeting the claustrophobic images of his sexuality as the trees bend over a river, like wild men over a sleeping girl, mirroring themselves (740–80).

The effort to disown by the act of transmission and appropriation achieves a parody of both Shelleyan narcissism and Wordsworthian self-transcendence. In the latter part of *Pauline*, the travesty shifts abruptly from *Alastor* to 'Tintern Abbey'. Since the imitation of Shelley's strategies leads to narcissism in the passage on the underground river, the poet makes a counter-move from self-enclosed confinement to pure air. Words-worth's 'living air', the transcendent universe of 'Tintern Abbey', in which self and other are inseparably fused, is invoked: 'Air, air, fresh life-blood, thin and searching air,/The clear, dear breath of God that loveth us' (788–9). But the 'Blue sunny air' (785) becomes the home of an anthropomor-phised cloud, a dead whale, picked by birds. Paradoxically, anthro-pomorphised life is literally death.

Wordsworth's anthropomorphism is no better than Shelley's narcissism as an account of consciousness and the relationship of self to external world. The *Pauline* poet reverses the movement of 'Tintern Abbey' by refusing the 'sleep' of the body (812) in a pastiche of Wordsworth's 'laid asleep in body'. To suspend sense in order to become a 'living soul' is too high a price to pay.[18] There is an attempt to reconstruct new values out of 'Tintern Abbey' through the act of transmission. When the *Pauline* poet moves *back* from transcendent experience to the populated smoking cots and cottages which he sees around him, he is returning to the human landscape from which Wordsworth escapes. But the cottages begin the movement *towards* pure consciousness and release in 'Tintern Abbey'. The *Pauline* poet reverses Wordsworth's movement and seeks to be enclosed in 'living hedgerows' (806) (Browning may have known that these were the results of enclosure in Wordsworth's time) and the political realities around them implied in the signs of human activity, economy and labour. He sees the Wordsworthian release as political retreat. Elements of the introduction to 'Tintern Abbey' are subtly reconfigured to enable a new content to emerge, a substantive human presence and the social world, which super-sedes the potentially anthropomorphised landscape of Wordsworth's poem.

But here the undermining nature of transmission forces itself upon the text. If the rhetoric in which expressive subjectivity straightforwardly sup-plies the categories of description is rejected, the secondary propositions which supersede this are equally subject to displacement and critique as dubious transmission. The result is that historicity is continually substi-tuted for belief. *Pauline* is made up of discontinuous, contradictory phases. That 'I am not what I have been' (192), and not 'what I once was', is reiterated. The 'narrative' is like the multiple texts of Schleiermacher's *Luke*, each told by different voices. While this strategy diminishes the ownership of one textual voice by another it also becomes an incoherent, unauthoritative editorship itself. It bears 'strong internal marks of improbability'. The daemonic 'biblical' text turns against itself.

The poem arrives at an impasse. If the strategy of transmission reconceptualises the beliefs of Shelley and Wordsworth as ideological forms of thought appropriating the world, then its own postulates are ideological fictions too. Fox saw the later, reactionary Wordsworth and Coleridge as renegade poets who betrayed revolutionary principles. The *Pauline* poet is a renegade poet in a double sense and *knows* that he is so in a way that the earlier poets did not. He has had their example before him. He reneges on the idealist Shelley and the prereactionary Wordsworth and he reneges on the principles of Fox. The 'science of mind' is for Fox a social principle, and gives poetry a political base. It endorses self-extension as the act in which thought grasps thought with thought in order to apprehend experience other to itself. Without this ground of projection, Fox says, forms of the self return to haunt it like Frankenstein's monster.[19] The *Pauline* poet abolishes this ground. Thus the political dream haunts it as fiction or monster. The 'key to a new world' (415), a political programme, is negated. Utopian, filtered through idealist rhetoric ('the muttering/Of angels' (415–16)), it is recognisably the programme of democratic reform envisaged by the *Monthly Repository*. 'I was vowed to Liberty' (425): a universal democratic politics of 'the people', or 'mankind', peace, pacifism, the transformation of values through emotion; a programme for the study of 'real life', a sociological analysis of 'Men, and their cares, and hopes, and fears, and joys' based on 'theories' which were 'firm', that is, the psychology of association (441–4), all these are abandoned. They denote the Benthamite pragmatism allied to Utopian values which redefine the greatest-happiness principle – 'How best life's end might be attained – an end/Comprising every joy' (446–7). Invoking the model of sexual power (the master poet was to be to mankind 'as thou to me, Pauline' (407)), the *Pauline* poet describes an impossible ideal.

> A key to a new world, the muttering
> Og angels, something yet unguessed by man.
> How my heart leapt as still I sought and found
> Much there! I felt my own mind had conceived,
> But there living and burning! Soon the whole
> Of his conceptions dawned on me; its praise
> Lives in the tongues of men; . . .
>   I was vowed to liberty,
> Men were to be as gods, and earth as heaven.
>   (415–20; 425–6)

But why are these ideals thrown over? Fox on Coleridge helps to explain. 'It is a pitiful compound of cant and sophistry', Fox wrote, in the *Westminster*

Review in 1830, of an earlier renegade, Coleridge, who had retracted a radical attack on the repressive regime of William Pitt. The 'Apologetic Preface', added at a later date to the 'War Eclogue' (1796), attempted to obliterate Pitt's crimes on those who had been 'insulted, plundered, oppressed, demoralised, starved, slaughtered by wholesale'. Fox's 'strong emotions of disgust' arose because he accused Coleridge of wishing away the historical realities of the Pitt ministry and its relation to the French Revolution.[20] The Coleridge Preface fictionalised these realities by seeing them as imaginary forms, *representations* rather than events. In exactly the same way the *Pauline* poet fictionalises beliefs and constructs them as representations. And the corollary, a consequence the literal-minded Fox did not follow, is a commensurate fictionalising of the self. The betrayal violently acknowledged in *Pauline* is not so much the traumatic break with the past as its consequences. The poem gives up, not a particular set of political beliefs, but the very notion of belief. The deconstruction of belief does not swing from radicalism to reaction but from the radical dream to nothing. When all beliefs become representations it seems impossible to ground them. Browning has reached the early Tennyson's position by a different route, but takes no pleasure in it.

If the confessional poet of *Pauline* struggles to reverse Shelley and Words-worthian bad faith by returning to a new, realistic politics, the analytical poet who restructures confession and relativises it as symptomatic state-ment has nowhere to go. The effort to go behind itself isolates conscious-ness. *Pauline* swings between violent extremes of exultant power and despair, conditions which belong to one another as the self is progressively fictionalised and experienced as alone and private. It is figured in paranoid images of imprisonment and enclosure where the private self is manifested as the discontinuous consciousness. Deprived of relationship, it seizes on a model of human relationships constituted by the privatised bond of sexuality. Pauline, as lover, stands in for Dorothy Wordsworth, a sexualised form of the sister addressed at the end of 'Tintern Abbey'. The condition of posthumousness makes it difficult for the poem to end because in one sense it has already ended. It looks forward to literal death: 'For I seem, dying, as one going in the dark/To fight a giant' (1026–7).

All these possibilities are inherent in the Romantic texts which Browning so knowingly deconstructs, but in *Pauline* he took them a stage further and created a seminal, experimental Victorian poem by recourse to the strategy of the 'corrupt' text which is both deviant and inauthentic. The 'editorial' process converts the immediate experience of autobiography and confession into a second-order activity as it is being written so that it opens up the possibility of critique. This risk-taking strategy opens up enormous prob-lems which *Pauline* itself recognises, but like Carlyle's *Sartor Resartus* (1833–4), another innovative, 'edited' text, it asks political questions about the nature of interpretation through the very structure of the poem. And to have a woman edit the text is to bring together the questions of transmission, textuality, power and gender at one stroke. The strategies of *Pauline* were to be refined and reorganised in Browning's later poetry and in the work of other poets. Its triumph is to turn the second-order status of the work into a form of analysis. However, one logical conclusion of expressive, subjective experience turned self-reflexive lyric is that it sings its own alienation as abstracted commentary on the forms of the historical self, a poetry deprived of content. This is what worried Fox and Mill. The project of Browning's work in the next decade was to find a way of returning to a content, of writing radical poetry without foregoing the strategies of the self-conscious analytical critique which *Pauline*, for all its problems, had discovered, the strategy, in fact, of problematising the text.

A solution to this difficulty existed in a robust radical theory of drama being explored by Fox and a less robust liberal definition of poetry as drama expressed by Mill, both in the *Monthly Repository*. Drama is a shared, public form. It is politically open because it is not monologic and authoritarian. It must be analytical and it must be ideological critique because the interplay of relationships is not created through expressive form but through actions from which the dramatist is dissociated. With characteristic virtuosity Browning learned how to make the textualising strategies developed in *Pauline* become the *substance* of drama. The self-reflexive expressive poem *internalises* its status as commentary and conceals its textuality and ideology. The drama *externalises* these things, brings them into the light, and makes them work for it. Later Browning discovered how to create the lyric *as* drama and to make the subjective lyric become the opposite of itself as the lyric came to be the open object of scrutiny at the same time as it was closed expressive utterance. The dramatic monologue is literally two things at once, lyric and drama concurrently. The risk-taking element in this double form, and risk is always necessary to Browning, is that each poem within the poem, lyric and drama, has a dangerous edge of ambiguity and instability, so that the interface is never clear – it is never quite clear where lyric is displaced into drama, or where drama is dissolved in lyric feeling. The questioning of form becomes a questioning of content. But this is to anticipate. Browning's route to this play with genre was circuitous and extraordinary and this circuitousness is the theme of the present chapter. First, however, his discoveries can be clarified by looking at the alternatives to the confessional form of *Pauline* which were available in the poets Fox published in the *Monthly Repository*.

ALTERNATIVE RADICAL POETRY AND ITS PROBLEMS

One alternative was the Shelleyan lyric. Fox's enthusiasm for Shelley prompted him to publish poems clearly derived from Shelley by Sarah Flower and William Bridges Adams, but the poet he promoted in particular was John Wade. A glance at some of his work suggests why Browning eschewed directly Shelleyan models. Wade's poems are imitative, moralised pastiche. Here, for instance, he attempts to capture the incandescent rhapsody of Shelley's odes, and their quick mobile fusion of categories, by celebrating the glow-worm as an example of the lowly creature which can nevertheless shine with its own natural, self-created light and withstand the storms and tempests of the world (presumably an allegory of the violence and suffering to which the poor and deprived are subject). Even the best of poets would find it hard to begin with an ecstatic apostrophe to the glow-worm's sexual desire. Uncertain quantity and awkward handling of Shelley's abstracting, idealising vocabulary – the exigencies of rhyme force him to match 'dampeth' with 'lampeth', i.e. to shine – produce an unconvincing celebration of the creature which 'Gleams – as in our fierce world, sweet innocence and worth' (stanza x). Some stanzas illustrate the uneasiness of Wade's attempt to imitate what was commonly described as Shelleyan mysticism.

> Drop of dewy light! –
>   Liker dew than fire,
> Lit to guide the flight
>   Of thy mate's desire, –
> Thou lookst a fairy robed in a moonbeam's attire.
>
> In thy leafy network
>   Thou, enshrined, dost glow,
> And a beamy fretwork
>   O'er its verdure throw, –
> Thou little spirit of light, green-paradised below! . . .
>
> Eyes which Sorrow dampeth
>   With the grief of love,
> That in beauty lampeth
>   Thro' their lashes, wove
> With crystal tearwork, beam like thee in dewy grove.[21]

Interestingly, Wade's poem ends with that self-reflexive movement, which preyed upon *Pauline*, and concludes, not with working-class endurance but with the poet's lasting power. As in Shelley's 'Ode to a Skylark', the tempest can be pierced 'As thro' the storms of time the poet's balmy verse'. Not Wade's, however. Wade's poetry becomes more interesting, and more complex, when it debates the anthropomorphism it takes for granted in the poem to the glow-worm. 'The Life of Flowers', published in 1834, which may be an address to the Flower sisters, Fox's wards, dramatises a conversion to the possibility that the external world possesses independent spiritual and emotional life. The plucked flower's 'thoughts and dreams' (stanza iv) may be damaged by the rationalist's refusal to assent to their mystery. The consonance of world and self, the problem of attributing the subject's categories to the world of objects, is dealt with thoughtfully in spite of being seen in emotional and not epistemological terms, and in spite of the mannered adjectival formations – 'nectarious kindred' – and the personifying process which makes dew drip from God's eyelids.

> and the heart-companionship
> Of their nectarious kindred, that reveal
> Their souls to sunlight, and with fragrant lip
> Drink the abundant dews that from God's eyelids drip.
>
> (i)[22]

In 'The Copse', published in 1835 and dedicated to Lamartine, Wade recognises that the external world 'answers' to whatever mood the self projects on to it and guarantees both political pessimism by demonstrating that it can tear itself to pieces and optimism through its continuity. The poem is arranged as an open-ended dialogue.

> 'From the music round us voicing
> I but gather sadness;
> Thou sittest on a tree uprooted,
> Which shall no more be leav'd or fruited;
> Those minstrel birds, the bird of prey,
> Or winter and its want, shall slay;
> Those insects are each other's slaughter;
> And the sweet music of the water,
> Yon emerald cavern's mystic river,
> The falling earth strikes dumb forever!'
>
> I would reply; but hark to that pure strain
> Those wiser birds, sing in the boughs again![23]

Here are the preoccupations of *Pauline*, which were addressed through the examination of *Alastor* and 'Tintern Abbey'. The subject is either trapped in its categories by appropriating nature for its ends or displaced by the independence of the external world. If it is displaced, the consequence is not only that the consonance of subject and object disappears, but also the materials for making analogies and ordering relationships. Deprived of the rhetoric of consonance the self is left in an empty universe. Browning's wary handling of humanised nature circumvents the difficulties of this rhetoric but it remains one of the central problems of Victorian poetry because it confronts major questions, the status of knowledge and perception and the mode in which symbol and representation take place. Interestingly, Wade's derivative Shelleyanism exposes these difficulties sharply.

The poems by Sarah Flower and William Bridges Adams are important for the way in which they develop and politicise elements of Shelley. One can see in them the shift from exposition to commentary, and from idealised sexual relations to the analysis of the constructed nature of femininity in contemporary culture which one also finds in *Pauline*.

Sarah Flower's 'A Dream', published in 1832, is a sombre and rather beautiful account of a congregation of people of all racial and religious types, heathen and Christian, who gather in a temple which emerges in a surreal way from a wilderness and a labyrinth. The packed tribes wait for revelation, but when a radiant angel utters what the congregation calls '*Truth*', a word without a content, 'I awoke'.[24] The *Monthly Repository* had run a series of articles on Herder which stressed the varieties of religious forms as forms of culture, evolved in different historical circumstances, and even formed by different geographical and climatic environments, and the poem assimilates this to the strange, crystal agnosticism of Shelley's 'Triumph of Life' (1824).[25] What is clear is that Christianity has no privileged status over other myths. The poem can comment on the nature of mythic thought as a mode of representation, but cannot assign a meaning to 'Truth' or become an exposition of it. William Bridges Adams's 'The Vision. A Dramatic Sketch', published in 1835, is a kind of literalised *Epipsychidion*. The speaker is in a suicidal condition without being able to die. He speaks of the carnage of misplaced revolution and is saved from despair by a woman. It is women who will achieve the work of 'hastening man's progression' and 'will to work'.[26] Unfortunately, he is beset with a succession of phantom women who are all profoundly disabled because they fulfil the social prescriptions of femininity. One anticipates Browning's 'Porphyria'. 'Her long fair hair/Twines in symmetric tracery' – is sexual but without sense: one craves protection, 'fondly clinging', and is subservient, but without 'high thoughts' or 'expanding mind'; one is a child-butterfly, another is dependent for her identity on dominating men, but without passion. Adams's chorus line of Victorian feminine types is hardly the soul within the soul intended in *Epipsychidion* but it is remarkable for the specific detail of its critique and the frank understanding of the relations of gender and power. It turns the tables on Shelley in the end by concluding toughly, 'There is no bait like a woman'.[27] These are the shadows of women and they will only transform the male world by changing themselves in and through the material circumstances of society – 'You must use earthly means'. The idealism of *Epipsychidion* gives way to materialism.

The other radical alternative for Browning was directly interventionist political poetry which attacked abuses and lampooned contemporary events. Fox regularly published the bitter protests of Ebenezer Elliott, the corn-law poet, and later the violent political burlesque of R. H. Horne. But there were real problems about becoming a political poet of this kind. Fox reviewed, and warmly praised, the poems of Ebenezer Elliott in 1832. But he used them as an opportunity to consider the ideological problems of radical writing. As we have seen, he makes a distinction between poetry as essence and poetry as cultural product. The possibilities of poetry are inherent in human nature, but poetry will take different forms according to the historical situation, nationality and *class* of the writer. This account of the ideological nature of poetry transforms Shelley's image of the lyre responsive to external forces into the 'well-strung harp' which responds to social environment. Fox then goes on to look at the class-based élitist traditions of English poetry.

> A thought or an expression is poetical, exactly in proportion to its power of calling up . . . associations. This power must evidently be varied by the peculiar mental habits of those who read or hear. There is much and noble poetry in our language, which only exists for scholars.[28]

The advantage of a tradition is that it can use its own past to consolidate its power – and power is never far from Fox's mind. Such poetry 'is like the combination of mechanical powers. It invests one man with the strength of many'.[29] But the poor cannot respond to such poetry, and they have been deprived of a tradition of their own, although there does exist a hidden tradition in the Bible, the hymn book and *Pilgrim's Progress*. It is the problem of popular culture and powerlessness. How can the poor create a poetry of their own? The poetry of the poor exists abundantly, witness Crabbe, but, 'It is poetry concerning the poor, but neither by the poor, nor for the poor. . . . The poetry of the poor should be something more than this. It should be the language, not of the observant and pitying gentleman, but of humanity in poverty, pouring forth its emotions for its own gratification'. A genuinely egalitarian radical poetry of poverty will be produced by the poor and the working classes themselves, and will include the scenery of the workhouse and the factory and the wrongs suffered by the working class. Fox is not advocating social realism (which would be the patronising poetry of the gentleman looker-on) but the passionate poetry which returns to 'the sorrowing or joyous cry of intellect', which was the possession of popular culture before the 'distinct articulation of science', and, he might have added, of class, restricted the nature of poetry.[30] There is more than an atavistic nostalgia for a presocial condition which has analogies with the Apostles' search for a unifying myth born before the birth of consciousness, but Fox's analysis is emphatically in terms of class. The review follows the exposition of Herder's thought earlier in the year, which began with Herder's theorising of the nature of popular literature. Herder had a power,

> almost peculiar to himself, of seizing the spirit of a particular litera-ture and of a particular state of society. . . . He thought with Bacon that a ballad or a legend often more faithfully indicated the current of popular feeling, and were better worth studying by the historian

of mankind, than the graver productions which are less impregnated with the spirit of the age, and in which the cold, technical exercise of the intellect has repressed the free and natural outpourings of the heart.[31]

However, Fox differs from the Apostles by turning his back on myth and sharply politicising the issue of popular poetry by insisting on its class consciousness. Working-class poetry 'must emanate from men who remain surrounded by the scenery, partakers of the privations, subject to the wrongs, real or imaginary, and animated by the passions and hopes, which belong exclusively to poverty'.[32] Thus new, not old, forms of radical writing will appear. Significantly he allows that real or *imagined* wrongs must be expressed in the ideology of the poetry of oppressed labour. He praises Elliott's 'The Death-Feast' for its fusion of politics and feeling. This poem tells the story of Jane suffering from consumption, orphaned and unemployed, and her young brother, who die a pauper's death.

> His watery hand in mine I took,
>   And kissed him till he slept:
> O, still I see his dying look!
>   He tried to smile, and wept!
> I bought his coffin with my bed,
>   My gown bought earth and prayer;
> I pawned my mother's ring for bread,
>   I pawned my father's chair.[33]

The 'watery hand' suggests the tears, and the dissolution, which are the boy's lot. Elliott's account of the progressive stripping of the minimal property which sustains life and affirms family identity is masterly. The consuming of possessions goes on concurrently with the boy's death from consumption as the need to bury him decently denudes life itself. The poem sharply underlines that the *materials* of life support the religious institutions which sell 'earth and prayer', a grave and the burial service, to the poor. The exchange of a bed for a coffin, places of rest for the living and the dead, marks the progressively contracting space allowed to the living, and suggests that the only exchange the poor can make is the exchange of life for death. Memory and family connection is consumed as ring and chair are sold. This poem is typical of the innocent-seeming pathos but bitter ironies of Elliott's poems. An extract from an anonymous work, 'Sunday. A Poem', published in a review in the *Monthly Repository* in 1835, engages with social critique but is nothing like so violent as Elliott's poetry. It begins with the innocuous assertion that the poor and rich alike can enjoy the physical, natural world, but the words 'Breakfast' and 'sup' disclose the contradictions of such assumptions. The rich can digest the scene aesthetically, the poor may well live on thin air.

Breakfast with Nature: flowing to the brim
With the first purple day-draught is her cup,
And from it poor and rich are welcome all to sup.
The mighty sun has risen![34]

Elliott's 'Songs for the Bees', a black study of the disintegration of the poor, published in 1836, deploys harsher ironies. Here the deserving poor are shown preparing for Sunday, a day of rest, by labouring unremittingly at domestic tasks.

Tomorrow will be Sunday, Ann,
Get up my child with me,
Thy father rose at four o clock
To toil for me and thee. . . .

So let us shake the carpet well,
Then wash and scour the floor,
And polish thou the grate, my love,
I'll mend the sofa arm.[35]

Such poetry is very near to the robust popular tradition of the urban broadside ballad of whose existence Fox seems to have been unaware. He may have ignored it because it appeared to be oral rather than written poetry (it was actually a mixture of both) but in fact it came very near to being the popular ballad so praised by Herder and respected by the *Repository*. Ironically, class blindness probably prevented its existence from being recognised, however much such writing was respected – indeed, desired – in theory. Ebenezer Elliott had a precursor in the Sheffield poet, Joseph Mather (1737–1804), who attacked the oppression of a master cutler in language Elliott was to develop: 'That monster oppression behold how he stalks/Keeps picking the bones of the poor as he walks. . . . That offspring of tyranny, baseness and pride,/Our rights hath invaded and almost destroyed'. Poets and chaunters selling their poetry in the streets were common in cities until mid-century. Some of their names are known – 'Blind Willie' Purvis (Newcastle), Reuben Holder (Bradford), who sang of the new poor law as the 'Starvation Law' of the 'British Bastilles', and Tommy Armstrong (Durham), the 'Pitman's Poet' – but even when their names are not known the themes of protest are held in common, as will be seen at a later point in this discussion. Rent day, making do on 15 shillings a week, satires on the 'march of intellect', factory conditions and emigration are frequent topics of broadside writing.

It is hard to see, however, how a middle-class radical poet outside working-class experience such as Browning could write popular lyrics of this kind without showing the condescension of the gentlemanly looker-on which Fox deplored. This was Browning's central problem, as *Pauline* indicates. The return to the cottages of 'Tintern Abbey' is a hard move to make.

One way of circumventing this problem was to write a poetry of protest which does not pretend to participate in the poor's misery but which exposes their exploitation and the contradictions of society by having recourse to *drama*, the supreme analytic form for Fox, as we shall see. R. H. Horne produced a burlesque, 'A Political Oratorio', published in the *Monthly Repository* in 1835, whose comedy reaches a savage, Brechtian intensity. It is a libretto for a comic opera in which trade unions and the forces of oppression, interpreted as 'priests, lords, kings', argue out their case in songs which expose ignorance and prejudice.[36] One chorus delineates the dilemma of a working class which has been trained not to have recourse to revolution, but which is nevertheless oppressed by a class who 'live by us'. A chorus of peers celebrates hereditary wealth with mindless zeal, accompanied by a trumpet obligato (fox-hunting music) which resolves itself into the indiscriminate baying sounds of the upper-class voice. When they ask whether hereditary peers must relinquish 'large tax. . . . Because men starve' the people, carried away by customary deference, inadvertently agree with them. These extracts from Horne's poem sharply contrast with the reactionary blank verse of Taylor's poem against trade unionism, *Philip Van Artevelde*.

> Semi-Chorus II
>
> Led by the Central Committee of Trades' Unions
>
> Is not the labourer worthy of his hire?
>   Thus do ye teach us every Sabbath morn;
> But what we're worth we never can acquire,
>   Since, with our wages, ye yourselves adorn!
>   We want no revolution
>   Of violence and strife;
>   We ask a fair solution
>   Of the problem of our life.
>   You live by us, are hous'd and cloth'd;
>   Why should we wander ragged, hungry, loath'd.
>
> Semi-Chorus III
>
> Led by three Poet-Mechanics
>
> We do not seek, as priests aver,
> Back'd by hereditary star and spur,
>   To rob the *sea* of whale or whiting;
>   But we claim justice to the letter!
>   We want no civil wars or fighting –
>   We *now* know better.

GRAND CHORUS OF TRADES' UNIONS

A right we claim from nature
  Beyond all priests, lords, kings,
Of having large inheritance
  In the wealth that labour brings!
A right in social state we have
  As well as priests, lords, kings. . . .

Chorus of Peers

With trumpet obligato

Tank! tank! too-too! Rise, souls of fire,
And let each peer with lofty ire
Think of the glories of his sire,
And make these slaves their folly rue
In chains of carnage! – *tank*! *too-too*!

Trank-titty-hank! – Shall ages gone,
And honours left, from sire to son,
Be by our vassals trampled – won –
And blown away like dust and flue?
Never – no, never! *tank too too*!

  Must peers – *trank hank*!
  In stellar rank,
Heed baying hounds – *tra ting, too-too*!
  Relinquish – *hank*!
  Large tax – *trank trank*!
Because men starve? – *hank hank, too-too*!

(Shouts of applause, in which the people join, carried beyond themselves
by its excellence.)[37]

A chorus of paupers follows, singing of the charity soup – which is deducted
from wages.

Significantly, Horne's poem is called an 'Oratorio', as if in direct disagreement with a distinction Mill made between the 'sincere' poetry of
dramatic soliloquy and the untruthful poetry of public oratory in the two
articles on poetry in the *Monthly Repository* of 1832. Horne, known to both
Browning and Elizabeth Barrett (he wrote on both poets in his *New Spirit
of the Age*, 1844), explored the possibilities of a popular poetry throughout
his career and was deeply concerned with the problems of drama in
England. He wrote three articles on drama in the *Monthly Repository* and
translated A. W. Schlegel's *A Course of Lectures on Dramatic Art and Literature*
in 1840. I shall return to his work, and that of Talfourd, and their
democratising project.

Horne's ideas belong to one of two concurrent but quite incompatible political theories of drama, dramatic poetry and its ideological significance as a democratic form in the *Repository*. Browning's work is in subtle and dissenting dialogue with both. One is the egalitarian and radical theory of Fox, with which Horne is aligned. The other is Mill's liberal, paternalistic account of poetry as drama. In 1836 Browning published two poems (renamed in 1842) in the *Repository* which became the axis on which his career as a poet turned. These were 'Porphyria' (later 'Porphyria's Lover') and 'Johannes Agricola' (later 'Johannes Agricola in Meditation'). They are described as his earliest dramatic monologues, but the formal description is less important than the epistemological and political leap they represent. They are literally a leap into another language. They seem to have emerged directly out of Browning's deep disagreement with Mill's judgements and the challenge to the poet as gentlemanly looker-on addressed by Fox. They enabled Browning to write a new kind of radical, analytical poetry and solved the difficulties explored by *Pauline* in an ingenious and complex way, even though they created new ones. As with Tennyson's *Poems* (1832), the politics of the monologues of 1836 initiate the founding rhetoric of Victorian poetry and its problems, conservative and radical. Hence they form the subject of the following chapter, where they are used as exempla.

5

THE POLITICS OF
DRAMATIC FORM

To begin with Mill, Browning's poems, 'Porphyria' and 'Johannes Agricola', constitute a running dialogue with his ideas. The two *Repository*
monologues emerge as parodies of his aesthetics and their politics. They
draw out and expose the implications of Mill's thought with devastating
rigour and virtuosity. Mill's apologetics, 'What is poetry?' and 'The two
kinds of poetry', make a fundamental distinction between two kinds of
knowledge.[1] One is the knowledge granted by expressive feeling and
psychological experience. The other is the knowledge granted by the scientist. The poet describes the lion affectively through the emotions, the
scientist neutrally, abstractly and literally (the lion becomes a locus classicus of Utilitarian aesthetics, making an appearance in George Eliot's
famous justification of realism in *Adam Bede*, 1859).[2] Hallam had granted
knowledge to the poet of sensation as well as to the poet of reflection. In
denying the poet knowledge Mill effectively removes poetic knowledge into
the post-Kantian realm of the aesthetic, cut off from discursive rationality
and instrumental activity. But, despite his emphasis on emotion, the representation of the poet's lion must take place without self-conscious displays
of subjectivity. This was the ground of Mill's objection to *Pauline*. His
attack on its morbid self-consciousness this side of madness is perfectly
consistent with his belief in expressive emotion. Like Fox, he believed that
the poet educates feeling, but unlike Fox he believed that poetry educates
by belonging to the domain of private feeling and not by negotiating the
public world of power. His distinction between the poet of nature (Shelley)
and the poet of culture (Wordsworth) rests on his belief that the drama
of expressive presentation actually transcends the immediate social order
and has its own form of truth. The poet of nature frees feeling and
emotions, returning a refreshed and purified experience to the society from
which he has escaped in order that the social can have access to a new
aesthetic order, a harmonised and healthy order, which becomes a form
of control on excesses of emotion.[3] Here is initiated the idea of poetry as
therapy, an alternative poetics which attempts to erase the political by
proposing to cure the neurosis of social division rather than to analyse it.

This view was to be influential in the nineteenth century, from Arnold to the later Morris. Mill, borrowing from the ideas of Dugald Stewart, preferred the lyric experience which was 'synchronous' (he speaks of using the language of the philosophers) because it *orders* feeling.[4] Random, sequential associations interfere with the pure experience, whereas synchronous, instantaneous experience controls and shapes emotion.

The purest form of expressive lyric is feeling *dramatised* as 'soliloquy', but this drama is not a public transaction between actor and audience. The distinction between poetry and 'eloquence' follows. Whereas the orator is the self-conscious scientist of feeling, publicly manipulating emotion and using psychological states instrumentally in the cause of action, or influence, the true poet is unself-conscious and alone with his affective, emotional condition which never goes beyond itself. 'All poetry is of the nature of soliloquy'.[5] All poetry is a construct, a representation, but the poet of soliloquy eliminates the evidence of its own construction.

> [Poetry] is feeling confessing itself to itself, in moments of solitude, and embodying itself in symbols which are the nearest possible representations of the feeling in the exact shape in which it exists in the poet's mind. Eloquence is feeling pouring itself out to other minds . . . poetry . . . is soliloquy in full dress, and on the stage. . . . But no trace of consciousness that any eyes are upon us must be visible in the work itself. The actor knows that there is an audience present; but if he acts as though he knew it, he acts ill . . . he [the poet] can succeed in excluding from his work every vestige of such lookings-forth into the outward and every-day world. . . . But when he turns around and addresses himself to another person; when the act of utterance is not itself the end, but a means to an end . . . then it ceases to be poetry and becomes eloquence.[6]

Poetry is '*heard*', eloquence is '*over*heard'. Inward-looking, private feeling, Mill says, apparently with enthusiasm, approaches almost to 'monotony',[7] and goes on to extend his distinction between poetry and eloquence to opera. With this formulation, constituting poetry as private production, Mill seals a distinction between poetry and the external world which, defining the poetic as the solitary work of the speaking subject over and against communality, was to have consequences for the rest of the century. It is a poetics of exclusion. We are back with the claustrophobia which *Pauline* struggles against. The poetics of exclusion generates a politics of exclusion or enclosure as the speaking subject in his or her private cell of subjectivity communicates if at all by accidental empathy. No audience is required, and the isolated lookers-on gain no knowledge except that of an equally isolated and dissociated psychological condition.

The two monologues, printed originally as 'Porphyria' and 'Johannes Agricola' (later their order was reversed and their titles extended), come into being as analytical experiments in the logic of Mill's closet poetics. Significantly they were later called 'Madhouse Cells'. They are a parody of the private utterance overheard rather than heard, the drama of soliloquy 'unconscious of being seen'. Nothing Browning had done before has their concentration and economy. Through them the fallacies of the poetics and politics of exclusion are explored. They achieve what was not achieved in *Pauline*, the poem which is simultaneously expressive utterance *and* reversed as objectified feeling, so that the speaking subject is at once self-analytical and capable of being the object of analysis which goes beyond the self. The parody of Mill's drama points up the central element of drama which is excluded in soliloquy: these poems are about acting and *taking action*, the construction of roles and their connection with volition and agency which relates people to the world. Browning takes those areas which were coming progressively to occupy the status of private experience of the self in his culture – sexuality and religion – as test cases. These were, in fact, the experiences which Mill was later to say were outside the jurisdiction of public morals.[8] The poems chart 'conditions of extremity'. 'Porphyria' narrates a fictional episode in which a sexual murder takes place as the woman named in the title arrives on an illicit visit to her lover. The title of 'Johannes Agricola' refers to the historical character who was an extreme Antinomian in believing himself to be one of the elect. Johannes Agricola is not required, so he argues, to act. Alone with an (almost certainly imaginary) lover, alone with one's God, this is the logical conclusion of Mill's solitude. The cold and greedy violence of these monologues establish a privacy in which the external world disappears. Where Tennyson depicts a self alienated and excluded from the world of choice and action, Browning depicts its opposite but dialectically related experience, a condition in which the private encroaches on and absorbs the public world to the extent that the public world is non-existent. The ultimate action for Porphyria's lover becomes the choice to kill: 'surprise/Made my heart swell, and still it grew/While I debated what to do./ . . . I found/A thing to do . . . /And strangled her' (33–41). Johannes Agricola lives in a world where to act is unnecessary because God has predestined all experience; 'I lie where I have always lain,/ . . . God said/This head this hand should rest upon/ Thus, ere he fashioned star or sun' (11–20): 'Be sure that thought and word and deed/All go to swell his love for me' (26–7). The self 'swells' in both poems, to exclude all else.

The critique of overheard drama raises a number of crucial problems. If the soliloquist is solipsist, speaking to himself, who is the addressee of private poetry? A relationship with a looker-on or an audience is excluded so that no space for dialogue can exist. Both monologues are remarkable for the silencing of the voice of the other as the speakers live in a world without reciprocity to the extent that their own speech is almost redundant too. Porphyria 'called me', but 'no voice replied' (15): and the poem ends,

'And yet God has not said a word!' (60). God predetermines every word for Johannes Agricola, so that his own praise of God is unnecessary, for God is speaking to himself through him. The syntax here points two ways as the infinitive verb makes it unclear whether it is God or Agricola who engages in the act of blessing: 'ful-fed/By unexhausted power to bless' (41–2).

The solipsism of expressive emotion privately experienced leads to another consequence – mania, delusion, paranoia and visions of total power as the speaking subject relinquishes relationships. When Porphyria enters, dripping from a storm, and proceeds to undress and seduce her strangely passive lover, it is not clear whether or not she has been conjured by the fantasist's dream of a seduction which is at the same time a form of mothering. He watches his seduction as he watches the process of stripping.

> Withdrew the dripping cloak and shawl . . .
>   let the damp hair fall,
> And, last, she sat down by my side
> And called me. When no voice replied,
> She put my arm about her waist,
> And made her smooth white shoulder bare,
> And all her yellow hair displaced,
> And, stooping, made my cheek lie there,
> And spread, o'er all, her yellow hair,
> Murmuring how she loved me.
>
>   (11, 13–21)[9]

The enclosing curtain of hair recalls *Pauline*, but this poem explores power and mastery in sexual relations with far more intensity. If the speaker is actually indulging in sexual fantasy he gains power and mastery over his seductress in imagination because she is his object. He does not speak, not from catatonic passivity, but because of a sense of control: the fantasist has no need to participate in human discourse with the productions of his fantasy. She is literally not there. Porphyria's voice is his ventriloquism. As he repeats but reverses her seduction by taking charge of the strangled woman, the depersonalised female body changes to 'it'.

> I propped her head up as before,
> Only, this time my shoulder bore
> Her head, which droops upon it still:
> The smiling rosy little head,
> So glad it has its utmost will,
> That all it scorned at once is fled,
> And I, its love, am gained instead!
>
>   (49–55)

The ambiguity of the reversible possessive 'its' in 'its love' points up the blurring of subject and object in fantasy. The speaker is both possessor and possessed, for 'love' both owns and is owned by 'it'. The same process goes on in 'Johannes Agricola' where Johannes is an object of God's 'content' (30) by loving him and literally the 'content' of God's love itself. Logically he *is* God.

A second consequence of solipsist soliloquy is the emergence of private contracts which come about directly as a result of the speaker's belief that they are exempt from public contracts and institutional agreements. Their contracts become a parody of legal and socially agreed definition. Definition, in fact, becomes an entirely private matter. Porphyria is the sexual property of another man but desires another contract, to 'give herself to me forever' (25). Johannes Agricola places himself and his relationship with God outside the sordid bargaining process involved in the economics of praise and good works expressed essentially as an economics of *repayment*. He refuses to 'bargain' (59), 'paying a price' (60) of praise, but he can do this precisely because God has already made a prior bargain and invoked legality to ensure his election – a guarantee and a 'warrant' (33), 'irreversibly/Pledged' (29–30) – God 'pays him off' as Mill said of *Pauline*. The vulnerable and suspect status of public contracts, and the equally vulnerable status of identity when it deems itself exempt from them, is exposed in these negotiations. Johannes speaks of the non-elect forced to 'win' (47) God's love, thus turning contract into a wager and identifying God with arbitrary chance, or worse, with the idea of competition. So a further question emerges – what is a law if it applies to some people and not others, or if there are two kinds of law for different kinds of people?

Lastly, solipsist soliloquy carries in its train, following on from madness and the dissolving of the notion of contract, the abolition of time. The speakers exempt themselves from temporality and history because their actions need not take place as a causal sequence. Mill's objection to the successive experience is taken literally, and it becomes clear that the 'synchronous' experience is incoherent. Agricola speaks in the present tense, and the monologue is held together in simultaneity by the ironical reiteration of 'I lie': I stay in the same place and I am untruthful. The arrest of temporality occurs because there is no need for agency in a preordained world – 'I lie where I have always lain' (11). God bade him '*grow*/Guiltless forever' (22–3) (my emphasis) but growth depends on becoming, and becoming cannot occur if futurity has been attained already, as the beginning of the monologue implies – 'For in God's breast, my own abode . . . I lay my spirit down at last' (8, 10). God's breast is his dwelling place, but as his abode and God are identical, again, logically, he is God. The intention ('For I intend to get to God' (6)) has already been pre-empted in the fact of predestination. Thus Agricola has no past, but his exemption from temporality actually depends on assuming that the rest of the world is not exempt. Temporality is there to define his freedom from it. The physical universe of suns, moons and stars which his mind cuts through to God is overcome as if it did not exist, transcended or 'passed' (9). But transcendence is only possible if the material world of process, capable of 'passing' into death, exists. The crowds of passionately believing men, women and children God has 'undone' (54) before the world began are ruthlessly condemned to 'striving' (50) in time, in order to be transcended by the elect Johannes Agricola. The incoherence of the doctrine of the elect, not to speak of its political implications, points remorselessly to the incoherence of Christian notions of heaven and hell.

'Porphyria' works as a successive narrative, but by the end of the poem the events have turned into the 'synchronous' totality of a retrospect – 'And thus we sit together now' (58). If the poem is a memory, the speaker has a past. If it is a fantasy nothing has happened – 'And all night long we have not stirred' (59). Delusions invent an illusory temporality which is quite independent of historical time. God cannot intervene in imaginary time and withdraws from it. Hence he 'has not said a word' (60). The monomaniac hubris of these two monologues works in contrary motion one to the other, but with the same result. In one, God and creation are indistinguishable because time has been abolished. In the other, God has disappeared because time is imaginary.

The derangement of these monologues comes from Browning's remorseless understanding of the structural problems which arise from the expressive poet's abolition of externality, of agency and action, time, and above all the obliteration of the reader. The characters obsessively read themselves, and if we understand the poems in terms of expressive psychological moments, they effectively suppress the fact that they are being read or 'heard'. They obliterate the active, critical presence of the reader because they obliterate their status as *texts*. So what of the politics of 'heard' poetry, or drama? Through Fox's alternative theory of drama as oratory, as an open, public transaction in which the work, like the actor who recognises the existence of his audience, declares itself as oratory and ideology, it is possible to turn these poems around and to see them as psychological texts rather than psychological expositions or expressions, a second poem created with exactly the same words as the first. This takes us some way into the extraordinary complexities opening out in Browning's work. But in these poems Browning took on a double debate with both Mill and Fox, and a reading of them is not complete without an understanding of the way in which they begin to reach towards another poetics. It is this which enabled Browning to become a political poet, not because he wrote directly of radical problems, but because it released him into the possibility of making a cultural critique in terms of the structure of the monologue itself. If a direct, working-class-based political poetry was closed to him by virtue of his middle-class status, he could write poetry which became cultural critique by presenting and dramatising a politics of poetics. For 'Porphyria' and 'Johannes Agricola' constitute a politics of Mill's poetics. They achieve this by engaging with further strategies which

141

go beyond the tactics of the immediate lampoon. What these are can be derived from Fox's understanding of 'heard' poetry.

Fox's writing on literature constitutes a conscious and deliberate effort to develop a *Utilitarian* and radical aesthetics. While this rests on a fundamental politicising of all literature there is simultaneously, as has been said, a sustained effort to deepen, expand and enrich the Benthamite concept of pleasure through a less mechanistic reading of the process of association than was customarily identified with Benthamism. It is through dramatic poetry that the poet exercises 'one rich ministry of pleasure'. Where the legislator, philosopher and divine must postpone pleasure and fulfilment in different ways the poet 'seizes upon the soul' immediately.[10] Indeed, Fox vigorously defended Bentham from the charge of narrow mechanistic thought. Though Mill depoliticises his expressive poetics, and is otherwise very different from Fox in his aesthetic thought, he shares in Fox's project to explore a new, associationist theory of poetry. But Fox's theory of poetry was fully dramatic and public where Mill's interest was directed to private soliloquy and opera. Significantly, Horne describes opera as the concern of the élite and aristocratic in the impassioned call for the reform of contemporary drama and the economic stranglehold of patent monopoly which prefaces his translation of A. W. Schlegel's lectures on drama. Which class, he asks, responds most to drama? Opera is an aristocratic pursuit comparable to the fighting of mock medieval battles, as in the farcical revival of tournament by Eglinton.

> Is it the aristocracy? They prefer the opera, the scenery, the wardrobe, the heroic Eglintonian pageantry. Is it the middle classes? They are the very followers and only supporters of the true drama. Is it the working classes? The large minority delight in the impassioned drama, and humbly reverence its power: the majority flock to the external shows.[11]

Fox's development of a Utilitarian poetics goes hand in hand with his attention to drama. If the prerequisite of the poetry which 'influences the associations of unnumbered minds' is that it is 'oratorial', open and 'heard' as a public transaction, then it must be rhetorically self-conscious and aware of itself as text and as ideology. In a remarkable passage on preaching, Fox speaks of the presentation of doctrine in preaching which must go on in detachment from the minister's subjectivity, which must go on, indeed, even when his own feelings are not identified with what he says. He compares his work to that of the actor, who deliberately manipulates and constructs a role and generates emotion through it.

> On certain days, nay, at certain hours, and even minutes, he is bound publicly and solemnly to tell his God that he is in a particular state of mind and feeling, when perhaps he is in a very different state of

mind and feeling. He modulates his voice, as he reads the liturgy, to the emotions of reverence, contrition, supplication, thanksgiving, sympathy etc; but who is so totally ignorant of the human mind as to imagine that these emotions either do or can arise within him at his bidding, and in their prescribed order of succession?[12]

So though these poetics are based on a theory of emotion they are not based on complete psychological identification with feeling on the part of either author or reader but on an analytical, detached, dramatic rendering of feeling in which there is an active, critical participation on the part of the audience. Poetry tasks the 'intellect' as well as the 'senses' because it makes use of 'the science of mind', that is, the discoveries of associationist psychology. Such analytical poetry is democratic in three ways. In the first place, it is democratic because it either contains or is structured in terms of *dialogue*. Fox insists that all poetry is dramatic even when it is not dramatic in form. Mental phenomena are externalised as events so that they are the equivalent of a set of incidents which can be publicly examined and mediated. 'Then a poem, however short, should be a narrative, or a drama, and have something of that sort of interest, and consequently of pleasure, which we experience in being conducted through a chain of events to a catastrophe'.[13] The drama may be constructed out of the associative process itself, not 'the current of outward circumstances' but 'that of the phantoms which are ever passing in long procession through the brain'. A poem may be dramatic without the existence of literal dialogue, but there *will* be a dialogue constituted by opposition and conflict within thought and feeling. 'By dramatic we do not mean that the poet should have recourse to personae and dialogue; but he should at least employ those defined and contrasted feelings which will, in very narrow space, shadow forth the strivings of the external and literal drama'.[14] The radical aesthetics of drama turns on the existence of dialogue or its equivalent because it is in dialogue that there is space for debate within the text and between text and reader. Moreover, it is only through dialogue that there is the active possibility of *change*. Schlegel based his definition of drama not on the fact of conversation between characters where 'the poet does not speak in his own person', but on the presence of dialogue. 'It is dialogue', Schlegel says emphatically, which is the very foundation of drama, for this *changes* us as intellectual and moral beings.

> When the characters deliver thoughts and sentiments opposed to each other, but which operate no change, and which leave the minds of both in exactly the same state in which they were at the commencement; the conversation may indeed be deserving of attention, but can be productive of no dramatic interest.[15]

Drama, then, refuses to 'leave the mind . . . in exactly the same state' as it was at the start. That is its essence. And inherent in this is action, action as energetic, non-passive involvement, as well as literal action, for action is 'life itself'.

The second democratic aspect of analytical drama is consequent again on the poet's access to the 'science of man', associationist psychology. The dramatic poet, as Fox says in his essay on Tennyson, can project himself into the subjectivity and associative complexity of any psychological state. But he will be particularly concerned with analysing the 'modern' psychological condition. Hence he abrogates the epic of Troy as against the French Revolution as the materials of poetry. But it is important to see here that Fox is not simply asserting that the modern reader is given access to contemporary subjects. He includes the open inspection of political events within the provenance of the science of man, but such topics are the result of a deeper analytical purpose. This is the exploration of psychological conditions as historical entities, as the product of different forms of culture: 'the whole should be based upon a profound knowledge of human nature, its constitution and history, its strength and weaknesses, its capabilities and its destiny; and where there is this science of man in the poet's mind, its existence will be ever felt'.[16] The poet has access to a radical historical and cultural analysis in which particular associative configurations occur at particular moments in history. Poetry is critique. Here poetry becomes a form of knowledge reached through the emotions and the critical intellect. 'It is an essence distilled from the fine arts and liberal sciences; nectar for the gods. It tasks the senses, the fancy, the feelings, and the intellect, and employs the best powers of all in one rich ministry of pleasure'.[17] Where Mill made a distinction between poetry and science or knowledge, Fox puts the two together.

Lastly, dramatic poetry is democratic because it deals with objectified materials which are capable of eliciting a responsive associative train in readers, who can corroborate or dissent from its delineations by reference to their own experience and build new patterns of association from the poet's explorations. This is very different from the disruptive, subversive function that the poet's breaking of associative patterns achieves in Hallam's aesthetics. Fox's poet and reader proceed by negotiation, Hallam's poet–reader relationship proceeds by a series of non-rational ruptures. Mill, of course, does not make provision for a relationship at all. For Fox the objectified representations of poetry are to be as *material* as possible. The poet 'must give us pictures'. It is impossible for language to produce 'actual' pictures but the poet must enable the reader to come to an independent mental representation of external things and develop 'new combinations' by appealing to the physical experience of the senses. 'His words should be such as are associated with the most common and most vivid recollections of those external objects whose presence most gratifies the senses'.[18] Here is an attempt to formulate poetic realism at the same time as recognising that the world is mediated through representations, and the ever present possibility of new representations.

Fox's curious combination of Benthamite materialism and rational philosophy of pleasure with Coleridgean idealist passion is strange. He can say that the finest poetry 'almost identifies poetical with religious inspiration' and almost in the same breath speaks of the poet in terms of the crudest psychological and social engineering: 'A great master of the art can play upon the nervous system, and produce and control its vibrations as easily as the well-practised performer can try the compass and power of a musical instrument'.[19] Thus democratic negotiation and a preoccupation with power belong uneasily together.

What did Browning take from Fox and what did he reject? There is no doubt that he was experimenting with the dialogic drama of externalised psychological narrative in 'Porphyria' and 'Johannes Agricola'. There are times when he describes his analytical procedures almost in Fox's words. In the preface to *Paracelsus* (1835) he claims that his poem is an attempt to 'reverse' the usual procedures of writing so that the literal external conditions of action are displaced by an analysis of the subject's internal drama. In *Strafford* (1837) he speaks of analysing action in character rather than character in action. In fact in the process of dialogic objectification Mill's expressive poem becomes the anti-expressive poem. In 'Porphyria' and 'Johannes Agricola' Browning relies on the hermeneutic shock created by the absence of dialogue. Characters so patently talking to themselves force a conscious intervention, force the reader to be aware of his or her exclusion and simultaneously force that awareness into a consciousness of *reading*, understanding the poem as the object of analysis and thus as ideology. So the structural relationships set up in the poems themselves become a political paradigm of change through an evolving, participating dialogue with the protagonist. Subsequently Browning refined the dialogic process and made it more complex by introducing a silent listener within the monologue itself, so that the poem is doubly a text, but the rudiments of this structural politics are all here in these early poems. Dialogic action declares power relations and thus their presence becomes one of the factors included in the process of analysis. In these poems the very extremity of the speaking subject's will to power and possession – one speaker virtually worshipped by God, another by his lover – is enough to indicate the implications of the act of appropriating which conceives the world as that which harmoniously answers one's own needs. The storm at the start of 'Porphyria' both echoes the speaker's mood with its vexation and 'spite' and yet he enters into a kind of power struggle with the elements conceiving their very animation and aggression as turned against him. This is an example of the way in which acts of mind are seen as a drama of changing events in dynamic relation to the reader.

It is clear, too, that Fox's understanding of political poetry as cultural critique, in which psychological states are rooted in history, is at work in these poems. The de-institutionalised private union with God, the curious reversal in which the self as God worships the self, the translation of this in an economics of relationships which is both repudiated and exploited in a contradictory way by the speaker, all this is an analysis of cultural forms in which experience is implicated in ideas of payment. Similarly, in 'Porphyria', the displacement of sexuality outside the institution of marriage, as the illicit affair becomes the consequence, the mirror image of licit, contractual union, is a brilliant social analysis of the way in which marriage and adultery are bound together in bourgeois society. So, too, is the objectification of the woman's body. A. W. Schlegel thought of the modern, romantic drama as a drama about dividedness and about the distorted desire which emerges from such alienation. The division of labour and the objectification of commodity occur in psychological forms. Browning's poem is a study of alienated desire, literally the desire for an object, a dead object. It is a cultural fantasy produced by social organisation. Whereas in Mill's terms these would be the expression of diseased subjectivities, in Fox's terms the poems would be a commentary, a critique of constitutive modern structures, religious, economic and sexual, which create diseased subjectivity and the madness of individualism. The reader is forced from one kind of recognition to the other, from the perception of diseased subjectivity to an analysis of its cultural form, because the poems parody expressive lyric.

It is Fox's account of realism, and the attempt to account for representation, which is least developed in his theory. The 'mental reproduction' of reality in 'new and becoming combinations' leaves the poem unanchored in the material world and is in danger of returning representation to solipsist subjectivity. It endorses that curious split in Fox's work between an assent to imaginative construction and positivist, technological instrumentalism. Browning's work, on the other hand, seems to develop very arrestingly and agnostically the whole problem of representation. There was, however, a paradigm for the work of art as pure construct. It is Bentham's theory of fictions. Fox may be dealing tentatively with the paradigm when he talks of 'new' combinations, though the question of direct influence is much less important than the nature of this model of fiction, which was certainly available at the time. Bentham's theory of fictions grants the work of art the status of cultural construct. The possibility for conscious investigation of representation *as* fiction is built into his theory. At the same time it is a model which enables the artist to speculate on the nature of the kind of intervention an imaginative construction makes in the world. It invites more complex and problematical political questions than Fox asked. Above all, it provides for a theory of poetic language. So one can see Browning's poetry developing a Benthamite poetics beyond Fox's theories.

146

THE DRAMATIC POEM AND THE THEORY OF FICTIONS

Browning never failed to acknowledge that the materials of art are the representation of 'external' objects, or objects where general cultural agreement about their representation exists. Thus the work of art is democratic because it is open to inspection and analysis, as Fox saw. To anticipate a prose work of 1851, Browning's prefatory essay to a collection of letters he supposed to be by Shelley, this is the ground on which the 'objective' poet is formed. There is, however, a more decisive and sophisticated shift from realism to representation than in Fox's work. The objective poet stays within the world of received and *experienced* representation. He can 'reproduce things external [either the scenic universe or the human heart and brain] . . . with an immediate reference, in every case, to the common eye and apprehension of his fellow men, assumed capable of receiving and profiting by this reproduction'.[20] Either he produces an 'intelligible whole' for inexperienced readers, or he provides material for 'corroboration' and amplification by more adventurous readers.[21] Readers, indeed, are in a position of critical awareness. They not only corroborate but actively bring their own imagination and intelligence to a reading and *develop* it. This must be the only guarantee of the real, and constitutes a democratic poetry which brings the active reader's interpretative power to the poem. Browning's account of the objective poet's work allows for access to the poem by Fox's uneducated readers. The poor for whom the middle-class poet cannot, according to Fox, write effectively, are granted a participatory role. The objective poet's art is Browning's attempt to ground poetry in common representations and to reclaim an area for the ideologically disabled middle-class poet. The objective poet is objective because he allows for his work to be a critique and become the object of a critique.

We 'covet' the objective poet's biography because he is necessarily detached from his material. The objective poem is 'substantive', 'projected from himself and distinct'.[22] Such distinctness is a way of precluding that appropriation of the external world from which Fox's account of psychological projection is not free. The coveted biography is eliminated. True to the *Repository*'s belief in drama as the only ideologically liberating form, Browning writes that objective poetry 'is what we call dramatic poetry', when 'even description, as suggesting a describer, is dispensed with'. Thus the reader is forced to hear, not overhear, a substantive and public poetry. 'The man passes, the work remains'.[23]

Having established the dramatic poetry which is available to critique, Browning seems to undo this work by reintroducing Mill's 'overheard' private *expressive* poet in his account of the 'subjective' writer. We 'necessarily approach the personality of the poet' and read biographically because such subjective poetry is the 'effluence' of unique vision. This move is baffling until we look again at the Platonic terms of this description. It is an attempt to look much more rigorously than Mill at the structural part played by the subject in the creation of a work of art. For of course it is not possible to eliminate the psychology of the writing subject in art, and nor is it desirable. But the utterance of the poet is precisely not the inward monody of pure feeling: 'the *Ideas* of Plato, seeds of creation lying burningly on the Divine Hand – it is towards these he struggles': 'Not what man sees, but what God sees'.[24] The objective poet sees and portrays what *man* sees and stays within the limits of the human subject. The subjective poet – and there is a Promethean impudence here – struggles to create as *God* creates. He is supremely external and analytical and deals with the constitutive elements of experience and not with superficial expressive forms. His art is a construct, one of 'the primal elements of humanity' and not a 'combination' of experiences.[25] The analogue of God's mind is the human mind and its *fictions*, pictures 'on the retina of his own eyes'.[26] The subjective poet is Browning's effort to allow for the existence of what Fox barely conceived, constitutive fictions.

The work of the subjective poet has always been seen by Browning's interpreters as the rendering of an inner life, of human essence over and against a history. As we shall see by turning again to the two *Repository* monologues, Browning was never free of casuistry and is prepared to run the risk of his theories by exposing them as casuistry. But here Browning claims that the subjective poet is immersed in history. Not only do the poet's imaginative fictions intervene in history but they must be constructed on the model of Plato's 'Ideas' out of the human mind and its experience which is 'the nearest reflex' of divine mind. Mind does not transcend itself because mind itself is the model for the creation of fictions. On the other hand, mind is not at the mercy of its own psychological experience either.

Browning is in a complex dialogue with Mill and Fox which involves him in both displacing and recentring the subject. Mill's unified expressive subject turns out to be the fragmented victim of psychological moments. If Fox's solid, analytical dramatic poetry is invoked to redress the privacy of Mill's poet, that drama is now displaced from the immediate external world to become a function of shared *representation*. What a representation can be is further sophisticated by the introduction of the idea of fictions. As Browning makes clear, objective and subjective forms are never produced as pure forms distinct from one another. But it is fiction, rather than the subject itself, which is at the centre of art. It is characteristic of Browning's restless deviance that the introduction of fictions makes a genuine political poetry at once harder to achieve and more possible. And it is absolutely typical of him that in the notion of the fiction as it is explored in the *Repository* poems, he chose the most politically disreputable and least credible model to hand in radical circles, the dangerous power of the legal fiction. For it is in the legal fiction that the concept of fiction was circulating at this time, the legal fictions which Bentham had condemned as despotic and tyrannical, the tools of power and injustice. And moreover he had associated legal fictions with the corruption of language. It is no accident that 'Porphyria' and 'Johannes Agricola' are obsessed with legality and the guarantee of contract which turns out to be exploited for private power, or that legalism and language are explored together.

As 'objective' poems, 'Porphyria' and 'Johannes Agricola' are immediately apprehendable as 'intelligible wholes', melodramatic and vivid representations of madness and psychosis. The *logic* of psychosis and its cultural significance is laid bare for the reader who wishes to develop and explore the nature of madness. Here Browning's readings are consonant with Fox. As 'subjective' poems, going further than Fox, they represent the fictions of madness and become explorations into the status and language of fictions themselves. And it is here that Browning places the fiction at the most dangerous edge of casuistry. The importance of this is that it is a casuistry from which Bentham himself was not free, for he recognised that human language finds it impossible to do without fictions. 'Porphyria' and 'Johannes Agricola' are experiments in the concepts he termed first-order fictions, love and God. Real entities are those things which have a correspondent image in experience. Fictional entities, love and God, are those things which do not have correspondent images in experience, and that is their problem at the same time as it can be their justification.[27]

In the review of Coleridge in which Fox developed his political aesthetic, he refers to a radical Utilitarian defence of Bentham in the *Westminster Review* which disputes conservative readings of Bentham. The article quotes liberally from Bentham's writings and concentrates on his attack on legal language and fictions. It demonstrates conclusively that the law for Bentham was the crucial institution because it is where conservative oppression manifests itself openly and issues directly in action and control. Mill's famous defence of Bentham as a codifier, on the other hand, in the essay to which I have referred, weakens the violence and political intensity of Bentham's attack on despotism. The writer of the Bentham article is at pains to show, first that Bentham condemned legal language because its eloquence was *aesthetic*, and secondly that legal fictions are the product of this aesthetic language. Forms of words are substituted for arguments (one example is the speaker who, like Johannes, says 'I am of the number of the Elect') and forms of words begin to have an autonomous life of their own which depends on 'the music of the maxim, absorbing the whole imagination'.[28] They prevent the listener from perceiving 'the nothingness' of a statement. Nevertheless, this 'nothingness' perpetrates actions. For legal fictions are constructions of events which substantively effect people's lives, making the innocent guilty and the guilty innocent. The writer means not merely chicanery and quibble but the train of precedent and legalism which actually result in contradictions in the real world, such as the acquittal tax on the innocent.[29] So fictions *intervene* in the world however aesthetic they may seem. To fight them we have to behave as if they were true. The writer savagely derides as conservative a reading of Bentham which actually justifies legal fictions aesthetically on the grounds of their internal coherence, and characterises it as mere 'sport' – 'the construction of an independent system artificially deduced out of its own technical principles etc'.[30]

'To be spoken of at all, every fictitious entity must be spoken of as if it were real', Bentham wrote elsewhere.[31] 'Nothingness' fictional entities might be, but they are essential to language and the process of conceptualisation. 'Every fictitious entity bears some relation to some real entity'.[32] Fictions are entities for this reason. They have an analogical base in physical and psychical experience but cannot be reduced to it. They cannot be translated or substituted for a real entity – words such as God, love, soul, are examples. But by exhaustive redescribing, metaphorising and *linguistic* substitution you can point to the fictional entity by reference to the real entity and demonstrate the structural relationship of the fictional to the real entity. This is a subtle route through the philosophical extremes of nominalism and realism, the independence of language from the world, and the referentiality which ties words to things. It neither consolidates pure representation nor identifies the sign and the thing signified. Curiously, its advantage to an artist is that it confirms the necessity of fictions and places them as central to the process of thinking, in spite of the discreditable purposes to which they may be put. Moreover, it asserts that fictional constructs intervene substantively in the world and affect choices and actions however fictional they may be. They are as enabling as they are disreputable. Lastly, the theory of fictions is a theory of language, which sanctions the ceaseless productions of language (as paraphrase, metaphor, metonymy) not as rhetoric but for the purpose of clarifying the structural relationships fictional entities bear to real entities. Bentham wrote:

> To language, then – to language alone – it is, that fictitious entities owe their existence; their impossible, yet indispensable, existence.[33]

It is a justification for a poetics. Ironically, this theory of 'nothingness', which evolved from an attack on the dishonesty and violent power of the law, *is* an aesthetic theory. It is a successful aesthetic theory. It is a successful aesthetic theory simply because it was an attempt to explain and understand the *effectiveness* of fictions. For Bentham it would be ineffectual idealism in the face of the law's fictions to assume they could be spoken of as if they were not real. The importance of the theory lies in Bentham's willingness to speak of a fiction 'as if it were real'. It is a flagrantly, almost perversely, paradoxical theory.

It is a short step from legal to aesthetic to psychological fictions. The importance of a theory of fictions to Browning is that it provides him with an account of the imaginative construct which is an intervention in the world and which escapes from solipsism and a subject-centred discourse. It also produces an account of poetic language in terms of definition and demonstration which depends for its being on abundance, on repetition and redescription in the public forum. The truly poetic language is a forensic language, is a product of legal debate. Both the form in which a fictitious intervention occurs in the world of choice and action and the way in which its language evolves secure a truly public, politically open situation in which questions can be investigated without mystification or the exploitation of power relationships. But more significant than all this, a theory of fictions is important because it is paradoxical. Browning's poems are not demonstrations of the nature of the fiction, but, like every-thing he did, a sceptical enquiry into it. Hence they are test cases of his own and Bentham's fictions, explorations of the casuistry which treats a fiction 'as if it were real'. At one and the same time this is firm political ground, and ground which gives under one's feet.

Agricola's fiction, that he is one of the elect, appears to concern only himself and God and yet it involves a ruthless rejection of other kinds of worshipper. Its exclusiveness has a substantive function in shaping his relations with the world. 'God' is a fictional entity at what Bentham calls 'the first remove', formed, presumably, on analogy with its noun 'man'.[34] Not only does God have human characteristics, such as anger and pride, but He is more human than Agricola, possessed of a past, planning and determining the future, exercising arbitrary power, expressing emotion, capable of the energy of thought and calculation. He performs all the functions Agricola has abrogated by resorting to passivity. This is the logic of treating God as if He were 'real', exactly like a human being. Agricola's mind creates God in his own image of despotism. Fictional entities, Bentham says, often control, dominate and organise our understanding of real entities, as if the fictitious body were a stake, and the real body a beast tied to it.[35] The connection between a word and its import is 'alto-gether arbitrary' but coercive. That is why war 'with all its miseries' emerges from language itself.[36] The blasphemous irony of this monologue is that Agricola is only doing what Christians ought to do in thinking of God as 'real'. The reader can only enter the complexity of the fiction by entering into the poem as if it were 'real'.

The remorseless process of sceptical exploration is directed to another problem in 'Porphyria'. What is the status of the 'murder'? If it is imagin-ary, what is the difference between a fiction and fantasy or delusion? And how does each materially intervene in the world? For they all seem to work in the same way. What is the status of an *imagined* or fictional action? Such 'actions' do not appear to impinge on the world and yet the conviction that something has 'happened' has to be dispelled by treating it 'as if it were real' – that is to say, to disprove anything, its possibility has to be taken seriously. The morbid violence, the intensity and extremity of feeling is substantive, produced by and producing the fiction. Porphyria's lover, however mad, has to be initially granted belief, and there is some strange sense in which the murder *is* in existence with the contemplation of its possibility, particularly as truth might be stranger than fiction. The pure idealism of the fiction is constantly shown to have material effects on the world in the most disturbing of contexts. In fact, fictions and the language of fictions, since they impinge on and create action, are crucial to political life, and indeed to all experience. Browning did not so much directly politicise his material in these two monologues as begin to write a politics of fictions.

In words which recall 'Porphyria' in an eloquent analysis of the contiguity of fiction and hallucination, Browning considers in the case of Shelley whether 'the idea of the enamoured lady following him to Naples, and of the "man in the cloak" who struck him in the Pisan post-office, were equally illusory, – the mere projection, in fact, from himself, of the image of his own love and hate'.[37] He quotes Shelley himself – 'To nurse the image of *unfelt caresses*/Till dim imagination just possesses/The half-created shadow', and adds, 'of unfelt caresses, – and of unfelt blows as well?'[38] The 'unfelt caresses' of Porphyria and their problematical status reappear in this essay, written nearly fifteen years later. Porphyria may be a projection of 'his own [the lover's] love and hate', but before we can discover whether this is an 'entity' of fiction or a hallucination the poem has to be read seriously, and in this way it has already intervened in the world. The strange syntax of the later title, meaning the lover *of* Porphyria and the lover *possessed* by her, suggests how the 'fictitious' erotic 'body' ties meaning to the stake.

The discovery of the fiction and its potential for a new poetics and a new poetry was of critical importance to Browning. It also led to a politics which stems directly from an account of consciousness and human action, for paradoxically the idealism of the fiction may *determine* action. In the *Monthly Repository* of 1835, Horne spelled out the problematical relationship between consciousness and politics through a discussion of Hazlitt's *On the Principles of Human Action*. 'Mind is the only criterion of all things; the only type and proof of reality; the only measure of creation. . . . The only fixed datum for metaphysical speculations, is consciousness'.[39] Even though, as Hazlitt says, 'self' is a fiction, 'this fine illusion of the brain and forgery of language' grounds human action.[40] Consciousness is constructed from memory and memory is a series of constructs. It is through the fictions of memory that the fiction of the future is established. The future is a projection of memory.

> And in truth, it requires a considerable effort of abstraction clearly
> to distinguish and separate the objects we frame for the future,

from those we have been conscious of in the past; so much are our imaginations mixed up with memory. In some cases this almost amounts, speaking abstractedly, to a solecism. I contemplate a statue or a figure, in imagination, having heard of it only: a few days after, I contemplate as near as possible the same idea, i.e. the memory of a former or past imagination. Is it not then a reasonable paradox, that the future is often unconsciously identified in the mind with the past?[41]

We can already see Browning's great epistemological lyrics of the 1850s in these speculations. Horne goes on to ask what '*real* interest' he could have had in the statue if he sees it in reality and discovers it to be quite different from his imagination. And yet knowledge of the existence of the 'real' statue makes possible his imaginary construction of it. Such epistemological speculation, he claims, is not ideal, for it affects the sphere of moral and practical action. For 'The Sun of hope is a fiction which the wisdom of the Creator has implanted in our minds with all the force of anticipated reality'.[42] All action is the product of the repetitions of the past in consciousness and a product of imagination. Belief in political action must depend on a projection in which the 'past wrongs' of a people are redressed through that mental process which identifies the past with the future. So action is based on a risk. This principle of action is at once utterly sceptical and completely affirmative. Consciousness only guarantees that 'Man stands like a speck upon a progressive point, between two eternities'.[43] And yet this negation of certitude must be the very ground on which action, and the future itself becomes possible. In 'Porphyria' and 'Johannes Agricola' Browning began a formative experiment, the exhaustive agnostic exploration of the risks of fiction.

The essays of Fox and Horne can be seen as markers for the formation of a new kind of Victorian poem. The different, oddly discrepant pressures of radical Utilitarian aesthetics, Shelleyan idealism and a Benthamite concern with fictions, combined to make possible the dramatic lyric or what has come to be known vaguely as the dramatic monologue. From Fox came a conviction of the ideological necessity of drama and a programme for drama as externalised conflict objectified as the materials for democratic participation. From Horne came a belief in the central structural importance of dialogue and an epistemological concern with the importance of the fiction or construct as the determinant of action. And behind both is the presence of Bentham. In Browning's work all these possibilities for a poetics and practice are opened up sceptically as problems. But his heard drama, originally in a parody of Mill's overheard drama, shifts the poem from psychology to epistemology and the textual complexity of the fiction. The possibility of agency and the structure of consciousness itself are at stake in the status of fictions. Browning's poetry becomes a dare with the status of the fiction, an analytical process which ceaselessly investigates the nature of utterance and its representations and their cultural meaning. Included in his poems is an understanding that they are made of language and that though they pretend to be speech, they are writing – not actually heard, but read. We read them self-consciously as texts. But it is through this process that they become forms of knowledge rather than the expressive emotion which Mill distinguished from truth. They belong to Benthamite science rather than liberal feeling.

The possibilities of the dramatic lyric came slowly to Browning. His contemporaries were preoccupied with political drama in the form of plays, and his attempts to become a dramatist and to write plays for the theatre continued until beyond the mid-1840s. Later, Browning's instinct for what was radical in the dramatic was reinforced not only by the Benthamite fiction but by a new account of oppressed consciousness which was ultimately to be described by Ruskin in *The Stones of Venice*. William Morris, directly in touch with Ruskin, became the practitioner of what Ruskin termed 'Grotesque' art. I discuss this new theory of radical poetry in connection with Morris in Part II. But when people described Browning as 'grotesque', as they frequently did later in his career, they implied a social theory of art which sees the longings, deviancy and violence of the grotesque consciousness as the product of the distorting nature of Victorian society, and particularly of oppressed labour. Certainly, Browning's poetry was transformed when he was able to work in the grotesque mode rather than in formal drama.

The plays, though not as frightful as some people believe, are not as successful as other works. *Paracelsus* (1835) began the move to drama, and seems to be a first attempt to redress Mill: Paracelsus, paralleled throughout with Luther as a liberating power, chooses to stand on knowledge rather than love and feeling, though it is the dichotomy itself which is under attack. *Strafford* (1837), the play which so exasperated Macready, was clearly written with political intent. Seventeenth-century politics were interpreted in terms of the nineteenth-century struggle for democracy. Browning's Strafford is a single-minded royalist who cannot understand the complexities of a new situation which demands an understanding of the working of a parliamentary system. It is actually more muted in its condemnation of Strafford than John Forster's *Life*, which Browning helped to complete, and it is typical of Browning's detached interest in equivocation and his refusal to take a standard radical line that this is so.[44] However, a comparison with the reactionary *Philip Van Artevelde* makes it clear that it is a very different kind of political play.

Though the later plays were more daring, much the most radical plays at this time were being written by Thomas Noon Talfourd. On classical themes, static, starchy and undynamic, but with a clear political implication, they deal directly with slavery, despotism and the exploitation of privilege. In *Ion; A Tragedy* (1836), the protagonist struggles against tyranny and becomes king on condition that republican democracy be established at his death.

> Swear to me
> That ye will seek hereafter in yourselves
> The means of sovereign rule: – our narrow space,
> So beautiful, so bounded, so compact,
> Needs not the magic of a single name
> Which wider regions may require to draw
> Their interests into one; but, circled in
> Like a bless'd family by simple laws,
> May tenderly be govern'd; all degrees
> Blent into one harmonious frame may glow
> A living form of beauty, free to smile
> In generous peace, or flash with courage bright,
> If tyranny should threaten. Swear to me
> That ye will do this![45]

Assent being given, Ion, demonstrating idealism but extraordinarily little political sense, promptly kills himself to bring democracy about. His mistake is to see democracy as a *future* state rather than attempting to bring it about in the present.

Though Horne was committed to drama, his most successful political poem was an epic, *Orion* (1843), which obeys Fox's principles in the sense that it portrays a series of powerful conflicts which can be, as Horne's preface remarks, 'perfectly intelligible to all classes of readers'.[46] It is 'an experiment on the mind of a nation' and its price, a farthing, indicates the attempt to reach a wide audience.[47] Effectively, Horne's epic is about 'the principles of action'. Orion the giant, who represents the enchained energies of the oppressed, goes through a series of experiences (and mistresses) which include orgy, famine, revolution, blindness and social reconstruction, though he is doomed to hope rather than achievement. The poem is an attack on mindless labour and exploitation. 'Toil' is 'Unvaried, ending always in itself'.[48] The power to change the conditions of labour is almost impossible to gain.

> Clearly I see this,
> And know how 'tis that toil unequally
> Is shared on earth; but knowledge is not power
> To a poor man alone 'gainst all the world,
> Who, meantime, needs to eat.[49]

Orion confronts the power-loving Akinetos and the reactionary Encolydon who is 'Hater of all new things' and 'Stood'st in improvement's doorway'.[50] The answer *is* action, though not revolution. Change seems to depend on mind, not on the pure 'principles of thought' expressed by Orion at the start of his progress, but on the constant reconstruction of consciousness. The symbolic blinding and regaining of sight – one man's mind and thought can 'like a star go out' – is the obliteration and reconstruction of belief, the 'star' of fiction.[51]

Horne's poem, even though it attempts to bring the classical epic into the provenance of popular poetry, is not innocent of being the product of the middle-class, gentlemanly looker-on. Orion, indeed, seems more like that figure at times than the giant strength of an exploited populace. *Orion* is not without its anxieties, just as Browning's poems are not. Browning sought ingeniously to find an authentic form, through *Sordello* (1840) with its tangle of epistemology, politics and poetics, and *Pippa Passes* (1841) with its looser dramatic form. It is the story of a factory girl who is unaware that her song, or fiction, impinges on others and transforms their actions. She is unaware that the intervention of her song actually affects her life too. Interestingly, the poem begins with Pippa's celebration of sunrise, glancing back to the ironies of 'Sunday. A Poem'. The Browning of the 1840s is as uneasy as Tennyson is, though for different reasons, as the acted drama he wrote failed to find a popular audience. He turned tentatively to dramatic lyric in the cheap pamphlets of *Bells and Pomegranates* (1841–6) and to poems with a context in the civil war, but these also failed to find a substantial readership. He was an experimental poet throughout his life, but the experiments of the 1840s are anxious, undirected works in spite of their daring.

In the end, both Tennyson and Browning settled for being middle-class poets, in order to be heard rather than not heard at all, one in England, one as an ex-patriot. Their major work is often seen to belong to the 1850s. However, it is impossible to overestimate the intellectual importance of the early period. The poetics of conservative and radical thought were formative. They created the possibility of a founding rhetoric for Tennyson and Browning which addressed cultural and ideological questions of fundamental significance. They also created the terms in which subsequent poetics and poetry evolve. Later writers select, reconfigure and synthesise elements of the founding aesthetics in different contexts. In both groups the double poem emerges in all its complexity from opposite political theories. The topics of the Tennyson debate, mythic structures and the nature of culture, the poetry of sensation, poetry and sexuality, the Tory Wordsworthianism of common feeling, Taylor's anti-anarchic, rational morality, the poetry of affective moral empathy, reappear in new forms to the end of the century. The topics of the Browning debate, the nature of an interventionist political poetry, poetry and class, poetry and feminism, the expressive psychological poem, the poetry of therapy, the critique embodied in dramatic form, the status of fictions, reappear, though never with the sharpness with which they were evolved earlier, and never with the radical edge of the first decade of Browning's work. Arnold and Clough, the so-called

Pre-Raphaelites, Swinburne and others, make new syntheses of these explorations, as did the women poets of the century. Sexuality, power and language reappear as preoccupations. A study of the early decades of Victorian poetry leads to an understanding of the anxieties of the century and the sophisticated response they called forth. The great critical effort, as Arnold would have said, of the 1830s and early 1840s, is indeed a crucial moment in the century.

It was perhaps a critical moment in poetry and aesthetics because the great critical effort of these early years struggled to evolve new concepts to describe and articulate a changed political situation which had emerged definitively with the consolidation of industrial society at this time. What has been called the aesthetics and politics of civic humanism in the late eighteenth and early nineteenth centuries could not be adapted to a new economic and social structure.[52] A different theory of art and politics responding to perceptible changes in social and economic organisation began, with difficulty, to be developed among both post-Benthamite and post-Coleridgean groups. Civic humanism had assumed that the model of a republic of taste or letters could be sustained as a reasonable account of the relations between artist and audience. Anyone capable of *governing*, capable of taking on powers and duties in the state, was deemed to belong to this 'republic' of taste. Thus the idea of the 'public' was restricted to this closed and highly selected body of male participants in the ruling hierarchy. One of the results of this definition was that art was placed firmly in the public sphere, subject to the same responsibilities and judged in the same terms as other public enterprises. But civic humanism crumbled under the pressure of an economic order which necessitated competition rather than the ideal of an organic hierarchy based on shared accounts of responsibility. The division of labour forced an increasingly fragmented, individual and privatised account of both work and art to displace the earlier ideals of 'public' cohesion. The growing recognition of the formation of a mass indus-trial working class destabilised and made obsolete the classical definition of the shared and privileged 'republic' of taste among ruling-class equals.

By the time Talfourd attacked Hazlitt for his anti-democratic definition of the aristocracy of taste, civic humanism had collapsed under its own weight as the republic of taste became indistinguishable from the aristoc-racy of taste and its private pleasures.[53] The struggle of the 1830s and 1840s was to define a new public account of the aesthetic, its provenance and its function: the discursive shift, indeed, can be seen in the change from a terminology of the 'public' to a terminology of the 'people', from the hierarchical presuppositions of Burke to the cultural and racial analysis of writers such as Schiller and Herder.[54] Herder, as we have seen, provided interpretative possibilities for both conservatives and radicals. Each could theorise from him a more inclusive account of popular culture, cultural identity and race and nation which, almost for the first time in the

157

discourse of literary production, conceptualised that mass which belonged neither to the aristocracy nor to the middle classes. The new situation required a new language, and this was forged during the early decades of the nineteenth century. The people, the common people, the poor, the crowd (the word used in Browning's *Sordello* to designate a mass audience), the populace, the peasantry, the artisan, the labourer, all these words were given a new semantic range during this period; the Fox and Hallam groups were continuing the work of definition in their own ways, work which had been begun by Blake, Wordsworth and Coleridge and which was to be further elaborated by critics as different as Ruskin and Arnold. We shall see Arnold later telling Clough with mock amazement how implausible the notion of the 'people' seemed to him.[55]

Hallam's theory of the unifying myth which healed the division of labour and assuaged class bitterness by replacing it with the collective imagination, and Fox's attempt to work out a theory of genuinely democratic dramatic poetry, both constituted a 'critical effort' to deal with what was perceived as a crisis in class and social relations and a corresponding crisis in the nature of literary production. Interestingly, however different their politics and their solutions to the problem, they were at one in their diagnosis of oppression. Tennyson mythologised and to some extent occluded oppression in poems such as 'The Lotos-Eaters': Browning's critique was more overt. The 'Cavalier Tunes' of 1842, for instance, cavalier both politically and morally, commemorate the revolution of 1642 by representing the careless confidence and assumptions of power and the right to rule among the landed interest, synonymous with the royalists; and in 'Incident of the French Camp' (originally 'Camp'), the second burial of Napoleon is attacked. In poems of 1845 (in *Dramatic Romances and Lyrics*), such as 'The Lost Leader', attacking Wordsworth's acceptance of the laureateship, and 'The Englishman in Italy' (originally 'England in Italy'), which ends sharply on the gravity of the corn-law debate, he continued to make explicit political allusions.

Both groups share an understanding of oppression with the working-class poetry of the period, and this may have been the only time in the century when middle-class and working-class poetry ran almost *pari passu*. Protest against pauperism, industrial conditions and factory labour are common in broadside songs. The refrain of 'The Pauper's Drive', with its ironical play on 'owns', points to the collapse of social and family relationships when property relationships supersede them: 'Rattle his bones over the stones,/He's only a pauper whom nobody owns'.[56] A poem such as the 'Collier Lass' demonstrates the way working-class labour maintains middle-class life:

> By the greatest of dangers, each day I'm surrounded,
>> I hang in the air by a rope or a chain,

The mine may fall in, I may be killed or wounded,
    May perish by damp, or the fire of a train.

And what would you do, were it not for our labour?
    In wretched starvation our days they would pass
While we can provide you with life's greatest blessing,
    O do not despise a poor collier lass.[57]

It is possible to see the generic relationship between Ebenezer Elliott's writing and Manchester hand-loom-weavers' songs of protest about the factory system. John Grimshaw's bitter refrain, 'You tyrants of England, your race may soon be run', in his 'The Hand-Loom Weavers' Lament', and the anonymous attack on factory regulations 'Where high build chimneys puff black clouds/And all around the slaves do dwell,/Who are called to labour by a bell', share a quality of fierce resistance to conditions created by the powerful.[58] On the other hand, it is necessary to be cautious in comparing Elliott's work with the broadside ballad. Elliott in fact made money out of the industrial system and deliberately addressed his poem to the 'Bees' or professional middle classes rather than to the working class. In some sense he represents the dilemmas of the consciously literary working-class writer and these explain why the preoccupations of middle- and working-class writing fracture during the century, as Fox always saw they might. While the middle-class writer was uneasily aware of the necessity of gaining access to a wider public whose existence and power was only just beginning to be recognised, the working-class writer knew that there was always a danger of alienating middle-class sympathy. If, as in trade-union songs and, later in the period, in Chartist poetry, a powerful class identity was asserted, making a sharper analysis of the structures which maintained economic conditions as they were, the common bond of understanding and outrage between classes could dissolve, as middle-class interests were threatened. Pity and outrage are always easier to produce than analysis. It is interesting that Elliott disapproved of the Chartist movement and dissociated himself from it.[59]

We can see, nevertheless, that a longer tradition of satirical and burlesque working-class protest poetry than Fox acknowledged continued into the early 1840s, when it met a kind of polemical poetry developing from Chartism (discussed in the next part of this study). By then working-class poetry was attracting guarded middle-class attention, treated as a new phenomenon, perhaps, because the aristocratic patron of the self-taught poet of the early years of the century was giving way to the subscription list and a different economics of publication and dissemination. Middle-class critics tended to construct artisan writing in terms of a romantic 'Burns' tradition, rather than taking a stand for a genuine working-class poetry, as Fox did.[60] Thus in many ways they muted and distanced its sharpness. However, poets such as Alexander Rodger and Samuel Bamford, the Manchester weaver and early radical, whose writing goes back to the first two decades of the century, wrote with an irony which is later taken up in the work of William Thom and W. J. Linton. Thom's 'Whisperings for the Unwashed' (1844), describing the weaver 'Supreme in rags' weaving in tears 'The shining robe your murderer wears', with its intermittent chorus, 'Rubadub, rubadub, row-dow-dow!', and Linton's 'Bob Thin, or the Poorhouse Fugitive' (1845), another weaver poem, with its fierce itemising of poor-house rations in the "regulation" human stables', inherit the irony of Rodger's 'George, the Regent's, chaste and wise,/Castlereagh's an honest man,/Southey tells no fulsome lies,/England's free – likewise Japan'.[61] R. H. Horne's 'Political Oratorio' is an attempt to expand middle-class writing to include this subversive satiric energy. Samuel Bamford, whose writing career spanned forty years, continued to write subversive lyrics into the 1860s. The cheerful cynicism of his 'The Landowner' (1864), who reckons that the influence of family connections and power in the army, the church and court cannot be given up without immoral irresponsibility, is recognisably in the tradition of Rodger's work: 'To leave good things behind we find,/Is sin of high degree,/I'll sin for nobody, no not I./Whoever may sin for me'.[62]

It is significant, however, that though Bamford was a committed radical, suffering imprisonment more than once in his early years, he explicitly censored his volume of 1843 on the grounds that 'exciting public interest' in contentious topics makes it impossible 'to forget and forgive' class conflict, even though it might 'disappoint some over pertinacious friends'.[63] Bamford wrote union songs which in some ways differ little from Chartist songs in their powerfully generalised rhetoric – 'When woe, and want, and tyranny/Shall from our isle be swept away, – The grand epoch of liberty/Awaits a faithful Union' – but he refused to associate himself with Chartism.[64] For him 'freedom' signified 'reform', just as 'patriotic fire' ('Union Hymn') signified the united *legal* activity of combination.[65] What could be seen as ultimately directed to the good of all classes, promoting solidarity in and between classes through constitutional and legal action, drew his support. The logic of Chartism seemed to be different: it seemed to entail a divisive class aggression and an operation outside the law, from which he recoiled. The cost of class alienation seemed too much. Even the terminology of his 1843 Preface is uncertain, making reference forthrightly to 'the working classes', but softening this to 'the labouring class', and 'the working man'.[66] This uncertainty is important because, as will later be seen, it is typical of a number of poets. Though on occasions he could develop a rhetoric of bitter, apocalyptic critique, it was never used in the Chartist cause. He reprinted some earlier polemical poems in 1843, but his account of the poor engages pity and affective feeling rather than forming the social analysis which is so vigorously made in his autobiographical writing. Here, the poor woman's 'nook' is not a place of safety by a fire but a freezing doorway whose shelter is insecure, and to which she has no right. The urban context deeply ironises the pastoral associations of 'nook', but the poem is lyrical rather than analytical.

> God help the poor! An infant's feeble wail
> Comes from yon narrow gate-way; and behold,
> A female crouching there, so deathly pale,
> Huddling her child, to screen it from the cold!
> Her vesture scant, her bonnet crush'd and torn;
> A thin shawl doth her baby dear enfold:
> And there she bides the ruthless gale of morn,
> Which almost to her heart hath sent its cold!
> And now she sudden darts a ravening look,
> As one with new hot bread comes past the nook;
> And, as the tempting load is onward borne,
> She weeps. God help thee, hapless one forlorn!
> God help the poor![67]

Elliott and Bamford exemplify the instability of a momentary convergence of working- and middle-class perceptions in the 1830s and 1840s. But although it would be true to say that there was always a divide between working-class and middle-class poetry, the resilience and expressiveness of urban poetry and the industrial ballad in particular is often remarkable. Middle-class poets from Tennyson to Kipling often seized upon (and plundered) the ballad as a way of reaching a popular audience, as other poets appropriated dialect writing or the satire and stoicism of later music-hall songs. But this was a one-way passage: self-taught artisans who adopted consciously literary forms and language tended to be ignored by the middle class and estranged from their own class because their non-literate audience was unable to read their work. A poetry which crossed class boundaries was never sustainedly arrived at by either middle- or working-class poets. The extraordinary excitement of new theory and cultural analysis in the 1830s and 1840s was not matched by a commensurate practice. Only Ruskin, as we shall later see, understood why. And perhaps this failure partly explains why the aesthetics which was to dominate the century was a liberal aesthetics which modified its precursors, as Mill's concentric middle-class circles began to intersect, rather than the specifically conservative or radical thinking of the early decades. But if this was a 'critical effort' that failed, it was still a formative effort: the circles never quite converged into a liberal poetry and poetics. A radical and conservative tradition continued to coexist throughout the century, challenging one another and 'centrist' liberal theory. Subsequent chapters of this book concentrate on moments when poets were confronted with, and made, crucial aesthetic and political choices.

161

Part II

MID-CENTURY: EUROPEAN REVOLUTION AND CRIMEAN WAR

Democratic, liberal, radical and feminine voices

6

INDIVIDUALISM UNDER PRESSURE

God, by a sudden visitation, has withdrawn from the income He yearly sends us in the fruits of His earth, sixteen millions sterling. Withdrawn it, and from whom? On whom falls the loss? Not on the rich and luxurious, but on those whose labour makes the rich man rich and gives the luxurious his luxury. Shall not we then, the affluent and indulgent, spare somewhat of our affluence, curtail somewhat of our indulgence, that these (for our wealth too and for our indulgence in the end) may have food while they work, and have work to gain them food?

(Arthur Hugh Clough, on the Irish Famine of 1847)[1]

I trust in God that feudal industrial class as the French call it, you worship, will be clean trodden under. . . . Tell Edward I shall be ready to take flight with him the very moment the French land, and have engaged a Hansom to convey us both from the possible scene of carnage.

(Letter of Matthew Arnold to Clough, 1848)[2]

But in spite of all the success I have had, I have not failed to be conscious that the art I have been helping to produce would fall with the death of a few of us who really care about it, that a reform in art which is founded on individualism must perish with the individuals who have set it going. Both my historical studies and my practical conflict with the philistinism of modern society have *forced* on me the conviction that art cannot have a real life and growth under the present system of commercialism and profit-mongering. . . . About the time when I was beginning to think so strongly on these points that I felt I must express myself publicly, came the crisis of the Eastern Question . . . it seemed to me that England risked drifting into a war which would have committed her to the party of reaction: I also thoroughly dreaded the outburst of Chauvinism which swept over the country, and feared that once we were amusing ourselves

with an European war no one in this country would listen to anything
of social questions.

(William Morris, Letter to Andreas Scheu, 5 September 1883)[3]

Clough, Arnold and Morris are effectively a second generation of Victorian
poets. But there is an oddity about this, for their most creative work spans
a very short period. Tennyson and Browning continued to write into the
latter half of the century, well after two of the three poets discussed here
had ceased to produce, and certainly after their most interesting work.
Strangely, the young are superseded by the old. And yet Clough, Arnold
and Morris are marked by entirely different historical circumstances, circumstances to which indeed Tennyson and Browning responded also; but
they did not confront these during the formative periods of their writing
lives in the way that the younger poets were compelled to do.

The writings which head this chapter indicate the 'repeated shocks' of
change which Arnold was to describe in 'The Scholar-Gipsy', the domestic
shocks of mass hardship and the Chartist movement with which Clough
and Arnold grew up in their twenties, the European shocks of the revolutions of 1848, which met their late twenties, and the experience of the
Crimean war, which occurred in their early thirties (1854). This war,
responding as it did to the power struggles between Russia and Turkey
which threatened, among other things, Britain's trade routes to India,
shifted the focus of international politics beyond western Europe. Morris,
who was in his twenty-fourth year when the Crimean war began, refers in
his autobiographical piece to a later resurgence of the Eastern question
(1877), which was to have repercussions to the end of the century and
beyond. The shock which was to shape the imaginations of these poets
was the movement, in the space of half a dozen years, from revolutionary
uprising in Europe to a reconfiguration of colonial power. The distant
spaces of the Caucasus and the east were brought nearer: the materials of
myth for the younger Tennyson in the 1830s, they became, two decades
later, the places where you fought. The internal political struggles of the
British Isles, the battles in Europe, which so fascinated Clough and disturbed Arnold, were not contained by Europe but extended to war beyond.
It is not surprising that an insistent figure of battle and the estranging
spaces of the sea should dominate the poems of both Clough and Arnold.
The tropes respond to literal conflict and disclose unease about the shifting
and amorphous definition of national space and frontier, the uncertain
delimitation of racial boundary and relationship. In their wake they carry
uneasy questions about the meaning of manhood and of action.

All but a few of Arnold's important poems appeared within this short
period. They are concentrated in three volumes – *The Strayed Reveller and
Other Poems* (1849), *Empedocles on Etna and Other Poems* (1852) and *Poems*
(1853), which was prefaced by an assured and controversial essay retract-

ing the positions of the earlier work (Arnold withdrew both early volumes from circulation) and attempting to redirect the course of poetry and poetics. Other volumes followed in 1855, 1858 and 1867, but it is arguable that they were shaped by the earlier years. Only two volumes of poems appeared during Clough's lifetime, *Ambarvalia*, which included work by Thomas Burbidge (1849), and *The Bothie of Tober-Na-Vuolich* (1848), written after the *Ambarvalia* poems and originally entitled 'Toper-Na-Fuosich' (the title was changed because Clough discovered that it had obscene implications). Though *Amours de Voyage* and *Dipsychus* were respectively first published in full in 1858 and (posthumously) in 1865, they were written over 1849–52. William Morris's *Defence of Guenevere and Other Poems* was published in 1858, four years after the Crimean war began; it was the first volume of poetry to be associated with the Pre-Raphaelite Brotherhood, which formed earlier in the decade.[4]

These works, clustering within ten years, are marked by more than the shocks of change and the shift in the political centre of gravity in Europe: their authors lived and worked in Britain. Browning became an ex-patriot in 1846; Tennyson was not economically dependent on a career in the professions to support his poetry-writing. On the other hand, Clough, son of a Liverpool cotton-merchant, ultimately took up a post in the Education Office. Arnold, son of the head master of Rugby, became an inspector of schools in 1851 after a period as Lord Lansdowne's secretary. Both entered a growing bureaucracy of civil servants and government employees.[5] William Morris, son of a city broker, did not enter the world of commerce because he was left comparatively rich by the death of his father (1847). But he articled himself for a short period to an architect (G. E. Street in Oxford), and eventually set up his own (admittedly unusual) manufacturing firm in 1861. Morris was younger than Clough and Arnold by over a decade, but like them he wrote during this crucial period. All three were educated in public schools, which were beginning to educate men for a wider range of professions than the traditional legal and clerical professions open to the middle classes earlier in the century. All three were educated at Oxford. Their poetry discloses immediate concerns with political and economic questions and an extraordinary tension about these questions.

All three were aware of class conflict and revolutionary feeling in England. It is tempting to see Clough as the poet who continued the post-Benthamite analysis of Browning and the *Monthly Repository* formation, and Arnold and Morris as the bearers of a post-Coleridgean poetic tradition. But this, though neat, is not what happened. Clough significantly altered the aesthetic basis of a radical, dissident poetry, though in continuing to search rigorously for a democratic form he is nearest to the formations of the 1830s. Arnold repudiated both intellectual traditions, but conflated elements of them both in an essentially liberal, therapeutic account of poetry as a way of escaping from the symptoms of cultural sickness and

167

alienation. The poetry of sensation is a repressed element in his work. Morris has affiliations with Hallam's aesthetic, but not with its conservative politics. The poetry of sensation and its defamiliarising strategies are taken up to disrupt, not the 'usual' expectations and themes, as Hallam called them – morals, love, religion, ambition – but to explore the revolutionary implications of disruptive material which is already taboo, already fragmented and deranged. Morris used the poetry of sensation to evolve a profoundly radical and subversive form of writing. In fact, the procedures of the two earlier writers, Tennyson and Browning, become, in different ways, materials for contemplation, become thematised by the second-generation poets. So if the sense of a self-conscious second-order exploration is present as one reads the work of Clough, Arnold and Morris, that is part of their project, as Mill's 'concentric circles' intersect, overlap and change their orbits. Though it is possible to see a radical and conservative tradition continuing beyond the work of Tennyson and Browning to the end of the century, the clarity of the early formations is far less evident. So this later poetry is post-revolutionary, post-technological, post-teleological and post-Kantian in a different way than that of the work of the 1830s. The implications for poetry of 'movable types' and the alienated sign in the context of the late 1840s and early 1850s, and its structural relationship to the circulation of language, money, labour, are different. Sexual politics take another form. The double poem takes on a more uncertain existence than it did in the sure experiments of the early Tennyson and Browning. The question of representation is more tentatively explored as a gap between sign and meaning; language becomes that which possesses an independent life eluding consciousness. It is seen as that which makes communal understanding impossible by its inherent ambiguities and fatal capacity to invite misprision.

In his Preface of 1853, in which he rejected his *Empedocles on Etna*, and which changed the ground of critical debate, Arnold speaks of his present time in terms of Babel: the poet confronts 'the bewildering confusion of our times': 'A host of voices indignantly' defend the present age: but

> The confusion of the present times is great, the multitude of voices counselling different things bewildering, the number of existing works capable of attracting a young writer's attention and of becoming his models, immense. What he wants is a hand to guide him through the confusion, a voice to prescribe to him the aim which he should keep in view.[6]

Pre-eminently, of course, there was Clough's oppositional voice, counselling him, not only in private, as Arnold indefatigably counselled Clough, but in public too. Just before Arnold embarked upon the writing of the 1853 Preface, Clough had published a severe critique of Arnold's first two volumes in the *North American Review* for July 1853.[7] Then there were the

168

voices of the older contemporary poets, politically at opposite poles, Tennyson and Browning. There were the discordant voices of Wordsworth, Coleridge, Byron, Keats and Shelley from the recent past, though for the Arnold group Shelley's importance had dropped away, and it was the damaging, toxic influence of Keats which offended Arnold.[8] Wordsworth's *Prelude* had been published as recently as 1850. Not only had the poet of early Romanticism and the French Revolution become, disconcertingly, a Victorian poet, but the *Prelude*, though composed before *The Excursion*, followed its publication by a considerable period, and so the Wordsworth known to earlier Victorians as the poet of *Lyrical Ballads* and *The Excursion* had to be reassimilated. *Death's Jest-Book*, a darkly resonant work drawing upon Elizabethan and Jacobean drama for its morbid and strangely disturbing lyricism, was published posthumously in 1850 after the author, Thomas Lovell Beddoes, committed suicide. Beddoes, whose major work falls in the 1820s, was another Romantic poet whose work returns to shadow the 1850s. For Arnold a diseased and frenetic subjectivity had erupted in another form also, in the work of a group of actually very disparate poets nicknamed the Spasmodic School, P. J. Bailey, Sydney Dobell and Alexander Smith. Bailey reworked Goethe's *Faust* in a series of poems amalgamated into the on-going *Festus*, a composite which first appeared in 1839. *The Roman*, Dobell's political poem, written to champion oppressed Italy and to further the cause of Italian unity, very different in fact from the abstract, cosmic metaphysics of Bailey's poem, appeared in 1850. A later poem, *Balder* (1854), has some affinities with Alexander Smith's *A Life-Drama* (1853), a poem which interested Clough. Smith and Dobell published jointly a volume of poems on the Crimean war (1855).[9]

The poetry of the Spasmodics, that of Alexander Smith in particular, surges with Keatsian excess and Shakespearean fecundity and uses the diction of superfluity to explore political questions, sexuality and marriage. The fervour of ridicule they for the most part aroused (Clough was an exception) is almost equal in intensity to the excess they were credited with: 'it is *fantastic* and wants *sanity*', Arnold wrote of contemporary poetry, in the second edition of his *Poems*.[10] For the Spasmodics were a threat to the dominant literary culture, a threat because they seemed out of control, a threat because their social origin (Dobell was a wine-merchant's son, Smith a Glasgow mechanic) gave them a doubtful and ambiguous status, a threat because they disclosed political problems and the tensions of sexuality and marriage without the distance they are given in Arnold's work and even that of Clough. In fact, their work exists in strange, turbulent parallel to the texts of these poets, like a dream work.[11] Dobell's *Balder* (1854), invoking the powers of hell and dealing with the euthanasia of a suffering wife, is like a conflation of Arnold's *Balder Dead* (1855), where the powers of the underworld are negotiated, and *Tristram and Iseult* (1852), where a virtual suicide pact ends the poem. *Tristram and Iseult*, where the lover is divided between different kinds of love for two women, has affinities with the confused loyalties of Smith's 'A Life-Drama', in *Poems* (1853). As in Dobell's *The Roman* (1850), Clough takes Italy for his theme in *Amours de Voyage*, and like Bailey, he reworked Goethe's *Faust* in *Dipsychus*, a poem of the early 1850s. Only Morris seemed to be able to gain fruitful access to the intensity of Spasmodic poetry.

Only Clough seemed to be aware of voices even beyond those of the Spasmodics. The Spasmodics did not quite fit into the conventional categories which both described and maintained some poets on the margins of literary culture, and perhaps this is why they were so disturbing. They were not all self-educated artisans, nor were they that anachronistic grouping, peasant poets. Clough heard the voices, confusing though they may have been, of working-class poets, Chartists and radicals. Though the phrase Fox had used to classify a new kind of writing, 'the poetry of the poor', helps to limit the perception of such a group by confining them to the very category which attempts to recognise them, it is clear that Clough attempted to assimilate their significance. It is an irony that one of these poets, Thomas Cooper, anticipated the subject of Arnold's *Empedocles on Etna* in his *The Purgatory of Suicides* (1845). Though short-lived as a movement, Chartism created a surge of poetic energy among working-class writers which drew partly from the radical rhetoric of poets such as Samuel Bamford and partly forged a new language of its own. Bamford continued to publish in this period (with *Poems*, 1843, as has been seen), but poets such as Thomas Cooper, Gerald Massey (who subsequently swung to reaction with the Crimean war), J. B. Leno, Robert Peddie and Ernest Jones, to name a few of the most prominent, evolved a powerful oppositional political rhetoric. Also heard faintly by the middle-class writer, and interpreted rashly (both then and now) as conservative forces, were the self-taught poets who worked in another tradition of literary language and often pastoral verse which used the dominant language and diction of educated poetry – though it often tended to be the language of eighteenth-century poetry – for their own purposes. The group round Bamford in Manchester, for instance, among them Elijah Ridings, J. C. Prince and J. B. Rogerson, used the diction and genres of 'educated' poetry, as Bamford himself did, following an earlier generation of self-taught poets. As the titles of their volumes indicate – John Nicholson's *Airedale in Ancient Times* (1825), Stephen Fawcett's *Wharfedale Lays* (1837) (both Bradford poets) and William Heaton's *The Flowers of Calder Dale* (1847) (Heaton was a Halifax poet) – pastoral is all-important to many writers. But pastoral serves a number of purposes, just as it does in Clough's eminently Theocritan and dissident pastoral, *The Bothie of Tober-Na-Vuolich*. It would be rash to equate the conservatism of Robert Story, whose *Poetical Works* were published in 1857, with that of the earlier John Nicholson, just as it would be inappropriate to see in the Manchester group a pastoral quietism comparable with that of Matthew Arnold. In fact the more they adopt middle-class writing conventions, the less like middle-class writers these poets really are.

But there was one voice which neither Arnold nor Clough could have heard in the 'Babel' of the mid-century: this was the voice of John Clare, a forgotten poet assigned to an almost forgotten category, the peasant poet. Clare, confined to an asylum from the early 1840s, continued to write throughout this period. Officially deemed to have lost the 'sanity' Arnold required of poetry, he nevertheless wrote in a pastoral mode. Clare's pastoral and the educated pastoral of Arnold's 'The Scholar-Gipsy' and 'Thyrsis', poems which Arnold hoped could become a therapeutic antidote to the 'confusion' of the nineteenth century, strangely reduplicate one another. And Clare wrote also of those experiences anxiously contemplated by Arnold and Clough, the loss of love and manhood.

The importance of Clough, Arnold and Morris lies in the way they attempted to negotiate the 'confusion' of the mid-nineteenth century. There were, as the poetics and politics of the 1830s and 1840s suggest, sophistica-ted accounts of power, ideology, class, representation, language and gender available to these later poets, but all three modified the tenets of the post-Benthamite and Coleridgean formations in different ways. All three appear to confirm Hallam's analysis of the position of the poet in modern culture: that his work will be isolated from 'community of interest', that it will be 'a reaction against' the 'general impulse of the nation', that 'the change in the relative position of the artist to the rest of the community' will create a fatal dualism. The 'return of the mind upon itself', he said, reinforces a split which is both cause and effect of the conceptualisation of a subjectivity in opposition to a resistant externality.[12] For Hallam, such alienation, the negative double of affirmative, competitive individualism, could be circumvented by 'magic', the access to the cultural possession of myth through the poetry of sensation. Morris found a way of negotiating this, as I have said, despite belonging to a coterie with very different interests. But rather than performing an analysis through myth by *making strange* the forms of their culture, as Morris did, Clough and Arnold per-formed an analysis of the *estranged* subjectivity of the artist and intellectual. Rather than making an analysis of the imaginative fictions of communal experience, one of the solutions evolved by the Fox group, they consented, in different ways, to a fiction of alienation. It became their myth, a myth from which they struggled to free themselves. Such a myth is a kind of inverted individualism, a form, ironically, of the ideology of the isolated psyche seeking a private gain which they both saw as the vice of Victorian society. So they are both poets of the unhappy consciousness, both analys-ing that condition only in the terms of the unhappy consciousness itself. Stoicism and scepticism, Hegel's dialectically related states, those comp-lementary strategies by which consciousness deals with its aloofness from substantive experience and only succeeds in abstracting itself further, are inherent in this peculiarly alienated individualism.

Their efforts to contend with this dilemma, and with one another, register not only the personal and complex disagreements of an intimate but painfully cooling friendship, but a particular cultural moment. Both, in public and in private, in poetry and in prose, obsessively accused each other of the same faults. Clough's 1853 review of Arnold's work and Arnold's 1853 Preface each represent, one openly and the other covertly, a critique of one another's work. But they both describe the same deficiencies. They are complementary poets rather than being in opposition to one another. Both write as if the other is looking over his shoulder. After considering Arnold's capacity for 'reflecting, pondering, hesitating, musing, complaining' in his review of 1853, Clough turns to contemporary cultural analysis:

> There is something certainly of an over-educated weakness of purpose in Western Europe – not in Germany only, or France, but also in more busy England. There is a disposition to press too far the inner and subtler intellectual and moral susceptibilities; to insist upon following out, as they say, to their logical consequences, the notices of some single organ of the spiritual nature.[13]

The survival of poetry depends not on a poetry of the past – 'Not by turning and twisting his eyes, in the hope of seeing things as Homer, Sophocles, Virgil, or Milton saw them' – but on a strong commitment to the modern situation, by 'steady courage and calls to action'. The strategy of the review is to present a resilient stoicism in the face of 'timid self-culture' and scepticism.[14] By implication Arnold is the doubting sceptic who, in a non-teleological culture given over to the conditional nature of post-Kantian representation in 'the modern German religion' with its 'transcendental doubt', is disabled, and unable to understand community, the wants of 'ordinary people' and 'positive matters of fact'.[15] (And for Clough, as we shall see, 'ordinary people' included Chartists as well as middle-class readers: 'calls to action' involve bourgeois and working class.) But Arnold begins the Preface of 1853 with just such a repudiation of scepticism:

> What those who are familiar only with the great monuments of early Greek genius suppose to be its exclusive characteristics, have disappeared; the calm, the cheerfulness, the disinterested objectivity have disappeared: the dialogue of the mind with itself has commenced; modern problems have presented themselves; we hear already the doubts, we witness the discouragement, of Hamlet and of Faust.[16]

The characteristic historiographical sweep through classical to Romantic experience, designated, in one of Arnold's most perceptive phrases, as the movement to the debilitating 'dialogue of the mind with itself', reclaims the stoic ground Clough had swept from under him and locates it exactly where Clough had seen the retreat into scepticism to begin. It is probable that Arnold had not seen Clough's review when he began work on his Preface, but the disagreements between them were well enough known. By implication Clough, whom Arnold had accused of being too content to 'fluctuate', is the sceptic suffering the damage of the modern consciousness.[17] In a world torn with political struggle, where estranged labour separated from nature gives expression to revolutionary turmoil – 'Man's fitful uproar mingling with his toil' ('Quiet Work', 1848, 10) – the complaining 'millions', he later told Clough, do not 'want' the deracinating political, intellectual and psychological reflection to be found in the now rejected *Empedocles*.[18] They want, not the representation of themselves through 'ordinary' 'matters of fact', but the representation of a classical and therapeutic composure itself. The 'mortal millions' ('To Marguerite – Continued', 1849, 4) living *alone*, the 'swarms of men' ('Stanzas in Memory of the Author of "Obermann" ', 1849, 176) who threaten to dissipate themselves in action, conceived as an undifferentiated flow of humanity, exert a terrible pressure on Arnold's poetry. And in these depersonalised crowds are included not only the working and middle classes but also that threatening influx of strangers and aliens from beyond Britain and Europe.

Despite very considerable political and intellectual differences which were to be extremely important in the shaping of their poetry, Arnold and Clough analyse their situation in the same terms. The ground of scepticism and stoicism changes places so bewilderingly because in and between their work the two terms collapse into one another and cannot be kept apart. At a deeper ideological level they share these categories, and only differ in the content they are prepared to attribute to this seeming opposition. Clough can write with a painful, demythologising rigour, 'Christ is not risen!', and assent to the rational fictions of Strauss ('Easter Day – Naples, 1849', 5): Arnold can utter a threnody on the lost myth of Christianity as the 'sea of faith' ebbs in 'Dover Beach' (21); Clough can portray the equanimity with which a woman considers the transience of sexual loyalty ('Les Vaches') and Arnold can attempt to remain aloof from a feminine sexuality 'mined by the fever of the soul' ('A Farewell', 1849, 22), but in both stoicism becomes a form of scepticism and scepticism a form of stoicism. Both poets confront an opposition between isolation and involvement, aloofness and commitment, self and society, the ideal and the real, being and knowing, cheerfulness and depression. The attempt to resolve these antitheses tightens their hold rather than loosens their authority. This is not so in the work of Tennyson and Browning a decade and a half earlier. For the account of consciousness explored by Clough and Arnold had a narrower epistemological basis than those available to poets of the earlier decades: it derives from an ethical and individualised account of selfhood, a buried, secret but discoverable integrity of being which could be the measure of experience, a separate self to which above all one could be true. Lone voyagers both in an existential sea, Arnold confronts its emptiness by internalising the voice of nature – 'Resolve to be thyself; and know that he,/Who finds himself, loses his misery!' ('Self-Dependence', 1849, 31–2); Clough confronts its fluctuations by trusting that the different selves which have been severed to sail on separate courses can obey the compass which reunites them – 'To that, and your own selves, be true' ('Qua Cursum Ventus', 1849, 20).[19] The pursuit of true individual selfhood, however, the poising of the solitary consciousness in the honourable integrity of stoicism or the honourable openness of scepticism, maintains an opposition between the self and the world and perpetuates the oppositions it seeks to resolve. This is the nature of the 'individualism' Morris deprecates in the quotation at the start of this chapter.

The strategy of abstraction, moreover, can become a compulsive formal ploy rather than a moral activity and it becomes increasingly difficult to find a content for the oppositional terms by which the self defines its relationships. A strategy for dealing with experience begins to take precedence over the particularity of experience itself. All thought is about experience rather than being experience. This is what Arnold meant by the dialogue of the mind with itself. This is why Clough makes the common-sense uncle in the Epilogue to *Dipsychus* complain about the disabling opposition which places the 'over-tender conscience' over and against 'the world':

'I quite agree that consciences are often much too tender in your generation – schoolboys' consciences, too! As my old friend the Canon says of the Westminster students, "They're all so pious." It's all [Thomas] Arnold's doing; he spoilt the public schools . . . the old schools . . . were in harmony with the world, and they certainly did not disqualify the country's youth for after-life and the country's service'.[20]

The pragmatic uncle is right. The self which experiences a split between the 'true' self and the world will be troubled about the nature of action. What constitutes effective action, where it lies, is a preoccupation elevated to an ethical and philosophical principle in the poetry of Clough and Arnold. Each attempts to retrieve the self for action in an attempt to close the gap between the reflexive self and the world. This manifests itself in Clough's 'call for action' in the contemporary political world just as it is manifested in Arnold's repudiation of intervention, which is to be replaced by an exploration of the 'great human actions' of the past. For both poets action is figured as combat or battle. But it is here, for both of them, that the trope of battle discloses a contradiction in the individualism it both

174

expresses and seeks to assuage in meaningful communal action. For the battle precisely undoes meaning and certainty in action. Its ground shifts, actions signify ambiguously. It is ethically compromising. It is the site of further isolation and solipsism, and, commensurately, deep sexual doubt and unease about one's male sexuality. Individual action and communality dissolve simultaneously. Moreover the independent striving for self-fulfilment becomes the counterpart of a more ignoble condition. At the end of 'Dover Beach' Arnold recalls a crucial text for Oxford intellectuals, Thucidides' account of the battle of Epipolae, a night battle in which the Athenians, not being able to tell friend from foe, fought one another.

> And we are here as on a darkling plain
> Swept with confused alarms of battle and flight,
> Where ignorant armies clash by night.[21]
>
> (35–7)

This is a double reference, for it looks back to Clough's image of the same battle in *The Bothie*.

> What are we to resist, and what are we to be friend with?
> If there is battle, 'tis battle by night: I stand in the darkness,
> Here in the mêlée of men, Ionian and Dorian on both sides,
> Signal and password known; which is friend and which is foeman?[22]
>
> (IX, 50–3)

Both poems reach back to another significant reading of this crucial text, Newman's. In a sermon of 1839 Newman had pointed to the ambiguity of contemporary intellectual debate: 'Controversy . . . does not lie between the hosts of heaven . . . and the powers of evil . . . but it is a sort of night battle, where each fights for himself, and friend and foe stand together'.[23] Shockingly, Newman invokes the aggressive language of economics and competitive *laissez-faire* individualism to describe contemporary intellectual life, and aligns the aesthetics and ethics of independent self-culture with it. And thus spiritual individualism becomes a form of the economic individualism which both Clough and Arnold saw and deprecated in 'busy' England. Spiritual individualism is always in danger of collapsing into the very economic processes which both scepticism and stoicism seek to resist by standing aloof in self-sustaining isolation. 'Each fights for himself': not only are the strategies of scepticism and stoicism identical in maintaining the dualism between self and world, but they also find themselves soiled by what Arnold called, in 'Stanzas in Memory of the Author of "Obermann"' (1852), 'The hopeless tangle of our age' (83), as isolation becomes the counterpart of the pursuit of private gain.[24] Self-culture becomes not the opposite but the twin of private gain. Thus the poetry of Arnold and Clough discloses and seeks to analyse a crisis in individualism. But because the analysis is often carried out within the terms of individualism itself both poets discover limits to their project. Their problem was to escape from the constraints in which they were entangled and to find new terms. Both poets made strenuous efforts to do this – great critical efforts, indeed – but such an escape frequently meant escaping from one another.

'Which is friend and which is foeman?' Because stoicism and scepticism become forms of one another and are not really in dialectical opposition Clough and Arnold define themselves against one another in an almost compulsive way. Clough calls for a movement from fastidious scepticism towards life and action. Earth, the solid ground, the visible solidity of building and city, dominate his poetry. Arnold calls for a retreat from the damaging introspection such scenes call forth to the cool rural slope, the hill, the mountain, an ascent to the overview. Clough's social and empiri-cally subsistent architectural structures, which register the poet's capacity to remain within the existing conditions of experience, are displaced by the ideal form of Arnold's aesthetic category, a formal *architectonicé* which shapes experience from without. But since both movements depend upon a view of the self as *external* to the scenes they either enter or depart from, a private self transcending its privacy by immersing itself in action or losing itself in the overview, it is no surprise that the necessity to differentiate and to distinguish between each other becomes for each poet an ideological as well as a personal project.

Arnold wrote poems to Clough either posthumously, as in his elegy, 'Thyrsis' (1866), or while he was alive, particularly in the year of European revolutions, 1848. 'The World and the Quietist', the two sonnets 'To a Republican Friend', 'Religious Isolation' and 'Quiet Work' are all from this period. All thematise the radical's misprision of the quietist's account of history, culture, politics, labour and its 'Wide Prospect' ('To a Friend', 3).[25] But stoic firmness itself involves a misprision of the radical sceptic's morbidly scrupulous need to 'fluctuate', as he told Clough in a letter. 'People try to force their opinions on others in order to convince them-selves', Arnold wrote in a telling letter to his sister.[26] Both poets try 'to convince themselves' of their difference. And it is the indirect strategies by which they defend and protect themselves against one another which are most significant. Yet while each poet's *oeuvre* sometimes seems like a mass-ive reply to the other, a dialogue to the death and beyond it, the defences reveal and conceal a sense that the other is a repressed form of himself, that each man meets his own image in the other. Thus the poems double, invert and split versions of the same content, often introducing misprision in the effort to avoid it.

The poems offer replies – *Sohrab and Rustum*, for instance, constitutes a reply to *The Bothie* – but both are engaged at a deeper level with the trope of war as manhood. Gender, intellectual self-culture, culture, art and the meaning of history – for it is the status of history and the classical tradition, its authority and signifying power, rather than the authority of myth which is important for these poets – are all problematical themes. Clough's commitment to Keats, whom Arnold deprecated, appears, longingly rejected, in the chill, gelid diction – like a Keats on ice – of the young poet Callicles in *Empedocles on Etna*. The weight of Empedocles' resignation is redefined as timidity and sexual failure in Clough's *Dipsychus*. The timid self-culture of *Dipsychus* returned upon the dead Clough in Arnold's 'Thyrsis' as that which 'made him droop' (47). In Arnold's 'Consolation' (1853), the 'Grey time-worn marbles' (16) of the Vatican withstand in their permanence and 'noble calm' (25) the assault of modern warfare as the French storm Rome in the last days of the Roman Republic (1849).[27] Ironically, Clough's letters seem to have prompted this reference, but in *Amours de Voyage*, where the siege of Rome is the context for a love affair, it is the chance to see these very Vatican marbles which destroys the growing love between Claude and Mary Trevellyn, so they are the source of the breakdown of relationships rather than 'noble calm'. Claude reneges on his promise to accompany Mary's departing family – and on sexuality and marriage too – using his special permission to view the marbles as an excuse for remaining. Claude meditates on stoic resignation, much as Arnold in 'Courage' (1852), where the raised arm of Cato signifies the implacable resignation of the suicide. In *Amours de Voyage*, however, the figure of the raised arm reappears but its signification is undermined and ironised, indeterminate and doubtful. It must have been the bitterness of these complex negotiations which made Clough take the name of the woman to whom Arnold's anguished 'Marguerite' sequence is addressed, Mary Claude, and split it between the failed lovers, Mary and Claude.[28] Mary waits hopelessly in Switzerland, the scene of Arnold's love affair, for the 'little lake steamer' to bring Claude at the end of the poem. He never arrives. The name of 'Marguerite' was a close-kept secret and has only been confirmed fairly recently. That Clough's need to debate aesthetics, politics and sexual politics led him to conceal and reveal such a secret 'signal and password', as in the betrayals of *The Bothie*'s night battle, testifies to the ideological tensions of a deeply ambivalent antagonism and friendship.

These tensions, and a divided and difficult analysis of the individualist ethic, are at their most complex in the long poems written by the two poets, Clough's *Bothie*, *Amours de Voyage* and *Dipsychus*, Arnold's *Empedocles on Etna* and *Sohrab and Rustum* in particular. A discussion of these poems forms the next part of this study.

7

THE RADICAL IN CRISIS:
CLOUGH

The Bothie of Tober-Na-Vuolich, a poem in hexameters subtitled 'A Long Vacation Pastoral', surprised Clough's friends. Since he had recently resigned his Oxford fellowship on supposedly religious grounds (he could not subscribe to the Thirty-Nine Articles), while the Tractarian controversy was at its height, it seemed likely that he would produce a theological poem.[1] It is, however, at once Theocritan pastoral, mock epic and modern verse novel. Though there is a concealed theology in the poem, as will be seen, it has little immediately to do with the Roman tendencies of High Anglicanism. What there is of Tractarianism seems like a parody of it, and it seems possible that, once liberated from Oxford, Clough was able to make a critique of the Oxford milieu. It is a study of the upper-class radical and intellectual. In Scotland with his tutor and an undergraduate reading party, Philip Hewson – student, Chartist, poet and enemy of the upper-middle-class conventions surrounding sexual relationships and marriage – becomes involved, out of a combination of lust and theory, with a working-class servant girl, Katie. He then veers towards a flirtation with the aristocratic Lady Maria and finally finds himself, his integrity and a wife, in Elspie, the crofter's daughter. In many ways it is a more realistic version of the genre of rustic 'daughter' poems of Tennyson, Sterling and William Allingham, and, like them, discloses a real anxiety about the sexual feelings and demands of women in heterosexual relationship. Its brilliance, however, does not arise from its direct social realism and confrontation of class, or its willingness to 'study the question of sex', as one of Philip's friends puts it;[2] nor does it arise from the innovation which made it one of the earliest verse novels. What Clough did was to evolve a form to which a politics was intrinsic and a language which was necessarily a democratic language. This meant entirely reshaping metrical structures and diction as they were commonly used in English poetry.

Though he was later generous to *The Bothie*, praising its 'rapidity of movement, and the plainness and directness of its style', in the lectures *On Translating Homer* after Clough's death, this testimony may have been a reparation for Arnold's strong and strongly expressed dislike of the poem in 1848.³ Then, it seemed the slave of the *Zeitgeist* and the contemporary rage for superficial topicality. But Arnold's subsequent praise of Clough's style does not really register the significance of the poem's language. One can best address this by returning to Clough's account of Alexander Smith's poetry in the review of *A Life-Drama* in 1853.

Though it is clear that Smith's poetic language is implicitly ideological in form, it is not the democratic language Clough sought. He praises Smith for a poetry which arises from the life of the modern city, the 'crowded, busy, vicious and inhuman town' (though he exaggerates the extent of Smith's urban imagery), but he dislikes its metaphorical excess. He saves this criticism until after he has dealt with the etiolated classicism of Arnold's diction, so that Arnold's language looks epicene by contrast with Smith's diction. Nevertheless, his attack on Smith is fierce and is offered with some of the coarseness Clough detects in his subject, as a certain snobbery elides Spasmodic poet and clerk (Smith was actually a lace-pattern designer).

He writes, it would almost seem, under the impression that the one business of the poet is to coin metaphors and similes. He tells them out as a clerk might sovereigns at the Bank of England. So many comparisons, so much poetry; it is the sterling currency of the realm. Yet he is most pleased, perhaps, when he can double or treble a similitude; speaking of A, he will call it a B, which is, as it were, the C of a D.⁴

Arnold and Clough concur here (one is tempted to say, for once) in an attack on such excess. In the 1853 Preface Arnold deprecates the poetry which ignores form and produces 'a shower of isolated thoughts and images'.⁵ It is clear that he is thinking of Smith, for he quotes David Masson's approving review of Smith with hostility and denies that a subjective poetry which, in Masson's words, presents 'A true allegory of the state of one's own mind in a representative history' is an adequate form for modern poetry.⁶

Why this concerted attack on a relatively harmless derivative Keatsian mode? Why the refusal of metaphor? It is the *economic* element of *exchange* in the metaphorical language of expressive poetry which offends Clough and, by implication, Arnold too. Expressive accounts of language and experience presuppose that inner experience occurs prior to language and subsequently seeks its equivalent in words. Metaphor is an extension of this process.⁷ Metaphor *coins* words and turns language into a currency by turning one expression into an equivalent term and exchanging one term for another. But since expressive language is a psychological language, and words are merely the proxy form for a psychic condition, a representative 'allegory of the state of one's own mind' simply returns one to the inner subjectivity of the self, because the outer shell of language is merely the equivalent of subjectivity. Moreover, the self makes capital out of itself, like a linguistic entrepreneur; it can 'double or treble' its linguistic profit

179

in the production of metaphor. In fact for Arnold and Clough metaphor is the ideological form of economic individualism where each man 'fights for himself', a form too close to the spiritual individualism of their own presuppositions to be comfortable. It is also an alienated language, for with the progressive movement from A to B and then to C and D words depart further and further from their primary meaning. They are the epitome of Carlyle's movable types, an estranged language of interminable substitution, like the marked piece of leather which stands in for the object of barter. Finally, expressive metaphor is logically a private language, for if words are merely a subjective correlative, so to speak, of an internal condition, then the sign has no communal value.

It is important to see that the analysis made by Clough and Arnold actually presupposes and consents to expressive theory even while it contends with its implications. It assumes the dualism between inner and outer on which the expressive model is founded. In their attempts to resist the language of expressive individualism they both close off metaphorical language as a form for modern poetry and both are left seeking an alternative. There were other ways of thinking about metaphor, but because their critique was in the terms of the expressive model of consciousness they were forced to abandon such ideas. For instance, Hallam's account of metaphor as an essentially analytic form, reconfiguring the relation between subject and object and making strange experience through the agency of the mythic language of sensation, went unrecognised by them. It is interesting that they did not mount Sir Henry Taylor's conservative critique either. While he saw metaphorical language in terms of sexual licence and revolutionary anarchy Clough and Arnold rather see it in terms of febrile productivity and madness. Sydney Dobell, the theorist of the Spasmodics, did produce a defence of metaphor based on the internal capacity of language to transform itself. He argued for a complex form of interaction and metaphoric transformation within language in a highly sophisticated reading of the expressive model. His basic premise, however, is the expressive model: 'To express a mind is to carry out that mind *into some equivalent*'.[8] On this reading the solipsist expressive poet is Mill's poet talking to himself, overheard rather than heard. Even if a method of displacing 'inner' experience into the 'equivalent' of language is found, the poet is still meditating on his internal condition.

There were few challenges to such linguistic dualism in the 1850s. Arnold and Clough were compelled to find a way round it. Arnold argued that the poet effaces himself by confronting objective actions where language as a medium almost disappears. Clough found another way. He evolved a radical language, not by inventing a notional 'common', universally accessible speech abstracted as a norm, nor by inventing a condescending imitation of the language of the poor, but by enabling language to become the object of democratic investigation. This is a democratic account of language because it explores speech as it is determined and organised by and in specific social groups. Language thus becomes the communal, social possession formed by particular groups, whether it is the possession of undergraduates or aristocrats. As such the authority of the language spoken by particular groups can be seen to be the function of their place in a social structure. This meant that the codes of specific groups have to be seen as a dialect, whether their place in the social hierarchy ranks high or low. Because each dialect is theoretically of equal status with another, the dominance of one group's language is not intrinsic to it but derives from external factors. Such a politics of language makes for a precise and self-conscious examination of language and power. This is more exact than the project of Browning and the Fox group, which it resembles, though the idea of dialect certainly extends the radical implications of the Fox group's ideas.

In order to register the variety of languages, Clough had to find a form sufficiently flexible to enable each group's language to expose and to act as a control on the other. He found what the uncle in the Prologue to *Dipsychus* described as 'hurry-scurry anapaests' (2), but what were in fact supremely modern hexameters. He is often thought of as the poet who introduced the cadences of speech rhythm and the 'ordinary' language of the speaking voice into Victorian poetry. But by the logic of his project there is no such thing as 'ordinary' language (he was pretty sceptical of Wordsworth's claims to be producing this): every language is extra-ordinary, a special variant or form.[9] And because it is special, every language is the material of poetry, which is given the status of the language of the special language in our culture. Clough is not the prosaic poet of the 'low' style or bourgeois Victorian speech; he is the poet of extraordinary language, which he explores with unique virtuosity. Exploiting the versatile stress pattern of the hexameter, *The Bothie* makes eloquent such language as 'You couldn't properly say our eyes met' (IV. 131), or 'Venting the murderous spleen of the endless Railway Committee' (I. 67), differentiating the stress and cadence of individual phrases with an exactitude which makes each utterance unique. And it is in his celebration of the uniqueness of all utterance that Clough's greatness lies. *The Bothie* liberates poetry into a new understanding of the potential of language.

It comes as no surprise that *The Bothie* begins with a crucial linguistic ceremony – the making of public speeches. It is a political ceremony too: a dinner concludes the Highland games, and this is a symbolic, exclusively male gathering, at which the representatives from the existing hierarchy of rulers and ruled, from Scots peasants to the English aristocratic landlord, meet to consolidate the status quo. They make patriotic speeches. 'Three-times-three thrice over' (I. 86), in a haze of toddy and enthusiasm, the party toasts 'Queen, and Prince, and Army, and Landlords all, and Keep-ers' (I. 87) – themselves. Clough makes no attempt to reproduce Scottish speech here or anywhere in the poem. This silencing of the indigenous language is deliberate. For he is portraying a Scotland dominated by the English and an anglicised ruling class. The visiting group of under-graduates are toasted benignly as 'the Strangers', and the poem is partly about the irresponsibility of the holiday stranger who treats the environment he has entered in an unscrupulous and insensitive way. But Sir Hector, the genial host and great local landlord, is another kind of alien, one of the class whom Arnold, with his capacity for the supremely arresting phrase, was later to call the 'Barbarians' in *Culture and Anarchy* (1869).[10] The poem begins with the final ceremony of the games, a fancy dress parade, significantly a recent innovation. Peering at the clansmen like specimens through lorgnettes, the female nobility adjudicate, 'Turning the clansmen about, as they stood with upraised elbows' (I. 8), and 'fingering kilt and sporran' (I. 9). The comic bravura, the mood of the whole poem, does not disguise this indignity. Indigenous tradition and dress, the critical differentiating marks of a culture (Scottish national dress had been banned until the early part of the century), have become a historical pageant.[11] There is at once a suggestion both of the denial of the men's sexuality and a covert enjoyment of it as an object of contemplation as kilt and sporran are fingered.

In a lecture on Dryden written after this poem, Clough argued that Dryden transformed the English language. It was no longer necessary to understand Latin to gain access to it; it was 'easier' to write and to read. Dryden 'organised the dissolving and separating elements of our tongue into a new and living instrument' which became a communal possession.[12] 'You may call it, if you please, a democratic movement in the language'.[13] Dryden succeeded he implies, for Clough was a patrician democrat, because he effected 'that aristocratic reconstruction which pertains to every good democratic revolution'.[14] With the dissemination of the written word in newspapers and the mass production of print, another democratic revolution is occurring: 'There has been a kind of dissolution of English, but no one writer has come to re-unite and re-vivify the escaping components'.[15] He makes a careful distinction between a 'popularised' language (a good thing) and a 'vulgarised' one. His argument is partly a familiar and relatively conservative one – there is no 'standard' – but his emphasis is on the difficulties of communication in a community which no longer shares a diction. It is a language which cannot mediate the new thought and 'events' of the nineteenth century. Lack of information, division and fragmentation are enemies to democracy. But what is clear is that English is now a language of 'escaping components', all incomplete, no one of which has authority. *The Bothie* exploits this lack of authority to make a social analysis.

The Bothie makes no attempt to homogenise and 're-unite' the language. Instead it performs an exuberant analysis of these 'escaping components'

182

as they belong to different groups and subgroups, different social 'components': and this must include, of course, a self-conscious analysis of the writer's own narrative style, for the poet, too, belongs to a particular subgroup with its own linguistic conventions. Such an enterprise deconstructs the power of the authorial narrative voice. This is a necessary project, for *The Bothie* is intensely concerned with a critique of language and power. Though there is no authoritative language there is no doubt that there is a politics of language, as Elspie so poignantly realises when she confronts the immense social difference between herself and Philip: 'and all those indefinable graces/(Were they not hers, too, Philip?) to speech and manner, and movement' (VIII. 8–9). Social class inflects speech and informs even an individual's movements. The parenthesis, an authorial parenthesis within what is already authorial narrative, is arranged as if to dissociate a more egalitarian view from the class assumptions of the main narrative – 'Were they not hers, too, Philip?' But – and this is where the qualification of the poem's narrative voice is brilliantly organised through syntactic structure – the egalitarian remark *has* to be ideologically bracketed. For though Elspie's 'graces' of speech and manner are just as powerful as those of Philip, and just as beautiful to him, this is a private perception. They are not perceived socially as being so by virtue of Philip's class superiority – and they are not perceived to be so to Elspie herself. The poem makes a running investigation of the power invested in this superior speech and of the classical languages in which it is trained. The 'vocabular ghosts' derived from the 'lexicon-limbo' (II. 224) of Greek and Latin dictionaries which are the 'signal and password' of a particular group exert a material pressure on it and on other people.

The poem begins with a mock-heroic ceremony of dressing for dinner in the coded language of the undergraduate group, specifically described as a 'dialect' (I. 29). It is a language of slang – '*Shady*', '*topping*' (124) – and mock-patrilineal naming in Homeric epithets – 'the lively, the cheery, cigar-loving Lindsay' (I. 31), 'Arthur, the bather of bathers' (I. 33) and, later in the poem, 'the glory of headers' (III. 58). The mock-heroic epithets extend to articles of dress, the waistcoats which are the equivalent of heroic armour – 'waistcoat work of a lady', 'Waistcoat blue, coral buttoned' (I. 25, 41): waistcoats as articles of display, Clough said, in the retrenchment speech which begins the chapter before this one, were the emblem of wealth and conspicuous consumption for the rich undergraduate.[16] The bonding of this private heroic language, based on coterie access to the classics, is directly juxtaposed with the categories of the public language of class hierarchy which does not operate so playfully – the postman calls Hobbes 'His Honour' because of his tenuous connection with the aristocracy. At the dinner the narrative moves in ascending hierarchy, through peasant, gillie and keeper, Catholic priest and Protestant minister of the established church (who are allowed to share the Grace to maintain social

183

cohesion), gentry, Guardsman, MP, marquis and earl. The dinner is a display at once of class generosity and class privilege as peasants answer the speeches of 'flattering nobles' (I. 105). Clough sets two kinds of aristocratic 'Barbarian' language against one another and against the private coterie speech of the 'Strangers'. There is the incoherent goodwill of Sir Hector, 'unsuspecting of syntax' (I. 96), like a 'speat' or flood, or a circus rider at 'Astleys or Franconi's' (I. 90, 92) (Clough mingles Scots dialect and popular allusion to indicate Sir Hector's chaotic demotic rhetoric) in 'grammar defying' (I. 88) form: 'There was a toast I forgot, which our gallant Highland homes have/Always welcomed the stranger' (I. 13–14). But there is also the unashamed rhetoric of the Marquis of Ayr, packed with the clichés of privilege: 'Floundering on through game and messroom recollections, . . . Anticipation of royal visit, skits at pedestrians [the reading party are pedestrians],/Swore he would never abandon his country, nor give up deer-stalking' (I. 100, 102–3). In other words, he will maintain the fiercely restrictive and punitive game laws.

Philip Hewson, the Chartist sympathiser, hater of 'Feudal tenures, mercantile lords, competition and bishops,/Liveries, armorial bearings, amongst other matters the Game-laws' (I. 127–8), replies to the toast. His speech is a high mock-heroic satire. The persistent martial image of the speeches is taken up and sophisticatedly ironised, as the 'feeling of manhood' (I. 144) is associated with the historic battles fought between Scots and English, now misunderstood by the company to celebrate mutual patriotism, and received with cheers which do not comprehend the irony – 'feet stamped, a glass or two got broken' (I. 157). Philip's alliterative speech, turning the clichés of battle against themselves, ends with an aggressive disclaimer intended to undermine the speech's inflated effect with political outrage in case the irony has been misunderstood: 'I have, however, less claim than others to this honour,/For, let me say, I am neither game-keeper, nor game-preserver' (I. 160–1). But a confrontation does not take place. This deliberate outrage of hospitality goes unrecognised – it is not *understood*. Inebriation, and the unthinkableness of radicalism in such a context, are partly responsible for this. But essentially Philip's is a coterie discourse, with a doubleness which is not accessible to other groups, but simply confusing in its ambiguity. The intellectual's irony is not a generally understood 'password'. What is the status of this doubleness if it can make no real intervention in politics or causes confusion when it attempts to intervene? This is a pressing question, particularly because the narrative style of the poem partakes of exactly the ambiguity of speech and mock-heroic practised by the undergraduate party. It is a dialect, proclaiming itself to be so. Mock-heroic is inherently ambiguous because it undermines, but nevertheless invests its subjects with a certain largeness derived from the high style. However, its inflation becomes a way of criticising itself. In *The Bothie*, it becomes a way of declaring that the narrative voice is not detached, but implicated in the problems it seeks to analyse.

But how does the doubleness of the narrative style enable a democratic access to the poem? 'The novelist does try to build us a real house to be lived in', Clough wrote in his review of Smith and Arnold. To be 'widely popular, to gain the ear of multitudes, to shake the hearts of men, poetry should deal, more than at present it usually does, with general wants, ordinary feelings, the obvious rather than the rare facts of human nature'.[17] This is reminiscent of Fox's belief that poetry can influence the 'associations of unnumbered minds'. But for Clough a truly democratic and non-élitist poetry no longer carried out the analytical project of exploring modern psychological conditions, the *structure* of modern consciousness. Poetry must deal with external things, with the 'palpable things with which our every-day life is concerned'. Above all, it must deal with and transform *work* and give it 'significance', the 'dirty' and 'dingy' labour and 'limited spheres of action' to which modern experience is restricted.[18] It is clear that Clough intends to suggest that this overwhelming sense of limit in work is experienced both by the factory worker – the Glasgow mechanic such as Alexander Smith – and by a middle-class writer such as Arnold – and himself. Both are alienated in different ways. So art has to do not with great human actions but limited ones, not past events but contemporary ones. Clough's belief that his poetry could encompass the interests of bourgeois and working-class readers may seem optimistic and unrealistic, but his *intention* is clear. More important, perhaps, there is a certain restriction here to a generally recognisable social realism which is in many ways limiting, because it remains with the external content of contemporary life rather than the modern structure of consciousness advocated by the Fox group, and can seem to restrict the content of poetry simply to the externals of contemporaneity. But Clough's emphasis is on the transformation of 'palpable' experience rather than the direct representation of it. This is why, though it has the solidity and substantiveness of a novel, *The Bothie* is not simply a *Bildungsroman* in verse. And this is why, despite the chastening training in discipline and moderation undergone by Philip, the poem's language does not evolve towards a commensurate simplicity. It retains its doubleness, and indeed attains a systematic and structural ambiguity by the end of the poem. For it is only through the linguistic inventiveness of ambiguity that transformation is possible. And it is through linguistic inventiveness that Philip solves the problem of political action and intervention. Moreover, ambiguity is a way of displacing power, your own and other people's. By offering two possibilities of meaning rather than one it disconcerts expectations by demonstrating alternatives.

The attainment of a 'familiar' language does not mean the reproduction of 'our rambling talk'. In the essay on Dryden the ideal democratic language is 'fluent, yet dignified; familiar, yet full of meaning'.[19] A proper, unalienated language is a *usable* language because it is expressive and because its simplicity does not exclude complexity. That is why it can be 'full of meaning'. True poetic language transforms the familiar by giving access to a recognisable diction in a form which *reconstructs* the words of our 'rambling talk'. Exact and literal, rarely investing in the estranged language of the individualist metaphor which retreats into a private diction by departing from primary meanings, the gravitas of Clough's lyricism dares to repeat directly the commonplace adjectives which *say* rather than *suggest*, and to transform them into unique and subtle cadences. These are often the stock, unspecific fillers which have lost their resonance and simply convey a general meaning. In the following passage describing the natural bathing-pool discovered by the party of students, Clough redeems the resonance of the formulaic word, 'Beautiful'.

> But in the interval here the boiling, pent-up water
> Frees itself by a final descent, attaining a bason,
> Ten feet wide and eighteen long, with whiteness and fury
> Occupied partly, but mostly pellucid, pure, a mirror;
> Beautiful there for the colour derived from green rocks under;
> Beautiful, most of all, where beads of foam uprising
> Mingle their clouds of white with the delicate hue of the stillness.
> Cliff over cliff for its sides, with rowan and pendent birch boughs, . . .
> Here, the delight of the bather, you roll in beaded sparklings,
> Here into pure green depth drop down from lofty ledges.
>
> (III. 34–41, 47–8)

The rediscovery of the supple and varied cadences of 'Beautiful' is made possible by the free stressing of the hexameter (the spondees are mostly stressed rather than quantified) and by a subtlety of phrasing. The first instance of the word (38) expands and articulates the three syllables as they follow the stresses of the spondee and flow into the regular 'there for the': the slight irregularity which results in the stress falling upon 'green' and '*un*der' substantiates the quality of what *is* beautiful – '*green* rocks *un*der'. The recurrence of 'Beautiful' in the next line, followed by a pause and the syncopation of an inverted stress – 'Beautiful, most of *all*' – has the effect of slightly hurrying the syllables of 'Beautiful', which seems qualitatively almost a different word, now dislodged into a slightly different set of sounds with another pattern, sounds which move at a faster pace, accelerating with the 'beads of foam' at the end of the line. Clough's is in fact a highly adjectival style rather than a metaphorical one. Adjectives either become nouns – 'sparkling' – or else they are attached to abstract nouns which become, as a result, experienced almost physically – 'stillness' can possess a 'delicate hue'. A depth, like a rock, can be 'green'. The solidity of his language – for it is sturdy as well as subtle – comes from his habit of attaching general adjectives to concrete nouns or very specific

186

adjectives to abstract nouns. This makes one re-experience both common and Latinate words with a weight and force which goes unnoticed in familiar language. The different inflections of 'Beautiful' achieve precisely such a re-experiencing of words. It is an irony that Arnold used this word when he complained of the deficiencies of Clough's writing – 'a growing sense of the deficiency of the *beautiful* in your poems'.[20]

Clough is often thought of as the poet of the colloquial style, the casual, conversational rhythms of the speaking voice. It is true that his poetry is receptive to an enormous range of intonation and vocabulary – he keeps nothing out. But it is tightly disciplined, exacting eloquence from the most unimportant particles and phrases. And because his work is acutely sensitive to the special codes spoken among particular groups, and because it persuades towards a re-experiencing of words, it effectively dissolves the category of the normal in language. In the description of the bathing-pool, the physical, bodily pleasure given by the words themselves renews the familiar experience of bathing and transfigures it in that sacramentalism of the everyday to which Clough was so committed. It denotes the physical release and exuberance felt by the young men when they are released from their classical studies. But though they have abandoned 'the musical chaff of old Athens' to slumber, forgotten and obliterated in Liddell and Scott along with their meaningless labour (II. 222), 'Weary of Ethic and Logic, of *Rhetoric* [my emphasis] yet more weary' (II. 269), the diction of the bathing passage freely mingles classical diction and allusion with familiar phrase. It is not inartificial. As he makes clear in his essay on Wordsworth, Clough was not aiming at an abstracted common language of men. For though we may recognise the familiar, men do not have a common language in the nineteenth century. The classical allusion is there partly to suggest that classical education earns the men the privilege of bathing so freely. They cannot escape it and neither can the narrative voice. It is there also to introduce an element of allegorical doubleness – 'pellucid, pure, a mirror' (I. 37): 'left alone with yourself and the goddess of bathing' (I. 45). Here there are hints of Narcissus, in love with his image in the pool, and Diana, discovered naked by Actaeon, as she bathed. The self-involved exuberance of this group, and the physical energy of their sexuality, their homoerotic feeling for one another mingling with erotic fantasy of the feminine, is conveyed through classical analogy. Here homosocial bonding does not, for a moment, include anxieties about heterosexual feeling. A 'lady', says the narrator, could 'step' the narrow passage leading to the pool (I. 29), a goddess who has not yet turned her hounds against the male viewer.

With this analogy another element is introduced into the dialect, or dialects, of *The Bothie*. Running through it is an analogical allegory, and this is what makes it a double poem. Rather than the conspicuous consumption of metaphor, Clough uses the clear parallelism of allegory to

187

explore the intimately related themes of work and sexuality. At the end of the poem, when Philip and Elspie are departing for New Zealand, Hobbes writes a letter expounding an application of the biblical story of Rachel and Leah, swearing by Origen, the early Christian (and unorthodox) exegetist. '*Which things are an allegory*, Philip,/Aye, and by Origen's head with a vengeance truly, a long one!' (IX. 186–7). The allusion to Rachel occurs first in the second book, when the men have their argument, prompted by Philip, about the superior beauty of working women, and is concluded by Hobbes's letter. The Rachel allusion works like an inverted Tractarian aesthetic. It is not the concealed and secret double meaning, working by subterfuge, recommended by Keble. The ironic reference to Origen signals a dissent from Tractarian aesthetic.[21] It is an open allegory, clear and accessible. It is important that Clough chose a biblical allegory rather than a classical one: the biblical allusion would be more widely understood, the classical analogy would be understood only by an educated class. The poem is deeply uncomfortable about the kind of 'work' the study of the classics represents. Lindsay calls the cottage in which the men pursue their 'dreary' and irrelevant classics 'the shop' (II. 230) with a certain irony. It is a factory for the training of a class who will wield power, and yet its influence is oddly indirect. Philip gets a First but goes off to New Zealand after being trained in manual labour by Elspie's father. Lindsay, his vehement Tory opponent, is 'plucked almost' (IX. 116), but stays in his class, like the others. Clough later attacked the narrowness of classical studies at Oxford, and the poem is uneasy about their status, aware of their narrowness, unwilling to abandon them.[22] Certainly it is not the classics which provide material for analogy in the poem, but architecture (the solid 'house' such as the novelist enables us to inhabit), buildings and the Bible. For the poem is not only an allegory but *about* these things as the material for allegory. Philip moves from a closed, élite Tractarian allegory to an open, democratic allegory.

When Philip condemns the affectations of middle-class girls, 'pink-paper' comfits (II. 63), and confesses that his first sexual feelings were aroused by the sight of a working girl uprooting potatoes, endorsing this with references to Rachel, discovered by Jacob watering cattle, and Tennyson's Dora in 'The Gardener's Daughter', he attributes to women genuine sexual desire and independence. With the knowing self-consciousness of an in-group, and with the impulse to joke in order to shy away from class and sex, they take up Arthur's suggestion that Philip is a 'Pugin of women', writing '*The Laws of/Architectural Beauty in Application to Women*' (II. 137, 144–5). A. W. N. Pugin had produced a number of works on Gothic architecture in the 1840s.[23] Part of the High Church movement, he advocated the Gothic style for church architecture (following his father, A. C. Pugin), but based his recommendations on an analysis of a movement from a 'pure' early primitive to a decorated and finally debased and

188

flamboyant style which reflected the decadence of belief. The transposition of this cultural analysis to sex and class is made with satirical linguistic inventiveness: the 'sculliony stumpy-columnar' progresses to the 'Modern-Florid, modern-fine-lady' (II. 147, 153). But the private joke exposes the superficiality of Philip's thought; he is infatuated with style – 'the removal of slops to be ornamentally treated' (II. 141) – and, thinking as he does of the woman 'Serving' (II. 77) the man, he is still trapped within a hierarchical account of class and sexual relations – and a thoroughly masculine one. The intellectual joke betrays a closed mind on the part of all the participants in fact. Lightly and brilliantly though it is handled, it is the coterie rhetoric of privilege and is of the same order as Philip's ironic battle speech, the produce of 'common-room breakfasts' and Trinity wines (II. 121), a 'password' for the educated.

By the time Philip accepts Elspie's less extravagant parable for relations between men and women – and classes – as an arch made by two equals, and her analogy of the tidal river for the overwhelming – and disturbing – flood of sexual feeling (VII. 99–140), he has come a long way. He has revised his belief that women are solely responsible for prostitution and has recognised that the luxury of the rich depends upon the exploitation of the poor. He has decisively redefined the tutor's careful, moral advice, now certain that his ethical individualism concerning duty and self-culture is effectively a form of the cruder admonition, 'Every one for himself' (IX. 68). As Clough's respectful but critical essay on Newman makes clear, the tutor's advice is a modified form of the principles of truth to self that he found in Newman.[24] Philip dissents. He is ready to think of a great city irradiated with sunrise – its 'unfinished houses, lots for sale, and railway outworks' (IX. 106), a child waiting by scaffolding with breakfast for her workman father – and transformed with feeling. This is an allegory of the resurgence of democratic feeling and sacramentalises the familiar. What he has done is to take the principles of Tractarian aesthetics and democratise them by turning them upside down. For Keble natural objects become a type of the divine, but for Clough human objects become a type of the divine. This implies a consent to action and a social responsibility involving a commitment to *change* which is outside the concerns of Tractarianism.

Newman's *Tract 90* on the compatibility of the Thirty-Nine Articles with Catholic doctrine had appeared in 1841. Perhaps one of the great triumphs of the poem is to make its central allegory depend on an examination and redefinition of the premises of *Tract 90*. Clough boldly reclaims its theological language for an exploration of sexuality and politics. By doing this he is able to expand the allegory which shapes the poem and to hold up the status of allegory itself for inspection.

The 'High Church', élitist allusions of the Pugin joke modulate into a further contemplation of Tractarian symbol when Philip, guilty and remorseful, but essentially in bad faith, laments his desertion of Katie the servant girl. He hopes that she understands that he is with her in spirit, mixing 'inner essence with essence' (IV. 42): 'Spirits escaped from the body can enter and be with the living' (IV. 40). In other words, Katie must experience the *real presence* of Philip's sexual love, despite his absence. For Newman the real presence of Christ in the Eucharist, and the doctrine of transubstantiation (one of the Articles to which Clough did not subscribe when he resigned his fellowship), is a crucial theological problem. It is qualitatively different from physical, material presence, for the body 'sets bounds to its approach towards us'. The 'presence of spirit with spirit', on the other hand, is experienced with absolute immediacy; it is 'the most intimate presence we can fancy'.[25] This is the language of love, and Clough's poem is extraordinarily percipient in its recognition that it is in theology in the nineteenth century, that the language of both spiritual and sexual love is to be found, the latter by its very omission in Newman's thought. But again, *The Bothie* inverts Newman's priorities. It is physical presence for which Philip yearns, and his belief in spiritual union turns out to be solipsistic, for Katie is happily dancing with another man while he is lamenting. With a blasphemous materialist empiricism the poem makes the body essential to relationships, as it is for Philip and Elspie, who condemns his idealisation of the Highland community as unreal – 'People here too are people, and not as fairy-land creatures' (IV. 120). It follows that political commitment to action in the material world is the effective course if spiritual reality *follows* upon material presence rather than preceding it.

But what is the real, and what is presence? Clough's text does not appropriate Newman's language by crudely reversing it however robust his confrontation with it and his refutation of Newman's analysis of the secondariness of the material. *Tract 90* is a disquisition on invisibility, on the meaning we attach to objects; it is a discourse on symbol, in which significance is attached to external things, which become a visible embodiment of the divine. Ultimately the only guarantee of the reality of symbol is the sceptical ground that we *experience* it as such. Thus Philip, in inverse but parallel antithesis to this thought, experiences his marriage to Elspie symbolically as a conversion to the real: the great city is symbolic of the renewal of democratic meaning; the emigration to New Zealand is a symbol of transformed social commitment, a new realism. But Hobbes's allegorical letter lays bare the sceptical ground of such realism and in doing so turns the whole poem into a radically ambiguous text. Using the biblical story of Rachel and Leah – 'Rachel we dream-of at night: in the morning, behold, it is Leah' (IX. 179) – he reminds Philip that marriage, and experience itself, is 'bigamy', a 'duality, compound and complex' (IX. 169). The disappointing reality of Leah displaces the real fulfilment of Rachel for Jacob, and the two women constantly displace one another in his life. Hobbes does not simply mean that the longed-for ideal is displaced by the real, or that appearance is deceptive. He means that we cannot assign a permanent meaning to any experience: real and ideal, literal and symbolic, these are terms whose meaning will change and displace one another as circumstances change and redefine them. They have a relative value in relation to one another. Representation will change as its ground changes. We may need the notion of the 'real' to live with, whether that 'real' chooses to grant priority to the spiritual or the material, but that 'real' is a deeply ambiguous entity with no intrinsic content, depending as it does on the guarantee of subjectivity to invest it with invisible value. Thus our actions are not invested with certainty any more than our choices are.

Hobbes's allegory both affirms and deconstructs what we might call the materialist Newmanism of *The Bothie*. It is there both to protect and undermine the poem. Accordingly, Philip's decision may constitute a bold political realism, or it may be a quixotic and romantic idealism. The poem may be a kind of non-political pastoral romance, as the Virgilian epigraphs to many of the books suggest. The departure to New Zealand may be an initiation of and into genuine change, or it may be an escape from the hard material realities of a class-bound England, as ideologically suspect, in its movement to a colony, as any colonialist venture. Elspie thinks of Scotland and its culture as similar to the Peruvian Indians conquered by the Spaniards and simply 'weaker' than they (VIII. 84). New Zealand is not exempt from this description. Scotland here figures the oppressed colonial other. Philip remains in uncertainty. His cry, 'O where is the battle?' (IX. 62), remains unanswered. The ground of action and its representation appears to dissolve. Language itself becomes ambiguous, 'a duality complex and compound', as 'signal and password', the codes which we can trust and recognise, are betrayed. And here Philip means not only the inherent ambiguity of language but the betrayals of the exclusive language of power. Its secrecy has become deceptive and has betrayed itself; at the same time it has also become 'known' and open to misuse, propagating deception. The language of power has a Keble-like duplicity.

Yet here, with Clough's astonishing capacity to relativise the text's statements almost as they are being made, the poem turns around on itself and makes a double statement. If a private code can be misused it can also be *used* once it has been disseminated. The language of privilege can never be the same when its exclusiveness is broken. As if to salute this actuality and the breakdown of this exclusiveness, Philip's battle imagery, so persistent in the poem, alludes not only to the mock-heroic but to another area of writing in English where the battle really did mean something certain and where martial imagery had its own justification: he alludes to the imagery of struggle in radical, Chartist poetry, where action and toil have a certain meaning. The poem alludes to the themes common to radical and Chartist poetry – the vindication of lowness, the weakness

191

of the oppressed poor, the dependence of the rich on the labour of the poor. Hobbes quotes a Chartist song ironically – '*So the good time is coming, or come is it?*' (IX. 151). Philip, however, with a kind of deference, takes up the familiar battle imagery of poets such as Gerald Massey and Thomas Cooper: 'The time shall come when Wrong shall end, . . . Toil, brothers, toil, till the work is done – /Till the struggle is o'er and the Charter's won!' His 'where is the battle?' takes up the imagery of struggle and action but implicitly contrasts the uncertainty of the middle-class radical with the certainties of the Chartists, who may have seen 'mess and dislocation' (IX. 64) in society but knew what they needed, and who were evolving their own campaigning language of protest to affirm themselves and to gain middle-class recognition. They were using the weapon of language to affirm a sense of community, whereas Philip has left his coterie group, which seems to be complicit with power and privilege. Thus the doubleness of Clough's allegorical writing both affirms Philip's questioning and offers a critique of it. It is unremitting in its exposure of the dilemmas he experiences and makes an analysis of the problems of an intellectual caught in an individualist culture with an intransigence only slightly masked by its buoyant good humour, its warmth and its liberating wit. Of all Victorian poems it is probably the most overtly politically committed, just as it is the most disturbingly sceptical poem of the mid-nineteenth century.

The Bothie was published at the Chartist movement's apogee and in the year of the revolutions of 1848. As the Chartist movement fragmented, its poetry changed in character. Up to 1848 a poetry of protest, exhortation and millennial confidence was dominant. Martial imagery, certainty in the necessity of struggle and action and a shared definition of manhood and agency create a remarkable bond between different poems. After 1848 such poems are harder to find. Ernest Jones, for instance, the only poet to retain a life-long commitment to Chartism, turned from song and ballad to narrative poetry and satire after 1848 in work which increasingly analyses the possibility and difficulty of effective action and the ground of male power and authority. It is interesting that this shift coincides with a similar intensification of the theme of masculinity, manhood and action in Clough's work, in both *Amours de Voyage* (completed by 1850 but first published in 1858) and the unfinished *Dipsychus*. It is as if the more affirmative elements in *The Bothie* and of Chartist poetry dissolve under pressure of reduced expectations and the failure of revolutionary change to manifest itself.

It is remarkable how frequently early Chartist poetry invoked a definition of manhood to enforce optimistic solidarity. This definition was protected against the erosions which are to be found in Clough's poetry because it is a discourse of manhood which contrasts universal man with the enforced subhumanity of the slave and collocates manhood and brotherhood as a morally indissoluble pairing. W. J. Linton (1812–97), for instance, writes of 'Man, the poor serf, by kings and priests long hounded. . . . Tyrants and priests! *we* need not *your* support. . . . We claim Man's equal rights; we will no ruin/Even unto the robbers'.[26] In a Chartist 'Hymn', John Henry Bramwich began with 'Britannia's sons, though slaves ye be, God your Creator made you free', and ended, 'All men are equal in His sight – /The bond, the free, the black, the white; – /He made them all, – them freedom gave – /*He* made the man, – Man made the Slave!'[27] An anonymous song to O'Connor, the Chartist leader, 'The Lion of Freedom', has a battle refrain – 'We'll rally round' – and speaks of O'Connor as 'the terror of tyrants, the friend of the slave,/The bright star of freedom'.[28] Gerald Massey wrote of the 'Soldiers of Freedom' and the 'battle for liberty' – 'Old earth yearns to know that her children are men'.[29] Here, however, 'men' suggests virility and power rather than brotherhood, and it is perhaps the potential within the battle image for the expression of violent militarism and phallic power which makes it such a dangerous and equivocal image except in the hands of exemplary writers of great integrity, such as W. J. Linton, whose 'Hymns to the Unenfranchised' contrast with Massey's violence.[30]

Much has been written about the 'collapse' of Chartism, a movement when the working class took writing as well as organised action into their own hands in an affirmative way. There were conflicts and strains within this body of writing (women, for instance, though they published poems in Chartist newspapers, are not strongly represented in Chartist accounts of 'brotherhood'): but it is important to salute the achievement of its critique. For a brief period Chartist writers evolved a genuinely *public* rhetoric of collective action and affirmation and a genuinely social rhetoric of community which derived from their own traditions – the ballad and refrain, the marching song, the Bunyanesque hymn, biblical imagery.[31] The verse was simple and accessible but firm and powerful verbally. It is worth remembering, to understand the variety of this poetry, that poets who contributed songs to the movement were poets both before and after it dissolved as an *organised* movement. Though the unique rhetoric of solidarity is hard to find again, many poets went on publishing protest poems. J. B. Leno, who refused to mourn the passing of Chartism, insisted that it took other forms subsequently – 'True, as a movement it died out; but it died to live again'.[32] He published protest poems up to 1861 and beyond.[33]

Radical and corn-law poetry often used a general, biblical, millennial and apocalyptic imagery. Chartist poetry drew on this also. Samuel Bamford, for instance, ends his 'The Labourer's Orison at Sunrise' with this apocalyptic challenge to oppression:

> And change you like the feather'd snow,
>   The melting sun hung o'er it;
> And whirl you as the wind doth blow
>   The desert dust before it![34]

193

In his 'Anti-Corn-Law Lyric' J. C. Prince had used a simple refrain, 'Give us bread!', and asserted that 'The Lord shall lift His mighty hand' against oppressors 'Till they shall feel and understand'.[35] But both the rhetoric and the programme of Chartist poetry was different. It was necessary to generalise and secularise biblical imagery because the stress was on human agency and not on divine intervention: it was necessary to evolve a rhetoric of power to energise and enable, a rhetoric of revolution and change which did not threaten immediate violence (or at least concealed its possibility) by shifting the mobilisation of force to an indeterminate, utopian future. At the same time the power of organised force had to be stressed. Unlike corn-law lyrics, Chartist lyrics do not stress the need to 'understand', or the need for empathy on the part of employers and oppressors: rather they stressed the need for *change*. Above all, because songs would be learned and sung by the illiterate they could not be burdened with literary device. Perhaps the greatest achievement of Chartist poetry was to avoid a personal language of oppression in favour of an impersonal language of hope and energy. Here Thomas Cooper's 'Chartist Chaunt' stresses, not pity or divine intervention but power and human possibility:

> Truth is growing – hearts are glowing
>   With the flame of Liberty:
> Light is breaking – Thrones are quaking –
>   Hark! the trumpet of the Free![36]

The simple metaphor of light 'grows' as Truth is said to grow, moving from the glowing heart of the individual, the flames of general principle, to a universal dawn. The trumpet of the Free sounds an apocalyptic moment, but it is also a battle cry, a call to action. The internal rhyme establishes relations of cause and effect: hearts both glow and *grow* with Truth; thrones are quaking as the light of Truth and Liberty breaks – they are also, quite unequivocally, *breaking*. The affirmative present tense and the impersonal rhetoric set up firm antitheses between the powerful and the oppressed, but it also challenges those 'Thrones' to participate in and recognise a new freedom where relationships of power are subsumed into a new, millennial order. Clough's 'Say Not the Struggle Nought Availeth', with its images of toil, light and growing possibility, is clearly modelled on the rhetoric of Chartism.

Firm antitheses – between tyrants, priests and slaves, peer and peasant, cottage and throne, industrial lord and labour – and clear symbols of oppression – mitre and crown, crown, cross and sabre – provide lucid contrasts and *alternatives*. 'And now we'll be – as bold and free,/As we've been tame and slavish'. Ernest Jones's 'A Chartist Chorus' puts alternatives uncompromisingly, savagely adapting biblical imagery – 'Our lives are not your sheaves to glean – /Our rights your bales [these are cotton lords] to barter'. Nevertheless, the challenge to the existing order asks not for the

simple defeat of oppression but for new relationships: 'But let be seen –
some law between/The giver and the taker'.[37]

J. B. Leno is particularly adept at the handling of antitheses and oppositions which are then restructured to accommodate a new order. Here the
solidarity of 'Old England' is appropriated for the manual labourer, and
patriotism becomes elided with the dignity of labour, as 'foes' and 'few'
and 'sword' and 'Wealth' become aligned with exploitation, and 'many',
'Man', 'food' and 'plough' become aligned with the solidarity of labour;
and it is *labour* which represents 'Old England':

> God speed the Plough of Old England!
> God speed the Plough of Old England!
>   Perish their foes if there's any!
> The sword may win wealth for the few,
>   But the plough raises food for the many.
> Prosper the man at its handle,
>   Succour the beast in its gearing;
> God speed the plough and Old England,
>   And ripen the food of its rearing![38]

In the third stanza 'wealth' is redefined as the harvest, which is carried
by the reapers themselves to 'poor-land', the real England of the cottage
rather than the palace. Leno can strike out the millennial images of Chartism with authoritative confidence. In 'Song' for instance, he brings
together the image of 'Titan' power and struggle with Moses striking the
rock – 'He has smote the rock in the desert wild,/And the waters leap
bounding forth'.[39] In 'Words of Hope' he creates a Chartist grand style,
exacting power from the familiar oppositions which always risk, but avoid,
banality, in the best tradition of this writing, appropriating the Christian
ideas of advent and sacrifice and secularising them boldly: 'The wisest of
earth's children,/The great among the great,/In the darkest age of history/
Foretold a "New Estate"./Saw unborn golden ages/With microscopic
mind,/And died to seal their advent/And the freedom of mankind'.[40]

The risk of Chartist poetry was that it could always tip over into
didacticism, sentimentality or violence, simplifying or blurring the rigour
of the deliberately banal material it worked with and generally transformed.
This can happen in Leno's work. His 'Cease not to toil' becomes a moralis-
ation on the importance of work and labour, and, in its effort to break the
rich/poor antithesis and to make a new alignment between *all* who work,
it becomes a campaign against the lazy workman rather than the idle rich
– 'He who spurns labour should never be fed'.[41] Leno's optimism, manifested in such songs as 'Song of the Spade' or the chorus of another 'Song',
'You can't judge a man by the coat that he wears', often takes on the
simplicity of enforced cheeriness.[42] He was perhaps too much aware 'Of
hearts surcharged with care' ('Words of Hope'), to maintain the fine

balance of Chartist rhetoric. This may be why he turned increasingly to subjective, expressive poetry of direct social comment, and why, in the 1860s, he moved to a poetry thematising the illusory dream of the future and the reassuring memory of a rural past.[43] In the 1850s, however, he produced some sombre and resonant poems. 'Herne's Oak', the title poem of his volume of 1853, is a sinister and very complex allegory of suicide and storm which permanently changes the nature of the tree, the symbolic oak of England, as if the suicidal 'lord' who hangs himself there creates a universal death wish.[44] 'The Ruined Tower' exposes the minute change which undermines a whole edifice from below: 'How one decaying stone may sap a tower'.[45] It is as if the energies of solidarity cannot really arrest the inexorable crumbling of the social fabric. His 'Song of the Slopworker' was frequently reprinted (and in 1861 accompanied by a police report demonstrating the poverty of the garment-finisher forced to steal in order to survive).[46] It is the utterance of an utter destitution, physical and spiritual destitution living on the verge of suicide: 'And yet 'tis strange I've lived so long/On poisoned air and tear-steeped bread!/'Tis strange, indeed, I've not sought Death,/But stranger he never found me'. These are poems of deep social mourning, rendering hopelessness in the images of starvation and cold, the images of the lost soul: 'A desert bounds my view today,/A sea of ice tomorrow!'[47] The psychological 'feeling of depression' which Arnold defined as the malaise of the 1850s is experienced here as the fixed despair and suffering of oppression incapable of being remedied. It is the result of a material condition, not the alienation of the intellectual.

Clough's Philip Hewson becomes intensely guilty about the fate of coal miners and other exploited workers (*The Bothie*, V. 51–79), but, as Philip himself recognises, he only knows about them, and can avoid even seeing them if he wishes. This could not be so for Chartist writers, and thus working class and middle class write from quite different centres of experience. Philip sidesteps Chartism by emigrating. When the immediate force of their movement died, most poets directed their energies elsewhere. Leno continued to write poems of protest but these modulated to more lyrical narrative, as we have seen.

Massey, a violent supporter of Chartism, became increasingly conservative and turned to an equally violent but incompatible support of the Crimean war. His is an extreme case, but exemplifies the plight of the self-taught artisan poet in particular once Chartism dissolved as a political movement. Linton turned to the Italian question and Cooper ultimately to religion as a way of redirecting and re-forming creative energy. Ernest Jones, on the other hand, unlike most writers in this movement an educated, middle-class man, continued to write, but directed his critique beyond Europe to colonialism and imperialist exploitation. In answer to Clough's Philip Hewson he would have said that there was still a battle to be fought. His 'prison-song', *The Revolt of Hindustan; or, The New World*, revised and republished in 1857 after the Indian Mutiny, is a fierce attack on economic exploitation beyond Europe in the name of civilisation. 'We civilise, reform, redeem!', the colonialist argues; but, 'You sent out Bishops in your battle-ships', the poet answers.[48] Colonial exploitation mirrors exploitation at home – hence the logic of emigration, where the state displaces its poor into the colonies. Where emigration is the subject of ambivalent feeling in Clough's poem, it is the object of violent satire in Jones's: 'Then cried those subtle gold-kings, one and all;/"The cure is found! The COUNTRY is too small!/Here's not enough your greedy maws to sate:/TO SHIP! TO SHIP! *You Paupers, emigrate*!/We'll grant free passage! aye! we'll even pay!/So that you'll but be still and – go away!" '[49]

Jones's poem, 'written by me in prison, with my own blood, on the loose leaves of a torn Prayer-book, in 1848 and 1849, while denied the use of writing materials by the prison authorities', is a measure of the extent to which the interests of middle-class poetry and poetry committed to specific political programmes and to working-class movements diverged.[50] Even 'Citizen Clough' (as his friends called him), with his sympathetic radicalism, does not put the issues as sharply as Jones, the working-class sympathiser and Chartist leader. Where early Chartist writing offers a definition of 'Man' which will include all classes in universal freedom, Jones saw that middle- and working-class interests were increasingly antagonistic. In his volume of 1855, *The Battle-Day: and Other Poems*, he wrote about the game laws and factory conditions hinted at in *The Bothie*. In 'Leawood Hall: A Christmas Tale', an unemployed labourer is killed by his landlord's bullet after poaching for his starving family; in 'The Factory Town' the factories employing men, women and children burn 'lurid fires' through the night – 'E'en Etna's burning wrath expires,/But *man's* volcanoes never rest'.[51] Here 'man' is the oppressor, the factory-owner, and the workers are souls in hell. True to his non-Anglocentric vision, Jones wrote on Russia and on Italy in 'The Cry of the Russian Serf to the Czar' and 'The Italian Exile to his Countrymen'. But most remarkable, and most indicative of the strains of political poetry, is his study of leadership in the title poem, 'The Battle-Day; or, The Lost Army'. It is in this poem that Jones explores the problem of agency and collective action, and it is here that his anxieties converge with those of Clough, even though his ideology does not.

Taking up the theme of the ambiguity of the word or signal in the supposedly collective action of battle, the mistimed utterance, the unuttered affirmation or 'password', which was being explored earlier in *The Bothie*, Jones's poem achieves an uncanny double critique. A commander in the thick of battle, Lord Lindsay's nerve and judgement fails. Suddenly overwhelmed with doubt, he is unable to give the battle cry or the appropriate signal for action. He 'marked the turning of the flood',

And thrice he raised his arm on high,
Thrice turned to shout his battle-cry;
And thrice the gallant impulse dies
To fears that throng, and doubts that rise; . . .
And every brow is turning pale!
They have the heart but lack the word:–
Broke from Lord Lindsay's lip no cry,
Flashed no signal from his eye,
He neither spoke, nor signed, nor stirred,
He thought but: '*Should they fail!*'[52]

Jones had been deeply involved in the agonising and divisive physical-force debate among Chartists. In 1848 he wrote, 'Because I advocate Physical organisation, I do not advise a physical outbreak'. Chartists should be prepared against attack, but – and this is what made the argument morally ambiguous – might be compelled to fight 'if moral means fail'.[53] Lord Lindsay's moral and physical leadership collapses, but both are ambiguously part of one another. And ultimately his failure is a failure of language as troops 'lack the word'. What constitutes the ground of action, whether the failure to act is to be attributed to cowardice, misjudgement or sensitive recoil from battle, how far a single man's doubt propagates collective despair, whether there is an inevitable 'moment' when success recedes ('It *was* the moment – and 'tis past!'), the importance of shared language to action – all these problems converge on Lindsay's action, or non-action.[54] Jones is clearly meditating the collapse of revolutionary energy in Chartism and the disintegration of its leadership. But because the symbol of revolutionary action is the 'manly' action of battle, the image serves another purpose. The unnamed battle, with its battery flames, its 'living pavement' of soldiers ready to be crushed by 'red advancing hell', is a modern battle, a Crimean battle, where the soldiers who would have been revolutionary forces are sacrificed to the 'flambeau' of the 'cannon-blast'.[55] The overwhelming failure of a ruling class is thus mapped onto the failure of revolutionary action without really matching it in a way which makes both causes disturbing and ambiguous: troops are needlessly sacrificed both in a good cause, social change, and in a bad cause, European hegemony in the east. The legitimacy of the use of force, and its human cost, in both contexts, Chartist and Crimean, is questioned, and what really constitutes the manly and the heroic is made problematical and contradictory. But what is brilliant in Jones's poem is its capacity to show how revolutionary energy can be deflected into war abroad, and how that war itself is conducted by an impotent ruling class.

The 'thrice raised arm' of Jones's poem, symbol of masculine power and phallic assertiveness, was, interestingly, the motif Clough chose to use and ironise in his analysis of the failure of the intellectual in his European

198

poem, *Amours de Voyage*. This poem probably shows Clough at his greatest point of virtuosity. It is a highly sophisticated and self-conscious study of elegant nihilism, as Claude, inadvertently war correspondent from Rome to his friend, Eustace, and inadvertently a lover, grapples with both roles. *Dipsychus*, or 'the double-minded', is perhaps ideologically the toughest of these long poems. The main character of the title is in conflict with an oxymoronically materialist 'Spirit' who is both his opposite and his double. Since the two poems expand on the more complex *Bothie*, they can be discussed more briefly.

Amours de Voyage brings the crisis of the intellectual together with the crisis of European liberalism, when the Roman Republic was attacked by the French in 1849. It is written in letter form, and this epistolary form textualises the poem, achieving a self-qualifying narrative very much more economically than the mock-heroic of *The Bothie*. It recalls Goethe's *Roman Elegies*, which contrast with the inhibited Claude in love. It also recalls Goethe's novel, *Elective Affinities*, with its meditations on 'juxtaposition' and the accident of chance meetings in love. The letter form decisively marks off the different dialects in the poem, and differentiates the language and values of speakers, particularly the frivolous conventionality of Georgina, sister of Mary Trevellyn, whose family prompts Claude to react snobbishly, seeing them as would-be-cultured Philistines. The mother 'Grates the fastidious ear with the slightly mercantile accent' (I. xi. 212). Since each letter is modified and realigned by the next, there is no authoritative narrative voice in the poem. It becomes a series of documents which the reader edits – and re-edits – as one letter succeeds another. Lastly, the letter form, meant for communication, paradoxically discloses the solipsism of letters as Claude writes to himself, producing a version of the dialogue of the mind with itself.

This study of detachment is not entirely free of the infinitely self-qualifying scepticism it portrays. Claude's habit of changing ground emotionally and intellectually has its literal counterpart at the end of the poem as he evacuates from Rome, almost evacuating the poem of content as he does so: 'Eastward, then, I suppose, with the coming of winter, to Egypt' (V. x. 205). 'I suppose' here can refer to the phrases which both precede and follow it, tingeing both with doubt. *Amours de Voyage* approaches the condition of a modernist poem, a self-reflexive poem without closure, dwelling on its self-reflexivity. It has often been compared in this respect with T. S. Eliot's *The Love Song of J. Alfred Prufrock*. It attempts to make a critique of such a condition, but what retrieves it from the endlessly self-qualifying narrative is the desperate poignancy of the loss it portrays, as Mary waits and Claude frantically searches the bewildering number of possible routes Mary and her family may have taken from Rome, to no avail – image of the confusion of alternatives which open out when you have decided not to decide.

Claude's two preoccupations, the meaning of Rome and the meaning of action, intertwine. There are three Romes in the poem. There is the Rome of the magnificently questioning, elegiac lyrics which preface each canto, the Rome of a continuous classical tradition, the product of an act of imagination, but a coherence longingly imagined as the lyrics invoke continuity with a past where there existed 'a land wherein gods of the old time wandered' (I. 3). Then there is the litter of history and the layers of successive and irreconcilable cultures in the present '*Rubbishy*' Rome, an archway and two or three pillars, 'All the incongruous things of past incompatible ages' (I. i. 22). Lastly, there is the political entity of the Roman Republic and the invasion by the French: 'Will they fight? They say so' (II. iii. 48). As the tentative love affair progresses, Claude begins to respond to classical sculpture, the 'immutable manhood' of the 'marvellous Twain, that erect on Monte Cavallo. . . . Stand with your upstretched arms and tranquil regardant faces' (I. x. 186, 188). But such manhood is only immutable when it is aestheticised and safe in the past. The 'upstretched' arms of the tranquil pair are recalled in a later test of modern manhood when Claude sees, or thinks he sees, a man killed. 'You didn't see the dead man? No; – I began to be doubtful' (II. vii. 192). 'Doubtful' that the event took place, and *alarmed*; the man was said to be a priest and 'I was in black myself' (II. vii. 193). Despite the comedy the 'event' is sickening in its confusion, ambiguity and brutality, not the least because it undermines the idea of coherent action altogether. The hacking, chopping swords are 'In the air once more upstretched! And/Is it blood on them?' (II. vii. 184–5). The event fragments into a series of discrete, unconnected perceptions of doubtful signification. Both action and manhood are deconstructed here. Later in the narrative the glorious statues are again recalled when Claude remembers a victorious sense of agency as he stood 'uplifted' on the poop of the vessel carrying him to Italy. But the moment goes, and he resigned himself to the fluctuation of the sea: 'I swayed with the poop' (III. ii. 55) unlike the 'erect' statues. Not only is agency equated with phallic power, but it seems to be something one can obtain only in imagination. He commits himself to the 'aqueous age', or to evolutionary determinism, to the sea where primary life originated and where agency is defeated.

The dispersal of the Victorian double poem into the self-reflexive poem in *Amours de Voyage* is perhaps a necessary consequence of its deconstruction of action and manhood. But there are two possible readings of Claude's condition, and the poem makes efforts to turn his fastidious self-examining utterances around to be the object of examination and critique in their turn. On the one hand, there is an ethical reading of Claude's experiences which is internal to his own subjective experience: a modern Hamlet, he loses an opportunity for engagement, literally, by failing to make his offer of marriage and by accepting instead the 'offer' of a view of the classical marbles. On the other hand, he is the object of a serious critique of the ideal of action and manhood, and this logically involves a rejection of the terms of bourgeois marriage (and the economic structure on which it is founded), which depends on those ideals and resists the redefinition of it which both he and Mary wish to make. Georgina's tactless manipulation of Claude into the conventional role of suitor scares him off, but effectively reinstates those ideals. Clough abandoned much material on the difficulties of entering the professions and on the options of emigration. But these do not have to be included for us to see that the poem is an examination of the values of the educated, redundant intellectual in crisis, whose relation to bourgeois values is deeply problematical.[56]

Dipsychus continues this theme. Dipsychus is split within himself, constantly examining the purity of his motives. But he is also split between the Spirit's crude materialism and his own idealism. So the poem fractures in several ways. The lampooning style of the Spirit's verse recalls, not only Goethe, but the mode of radical poetry and certainly that of the early R. H. Horne: 'They may talk as they please about what they call pelf. . . . But help it I cannot, I cannot help thinking/How pleasant it is to have money, heigh ho!/How pleasant it is to have money' (scene V. 131, 133–4).

The poem is generally seen as a dramatisation of Victorian doubt. It is certainly that, but, as one comes to expect of Clough, a dramatisation of a complex kind. It begins with a quotation from the refrain of a powerful earlier poem, 'Easter Day – Naples, 1849' – 'Christ is not risen!' That poem laments the end of a teleological universe in the *literal* terms of Christian myth, but it is followed by a strong humanist reinstatement of those truths which ironises the need to cling on to the earlier forms of the myth. *Dipsychus* appears to be a reinvestigation of this humanist position and its implications. The ground of some of the iconoclastic earlier poems, such as 'Duty – that's to say complying' or 'The Latest Decalogue' – 'Thou shalt not kill; but needst not strive/Officiously to keep alive. . . . Thou shalt not covet; but tradition/Approves all forms of competition' (II. 2, 19–20) – is given a new context in the conflict between what is termed in the Epilogue 'the tender conscience and the world'.[57] In the Prologue the conservative uncle of the author complains that there are 'three or four ways of reading' the hexameters, 'each as good and as much intended as the other'.[58] His own speech is capable of the same reading, for though he means the regularity of the metre, what he says can also apply to the meaning of the lines. And there are certainly at least two ways of 'reading' the relationship between the Spirit and Dipsychus. One is as the temptation to succumb to the brute materialism of a cynical and competitive society. The other is as a study of a fastidious and self-involved morality which requires the common sense of the Spirit to come to terms with itself. The Spirit sees that a purely ethical concern with doubt can remain with an idealism which has no issue in conduct: he sees, encouraging Dipsychus to consort with the prostitutes with which he is so obsessed, that his purity is a form of prurience; he also sees that a refusal to opt for any kind of occupation on the grounds that it will compromise morality is to evade any form of action, and that Dipsychus' conscience is ultimately disabling. But this view is a simple inversion of that of Dipsychus. The Epilogue indicates the ground of another reading when the author remarks that 'the Spirit in my poem may be merely the hypothesis or subjective imagination formed' – but the uncle brushes aside such pretentiousness.[59] Yet the author's remarks here seem to suggest that he is concerned less with the way idealism and materialism conflict than with the significance of the *opposition* itself. The Spirit is precisely a 'Spirit' because he is a projection of the idealist consciousness, and once it can be seen that Dipsychus and the Spirit are doubles of one another, another reading opens out as they become dialectically related: the Spirit's brute materialism is the other face of idealism; the self-cancelling abstractions of idealism are the other face of materialism, as both call each other forth. They are not alternatives but forms of the same thing, as idealism becomes the aestheticised form of materialism. This can be seen by the end of the poem, when Dipsychus has entered the law – and moral compromise.

Clough was composing the poem over the years which included the Great Exhibition, one of the high points of Victorian confidence. This enters the poem by implication in an increasing emphasis on consumption and affluence in the words of both characters. Dispersed, prolix and unfinished though the poem is, it marks the last phase of Clough's original explorations. *Mari Magno*, another unfinished poem, a series of modern tales (there are fragments of a poem on the Crimean war) on the model of Chaucer's *Canterbury Tales*, was first published in part in 1862 after his death. It is as if he is attempting to rework and domesticate the earlier preoccupations. Though they contain some arresting material, they are written with a sobriety which makes them less demanding than the earlier work. In a different sense than Arnold meant in 'Thyrsis', the extraordinary energy of the earlier work had 'drooped'.

Clough made a serious attempt to write political poetry and to extend the idiom of middle-class writing. Though Browning continued to experiment, the radical tradition takes new directions as the century goes on. The Pre-Raphaelite poets gathered around *The Germ* admired Clough (Dante Gabriel Rossetti's 'Jenny' is a poem in his social-realist vein), but Morris chose to approach the political more indirectly by adapting the poetry of sensation. Political poetry did appear, but it does not possess the remarkable linguistic experiment which made Clough's work so much more than the limited topical poetry Arnold deprecated. Perhaps the most interesting middle-class political writing on topical issues arises over the Irish question. For Ireland, like Scotland, figures colonial oppression and the insoluble problems of exploitation.

William Allingham's *Laurence Bloomfield in Ireland. A Modern Poem* (1864), subtitled 'A Modern Landlord' in the second edition, is a verse narrative which resembles *The Bothie* in some external details. A combination of pastoral and sociology, it describes the attempts of a liberal and fair-minded landlord, who believes in peasant ownership if conditions are right, to divest an enclosing and evicting land agent of power. It aspires to a neutral analysis of a complex and confused situation, however, and though written with enormous sympathy for the Irish, it ultimately lacks the commitment of *The Bothie*. Bloomfield meets an astonishing range of bigotry among the landowning gentry, encounters the conservatism of the priest-hood and the cynicism of Protestants. He sees the systematic exploitation and starvation of the poor and the inevitable resort to political extremism and murder. His own policy of clemency leads to violence. Allingham's picture of cruelty and oppression is graphic, particularly the eviction of the whole village of Ballytullagh, and contrasts with the resilience of popular life (girls dressing for the local fair use the pool as a mirror). If the poem moves to a rather unconvincing pastoral gesture of hope at its end in transfigured Irish landscape, this is not before some important analyses have been made, which are certainly bolder than those of his other poems.

If Allingham dealt with what Clough would have called 'positive matters of fact', it is clear that he found difficulty in accommodating the heroic couplet to them. But he can be graphic on the landscape of poverty: a lane straggles

> To form the street, if one may call it street,
> Where ducks and pigs in filthy forum meet;
> A scrambling, careless, falter'd place, no doubt;
> Each cottage rude within doors as without;
> All rude and poor; some wretched, – black and fair
> And doleful as the cavern of Despair.
>
> (V. 25–30)

He can be incisive even when his writing leans to abstraction. The rebel Neal broods on

> The narrow toils and hardships of the poor,
> Which no kind hand assists them to endure;
> For rich and poor, contrasted lots at best,
> Here plainly mean oppressors and opprest.
>
> (VI. 17–20)[60]

Though there is no intrinsic reason why topicality should guarantee a probing political and social analysis, a poetry of protest, it is clear from the work of Clough and Allingham that they felt that it did. It is interesting that Aubrey de Vere, a contemporary of Allingham, chose to embody a

203

more conservative view of Irish history in the form of myth and legend. He did write directly of 'English Misrule and Irish Misdeeds' in 1848, but apportioned blame to Ireland in a way Allingham did not. His *Inisfail: A Lyrical Chronicle of Ireland* (1863) is an attempt to place Ireland as the bearer of authentic religious tradition. His 'The Irish Slave in Barbadoes' takes up Allingham's themes in a very different way, just as 'The Infant Bridal' (1855), the legend of a child marriage, may be an allegory of exploitation. His theory of poetry as dramatic projection, though it looks like the view developed earlier by Fox, is actually an account of spiritual embodiment in the material, a Catholic aesthetics in intention (de Vere became a Catholic in 1851), very like that criticised by Clough in *The Bothie*.[61]

Though with far less sophisticated accounts of power, ideology, consciousness, class, representation and language than the formations of the 1830s, the work of Allingham and de Vere bifurcates rather as those traditions do. Allingham followed, as did Clough in a modified way, the Benthamite concern with critique in his long poem on Ireland, though his work also leaned to the Tennysonian idyll, as will later be seen (and this warns us against erecting a rigid account of poetic tradition). De Vere followed the Coleridgean concern with art in terms of mythical construct. But Arnold developed neither concern and intransigently turned his back on both even when he remained more of a Coleridgean and idealist than Clough.

8

THE LIBERAL IN CRISIS: ARNOLD

It is tempting, when reading Arnold's side of the correspondence with Clough in the late 1840s, with its elegant brio, wit and hurtfulness, to align him against radical poetry and with an oppositional Coleridgean position similar to that of the Apostles in the 1830s. But this would be to misunderstand the many important differences between Arnold and the earlier Apostles and his attempt to recentre poetry in a moral tradition in the new circumstances of the mid-century. In fact, he rejected both traditions and actually conflated them, reading them both as the continuance of a deeply damaging aesthetic theory and practice deriving from the Romantics. There was warrant for this in the Apostles' theory of sensation and in the Fox group's preoccupation with emotion, but neither group, with the exception of Mill, advocated the unmediated transmission of a subjectivity or the overflow of feeling in poetry. Both found ways of turning the exploration of subjectivity into the material of critique and investigation, either through drama or through the 'sentimental' poet's mediation of naive material. To turn to Arnold's correspondence with Clough is to see him evolving the ethical aesthetic of the great human action of the past which was to emerge in the 1853 Preface, excluding those many importunate 'voices' of the nineteenth century from the homogeneity of the Grand Style. That this was no simple matter can be seen from the conflictual anxieties of 'The Forsaken Merman' (1849), which can form a context for Arnold's correspondence with Clough.

In this poem importunate voices call to Margaret, who has already made the choice of living in the sea envisaged in Tennyson's 'The Mermaid' – and reneged on it. The 'babel' of voices, indeed, call over one another with different messages in the anapaestic forms which are made to represent a confused toss and surge of feeling like the tossing waves of the sea. The forsaken merman urges his children to 'Come away' from the shore, and as he calls them the children make a last effort to call Margaret from the town in which she now is. They look to the land rather than to the sea, torn between the father's conflicting instructions. Margaret, too, has been at the mercy of conflict. The 'far-off bell' from 'the little grey church on the windy hill' (71) has called her to Christian worship and the saving of her human soul. She regains her soul, her kinsfolk and her work. The church is the only authoritative moral imperative in the poem, but it disrupts all other relationships.

> Singing most joyfully,
> Hark what she sings: 'O joy, O joy,
> For the humming street, and the child with its toy!
> For the priest, and the bell, and the holy well;
> For the wheel where I spun,
> And the blessed light of the sun!'[1]

She spins in isolation, but nevertheless in a community, rather like a Lady of Shalott in reverse, having chosen, not fulfilment but abstract moral authority, not arousal but amnesia. But conflict is embedded in conflict in this poem, for her choice does not result in the eradication of contradiction. She has chosen, not between isolation and community, but between two kinds of isolation, two kinds of community and *affiliation*. The 'child with its toy' is not hers. Mature sexuality and the mothering of children lie in the sea. *Work* and domesticity are split between two places ('The youngest [child] sate on her knee' (52) when the church bell sounded). The child now seems to her an alien with 'cold strange eyes' (106) and the merman is forced to adopt the role of mother. The merman and his children, climbing over the church graves in search of Margaret, seem like a sinister invasion of miscegenated, subaqueous creatures on land. The terrible cost of exclusion, which forces such distorted categories upon both perceiver and perceived, is the result of Margaret's original alienation from the land. But alienation is always a double process. The estranged person can neither return to the community which has been left nor *back* to the same position of estrangement in the sea. For both 'places', and the people in them, have been materially altered. The moral imperative is no longer clear. Margaret's estrangement effects a multiple alienation, of herself and of those around her. That is why both merman and human 'mermaid' are 'Forsaken' in the double meaning of having been deserted and having given up something. Not the least of this poem's strange power comes from the slight unconscious shock of the title, where the more conventional 'forsaken mermaid' is displaced by the 'forsaken merman'.

'Hang this thinking!' (*Amours de Voyage*, III. x. 207), Claude exclaims, and Dipsychus thinks of himself as sick with thought. Arnold's work never wishes to commit itself to this 'strange disease' of modern life (as the famous phrase of 'The Scholar-Gipsy' (203) has it), but is continually aware of the *results* of its over-reflective, alienated conditions. He is the poet of cultural displacement, the refugee fleeing the 'infection' of fatigue, doubt and 'mental strife', but always between two worlds, like Margaret or Senancour's Obermann. He is most successful, less when he attempts the poetry of therapy for this condition, but when he writes of the psychological stress it engenders, despite his belief that to describe division is to concede to defeat. Always seeking secure ground free from the tracks of occupation, his isolation makes him hyperconscious of the intruding footsteps of alien beings – the 'heavy tread' of the 'new-waked clown' (181) or Shepherd in 'Resignation', after whom 'the wet, flowered grass heaves up its head' (185), or in the tracks of the persistent Callicles in *Empedocles on Etna* – 'One sees one's footprints crushed in the wet grass' (I. i. 14). Solitude, after all, is predicated on the people you escape from. Arnold's poetry is at its most intense when it lets in these culturally dislocating forces. It is heavy with territorial reference at these moments, the boundary or limit of field, sea, land, European mountain or stronghold, occidental plain or desert (Margaret's church on dry land, for instance, and the subaqueous world). From the prize poem 'Alaric at Rome' (1840) to *Sohrab and Rustum* (1853), armies tramp through his poems in successive waves of cultural invasion – for instance, Moslems, Crusaders, Goths, Huns ('Resignation'), Tartars, French, Arabs ('Consolation'), Tyrian traders, Greeks ('The Scholar-Gipsy') – or one form of thought displaces another, as the sophists displace Empedocles.[2] Arnold becomes the truly modern poet he never really wished to be when he encounters these historical forces in *Empedocles on Etna* (1852) and *Sohrab and Rustum* (1853). The ethical, stabilising poetry of joy he wished to create reverses itself, and he becomes the European poet whose cultural boundaries are threatened with dissolution. Whereas Clough (except in *The Bothie*) rarely goes beyond Europe, Arnold is always aware of the threatening or mysterious East, and while Clough uses the choice or discovery of the route or pathway as an analogue for experience, Arnold's preferred model is the territorial margin and the problematic affiliation with family, creed or race. How these work in the two long poems can best be seen after the evolution of Arnold's early thought is described. For though he objected to Clough's politics and aesthetics, he made a serious attempt to evolve a poetry which would be accessible to what he called 'the complaining millions of men'. If in Clough we see the radical in crisis, in Arnold we see the liberal in crisis.

In his explosion over the publication of Keats's letters after September 1848 – 'What a brute you were to tell me to read Keats' Letters' – where the passion should not be lost in the comedy, Arnold associates Keats with Browning and Tennyson alike.

> What harm he has done in English Poetry. As Browning is a man with a moderate gift passionately desiring movement and fulness, and obtaining but a confused multitudinousness, so Keats with a very high gift, is yet also consumed by this desire: and cannot produce the truly living and moving, as his conscience keeps telling him. They will not be patient neither understand that they must begin with an

idea of the world in order not to be prevailed over by the world's multitudinousnes: or if they cannot get that, at least with isolated ideas.[3]

Tennyson is thrown in with Browning and Keats 'et id genus omne': if people cannot read Greek, this famous letter continues, they should read nothing but Milton and, tellingly, 'parts' of Wordsworth: 'the state should see to it' (as Arnold later did his best to make it).

Here we see the beginning of Arnold's long and ultimately successful attempt to recentre English poetry in a moral tradition. But more important for the moment is his elision of Keats, Browning and Tennyson and his misprision of them as simplistically expressive writers in order to do so. His refusal to differentiate between them comes from his belief that both the poetry of sensation and the reflective poetry of political analysis spring from the same roots and can be brought under the same head as part of a destructive cycle of intensity and ennui which is endemic to Romantic art and which belongs to what is essentially a psychological poetry, whatever the superficial difference of form. Arnold has done his work so well that his subsuming of all Romantic poetry into a psychology of expressive feeling remains as a powerful account of such poetry. And Tennyson and Browning are both subsumed into 'Victorian' poetry, their differences of politics and aesthetics ignored. In his commentary on his own poem, 'The New Sirens', a few months later, he diagnoses the seductions of modern poetry as an intensity which leads to the '*alternation* of ennui and excitement'.[4] The pure subjectivity which he later saw as the vice of his own poem, *Empedocles on Etna*, is foreshadowed here: the dangerous jouissance of introspective feeling has begun. Movingly, the intensity of the Keats letter produces a syntactic slide in the confession, 'I have had that desire of fulness without respect of the means, which may become almost maniacal'. 'Maniacal' describes both the desire of fullness and the intense frustration of the condition of being without respect of the means to achieve it. The Arnoldian repression of the different Browning/Tennyson formations and his misprision of them comes from a complicated source.

In the one-sided correspondence with Clough which remains (it is somehow sadly typical of the relationship that only Arnold's letters survive), one sees a progressive retreat from a shared political and aesthetic excitement to distance (is it ennui?) culminating in Arnold's refusal to write a prefatory memoir to Clough's poems after his death.[5] Steadily one sees Arnold dissociating himself from Clough's radical politics. The will to depoliticise results in a sustained attack on the place of reflective thought and analysis in Clough's poetry. The need to divest poetry of politics becomes a will to ahistoricise and a rejection both of the idea of ideology (we see the thing without the name in the work of both Fox and Clough) and of the idea of myth. Ideology becomes a relativistic *Zeitgeist* or time spirit which because relative is seen as superficial. By the time Arnold wrote his Preface of 1853, rejecting *Empedocles*, myth was no longer the changing configuration of interpretative symbol and sensation it had been for the Apostles. It was either thinned to the consistency of allegory, the form which Coleridge called phantom proxy, as an 'allegory of the state of one's own mind' (a mere substitute for psychology), to which he was hostile, or hypostatised to a timeless story of great human action, of which Arnold approved. He found his way to 'the beautiful', the deficiency of which he noted in Clough's poems, but it was not that of the poetry of sensation. In fact he abandoned a theory of representation and language and adopted instead a theory of style. And style was to produce 'grand moral effects' by its limpidity, its capacity to *be* an ethical state rather than to represent one.[6]

The letters to Clough make complex and painful reading, not the least because Arnold was pained by them himself. The supercilious cruelty with which he greeted Clough's poems – 'I have had so much reluctance to read these, which I now return that I surely must be destined to receive some good from them' – was quickly followed by a retraction.[7] The move to the stoicism of the *Bhagavad Gita* was not an easy one and the withdrawal from Clough can make agonising reading. Something of this comes out, not in the declared elegy on Clough, 'Thyrsis', but in 'Dover Beach', surely as much a love poem to him as the occasion of Arnold's marriage, which accomplished an effective separation. The 'clash by night' there alludes to Clough's *Bothie of Tober-Na-Vuolich* (IX. 51–4) and Thucydides' description of the confused battle of Epipolae, as we have seen. Like the waves on Dover beach, the phrase 'neither joy nor love' washes over the earlier words 'Ah love, let us be true/To one another', and obliterates them. The letters are full of half-frivolous endearments which prefigure the tragic sense of loss in 'Dover Beach' – 'You will not I know forget me' (Letter 32, 23 September 1849), 'Adieu and love me' (Letter 37, 9 April 1852). If these lines (29–37) were written in late June 1851, as Kenneth Allott's *The Poems of Matthew Arnold* suggests, the friendship with Clough would have been in Arnold's mind.[8]

But whatever underlies Arnold's great poem, it is clear that the struggle over Clough's aesthetics one sees going on in the letters is concurrently a political struggle. Arnold's suspicion of Clough's depth-hunting attempts to '*solve*' the universe in his poetry, his 'growing sense of the deficiency of the *beautiful* in your poems', is well known.[9] But this commentary is mingled almost inseparably with Arnold's sceptical and ambivalent response to the French revolution of 1848. The discussion of the 'beautiful', for instance, is immediately followed by news of the National Guard quoted at the beginning of Part II of this study: and 'I trust in God that feudal industrial class as the French call it, you worship, will be clean trodden under'. Though he was willing to consider the redistribution of wealth under capitalism and an 'apostolic capitalist' who did not live 'like a colossal

Nob', he thought that Carlyle's 'Gig-owning' aristocracy had received only a 'please God, momentary blow'.[10] The scepticism progresses: on 6 March 1848 he has no faith in the people and then, in a letter dated as possibly 24 March, he expresses doubt in the very concept of the *'people'* as a category.[11] This culminates in a fierce letter of (probably) November 1848 attacking Clough's *The Bothie of Tober-Na-Vuolich* and the Oxford clique who 'rave about your poem'.[12] He admits to bitterness towards Clough and 'the Time Stream in which they and he plunge and bellow' and describes a retreat to the solitude of Senancour's Obermann – but not before this practitioner of the 'oriental wisdom' has uttered a bellow of rage himself.[13] So the tensions of politics and poetics are deeply involved in these letters.

The inexorable distancing from Clough is accompanied by a search for withdrawal from these 'damned times'.[14] The philosophy of detachment sought in the *Bhagavad Gita*, 'abandoning the fruits of action', a 'supreme step', leads to a new aesthetic.[15] Though Arnold is concerned with the lack of the beautiful and of pleasure in Clough's work, this new position is no more related to Hallam's poetry of sensation and its subversive workings than Arnold's belief that poetry must subsist 'by its *contents*: by becoming a complete magister vitae as the poetry of the ancients did' is related to the probing work of reflective thought he saw in his friend's poems.[16] He explicitly excludes the poetry of 'exquisite bits and images' associated with Keats and Shelley from his new concept of style, a term which increasingly preoccupied him in the letters after 1848.

What, then, are 'the grand moral effects produced by style'? What is the beauty which is not Hallam's beauty, the plainness which is not Clough's plainness? The function of the grand style is to 'compose and elevate the mind' ('compose' here suggests a therapeutic calm) by producing moral effects, not statements, by expressing 'character', not 'mind',[17] by *satisfying* 'religious wants', not by *expressing* religious wants.[18] Were it to be anything else, it would violate detachment and return to the vulgar striving of commitment. The elevation of the grand style raises one above action, thought and feeling and stands over and against history, with its alternation of excitement and ennui.

'The trying to go into and to the bottom of an object instead of grouping *objects* is as fatal to the sensuousness of poetry as the mere painting, (for, *in Poetry*, this is not *grouping*) is to its airy and rapidly moving life', Arnold wrote to Clough.[19] 'Grouping', a totality which is a stance, an attitude, a gesture, a totality which *is* the liberated composure it seeks to produce and not the fragmentation of consciousness in ideas and feelings, this is the moral effect of the grand style. Such a disinterested free play of mind *is* moral and religious without having to explore morals and religion. Arnold's later preference for the great human action and its seeming objectivity derives from the same interest in 'grouping objects'. To configure a past action as a unified whole is to imitate the composure such unity produces rather than to represent the processes of action. His advocacy of the great human action has an anti-subjectivist purpose, but as soon as that action is contemporary we are immersed in subjectivity once again, and so almost any 'great' action of the past is preferable to the present because it escapes instrumentality and immersion in destructive, partisan passion. It is interesting to reflect that the Preface appeared (1853) when England was approaching the Crimean war.

Kant's category of the aesthetic, of course, is behind Arnold's grand style. The freedom which subsists in the disinterested play of mind over the object, its severance from the practical and instrumental, this is familiar Kantian ground. Arnold's grand style, standing over and against morals and religion but nevertheless *being* them, transcending the inessentials of politics and passion, achieves the detachment of Kant's aesthetic while associating it with ethics, something about which Kant was far more doubtful. Indeed, Arnold's grand style *is* the aesthetic. It *enacts* the aesthetic state, the end product, the work of art's results, rather than working on the experiences which produce that result. Hence its concern with effects. And for all its repudiation of psychology it is effectively a psychological theory of art as calm, as therapeutic composure and unity. It is also a formal theory, not so much because it is formalist, but because it is concerned with the abstract condition of composure rather than with the elements which create it. The cool, gelid effects of Arnold's own poetry, striving for the blanched landscapes where composure lies, sometimes all too poignantly freeze the 'airy' spirit of life he sought in the free play of the aesthetic state. What remains is a stance, a gesture, an attitude.

A concern with objectified action seen as a totality developed 'as a group of statuary, faintly seen, at the end of a long and dark vista' emerges into the light, and a language of the utmost simplicity, becoming like that of the ancients, 'more independent of the language current among those with whom they live', are Arnold's defences against expressive subjectivity in the 1853 Preface.[20] This was to create 'a steadying and composing effect' upon the 'judgement'.[21] Mill's soliloquist has been turned inside out and made to oversee an action rather than being 'overheard', responding to the effect of catharsis rather than experiencing its process.

Empedocles, analysing his condition and expressing his despair in solitude (as Arnold conceived Clough to be doing), is 'overheard' by the young poet Callicles, who occupies the slopes of the mountain, and cannot pass to the eroded, scorching heights like the older poet. His condition is thus exactly that of Mill's poet. In spite of Arnold's rejection of it, the poem is one of the great nineteenth-century studies of the despair of solipsism. Empedocles, aware of his isolation and yet conscious that his condition has no boundaries, because pure 'thought' (II. 345) has no limit, experiences the contradictions of solipsism. He is aware that he has lost

211

the capacity for joy (II. 240–4) both in thought and society, but the perception itself creates a split between being and knowing which reintroduces the fragmentation of the unified consciousness. If self-enclosure 'fencest him from the multitude' (II. 211) it provokes the question, 'But can life reach him?' (II. 210). And this in turn leads to the perception that the self conceived without relation to the other has no 'fence' – or defence – from himself as the sound of torrents and 'the beating of his own heart' (II. 214) mingle without distinction. This recall of Tennyson's 'The Lotos-Eaters' in the idiom of Wordsworth's *Prelude* (very recently published in 1850) amalgamates the poetry of reflection and the poetry of sensation and uses both to suggest estranged labour and estranged thought. For the irony of Empedocles' situation is that his own analysis leads him ever further from the solutions proposed in it. In the grating philosophical liberalism of I. ii, his solution to the Wordsworthian 'burden of ourselves' (128) is not to depend on the authority of an illusory God or Nature or intellectual or political systems: we have no *rights* (I. ii. 155) except those that man invents himself; in an intransigent universe there is only the individualist's stern ethic – 'To work as best he can' (II. 269). Yet this combination of modernised Epictetus, Spinoza and Senancour does not enable him to deal with scientific knowledge, history or culture, as the cumulative literature of cultures grows overwhelming, no longer a palace of art but a massive library: 'The mass swells more and more/Of volumes yet to read' (I. ii. 333–4). The 'o'er laboured Power' of evolutionary growth is indifferent (I. ii. 290–6) to this deadness and grows old with human culture. Finally, language collapses as it becomes irrelevant and redundant and a split between name and referent opens out (I. ii. 331). Neither abstract nor mythological language will work. The abstracting tendency of Empedocles' vocabulary creates such general categories that it almost becomes a non-specific language which escapes particular meaning. The mythological commentaries of Callicles, lyrics on classical legend which are analogues of Empedocles' situation, are misinterpreted by him. The way is open for endless misprision.

It is through Callicles and the primitive myths of the unified consciousness that the critique of Empedocles is made. But the poem also turns round and dramatises the limits of Callicles through his mythic language. The friction between these lyrics and the speeches of Empedocles makes the poem possess that doubleness of content which we have seen being evolved in different ways in the work of Tennyson, Browning and Clough. The dramatic form adopted by Arnold enables the poem to go beyond the limits of both speakers' consciousnesses and opens them up for analysis. In the 1853 Preface Arnold quotes Schiller's remark that all art is dedicated to joy. Like Hallam, he was searching for a means of overcoming the split consciousness of modern European experience. But by 1853 the transcendence of this condition means eliminating conflict rather than re-entering into the experience of the naive poet and exploring the difficult act of assimilation undertaken by the sentimental poet. In *Empedocles* this act of assimilation is attempted and fails, as Empedocles interprets the mythological experience of the naive poet of joy, Callicles, in a *literal* way, undoing mythic thought and distancing himself from it so completely that he is incapable of understanding it.

In simplifying the nature of Callicles as the voice of spontaneous, pre-intellectual lyric feeling Empedocles blocks the way to understanding him, for Callicles is already, as it were, a reconstructed mythic poet, sceptically refusing to see the cure worked by Empedocles on the woman Pantheia as a 'miracle' (I. i. 133–40) in a forcefully rational speech to Pausanius, follower of Empedocles. (In this exclusively male colloquy Pentheia and her resurrected body are hints of the absent feminine, disregarded by both old and young poet.) He diagnoses Empedocles' condition as a deep psychological sickness for which neither 'the times' (I. i. 150) ('These are damned times', Arnold wrote to Clough, we remember) nor the sceptical sophists are responsible.[22] To allay this condition he sings of Achilles instructed by the Centaur (I. ii. 57–76), of the flight of Cadmus and Harmonia, changed into serpents to escape the calamities of Thebes (I. ii. 427–60), of the rebel giant Typho, buried under Etna, and of the easeful gods who have defeated him (II. 41–88), of the competition of Apollo and Marsyas (II. 129–90), and at the end of the poem, after Empedocles has committed suicide by throwing himself into Etna, the departure of Apollo to Olympus (II. 417–68). There are reminiscences of Keats and Tennyson in all these songs (most particularly references to *Hyperion* and the over-throw of Saturn and to the Epicurean gods of Tennyson's 'The Lotos-Eaters'). By inference Callicles is a sort of Browning, too, as Empedocles' lines recall part of Browning's 'Saul'.[23]

The first two songs are myths of cultural transmission which come before and after Empedocles' long analysis of modern knowledge and consciousness in I. ii. The first song refuses Empedocles' individualist epistemology by insisting on *shared* transmission and the second recognises its breakdown (Cadmus invented the alphabet, and thus the self-conscious-ness and abstraction of writing becomes the seed of discord). There is both a positive and a negative solution for this – either transformation and change or escape – but Empedocles ignores both and assumes that Callicles is commenting on his own status as exile and wanderer (I. ii. 477) among 'revolutions' and change (I. ii. 472). He sees the Typho myth as the defeat of great qualities by 'littleness' (II. 93), or, implicitly, democracy. He sees the defeat of Marsyas, Pan's candidate, as the sign of Apollo's unbearable isolation and resigns his own Apollonian trophies in recognition of defeat. But there are also quite different possibilities in these lyrics. Cadmus and Harmonia can only abandon conflict by the unacceptable strategy of abandoning language and becoming 'placid and dumb' (I. ii. 460) in the

'untrodden' (I. ii. 455) mountain ways. Quietism, in other words, is dumbness. Typho's terrible punishment came about because he challenged the
legitimacy of the authority of the ruling gods. And the challenge was
necessary. Like 'The Lotos-Eaters' the Typho story is a myth of repression.
Callicles' songs become increasingly violent. Marsyas is torn to pieces in
the violent defeat of the energies of Pan, the defeat of one poetic form and
language by another. The possibility of political violence and the consequence of its repression both at home and in Europe are surely present
here. And thus the double poem emerges in these different readings. The
problem with Empedocles is that his solution is detachment, the problem
with Callicles is that he sings of these things *uncommittedly*, and so both
figures are in retreat.

It is fascinating that Thomas Cooper's section on Empedocles in his *The
Purgatory of Suicides* (1845), written while he was imprisoned in Stafford
gaol for political, Chartist 'crimes', is a subversive, demythologised reading
of the story. Despite his desire to impart knowledge to his kind Empedocles
is accused of deceiving men with fraud because he wished to be seen as
a god. That is to say, Cooper's Empedocles is the figure of mystifying
power. Cooper's Empedocles uses the same images as Arnold's – 'poor
shipwrecks we' (Cooper):[24] 'our souls. . . . But with the winds must go' (I.
ii. 93–4) (Arnold) – and both poets use very nearly the same stanza form,
Cooper the full Spenserian stanza and Arnold, for Empedocles' speech, a
kind of sawn-off Spenserian form. Cooper, a flayed, protesting Marsyas,
enters unawares into a poem which recognises the anguish of maintaining
an Arnoldian politics of detachment. But there is no doubt that for Arnold
Marsyas is a loser.

Cooper's massive poem, one of the major achievements of Chartist
poetry, was well known. It is a measure of Arnold's need to erase the very
notion of political and social conflict that it figures almost mockingly as a
repressed element in his own *Empedocles*. *The Purgatory of Suicides* is a vast
modern myth, a new working-class cosmogony, challenging classical and
Christian orthodoxies by appropriating the epic (for Arnold the bastion of
privileged European culture), fusing epic with a Dantesque visit to purgatory, and rewriting history and political relations in a 'historical romance',
as Cooper calls it, which is an attempt to reconstruct knowledge. It is
explicitly shaped by his 'political struggles' and we should not forget that
part of its title is *A Prison-Rhyme*.[25] The normally soft cadences of the
Spenserian stanza are wrenched and welded into an iron substructure as
a series of debates takes place between personages such as Empedocles
and Cleombrotus (Book II) and Castlereagh (the epitome of oppression
since Shelley's 'Masque of Anarchy') and Judas (Book III). The poem is
an analysis, not of intellectual despair, as in Arnold's poem, but of collective political despair, and the reasons for it. It begins and ends with attacks
on oppression and exhortations to action in the millennial rhetoric of

Chartist writing, versifying Cooper's own speech on the occasion of the Hanley strike on 15 August 1842:

> Slaves, toil no more! why delve, and moil, and pine,
> To glut the tyrant-forgers of your chains?[26]

Book 10 rises to a crescendo in an onslaught on reactionary power and the military figures of British victories in modern Europe which have used the poor as cannon fodder.

> While feverous Power mocks the weary sun
> With steed-throned effigies of Wellington,
> And columned piles to Nelson, – Labour's child
> Turns from their haughty forms, to muse upon
> The page by their blood-chronicle defiled;
> Then, bending o'er his toil, weighs well the record wild.
>
> Ay, they are thinking, at the frame and loom;
> At bench, and forge, and in the bowelled mine;
> And when the scanty hour of rest is come,
> Again they read – to think, and to divine
> How it hath come to pass that Toil must pine
> While Sloth doth revel; how the game of blood
> Hath served their tyrants; how the scheme malign
> Of priests hath crushed them; and resolve doth bud
> To band, and bring back the primal Brotherhood.[27]

Consonant with Cooper's belief in the necessity to 'think and to divine', this is a philosophical poem in which the 'million' succeed 'By will – and not by war'.[28] The synchrony of purgatory enables him to bring together events and people from different times so that a strenuous dialogue, not of the mind with itself, but between clashing histories, can take place. The unifying device of suicide is literally eccentric, because suicides have chosen to place themselves in 'self-exile', outside the circle of those who have found the world bearable, and thus can be expected to exist in a critical and self-conscious relation to it: and by a grotesque logic, suicide is the great intellectual leveller, since all are motivated by forms of scepticism. This enables Cooper to anatomise the dialogue between two kinds of despair in the Judas/Castlereagh debate. Judas, stronger in moral despair than the weak and reactionary Castlereagh, drives him off. This clears the ground for an analysis of the cycle of reaction arising from the French Revolution and its impoverished rationalism (Book V): it is vital for Cooper to see how one potentially liberating movement failed. But the ground of his critique of European politics is the Empedocles dialogue, and since this debate, a kind of intellectual burlesque at one moment, part cumbersome, grimly resonant ratiocination, sometimes rising to an austere polysyllabic

215

rhetorical intensity (its own grand style), is so different from Arnold's version, it is important to see what the poem is doing here. For the Empedocles debate constitutes a critique of the classical thought which grounds European history.

Empedocles and Cleombrotus, old sage and youth, are locked in debate through 'ages of thought' at the same time as being doubles of one another, since they are bonded by fanaticism: one cast himself into fire, one into the sea. If Empedocles, called a 'charlatan' (stanza 27) by the youth, fraudulently assumed godhead to lead a populace towards morality by adding a 'tinge of mystery' to 'moral lessons' (stanza 36), Cleombrotus fraudulently deceived himself by promise of an ideal platonic world beyond the material one – 'Thou . . . wert maddened with desire/To realise some pure hypostatis/Platonic dreamers fable from their sire'.[29] This passage, typical of Cooper's rhetoric, in which the awkwardness is part of the intensity, is a key to the nature of his exploration of the status of thought. Empedocles wonders why men err from the satisfying pleasure of pure thought into the immoral use of power and Cleombrotus wonders why he was lured to pure thought by some 'vaguely imagined good' (stanza 51). Twinned as they are, they are attracted to oriental detachment and quietism as a form of liberation into pure thought and persuade Calanus to unlock the 'mystery' of 'Existence' (stanza 58) through Indian philosophy. But Cooper ingeniously describes their response to thought in the metaphorical terms of fire and sea, as if thought can never be free of the emotional and physical or *material* conditions in which it is experienced: Empedocles felt 'consuming fire' daily 'in my veins' (stanza 35) to rescue his people from debasement: Cleombrotus experiences, in language which takes an inexorably passive downwards movement, 'A tide of thoughts: and o'er my spirit flows/Wave after wave, bearing me, nerveless, from/My fancied height: as when, by acheful throes,/Self-castaway, the shelving rock I clomb' (stanza 38).[30] The Indian sage, after condemning the restlessness in which 'Our being is a contest and a strife/Of self with self . . . struggling to be free' (stanza 85), dissolves into 'doubtings void' (stanza 87). The transcendence of conflict seems to lead to further doubt. Through this tripartite colloquy Cooper suggests – what Empedocles and Cleombrotus are unable to see – that the pursuit of a 'hypostatis' of 'pure' abstract thought free from the impurities of moral, emotional and political experience and its material immediacy, free from experience which affects the 'veins' (Empedocles) and 'nerves' (Cleombrotus), is an illusion. We 'add unto our fetters' (stanza 83) if we believe this: we are 'fools!' It is a fallacy that we can live without 'contest and strife' within the being. Even his suicides are doomed to repeat the 'strife/Of self with self' without historical movement or change.[31] The unchanging permanence of abstract classical thought is stultifying, just as the 'oriental wisdom' beloved of Arnold is unsustaining. The dialectical 'contest and strife' inherent in thought is, for the truly political writer, Cooper suggests, perpetually redefined in different historical situations.

Nothing could be further from Arnold's dread of hyperactive reflection than this perpetual conflictual redefinition of the content of thought as real dissidence. Cooper's huge and turbulent poem stands as a critique of this retreat into the politics of liberal detachment. *The Purgatory of Suicides* both thematises and represents through its structure the politics and poetry of struggle which Cooper won so dearly. Arnold's epic, intended as an exemplary poem of the great human action, *Sohrab and Rustum*, took a very different form.

The effort to create a composing action and to seek a pure diction consonant with the unifying grand style is increasingly apparent in Arnold's poems after 1853. The grand style in its simplicity was intended to be *universal* and thus generally accessible, enabling the moral effect of poetry to be widely experienced. For Arnold, though no democrat in poetry, had the liberal's need to disseminate the values of high culture. The problem with such diction is that it is a selective, hypothetical style and thus becomes the pastiche of a notional purity, a memorial to a unified language which exists as an idea, a linguistic 'group of statuary' contrived of the habits of chaste dictions derived from touchstone poets of different ages – Homer, Milton, Wordsworth. It is deliberately Parnassian, as Gerard Manley Hopkins would have called it, often building its own tomb, like the woman in 'The Church of Brou' (1853). After 1853, indeed, many of Arnold's poems were memorial poems – to Clough, to his brother, to Rugby Chapel, to Wordsworth, the Brontës, Heine, Senancour and, it is tempting to say, to himself.[32]

Sohrab and Rustum might seem to be one of these memorials, but it could also be seen as Arnold's last major modern poem despite itself. The huge armies of the eastern troops, Tartars and Persians, gather on the open plains of the Oxus to participate in a 'great human action' by watching the single combat between the 'Tartar' Sohrab and the Persian Rustum – but what could be more modern than this? The historical context of Arnold's writing was the collapse of the Ottoman empire, the insecure status of Afghanistan and the new alignments of Britain, France and Russia, *the* nineteenth-century problem. The Crimean war was two years away, but the eastern question already cast shadows at the beginning of the 1850s. After the European poem, *Empedocles*, Arnold returned to the theme of territorial dissolution, uncertain affiliation and legitimacy, and with it to a questioning of the idea of manhood, as Sohrab, seeking out the father who kills him without knowing of the relationship, proves that he is neither girlish nor the girl Rustum believes he fathered. Researched from the work of orientalists (Sir John Malcolm's *History of Persia* (1815) and Alexander Burnes's *Travels into Bokkara* (1834)), taken from a story by Sainte-Beuve who translated Mohl's translation of Firdausi, assimilating orientalism to the European classicism of Homer's *Iliad* and then attempting to orientalise that, the transmission of Arnold's poem reproduces the confused affiliations it describes.[33]

Like the battle of Epipolae in 'Dover Beach', this is a poem where 'ignorant armies' clash, this time because parent and child do not know to which side each belongs, or whom each is fighting. Language is not so much betrayed (as in Clough's *Bothie*), as mystified. The meticulous epic naming of the components of the troops of both sides, an attempt to master and order the different groups which comprise allegiance, contrasts strongly with the confusion of naming of which Sohrab and Rustum are the victims, though even here the Miltonic lists confuse and blur difference of race, nation and loyalty when the 'Ilyats of Khorassan' are ranged with the Persians, but 'Tartars they seemed' (137–8). Rustum, indeed, cannot accept the truth through language but only from the mark pricked by Sohrab's mother on the arm of her child (655–60), the 'proper sign' (687) of family relationship. In a reworking of the oedipal legend, Rustum the father inflicts the patriarchal wound of separation, though the two men are bonded together in despairing individual heroism before Sohrab dies.

The poem's deep unease about patriarchal arrangements, which come to symbolise the permanent structures of bourgeois society, expresses itself in the inset similes, which seem to constitute the exquisite, but redundant ornamentation Arnold wished to avoid. These are concerned with family or trade or class, the culturally unsettled elements which increased the vulnerability of a Europe further threatened by the opening up of Tartar space. The similes in fact confuse gender and family relationship: at the crucial moment of revelation Sohrab and Rustum are compared to a pair of mated eagles, male and female (556–75); at the first encounter Rustum is compared to a woman of high social class watching the 'drudge' who makes the early morning fire and, in a Wordsworthian moment transferred to urban poverty, 'wonders how she lives' and what her 'thoughts' may be (307). This Wordsworthian, British, urban and class-aware simile is one of the strangest interpellations in this 'oriental' poem and indicates the stress its cohesion is under. And both participants, Rustum as mistress, Sohrab as slave, are converted into women. The pastoral corn of England as an image for Tartar joy in Sohrab is set against Persian fear, like the insecure pedlars crossing vertiginously under the Indian Caucasus (154–69), strangely interdependent images subliminally aware that Britain's threatened trade routes and her corn fields depend on one another. The heroic tragedy of Sohrab's death is associated with a poignant domestic scene, a piece of genre painting in which Sohrab is compared to the soiled white violets thrown aside by children as they are called to the protection of their nurse (842–7). It is not so much the oddity of the bourgeois reference which strikes as the scene of protection, nurture and intense vulnerability it calls up. A vulnerable English culture seems to lie wounded and in haemorrhage by Oxus, the river which at the end of the poem is deflected from Europe into the landlocked Aral sea in one of Arnold's most unsettling images of blocked energies. *Sohrab and Rustum* registers the uncertainty of the double poem in Arnold's work. It expresses a heroic individualism and appears half willing to make a critique of it. Yet this critique is discontinuous, without the systematic ambiguities one finds in other poems, and particularly in *Empedocles*. A threatened hegemony, a confusion of inside and outside, where the invader from without elides into the conflict from within, the dispersal of power through misprision, where male energy is contaminated and dissipated – these undermine the poem, and with it the diction of the grand style which is meant to legitimate unproblematical wholeness and sustain energy.

Arnold was acutely aware of the difficulties of writing in a time when the poet was on the margins of culture, and of *justifying* writing to an unsympathetic community. He was as toughly aware as Hallam of the problems of making claims for poetry. His defence, a moralised aestheticism, the beautiful as ethical, is canny in the sense that it prevented poetry from being a commodity while introducing the moral as a form of 'use'. The fallacies of the Preface, its depoliticised stance and the repression of Clough's work its values virtually ensured, should not prevent one from seeing it as the brilliant manoeuvre of a principled liberal in a tight spot. His poetry is compelling because it recognises the strain and difficulty of his enterprise and the confusion of the voices he encountered. He is actually a much more uncertain writer than Clough. His terror of infiltration, contamination and emasculation, from within – by effeminate poets, by women, by the masses or by his own troubled consciousness – and from without – by foreign trade, by European revolutionaries or by the alien hordes of non-European civilisations which come up from the sea like the rejected merman – was matched by his fascination with the sources of cultural dissolution. So much so that where Clough could ask where the battle was, Arnold wondered who the alien really was. The poet of wholeness and centrality was never sure where the centre was. Who is alien to whom? The merman or the little village? The Scholar Gipsy, affiliated with his exotic nomads or the bourgeois and Oxonian culture he flees? Sohrab or Rustum? His anti-poet is not really Clough but a poet who met the same problems at the other end of the social spectrum and negotiated them differently, John Clare.

The formative time of Clare's work falls in a much earlier period than that of Arnold but he continued to write in the asylum years and there is an uncanny meeting point between them. Both write of dislocation and isolation, both are fascinated by Gipsies, traditional outsiders of the culture, both negotiate a bewildering number of poetic voices and traditions, Keats, Wordsworth, song, ballad and political lyric – and both are acutely sensitive to spatial boundary and limit. They even hit the same phrases and cadences: 'Where there is neither sense of life or joys', Clare wrote in 'I am'; and 'a void – nor love nor hope may fill' ('Dull must that being be');[34] 'Dover Beach' evokes a world where there is 'neither joy, nor love, nor light,/Nor certitude, nor peace, nor help for pain' (33–4). But it would be right to argue the speciousness of this superficial resemblance. The interest of this analogy comes from the way two very different poets struggle to use conventions available to them. For Clare the conventions of solitude and the pastoral are anomalous in a context where, though the wise 'plan' of 'The Bible says that God is Love', its 'contradiction puzzles me' ('Letter to Miss B.'). The comparison is further complicated by the fact that poets such as Clare, after the narrow nineteenth-century term 'peasant poet' was abandoned, were assimilated into a newer tradition of the centrality of simple rural Englishness which Arnold's need to find a centre for English poetry has helped to define.[35]

A reading of Clare which does without these categories is beginning to discover the complexity of his work. We can be astonished by a poem such as 'Enclosure', which disrupts the carefully arranged hierarchical sequences of the eighteenth-century prospect poem by taking the eye into extended space and colour.[36] It adapts Wordsworth's 'Tintern Abbey', itself an adapted prospect poem, to extend limit – 'And lost itself, which seemed to eke its bounds,/In the blue mist the horizon's edge surrounds'. Clare uses the vocabulary of infinite space and boundlessness to make the political point that there should *be* no bounds. In Wordsworth's poem orchard-tufts 'lose themselves', but in contrast to Clare the land is marked off from 'the quiet of the sky'. Wordsworth's vocabulary of memory in 'Peel Castle' is put sharply against brute economic transformation in Clare's poem: 'And hath been once as it no more shall be./Enclosure came'. Keats's 'might half-slumbering on its own right arm' and the end of 'Ode to a Nightingale' are invoked to demonstrate the restriction put upon imaginative possibility and action, as the poet's visions are giants 'bereft' of limbs and the poem ends with devastating realism; 'And find too truly that they did but dream'. The diction of Pope's 'Epistle to Burlington', a poem about landscape gardening among the rich, is redirected to the 'garden-grounds' of enclosure, where, instead of the luxury artefacts of statues facing one another, one discovers 'Fence meeting fence'. This is a moment in which Clare takes the literary language of two traditions, eighteenth-century and Romantic, and forces upon it the significance of material change, using it to register ever decreasing space.

If Arnold's 'Thyrsis' and Clare's 'Dull must that being be' are considered together (both poems which use the pastoral to explore loss and memory and to retrieve loss, a familiar Romantic pattern), the different possibilities they found in the pastoral convention – perhaps were forced to find – become apparent.[37] The difference is not simply between an educated, overloaded artificial language and an 'untrained' simplicity and directness, between classical reference to Corydon and Demeter and 'The scenes and objects that his childhood knew – /The schoolyard and the maid he early loved'. For such an opposition underrates the seriousness with which both poets used the pastoral and its *conventions*. Though Clare's remarkable brevity – 'The grass that e'en till noon retains the dew' – contrasts with Arnold's expansive lists of flowers, it is clear that he is assimilating a literary mode, just as he does when he uses the language of 'scenes and objects' from the tradition of descriptive poetry. The solidity and pressure of his lines contrasts strongly with the elaborately stressed syllables in Arnold's poem, but they are handled with subtlety and confidence. Nor is it either that Clare is experiencing the countryside at first hand, that in the strangely universal language of the pastoral he *could* have been one of the 'country-folk' with whom the educated Thyrsis poet makes 'acquaintance'. Both participate in the Romantic movement of estrangement from an earlier environment, but it is in the definition of this that they fundamentally differ. And this creates a fundamental difference in their language and diction. Clare writes of the 'map' of boyhood, and both poets map out space. But whereas Arnold figures a return to slopes, ridges and hills, and, in spite of his wandering state – 'Quick! let me fly, and cross/Into yon farther field' – discovers reorientation in the rediscovery of the 'signal-elm', the movement of Clare's poem is quite different. It progresses from the familiar demarcations of a community, 'sunny wall' and 'old elms', to a more vulnerable reconfiguration of those elements where *exposure* is stressed – hedges, walls, 'And hollow trees that sheltered from the blast'. He can never return except in the mind even to this. Existing in 'unknown solitude', a solitude never before experienced and a solitude unknown to those who once knew him, he has gone beyond an earlier condition. The poem contrasts, with stark and subtle irony, for there *is* really no contrast, his 'home', made at different times in stately palaces and in the 'Gipseys camp', and the state of being a mere 'tennant' in hall and cot. This is an account of exile, but it also radically questions the meaning of 'home', a security which cannot be found in hall or camp and which seems to be defined in terms of financial safety and public, *social*, recognition, both of which are denied to him. The idea of 'home' is further modified when it becomes a metaphorical possibility only – 'Parted from one whose heart was once his home'. As in Arnold's poem there is a process of retrieval, but there is no 'home', only the knowledge of a one-sided love, a relationship to the lost lover which reflects the one-sidedness of the tenant's position. Arnold, figuring estrangement as the *voluntary* retreat from a group of noisy fox-hunters (the 'Barbarians' of his later prose), retrieves a symbolic transcendence from the material landscape, the signal elm. Clare, progressively subject to *enforced* exile, cannot find symbolic material even in the physical landscape, but only in his own mind, which is all he is left with. Arnold's 'signal-elm' makes cultural signals quite different from those of

221

Clare's 'old Elms'. One could say that properly the elm is a materially different tree for both poets, a different sign. One elm is a private, coded symbol of hope to which the solitary gives us access. The other elms are the sign of a community from which the poet has been excluded for ever. The difference between the threnody of one poem and the despair of the other is the crucial difference between the intellectual and emotional conditions of *alienation* – and of *dispossession*. Neither poet chose that condition. But it did mean an active choice of language and convention to analyse the situation in which they found themselves. If Arnold attempted to circumvent the moral difficulty of being a latter-day reflective poet, Clare did not choose to be a naive poet. A register of these different conditions is their analysis of manhood. For Arnold, and for Clough, the burden of masculinity and the self-sustaining strength, power and aggression it seems to demand are experienced uneasily, as a condition which isolates even when it commands respect. When Clare wrote, in the 'Letter to Miss B.', that he could not be a 'man', he meant not only that he could not act upon his sexuality, but that he was deprived of recognition, choice and agency, and that he had no public or private identity. What it is to be a man is radically different for the middle-class and the working-class poet.

Clare's ability to reconstruct and reinterpret the language – or languages – of pastoral to form his own account of property and manhood is an implicit challenge to the possibilities and conventions of poetic diction and pastoral. Is his work an exception? Clare, of course, was a rural poet. It is often thought that the abundant use of pastoral among urban working-class poets belongs to an essentially conservative tradition of detachment from immediately activist and political verse which could be said to form a shadowy quietist counterpart of Arnoldian values. But some caution is required here. Looking back to the first section of this book it will be remembered that there was a conservative and a radical reading of the significance of landscape poetry. While John Wilson reminded Tennyson that landscape poetry would provide him with the continuity and anchorage of an objective, external world of tradition and rural simplicity, Talfourd had argued that landscape poetry was truly democratic because the writer was free to construct his own associations and cultural meaning from the external world, free from conservative associations and independent of oppressive conventions.[38]

Working-class pastoral actually moves in both directions, but it is important to remember that poets worked in a number of genres, and that pastoral was adapted to serve a variety of purposes. There was a deep respect for 'educated' forms, but this did not preclude a highly independent use of them. It is striking that Samuel Bamford's first prison poem is, unexpectedly, an eclogue, not an overt protest poem or a satirical attack on oppression. It is a supremely controlled and quiet poem, an antiphonal lament between two imprisoned rustic figures.[39] One figure, 'prostrate', laments the loss of the 'vernal meadows' and the 'waving grove' of his home. The other figure, 'erect', fiercely attacks his condition: 'By tyrants hunted like a beast of prey', he is denied 'domestic joys' and his 'lowly cot'. He asks for protest on his behalf and for representation: 'Oh! shall no English man with kindling eye/Speak loudly, loftily, unto the throne?' But the final words of comfort are spoken by his friend: 'The clouds of night around the hills descend,/The shepherd driveth home his fleecy care;/ Come calm those fierce emotions, dearest friend'. What a cursory reading could interpret as defeatism is actually a consummate use of diction for complex purposes which reactivate the conventional metaphor, the artificial and in many ways obsolete eighteenth-century circumlocution, 'fleecy care', meaning flock of sheep. The logic of the metaphor means that the protesting figure is being asked to shepherd his 'fierce emotions' to provide a 'home' or protection for them. But the noun 'care' is given a wholly new application because two meanings converge to make it both metaphorical and literal, as the care of a flock elides into the terrible 'care' of the imprisoned consciousness. The friend's sensitivity and understanding come to redress and assuage the 'fierce emotions' of his companion, but his diction recognises just how intense suffering is. And the protester is not being asked to eliminate his emotions, but to give them a home, a base, to try to live with them, to protect himself by protecting them, even though he is in prison, and far from his actual home, the context in which he might normally be able to achieve calm. His oppression is recognised even when he is being asked to transcend it.

Bamford was not alone in his capacity to bend pastoral to his own condition. Another example would be Stephen Fawcett, who uses poetic diction juxtaposed with stark plainness to achieve a double mood of simultaneous freedom and threat. In his 'The Daffodil', for instance, a single line creates a sense of liberation – 'The fleecy light cloud flew' – and vulnerability – 'and the blighting east wind blew'.[40] Nor is Bamford alone in emphasising, as Clare does, the importance of 'home'. If this seems a mimicking of bourgeois sentimentality and the Victorian obsession with domestic virtues, it is worth pausing to see how the trope of home functions in working-class poetry.

Bamford himself remarks on the importance of the thematics of 'home' in his 1843 Preface. He offers a conventional argument – that a response to home is universal, that shared understanding enables different classes to bond and understand one another (an appeal to the middle-class reader); but he also puts forward another case. 'When coldness or repulsion meet us out of doors, what more natural than that we should turn to those who always make us welcome at home? What more becoming? What more manly or womanly subjects for verse, than our own firesides, and their dear and consoling associates?'[41] The private space of home, in other words, is where the working man and *woman* are free, not because it is private but precisely because it is truly social. This is where he and she (and Bamford deliberately puts women on an equal footing) find recognition and respect. Home is the place where identity is discovered, and because in it you are free, the *complement* of a poetry of the home is a poetry of nature, where, in solitude this time, the same expansion and sense of autonomy can be gained. The use of pastoral is often seen as a way of gaining middle-class recognition: it may have been, but it was also a way of asserting independence, a way of using the democratic space of the visual to order one's relations to the world both in space and time. This may be why so many pastoral poems move from the local scene and affiliations into history, reworking national history and reconstructing it into a new explanatory myth which accounted for the lives of the artisan. Such myths emancipated poets from the confines of their immediate conditions. Fox's belief that the poor should write of the factory and the workhouse is humane but restricting: Bamford, for instance, brought up in a workhouse, did not write poems about it. The myths evolved were not, except in a few cases, the unifying national myths envisaged by the Tennyson group: they were forms of explanation which included working-class writers in the past.

  Elijah Ridings, one of the prolific Bamford group in Manchester which included Charles Swain and Thomas Cleaver as well as Prince and Rogerson, provides a good example of the way a poet could move from home to history to pastoral in a single poem in 'The Remembrance – or, The Englishman's Home'.[42] He begins with the explicit intention of making poetry of his early home – its hams, flitches of bacon and fresh oat cakes – thus bringing not only an atavistic delight but also the 'social love' of home into the public sphere.[43] The poem is part autobiography, part a history of the autodidact's reading – 'Sweet is thy pastoral pipe, Theocritus' – and part admonitory political commentary.[44] It argues that England's laws are sufficient to protect the working-class 'freeman' now that reform has been achieved: 'the good old laws' are 'a guarantee of justice unto me', and thus there is no need for the 'faction' of Chartism to claim the rights of the aristocracy.[45] This conservatism is more complicated than it looks, however, and less trustingly bland. Reformist extremism, he argues, divides the solidarity of the working class. In early reforming campaigns, 'Many forsook *us* [my emphasis] for the other side', the side of reactionary conservatism.[46] Ridings establishes the myth of the independent 'freeman' in order to mute class conflict, but he was aware of the ideological cost of this position. Another poem, 'The Return: or, The Temptation', uses a remarkable Goethe-like Faustian dialogue between a poet and Mephistopheles to argue a conservative position which is constantly deconstructed by Mephistopheles. When the poet asserts his commitment to religious truth, Mephistopheles argues that this is a form of mystification which lays the way open for exploitation, because religious institutions live off the poor man's labour as much as any others: with considerable sophistication, religious truth becomes at once the apple of temptation and the classical fruit which turns to ashes.

> While man is seeking for religious truth,
> Which, like the apples on Asphaltes' lake,
> When tasted, change to ashes in the mouth,
> The cunning priests are revelling in the sweets
> His labour hath produced. Ah! simple man![47]

The poet has no other answer to give than that he will *be* a simple man, knowing the ideological risks he is taking. This poem, uncannily resembling Clough's *Dipsychus*, and roughly contemporary with it, has a more sophisticated understanding of ideological choice than that poem.

Like Elijah Ridings John Critchley Prince explicitly warns against violence, faction and the 'anarchy' of 'Judas-like' demagogic leadership, often in Miltonic rhetoric of which these impressive lines are an example: 'Awake!/In pity to yourselves, beware/Of battle-breathing knaves,/Who raise their voices in the air/To congregated slaves' ('A Call to the People').[48] His strong support for Victoria ('My Country and My Queen'), his campaign of temperance poetry, his advice to 'Labour' to work through education and intellectual progress in concert with economic progress, all suggest a cautious conservatism which deprecates change: 'Commerce, send out thy multifarious prow/Laden with goodly things for every land;/Labour, uplift thy sorrow-shaded brow,/Put forth thy strength of intellect, and hand,/And plenty, peace, and joy may round thy homes expand' ('A Rhyme for the Time', 1847).[49] But both Ridings and Prince saw fundamental social change as a utopian possibility. In 'The Remembrance', Ridings envisages a new economic arrangement which will enable a just expenditure among both governors and governed, so that all 'live on what the people can afford'.[50] Prince considers the redistribution of wealth to provide resources for the poor. In 'An Appeal on behalf of the Uneducated', he writes, 'Give back a portion of your ample store,/To purchase wholesome knowledge for the poor'.[51] That this is not mere charity can be seen from his 'The Waste of War' (1855), where he writes in a visionary rhetoric of the cost of war, which could (with reminiscences of *Lear*) 'clothe each ragged wretch', and finance land, homes, schooling and higher education and art: 'Give me the gold that War has cost,/In countless shocks of feud and fray,/The wasted skill, the labour lost,/The mental treasure thrown away'.[52]

In the context of such thought, what has been described as the escapist and 'Parnassian', consciously literary poetry of pastoral and rural retreat, can serve a number of purposes. It can be, and generally is, a retreat, but pastoral always presupposes the existing world, against which its conventions are measured – what Prince recognised as the 'degrading', 'brutalising' condition of industrial exploitation in 'An Appeal' – and thus it has the function of critique simultaneously with its idealisations. In Prince's 'The Poet's Sabbath', the outworn eighteenth-century poetic diction is used to stress two things – space and abundance. 'My foot is on the mountains, – I am free,/And buoyant as the winds that round me blow!', he writes, hinting at Wordsworth.[53] The poem gradually unfolds two kinds of space; one space is natural space, but space as a spontaneously *constructed* architecture which provides boundless protection, support and the foundations of a natural 'home'. The conventional words of poetic diction, 'dome', 'canopy', 'enamelled floor' and 'pavement', are reconfigured to describe a bright and incandescent world which is also constructed from mobile and changing elements:

> Man cannot stand beneath a loftier dome
> Than this cerulean canopy of light –
> The ETERNAL'S vast, immeasurable home,
> Lovely by day, and wonderful by night!
> Than this enamelled floor, so greenly bright,
> A richer pavement man hath never trod;
> He cannot gaze upon a holier sight
> Than fleeting cloud, fresh wave, and fruitful sod –
> Leaves of that boundless book, writ by the hand of God![54]

Humanly made space, on the other hand, is shaped by 'gigantic Commerce', its proliferating constructions subordinated to the needs of wealth: 'As yet gigantic Commerce had not built/Cities and towers, and palaces of pride'. Prince populates these buildings with a 'throng' of personified figures which become a dehumanised and abstract list of psychological, moral and physical conditions – 'Crime and Remorse, Disease, Despair, and Pain'. Not homes, but 'vast abodes', impersonal spaces, these are nevertheless overcrowded and claustrophobic, containing shocking and arbitrary contrasts – 'Where Wealth and Indigence stand side by side'.[55] These abstractions are given intense life because the sound affinities weld words together as if in a cause–effect pairing: wretchedness/wealth: guilt/indigence. The opposite of 'gigantic Commerce' with its proliferation of 'wretchedness' in proportion to 'Wealth', is 'spontaneous Plenty'. Plenty, encompassing as it does the products of the natural world and the creations of human labour, is a generative and fertilising agency for Prince and points to an unalienated condition of 'mighty brotherhood'. Plenty distributes riches to the 'universal feast' with 'equal hand': another subtle reactivation of poetic diction takes place here; 'equal' has the primary meaning of 'impartial' or 'just', but these meanings call up the political sense of 'equal', suggesting the social arrangements most likely to produce 'Plenty'. Plenty's equal *hand*, another eighteenth-century metonymy, also reminds us that, however 'spontaneous', plenty is both produced and directed by human agency, produced by the worker or the 'hand', distributed through human powers. Prince's diction discloses a fecund, active and mobile world, a natural, unrestricted wealth and productivity constantly reproaching by implication the economy of the world of 'Commerce'. It is interesting that he was attracted to Keats's poetry, which he discovered as a mature poet. He characterised Keats's work as 'luscious', and its sense of abundance and commitment to *pleasure* clearly attracted him.[56]

It is easy to assume that this poetry is caught up in a hegemonic literary language which conspires to perpetuate the very oppressions it attempts to undermine. But on the contrary one is aware of a constant struggle with a medium of poetic diction, and the attempt to use its authority at the same time as wresting from it the potential for critique and above all, perhaps less expectedly, the possibility of *pleasure*. It is as if the capacity for mental and physical pleasure is what really assures these poets of their capacity to emancipate themselves from the conditions and limits forced upon them and to vindicate themselves as men. The pleasure is a pleasure of resistance. It affirms 'brotherhood' and dignity (and even the dignity of women – Ridings and Bamford celebrate the powers of women[57]). To the extent that he saw the importance of pleasure, Arnold was right about the needs of the complaining 'millions' of men – but he did not see that struggle was bound up in pleasure. Pleasure was an index of the capacity to overcome the indignity of Burke's description of the labouring classes as – a description Bamford remembered bitterly – the 'swinish multitude'.[58]

It becomes possible to discriminate the politics of these pastorals from poet to poet. Prince writes in the tradition of John Nicholson, an earlier poet, whose *Airedale in Ancient Times* (1825) celebrated an idealised heroic past, and an age where the feudal bounty of the 'lib'ral lord' ensured the absence of poverty – 'At little rent some acres each possess'd'.[59] Like Prince's, it is a world of natural fecundity: 'And plum trees bended with the sable store'. The 'ills which crowded population brings' are absent.[60] But unlike Prince's world it is ordered from above. Valleys 'smile' with 'Commerce', which is allied with the natural world rather than in opposition to it.[61] And, significantly, the landscape is described in terms of the aristocratic Burkean sublime, becoming itself an aristocratic habitat: 'Projecting masses to the clouds are pil'd,/And grandeur revels in her palace wild'.[62] In other poems Nicholson writes of the evils of poaching ('The Poacher') and the suffering of the poor in the workhouse ('On Visiting a Workhouse'), suffering created not by social conditions but by family neglect.[63] William Heaton's much later *The Flowers of Calder Dale* (1847), written very much in imitation of Nicholson, repeats the celebration of commerce and order, but with an intense unease: where Nicholson saw hierarchy and stability, Heaton portrays a threatening world, where rocks, no longer sublime, are 'haggard' and 'furrow'd', where the 'bright golden bloom' of the furze is counteracted by – a disturbing chiasmus – the 'sear buds' of the broom. An emblematic *'naked'* tree signifies the transformations of age – 'burthened with care'.[64] It is not difficult to find the source of Heaton's disquiet: insecurity is figured through the loss of *home*; one of his most impressive poems is 'The Emigrant's Farewell' – 'I am bound o'er the salt wave to a foreign land'. The resonance of 'bound', which calls out the meaning of purposeful action *and* enforced action, is characteristic of Heaton, who stresses the verb 'must' throughout his first stanza – 'Farewell to the place of my birth! I must leave thee;/The ship's on the wave that must bear me away'. The ship's sails, associated with authority as well as with the inexorable necessities of the tides, 'forbid' the exile to stay.[65] Arnold's 'estranging' sea is here given a social as well as an existential meaning. Heaton wrote poems to the conservative figures of popular imagination – Wellington, Peel's widow and Wordsworth – but the inflection of his conservatism is different both from that of his predecessor, Nicholson, and his contemporary, Prince.

The language of natural description serves many political and psychological purposes. Bamford, for instance, uses it to register struggle. His 'Hymn to Spring' asserts the difficult, but energising power of change as spring, with its 'storm-blown hair' reminiscent of Shelley's 'Ode to the West Wind', is welcomed: 'Thou bringer of new life,/Welcome thou hither!/Though with thee comes the strife/Of changeful weather'.[66] Rogerson, in 'A Voice from the Town', the title poem of his 1842 volume (extracted and called 'Nature' in his collected poems of 1850), polarises the remote dwellings of man and the luxury of the natural world and celebrates the 'delight' of 'rural objects'. He stresses both plenitude and sensuous luxury: 'The azure bells that deck the verdant hedge;/The primrose with its pale and sunny hue;/The rich-hued violet with its eye of gold,/Gleaming like jewels in a velvet fold'. But the luxury is also the luxury and artifice – rich-hued, gold, velvet – transposed from the ornament and commodity of the social world. As if in recoil from this knowledge, the bare trees seem to him to be 'animate', and 'Each branch hath seem'd a hand to supplicate' for the return of summer to 'feed' them with 'blessed', unmanufactured, natural sun and dew.[67] In yet another figure of the signifying tree, this poet returns upon the social world and the lack he had repressed and acknowledges the needs of those who 'supplicate'.

Even the cruder language and simpler conservatism of Robert Story, always anxious to keep 'the Spirit of Change' in check by the 'Spirit of Caution' ('When Freedom made This Constitution Ours'), whose account of pleasure is simpler and more moralised than that of the poets so far discussed, can light up in landscape poems such as 'Ingleboro' Cave' (1840).[68] Here he finds the natural riches and the illusions which do not deprave, the 'gem-studded ceiling', the 'columns of crystal' and the floor of the cave revealing 'A pure water-mirror that doubles the scene'. For

the most part, however, Story's belief that good cheer, pleasure and morality are natural and unproblematical allies for the working man, his enthusiasm for 'the old War-flag' (1854) on the advent of the Crimean war[69] and
his attempt to sustain the myth of merry England even on the battle field,
produce writing which is far less subtle than that of his contemporaries of
the late 1840s and 1850s. Consider 'Sebastopol is Low!' (1855):

> Hark! heard ye not these boomings,
>   Repeated deep and slow?
> 'Tis the voice of Freedom's triumph –
>   It is struck – the glorious blow!
> And all through merry England
>   Brave songs, to-night, shall flow;
> For the last assault *is* over,
>   And Sebastopol *is* low![70]

The war, indeed, divided writers with an allegiance to the working class
as deeply as it divided middle-class writers. Story, praising Louis Napoleon's coup d'état in an ode addressed to Tennyson, followed this up with
a series of poems on the war, which became at times as bloodthirsty as
the work of Gerald Massey: 'Saw ye the wave that rolled purple with
blood?', he wrote, in 'The Battles of the Baltic', in words which recall the
'voluptuous blood' of aggression celebrated by Massey.[71] The logic of a
rhetoric of freedom and united manhood which had consolidated Chartist
poetry seemed to some to imply the logic of patriotism – it is almost as if
the rhetoric of Chartism becomes pathologised in a literal war. J. B.
Leno, who worked so strongly with images of strength, freedom and unity,
celebrated the victory of Waterloo, an event which becomes for many poets
an analogue of the Crimea,[72] with a dangerous triumphalism. William
Heaton, on the other hand, wrote of the suffering and fear of a deserter
in the French wars in 'The Old Soldier' (1857), implicitly criticising the
cruelty of war: 'The snow all around me was covered with blood,/'Twas
the blood of the foe and the friend;/I made a retreat from the spot where
I stood,/For fear did my footsteps attend'.[73] Others, however, were far
more unequivocal than he in their condemnation of war in the Crimea.
Ernest Jones, J. C. Prince, Sydney Dobell and Alexander Smith, all very
different poets, opposed it. Two magnificent sonnets by J. C. Prince and
by Sydney Dobell suggest how strong feeling was.

> 'Tis strange, profanely strange, but men will stand
>   Upon some spot of blighted happiness,
> Where the Omnipotent's mysterious hand
>   Has fallen with disaster and distress,
> And they, perchance, will question His just laws,
>   Wax grave, and sigh, and look demurely wise,

As if, poor fools! they could arraign the Cause,
　And see with Wisdom's never-failing eyes!
But let them saunter o'er a battle-plain,
　Still red and reeking from the recent strife,
Where, spurred by lust of conquest and of gain,
　Relentless heels have trod out human life,
And they will prate of greatness, glory, fame!
　God! how Thy creature man insults Thy holy name!
(J. C. Prince, 'A Thought on War', *Autumn Leaves*, 1856)[74]

Last night beneath the foreign stars I stood
And saw the thoughts of those at home go by
To the great grave upon the hill of blood.
Upon the darkness they went visibly,
Each in the vesture of its own distress.
Among them there came One, frail as a sigh,
And like a creature of the wilderness,
Dug with her bleeding hands. She neither cried
Nor wept: nor did she see the many stark
And dead that lay unburied by her side.
All night she toiled, and at that time of dawn,
When Day and Night do change their More or Less,
And Day is More, I saw the melting Dark
Stir to the last, and knew she laboured on.

(Sydney Dobell, 'The Common Grave', 'Sonnets written in
1855')[75]

It is not surprising that those in and close to the working class should
have felt so strongly, and written so directly, about the war, for it was
their war. 'I passed some recruits the other day, and a man looking on
said "They'll all be killed, every man Jack of them. I'm sorry for it – "',
Clough wrote to C. E. Norton on 18 November 1854.[76] He saw the war,
coolly, as the primary concern of the 'peasantry' and the British aristocracy
because it was an attempt to maintain the hegemony of the aristocracy,
using the labourer to do so. When the war was won, he wrote,

Our Aristocracy will last now, I suppose, till another great War
comes and forces the trading and manufacturing classes to take to
fighting. At present our officers come from the gentry and our soldiers
mostly from the peasantry or at least the day labourers, much in the
old feudal manner.

(Letter to Emerson, 14 September 1855)[77]

Clough makes a running commentary on the war in his letters, partly
because he was related by marriage to Florence Nightingale. Arnold,

strangely replicating the doubts of *Sohrab* around the effeminacy of his hero, joked that the vanity of the officer class and their dressy uniforms would make them incapable of war.[78] Because they were detached from the immediate physical demands of war, Clough and Arnold were necessarily more aloof from it at the level of conscious discussion than working-class contemporaries for whom it meant literally life and death. Their doubts about manhood, battle and territory, though deeply structured by the dissolution of post-1848 Europe and its politics, were expressed as existential doubts, ambiguities and repressions which were constantly sliding into trope: they were real enough, but working-class response to the same things was necessarily more absolute, direct and immediate, and was expressed either as fervent idealisation of war or fervent protest and resistance. Only William Morris found a different way of dealing with these problems, a paradoxical way, which enabled him to write about the war without even mentioning it.

9

A NEW RADICAL AESTHETIC

The Grotesque
as cultural critique:
Morris

William Morris's *The Defence of Guenevere and Other Poems*, a revolutionary work in Ruskin's sense and probably in ours, was published in 1858, some years after the innovative periods in the work of Arnold and Clough. Yet Morris belongs here because like them he contends with an individualist and expressive account of poetry and dissents from it. But whereas they orientate themselves through redefining a classical tradition, Morris deliberately aligned himself with what might be called a 'gothic' reading of culture. This early volume, with its debts to Froissart and Malory, is often seen as an anticipation of the 'medievalising' mode of Pre-Raphaelite poetry which came into prominence in the 1860s; or its Arthurian themes are seen to assimilate it to Tennyson's *Idylls of the King* which began to be published in 1859; or it is elided with the relaxed prolixity of Morris's own later work in *The Earthly Paradise* (1868–70). This later poem, however, is quite unlike Morris's first volume. It is a cycle of alternating classical and Teutonic legends, and advises its readers to 'Forget six counties overhung with smoke' and to retreat into the past or to an idealised past. In it Arnold's poetry of moral composure and consolation seems to have modulated into a source of therapeutic beauty to redress the damage done by work in an industrial society. But *The Defence of Guenevere* is none of these things. It has no precedent or sequel. Its boldness lies in its seizing of the possibilities of myth and legend which had been theorised through the post-Coleridgean and conservative tradition and redefining them for a radical aesthetics. If Clough is the democratic poet of contemporary realism and Arnold the liberal poet of the history of objectified action, Morris takes myth, the most potent material for conservative poetics, and rethinks it for a different politics. A fresh account of work, gender, consciousness and language shapes this volume. In a deceptively simple language, without density, but with a highly energetic and laconic compactness, it is written with remarkable innovative freedom which extends to both metrical experiment and narrative condensation. Overlaying narrative with drama,

232

with internal monologue and with lyric and ballad refrain, it makes temporality and utterance problematical and enigmatic by exploiting the multiple disjunctions between different forms. Brilliance of colour and intensity of optical detail detach the act of vision and perception from other experience, force them into hyperconscious significance, and make it necessary to consider what the nature of *seeing* is. Where Tennyson defamiliarises associative patterns, Morris dissociates vision by aberrant distortion and selection.

These procedures emerge from a dialogue with Ruskin's social and aesthetic theory and in particular with his account of the 'Grotesque' element of gothic art, in *The Stones of Venice* (1851–3). Here Ruskin elaborated an alternative to Arnoldian positions. Morris, of course, wrote under the spell of Dante Gabriel Rossetti and was closely associated with the Pre-Raphaelite group: as a comparison between Rossetti's 'The Blessed Damozel' and Morris's 'Rapunzel' suggests, there are strong affinities between them.[1] But Morris seems to have cut his way through some of the confusions of Pre-Raphaelite thought, helped by Ruskin who, before he met the group, had defended Pre-Raphaelite painting in letters to *The Times* in 1851 and 1854, and had probably managed to give there a more coherent account of Pre-Raphaelite principles than they could themselves.[2] Morris's reading of Tractarian literature, of medieval texts, of Benjamin Thorpe's *Northern Mythology*, and his passion for gothic architecture, was given a political focus by Ruskin which is not immediately apparent in Pre-Raphaelite writing in *The Germ* (later *Art and Poetry*) or in the journal which Morris himself supported, *The Oxford and Cambridge Magazine*, periodicals which had a short life and a restricted coterie readership in the early 1850s.[3] But a brief consideration of the principles of *The Germ* and its relation to Ruskin does indicate where Pre-Raphaelite thought and that of Ruskin intersect.[4]

The Germ (1850) was prefaced by W. M. Rossetti's sonnet which asserts that the cardinal principle of all artistic creation must be to ask the question, 'Is this truth?' Accordingly, the aesthetic of *The Germ* has often been seen as a call for a return to 'nature', a claim made by all new movements, and, helped by a frequently confused and contradictory exposition in the articles of *The Germ*, one which it is easy in this case to dismiss.[5] W. M. Rossetti, writing under the pseudonym John L. Tupper on 'The subject in art', in the first and third issues of January and March 1850, seems to be having it both ways: 'A writer ought to think out his subject honestly and personally, not imitatively, and ought to express it with directness and precision; if he does this we should respect his performance as truthful . . . individual genuineness in the thought, reproductive genuineness in the presentment'.[6] This looks like an attempt to square the expression of an inner subjectivity with accuracy of external representation, and an idealist and a mimetic theory consort uneasily. The same is true of Dante Gabriel Rossetti's prose piece, 'Hand and Soul': 'In all that thou doest work from thine own heart, simply'.[7] W. M. Rossetti's subsequent gloss, that the piece is about painting what 'your own perceptions and emotions urge you to paint', rather than didactic topics, as a way of affecting 'the mass of beholders', compounds the problem.[8] But it is a comparatively bold and innovative attempt to formulate a number of new principles: to move away from expressive theory by attempting to extend a *visual* theory to language and poetry in general, to move away from the terms in which the 'subject' in art was being discussed by assuming that, just as in painting, no object is *intrinsically* more suitable than another for depiction in the literary text, and to claim that such an art has social implications – it can reach all classes if it attends to 'the semblance of what in nature delights'.[9] This was something the Rossettis never lost sight of. W. M. Rossetti published *Democratic Sonnets* in 1907.

The word 'semblance' denotes the shift being made in Pre-Raphaelite theory: it is a rudimentary attempt to move the ground of discussion from expression to *representation*. In *Modern Painters*, the first two volumes of which had appeared in 1843 and 1846, Ruskin insisted on the fallacy of mimetic fidelity to the detail of the external world; instead the educated eye of the trained and exact vision, a democratic vision because seeing is the fundamental capacity of us all, paints the *experience* of what it sees as faithfully as possible.[10] Such an account of representation makes self and world indispensable to one another and avoids the one-sidedness which gives primacy either to the human subject or to objects. Hence the rather clumsy attempt we have seen W. M. Rossetti making to hold subject and object in equipoise. But hence also his constant emphasis on the importance of physical, sensory excitement and arousal as well as mental excitement, on response to the external rather than expression, and his belief that any representation contributes to 'the general happiness of man', 'however wild' – even hangings and executions – as long as their handling is consistent with 'rational benevolence'.[11] Hence F. G. Stephens (also known as John Seward) could argue that 'Closer communion with nature' and 'exact adherence to all her details' was liberating to the eye because all that exists in the external world is open to representation.[12] His instance is early Italian painting, but such painting is a model because of its procedures rather than being a style to copy.

The reason why *The Germ* looks eclectic, holding together a Benthamite language of 'rational benevolence', a certain aestheticism and even an element of redefined Tractarian thought, can be explained by its attempt to bring the post-Benthamite and Coleridgean traditions together on the ground of visual representation, fusing the aesthetic of the poetry of sensation with a democratic art. It is significant that W. M. Rossetti reviewed Clough's *Bothie* enthusiastically with a real understanding of its project (he thought, on the other hand, that Arnold's interest in antiquity suggested that he was 'no longer young': Arnold was not yet 30), and that Browning's *Sordello* was vigorously defended – 'Read Sordello again'.[13]

The idea of representation through the visual and, by extension, the verbal sign, is the strength of Pre-Raphaelite thought. It returns to an interest in language which was the possession of earlier decades. For despite the very considerable production of theories of poetry at this time, the framework of expressive theory to which they belonged made form and language a curiously superfluous attribute of poetry. E. S. Dallas, for instance, democratic because he believed that the poetic faculty was common to all men and because a non-didactic poet 'is no preacher of the law, he reads no riot act', was constrained in his avowedly Kantian and idealist account of representation by his understanding that the poet projected internal experience into form.[14] Feeling comes first, expression follows as a secondary manifestation of feeling. The link between the manifestation of feeling in language and primary feeling is mysterious because feeling is involuntary and unconscious and therefore unknowable, a private, psychologised Kantian noumenon behind the appearance of language. This psychological account of poetry takes different forms in the 1840s and 1850s and crosses political and religious divisons. One finds it in Keble's Oxford Lectures on Poetry, where the pressure of feeling builds up to the point of madness unless it can be displaced indirectly into symbol. Language is seen rather as a barrier to be crossed than as a representative structure. In fact, for Keble language conceals rather than represents.[15] One finds such a view being disseminated in F. W. Robertson's *Two Lectures on the Influence of Poetry on the Working Classes* (1852). Because the source of poetic feeling is unconscious and 'uncalculating', it can only be given indirect expression in external form in symbol which is mysterious and ultimately inadequate, finding 'finite words for illimitable feeling'.[16]

Ruskin sharpened Pre-Raphaelite aesthetics by developing a notion of representation as the mediation between experiencing self and the world, by formulating an account of Grotesque art in a way which enabled it to open up possibilities for a new kind of myth, and by making the form of art materially dependent on the kind of *work* undertaken in a society at any given time. Art is a form of labour and does not exist over and against work. In a modern society, he believed, it is thus available to management and organisation by the state, as is any sensible political economy.[17] His thought enabled Morris to produce a book of poems exploring the modern Grotesque (for the Grotesque is not confined to its particular historical manifestation in gothic Europe), exploring the ways in which modern poetic form and consciousness are materially shaped by the form and nature of work in nineteenth-century society. Its medieval content, ballad and folk lyric, are not a simple proxy or disguise for contemporary conditions. Nor are they even a form of analysis conducted by the latter-day

235

reflective poet on naive material to expose the modern condition, for that would be to grant the poet a certain exemption from history even as he analyses his condition. As Walter Pater remarked much later of Morris's subsequent work, but in words more apposite to *The Defence*, this poetry uses that of a past age 'but must not be confounded with it'.[18] The poems are not concerned either directly or indirectly with work or politics. Instead they are an attempt to *be* the form in which modern consciousness shaped by work and labour sees, experiences and desires, to be what it imagines and the myths it needs to imagine with. Its assumption is that a modern consciousness needs to imagine the past in this way, not that the past will be a tool for analysis. For, as Pater saw, this 'past' is 'no actual form of life' but a sublimated form projected above but produced by the 'realities' of another historical situation, the nineteenth century.[19] It is significant that the last poem in *The Defence* is entitled 'In Prison'. These poems inhabit the enclosing perspectives of the modern consciousness which sees only 'the loophole's spark' and hears the wind beyond. Its reading of signification and the visual sign, the banners which flap 'over the stone', seen, but above and beyond the beholder, is conditioned and made problematical by the narrow loophole.[20] One of the conditions of the Grotesque, Ruskin says, is distortion, the gap between imagined possibility and realisation.[21]

A little more needs to be said about the Grotesque as cultural critique before *The Defence* can be discussed. The Grotesque is not a sign of degeneration or decadence. Indeed, it is the vital possession of a healthy culture and takes different forms in different periods. A key to the modern Grotesque is Ruskin's comment on Holman Hunt's painting, *The Awakening Conscience*. He rebuts the charge of slavish detail, saying that the Pre-Raphaelites aim to paint what is possible within the field of vision. But Hunt's picture, and the intensity and minuteness of its depiction (a girl starting up from her lover's knees as they sit before the piano), pose a problem, and Ruskin's argument is precisely that the picture problematises vision and makes it aberrant because

> Nothing is more notable than the way in which even the most trivial objects force themselves upon the attention of a mind which has been fevered by violent and distressful excitement. They thrust themselves forward with a ghastly and unendurable distinctness, as if they would compel the sufferer to count, or measure, or learn them by heart.[22]

One thinks of Galahad's vision of drops of melted snow on his steel shoes and 'bunches of small weeds' between the tiles of the floor he stares at in 'Sir Galahad, a Christmas mystery story'.[23] In 'King Arthur's Tomb', Lancelot measures the walls he rides past as a way of both remembering and of repressing memory.[24] The rider in 'The Little Tower' measures time and space by landmarks which are psychological defences but which turn into real defences when he besieges the tower, and ransacks the materials of the landscape he has passed to provide barriers and armaments.[25]

Such intensely perceived detail, however, has more behind it than the psychological justification by which we might defend, for instance, Tennyson's 'Mariana' (though it is significant that this, like 'The Lady of Shalott', was a key poem for this group).[26] In *The Stones of Venice*, in his chapter on 'The nature of gothic', Ruskin associated the Grotesque of gothic with a 'Disturbed Imagination'.[27] He thought it important enough to devote a whole chapter to it in the third book, and in his own very gothic, detailed and idiosyncratic way he makes it clear that the 'Disturbed Imagination' is one of the essentials for the possibility of a properly free, democratic art. He arrives at this paradox through an argument which is often misunderstood.

To begin with, his view of gothic is more complex than that of Pugin, who saw a movement from the pure morality of a nobly organised feudal society to religious decline reflected in cultural artefacts.[28] Likewise he differs from Carlyle; though he sees the ignoble form of the Grotesque as a sign of the decadence of Venetian religion, he does not concur with Carlyle in believing that there was ever any ideal feudal society of the past.[29] Gothic architecture occurs at a time when work and art come together, when the workman was allowed, within the constraints of the social organisation, a limited measure of freedom and spiritual autonomy. Thus the gothic may be a reflection of such freedom but it is also an art of *resistance* to bondage, of the religious principle and 'revolutionary ornament', a moment when the individual consciousness gave material form to art within a corporate social organisation and found a way of representing certain attributes of freedom.[30] Savageness, or energy, Changefulness, or a subtle and flexible refusal of the servile principles of order, Naturalism, or a celebration of fecundity, Rigidity, or an assertion of will and independence, Redundance, or a love of excess and generosity, are all possible forms in combination with the Grotesque. The gothic artist was in bondage, but could give form to this bondage in a way that the modern operative cannot in the division of labour – 'It is not, truly speaking, the labour that is divided; but the men'.[31] Then follows the frightful account of the slavery of the modern glass-bead-maker, hands trembling with a fine palsy created during the incessant action of cutting glass rods, so that work mimes and becomes a form of illness in itself.

It is the Grotesque which affords one of the few modes of self-representation for modern slavery and one of the few forms of representation in cultural production. For the Grotesque, springing from the imagination, is a form of play and the form taken by the play instinct. Because play is a reaction to work and thus a disturbance or movement of the mind it must take a fanciful or distorted form (the analogy is with the displacement of the Freudian joke). But the kind of play we can exercise *must* be conditioned by the material circumstances of our work – a typically paradoxical but logical gothic formulation which politicises play. It is not *free* play, in Schiller's sense. At this point Ruskin's divisions and subdivisions proliferate and often disguise the dialectical nature of the Grotesque and its ideological significance. The Grotesque can take a wholly ludicrous or fearful form and both forms can be culturally healthful or decadent. There are four subforms of Grotesque, which attempt to account for the organisation of work and the economic structure in different societies (free, aristocratic, post-feudal and capitalist–industrial or slave societies: though these are not exact, since Ruskin's point is that very different structures can produce equivalent forms of exploitation and that at times all four kinds of play coexist in the same society). Only two need concern us. There is the Grotesque of those forced to play, with the release of a kind of fantastic extremity in reaction to the captivity and imprisonment of labour. Such release, 'whether in polity or art', Ruskin comments, cannot be exaggerated in importance, clearly believing that this maintains the stability of the bourgeois state.[32] There is the Grotesque, always taking the form of the 'Terrible', of those who cannot play at all, either from pride in status, or from repression, or because they are 'utterly oppressed with labour' – like the glass-bead-makers.[33]

It is the last form of the Grotesque which preoccupies him, the Grotesque of those who cannot play, for this is at least a means of giving negation and oppression representation. This Grotesque is forced to experiment with the terrible in an irregular but mystified way, unable to explain it (presumably because oppressed consciousness cannot understand the conditions of oppression), and is characterised by both love and fear of God (dialectically related feelings, where lack is displaced and returns to God as fullness either of desire or dread). Extravagant and distorted excitement and intensity result from the apathy of oppression ('he is stone already') which forces itself to feel.[34] Satire and vulgar humour (the dialectical opposite of apathy) which *need* the proper aggression of indecency to represent the protest against oppression are further manifestations of the terrible Grotesque. The terrible Grotesque is the form taken by working-class protest. But in the nineteenth century, Ruskin says, it can only be represented in daily language and not in art because 'the classical and Renaissance manufactures of modern times' have 'silenced the independent language of the operative, his humour and satire'.[35] It is now only the *object* of study by middle-class authors such as Dickens. In poetry, perhaps, the work of poets such as Thomas Hood would be analogous to this middle-class research into the working class. Not a working-class poet, not quite Fox's gentlemanly looker-on either, but speaking for working-class suffering in poems like 'The Song of the Shirt' or writing popular satirical lampoons such as 'Miss Kilmansegg and Her Precious Leg' (1841–3), the story of a woman whose money takes the literal form of prosthetic aid in the shape of a solid gold leg, with which she is eventually killed by her husband, Hood is to some extent a ventriloquist for the working class.

The third and for Ruskin possibly the most important category of the enslaved Grotesque is 'diseased and ungoverned imaginativeness', and a wildness of the 'mental impressions' (one thinks here of the analysis of Hunt's picture). Disorder is the embodiment of the sense of failure and incompleteness of the 'human faculties in the endeavour to grasp the highest truths'.[36] It is the condition of the enslaved mind which longs for transcendence of the material but experiences an incomplete transcendence. Ruskin's comment that this is a distorted form of the sublime helps to gloss his discussion here. The sublime moment is an experience of annihilation in the face of overwhelming external circumstance, but is actually invested with power when consciousness comprehends annihilation as meaningful. But different historical conditions govern the sublime and the Grotesque. Logically the conditions of the enslaved consciousness call forth a desire for meaning, for a transcendent explanation of oppression, but oppression itself resists the recuperation of this condition as meaningful and thus a wayward, deviant and fantastic perception is substituted for transcendence, the more fantastic the more the enslaved consciousness strives to overcome its conditions. Indeed, the more consciousness strives to find a norm or an ideal by which the aberrance of the Grotesque can be measured, the more its correctives turn out to become distortions in themselves. The result is the broken mirror of perception, a vision 'with strange distortions and discrepancies, all the passions of the heart breathing upon it in cross ripples, till hardly a trace of it remains unbroken'.[37]

This Grotesque takes the form of the fragmentation of dreams (which are akin to madness), visions and the displacement of symbol which registers a gap between the symbolic sign and what it represents. The symbol is either iconographically narrowed and literalised (used as if it were a rebus – the example Ruskin gives is Jacob's ladder) or else the sign is estranged and representation is seen as the *veil* of meaning, a meaning we cannot reach or penetrate (we might think here of those accounts of poetry discussed above which make language the inadequate embodiment of inexpressible feeling). Above all the terrible Grotesque manifests itself in superstition and the paralysis of reason and the overexcited fancy in the face of death. For death, disturbing 'the images on the intellectual mirror', is regarded with fear and trembling, with fitful and ghastly images, by the enslaved consciousness.[38] An obsession with death is the logical outcome of the oppressed condition for which the literal annihilation of death is its counterpart, and in the face of which it has no means of transcending itself.

All these forms of the Grotesque can manifest themselves in creative or debased ways. The presence of the Grotesque in its 'full energy' is possible even in conditions of oppression and its morbid but powerful energy is the mark of a particular kind of cultural power.[39] But again, Ruskin observes, workmen in present-day England are only allowed expression of the disturbed imagination in 'gesture and gibe, but are not allowed to do so where it would be most useful'.[40] That is, it is not incapacity but the social structure which oppresses working-class representation of oppression. Caricature is the vestigial form of the Grotesque generally available. But this tends not to be possible for the working class. One could instance the prevalence of parody and pastiche in nineteenth-century poetry in endorsement of Ruskin's analysis.

The importance of the theory of the Grotesque is that it is a theory of representation based on a social and not a psychological analysis, seeing psychological experience as determined by cultural conditions. In its gothic proliferation and comprehensiveness, cryptic and idiosyncratic formulations, odd categories and juxtapositions, in its need to totalise and systematise, in its moral indignation, it is easy to see it as a romanticised and anachronistic analysis of unestranged labour, as Ruskin's myth. Though elements of Ruskin's work can be interpreted in such a way, this would be a fundamental misreading. It is uncompromising in its understanding that the cultural production of a whole society and its consciousness will be formed by the nature of its dominant form of work. It does not see art in terms of progression or cultural continuity or a disinterested ethical tradition to which a way must be found of giving access for the underprivileged. It is stark here in its understanding that in nineteenth-century England the working class have been inhibited from actively evolving a form of art which belongs to them. On the other hand, it is unique in its understanding that in oppressed societies art is possible as a form of resistance and finds a cultural space for itself by making the representation of the Grotesque a form of analysis. It is alone at this time in finding an alternative to moral or psychological and individualist theory. Perhaps it owes something to Hegel's *Aesthetics*, where modern art is made structurally dependent on culture, and where the disjunction of form and idea is seen as the typical representation of modern consciousness, but the attention to labour, though Hegelian in essence, is Ruskin's original contribution.[41] *The Stones of Venice*, with the two lectures on *The Political Economy of Art* (1857), where Ruskin was concerned with the economic consequences of the integration of art into state organisation, and particularly with the possibilities of trade-union activity, form a political analysis with a coherence which was not to be seen elsewhere, even in the later prose of Morris. Bizarre, perverse at times, this is Ruskin's myth in the sense that it is an imaginative and passionate discourse.

In what sense is Morris's *Defence of Guenevere* in dialogue with Ruskin? In what ways might it be a' manifestation of the modern gothic or Grotesque? For Ruskin helps one to understand the extraordinary nature of Morris's experiment. At the same time Morris responds to Ruskin with some important modifications of his aesthetic. The Grotesque makes for the double poem because it is the embodiment of distortion. The poem becomes intrinsically a form dislocated by the aberrant vision, which simultaneously calls forth as an absence the possibilities from which it deviates. The representations of the disempowered consciousness constitute expressions of a subjectivity. But since those representations become a form of resistance for the oppressed, resistance embodies critique, as the disempowered discourse exposes the limits of its perceptions in its struggle to find meaning, limits imposed by its form of life. Morris explores these possibilities. One would also expect to find, in an exploration of the modern Grotesque, the experiences and forms which are constitutive for the consciousness which cannot play. We would expect to see, that is, less the portrayal of the condition of oppression than its own *representations*. It is important to see that in *The Defence* Morris is not dramatising the conditions of a remote medieval society in a state of oppression but finding this notional society as the one which the disempowered modern consciousness *must* create. It is the Grotesque creation of the longings of modernity, the representations of and by the nineteenth-century subject. So *The Defence* is an intensely analytical work.

Of the three forms of the modern Grotesque posited by Ruskin – the forms of a predetermined and involuntary apathy, of mockery and of diseased and involuntary imaginativeness – one would expect to find only two in the work of a middle-class poet such as Morris. For the representations of mockery belong to the dispossessed and deprived. However, the middle-class poet does ventriloquise the forms of a notional past populace in the sparse, terse, laconic ballad quatrain and the persistent refrain which Morris handles with such virtuosity, the reconstructed language of an imagined peasant class. The operative is present by omission in this poetry through one of Morris's most startling metonymic devices. The overdetermination of the hand seen in dissociation and isolation, and with almost hallucinatory intensity as a virtually estranged object, the woman's hand in particular, is everywhere in this poetry. The blood half-transparent in the hand as it is held to the light ('The Defence of Guenevere'), the veins which 'creep' in the hand ('Praise of My Lady'), hands caressing hair, face, lips, one another, clutching, waving. The hand is invested as erotic sign and yet the hand is also the sign of instrumentality and agency as it manipulates objects, often objects of consumption, cups and clothes, holds shields or swords in disturbing disconnection from the body. The 'hand', of course, names the nineteenth-century operative on whom depends the leisure for the construction of this world of castles and towers and gardens, sinisterly emptied of the signs of servility except for the soldiers designated by their weapons as 'Spears'. The emptiness becomes so insistent that it constitutes a Grotesque technique for revealing repression. The modern Grotesque *cannot* represent the worker who cannot represent himself except by omission.

The woman's hand leads to an important modification or extension of Ruskin's gothic here. The sense of lack which returns love or fear to God is directed towards women in this volume as well as to God. In 'Sir Galahad' a compensatory vision of the divine is granted to the knight, who seems specifically excluded from the sexual love experienced by Palomydes and Lancelot. The poem can be read as the transcendence of physical love by spiritual love, as the lesser knights, who have substituted sexual love for spiritual, fail: the poem ends, 'In vain they struggle for the vision fair'.[42] Or it can be read as the disturbed and deprived imagination's *substitution* of spirituality for sexuality as the neurotic intensity of Galahad's longing is displaced into the idealism which conjures the Sangreal and its attendant and subordinated female saints. Sexual longing and desire are scarcely absent from the poems, experienced with a consuming intensity by men for women and by women for men. The void of pathological sexual longing, which empties out the consciousness and fills the self with a sense of powerlessness and loss is the organising feeling in poem after poem. These are perhaps the great poems of desire in the nineteenth century. For Ruskin desire is the central experience of the enslaved consciousness and motivates the modern Grotesque, but by defining desire in sexual terms and introducing the question of gender, Morris takes Grotesque representation into different and problematic areas.

The taboo on overt reference to sexuality is everywhere broken. A sign of this transgressive movement is the unremitting and exaggerated visual concentration on women's hair, let down and flowing, a Victorian code for released sexual feeling. The position of women in these poems is contradictory and paradoxical. They are disempowered and passive, waiting, longing and dependent on vicarious male action for representation or nullified by male rejection ('The Sailing of the Sword', 'The Blue Closet', 'The Tune of Seven Towers', 'Old Love'). On the other hand, they exert a curiously coercive power, motivating violence even when they are seen as objects of possession ('The Judgment of God', 'The Gillieflower' of Gold'). They are horribly punished when they assert themselves ('Golden Wings', 'The Haystack in the Floods'), but they are involuntarily the *distorting* factors in the social structure in a way which causes profound suffering both to themselves and to men. The cathexis of frustrated passion in 'A Good Knight in Prison', which forces an almost deranged perception of colour and detail as the bee on the sunflower signifying sexuality assumes a disproportionate intensity, issues in appalling carnage when the opportunity to escape occurs. 'Spell-bound' restages repeated phases of mutual longing and separation in the present, the past, the past of that past, in hypothetical, remembered and immediately experienced narrative which insists that mutual suffering is the norm where relationships are pulled awry and deflected by a 'wizard', the superstitious figuring of distortion as magic by the Grotesque imagination which can only mystify explanation and make it fantastic.

The title poem of the volume, 'The Defence of Guenevere', both a protection or repression of her situation and a representation of her case, as the two senses of 'defence' suggest, epitomises the malfunctioning of Grotesque hermeneutics when women's sexuality is defined in terms of the deviating and distorting element. Both senses of the word 'defence' suggest displacement and this is what occurs. 'God knows I speak truth, saying that you lie': a lie is literally a distortion, and Gauwaine draws out a corresponding distortion in Guenevere.[43] She claims that Gauwaine distorts the truth by accusing her of adultery. Her love for Lancelot is a pure love and therefore not amenable to such a description; but her defence becomes progressively more deviant the more she offers a corrective to the 'lie'. She struggles with the contradiction between the intense spiritual importance attached to the liberating power of transcendent mutual passion and the equal importance attached to loyalty in wedlock. The paradox of the 'pure' woman is that the more she argues for the intensity and beauty of her experience, the more she has to repress its sexual nature and the more she argues for the purely legal status of her marriage the less she should have reason to do so if there has been no transgression of it. The more she argues that she has not transgressed the more transgressive she becomes. She is forced into dishonesty and misrepresentation because of the contradictions in which she lives. Guenevere sees her parable concerning the choice between two cloths, one red, one blue, as the representation of the complete ambiguity of choice and responsibility in a situation where the chooser is blind to the implications of her choice: but they are rather a representation of the complete contradiction between one interpretation of sexual loyalty and another. Guenevere's monologue is not in fact about an awakening conscience but about an awakening to incompletely understood contradiction, and that is why it is the title poem. For in this volume it is women who are most exposed to the contradictions of the consuming Grotesque desire for transcendence.

The numbness of being experienced by oppressed consciousness is redressed by a corresponding need for intensity in proportion to its numbness. Pater, inadvertently expressing the very desire for intensity which is the object of Morris's critical analysis, writes of the 'sharp rebound' in modern art to 'the elementary passions – anger, desire, regret, pity and fear'.[44] In Morris's volume this is not a return to simplicity but a Grotesque recourse and assent to violence. Extreme physical cruelty and torture meet Sir Peter in 'Sir Peter Harpdon's End' when he becomes victim instead of victor in an unexpected reversal. It is the counterpart of the end he had planned for his rival, as the title punningly suggests – his *aim* as well as his end or death. His aim goes awry and the peripeteia of his death becomes less a moral reversal or the occasion of pity and fear than an orgiastic exchange of violence. The recurrent violence in the book is either completely brutal – when Robert is defeated in 'The Haystack in the Floods', his enemies 'ran, some five or six, and beat/His head to pieces at their feet' – or it is romanticised, like the violent death of the dead lovers bleeding from wounds on horseback in 'Concerning Geffrey Teste Noire' – or it is aestheticised in the pageantry of single combat marked by emblem and favour.[45] This is not chivalric but Grotesque combat. The fighter in 'The Judgment of God' is urged by his father to cheat by deflecting the gaze of his opponent: 'Swerve to the left'.[46] At the same time he represents single combat as a symbolic economy of simple and straightforward *exchange* between individuals, of blood for blood, right for wrong, which will terminate the endless cycle of revenge even though he knows that butchery will be the result whether he wins or loses. As if recognising the inadequacy of this analysis, his thoughts are deflected to the love of the woman he rescued from assault. Disregarding the fact that this was a communal rescue he rests his sense of truth – and identity – on the private compact between them, assuming that the public combat can be solved 'My father's crafty way'.[47] The breakdown of the ethics of single combat comes about from the separation of private from public ethics and identity: in the end the fighter's symbolic status does not synchronise with his actions. But neither can the private, compensatory lovers' compact be independent of communality or seen as a separate economy, for the lady was won in warfare, and belongs to the economy of public exchange, and, it is enigmatically hinted, belongs to the web of aggression which has issued in the duel.

Here Morris extends Ruskin's insights into the structure of oppression. The more complex the social origin and public responsibility for action becomes, the more complex questions of right and wrong, the more isolated the individual will become, interpreting all conflicts on the model of individual responsibility, assuming the paramount importance of his agency in the public sphere, which is supported by a mystified privacy. The model of single combat is not an adequate representation for the complexities of relations in social groups but it is the only one the Grotesque consciousness can arrive at. It is interesting that in the third volume of *Modern Painters* (1856) Ruskin introduced a typically indirect and two-edged commentary on the Crimean war. He acknowledged the importance of individual heroism and even appeared to glorify the crimson wave of carnage which occurred. But his main point is that such sacrifice could only be justified, not because it led to the defeat of the Tsar but to the realignment of Britain and France in the concord of civilised friendship and social bonds as their traditional enmity was abandoned.[48] The Crimean war, the first European modern war, reported and photographed and interpreted by modern media, turned out to possess a complexity far beyond the model of war as a single combat between nations, an understanding dearly bought by its carnage. This traumatic understanding is embodied in Morris's poems, as the Grotesque fascination with violence refuses to match the complexities from which it emerges. Violence is the Grotesque's over-simplification of the complexities to which the numbed consciousness cannot respond.

The longing for meaning, and the sense of the failure of perception in the oppressed state which calls forth an ever more wayward and pathologi-cal fantasy, mean that consciousness pours inventive energy into the vision and the dream, and into the symbol which either reveals too much of the literal or conceals too much of the noumenal. Representation registers a gap between sign and *meaning*. The protagonists of these poems in fact rarely dream ('Sir Galahad' and 'The Wind' are exceptions), but they are *in* the world of the dream. The terse, gnomic narrative is structured with the gaps, elisions and displacements of dream work, where objects are juxtaposed with startling vividness but without relational explanation in an unremitting and almost tiring metonymic intensity, isolated in space. Temporality contracts or expands with dream logic, a subsidiary part of the narrative suddenly assumes disproportionate importance, or it will be arranged as the interventions of multiple, fractured utterances. The poems inhabit an explanationless world, as actions, events and refrains mismatch with one another. The narrative of 'Concerning Geffrey Teste Noir', for instance, deviates from what seems to be the story of an ambush into a secondary tale of the discovery of dead lovers which then assumes primary importance – what really is 'concerning' the narrator is not Teste Noir but a woman's skeleton and the power of the woman both to disrupt and to confirm masculinity. That *women* die and become deeply implicated in masculine conflict haunts and disturbs him, as if the death of the woman's body signifies a special negation and horror. He remembers his father's horrified and horrifying reaction to the discovery of women's bones in the burning church of Beauvais, 'Between a beast's howl and a *woman*'s scream' (my emphasis).[49]

In 'Golden Wings' the causal relation between Jehane's departure from the castle, its destruction and her murder is never explained. The 'slain man's stiffened feet' of the final sinister line, protruding grotesquely from the 'leaky boat', may be those of enemy or friend.[50] The violation is presented without context, like the 'green' apples (another feminine symbol) which hang against the mouldering castle wall. Even brilliant emblematic and heraldic colour, the epitome of unambiguous signification, obfuscates and confuses. The insistent refrain of 'Two red roses across the moon', incorporating emblems of love and chastity, seems to bring opposites together and to assert the permanence of the signifying colours, gold and red. The refrain punctuates the narrative of a ride to and from battle (where routine slaughter takes place) and the return of a knight to his lady when he has victoriously cut down the enemies in their scarlet and blue. All the actions of the poem occur at noon, the decisive point of division in the day. Gold dominates in the last stanza – 'there was nothing of brown', the stains of battle, the colour of mundane experience, but also the colour achieved from mixing together scarlet and blue.[51] This, of course, is exactly what the slaughter has achieved, as the differentiating marks of opposition both within the enemy side and between it and the victors have been annihilated. The totality of annihilation which the dominance of 'gold' seems to require and the necessity for the conversion into 'brown' of all that is other to gold are immediately apparent. So too is the dependence of the refinement of the golden world on brutality. But gold, too, mixed with red, the colour of both love and war by the end of the narrative, would also become brown, and the *same* colour would signify both the alliance of gold and war and gold and love in a collapse of meaning which throws customary interpretations awry. Grotesque colour here poses a riddle of meaning, and Morris's poems often acquire the arcane and incomplete nature of the riddle, embodying the baffled and fantastic hermeneutic dislocation of the Grotesque consciousness.

'Rapunzel' and 'The Wind' are poems where Morris explores the Grotesque most elaborately. 'Rapunzel' shares the figure of the lady in the tower (Tennyson's 'The Lady of Shalott' and 'Mariana', as has been suggested, motivate many Pre-Raphaelite poems, indicating the intersecting circles of conservative and post-Benthamite thinking which Mill predicted would occur) with Dante Gabriel Rossetti's 'The Blessed Damozel', which was published in the second issue of *The Germ*. It is useful to compare the two poems, since Rossetti's poem works through an immersion in the Grotesque, whereas Morris's poem explores the Grotesque as resistance and objectifies it. Rossetti's poem rests on a simple yet bold reversal. Sensuous longing and physical desire are placed in heaven, itself a physical barrier, a golden bar or rampart, a bar which the bosom of the Damozel can make warm with her flesh, as in Keats's 'The Eve of Saint Agnes' the earthly Madelaine transfers warmth to her jewels. The lover, whose words occur in parenthesis to denote his separation, defines his separation in terms of infinite distance in space and time and the loss of a sense of materiality and physical reality. Rossetti, like Clough but far removed from his empiricism, is exploring the Tractarian orthodoxy concerning symbol. Ruskin, not without reason, had detected signs of Tractarian and 'Romish' thought in the work of the Pre-Raphaelites, and though subsequently assured of the contrary (the Rossettis were Anglicans) it is the case that this poem meditates the notion of presence and the symbol which takes the transcendent mystical body to be represented by the outward sign.[52] Newman had said in *Tract 90* that the material body sets 'bounds', like the Damozel's ramparts, to spiritual presence, and makes us think in terms of degrees of nearness or farness, unlike spiritual presence, which has nothing to do with physical measurement.[53] But the Damozel, who asks

246

for the intensity of earthly love in heaven – 'Only to live as once on earth/ With love' – is presented in a deeply physical and erotic way, and certainly makes the speaker aware of degrees of farness as she becomes unobtainable and distant in heaven.

The poem is asking in what way we perceive the mystical body through the physical body and how we invest the material with significance. The Damozel is literally invested, or clothed, with symbolic garments and emblems, three lilies, seven stars, a white rose. Her robe, 'ungirt from clasp to hem' both conceals and reveals her body.[54] It is only through material signs and analogy that the speaker can grasp her language, which is like the voice of stars, the song of birds, the sound of the bell, like and not like, concealing and revealing, steps on the 'stair' which leads from earth to heaven. But if these literal signs 'bridge' the gap between earth and heaven and reach the 'Occult, withheld' experience, there is a sense in which 'likeness' as an identity of mystical and physical simply returns us repeatedly to the material. The promised new knowledge is simply a form of the old, since we can only know through the physical. Hence the acute despair of physical loss which ends the poem: 'And then she cast her arms along/The golden barriers,/And laid her face between her hands,/ And wept'.[55] Once the physical presence of love is removed there is nothing. The poem is at once a passionate account of the necessity of the incarnation of symbolic meaning, when the seen guarantees the unseen, and a sceptical discourse on the idea of the transfiguration of the erotic by the mystical: there may simply be only the manifestation of the physical or the erotic in all its fullness. The 'robe' which is the physical body conceals and reveals nothing but itself. Thus there is no stair or bridge to the unknown, and the mystical body is a case of the emperor's – or Damozel's – new clothes, as the woman's body figures nothing but itself. Perhaps that is why, despite or perhaps because of its beauty, the Damozel can remind us of one of Rossetti's 'stunners'.

The problem with the occulted nature or symbol for this poem is literally a problem of *translation*. Because there is no reversible relationship between the seen and the unseen, because we necessarily start from the seen and not the other way round we are caught in material representation. When the Damozel is 'translated' to heaven, therefore, she becomes the more intensely perceived as physical and sexual being the more ethereal she supposedly is. With her disappearance the 'clothes' of the Carlylean symbol (for this is a highly eclectic poem fusing a number of discourses of symbol just as it fuses Crashaw-like extravagance and Victorian lushness) do not become infinitely renewable as, in the last stanza, the narration moves from the visible to the merely heard '(I saw her smile.) . . . (I heard her tears.)'. The poem ends with a parenthesis not placed *between* two linguistic structures but followed by a void. The intensity of affective diction – 'The light thrilled towards her' – seems to be motivated by an anxiety lest language should break down altogether when the last evidence of the Damozel's presence disappears: 'She ceased'.[56]

'Rapunzel', like 'The Blessed Damozel', takes the image of separation as its central figure, as Rapunzel's yellow hair creates a 'path' or 'stair', as the Prince and the Witch call it, between the tower where she is imprisoned by the power of the Witch and the ground below. As in Rossetti's poem, the body of a woman bears the full weight of symbolic meaning, but whereas Rossetti's poem is a discursive and reflective meditation on the symbolic conversion of the body, Morris presents Rapunzel's hair in mysterious metonymic isolation – it does not even belong to her as she is forced to let it down to the foot of the tower and turn it into a ladder at the Witch's instigation. The golden hair falls 'fathoms' below her, a word which allies with the 'waves' and 'ripples' by which it is described to suggest an amorphous substance out of her control. Like the iconography of Jacob's 'ladder' which Ruskin instances as a form of Grotesque symbol, it is seen with a narrow concentration and enigmatic intensity which literalises its function as stairway. Morris dramatises the fairy story in terse and laconic episodes and disperses the events between several consciousnesses so that no single perspective has authority. Rossetti's poem moves between two visual fields, that of the Damozel and the excluded speaker. Morris persistently triangulates relationships, seen variously from above or below by the participants – the Prince, the Witch, Rapunzel. The Witch's perspective changes constantly, magically belonging to the tower or the ground. Rapunzel invokes Mary and Saint Michael from the vestigial Christian tradition she brings to her defence: the Prince sees Rapunzel through the eyes of the court and through the song of a minstrel. The power of the gaze is not invested in a single vision but moves erratically as different perspectives intersect and diverge.

The golden hair, literally a mediating entity as demons or princes climb up or down it, becomes a symbol of mediation, but it is a fetishised symbol. The Victorian fetishising of hair as a sign of sexuality is clearly at issue here, but Ruskin had also used a related metaphor in *The Political Economy of Art* (1857) which is relevant. Speaking to a Manchester audience and using the idea of weaving as a metaphor for wealth, he talked of the 'golden net' of the world's wealth, entangling and destroying like a spider's web, or liberating when used in the social good. The price of anything never represents its value but 'the degree of desire' rich people have to possess it (in fact, he recommended coming off the gold standard for this reason).[57] Thus the net of money is a signifying system for Ruskin. The importance of the hair as fetishised symbol in the poem is not that it can be given a specific meaning but that it is implicated in desire and is substituted for different things in different ways. It is demonised as 'Devil's bats' swing on it like spiders; it is the object of struggle to the death as knights fight over emblems of it.[58] It is idealised as 'paths of stars' or a

248

'golden cord', or narrowly literalised so that it is used as if it *were* the object it symbolises.[59] Or it is seen, as the Prince and minstrel see it, as an obfuscating 'film' or 'veil' of gold, as Ruskin's Grotesque symbol which is experienced as veiling meaning.[60] The symbol becomes aestheticised, the opposite of literalisation, as the veil of representation takes on an independent life, creating reference out of its own distortions.

The minstrel sings of the hair as 'veil', as his refrain has it, existing ''Twixt the sunlight and the shade', made by the 'rough hands' of a warrior.[61] The veil is created by the illumination and blind spots of individual vision, but the gaze also depends on the immaterial but palpable play of light and shade in the external world. The song testifies to the complexity of the gaze and the meaning of the hair. The 'veil' of symbol is always, even here, subject to the individual's 'degree of desire'. The minstrel renames Rapunzel as Guendolen, and though she is liberated into a new language, naming the hare-bells as they become more specific than the 'blue flowers' seen from the tower (a subtle way of suggesting a new perspective), her name is imposed on her as much as the name of the Witch Rapunzel, which at least signified the double identity of light and shade. In the song 'Guendolen now speaks no word', and in the life of the court she is subject to the new social taboo of marriage.[62] The marriage is a protection, a happy ending, but an equivocal one. The Witch from hell forbids men access to her golden hair.

Rapunzel/Guendolen has the vision of the oppressed consciousness which cannot play. Even her tear is absorbed by the marble parapet's 'red stains' as if to emphasise her powerlessness (unlike the Damozel of Rossetti's poem who gives warmth to her golden parapet).[63] The Prince, too, though to a lesser extent, is subject. He can only gain access to Rapunzel when he has assumed the warlike identity urged upon him by his guardians in the 'council-hall', when he works rather than dreams. His identity, and that of Rapunzel, is created for him by the Minstrel's song. Even when he sings the song to 'express' his own situation he is mediating another's representation of himself. The oppressed consciousness's fascination with death is apparent after the consummation of love when he asks 'did you ever see a death?'[64] This abruptness is typical of the non-sequiturs of the poem, a curious question to ask after a consummation. Love and death seem to come to his mind as linked extremities, terminal moments which are the counterparts of one another.

Death broods over *The Defence*, a never repressed nemesis. The Blake-like, gnomic refrain of 'The Wind' asks questions of the life force and energy represented by the wind. Is it sad, kind, unhappy, in its blindness as it seeks out the 'lily-seed'? Its indifferent, predatory purposiveness seems to be not the opposite but beyond or the other side of the death wish, a pleasure principle without awareness of pleasure. This collapsing of opposites occurs throughout the poem, where all experiences, however discrete, are related in contiguity rather than difference. An orange, its juice, we later learn, like blood, lies on a green chair hanging 'with a deep gash cut in the rind', and it is not immediately clear whether the orange is an actual or a represented fruit woven into the cloth, art or life, for the dragons on the cloth 'grin out in the gusts of the wind', moved by action in the external world as if they may be living.[65] Memory falls into dream, love is displaced by death, as the inexplicable fantasy of Margaret supersedes memory. Margaret, dead under a bier of life-giving spring daffodils, seems to be associated with cyclical movement of the seasons, and thus with death rather than life, for spring is inevitably superseded in time by another season. Finally, 'in march'd the ghosts of those that had gone to the war', and it is not clear whether these ghosts are part of the Margaret dream or whether they 'really' approach the speaker in a waking vision.[66] In either case the ghost is ambiguous here, for a ghost can be the return of the dead or of the living who are ghosts of their former selves. Their heraldic colours, once painted by the dreamer, but now 'faint', and thus unreadable, are the antithesis of the brilliant and hallucinatory colour of objects at the start of the poem. Nevertheless, they are complementary, for a brilliant and fantastic intensity is one of the needs of the consciousness experiencing the faded sense of lack and numbness, of the person who cannot play, the male hysteria which belongs to the heart of stone. This, above all the poems, is Morris's Crimean-war poem. The ghostly return of the ghosts is a return from the death of war to a civil *society* of death.

Ruskin always insisted that the Grotesque was not a sick or degenerate form, though it could be under certain historical conditions. It is Morris's achievement that he analyses the Grotesque through its manifestations, simultaneously inward with and external to it, actively expressing its longings and at the same time analysing the structure of its determining conditions and politics. It is this which gives these poems the energy of resistance, whether it is in the need to break through oppression and escape as Rapunzel and Jehane of 'Golden Wings' attempt to do, or in the need to experience phenomena with extraordinary hyperaesthetic intensity. For intense feeling, grief and madness are forms of resistance rather than disease in Morris's texts. Thus he produces a double poem which both expresses and *reads* the Grotesque. Ruskin believed that the education of the eye was the essential democratic need, for 'the eye is a nobler organ than the ear' and through it we obtain or put into form 'nearly all the useful information we are to have about this world' (*The Political Economy of Art*).[67] He spoke of the distance of the verbal and the written sign in comparison with the ocular, though he was probably one of the first critics to think of the verbal, written and visual sign as texts. The Pre-Raphaelites are often thought to have brought the vividness of the pictorial into their writing, but rather they brought the problematical gaze of the Grotesque vision. Morris's reading of the Grotesque gaze is as much a verbal as a visual matter. The dream syntax and articulation of Morris's Grotesque, whether at the level of a single line or phrase or a syntagmatic sequence of narrative, require a double act of seeing and reading and are highly organised linguistically. Its simplicity is of the utmost sophistication because it is about misprision rather than mastery. His poems compel the reader to go through the processes of interpreting and relating, misprision and adjustment, actively, by refusing explanation and context for the transgressive and disturbing material they present. The associative process envisaged by Hallam and Tennyson commands assent and shocks by subterfuge. Morris's poems ask for dissent and shock by enabling a reader to see the distortions of Grotesque vision even while he remains within them. Popular, immediate, simple in form, democratically accessible, they nevertheless expose the 'ripple', as Ruskin called it, on the mirror. In this way they aim for the democratic self-education of the reading eye. It is interesting that in 'The Wind' Margaret is reading a text before she is so violently deflected by the dreamer.[68]

10

TENNYSON IN THE 1850s

New experiments in conservative poetry and the Type

FROM GEOLOGY TO PATHOLOGY – *IN MEMORIAM* (1850) TO *MAUD* (1855)

The gap between *In Memoriam* and *Maud* seems as decisive as the huge breaks and fractures Lyell sees as constitutive of geological structures in *The Principles of Geology* (1830–3). They belong to different kinds of history. To speak of them together appears to commit what Lyell described as the fundamental intellectual mistake of creating artificial connections between different geological phases by transposing the temporal sequence evident in one area of the world to fill in the break existing at the same time in another. All that they share is the fact of succession in time, and 'will therefore no more enable us to trace the signs of a gradual change in the living creation, than a fragment of Chinese history will fill up a blank in the political annals of Europe'.[1] Lyell's recognition of the culturally specific nature of experience and knowledge here is a reminder that *In Memoriam* and *Maud* were written in radically different historical circumstances. The watershed of the Crimean war, with the consequent reconceptualising of Britain's relation to Europe and of Europe itself, divides them.

Lyell's modes of 'gradual change in the living creation' are negotiated in the movement of *In Memoriam* itself, which uses the myth of geology structurally as well as absorbing its language. It is partly the incipient problems of this model which create a fracture that makes possible the new rhetoric of *Maud*. But this way of understanding the change from one mode of writing to another in terms of transition from the Tennysonian 'norm' of *In Memoriam* to an aberrant text, *Maud*, constitutes another kind of misreading. It is much more plausible to think of *In Memoriam* as the exceptional text. For this memorial poem to Arthur Hallam reneges on his principles. On one reading it abandons the poetry of 'sensation', which is the solvent of habit and the defamiliariser of ideology, and appears to turn towards the poetry of 'reflection' of which Hallam had been so critical. It

252

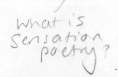
What is
Sensation
poetry?

seems to be abandoning the culturally marginalised status of the poet axiomatic to Hallam and making a bid to be 'universally agreeable', taking for its primary subject 'the *usual* passions of the heart. . . . Love, friendship, ambition, religion, etc. . . . matters of daily experience', all of which Hallam had deprecated in his review of Tennyson's early poems.[2] It even seems, with consummate duplicity, to be dealing with the 'usual' passions 'in a simple state', using without disruption the existing 'forces of association' which are 'ready to work in these directions'.[3] Hallam's death seems to have made necessary a memorial poem which would transgress all his propositions by dealing with love, friendship, religion (and perhaps even ambition). *Maud*, on the other hand, returns to the poetry of sensation, to an attack on ideological formations, to Hallam's belief that consciousness is constituted by discontinuous fragments of sensation connected by the 'ligature' of thought, to his belief that sexuality and libido are at the centre of existence, and that the image of the God of love in which man is created must mean that the intensity of love and passion is subsumed into sexuality.[4] And it manages to make all these things work towards a politics scarcely envisaged in *In Memoriam*.

But if *Maud* returns to the concern with consciousness (with its concomitant interest in non-rational conditions and madness) and to the concern with subversive conservative politics evident in the 1830s, it does so in cultural conditions which had fundamentally changed in twenty-five years. For one thing Hallam's marginalised poet was becoming institutionalised in the vocabulary of madness, as the controversy surrounding the Spasmodic poets, Alexander Smith and Sydney Dobell in particular, is witness. 'Rant', 'Bedlam', 'epilepsy', 'lunatic', were common epithets. 'My brain is whirling like a potter's wheel': *Firmilian*, a parody of Spasmodic writing, enunciates the connection between pathology and poetry.[5] At the same time, the clinical categories of the new discipline of psychiatry assimilated the language of literary criticism. Henry Maudsley's *The Physiology and Pathology of the Mind* (1867) uses a strangely aesthetic terminology, *Neurosis spasmodica*, for 'the tyranny of bad organisation', and associates linguistic tropes, punning and the double meaning of ambiguous words, with madness.[6] In the discourses surrounding the Crimean war there was a tendency to speak of both peace and war in terms of cultural pathology, and so *Maud* or 'Mad' negotiates political stakes in the definition of madness.[7] And since one of the signs of madness is the madman's belief that his account of things is self-evidently 'true', to claim the truth becomes a problematical act.

The trauma of grief in *In Memoriam* occasions the madness of contradictory states in which 'calm despair and wild unrest' (XVI) are perceived to coexist, but this is diagnosed as a private tragedy.[8] Its public dimensions are generally theorised in metaphysical terms; or else the huge, impersonal movement of geological time is invoked both as analogy for the frightful break in continuity occurring with death and as a mode which provides, literally, residual comfort. For the geological model makes it possible to reconstruct continuities out of rupture itself, as the massive diachronic subsidence and shift of deposits from one era to another creates an 'economy' (Lyell's word) which destroys in one place and repairs with the residues of a former age in another. The poem, or at least the poem requiring a reading which is 'universally agreeable', lyricises the constant flux of displacement which is both undermining and reassuring. The sea's movement will 'Sow the dust' of the great continents of futurity: 'The moanings of the homeless sea,/The sound of streams that swift or slow,/ Draw down Aeonian hills, and sow/The dust of continents to be' (XXXV). In organic continuity seas sow dust in which the sown seed grows, the seed both of crops and future races and cultures. Geological process is associated with the marvellous and uncanny and yet assimilated into a seemingly reassuring economic pattern of exchange and transposition. 'There rolls the deep where grew the tree. . . . There where the long street roars hath been/The stillness of the central sea' (CXXIII). Here the equanimity of exchange is satisfying because of its not-quite-symmetry; sea supersedes tree, city supersedes sea, and though the 'roars' of the street carry a residual sound deposit from the 'roll' of the deep the tree carried along in s(tree)t is not quite recuperated, and not quite suppressed, by the city. Continuity and displacement achieve an always precarious but just demonstrable equipoise. Thus although the text repudiates the facile economy of loss and gain, refusing to see loss as an investment recuperated in the future, the 'far-off *interest* [my emphasis] of tears' (I), there is, or seems to be, to use Freud's words, an 'economics of pain' in mourning equivalent to the consolatory redistributions of the earth's matter in geological process.[9] The self's relationship to the world is redistributed as it gives up, at some, though not at all points in the poem, a longing to incorporate the dead.

Lyell's writing, to which I will return, paradoxically encourages a grasp of slow process (though not a teleology of it) by describing the passage of millions of years in a way which makes geological movement rise and fall with great rapidity. 'If we are lost in conjectures when speculating on the ages required to lift up these formations to the height of several thousand feet above the sea, how much more remote must be the era when the same rocks were gradually formed beneath the waters!'[10] It is the extraordinary movement of this rhetoric which *In Memoriam* registers. In *Maud*, on the other hand, geology as fluid process and change has hardened and atrophied like Ruskin's stony nineteenth century. It returns in the local squalor of the hollow, pit or quarry where suicide or murder occurs and stones are human weapons. It is metaphorised as leavings, unassimilated shards, residues and the impacted stone of the nameless narrator's heart. Maud's cold 'clear-cut face', 'icily regular, splendidly null' (I. ii. 78, 81), cut like a jewel, or the 'glassy smile' (I. vi. 238) of her brother take on the inorganic attributes of the geological product worked by human labour. The profiteering grandfather of Maud's newest suitor bequeaths a coal-mining fortune plundered from labour underground: 'And left his coal all turned into gold' (I. x. 340). The trope in which coal turns to lumps of gold registers the troping nature of profit itself, in which resources become the subject of economic exchange and imaginary value. The organic world of natural growth is endowed with the imaginary value of inorganic matter 'turned' to jewels in a deranged ecology: 'A million emeralds break from the ruby-budded lime' (I. iv. 101). This reversal of organic into inorganic in the process of consumption appears in the crucial example of the exploitation of the poor: chalk and alum and plaster are sold to the poor as bread, and geological residue, refined to a spirit of murder, 'works' like yeast in the means of life so that a double exploitation and alienation of human labour takes place. The structure of the pathetic fallacy, which had attracted Tennyson because the world answers to moral feeling and emotions, is 'turned' or troped against itself. The world is seen in terms of the artefacts of consumption and the categories projected onto objects become themselves the dead products, the end of a process of manufacture, returned to an inanimate world and seen with a hypersensitive, narcissistic intensity. When the larger movements of the world impinge they do not belong to the impersonal violence of selection but to a 'sad astrology' and a Schopenhauerian universe of intentional violence and mutually antagonistic wills.

> The mayfly is torn by the swallow, the sparrow spear'd by the shrike,
> And the whole little wood where I sit is a world of plunder and prey. . . .
> We whisper, and hint, and chuckle, and grin at a brother's shame;
> However we brave it out, we men are a little breed.
>
> (Part I, IV, 124–5, 130–1)

It is tempting to associate *In Memoriam* with 'normal' mourning and *Maud* with the 'pathological' mourning of melancholia according to Freud's distinction in his essay on 'Mourning and melancholy': this can lead to some insights but it can also obscure the nature of *In Memoriam* as exceptional text in the Tennyson canon by virtue of its very struggle to normalise itself. Understanding the struggle of *In Memoriam* is a prerequisite for understanding that of *Maud*.

The great complexity and incipient collapse of *In Memoriam*, which is called a 'contradiction on the tongue' (CXXV), emerges in its attempt to negotiate the mourning process through two different and antagonistic accounts of geological process which are continually disrupting one another. Each is associated with a theory of language founded on a politics and a teleology with quite different implications for the love which the poem is so desperate to celebrate and consolidate. One discourse is represented by the intensely reactionary work of Richard Chenevix Trench, whom Tennyson knew as an undergraduate and Cambridge Apostle, and the other by the subtly conservative Charles Lyell's *Principles of Geology*. A 'universally agreeable' poem obedient to Trench's principles is fused with an uncomfortable and transgressive text which opens up the problematical nature of Lyell. A massive double poem is the result. I shall consider how this double poem works, or rather, begins to pull apart, and how this creates a movement from the language of geology to the language of madness.

Trench's *On the Study of Words* appeared a year after *In Memoriam* in 1851 and was followed up with *English Past and Present* in 1855. The immediate ideological purpose of these works was to consolidate an account of the national language which offered a coherent understanding of national consciousness and consequently a rationale for the approaching Crimean war.[11] In *Maud* these theories disintegrate, but they appear to sustain parts of *In Memoriam*.

Trench's paradigms are responsible for those parts of *In Memoriam* which the reader hurries over with embarrassment. But it is important to see how these embarrassments arise. For Trench language is not the construction of 'arbitrary signs'. He argued that language is Adamic, even though in order to do so it was necessary to resort to a casuistical revision of Adamism: God laid down the fundamental principles of language which were then progressively developed by civilisations, particularly the English. The permanent roots of Indo-European linguistic formations discovered by nineteenth-century philologists enabled Trench to elide the idea of the buried root with the fossil, with a store of underground treasure and with the buried fragments of bone which are a clue to the essential form of the Cuvierian Type, the universal structures which enabled early geologists to believe that missing elements of form could be constructed by extrapolating from the nature of a single bone. Conveniently, such a geological type can be assimilated to the theological Type, the universals which are a teleological guarantee of permanence, and enable one experience to be seen in terms of another. Thus the possibility of analogy and symbol also arises from the fixed and universal type.

Leaning heavily on Emerson, Trench argues that our language is not simply 'fossil poetry', but 'fossil history' and 'fossil ethics' as well.[12] Using the idea of geological strata to constitute a hierarchy of change in which the earliest meaning is the truest and essential meaning of a word, he can say that the legitimate or originary meaning is embalmed in history and sanctifies the concept of ancestry. Access to the buried treasure of meaning is only through the past and it is always necessary to return to a fixed and univocal definition in order to keep language pure. The store of language has to be re-stored and desynonymised to prevent the unfortunate tendency of words to possess a downwards social mobility, producing meaning which becomes a degenerate form of the original. But if the social and racial purity of language can be maintained by vigilance this is also a treasure to be exploited, 'more precious than the mines of California'.[13] Treasure is elided with currency as the circulation of the national incarnation which is language opens up new dominions and empires of meaning through developing its legitimate roots. If a language can degenerate it can conversely conquer. A rationale for profit and colonialism emerges in the rejection of the 'orang-outang' theory of the growth of language from primitive to more complex forms. The language of the savage is the manifestation of a fallen state. Trench instances the 'brutal poverty' of the language of uncivilised tribes (the Bechuanas have no word for God or thank you).[14] Not to have a language is a sign of debasement and degeneration.

To be with 'no language but a cry' (LIV) is a shameful confession in these terms. The yew-tree poem configures roots, names, stones, bones, in a painful effort to 'incorporate' death into history and language, and fails (II). In fact, the poem reverses into a critique of Trench's categories as death or its symbolic representation, the yew, disperses and rapaciously ('graspest') engorges language and history. Roots trap bones and reach out to dislodge the stone monuments which in their turn ossify the naming processes of language. This calls out an equivalent in the self-murder of suicide which longs to become 'incorporate' or bodiless. The extraordinary pun of 'incorporate' also yields an opposite but reciprocal meaning, moving from the bodiless to the bodily as it discloses the atavistic desire to incorporate the lost object in the darkness of the yew cannibalistically as part of the self. The Trenchian requirement to repress double meaning actually doubles it and 'incorporates' it in the pun. The brilliance of *In Memoriam* is its capacity to assimilate an investigation of psychogenetic, linguistic and geological movements to one another. To research into what remains of both geological and human 'remains' is the project of the poem. The research into mourning is a research into history and culture.

The investigation of Trench's categories is not always so complex as in the yew poem though even at its crudest the text is always in dialogue with them. Nevertheless, to Trench may be attributed the insistent desire to fix and stabilise in the authority of the Type. The typing of language extends to include religious experience, ethics, history. A Christian typology of fossilised universals is ambiguously conflated with the geological type and produces a new kind of bourgeois social typologising. Hierarchies of class and gender are generalised as universal commonplaces. The undebased language which is committed to 'fitting aptest words to things' (LXXV) in desynonymised purity is analogous to the permanent type of Lazarus's sister whose faith can 'fix itself to form' (XXXIII). The God who can 'type this work of time' (CXVIII) creates a progressive, linear history in which degenerate forms can be superseded and 'man' can 'Move upward, working out the beast,/And let the ape and tiger die'. This sanctions a conservative ideology which condemns the destabilising of faith and 'form' in the revolutionary 'red fool-fury of the Seine' (CXXVII). Just as the fixity of the feminine type is associated with the pure form of religious faith, so the immutability of class comes together with the fixed category of the feminine; 'Like some poor girl whose heart is set/On one whose rank exceeds her own' (LX). Conventionalised types reinforce convention, or seem to, such as the waiting woman of section VI, whose colour 'burns' as she awaits the lover who is in fact dead; 'she turns/Once more to set a ringlet right'.

Such quintessential bourgeois sentiment is endemic to parts of *In Memoriam*. Though Tennyson's negotiations with it are, upon closer investigation, arguably much more complex than they seem, the strategy of the text is to present such moments as if they are simple and unproblematic. A moment's thought reveals that section VI is an almost ribald parody, with close verbal parallels, of Robert Montgomery's *The Omnipresence of the Deity* (1828) which Arthur Hallam had derided in his review of Tennyson: the shipwrecked sailor is not saved by a God prepared to save the drowning believer; the statement that death is common is uttered by a suspect witness – it derives from Hamlet's Gertrude.[15] Section VI is a double poem, but the expressive idyll masks the satire on domesticity. The text seems to long for the simplicity it betrays.

At the time *In Memoriam* was published Tennyson became interested in the poetry of William Allingham and, if Coventry Patmore can be trusted, enthused over Allingham's *Poems* (1850).[16] Allingham's work is reminiscent of the Apostles' much earlier interest in fairy mythology and the supernatural. 'The Fairies' ('Up the rocky mountain,/Down the rushy glen') appeared in this volume, which also explores a much weakened aesthetics of the poetry of sensation. Allingham is fascinated by the intense image in the mind, by feeling, emotion and memory, but these are assimilated into Wordsworthian commonplaces and didactic 'contemporary' idyll on the modern situation. Class, work, emigration, the poor, the industrial scene, are addressed in poems such as 'The Pilot's Pretty Daughter' (another of the numerous 'daughter-category' poems which seemed to cathect Tennyson and other Victorian poets), 'The Music-Master', 'The Emigrant's Dream', 'The Train'. In fact, Allingham had found a way of domesticating the poetry of sensation and contemporary politics by eliding both in the pathetic fallacy, much as Tennyson was tempted to do after 1842, in parts of *In Memoriam*, and well beyond this in later poetry of the 1860s. His work must have seemed to ratify those parts of *In Memoriam* which can be associated with conservative readings of language and politics and, more dangerously, to provide a model for the future. The overt political statements are temperate and moderate, but they constantly transcendentalise

258

economic situations either by making them disappear into a 'dream' which is immaterial, or by escaping from them into a dream, or by looking forward to a moment when all difference will be eliminated in a mutual and reciprocal merging of antagonistic elements, the poor with the rich, suffering with mystical serenity, human emotion with the sunset and sky. An insistent vocabulary of fusion, merging, mingling, embrace, recurs in his poems, in which subject and object solve their problems by becoming inseparable. An instance of this is to be found in 'The Pilot's Pretty Daughter', whose 'Sunday Frock' and 'stout but no-way clumsy shoe' give rise to contemplations of the love between classes and the impossibility of the power of love to 'raise' the poor to another social class, almost as difficult as raising the dead through love. 'Raise' is used in both these senses in the last stanza of the poem. It is fascinating to see the work of the pathetic fallacy attempting to 'join' the unassimilable other, the poor, with the rich and the stars in heaven under the unifying term of 'stedfast truth'. The pathetic fallacy confers human feeling on the non-human world, anthropomorphising and psychologising what is external to the subject. Allingham tends to search for a quality which appears to be held in common by subject and object in order that different categories can melt into one another. Here it is the 'stedfast truth' of the stars which subsumes the differences between rich and poor:

> Joined in my free, contented love
> With these fair gathering stars above –
> Before whose stedfast truth it seems
> That 'Rich' and 'Poor' are as the beams
> And shadows in the river streams
> That soon will sing thee into dreams.
> So passed the Pilot's Daughter.

In Tennyson's poem social difference is not solved so easily as this! There is still the 'poor girl' whose lover's rank exceeds her own (LX). Nevertheless, Allingham's ability to contain the subversive power of the poetry of sensation by confining it within the idyll narrative of external event and converting it to description rather than image, his capacity to summon the affective morality of landscape through the pathetic fallacy, must have seemed a tempting proposition: it was morally and politically safe and reassuring. Allingham had all the decent man's worry over social conditions (and as an Irish poet he was particularly concerned with emigration) but without expressing any indecent protest. He was, indeed, more overtly concerned with social comment than Tennyson in the early 1850s. But a glance at 'The Emigrant's Dream' suggests how the aesthetic of pure expressive feeling, into which the poetry of sensation had been converted, sidesteps social issues. The emigrant, 'Smothered in a shaking jail,/Driven by the wandering gale', too 'cramped' and too 'free', dreams of a thrush,

259

which gives him fresh hope for a time when he might have strength to surmount his fate. Hope here defers hopelessly, but this does not seem to matter because feeling has been evoked. The pure, wordless music of the thrush figures the projection of feeling onto the world, and its reciprocal response, without the mediation of language, which accomplishes an unbroken circulation of feeling between subject and object. In 'The Music-Master', another poem which is concerned with emigration, music, 'that flows through sense unstained with its alloy', is that wordless feeling akin to love which unifies through pure emotion.

Yet whatever Tennyson's interest in the work of a poet who seemed to be adopting the strategies he was exploring in his own poem, *In Memoriam* does not consolidate the bourgeois idyll or confirm the affective morality of the pathetic fallacy. It does constantly betray its own simplicities, in the first place by subjecting the idea of the pathetic fallacy to a fierce critique and secondly by invoking the non-progressive, non-developmental aspects of the geological model proposed in Lyell's work. I have discussed elsewhere poems such as 'Calm is the morn' (XI) and the Wye poem (XIX) as enquiries into the psychological lie of the pathetic fallacy.[17] Here I shall concentrate on the double poem created by the use of Lyell's theorising of change, which is in direct opposition to the conceptualising of the past to be found in the work of Trench. The two epistemologies run counter to each other. Section LVI, 'So careful of the type', is the central poem here. Section XXXVI, following on the Lazarus poems, prepares the way for the evolution poem. It is at one and the same time a poem about the power of the biblical story to convert both the poor and the non-Christian savage (a thoroughly Trenchian theme), and a poem which self-consciously uses geology as myth to dissolve the Christian legend into Feuerbachian fiction.[18]

The poem carefully debates the failure of philosophy, truth in 'closest words', and even poetry, in comparison with the dissemination made possible by legend, which is not an élite form, and can enter in at 'lowly doors'. With the deceptive equanimity of generalising pastoral so common in *In Memoriam*, it moves to the celebration of abstract types of worker, the reaper, the builder, the gravedigger, without whose labour the processes of life and death would not be supported.

> Which he may read that binds the sheaf,
>   Or builds the house, or digs the grave,
>   And those wild eyes that watch the wave
> In roarings round the coral reef.
>
> (13–16)

But there is a subliminal shock here, disguised by a seemingly smooth compatibility, as the familiar tasks of native England are juxtaposed with the action of another 'native', the unconverted primitive tribesman in the tropics whose 'wild eyes' gaze on the coral reef in incomprehension. The coral reef was for Lyell, and for Darwin too, the only visible instance of continuous development in the world. All other geological remains are evidence of displacement and cannot be read as continuity. The coral reef, building living matter on the stepping stones of its dead selves (section I implicitly refers to this), can be seen as the single, but for this very reason, precarious, example of unbroken continuity in time. Hence Lyell's fascinated but sceptical response to the formation of coral as a living exception, a virtual aberrancy of nature.[19] And in Tennyson's poem it is this precariousness and the erosion of 'the wave' which is uppermost – so another poem emerges. The savage nature, like the Chinese history wrongly interpolated into European time, cannot be seen in continuity with the pastoral figures delving the native English soil. Thus the continuity of the Christian myth breaks down. And along with it the highly unstable nature of the subjunctive, 'may read', comes into prominence. The English builder 'may' read the Christian story, if he is literate, or interpret it if he is illiterate, but what the savage may read in his culture is surely an unknown possibility. The poem undoes its earlier assurance: truth is 'embodied in a tale', a legend, a fiction or a lie. Truth, which is 'darkly' or obscurely apprehended, is in fact set in opposition to the 'name' of Christ, which is a fiction which circulates in a culture as money, 'current coin', or a currency with a fluctuating value, in a state. This is not Trench's buried treasure of primal meaning but a signifying system in which language carries fossil history, but not truth. Lyell often thinks of geological remains as a language created by the 'author' of the world. But he recognised that there is a gap between the inferences we make and the empirical reconstruction of geological process, that the meaning we give to it is arbitrary. This poem proves the greater sceptic here, seeing the Christian 'tale' as a human fiction constructing language or the 'Word' rather than being determined by it. Section XXXVI moves to a Feuerbachian account of belief as the projection of human categories, and culturally and historically specific categories at that, onto the world.

The difference between Trench's fossilising and Lyell's geology is the difference between a naive search for systematic continuity and the theorising of change. The same difference is to be seen between Chambers, the populariser of geological ideas and Lyell, who is epistemologically sophisticated.[20] To put Lyell by Trench is incongruous: it is to put an infinitely subtle intellect beside a superficial populariser, and it would not be necessary to make the comparison were it not that the double poem of In Memoriam implies the juxtaposition. It establishes continuities only to fracture them by understanding change in terms of breaks and discontinuities, the very opposite of linear progress.

Section LVI, ' "So careful of the Type?" ', one of the climactic moments of In Memoriam, envisages the obliteration of the human species, the end of its history, as the logical consequence of the fractures of 'scarpèd cliff and quarried stone'. It registers the paradoxical nature of Lyell's geology. For Lyell's charting of the ceaseless subsidence, upheaval, displacement and transfer of the earth's matter turns all geological evidence into material remains, the non-volitional posthumous monuments of past process. It posits a diachronic flux in which we can discover the manifestations of secondary causes, but not origins, an economy which demonstrates a pattern but no meaning and teleology – except the one we choose to give it.

The meaning Lyell chose to give what Tennyson was to call 'the dust of change' was that of the uniformitarian, slow continuity of change itself through time. This view of creation is agnostic enough. But in order to demonstrate continuity he had to consider the nature of change and to found his argument on the evidence of *discontinuity*. Simply because of the fact of flux itself it is impossible to see the coherence of geological structure which has itself been formed through the operation of chasms, breaks and gaps in time and space. The like formation has been sundered, the unlike and discrete juxtaposed in the eternity of the past.[21] Add to this that at any one point in space and time, multiple causes acting at different rates and subject to different conditions are the very essence of change, then it must be that though there may be continuity we do not *experience* change like this.[22] Lyell reiterates that we cannot see change at work, cannot be in possession of the subterranean workings which suggest from the 'decomposition of rocks, and the transportation of matter by rivers to the sea', that 'new strata' are being built 'beneath the waters'.[23] 'It should, therefore, be remembered that the task imposed on those who study the earth's history requires no ordinary share of discretion; for we are precluded from collating the corresponding parts of the system of things as it exists now, and as it existed at former periods'.[24] We cannot learn 'the living language of nature' by our 'daily intercourse with what passes on the habitable surface'.[25]

Though the principles of Lyell's great work depend on the Kantian a priori categories of space and time for their foundation, the epistemological *effect* of his argument is to dislocate these categories from the ordering power of the perceiving consciousness. Because he envisages a world continually in a state of repositioning, a shifting condition of mobility in which areas literally 'move about', the perceiving consciousness is in a corresponding state of repositioning.[26] It cannot fully comprehend what is acting on it and cannot act on the immediate evidence of its perception. It is not simply that it cannot trust its correlation of perception with the world: it is not in *control*. It is in a world of non sequitur, constructing and reconstructing phenomena which it cannot know. In a thoroughly Kantian manner it has to presuppose the categories of space and time in order to *represent* the thing in itself which it cannot ever know. *In Memoriam* itself works as a series of discrete repositionings, non sequiturs and continual rethinking and new representations of loss.

The radical decentring of the subject inadvertently achieved in Lyell's text is perhaps what causes him to insist so tenaciously on the permanence of the type. He rejects Lamarck's orang-outang hypothesis as emphatically as Trench. The possibility of hybrids, the monstrous births bred out of 'promiscuous' alliances between species, is also discounted. It is *not* the case either, that genera 'are mere arbitrary and artificial signs' invented for the purpose of classification; inventions, in other words, merely of the categories of language.[27] Yet Tennyson's section LVI, using the evidence of Lyell himself, reverses this argument and goes beyond it to the final collapse of language and the 'artificial signs' which designate the human species and which are used by the human species to designate itself.

Section LVI begins by refuting the poem prior to it and challenging its argument. ' "So careful of the type?" but no'. It is not concerned with the arbitrariness of natural selection but with the conceptualisation of the 'type', here the biological Type, but implicitly the biological Type elides with the theological Type and the categories of language or a text set up in type (the word allows a multiple pun). Section LV had retrieved comfort from the preservation of the Type but LVI abolishes this. Here Nature gendered as female is in conflict with a masculine God who may have been a fiction of the human species. The point is not that Nature is 'red in tooth and claw', for, the poem asserts, man has always known of this aspect of creation ever since he set up the loving God whose creed contradicts the evidence of the natural world. What is appalling for this poem is that the possible extinction of man as species follows upon the collapse of the idea of the Type which has sustained the notion of man as a distinct species. The Type is thus one of the 'mere arbitrary and artificial signs' of classification and nothing more. The poem certainly envisages the end of man, physically dispersed as mere material particles, 'blown about the desert dust,/Or seal'd within the iron hills'. The mourner of Wordsworth's Lucy poem can at least envisage the incorporation of the dead in rocks and stones and trees. The *In Memoriam* mourner sees the lost race both as indistinguishable from dust and hill and yet forever unassimilated, 'blown about', 'seal'd within'. By implication, this is also the fate of the dead Hallam, whose death provoked the enquiries into the death of a species. By implication, too, the process of mourning is blocked by such thoughts and made impossible by the inferences which follow in the final two stanzas. For there is worse to contemplate than the annihilation of the species, as the question 'No more?' suggests.

> No more? A monster then, a dream,
>   A discord. Dragons of the prime,

263

That tare each other in their slime,
Were mellow music, matched with him.

(21–4)

Logically, there may be nothing to mourn. The fragmented syntax, in keeping with the disintegration of categories which is envisaged, implies a number of meanings: 'a monster then, a dream,/A discord'. Both man and his God, the syntax allows, are monsters, the hybrids and monstrous births of arbitrary nature, and partake of its violence. They are the constructs of an insane dream which is both nightmare and fiction. They are creatures of discord or violence, like the clashing of musical notes, and, the third sense of 'discord' implies, they are the aberrant products of a *grammar* which is itself aberrant. For the collapse of concord implied in the disintegration of the Type is the collapse of categories which make thought and the construction of relationships possible. If the Type goes, the idea of difference on which language is based also disappears. 'Man' is not only the phantasmal classification of 'artificial signs' but the very arbitrariness of those signs ensures their instability and collapse. The undifferentiated, primeval world of the dinosaur (here classified as 'dragons' with the slippage which would characterise the untyped language) was a world of 'slime' in which attacker could barely be distinguished from what is attacked. The ambiguity of 'their' slime registers an undifferentiated world in which it is not clear what belongs to subject and object, to self and other, or to the environment. The language becomes like slime and collapses subject, object, time, space and gender in the final instability of 'match'. The beings of the primeval world 'Were mellow music matched with him'. In a brilliant indication of what would disappear with linguistic difference, the capacity for making relationships and correspondences, 'matched' means 'compared with'. The primeval world would seem harmonious compared with, if we could compare it, what would now be brought about. But in another equally brilliant pun 'matched' means 'mated', and the syntax brings into being a chain of miscegenation which would be consequent on the disappearance of the Type. The dragons would be sexually mated with an unspecified 'him': for a moment the syntax even holds out the miscegenated mating of categories, of music with a biological existence; but it also holds out the mating of monster with the God which would be itself the product of monstrous birth, and the mating of the monster with the untyped, post-linguistic 'man' of the future.

Logically, there would be no gender, or only one gender, that of the male. Since elsewhere in *In Memoriam* Tennyson happily uses the language of marriage and sexual love when he is speaking of the loss of a male friend, I do not think that what is shocking here is the 'mating' of men. It is the transformation of sexuality into unknown forms which is at issue. Sexual and linguistic differences seem here to depend on one another.

264

When linguistic difference collapses all difference collapses. The poem has reached the state Nietzsche hoped for but envisaged as a remote possibility: God goes when grammar goes.[28] And when for Tennyson God and grammar disappear, man goes too.

The final cry, 'Behind the veil, behind the veil' perhaps restores the poem to a more conventional hope for transcendental existence and revelation. It can certainly be read like this, just as the whole poem can seem to be a comparatively orthodox lament for the disappearance of God. However, for Lyell the 'veil' is the physical world of the earth's surface, which veils further manifestations of the material world from sight. The hidden forms of organic life, 'though now existing, are veiled from sight'.[29] We cannot see *through* the veil, but have to construct possibilities only from what we know of the physical world, out of the veil itself. The veil is not a medium *of* representation. As so often Lyell sanctions both knowledge and nescience.

The manner in which section LVI veers towards a more dangerous poem than it seems to promise is shared by a number of poems in *In Memoriam*. This is particularly noticeable in two unnoticeable poems on the institution of marriage placed before and after section LVI, 'How many a father have I seen' (section LIII) and 'O sorrow, wilt thou live with me' (section LIX). These, along with section CIII, a poem envisaging union with the dead Hallam, will form the last part of my discussion of *In Memoriam*. Before moving to these it has to be made clear what underlies the preoccupation with marriage in the poem. It is not simply that the marriage theme prepares for the attempted resolution of marriage in the final section. Rather, that itself is a sign of deeper concern.

Throughout the poem, Tennyson experiments with what he calls the 'double name' (section CXXI) and a double syntax which yields antithetical readings. The poem tests out the extent to which language can be freed from the univocal 'type' of meaning without becoming deranged. His fascination with systematic ambiguity (the first yew-tree poem is an example already discussed) discloses puns where metaphorical relations are responsible for producing opposite categories of meaning. Pun and metaphor become models of the hybrid, the bringing together of unlike categories. The hybridisation Lyell took pains to reject turns out to be at the heart of language. For Lyell the impossibility of the biological hybrid confirms the type, but its possibility just as easily confutes it. The sexual model, marriage, the embrace, union in love, that which mixes, as the land can 'mingle' with the 'bounding main' in section XI or as the fields and farms of section CII 'mix in one another's arms/To one pure image [or metaphor] of regret', becomes metaphor for the possibility of metaphor, correspondence and analogy. The hybridising process of metaphor both stabilises and dissolves categories. It legitimises their integrity by making possible the act of comparison between unlike things, but the transformation of metaphor also becomes the miscegenated union of different orders of being. For an anxious text which longs to make the mourning process one which both slowly detaches the consciousness from the lost object *and* also one which needs to see the mourner fused with what is lost, the strange miscegenation of metaphor is as enthrallingly beautiful as it is dangerous. If it holds out the possibility of the union and transformation of categories just as certainly as it marks their difference, its unstable manoeuvres presage the collapse into arbitrary signs which Lyell had worked so hard to avoid.

The authority for seeing the manifestations of language as a model of the union of sexual love may have been Arthur Hallam's understanding of God's love as libido, the most intense experience of passion. The 'word' correspondingly manifests the same pattern as love itself. There was also a more theologically orthodox and more limited sanction for such metaphorical structures in Keble's *Tract 89*. There Keble naturalises and stabilises the theological Type by suggesting that though natural objects are so 'fraught with historical difficulties' that each person may make symbols out of things permanently existing in the external world, common symbols can exist. A symbolic correspondence and exchange of attributes can arise between a cross and a tree, for example. Common objects produce associations held in common, but at the same time each person will have a poetry of his own, a set of 'associations' peculiar to him.[30] Though *In Memoriam* often works to create a network of common associations around natural objects, however (we can return again to the yew as an example), it often simultaneously undermines the fixity of the category and the projection of human feeling on to these. Section CI, about the departure from Somersby, envisages a world in which 'fresh association' supersedes and eradicates those of the earlier inhabitants. Indeed, it considers a subjectless world, in which the remains of the humanly cultivated environment, beech, maple, sunflower and carnation, act and react upon themselves 'unwatched'. No agency or cognitive centre exists to read the world, as communal memory and (by implication), language, die together. We are back with the universe of remains, albeit the delicate remnants of pastoral, opened out in Lyell's text.

The permanence of institutions and the language which sustains them, though not often remarked, is a preoccupation of *In Memoriam*. It follows from the enquiries set in motion by the supposition of multiple change and the elimination of human culture which geological theory can support. Since marriage, betrothal and the institution of the family become major concerns in *Maud*, it is important to see what is going on in sections LIII and LIX.

Section LIII begins with a bourgeois picture: 'How many a father have I seen,/A sober man, among his boys'. But such a family is founded, if not on prostitution, certainly on promiscuity. The poem deals with the social implications of the following sections LIV and LV in a typically veiled and tentative way: if that 'not a worm is cloven in vain' no longer holds (LIV), and if of fifty scattered seeds only one is brought to fruition (LV), it may be possible to 'dare' to suppose 'That had the wild oat not been sown' the 'hale' patriarchal figure of the first stanza of section LIII would have been subjected to an enforced continence. His capacity to reproduce, not only sons, presumably, but the institution of the family, would be endangered. Because the premises of the argument of LIII actually *follow* its conclusions in LIV, and because the sexual meaning is encoded in the 'double names' of circumlocution – 'barren' soil, the 'grain' by which 'a man may live' – the implication that sexual health and the survival of the family depends on sexual activity rather than continence is disguised. There are so many outrageous conventional and unconventional assumptions here (nothing is said about the women who make legitimate and illegitimate sexuality possible) that it is arguable that the poem is in thoroughly disingenuous support of the status quo. But the 'green' man-hood of the patriarchal male is itself disingenuous and cannot but question the 'legitimate' family here by bringing its structure into the open. A similarly deconstructive movement ends the poem, which reads two ways at once. The daring thoughts of the poem are not advice to give to the promiscuous. Rational thought, 'divine Philosophy', can overreach itself and become 'Procuress', interestingly gendered as a female pimp, for male evil. This would be a suitably orthodox conclusion were it not that in Milton's *Comus*, 'divine Philosophy' is not scepticism but the divine reason-ing which sanctions chastity.[31] In this reading the strict philosophy of chastity itself becomes the procurer of prostitutes as the ethics of continence lead to their violation by being too strict to bear.

Section LIX, partly a pastiche of the famous lyric of Catullus to Lesbia, returns to the idea of marriage and the question of gender with the same ingenuous diction. Here the women's part, largely repressed until now, enters fully into the debate. Like the reckless 'Nature' of sections LV and LVI (which perhaps owes her gender to Hallam's understanding of the sensuous life of women as being outside the restrictions of rational male law), 'Sorrow' is gendered as female. But here she is institutionalised and taken into legitimate wedlock, 'No casual mistress, but a wife'. In recog-nition of the poet's absolute union with grief, sorrow becomes 'half of life'. But here the poem takes an unexpected turn, emerging out of the recog-nition that profound sorrow is allied to the play of sexuality. The poet is a capricious lover, whose 'blood', or sexuality, and faithfulness – 'If thou wilt have me wise and good' – can only be subject to sorrow's 'rule' if she is as gentle as a new bride. Despite the guarded and subjunctive syntax marriage emerges as a play of power relations which can only be sustained if these are self-consciously *enacted* as 'centred passion' requires relief: 'But I'll have leave at times to play/As with the creature of my love'. These words bring together both the onanistic nature of sorrow, and the wife's ambiguous status as 'creature', subject, possession, plaything and thus a wife who plays the role of mistress. The ownership confirmed by marriage enables the poet to 'set thee forth', to set up the woman with the status of wife, but also, the strange ambiguities assert, to set up the woman like a kept mistress in perpetuity. As so often the last lines of the poem read in opposite ways, splitting the nature of marriage into private and public domains. 'Howsoe'er' the poet husband may 'know thee' (and *exactly* how this private knowledge operates is left unstated), the external world can 'hardly tell what name were thine'. If Sorrow is a conventional wife the poet has taken her to himself so intimately that her name is obliterated by his: she now *is* the poet. If Sorrow is a wife–mistress her independent identity is dominant and escapes the patriarchal name which designates appropriation. Language and naming are now brought directly into relation with institutions. Names are not intrinsic but controlled by institutions, which control identity.

The sophisticated virtuosity of this poem with its scene of personification is more complex than section LIII. The exuberance of the Catullus poem is rerouted towards an exploration of the passion of loss which becomes libidinal and begins to displace the manifestation of libido. The contradictions of mourning, which require grief to be an end in itself, which envisage grief now as a capricious separate entity, now as fused with the self, which require a self-conscious theatrical drama in order both to sustain itself and to provide the superficial play which makes sorrow bearable, these are all released in this poem. It is about the impossible, psychic condition of the perpetual night of mourning, which can be neither fully assimilated nor fully detached from consciousness. One needs to beware of forgetting this poem about grief when remarking the poem about marriage, and of assuming that the double poem will always be constituted by one sophisticated and one unsophisticated text. Nevertheless, in exploring how the process of mourning is blocked when loss is internalised, the text uses the internal contradictions of marriage to pursue the implications of grief. And in order to consider how identity is transformed by sorrow, it concludes that names transform identity, but that names are not fixed except by the power of institutions, which are highly artificial forms.

I have looked, of course, at one of the points of greatest turbulence in *In Memoriam*. Though the conclusions reached at all stages of its movement are always provisional and divided, it could be argued that poems such as sections XCV and CIII resolve some of the difficulties explored in LV and LIX by assuming an ultimate transcendence. Despite the return to 'matter-moulded forms of speech', the materiality of language, in section XCV, the poet achieves a visionary, longed-for union with the dead.[32] In section CIII transformed poet and muses sail into the sunset with the strangely enlarged being of Hallam who is figured as Christ. However, the intrinsic scepticism of *In Memoriam* qualifies such events. And since such scepticism motivates *Maud*, which does not take the way of transcendence (for there the supersession of the self by the 'higher' needs of the nation in war is implicitly denied), it is necessary to note the agnosticism of *In Memoriam*.

The elaborate allegory of section CIII leaves the 'veil'd' statue of Hallam behind in the hall of the earthly muses as they move to the mystical reunion with the dead. But, with the ingenuous cunning which the reader of *In Memoriam* begins to recognise, the memorial statue is hidden by the veil of representation, the mythic being of poetic language which must constitute all we can know of human art and history. Allegory is also such a 'veil', and thus the poem offers itself as a representation of representation, not as an escape into a new form of experience. It is an enquiry into the way representation can reorder experience, fusing the human image with the myth of Christ's love. Like the geological myth of section LVI it envisages the transformation of gender, literally taking the problem on board as the female muses beg for a passage on the departing ship. Interestingly it is they who create the songs of history, and they who are capable of engendering a fruitful androgyny as they become 'lordlier than before'. At this point in the poem the artifice of names and the collapse of categories this makes possible lead to transformation, and to new myths.

But the gap between the transformation of categories and their disintegration is a narrow one. Section LVI threatens the 'dream' or nightmare of insanity. Madness enters the poem earlier in sections XV and XVI and recurs in section LXX. Insanity occasions and is occasioned by the disintegration of language. Just as in Lyell's text the geological formation returns and revisits the same place in a different context and another time, madness revisits the text of *Maud*, bringing with it the derangement of language. In a famous comment Keble envisaged madness as a consequence of the poet's failure to give expression to feeling. His solution was the attachment of feeling to objects in the world, as we have seen. It is as if *Maud* is a study of the expressive theory of self as madness itself, where everything reflects the narcissistic desires of the speaker in a delusory way. The pathological disjunction of the unnamed protagonist's 'will', a recurrent word, and the exploration of sexuality and marriage, however, now take place in a different ideological context and another politics. The speaker's narcissistic desire for appropriation, for Maud to be to him 'lovely like a bride', to use the words of *In Memoriam*, occurs in the feverish overwrought period of the Crimean war. It is as if the mourning process of *In Memoriam* has been arrested at its early stage and turned morbid. In *Maud* the object of love is simultaneously loved and lost and the speaker's grief and aggression preys upon the loved object and its condition on to a similarly destructive universe possessed istic movement Freud noted in the mourning which has both erotic passion and war are brought together in fever

269

The shift from geology to pathology could occur for several reasons. The unfixing of the Type which we have seen at work in both Lyell's and Tennyson's texts produced the condition for the disordered conjugations of a deranged language, as has been seen. Following from this the permanence of truth collapses, so that it becomes a function of solipsism to 'hold it truth', and paradoxically a feature of mania to believe fixedly in the absolute reality of a particular proposition. The psychiatrist, Henry Maudsley, points out that this is often a 'proof' of madness. (In *Maud* the asylum contains people who believe unshakeably that they are princes or politicians.) Furthermore, the structure of geological process could be given an analogy in the structure of mind, and this psychological structure could be extended to the organisation of a whole culture. Lyell's account of geological change in terms of discontinuous fracture, where the formations of earlier and later periods millions of years apart coexist on the earth's surface, bears an uncanny resemblance to Freud's model of psychic formation as a city in which primitive remains coexist with highly developed buildings of a later period.[33] Lyell's epistemology can sanction a discontinuous consciousness, factured into moments of being, constituted by gaps. Just as important to psychiatry was the geological idea of concealed process, the energy at work *underground*. Concealed, irrational energies not apparent to the rational surface but continually threatening to disrupt it work like the 'vitriol madness' which 'flushes up in the ruffian's head' (I. i. 37). This parallels and can be sanctioned by Lyell's understanding of the hidden processes of the earth's movement which cannot be known. Such a model radically undermines the idea of the integrated, rational identity, though, as we shall see, one of the drives of psychiatry is to make that hidden energy overt and rational; when transferred to the social and political sphere it produces an account of repression in which the hidden energies of the oppressed classes threaten to disorganise and overwhelm the state. In fact, the self and society are always in a condition of potential anarchy. The anonymous 'hero', driven underground in fantasy, imagining himself pounded by the traffic above a shallow grave (Parts II, V), continually attempting to 'bury' his melancholy (I. i. 75), is aligned with the violence of the poor, 'hovelled and hustled together, each sex, like swine' (I. i. 34), and the underground miners exploited by the grandfather of his rival. He drags even Maud – mad, mud and 'mine', as he asserts, the woman who belongs to him and also, tropingly, of the depths – to his subterranean world. At several points in *The Principles of Geology* Lyell considers what the world would look like to a creature living underground in order to defamiliarise accepted propositions about the nature of the earth's structure.[34] *Maud* sees what the social and political world of British upper-class life looks like from underground. It defamiliarises this society, and its assumptions, about property, privilege and sexuality. Ownership of the 'ground' itself becomes a contestable matter, a context not only relevant to class privilege but to the nature of war, which is a struggle for ground.

The dangerous energies of *Maud* have always been difficult to place ideologically. The reactionary violence of the attacks on the peace party and the xenophobic celebration of war in Part III are particularly vicious. It all looks like a conservative writing wildly out of control. *Anti-Maud* (1855), by a 'Poet of the People', a satirical pastiche of *Maud*, assumes that Tennyson (who as laureate after 1850 had a prominent public position) is to be identified with the speaker of the poem.[35] It sees the war as a ruthless attempt to repress social protest by deflecting attention overseas: 'Drown the clamour with drums and fife!' The starving poor are used as cannon fodder and resources are directed away from improving their plight into a war economy. It sees the war as straightforward ideological and material exploitation and oppression. Addressing stanzas 10–13 of the first section of the poem, it attacks their picture of the degenerate poor:

There in the by-lane foul, where the air and the water is bad
And fever is never away, – women and children are crying for
food, –

Drown the clamour with drums and fife! The sinews of war must be
had –
Money and men, money and men; the poor man's earnings, the poor
man's blood!

The laureate, who is not 'ready to fight', but 'merely intends to write' (stanza 21), is incapable of understanding the real politics of the war, in which Russian wheat is wantonly burned instead of supplying desperately needed bread (stanza 16). The poem attacks the irrationality of a position which advocates war simply because peace does not produce ideal socio-economic conditions. It charts the blessings of peace – homes, schools, churches (stanza 14), the spread of science, art and education to the poor – 'millions of minds were fed' (stanza 16). Its analyses are magnificently lucid for it sees above all that the war hysteria of *Maud* is a condition of *disease*. It is bred of an irrational fear of being absorbed into the filthy degeneracy of the classes it fantasises as 'swine'. This is why the first stanza begins with the bathos of 'I hate the murky pool at the back of the stable yard' and ends with the complaint of Echo, 'I feel very unwell'.

Maud probably ought always to be read alongside this anti-poem because it is deeply ambiguous. But it is itself a form of parody and this complicates its status. Gerald Massey's *War Waits*, a volume of orgiastically patriotic war poems, appeared in 1855, the same year as *Maud*, though some similar poems had been published earlier in *The Ballad of Babe Christabel, with Other Lyrical Poems* (1854). Massey had begun life as a radical but he turned to a violently hysterical celebration of the war.[36] There is an uncanny parallel between the rhythms of these poems, and their blood-drenched, pulsating, sadomasochistic imagery, and those of *Maud*. Where Massey assimilates the discourse of sexuality and uses it in the service of the discourse of war, *Maud* reverses this and fuses the language of erotic passion with aggression and violence. Whether or not Tennyson had direct knowledge of Massey's work is not the point at issue here. He could not have seen the poems published in the same year as his own. What is important is that there is an intuitive recognition in the text that the privacy of sexual experience, with its powerfully affective language, is linked with aggression just as aggression is linked with sexuality. The effect of these elisions is to politicise sexuality and to sexualise war, questioning the roots of violence which they share. Such language implicitly investigates the psychopathology of war, and simultaneously asserts that passion and sexuality cannot be free and exist independently of cultural and ideological forms.

Tennyson's poem works as if it is reconfiguring the elements of Massey's war poems – the blood, the flush of battle, the fire and rage and wine of war, the rose of England, the lilies of France, the sanctification of English soil, the print of battle, the garden of the nation and above all the energising throb, pulse and beat of heart and drum, all these find a place in the supremely erotic language of *Maud*. The derangement of categories made possible by Lyell's epistemology enters disturbingly into the love lyrics as they absorb the rhythms of violence.

> Maud has a garden of roses
> And lilies fair on a lawn;
> There she walks in her state. . . .
> (I. xiv. 489–91)

The speaker's dawn visit to the garden gate – 'A lion ramps at the top,/ He is claspt by a passion-flower' – picks up the movement and some of the iconography of Massey's 'A Battle Charge', adding the British lion to it. Beside the Massey poem the lion and the picture of Maud walking 'in her state' seem less innocent. Maud's 'state' is a garden, a patch of ground. Massey envisages the garden as a battlefield, a symbolic patch of ground disputed by warring states.

> We have chosen a goodly garden,
>   Where our old Red Rose may blow!
> With bloody hands, eyes red and burning,
>   There the living our dead laid low!
> Shall the foe keep his Bacchanal triumph
>   Blood-drunken, and dance on the sod
> That is quick with the Flower of our nation,
>   In the name of the most high God?[37]

Maud's 'feet have touch'd the meadows/And left the daisies rosy' (I. xii.

434–5). Tennyson writes of the blushing world of erotic feeling conjured by Maud's footprints: Massey writes of England's 'footprints red with blood' ('The Battle-March', 2–5: 4). The speaker's heart is 'Ready to burst in a coloured flame' (I. vi. 208), he experiences 'the new strong wine of love' (vi. 271), his heart 'beat stronger/And thicker' (viii. 308–9), his 'pulses play' (xviii. 664) and in the climactic garden tryst of section xxii, 'Come into the garden, Maud', 'the soul of the rose went into my blood', and 'My dust would hear her and beat . . . /And blossom in purple and red' (882, 920, 923). To name only one poem among many by Massey, 'The Fifth of November at Inkerman' (25–32) is saturated in the same language. The 'fiery tide of war' reaches 'to the red roots of the heart' (26). England is a Bride wedded to the Bridegroom of War, a rampant lion on ground where wheels grind and feet trample, drums throb to the 'red-mouthed cannon's fiery tongues' (28). Men fight in the 'gory red' and 'fervent heat' 'With a royal throbbing in the pulse that beat voluptuous blood' (29). 'O but it is a gallant show, and a merry march, as thus/We run into the glorious goal with shouts victorious!' (30).

Massey's poems suggest that war is a gallant show in more senses than one. It is the theatre of the territorial imperative of imperialism. It requires representations or 'shows' which stir deeply irrational impulses. The erotic violence which plays around the hysteria of imperialistic feeling registers a new phase of British expansion. Here the rush towards the goal of victory is the assertion of sexual power. It is fascinating that in *Maud* the Tsar is seen as a violent father-figure subduing an 'infant civilisation' with 'rod or with knout' (I. iv. 147) who has to be encountered with violence. He is the parallel of the rival father-figure at home who subdued the protagonist's own father and made compacts over the infant bodies of Maud and her lover.

Maud's alliance with Massey, the voluptuary of war, may be read, of course, as a form of collusion rather than critique which does not by any means redeem the poem from the attacks of *Anti-Maud*. But in another reading the poem does turn the language of madness towards a critique of the politics which actually engenders war and madness. It is common to avoid the discomfort of *Maud*, as the Victorians did, by pointing to its dramatic nature as monodrama. It is seen as the dramatic exploration of a diseased subjectivity. But this is to turn the poem into a restricted case history and to eradicate or minimise the politics of the poem by seeing them as the excrescence of madness. The double poem of *Maud* is not quite like this. Rather the critique is of a structural kind, turning on the definition of madness itself. The speaker of *Maud*, looking at the world from the underground of madness, is excluded and oppressed, or believes himself to be. He is the alienated other of the privileged world he longs to join and mourns its loss. This enables the poem to look at privilege from the outside, but more importantly the society of the Hall, its land,

273

possessions, politics, power, entertainments, is defamiliarised, and alienated: in its turn, other to the speaker. By making the speaker a madman,
or at least a highly disturbed figure, the arrangements of privilege come
to seem no longer natural or inevitable. They begin to seem the products
of madness. This is particularly the case as the speaker constantly argues
that he is the *same* and as *sane* as the people of privilege. But for the
accident of a financial collapse he would be like them. So irrational and
rational come to be elided. We are back with the obliteration of difference
and the collapse of categories explored so persistently in *In Memoriam*.

The definition of madness disclosed in the text assumes the elision of
the irrational and rational, as did contemporary psychiatry. Matthew
Allen, whom, of course, Tennyson knew, bases his work on the premise
that the madman is *not* irrational. He is like rational people. His writing
substantiates Foucault's claim, in *Madness and Civilisation*, that advanced,
benevolent theory in the nineteenth century presupposed the rationality of
the madman.[38] His treatment consisted of kindness, persuasion, training,
discipline and self-control, and the lure of returning to 'normal' life in the
privileged house which marked the achievement of rational behaviour. In
fact, his *Essay on the Classification of the Insane* (1837) is not so much a
taxonomy of madness as an account of the spaces the insane should belong
to according to their degrees of rationality.[39] Madness is a space rather
than a condition, and certainly not a criminal condition as it was in the
eighteenth century. He describes civilised conversation worthy of the most
respectable gathering taking place in his asylum, which is for him truly
the 'home' or place of refuge of its etymological origin. But this normalising
of madness sends insanity underground, refusing to recognise it as a category, at the same time as it makes the madman morally and rationally
responsible for controlling his disease, a disease, however, which is deemed
not to exist. It is a form of degeneracy rather than a mental condition.
Foucault is quick to see the contradictions in such coercive kindness. The
madman becomes unbearably responsible for his condition. He is forced
to normalise himself because other people are like him and he is like
them.[40] His illness is either repressed or forced upon him as the result of
biological, or hereditary, determinism which in fact reinstates madness as
a condition outside the control of rational discipline altogether.

Allen adds a further deterministic element to his definition of madness
which has the effect of dissolving it into a larger cultural situation. Madness
is a social condition, an 'over-excitation, arising from our mad desires after
wealth, fame, and distinction', with its consequent disastrous social failure,
the 'overwhelming miseries of misfortune, poverty'. Sensitive persons
become 'victims' to the 'modes and amusements of fashionable life'.

> still we have reason to fear that we pursue the important duties of
> civil life, whether it be the weighty matters of legislation, or the

scarcely less responsible exercise of the learned professions, or what ought to be the binding and sweet influence of faithful dealings in trade, and our common intercourse with each other, in an improper spirit, and from improper motives, and not with that singleness and simplicity of heart for each other's good, which alone is useful and safe; which we could not fail to do, were we sufficiently aware, that in as far as we depart from this purity of spirit, our views of truth must be perverted, and our healthy vital energies, causing fever, paralysis, or some morbid state, and all our sympathies poisoned and deranged.[41]

This elementary but in many ways admirably liberal attempt at socio-economic diagnosis nevertheless has the effect of pathologising the arrangements of everyday life – madness can be explained rationally from cultural derangement and malaise. The effect is to pass on the responsibility for madness to an ever widening circle of agencies and to undermine, or open up, the definition of madness. If madness is a morbid form of the norm, the norm itself is always potentially morbid. Madmen are disorganised rational people, or society is regulated derangement. Such a collapse of terms means that Maud's brother can be called a 'madman' when he perpetrates a duel because his rage forces him to violate the law, just as the ruffian wife-batterer of the first poem is the victim of madness because he breaks the regulative arrangements of marriage. By the same token, the first poem in *Maud* makes peace into disorganised war, and war into organised aggression or regulated madness. 'Is it peace or war? Civil war, as I think, and that of a kind/The viler, as underhand, not openly bearing the sword' (I. i. 27–8).

It is exactly such crossing over of terms which makes the asylum, the place where the mad are cared for, a *home*. *Maud*'s project is to negotiate contradictions of a structural kind which occur when madness and the norm merge into one another and become conflated. Questions of agency and choice become paramount as the madman becomes painfully responsible for the madness which is at the same time society's madness. If society is organised madness, how is power and legitimacy maintained and what confers right on legitimacy? The poem's answer is to explore the nature of the *will*. The will as the imposition of legal power controls inheritance, and the distribution of property. The will in the personal, ethical and psychological sense controls a biological inheritance, the blood and the nerves of the physical being with which the speaker is so obsessed. These two senses of the law or will emerge in the first poem. One is the law of inheritance which makes the 'old man' who 'Dropt off gorged from a scheme that left us flaccid and drain'd' now 'lord of the broad estate and the Hall' (I. i. 19–20). The second is the act of self-control: the speaker vows to 'hold by the law that I made, nevermore to brood/On a horror

275

of shatter'd limbs and wretched swindler's lie' (55–6). The freedom of individual self-mastery is set against the brute power which has manipulated the laws of property. The death of the father and economic loss are seen as impotence – 'flaccid and drain'd' – and castration, the 'shatter'd limbs' of the dead father-figure as a phallic loss. The 'dreadful hollow behind the little wood', with its 'red-ribb'd ledges', becomes a destructive feminine symbol, the condition of being without. It is not surprising that violence is implicated in sexuality throughout the poem, for the erotic passion for Maud is one way of redeeming manhood, just as going to war is a form of self-mastery, a turning away from mourning. They are both ways of reasserting the will. There is a supreme irony in the poem's title. The named, 'entitled' woman is spoken for by the unnamed, unentitled protagonist, who wants to come into identity and legitimate being through her. At the same time the feminine signifies a condition of lack.

By the end of the poem the text investigates what is involved in the freedom of the will against the necessity of what is willed in the inheritance determined by the law and by biology. The second poem of Part II, 'See what a tiny shell', tries to bring the two into relation, and fails. The first part of the poem prepares for this moment by setting up a false dialectic between the will to privilege and power and the will to self-mastery. The more the speaker takes on the responsibility for rational control of melancholia to confront the powerful order of wealth and privilege represented by Maud and her brother the more he identifies with them, reduplicating for himself the structures of family and ownership which exclude him, and causing further melancholia. The attempt at self-mastery leads him further into irrational isolation, but at the same time his obsession with the life of the Hall has the effect of making that life itself manifestly irrational. Because it is reflected into a pathological world it cannot be seen in opposition to the speaker's violence but becomes a part of it. And the speaker in turn becomes an extension of that world. They become doubles of each other. Madness is not a contradiction of the life of the Hall but a confirmation of it. The Hall becomes the mirror image of madness, not its rational opposite.

The topography of *Maud* strangely reproduces the spaces Allen advocated for the classification of the insane. Two establishments, sufficiently separated, but in the same grounds, were to house males and females and the proprietor was to reside in one of these. He was to inspire the inmates with a zeal for rational behaviour by admitting them to his company as a reward for self-discipline. The rational come to the 'front' of the house, the less rational remain behind and hidden.[42] In *Maud* the spaces that matter are those of the speaker's 'home' and the Hall. He retreats into one and longs for access to the other. Though the speaker is excluded like a stranger, viewing Maud's cold, clear-cut face in a passing carriage, seeing the flash of a bridle as she and her brother ride with the suitor, looking at Maud at church with hungry voyeurism, both home and Hall are isolated from the village community (it is simply the place where he can meet Maud accidentally, as it were out of bounds), and from the *nouveau riche* towers of the suitor's abode. The excluded speaker is deeply complicit with the life of the Hall. He views the brother with dependent fascination, longing for fellowship: 'I longed so heartily then and there/To give him the grasp of fellowship' (I. xiii. 458–9). And though he is given the 'gorgonising stare' of the British upper classes, that stare is in alliance with his own 'heart of stone', just as Maud's 'null', stony face parallels his own 'set' 'flint'-like face (I. i. 31) and just as her blushes in I. viii and I. xvii reflect the feverish flush of blood in his own physical being.

The speaker is constantly situated at a boundary point in the Hall grounds, looking in from the outside, at 'the high Hall garden', outside the gate, outside the sleeping house, in the field below it. Imagining that he is only noticed for the sake of his vote, uninvited to the great political dinner and dance, he marks the barriers and points of exclusion which possessions and property can establish. And yet the estrangement is for him simultaneously a participation in privilege. Ownership and power over the *ground* fascinates him. He is delighted that a stream crossing 'my ground' carries a rose in its current 'born at the Hall' (I. xxi. 844) which he supposes to have been sent by Maud. In the triumphant lyric, 'I have led her *home*' (I. xviii), the certainty of feeling prevents the incipient questions from emerging: *whose* 'home', hers or his? The worst that can happen is that the 'solid ground' (I. xi) should give beneath one's feet and leave one *without* entitlement or security. His home, with its two servants, replicates the master–servant structure of the Hall. In the extraordinary, deranged lyrics of Part II which mark the movement from morbidity to insanity the difference is one of degree rather than kind. The poems are obsessed with spaces. The market place, the 'squares and streets' (II. iv. 232) are loathed spaces because they alienate him from the memory 'Of the old manorial hall' and its privileged enclosure. The living burial underground (v) simply reproduces the exclusion experienced earlier, but it too is an enclosure mimicking the confinement of both 'home' and 'Hall'. The movement to open war in Part III simply extends these relationships to foreign ground. The passion for ownership is subsumed in national identity – 'I have felt with my native *land*' (III. vi. 58) (my emphasis). Participation in the Crimean war is an attempt to foreclose the act of mourning in a final act of mastery which fuses self and nation, not loss of self but an extension of power and control.

A passionate concern with inheritance, genealogy and degeneration, which replicates the bourgeois family structure even when it proposes an alternative to it, is a parallel concern related to the consuming interest in ownership, land and the boundary which excludes. The speaker insists that he is cheated not only of a financial inheritance but of Maud herself,

subject of a marriage contract (I. vii, xix). Maud is 'my bliss' (I. xviii.
655), 'my Maud' (656), 'My bride to be . . . /My own heart's heart, my
ownest own' (672–3), a possession by a parody of legal right as well as
through the rights of love (I. xix. 722–6). In an inconsistent effort to evade
the lineage of patriarchy which actually confirms it by consolidating the
idea of descent, he attempts a Schopenhauerian account of inheritance by
proposing Maud's descent only through the mother's line, 'the sweeter
blood by the other side' (I. xiii. 477). Such infantilised fascination with
the mother, Maud's mother and his own, as the redeemer of patriarchy
makes the speaker's passion regressive and strangely participates in the
slide to a 'lower' form of life which he dreads. The 16-year-old Maud
envisaged in her plain riding habit or precociously seductive 'gipsy bonnet'
(I. xx. 805) plays out contradictory roles of child, bride and mother, acting
out the inconsistent needs of patriarchal ownership for both lover and
brother. The Gipsy bonnet, with its suggestion of degenerate ancestral
blood, hints at one of the continual threats to the speaker, the recognition
of degeneracy, inherited in his own mental and physical being, in Maud's
family, in the working classes, in man as a whole. The speaker is constantly
aware of his own hypersensitive nerves ('Prickle my skin and catch my
breath' (I. xiv. 524)) and the blood which made his own father rage and
rave. He attributes the degradation of deceit and 'inherited sin' to Maud's
family (I. xiii. 484), theft and lies to the servants and 'Jack on his ale-house
bench' (I. iv. 110) and baseness to man in general, 'Nature's crowning race'
(I. iv. 134). In the first poem the poor have reverted to the condition of
animals. Degeneracy is inherited by family and class, confirming a structure which is absolutely corrupt and absolutely fixed, yet somehow always
in danger of becoming ever more degraded. War is a way of arresting this
process, reaffirming the strength of Britain's ancient lineage – 'The glory
of manhood stand on his ancient height' (III. vi. 21).

These dreads and fantasies of a universally determined physical and
moral degeneracy are accompanied by a phenomenon of behaviour which
is equally hysterical and inconsistent – the assumption of absolute moral
responsibility for the condition of madness. Madness is a disease of the
will and the will can arrest the decay of biology. The need to be rational,
to 'keep a temperate brain', to be 'passionless' (I. iv. 141, 151), to repress
'morbid hate and horror' (I. vi. 264), to control the 'splenetic', 'rancorous'
'war with myself' (I. x. 362–4) and above all the need for a new manhood,
bespeaking both moral and sexual power and health to 'arise' in the self,
are paramount in the poem.

> And ah for a man to arise in me,
> That the man I am may cease to be!
> (I. x. 396–7)

Such a new man can arrest the dreaded slide to lower forms, the identification of the speaker with the swine-like classes, just as it can repress the outbreak of buried violence and anarchy which is a continual threat to political stability. In war we make good that power, Part III asserts, abandoning the 'old hysterical mock-disease' (III. vi. 33) of madness. By an ironic trick of syntax the imitation disease of madness gives way to the 'real' hysterical disease of war.

Yet a theory of reversible degeneracy and the belief in moral and rational responsibility for disease are incompatible. These are the contradictions of the false dialectic set up in the poem. Foucault sees the assumption of power as a pathological form of the 'apotheosis of the self' in the nineteenth century in which the imperative of rational responsibility for the self takes the form of paranoia.[43] The speaker's new 'man' of power is the equivalent of the madman who becomes a 'lord of all things', a 'statesman', a powerful 'physician' (II. v. 270–4). Interestingly the commonest instance of madness offered by Allen and Maudsley is this form of delusion. Allen describes a dissenting minister believing himself one of the elect, and a man who believed himself a genius – 'he was the greatest of men'. Maudsley remarks that the lunatic appeals to the evidence of his own consciousness for the truth of his hallucination or delusion. 'The only person who answers at all to the metaphysical definition of a self-determining will is the madman, since he exults in the most vivid consciousness of freedom and power'.[44] The apotheosis of subjectivity which calls for 'One still strong man in a blatant land . . . /Aristocrat, democrat, autocrat – one/Who can rule and dare not lie' (I. x. 392–5), to match the speaker's new powerful self is an irrational cultural delusion. The strong man is the double of the wife-battering ruffian of the first poem. He is the product of an ideology which celebrates the individual will at the same time as it dreads the degeneracy which undermines the will.

The decision to be 'one with my kind' in the higher life of nation and war (III. vi. 58), to be 'noble still' (55) and to find a name at last in the 'making of splendid names' (47) is a further manifestation of the apotheosis of subjectivity in delusion and not its transformation. A confirmation of this, if any is required, is the existence in Part III of the same compulsive linguistic patterns as those which occur earlier. The speaker discloses a libidinal fascination at the start of the poem with the mouth of the 'dreadful hollow' as erotic orifice reproducing *sound* which can be interpreted as he wills – 'And Echo there, *whatever is ask'd her*, answers "Death" ' (I. i. 4) (my emphasis). The same oral and aural image returns in the figure of the 'dreadful-grinning mouths of the fortress' (III. vi. 52) at the end of the poem. To mix 'my breath/With a loyal people shouting a battle cry' (III. vi. 34–5) is to make the universe the servant of desire in language. Echo invariably answers 'Death' because she ventriloquises the speaker's obsessions, just as 'breath' rhymes with 'death' (37) in the last poem. The unifying battle cry is a linguistic figment appropriate to a consciousness which conceives all language and communication as pure *noise*, 'hubbub', 'chatter', 'babble', unless it will answer to his own moods. Maud, so much an extension of himself that he cannot remember what he has told her, is 'Not her, not her, but a *voice*' (I. v. 189), a voice like Echo's to 'answer' to needs, and perhaps a delusory voice: like the rose which can be read as the secret sign of a private assignation; like the voices of the non-human world where mice shriek (I. vi. 260) and the beach screams (I. iii. 98), where birds call 'Maud' (I. xii. 414), where passionate flowers speak (I. xxii. 912–15). The poem mobilises the pathos of the pathetic fallacy to explore the linguistic solipsism of madness, another manifestation of the will to power.

If the madman is replicating society's madness, the assent to war is a further assent to madness. War is the product of a deranged society. The last two parts of *Maud* are often thought to chart the speaker's collapse and reintegration in recovery, but if they are read like this they become a successful attempt to conform to the war ethic.[45] They stand as an insane duplication of the incipient madness of Part I. Unlike *In Memoriam*, where a dialectical reading of collapse and recuperation is possible, *Maud* is not a dialectical poem. Its separate parts simply mirror each other. The question of the will becomes parmount for the last two parts of the poem. Is the assent to war a triumph of the self-determining will or is such an assumption of responsibility an illusion? The second poem of Part II, 'See what a lovely shell', brings the exploration of will into explicit relation with the speaker's condition as the 'tiny cell' (61) of the underwater mollusc, bearing an affinity with his underground state, becomes the object of contemplation. In its 'dim water world' it is another of Lyell's subaqueous creatures without knowledge of the upper world, of the geological and biological processes to which it is subject, or even that it may be a 'miracle of design' (56). It has an extraordinary resistance to shock and change despite its capacity to be 'crush'd with a tap of my fingernail' (69–70). When it was not 'void' of the 'little living will' (62) did volition enable it to have power over the environment or was it always subject to external forces? Has the speaker likewise, and we note the language of power, 'a spark of will/Not to be trampled out' (104–5)? Yet in a subsequent poem 'Will', one of the most non-univocal words in Tennyson's vocabulary, is used in its opposite sense as that to which one is subject rather than volition. The vision of Maud is a 'blot upon the brain', an internal phantom or even a physiological mark objectified, which makes the self subservient to it – 'That *will* show itself without' (II. iv. 201).

The shell poem is taking part in a debate about the psychological, philosophical and cultural significance of the concept of 'will' which preoccupied both idealists and materialists in the latter part of the nineteenth century. Interestingly, both use the mollusc or crustacea as analogue of the will.

On the lowest levels of animal life the motive is still closely related to stimulus: zoophytes and radiata in general, acephala among the molluscs, have only a feeble twilight of consciousness, just as much as is necessary to perceive their nourishment or prey and to snatch it when it offers itself. . . . Who will dream of freedom here?

(Schopenhauer, *Essay on the Freedom of the Will*, 1841)[46]

Organised as we are we can no more know about it than an oyster in its narrow home and with its very limited sentiency can know of the events of the human world.

(Maudsley, *The Physical Basis of Will*, 1880)[47]

In different ways both writers, the German idealist and the British empiricist, swing between the concept of will as necessity and will as choice. Rather than mediating between these notions Tennyson's text uses both accounts of will to open up questions about the nature of madness and war in a deconstructive movement which makes the status of the speaker's commitment to war finally problematical.

For Schopenhauer a war of antagonistic wills, a universe at war, is a biological necessity. Freedom is limited both by inheritance and the passions, insanity and mania being the most extreme. However, essence, not action, is the seat of the will. A man *is* what he does, but this can only be seen a posteriori and cannot involve intentional action. But it is precisely such a posteriori knowledge which liberates consciousness into an *idea* of the self. This can be turned against the determinations of the will. Freedom lies in reflexive contemplation rather than action.[48] There could be no freedom of action or choice in war, partly because transcendental contemplation constitutes freedom and partly because war is a condition of wills in conflict by necessity. To *decide* to fight would be a form of suicide.

With the same paradox that makes quietism the ultimate freedom of the will the latter part of the poem moves towards a gentler vision of Maud and her suffering. It accepts her as fate or necessity rather as Freud was to see the woman as law because she obeys the cycles of reproduction and death.[49] Maud's paleness and dumbness denotes the absence which is death. Yet the way of transcendental quietism is to live with death, and ironically presages more violent derangement, as the last troubled poem of Part II suggests, 'Dead, long dead' (II. v). Nor does the Schopenhauerian solution produce an adequate account of war. For peace and war are alike the undifferentiated war of wills elided without distinction, the conflation seen as both cause and effect of madness in this text. If this *is* a Schopenhauerian poem, and there are certainly elements which suggest so, Tennyson has transposed the universal conflict of will, in which both peace and war are subsumed, into an ideological critique. We must differentiate between the hero's compliance in an account of universal war from the analysis of the text, which sees the madness of the 'civil' life of the Hall as an extension of and double of the hero's madness and not its opposite, and the madness of war as a double of both.

Does the poem, then, anticipate Maudsley's oyster as will rather than Schopenhauer's mollusc? In many ways Maudsley adopts the impossible account of will which the text tries to negotiate, the threat of degeneracy coupled with the need for moral responsibility. In several works he argues emphatically against the freedom of the will and self-determining agency. Consciousness is not coextensive with mind. It responds to external stimuli but cannot know of 'pre-conscious' and 'unconscious' operations which are founded in physiological action 'which it receives unconsciously from other organs of the body'.[50] The influence of the sexual organs upon the mind is a prime example of such processes. Mind receives its life from the continuous cycles of repair and waste going on in the body. The most important part of our experience 'lies in the dark'.[51] Inheritance determines our nature, passed on from generation to generation. The 'anti-social conditions of one generation predetermine the social disintegration of following generations'.[52] Mania and monomaniac brooding are connected with the impairment of nerve centres whose 'solidarity' is undermined. Will is 'the character of every organ of the body'.[53] When physiological unity is damaged the 'dissolution' of the 'conscious ego' follows. A 'double or divided personality', each speaking in a foreign language to the other, occurs when a morbid growth 'lives its own life apart' physiologically and mentally, often resolving into 'two different and hostile unities'.[54] The threat to unity and 'organisation' haunts his work. And yet he maintains that it is civilisation and the development of human culture in time which can prevent decadence and the dreaded disorganisation. The responsibility for coherence is displaced from the individual to human history, which might be capable of opposing the unbecoming of genetic weakness with the becoming of integration. The dark physiological writing of the body in *Maud* seems to be retrospectively theorised here.

Maudsley, however, writing a peculiarly Victorian version of civilisation and its discontents, does offer, perhaps unawares, a way of deconstructing his theory of unity. As well as describing the disorganisation which the culture struggles to repair he does pay attention to the needs of those forces which lie 'in the dark', the 'latent energies' of 'secret and silent courses, in infra-conscious depths' which lie beneath the surface of national consciousness. Its traditions, opinions, institutions, open feelings, aims, find expression in 'disorderly volcanic upheavals' unless they are recognised rather than repressed. The 'ignorant ruler' 'despises' them, but 'great pulses' and 'great sub-conscious social forces explode . . . if too much or too long repressed'.[55] This expressive politics has revolution in mind. In *Maud* the displacement of frustrated social energy into war is analogous to the 'volcanic upheavals' and their terrible catharsis predicted by Maudsley.

The hero of Maud, experiencing the world from underground, yet living out the ideology of repression, colludes with the notion that war is the expression of national will and unity. Maudsley's writing, on the other hand, allows that it can be the ultimate pathology of will in which war becomes a representation for deranged energy. On this reading *Maud* is closer to *Anti-Maud* than its 'hero' knows. The implicit debate on the will makes the confirmation of war deeply problematical. The mysterious, sudden non sequitur of the hero's final triumphalism is sinister: repressed mourning erupts into the violence of national will and its apotheosis.

It is tempting to feel that after *In Memoriam* and *Maud* Tennyson never achieved anything of quite the same concentration again. Certainly both are double poems of extraordinary complexity. Both drive towards the 'unity' and 'organisation' which Maudsley was to value so highly: *In Memoriam* by evolving through the vicissitudes of trust in love as 'creation's final law', *Maud* by the need to be 'one with my kind'. Both sanction conservative, not to say reactionary readings, and both investigate the contradictions on which these are founded. The need for continuity in *In Memoriam* and the need for violence in *Maud* are subjected to a rigorous analysis. Their way of combining expressive writing with critique is perhaps unparalleled in the nineteenth century. Tennyson's capacity to be startling is evident in both, but the move from *In Memoriam* and the unseen workings beneath the earth's surface to the pathological geology of the self in *Maud* in which 'secret and silent courses' work darkly in the physiological cells and in the brain, creates a Victorian writing of the body which is startling in the extreme. The throbbing pulses and coercive rhythms of *Maud* live in the writing of the next decades even when Tennyson was deemed old-fashioned and conventional. *Maud*'s Victorian exploration of the unconscious, published the year before Freud was born, is not to be identified with his, but it initiates the exploration of hysteria with which Freud's work began and brings this together with cultural critique and ideology in a way which he did not. Interestingly, *Maud* studies a hysterical man; Freud, more conventionally and in accord with nineteenth-century preconceptions, worked with hysterical women. As in the early poems, Tennyson's conservatism leads him towards radical questioning.

11

BROWNING IN THE 1850s AND AFTER
New experiments in radical poetry and the Grotesque

When Louis Napoleon is found to cut the knot instead of untying it
– Ba approves – I demur. Still, one must not be pedantic and
overexacting, and if the end justifies the beginning, the illegality of
the step may be forgotten in the prompt restoration of the law – the
man may stop the clock to set it right. . . . Ba says . . . the
parishioners, seven million strong, empowered him to get into the
steeple and act as he pleased – while I don't allow that they were . . .
at liberty to speak their judgment.

(Letter of Browning to George Barrett, 4 February 1852)[1]

In 1846 Browning married Elizabeth Barrett and became an ex-patriot
poet, living in Italy until her death in 1861. *Men and Women* (1855) might
suggest, therefore, a decisive break with the past. The old radical formation
is left behind. Politics are displaced by aesthetics, public drama by private
lyrics of love. Idiosyncratic, bizarre, arcane, the language and structure of
the poems could signify a retreat into privacy. But, as the above quotation
suggests, Browning and his wife were intensely committed to politics,
European politics. In their perpetual political disagreements, Browning
always took a more radical line, as in the dispute over the coup of Louis
Napoleon in 1852. It is this 'European' progressivism which made conservative critics in England uncomfortable.

Mr Browning has lived the greater part of his literary life in Italy.
The colouring of his mind and the colouring of his work are alike
Italian. . . . If Mr Browning had studied England and the English
character as faithfully and successfully as he has studied Italy and
Italian character, his position as an English poet would have been
other than it now is.

This was how Walter Bagehot saw Browning, reviewing *The Ring and the*

284

Book in 1869. Tennyson, he said, 'is one of ourselves' in his Englishness, and implies that Browning, with his 'dramatic, intense, colour loving spirit', is not. *Pippa Passes* 'could never have been written in England'.[2] But *Pippa Passes* (1841) *was* written in England. It is an interesting error, suggesting that Bagehot's sense that Browning was not 'one of ourselves' and his willingness to see Browning as an ex-patriot came from a deeper unease with his work than insular worries about Italian settings. Browning to Bagehot is essentially a dangerous foreigner, hardly a gentleman.

Bagehot, indeed, had mounted a liberal/conservative critique of Browning before this which indicates how the ground of Unitarian and Dissenting criticism had narrowed and changed since the 1830s. He wrote for the *Prospective Review*, a Unitarian publication which began in 1845, and with R. H. Hutton he founded the *National Review*. Both editors were graduates of University College London, a Benthamite foundation which Browning had briefly attended in his youth, but in a deeply hostile study of Browning in a review of *Dramatis Personae* (1864), which he relates to the whole of his work, Bagehot, himself a Dissenter with banking connections like Browning's family, dissociates himself from Browning. Using a set of categories designed to redefine Ruskin's Grotesque art negatively as 'ugly reality', he relates Milton and Wordsworth to 'Pure' or classical art, Tennyson to 'Ornate' or Romantic art and Browning to 'Grotesque' or medieval art – though it is clear that Browning for him uses medievalism as a front for modern or contemporary art. Classical art is explicitly Arnoldian, the art of the pure Type, whole, unified, with 'invisible' accessories or verbal economy, an art which does not 'mutilate' its object. Milton's *Paradise Lost* belongs to the category of Pure art even though, significantly, Milton makes the Fall originate in 'a *political event*'.[3] Whereas Arnoldian Pure art is an antidote to anxieties rather than expressing them, Ornate art conceals its anxieties and disguises the unpleasing Type by loading it with superfluous and distracting detail. It is an art of 'accumulation' and 'aggregation' which is used to create a sense of mystery and illusion.[4] He quotes Newman on the alluring but factitious sense of mystery and illusion created by such poetry. A tree in the distance implies an unseen wood; a hill a vale beyond. Newman's own words are thus deftly used to turn Tractarian accounts of symbol, which are based on the assumption that language both conceals and reveals, against themselves as suspect and virtually erotic. Nevertheless in attempting to establish the pure, fixed, universal theological Type against the Grotesque, Bagehot, even though using the Type metaphorically, exploits its conservative propensities. It is the Grotesque art represented by Browning which comes in for Bagehot's full disapproval: it takes the Type '*in difficulties*', 'struggling with obstacles', 'encumbered with incongruities', portraying 'the distorted and imperfect image'. It is both the theological Type fallen into imperfection and the evolutionary Type 'in its minimum development', an art not of normal but 'abnormal specimens', barbarous, degraded and degenerate.[5] Bagehot's unconcealed repugnance is itself disturbingly neurotic. The poetry is un-English and is sexually disturbing. Just as soldiers get used to the reek of blood in battle, he writes, expressing an extraordinary physical nausea, so Browning's ingrained coarseness enables him to deal with his degraded material.

Within this hierarchy of categories Bagehot had some very subtle and intelligent things to say about both Tennyson and Browning, but the intensity with which he attempts to wrest the Grotesque from Ruskin is a measure of his political suspicion of Browning. It is clear that Pure art is high art, Ornate art, with its acquisitive aggregation of detail, is bourgeois art and Grotesque art appeals dangerously to the '*half* educated quality of readers' and their language, which has no norms and standards.[6] In unfixing the Type in the Grotesque, Browning is conceding to the debasement made possible by the wide dissemination of the printed word and popular access to it – Carlyle's movable types. Bagehot, with his fondness for the high Whig reviewers of the early part of the century, was uncomfortable about this, but his uneasiness and his reading of Browning in terms of the ideology of the Grotesque does suggest that conservative readers at least found political implications in his work, and that the ex-patriot poet did not abandon the cultural critique which belonged to his earlier work. Bagehot's article relies heavily on Arnold's 1853 Preface. The new liberal critique of Browning was aware of his subversive implications. Ruskin, on the other hand, claimed Browning for the gothic and the Grotesque. Although he had reservations about *Men and Women*, he said, significantly, that an earlier poem, 'The Bishop orders His Tomb at Saint Praxed's Church' (1845) anticipated 'nearly all that I have said of the central Renaissance in thirty pages of the *Stones of Venice*, put into as many lines'. He was writing in the fourth volume of *Modern Painters* (1856), published after *Men and Women*.[7]

Those 'thirty pages' are presumably the account of the decadence of the Grotesque with the emergence of Renaissance luxury in the last volume of *The Stones of Venice* (1853), where the pursuit of pleasure and family aggrandisement has subordinated work, and the degenerate Grotesque art of the culture which plays 'inordinately' has displaced the 'noble' Grotesque. The profound relevance of the cultural analysis of this chapter to the conditions of work and art in the nineteenth century has already been established. Thus in associating Browning with the politics of the Grotesque Ruskin was connecting him with the reconfiguration of a radical aesthetic which was going on round his own work, and acknowledging that this alignment was not necessarily one which involved direct influence but belonged to a formation of common ideas and analyses. The last volume of *The Stones of Venice* appeared while Browning was composing some of the central poems on art (for instance, 'Fra Lippo Lippi') in *Men and Women*, probably too late for a direct intertextual relationship. The

Brownings would have known the earlier volumes of *Modern Painters* more inwardly than *The Stones of Venice*.[8] But, like Ruskin himself, it is not necessary to argue for association by source (as one can in the case of Morris) to suggest that the poems of *Men and Women* belong, however independently, to a project akin to that of Ruskin. The title of the volume itself, suggesting the representation of the universal 'types' of gender, an appeal to our most general interests (so much so that critics often talk of 'Browning's men and women'), constitutes one of those deflections or obliquities associated with the Grotesque. For only a handful of poems are actually spoken by women. When women appear men speak *about* or *to* them as a feminine other. And the title actually declares the absence of the woman's voice. The conjunction gives men *and* women equal status and simultaneously subordinates women as a secondary category: men – and women. It points to that fascination with women which is everywhere in Victorian poetry and to their historic function as subordinates. The letter about Louis Napoleon's dissolution of the French Assembly which begins this chapter testifies not only to the Brownings' eager responsiveness to political events but to Robert Browning's continuing interest in democracy – to the extent of entering a democratic debate about it with his wife. In the 1855 volume he was writing about what intensely *concerns* men and women, not speaking *for* those not 'at liberty to *speak* their judgment' (my emphasis), but speaking out (something he had always admired his wife for) on questions of fundamental concern to the nineteenth century. Work, ideology, consciousness and teleology, language and gender, are just as much at the centre of his poetry as they are for Morris. And, as Bagehot realised, his very presence in Italy constituted a critique of 'British' culture. While Morris works inside the iconography of the Grotesque, producing poems of such accessible simplicity and immediacy that their critical significance is only gradually apparent, Browning exploits the Grotesque as a technique for exposing complexity.

The poem Ruskin so much admired, 'The Bishop orders His Tomb at Saint Praxed's Church', is based on a typical Grotesque procedure – the distorted perspective of restricted vision. The dying Bishop, surrounded by 'nephews', can only think of his magnificent tomb from the perspective of someone lying on it, just as he is lying on his deathbed. The irony is that from this position looking outwards into the church one could see precisely what a spectator in front of it could not see – but one would have to be dead, or one of the stone effigies on the tomb, to do so. The violent power of the gaze, a greedy appropriation of the aesthetic and the sexual, and a complete failure to imagine or comprehend death are conveyed through the limited comprehension of the gaze itself. The monologue combines, as do so many of the poems of *Men and Women*, what seem to be two incompatible and incongruous propensities, an extreme intellectual and epistemological sophistication and an extreme commitment to the voracious power of anarchic, libidinal emotion and desire. The oppressed Grotesque consciousness is here in a position of frightful desire, consumed by the will to power, a will to power in the sense Nietzsche understood it, which is the will to experience energy, as much as the need for dominance. A fantastic, ludic, intellectual complexity and the raw intensity of disruptive libido are not perhaps compatible with one another but they live together as elements of the Grotesque in Ruskin's analysis as the related forms in which the oppressed consciousness both responds to and resists its condition. These two elements often co-operate with one another in Browning's poems to mask and confuse his concerns but they do in fact lead to and constitute those concerns. They are not the superficial forms of an extractable content but often posit an intractable problem.

The extreme textual sophistication of the monologue or the dramatic lyric, a poem proposing itself as the immediacy of a speaking voice in dialogue with a silent listener but which is in reality a text, a written artefact, raises immediately the problem of its own and the reader's status by confusing speaking, which assumes a listener's presence, with writing, which assumes an addressee's absence. The form dramatises the hermeneutic problems in interpretation and communication. For the reliability of the speaking subject in relation to the silent listener is problematic and is itself a model of the relation between reader and text. The reader reads a text constructed out of a speaker interpreting himself to a listener interpreting him, but who is only to be inferred from the subject's speech. The monologue brings into being a quadruple hermeneutic relation at the very least, between speaker, listener, text, reader. There is an infinite regress of possible interpretative instability as the reader's own reading process is implicated in hermeneutic difficulty. If the dramatic form provides the lyric utterance with relations it cannot have within itself and opens it up to analysis, it is epistemologically on the dangerous edge, taking risks with its form by asking how meaning is constructed, and by extension, how both meaning and subjectivity are constructed in language. And, since language is a cultural artefact, as the Fox group well knew, the monologue always opens onto cultural problems.

The complexities of the monologue can be taken further, but for the moment enough has been said to indicate how the form raises some important political and teleological questions. If Browning's dazzling epistemological daring makes him a Derridean before his time, this is because the unstable text was an implicit presupposition of the biblical criticism which shaped the structure of *Pauline*. The monologue contracts and intensifies the huge metaphysical and philosophical concerns of the earlier poems by embodying them in its organisation and form. The dramatic form decentres both speaker and reader, questioning the authority of both. It dramatises but does not concede to the power relations of communication and interpretation, showing them in operation and enabling a democratic access to their complexities. It embodies the *structural problems* of power in its form and comprehends the reader within these problems. In developing the possibilities of the dramatic monologue Browning was consolidating Fox's view that drama was the essential political form, and by exploiting the limited perspective of the perceiving subject he was developing the Grotesque by building its distortions into the organisation of the poem, so that it cannot help but become a model of the relations between oppressed consciousnesses.

The monologue by its form becomes the political art of a post-revolutionary situation, where questions of power and democracy must be foregrounded. It is also a post-teleological and post-Kantian form. These implications will be expanded shortly, but here it is sufficient to point out that the monologue's assent to the problematical nature of the text and its 'truth', its refusal to grant authority to the word, is a deconstructive process which ultimately raises theological questions because it interrogates the possibility of absolute judgement and coherent subjectivity. Its form does indeed invoke the higher criticism. Similarly, because it is the representation of a representation in language it opens up a questioning of representation and the sign. We can only know the material phenomena of language in the monologue, the veil of representation, not what it represents, because the monologue is speech, not action, and writing, not speech. Indeed, Bentham's idea of fictions in relation to language makes this problem even more difficult, as will be seen. For if language represents that which is not an entity in the world its fictional status gives it an inherent insecurity. The language of the poems alternates between densely complex casuistry and paradox and the gasp or gap of inarticulateness, between overloaded, prolific heterogeneousness of vocabulary and extreme syntactic fragmentation and hiatus as if to foreground the problematic nature of the sign and the slide of meaning.

And yet concurrent with this sophistication and profoundly theoretical intellectual complexity is that violent energy of desire and feeling which spurts in the language of even the most subdued of Browning's poems – the colour of the autumn leaves in 'By the Fire-side', like a splash of blood, 'intense, abrupt', sums it up.[9] This deranged intensity seems to cut across the cerebral power of the poems and convert it to violence, melodrama or farce, producing a hybrid, mixed, impure form. Such intensity is not understandable simply by using the classification 'gothic', for though it conveniently classifies the poems in Ruskin's terms it does not yet provide an analysis of their energy. One can begin to approach Browning's work, however, by remembering that many of the poems are *about* energy, whether it is the overflow of repressed sexuality in 'Fra Lippo Lippi', the almost raucous religious rapture of 'Saul' or the grey, Chekhovian lassitude of 'Andrea del Sarto', where energy is there by virtue of the experience of its lack. David, liberated after projecting his own life and spirit into the

289

exhausted Saul, Fra Lippo Lippi, escaping from the imprisonment of the monastery where he is painting under duress for the Medici family, Andrea del Sarto, committing himself to the discipline of lifeless work in order to earn money to support his wife's extravagance (or so he justifies his absorption in consuming labour): in all these poems an excess or distortion of energy and libido is connected with its displacement from or in work. The oppressed consciousness which is forced to play as a release from the half-paralysing imprisonment of labour experiences play in extremity as the fantastic exercise of emotion and imaginative power. That which cannot play at all because utterly oppressed with labour experiences a violent sense of limit which issues in a correspondingly violent longing. Thus the phenomenological form of oppressed labour manifests itself everywhere in Browning's work, even when he makes no immediate contemporary reference to the post-technological world of the mid-nineteenth century. He does not describe alienated labour so much as the results of it.

But that world was also a post-revolutionary era, as Browning knew from his experience of Italy and France as well as of England. Ruskin thought of the Grotesque as a form of resistance and defence. In Browning's work the energies of the Grotesque not only manifest themselves in violent libido and desire but in frustration and aggression, or they issue in the *exercise* of oppression in power and domination, whether it is the sexual domination of 'Mesmerism' or the political and religious will to power in 'Bishop Blougram's Apology'. The revolutionary energies of the restricted consciousness and the energies called forth to repress these are alike the disorganised manifestations of *power* in a culture fascinated both with the excess and lack of energy. Thus the wayward and superabundant overflow of feeling in Browning's work is directly related to the cerebral and theoretical epistemological intensity – perhaps in this context it is the epistemophilic Grotesque intensity – of his poems. For both become a way of finding form for political, teleological, social and linguistic anxiety. But one's sense that the two aspects of his work pull apart from and subvert one another is correct. They do not collaborate with one another as they would in a unified 'classical' work. Nor does the analytical element of the poems act as a control on the expressive side. The cerebral element is too agnostic and investigative to do this, constantly examining the premises of its own structures and the ground of subjectivity. The primordial excess of feeling is too impersonal and Dionysian (it is appropriate to use Nietzsche's categories here) in its intensity to fall easily under definition. It is not, as Ruskin would have said, servile. Both analytical and Dionysiac urges share the same libidinal intensity. They struggle to make and unmake one another in the constant process of construction and reconstruction by which the Grotesque poems of the middle period are constituted.

The central project of *Men and Women* is the investigation of cultural fictions and the form in which they are constructed. The Benthamite fascination with the construct, with the fictional entity which may have no counterpart in the world but nevertheless intervenes in it, exercising a coercive imaginative pressure on thought and action, is developed in a remarkable way in this volume.[10] It explores a multiplicity of fictions and myths. As we have seen in the first chapter of this book, 'Love among the Ruins' is set at the beginning of the first volume of *Men and Women* as a crucial declaration. It points to the myth of myth itself, to the sustaining fictions of mutual passion and a corresponding belief in the unified consciousness prior to the cultural fragmentation which destroys myth and symbol. By eloquently and passionately undermining the processes by which this myth is constructed and exploring the way in which the unified subjectivity itself, at the mercy of language, is a fiction, the poem indicates the project of the volume. This is not so much to create a new mythos, a totalising fiction for and of contemporary culture, but to explore a multiplicity of modern ideological myths, fictions and forms of thought, and the conditions under which they are created. Thus the poems explore the fiction of the aesthetic, the teleological and the positivist or scientific consciousnesses as separate spheres, the split culture of the modern world. This investigation of fiction-making and representation is a Grotesque project of cultural critique because it recognises that fiction-making is a provisional and precarious process, bound by the limits of ideology, an expression of oppression unavailable for analysis by the speaking subject. But fiction-making is also a form of *ideological* creativity and inventiveness as well as being formed by ideology. And since ideology as the representation of imaginary relations is always being remade, no single fiction can organise experience. The Grotesque, with its pressure upon limit, its *play* with understanding, its sense of the gap between representation and its object and the disjunctions and discrepancies of consciousness, is a mode particularly suited for both rendering and analysing fiction-making.

Because the Grotesque is not a unifying mode, *Men and Women* is a fragmented and composite work, Ruskin's 'broken mirror, with strange distortions and discrepancies'.[11] It is a deeply historicised work, for the Grotesque's perception of incompleteness extends to modernity and historicises that. But it offers no one, coherent and unified history, merely a set of different and discontinuous histories, discrepant even when they overlap. The Victorian habit of seeing history in terms of related phases and stages of development (a simplified post-Hegelian interpretation of Hegel undertaken even when the Hegelian categories are abandoned), is not the habit of this volume. Ruskin's account of the Grotesque, to some extent Hegelian, is non-progressive. The monologue of the Renaissance painter, Fra Lippo Lippi, for instance, is juxtaposed with that of a musician of the Venetian Enlightenment, 'A Toccata of Galuppi's', almost as if the random euphony of the names relates them. Two modern love lyrics are followed by the epistle of Karshish, an Arab physician writing at the dawn of Christianity. 'Andrea del Sarto', belonging to the same historical period as 'Fra Lippo Lippi', belongs to the second volume of *Men and Women*. The biblical 'Saul' and the art history of 'Old Pictures in Florence' sandwich 'In a Balcony'. Browning is fascinated by moments of historical transition, but they are never the same moments. Similarly, he works with incompatible historical models and categories. In 'Old Pictures in Florence' he seems to be working with Hegel's categories of classical and Romantic art, exploring the early Renaissance painter's negation of the flesh and external reality. In 'Fra Lippo Lippi', on the other hand, he seems to abandon the Christianised neo-Hegelian theory of phases of moral and subsequently decadent art in the Renaissance, propounded by the Catholic Alexis François Rio and mediated by Anna Jameson.[12] This is overlaid with both Ruskin's ideas and those of Browning's friend Joseph Milsand on Protestant art.[13] The concern with deconstructing evolutionary history has behind it a concern with the progressivist models of pre-Darwinian theory. The poems resist a social interpretation of evolutionary processes in terms of progress, and are fascinated instead by the randomness of evolutionary operations.

The concern with discontinuous temporality and history is transposed to the investigation of consciousness. For instance, 'Two in the Campagna' begins stressfully:

> I wonder do you feel today
>   As I have felt since, hand in hand,
> We sat down on the grass, to stray
>   In spirit better through the land,
> This morn of Rome and May?
>
> (1–5)

Consciousness, what Horne and Hazlitt had concurred in calling 'this fine illusion of the brain and forgery of language', becomes its own subject in the drama of this lyric and makes subjectivity the content of the poem.[14] But consciousness seems to be the *product* of a multiple and discontinuous series of historical moments and temporalities, moments which the consciousness *itself* has paradoxically constructed. The words 'I wonder' interrogate a moment of consciousness which has occurred before the words are uttered.

The poem begins as if the speaking subject is breaking in upon itself, intruding upon its own consciousness at the same time as it attempts to break out of itself with 'I wonder do *you* feel'. But the status of the question is questioned because the fluid, open syntax and the complex movement of tenses avail it of several forms of question and several pasts and presents: Do you feel *now* as I have felt *today*? Do you, *today*, feel as I *have felt* in the past? Do you feel . . . since we sat down *this* morn? Do you feel . . . *this* morn as I have felt *since* (in time past) we sat down (once before)?

The status of the movement of consciousness, of the self as essence, its presentness and its pastness, is called into question. When and where *was* the past? Where and what *is* consciousness? Location, placing, history, time, space, are under stress. What 'Rome', that great cultural symbol of western civilisation, really is becomes problematical as the complexity of the question emerges – this morn of memories of historical Rome, this morn of Rome, the present. Consciousness, Horne said, is memory, the memory of memories, and the memory of projections into the future. But if consciousness is not simply the history of its moments but the product of the repetitions of the past, a multiplicity of temporalities, it becomes a fictional entity entangled in its own projections and categories.[15] (Stanza ii figures this in the image of the spider's web obstructing our 'path'.) Thought attempts to grasp thought with thought. On the other hand it is discontinuous, experiencing itself as gaps and breaks without connection (the dislocated and deranged syntax encourages this perception), outside itself, displaced and split off from its own content. It is the after-effect of memory or projection, experience which has gone before or beyond it. And the 'you' of the poem, the lover's lover, is as much a fiction of memory as the consciousness of the perceiving subject, and as much an after-effect of experience as his alienated consciousness. One remembers Marx's comment that experience is always *disappearing* in such an account of mind.[16]

It is in the discontinuities of the experience of the historicised consciousness that Browning locates the Grotesque condition, its sense of the gap between desire and the object, of the failure and non-correspondence of representation and the sign to what it represents. The poem moves to the crucial significance of volition and action for such a condition (as Horne did) but this will be discussed at a later point. For the moment the first stanza of 'Two in the Campagna' introduces further aspects of the dramatic lyric and monologue, and the nature of the double poem, which require discussion as a preliminary to a consideration of the cultural fictions which are at the centre of *Men and Women*. The significance of two poems concerned with art and culture, 'Cleon' and 'Fra Lippo Lippi', a poem concerned with belief, 'Bishop Blougram's Apology', and one making scientific and positivist readings of the world, the 'Epistle of Karshish', and of some of the love lyrics, becomes clearer after what we have learned to call the 'dramatic monologue' has been explored.

It is as well to have introduced the complexities of the beginning of 'Two in the Campagna' into this discussion, for its self-subversion and lacunae make it difficult to maintain what has come to be a conventional view of the monologue and of the history of Browning's poetry. It is often assumed that with *Christmas-Eve and Easter-Day* (1850) and 'Saul' (published in 1845 but completed for *Men and Women*) Browning announces a return to a qualified assent to Christian belief: simultaneously he begins to see the possibilities of the dramatic monologue in terms of the psychological case study which requires a moral and imaginative act of empathy on the part of a reader, who arrives at an ethical judgement informed by his or her inwardness with a psychological condition. In this reading Browning would be assenting to the expressive theory of the 'overheard' soliloquy promulgated by Mill, in which the reader overlooks a sawn-off play, a dehistoricised one-sided drama of the self spoken by one person. We are let in on Arnold's 'dialogue of the mind with itself'. Such a view has been discussed with varying degrees of sophistication (Robert Langbaum, for instance, claimed that this is the true 'empirical' form of the nineteenth century, giving the reader access to the facts of a case[17]) and the characteristics of Browning's new poetic category have been codified meticulously.

But it is arguable that the 'pure' dramatic monologue is an invention of the twentieth century. Browning wrote to Forster that he had written 'a number of poems of all sorts and sizes and styles and subjects' (5 June 1854), and seems to have thought of *Men and Women* as a composite and eclectic affair. As has been seen, there were many theories of the poem as drama in the nineteenth century, and though this may have been a peculiarly Victorian understanding of poetry, it encompassed lyric and narrative, as it did for Fox, for a poem becomes drama the moment it is conceptualised as not the poet's 'own' subjectivity uttering itself.[18] Browning's poems actually move through a spectrum, from unindividuated lyric utterance to speech of an almost overdetermined historical and psychological specificity. Such poems appear to encourage a literal reading as a transcription of autobiographical or biographical experience in which an authentic speaker offers a coherent narrative for investigation. But several elements of the poems should warn one away from such a positivist reading. The conscious historicity of the poems, available to the reader but not to the speaker, seems like a simulacrum, a fantastic mimicry and faking of realism, rather than a careful literalism. All this suggests that the Grotesque is operating as a technique: the skewed gaze of Grotesque perception, the invasion of libido and desire which registers a sense of limit, the sense of something missing, as representation is incommensurate with what is represented, and the consequent fragmentation of consciousness, which has been seen at work in 'Two in the Campagna', as the oppressed condition attempts to wrestle with self-separation – these are all structural elements in the poems. The poems seem to be presented as the scenes of restless secondary revision, an attempt to produce coherence, rather than as coherent representations in themselves.

Such characteristics have availed themselves of some sophisticated theoretical readings. Lacanian psychoanalytical reading and Derridean analyses of language have deconstructed the realist psychological reading of the poems.[19] Two important readings take Nietzsche as a reference point. And Nietzsche's attack on Schopenhauer's account of lyric, which he discusses in *The Birth of Tragedy* (1872), less than a couple of decades after *Men and Women*, is a reminder of the relevance of the Nietzschean project to Browning's work. In formulating the lyric as the alternation of pure, will-less selfhood, or 'knowing', with phases of interruption by 'the stress of desire' and 'willing and its strain', Schopenhauer was giving authority and epistemological centrality to an unproblematical, independent subjectivity as agent which does not, Nietzsche argued, exist. Such an identity, he said, is only an '*aesthetic phenomenon*', created by the play of projection and image and the need to find an 'author' of our being.[20] The psychoanalytical reading sees Browning's monologues as the defensive play of 'Travesty, camouflage, intimidation' and 'mimicry', strategies of the unconscious as it masks the unrepresentable nature of the object of desire and *invidia*. Since the scope of our own gaze is precisely what eludes us representation is never experienced as adequate to the object. Behind Browning's monologues is 'the desire of the creative mind for priority' over the precursor, the ultimate figuring of elusion. Elusion as illusion is similarly the movement charted in the Derridean reading. Language appears to be writing the self, establishing presence and bringing it into being: but since the sign is constituted by absence and its nature as substitution, the unified consciousness is undone simultaneously with its construction, and consciousness, always already posited in language, is always being abolished by the very things that bring it into being.

It is important to recognise the subtlety of such discussions, particularly as what they describe has an obvious affinity with elements of the Grotesque. However, both accounts turn the poems into a repetition of the same narratives – they are always about the same thing – and divest them of their specificity. The psychoanalytical reading returns the poem to an expressive form at a different level: *behind* the forms thrown up by the unconscious is the desire for origination. The Derridean reading reverses this: the originating self is an effect of language. What is omitted in these readings is a recognition that writing made as a textual artefact has a status rather different from that of a dream, and language organised as poetry, where the fact of its existence as language is foregrounded, is likely to be constructed with an awareness of linguistic complexity. The monologues invite deconstructive readings such as I have discussed almost ostentatiously, as the opening of 'Two in the Campagna' suggests. However, the complexities elicited in these readings are already seen as problematical by the poem itself. The movement of Browning's double poems immerses the reader in the forms and energies of the Grotesque and then requires a second reading when these are seen as phenomena for analysis. His poetry evolves a form which reflexively questions its own procedures. 'Two in the Campagna', for instance, moves to the problem of subjectivity and agency in a way which requires the reader to go beyond the limits of the speaker's consciousness. In this way it takes the deconstructive moment as a *political* problem. It makes the political problem intrinsic to the form of the dramatic poem. It is built into the very structure of the poem *as* a problem. This is particularly important for a reading of texts which explore the psychic condition when it is driven by the coercive power of ideological fantasy and asks for a democratic response to such fictions. For the problems of consciousness are not abstract epistemological dilemmas in Browning's work, as the deconstructive readings suggest. They relate directly (as Horne saw more than a decade before) to the political imagination by raising questions of agency and questions of interpretation. These affect both the text and its reader. The poem which turns around the utterance of a subjectivity and makes it the object of investigation asks a reader to move beyond the limits of the uttering speaker: but if consciousness is always entangled in the spider's web of its representations, so that what it perceives is an aspect of its own projections, it will be caught in a circularity of experience from which it cannot be retrieved. And if consciousness is the unstable after-effect of memory and language, it works in a perpetually ungrounded movement of representation which eludes common definition and shared categories. Browning's quicksilver syntax, and the slide of semantic definition registers that sense of the missing ground.

Nevertheless, the problem of circularity and ungroundedness *is* exposed as a problem for the speaking self in the monologue. It is also a problem for the reading process. The meeting point of text and reader and the act of interpretation becomes the convergence of two circularities and two kinds of ungrounded representation which are always eccentric to one another and which can never be brought to rest in a final reading. Ludwig Feuerbach, whose *The Essence of Christianity* (translated by George Eliot in 1854) seems to have helped shape 'Cleon', the monologue which begins the following discussion of individual poems, expressed this effective non-convergence as the aspects of circulating planets to one another:

> The Sun which lights and warms Uranus has no physical (only an astronomical, scientific) existence for the Earth; and not only does the Sun appear different, but it really is *another* sun on Uranus than on the earth.[21]

Feuerbach discusses the nature of the 'twofold life' of man as a reflective being in the circular terms which might describe the structure of a Browning lyric of the 1850s:

> Hence the brute has only a simple, man a twofold life: in the brute, the inner life is one with the outer; man has both an inner and an outer life . . . man *thinks* [my emphasis] – that is, he converses with himself. The brute can exercise no function which has relation to its species without another individual external to itself; but man can perform the functions of thought and speech, which strictly imply

296

such a relation, apart from another individual. Man is himself at once I and thou; he can put himself in the place of another, for this reason, that to him his species, his essential nature, and not merely his individuality, is an object of thought. . . . The consciousness of a caterpillar, whose life is confined to a particular species of plant, does not extend itself beyond this narrow domain . . . the conscious subject has for his object the infinity of his own nature.[22]

The confident rationalism of the higher biblical criticism proclaims this tautology of consciousness. The optimistic and undynamic nature of this view of the subject as its own object is at issue in 'Cleon', as we shall see, but the circularity which is created when the world becomes an extension of the self and the ungrounded nature of representation, puts substantial difficulty in the way of a democratic reading. It appears to presuppose that the portrayal of a tautologous and ungrounded experience will be appropriated in the terms of the reader's ungrounded and circular experience – the poem will always be 'another sun' to each reader.

Men and Women does not seek to solve these problems with Nietzschean jouissance, but they are confronted with robust acceptance and excitement. They are precisely the political and moral problems central to experience. Repeatedly they are built into the structure of the poems and declared as the *problematical* condition of experience and its reading. Almost all the important poems of this volume contain within themselves a paradigm of this problematical process. 'Fra Lippo Lippi', for instance, ends with an account of the religious picture to be painted at Sant' Ambroglio's to 'make amends' (343) for Lippi's sacrilegious conduct and art (345–92). 'Make amends' suggests both redressing a moral flaw and the classical sense of art as that which 'makes up for' the defects of the real and assuages unsatisfied desire. But as soon as the 'bowery flowery angel-brood' (349) is imagined – the parody of sentimentality cannot help suggesting a brood of birds or chickens – Lippi gets embroiled at Sant' Ambroglio's and in unsatisfied sexual desire by getting into his own picture.

There is a surreal, illusionist's delight in becoming part of one's own *trompe l'oeil*, evading the restrictions of the Grotesque vision by participating in it and staging it as illusion. Once incongruously part of the religious scene in monk's habit with 'the rope that goes all round' (104) (the rope that circumscribes, as the picture does, and the rope that throttles, the hangman's rope), however, the painter is subject to the conventions of the picture's world and frozen in it – 'Mazed, motionless and moonstruck' (364). But simply because it *is* a picture he can get out of it – he attempts, with 'blushing face' (embarrassment and lust) to 'shuffle sideways' (378): a sideways shuffle is all that one can attempt on a flat, one-dimensional canvas, but it also marks the obliquity of vision to which all perception is subject, in or out of art. Half in, half out of the picture, the painter of it ventriloquises the speech of the woman who is an angel in the picture, representing God, and the woman who is posing for the representation of an angel outside the picture. One object of the painter's creation speaks to another, God, and blasphemously reverses the order of theological creation by giving the power of origination to the painter – 'He made you and devised you' (373): a representation of God who makes man is told by an artist's creation that a man has represented God making man representing God. The return of representation upon itself is endless. But the painter does get out of the picture, and, 'all the doors being shut' (381), makes love – with the angel who is a woman representing an angel. The doors of the non-fictional church are closed (but of course it is a fiction of Browning's poem) against the outside world as the picture is closed against it. 'Iste perfecit opus' (377), says the 'angel' via Lippi or Lippi via the 'angel', outrageously appropriating the language of creation.

But the picture is not 'finished'. It has a special status as a deliberately made representation which sets it off from other forms of representation; it is a construction which can, despite and with all the limits of the distorted gaze of perception which construes it in terms of its own categor-ies of thought and experience, become the object of analysis – even if you have made it yourself. Nevertheless, the gaze is implicated in the picture, embroiled in it. Even when the painter has 'escaped' from the picture the closure which marks off painting from 'life' is incomplete. The picture has repercussions in experience. Its idealised representation both represses and arouses desire, transmutes it and produces it. Lippi plays 'hot cockles' (381) with the 'angel' in reaction to his own picture, and this has further social repercussions as the 'hothead husband' (383), inflamed with anger, desire and the rage of flouted legal possession, breaks through the closed doors of the church to claim his domestic angel in the house, asserting the property rights of marriage: an *imagined* scene about the *material* effects of imagination.

The ambiguous status of the constructed aesthetic object or fiction, its reflexivity and the embroilments of its circularity, its self-subversion and subversion, indirect or direct, its ideological nature and the repercussions it has beyond itself, all these are figured in Lippi's problematical inside–outside relation to the picture. He can get neither fully inside nor fully outside it. But what is clear is that as an object of contemplation the picture has entered the world. There is a double mediation between picture and world, world and picture in an endless reactive chain. In this Browning is extraordinarily faithful to his inherited Benthamite understanding of the fiction, and it is here that the democratic reading of ideological fictions is founded. No interpretation of a fictional entity which does not have relation to an entity in the world can be grounded, Bentham said. But in order to deal with it we must behave as if it is real simply because it has entered substantively into experience by existing at all. The importance and legitimacy of a fictional entity can never be fully established, but it is open to inspection because it can be considered in relation to known and analogous structures and categories. Yet this entails an exhaustive process of definition, redefinition and redescribing which perhaps can never be finalised; but as an exercise in definition it is essential if we are not to be at the mercy of our fictions. To however limited an extent we can attempt to be in possession of them. All social action and decisions depend on this. It is on such an arduous and exacting discrimination that a democratic reading depends. And Browning might have added that the reading is made with the fullest commitment of intellectual and imaginative energy, made by the capacity of the aesthetic fiction to arouse. In the morphology of the dramatic lyric the solipsism of the Grotesque is presupposed along with a belief in the possibility of endless redefinition. If the dramatic text requires the reader to formulate a problem beyond the limits of the speaker, the text hands back the unfinished problem of redefinition to the reader with its circularity understood, but with the possibility of an enriched understanding of what that problem is. This is a complex process, but there is no reason why the labour of a democratic art should be simple, just as it is a fallacy to assume that difficulty in itself makes a thought important. What it does is to make *language* central to Browning's enterprise. Paradoxically, if linguistic fictions are never exact, then the more exactly they are considered the more richly they can be comprehended. Language is at the heart of ideological misprision and creativity. Language, that indispensable and elusively ambiguous entity, is the material of our inexhaustible fictions, and calls forth all the resources of an equally inexhaustible hermeneutic process. The waywardly eclectic and omnivorously logophiliac inventiveness of Browning's poetry declares itself insistently, almost raucously, with a kind of ravenous energy which asks to be confronted.

Language, intervening in the world, is the prerequisite for action. The constructs of 'the forgery of language', Horne said, eliding memory with projection and projection with memory, are essential motivating factors in choice and action because their very fictionality opens up an imaginatively possible future. This imagined future is a linguistic moment, made unconsciously and riskily out of the repetitions of past thought and action, past memory and desire and past language, but conditioning the beyond, a fictional continuity made out of a radically unstable discontinuity but nevertheless providing the ground for action. No action, right or wrong, can occur without the creativity of language. For Browning the politically determining nature of language obliges an ever more passionately scrupulous response to it. The achievement of *Men and Women* culminates logically in the exhaustive redescribing of *The Ring and the Book* (1868). In 'Two in the Campagna' the 'floating weft' (15) of language and thought which are indivisible as both the materials of experience and the tools by which it

299

is analysed, moves always *beyond* the grasp of the speaker. The floating weft of the spider's web is both a thought process and the means by which it is grasped, but strangely the materials of retrospection seem to form in the future: 'Help me to hold it!' (11). The experience of thinking, but without its content, is rendered kinaesthetically as something 'touched' (6) but unknown and random. The thread touches the phenomena of perception, the historical artefact of the 'tomb's ruin' (14) and the biological life of the blind, green beetles in an orange cup, with all the intensity of the Grotesque vision. At the end of the poem the thread is 'Off again!' (57). The random and discontinuous way in which thought and language construct experience seems to make choice and the will an accident of improvisation, and this removal of ontological guarantees sanctions an assent to the 'primal naked forms' (28) of sexuality and natural life, with which experience seems analogous.

Nevertheless, the improvised will improvises a future: 'I would that you were all to me' (36). The subjunctive 'would' simultaneously signifies wishing and willing and cannot be uttered without hypothesising a forward movement into a possible future, even though it is constituted on an awareness of past and present lack. The poem moves into the present tense, and it is not clear whether the 'present' actions are ones which have turned into the past or postulate a future present where they will become immediately known as the past. 'No. I yearn upward. . . . Already how am I so far/Out of that minute?' (46, 51–2). The backward- and forward-looking adverb 'Already', encompassing then and now, now and when, consummately expresses the temporal ambiguity. How am I out of that good minute previously to it and beforehand, in advance of it? The 'wound' of love is to be explained by the form of this question, the knowledge that there is no present for consciousness, only a past and a future, for to utter 'already' is to place it in the past or the future. It is this experience, however, which marks off the weft of consciousness both from narcissism and from the *blind* biological life of the green beetles who live in physical immediacy with themselves, without the language which makes it possible to 'discern' (58) the discontinuity of knowing from itself by bringing into being the split which makes experience either behind or ahead. 'Only I discern –/Infinite passion, and the pain/Of finite hearts that yearn' (58–60). I merely, I alone, *except* that I discern . . . infinite passion: yearning presupposes longing in the future produced by the loss of the past. Simultaneously sceptical and affirmative, the end of the poem is a self-fulfilling prophecy predicting loss, on which is founded the continuance of love. The 'action' of love is reconstructed by the repetition of its loss and is paradoxically granted a new content – until the sense of a future disappears.

It is important to consider Browning's exploration of ideological fictions in *Men and Women* as poems intensely concerned with language and action, as the provisional myths of a kind of cultural secondary revision which invite and confound reading. Perhaps the most significant poems in the two volumes are the ones which represent the two fundamentally opposed cultural theories of the nineteenth century, gothic and classical, Ruskin's democratised aesthetic and the conservatising tendency of Arnoldian liberalism, 'Fra Lippo Lippi' and 'Cleon'. Just as he anticipated Ruskinian gothic, Browning may be said to have anticipated Arnoldian culture. The poems, two of the modern myths anticipated in 'Love among the Ruins', contain, like the first poem in the volume, disruptive elements; both are critiques, and indicate the uses to which the Grotesque vision can be put.

At issue in 'Fra Lippo Lippi' is the nature of a democratic art. Lippi's apologia is based on the claim that he has transformed painting with a new, accessible realism, and the related justification of aesthetic freedom which he associates with sexual freedom. Caught by the Watch while on the hunt for prostitutes after escaping from the toil of painting pictures for the Medici, he is forced into the defensive and trivialising role of clowning bohemian artist. It is this which begins to suggest the contradictions in which he is caught. The monologue is generated out of the will to verbalise of the compulsive talker and reverses the initial relationship of captive and captor. The demotic language of a common-sense view of art simultaneously attempts to sustain the privilege of private vision. Lippi's art is anti-didactic and anti-idealist and refuses the dualism imposed by religious authority and its coercive censorship – 'Paint the soul, never mind the legs and arms!' (193). As the fragments of popular secular love songs suggest, it is the subversive, carnivalesque art of the unrepressed body, but it reintroduces the dualism it seeks to solve by Grotesque oversimplification of what it means to paint things 'Just as they are' (294). Throughout this poem the Grotesque works by comic oversimplification which exposes both incoherence and the sheer difficulty of the issues Lippi raises. It is something of an achievement to have parodied and distorted *common sense*. Lippi argues that his views are obvious, but they are not obvious at all.

'You should not take a fellow eight years old/ And make him swear to never kiss the girls' (224–5). The 'Flesh and blood' artist knows the 'value and significance of flesh' (268), the richness and beauty of unrepressed sexuality and libido. Unrepressed art is a truly naturalist art, and a truly naturalist art is democratic, an art of the people, simple monks, 'good old gossips' (147), thieves, murderers. It is impossible to paint unless you have experienced what you paint, the real. The real means on the one hand sexual freedom and on the other an understanding of deprivation and poverty. The real is identified, however, with litter, with detritus, the leftover, the half-consumed reject which has already been stripped by someone else – 'Refuse and rubbish' (85); 'Fig-skins, melon-parings, rinds and shucks' (84); 'The bit of half-stripped grape-bunch he desires' (115); 'The droppings of the wax to sell again' (120); 'Which dog bites, which lets drop/His bone from the offal in the street' (122–3). The artist trains himself to snap up society's waste products and recycle them – and resell them – as art. 'To find its meaning is my meat and drink' (315). Art is fed by appetite. The insight that art and appetite are linked is skewed, however, because there is no necessary connection between aesthetic naturalism and libertarian sexual freedom, just as there is no necessary relation between the real and the scatological. Parodying this slapdash libertarianism, the text comes near to parodying Charles Kingsley's common-sense English Protestant view of the Catholic, ascetic early Renaissance art prior to Lippi's time. Such effeminate painting, Kingsley had argued, ignores 'the beauties of sex, of strength, of activity'. It is unmanly, and what was good in it came not from Catholic purity but a 'healthy layman's common sense'.[23]

The non sequiturs of the text point up the underlying sexual fear in the protestations of hubristic and voracious masculinity through Grotesque distortion. On the other hand, there is an equally powerful distortion working in the opposite direction, which is why this monologue swings between contradictory assertions.

> However, you're my man, you've seen the world
> – The beauty and the wonder and the power,
> The shapes of things, their colours, lights and shades,
> Changes, surprises, – and God made it all!
> For what? Do you feel thankful, ay or no.
>
> (282–6)

This exuberant and intensely felt celebration of energy and form comes out of nowhere, appearing almost inconsequentially. And yet this comes in the context of a quite different and extraordinarily aggressive account of art as defacement and defecation. The Lockean tabula rasa is displaced from the mind to the world and the expressive artist relieves his 'crammed' (143) mind by marking the blank space before him; 'the walls blank,/ Never was such prompt disburdening' (143–4). The artist voids pent-up emotion and images from his mind in a flagrant parody of the expressive artist's overflow of feeling. 'This world's no blot for us,/Nor blank' (313–14). Here the insistent defensiveness suggests that the world *is* potentially a blank to be blotted by the artist who has 'splashed' (324) a fresco in fine style. The ejaculatory imagery confirms Lippi's sense of himself as a 'beast' (270), the coded Victorian term for sexual licence.

The monologue is taking up here and playing with Ruskin's ideas in *Modern Painters* in a complex way. It filters a Ruskinian view of painting through a consciousness Ruskin specifically deprecated, and exposes the uneasiness of Ruskin's understanding of the universal appeal of the eye through an equally uneasy account of the importance of seeing. 'The beauty and the wonder and the power' (283) are Ruskin's categories. The first volume of *Modern Painters* (1843) establishes the 'pleasure' of painting through ideas of beauty and power, truth, imitation and relation. Ruskin insisted on the liberating power of the eye as a universal possibility: 'There is not one single object in nature which is not capable of conveying' beauty: that all art starts with 'the representation of facts'; and that 'it is in the power of all, with care and time' to respond fully to painting.[24] Throughout *Modern Painters* Ruskin claims that the pleasure and delight of the eye is the founding perceptual experience and that painting liberates the vision. Quoting Locke on the necessity of the mental apprehension of the materials of perception made 'on the outward parts', he says that because sight is so habitual, men can pass things virtually 'unseen', and speaks of the 'love' which comes from the 'acuteness of bodily sense' (Part II, section i, chapter 2).[25] On the other hand this generosity can shift into a highly restricted and authoritarian view of art. He deprecated the deception of 'imitative' painting which appeals to the superficial 'animal feelings' and responds to flesh colour and physical immediacy (II. i. 1).[26] The understanding of the high truth of painting is 'altogether intellectual' and requires constant cultivation and refinement if physical experience is to be brought under the moral nature which is independent of it. Celebrating the bodily sense, he reintroduces a split between body and mind:[27] celebrating a universal, democratic access to the visual he yet asserts the high authority of the artist's privileged vision.

Lippi appears to paraphrase Ruskin: 'we're made so that we love/First when we see them painted, things we have passed/Perhaps a hundred times nor cared to see' (300–2). But, true to the carnivalesque, Lippi's arguments (286–307) are actually an inversion of Ruskin's, and expose their equivocations by careless and self-contradictory simplification; Lippi's arguments expose the dualism of the insecure connections between art and morality and intellect and the concealed authoritarianism and idealism of the artist's private vision. If we paint things 'Just as they are, *careless* what comes of it' (294) (my emphasis), moral and spiritual truth follows automatically. We may not presume to 'Interpret God' (311) but the artist's observation itself is invested with ethical and imaginative authority – 'Make his flesh liker and his Soul more like' (207): more like *what?* the uncompleted comparative asks. The unfinished thinking exposes the problems of the status of the spiritual in representation. Similarly we may not 'reproduce' (298) (the art of imitation), or 'beat' (299) nature (idealist art) but the artist's private vision is paramount and can be 'borrowed' by his public: 'God uses us to help each other so,/Lending our minds out' (305–6). This economy of art ('use', 'lending') suggests generosity while re-establishing ownership. Paradoxically the Grotesque works with extraordinary linguistic subtlety as the language discloses the Ruskinian premises by the most precise distortions. Despite these 'Ruskinian' views Lippi shows himself earlier in the poem as a convinced imitative artist, enabling his viewers to experience the surprise of deceptive semblance (they

303

recognise the Prior's 'niece' (170)) from his painting in a way Ruskin would have deplored. Yet, in giving pleasure to an audience he thinks of with some condescension as 'simple' (168), he presupposes an élite cultivation as the prerequisite of true appreciation.

The monologue carries these inconsistencies into the contradictory psychology of the speaker – a demotic energy and generosity accompanied by the rage of the displaced artist whose very demotic pretensions prevent him from claiming the privileged authority of vision he desires. The monologue does not solve the problem of a democratic art but opens out its complexities. By exposing the comedy of Ruskinian democracy it returns to the great question of pleasure and its dissemination which had preoccupied Fox as an aesthetic and political problem. This monologue is dominated by the definition of one of Bentham's 'non-entities'. The soul, he said, has no existence in the world to which we can refer.

In this poem Browning explores the radical implications of Ruskin's theory of the Grotesque at the same time as suggesting that in practice his writing is not radical enough. But if the analytical Grotesque pulls awry Ruskinian aesthetics, and makes a political critique, distorting Ruskin both to assent and dissent from him in 'Fra Lippo Lippi', that poem could well be invoked to redress the dry sense of impoverished energy in 'Cleon'. Its speaker, an intellectual and aristocratic polymath writing to his patron prince at the end of Greek culture, just before the advent of Christianity, has been asked by his patron how his wisdom assists a confrontation with death – and responds with fastidious aesthetic disgust. Death is an obscenity which in an odd way comes alive for him in the chiasmus of 'quickening' horror (315). The oppressed consciousness, Ruskin said, is fascinated by death. Lippi acknowledges the 'grey beginning' (392) (the dawn, and the onset of enervation after the violent attempts of Grotesque consciousness to energise itself) but death dominates Cleon's sense of himself as a latter-day intellectual living in an era of decadent culture. The rigidity of pride as well as the paralysis of labour produces the consciousness which cannot play, one remembers, and Cleon celebrates the importance of aestheticised intellectual labour over and against brute labour even while the slaves on whom his freedom depends unload the luxury gifts sent by his patron which 'block my court at last /And pile themselves along its portico' (8–9): 'pile themselves' is a telling phrase, for the gifts are actually piled by the slaves, but a slave society depends upon a definition of physical work as degraded and upon the repression of the fact of that labour. His patron's architectural project, the building of a tower, does not 'engage in work for mere work's sake' (31). Slavery and power are at the heart of this most understated of Browning's monologues but this can easily be misrecognised because of the highly refined analysis of culture conducted by Cleon. The shock of the Grotesque technique here is to put Arnoldian classicism and its analysis of the decay of the modern

consciousness back into the historical moment when 'the calm, the cheerfulness, the disinterested objectivity' (1853 Preface) was, according to Arnold,
disappearing, and so to distort that 'objectivity' as to make it a part of
the decadence it analyses.

The vocabulary of 'Cleon' is a prophetic construction out of the values
of *Empedocles* and the 1853 Preface. Arnold's public concern with the critical
spirit, with adequacy, with how to live and with the nature of culture,
came after 1853.[28] Cleon, the dry, fatigued and hungry intellectual, is
uncannily invested with a prescient Arnoldian vocabulary: 'Within the
eventual element of *calm*' (42): 'let him *critically* learn/How he lives'
(216–17): 'Nay, so much less as that *fatigue* has brought/Deduction to it'
(244–5): 'life's *inadequate* to *joy*,/As the soul sees *joy*' (249–50): 'O King,
with thy profound *discouragement*,/Who *seest the wider* but to sigh the more'
(270–1) ('Arnoldian' terms are emphasised). The critique of Arnoldian
values turns on Arnold's analysis of the estrangement of the intellectual.
Pure knowing split off from the energy of pure being is the sickness of
Empedocles. This is also the condition developed into a syllogism rendering
the contradictions of consciousness by Cleon. The more he understands
the nature of joy the more he is cut off from experiencing it; the more
richly joy is seen and desired the more inevitable is his severance from it.

> What? dost thou verily trip upon a word,
> Confound the accurate view of what joy is
> (Caught somewhat clearer by my eyes than thine)
> With feeling joy? confound the knowing how
> And showing how to live (my faculty)
> With actually living?
>
> (278–83)

Hence the fatigue and pessimism: 'Most progress is most failure' (272).
Cleon's almost prurient sense of shock that 'actually living' can be confounded with knowing how to live, however, is deeply ironised, unlike that
of Empedocles. The contradictions he analyses are seen to be the product
of a further contradiction he cannot reach. Cleon's sickness is not the
sickness he analyses. The fundamental problem is that his view of consciousness and civilisation *predetermines* the split between knowledge and
being and produces a thin and impoverished understanding of what it is
to know and to be, inevitably creating the fracture it seeks to heal. This
is a cultural problem, as the social and political context of the monologue
suggests, related to the *acceptance* of a social structure which makes it
possible for the alienated unhappy consciousness to emerge. Its cycles of
negation are related to an idealist account of mind, and an idealist account
of mind is related to the structure of the slave society. Behind Cleon's
thinking is a Hegelian and evolutionary movement of development which
guarantees the master–slave relationship he accepts as fundamental to life.

305

And behind *that* is the class and colonial organisation of contemporary British society.

It is fitting that this monologue is a written epistle, for writing is detached from the recipient in a way that speech is not, and thus becomes 'the dialogue of the mind with itself' which Arnold saw as the sign of self-conscious modern subjectivity. But because it is presented as a letter, the dialogue of the mind is objectified for analysis. Moreover, the abstraction of writing, which betokens absence, is an alienated form of communication and registers the peculiar detachment of Cleon's mind. The more abstract Cleon becomes, however, the more he is concerned with power. In this monologue the Grotesque technique sports with forms of thought, idealist and evolutionary, disclosing them as cultural myths and exploring the logic of the free play of mind in which scepticism and pessimism become a form of oppression.

The monologue is organised in three phases of expansive movement, each of which turns back on itself, mimicking the tendency of developmental theory to define progressive phases of history in threes. In the first phase Cleon contemplates the Tower of Protus, and finds satisfaction in the transcendental labour of the free play of mind, omitting to remember that the Tower is built on the labour of slaves. This leads him to contemplate the movement of history as the development of mind, defining the intellectual improvement of his own refined and rarefied culture in a phenomenology which excludes material change. But though the present should include within itself the gigantic intellectual moments of the past (the best that has been thought and said in the world, Arnold would have said), his own era is a period of decadence: 'The soul alone deteriorates' (138). His is a culture of the 'composite' (65) and 'synthesis' (94), but paradoxically adds up to less than the parts of the past. He argues that it may not be possible to see the 'whole' of our culture (to see life steadily and see it whole is an Arnoldian ideal), because we are necessarily a part of it. And so the 'whole' fractures into parts estranged from one another, and leads intellectually to an eclecticism with no principle of origination in it. There is no Hegelian *Aufhebung* here, even though the pattern of thinking is Hegelian. But the conceptualising of culture in terms of a wholeness one can master creates the possibility of its opposite, fragmentation and impotence. Another paradox is that the idea of decadence is made logically possible by thinking in terms of progressive movement. This Cleon recognises, as he considers culture in terms of biological and evolutionary growth from primitive to complex forms, from the simple flower to the sophisticated hybrid. The crude idea of progress, when it is rarefied to the idea of refinement, becomes deeply pessimistic. He has taken the wild flower and 'dashed/Rose-blood upon its petals' (147-8) and 'driven' (149) its seed to fruit, achieving 'a better flower if not so large' (150). Such cultivation results in further alienation from external 'natural' processes. One is reminded of Empedocles and his sense that he is cut off from nature and evolutionary process itself. The violation of a lost simplicity indicates both the power of human culture and its impotence.

Meeting the sense of impotence at all points in his argument, he turns in the third phase of the monologue to the power of pure mind. And here he invokes an idealist epistemology whose structure determines alienation and simultaneously *justifies* a power relation which seems to redeem him from it. He puts the emergence of reflexive thought in evolutionary and Feuerbachian terms as a 'higher' principle of life. The brute cannot externalise himself to himself, Feuerbach said, cannot think, and is thus immersed in matter because it is dependent on the physical presence of things to recognise and fulfil its needs. But man thinks, and his 'true objective *ego*' is known in the object he creates; he is both I and thou. In a virtual paraphrase of Feuerbach Cleon declares the mind's self-awareness which releases thinking things from the world of matter which otherwise 'has them, not they it' (206). When man grows 'conscious in himself'

> We called it an advance, the rendering plain
> Man's spirit might grow conscious of man's life,
> And, by new lore so added to the old,
> Take each step higher over the brute's head.
> This grew the only life, the pleasure house,
> Watch-tower and treasure-fortress of the soul,
> Which whole surrounding flats of natural life
> Seemed only fit to yield subsistence to.
>
> (227–34)

The marvellous, unconscious energies of the natural world simply act (197–202) – the fish *strikes*, the shell *sucks*. The verbs are made intransitive to indicate the non-objectifying, non-reflexive life of brute existence. On the other hand, Cleon's sentences circle back on themselves, become tautologous, and duplicate the subject as object so that they fail to proceed to a new object: they include the categories of the subject in the object or they end with a preposition or infinitive which appears to seek a new predicate but doubles back to an antecedent one. The syntax is a Grotesque parody of the enclosure of pure mind which cannot move beyond itself, living in the tower of self, a parallel to that constructed by Protus, experiencing itself as tautology. Feuerbachian thinking is static and actually organises consciousness to confirm the split between knowledge and being because it presupposes a simple duplication of the self without considering the dynamic movement between consciousness and the world which mutually transform one another. The mind conceiving itself as its own object constructs a 'real' object from which it is forever excluded and which is always unreachable. Paraphrase becomes parody as the thwarted mind authoritatively abstracts its procedures for analysis and simultaneously

307

experiences a rage for unattainable sensuous fullness and energy. Hence 'the feeling of depression, the feeling of ennui', as Arnold called it, which pervades this monologue.

The high ground of transcendent thought and self-separation creates Cleon's isolation but also guarantees the master–slave relationship by defining the slave as the brute immersed in matter – the 'lower and inconscious forms of life' (226); 'Using his senses, not the sense of sense' (224) – and the intellectual aristocrat as one of an élite dedicated to pure mind. The static epistemology supports a static social structure. The slaves, at first seen, or rather not seen, as part of the black-and-white pattern of the geometrical paving in Cleon's portico, are seen purely instrumentally but are regarded with the fantasising of estrangement. They keep surfacing in Cleon's mind with the persistence of fascinated repression. In this most cerebral of monologues the intelligent and sophisticated arrogance has moments of dry hunger for the sensuous. The 'lyric' female slave who 'refines upon the women of my youth' (137) (the text allows that all women are slaves), her 'crocus vest' (15), the 'muscles all a-ripple' (299) on the male's back, introduce a sexuality which is both threatening and deeply desirable because to the exhausted Cleon, who sees slaves as objects, their energy seems unalienated. In fact their erotic power dominates him and thus they unconsciously reverse the power relations on which Cleon founds his life. In each phase of the poem they enter and disrupt. The ultimate condition of the man who oppresses is that he becomes ever more exhausted in the effort to maintain his power, the logic of a dialectic of power. It is Hegel and not Feuerbach who builds the master–slave *dialectic* into his account of self-consciousness. Feuerbach excludes it, and with it any account of inherent struggle in the processes of mind and the social processes to which mind belongs. The monologue grasps the essentially undynamic structure in which Cleon lives and thinks.

These two monologues, 'Fra Lippo Lippi' and 'Cleon', investigating the forms of thought and feeling which belong to the two great ideological myths of the nineteenth century, approach the oppressed Grotesque consciousness through the distortions of the Grotesque analysis, its restricted perspective, misprision and linguistic slippage. Democratic realism, élitist idealism, are alike the provisional and contradictory constructions of cultural fictions. The point of the monologues is that people *live* and experience them: imagination shapes and is shaped by them; they determine choices, and yet they cannot be extracted as 'pure' forms of thought and experience from the language and conditions in which they are produced. Ideology cannot get outside itself. But what we can do is to participate in the endless process of redefinition. There will always be, as the final poem of the volume indicates, 'One Word More'. Hence *Men and Women* produces discourses with immense fertility, overlapping but never isometric. Almost all the poems appear to be generated out of the two central monologues, but two monologues, 'Karshish' and 'Blougram', ask for some attention along with a group of love poems, for they all turn on a question fundamental to the production of fictions – what it means to *believe* anything.

'And then Christianity is a worthy *myth*, and poetically acceptable', Elizabeth Barrett Browning had written before their marriage.[29] 'Karshish' and 'Blougram' are concerned with the myth of Christianity at two different historical moments, its beginning and its end, AD 66, at the time of the Emperor Vespasian's invasion of Palestine, and contemporary England, where humanism and Catholicism are in debate. 'Did Christianity conquer a single philosopher, historian, or poet of the classical period? . . . The decline of culture was identical with the victory of Christianity', Feuerbach wrote in *The Essence of Christianity*.[30] The scientific consciousness of Karshish at a time of intense rationality is confronted with the 'miracle' of Lazarus: the sceptical consciousness of the Bishop, at a time of advanced positivist culture, colluding with gimcrack miracle – 'the Virgin's winks' (699) – is confronted with the problem of belief. Both are empiricists: ''Tis but a case of mania subinduced/By epilepsy' (79–80), Karshish theorises Lazarus's condition. 'State the facts,/Read the text right' (581–2) is the Bishop's knowing and ironic comment on the German biblical criticism which has actually made it impossible to read the text 'right'. In both, the monologue form attempts to deal with the irreducible instability of interpretation, where the speaker constructs the object in terms of his own categories, by including that irreducible instability as one of the 'facts' for investigation, with a distorting empiricism which attempts to outflank empiricism. The mastery of the empirical mode is encountered with its double in a parody of mastery. That the Grotesque consciousness can only be interpreted through the strategies of the Grotesque itself is what makes the deconstructive project so risky, always on the dangerous edge of collapse into the terms and categories uttered with such conviction and passion by the speaker. In both, the question of *definition* is at issue. For Karshish it is the extent to which experience can be included within his scientific categories; for the Bishop it is the definition of belief and unbelief.

Karshish assents to the scientific mode which determines him as external to and outside all phenomena, whether material or psychological. But objectivity is actually a passion and shapes his research into physical properties – 'Judea's gum-tragacanth/Scales off in purer flakes . . . exceeds our produce' (55–6, 58) – as much as it shapes the medical man's sceptical analysis of another objective phenomenon, the risen Lazarus. Lazarus, a man 50 years old, is in an autistic condition of detachment, strangely paralleling the detachment assumed by Karshish. But Karshish cites this condition as evidence of physical illness. Lazarus is indifferent to the Roman armaments which are building up to defeat his country. Karshish, assuming the value-free detachment of the scientist who is exempt from political and national boundaries, nevertheless interprets this indifference

309

as a sign of mania. Thus his detachment is founded on certain cultural norms. As he considers the case of Lazarus, attempting to assimilate the phenomenon into his own categories and terms of reference, these are strained to breaking point. His definition of madness is physiological (here Browning glances at contemporary physiological accounts of mind), but it attempts to assimilate a psychological condition. Christian experience is for him a form of madness, and the definition of madness opens up as a condition imputed to any state which cannot be culturally assimilated and which falls outside the experience we agree to be rational – but then rationality is open to definition as well. Madness and rationality become possible fictions.

At the end of the poem Karshish's mind makes more or less this kind of imaginative leap, as he attempts to displace the idea of power with the idea of love – 'So, the All-Great were the All-Loving too' (305). It is a moral leap, but it is projected within the terms of a positivist fiction, a Feuerbachian God projected from human love. It becomes a Grotesque fiction because the transforming possibility is arrived at through rational humanist thought, which may not comprehend an experience radically different from his own.

'Blougram', ostensibly an informal chat about belief over wine and urbane jokes about 'half-baked' (7) Puginesque gothic rosettes, is in fact, formally, a highly organised poem, and, unusual for the monologues at this stage, ends with a tail piece added by the poet. The poem has an illusory antithetical structure; at mid-point the Bishop moves from an analysis of unbelief and turns to belief – 'Believe – and our whole argument breaks up' (555). But the two halves of the monologue fall inwards to one another, section by section, mirroring one another as the arguments for belief parallel the arguments for unbelief (see, for example, the tenth paragraph matched by the twenty-first, 173 ff.; 647 ff.) until the last mirrors the first. Belief and unbelief reflect into one another, each becoming a form of and justification for the other. So belief becomes a mirror image of unbelief and not its true opposite. Unbelief is 'converted' into belief and by the same token belief is converted into unbelief. The Bishop is 'converting' Gigadibs the humanist, his opposite, but true to the circularity of projection, Gigadibs mirrors his own categories. The Grotesque turns this circularity against itself by ironising the Bishop's distortions of humanistic thought. If the religious idea represents the highest ideal of human thought it can also mirror its opposite, the lowest instincts of Manichean *invidia*, the 'hell-deep instincts' (990) of the Bishop described in the 'authorial' tail piece. None the less the tail piece does not actually clarify these, for its language slides, and opens up once again the radical instability of definition set in motion by the Bishop. He believed 'half he spoke' (980) and called truth by 'wrong names' (996) – but *which* half he believed is left undefined, just as 'truth' and 'wrong' are given no content. The tail piece is a sport

310

with hermeneutics and definition, a mirroring of the Bishop's procedures rather than a resolution of them. The Bishop introduces a radical ambiguity by defining Gigadibs's humanism as 'belief' and his own sceptical assent to Catholicism as honest 'unbelief', inverting terms which are inverted again when the monologue turns from the definition of 'unbelief' to 'belief'.

There seems to be a compulsive need on the Bishop's part to obtain mastery over the language of rational definition at the same time as definition is dissolved. Some of this turning of definition provokes a sharp rethinking of terms – a great deal that the Bishop says, perhaps the ultimate irony, actually *is* rational and probing: he lists conversion experiences with knowing irony, the sense of transcendence evoked by a sunset, a flower, a death, 'A chorus-ending from Euripides' (184) which attack us 'Just when we are safest' (182). These are generally the humanist's substitute for transcendence and attack us just when we are safest in belief, eroding certainty. But the sentence reverses these expectations; just when we are safest in agnosticism these sentimental, aestheticised emotions send us back to a suspect belief, 'the ancient idol' (189). Both sentimental humanism and sentimental Christianity are exposed. The slide of definition and syntax here is characteristic of the Bishop's rhetoric – for instance, the indeterminacy of the pronoun 'we', typical of the use of all pronouns in the poem. The emptying out of content is so insistent that the overt rationality dissolves and is displaced by a latent argument created out of figurative association rather than logical relations. It is important to see that many of the arguments are acute at a rational level. It is their juxtaposition and their context of emotion which distorts them. In order to 'read' the text 'right', we are forced back on the reading of an emotional subtext. Not the least of the virtuosity of this monologue is that it demonstrates the way in which the destruction of syntax and definition forces one into the miasma of the non-rational.

The chain of unmaking and self-undermining of meaning is inexorable and highly complex, but two important moments demonstrate the deeply reactionary sense of lack and *invidia* which works concurrently with the sophistication. 'Want' is a recurrently unmade word in the poem, want as desire, as aspiration – religious, political, aesthetic – want as greed, for power and for material goods, want as lack, deprivation and *invidia*, want as poverty and above all want as the lack of energy, the 'fire and life' (557) lacking in the 'dead matter' (558) of human consciousness. 'Want' is constantly 'converted' into its most negative possibilities as lack. At the turning point of the poem, when it swings round from the nature of unbelief to define belief, lack of belief is defined as belief: 'If you desire [i.e. *desire* and *lack*] faith . . . you've faith enough. . . . What else [but desire] seeks God? . . . what else seek ourselves?' (634–5). The syntax allows that not only do we ourselves seek God but that in seeking God we seek ourselves, which is to seek only the deprivation of want and desire. Speaking of the cult figures of the nineteenth century as 'believers', Napoleon and Shakespeare, the language manages to turn both into creatures of want indiscriminately, want either as the violently fanatical desire for power (resulting in 'The blown-up millions – spatter of their brains/And . . . so forth' (458–9)) or the creative artist's atavistic and consuming need for everything the world can offer, from material riches to the power of energy: 'We want the same things, Shakespeare and myself' (539): 'Enthusiasm's the best thing, I repeat;/Only, we can't command it' (556–7). The strategy of the Bishop's case is to 'justify' all forms of unbelief or want and then to demonstrate that they are paradoxical forms of belief, thus 'converting' unbelief into belief, which is another form of want.

The obsession with 'want' leads to a chain of aggressive figures of gross feeding and consumption (877–82), which for the Bishop is the real motive of action, and particularly the motive of Gigadibs, whose humanism disguises violent libidinal desire with timid rationalism, derided as the feebleness which does not recognise lack. The Bishop's language thus becomes a kind of consuming of or gross feeding upon his opponent as he sets about converting his opponent's ideas into his own image of experience – feeding is after all the most literal form of conversion. The idea of 'want' opens up another chain of obsessive figures connected with it – a terror of nakedness, exposure, stripping, cutting, flaying, castration, which returns in aggression. In the second half of the poem the 'lidless eye' (559) of 'naked belief' (648, paragraph 21) matches the earlier sceptical account of transcendence (paragraph 10) and redefines it as the horror of exposure. Similarly, the humanist's attack on dogma is seen as the ultimate stripping and negation – 'Linen goes next, and last the skin itself' (794, paragraph 28) – and echoes and exposes the fear of the earlier statement by being a mirror image of it: 'The naked life is gross, till clothed upon' (329, paragraph 14). The formulations of high theory, offered urbanely and sophisticatedly – 'Fichte's clever cut at God himself' (744) – turn out to figure the violence of castration. Such violence emerges politically in an intense assent to the necessity of repression: 'Suppose I own at once a tail and claws . . . I'll lash out lion-fashion, and leave apes/To dock their stump and dress their haunches up' (350, 352–3): 'the rough purblind mass we seek to rule:/We are their lords or they are free of us,/Just as we tighten or relax our hold' (756–9).

'Bishop Blougram's Apology' is often seen as a biased lampoon on Catholicism, but it rather suggests that the debate about it unleashes the most intense fears and fantasies. It is certainly a poem about political argument and reactionary debate, and extends the notion of 'belief' to include the account of human possibility which informs it – the Bishop's ideology is shaped by contempt and a narrow and impoverished understanding of possibility which is itself ideological. The Bishop's daemonic conservatism is a literalised, ecclesiastical embodiment of one of those *ministers* of 'pain, and fear,/And disappointment', the Furies, in Shelley's *Prometheus Unbound*, who force their victims to 'grow' like what they 'contemplate'.[31] The decay of language which exaggerates the Grotesque incommensurateness of representation to the point of travesty and nescience and exposes the irrational subtext is thus of crucial importance. The inherent instability of language is manipulated here for ideological purposes as the Bishop contends for the meaning of 'belief'. But if we are to have a chance to 'read' a text it is essential to a democratic reading that language is not deprived of signification. In showing that we can and cannot 'read' the Bishop's language the Grotesque treads the dangerous edge of the democratic interpretation.

The anxiety of reading is nowhere more evident than in the love poems – the ending of love turns on a 'word' (89) in 'A Lover's Quarrel' – and nowhere so agnostic, as the lover commits himself to endless reading and hermeneutics, which is also the endless production of fictions. The double reading is intrinsic to these poems, which present themselves as the most immediate utterances of longing. And yet they are founded on a constant remaking of the self and the self's object through unstable memory and desire. The Grotesque extremity of desire pushes them towards intensity and incompleteness. The lurking pressure of frustration endows an irritable sexuality to the objects onto which it is displaced – toadstools gaze voyeuristically at the mushrooms' 'coral nipple' (63) in 'By the Fire-side'. This poem, a hypothetical memory of a remembered event, turns into a double memory when the speaker returns to a supposed present, two experiences of the same event which turn out to be two different events and two different experiences, all of which are open to perpetual redefinition as the poem ends: 'And the whole is well worth thinking o'er . . . which I mean to do' (263, 265). This poem is built round a structural chasm. Memory returns to a present already reshaped by the experience of memory to reassure itself of its validity and almost begs for the continuance of love to be made possible – 'My own, confirm me!' (121). There is a fragility here as the woman is asked to confirm the man and his memories. The first movement of memory is towards a dead centre, the disused chapel to which the lovers walk. The 'second' memory leads, significantly, to the moment of union on the bridge leading away from the church. A bridge, both crossing and connecting, marks both transition and terminus. The 'one and infinite' (181) moment *is* 'one' only, for it takes place in the world of process as the water 'slips' (182) or passes over the rock and the west is 'tender' (183), charged with feeling, perhaps, but also vulnerable, as delicate skin is tender (so Browning transforms Keats's 'Tender is the night' in 'Ode to a Nightingale'). 'The lights and shades made up a spell' (189): 'spell' here means equally a short space of time and a magical transformation. The moment is infinite because it can be repeatedly transformed by memory.

The fiction is both the despair and the creativity of love. In 'Love in a Life' it is imaged as repeated search for the 'Heart' (4) or the 'centre' (12) of an experience, both words occurring at the centre of each stanza. But the rhyme scheme opens out and closes as the lover moves through successive rooms in his search for the woman, coming to rest at the centre of each stanza – ABCCC – but displacing the central rhyme to the end of the stanza – ABC – and forming a repetition which is another beginning. The woman is never known except by her effect on the closed environment of the house, the 'trouble' (5) behind her – a moving curtain, perfume, an evanescent image in the mirror – which leaves only the evidence of its pastness to be experienced as the cornice wreath 'blossomed' (7). The speaker attempts to catch up on a past which has, paradoxically, gone before him. But the effects of the woman's presence may well be the effects of his own mind, a fiction, the lover's pursuit of his own echoes which have effaced the woman he pursues. 'Heart' is ambiguously the lover's heart and his sweetheart. The strangely predatory word, 'hunt' (2), suggests that the 'trouble' is an attribute of the mind as well as the movement of a curtain. But the lyric goes beyond this to the way that physical spaces organise the lover's experience, each room closed off from the other, organising sexual relationships in terms of division and alienation and barrier. This minute poem suggests how the fiction of love is sustained by the material details of space and furniture – curtain, mirror, cornice – which create the 'trouble' and concealments of Victorian sexual relationships.

'Childe Roland to the Dark Tower came' is unlike anything else Browning wrote. But it was written the day before 'Love among the Ruins', the poem which was important enough to stand at the beginning of *Men and Women*, and perhaps fittingly ends a discussion of the 1855 poems. Created out of a hint from *King Lear*, reaching back to the chivalric world which Tennyson had already laid claim to, it is a symbolic and existential poem of a kind Browning rarely wrote. Yet it is a companion poem to 'Love among the Ruins' because it is a black, reverse exploration of the power of the mythos and the need for alternative myths. Some critics have seen it as the culmination of Romantic aporia in which all teleological and existential certainty has disappeared.[32] Yet the Grotesque makes this so obvious that it is worth considering other elements of the poem. The language is crude and violent and heavy with overwrought physical horror and hysteria. Sexual hatred and disgust emerge in a miasma of perceptual uncertainty: 'It may have been a water-rat I speared,/But, ugh! it sounded like a baby's shriek' (125–6). Language is unreliable. The knight is convinced that the leering old man's directions at the start of his quest are false, yet he leaves the 'safe way' for the 'ominous tract', which 'all agree'

(14) hides the dark tower. After that he walks a physical and psychological treadmill, repeating the same experience in a multitude of different and ever more violent ways. He attempts to impose the notion of the quest as on-going progress and achievement on experience, but it resists this formulation. The imagery is all circular, even if it may look superficially as if some progress has been made. A river is crossed, a landscape changes, but there is no change and no progress – 'And just as far as ever from the end!' (157). An appalling conflict, a 'mad brewage' (136), has taken place, but penned in a hollow where no footsteps can be seen leading out of or into the fight.

> Whose savage trample thus could pad the dank
> Soil to a plash? Toads in a poisoned tank,
>   Or wild-cats in a red-hot iron cage –
>
> The fight must so have seemed in that fell cirque.
>   What penned them there, with all the plain to choose?
>   No footprint leading to that horrid mews,
> None out of it.
>
>   (130–6)

Toads in a poisoned tank, wild-cats in a red-hot cage, these are images of atrocity, torture and sadism which seem the product of anguished and deeply violent fears and fantasies, as the notion of linear achievement actually creates a prison for the knight. He sees his quest in terms of an escape from the self, the search for revelation from without. But as he is forced further into the solitude of the quest, with hints of guilt and betrayal among the masculine band of peers, he is forced deeper into the disordered regions of his own isolation. Revelation of a kind is granted him. The plain dissolves into a bowl of mountains (another circular image) and he realises that 'progress' is impossible – 'you're inside the den!' (174). With this acceptance he recognises the irrational violence and hatred as his – the 'den' is an appropriate word for both the containment and release of violence. With the blowing of the horn comes the discovery of meaning – or meaninglessness – as he realises that he is upon the dark tower without having recognised it.

The 'meaning' of the dark tower and the blowing of the horn is the crux of the poem. Death, the ultimate comprehension of selfhood, an insight into gnostic meaning, all these are possibilities. And yet in its deliberate gesture towards meaning it defies meaning. Phallic, ugly ('round squat'), opaque and mysterious ('blind as the fool's heart' (182)), and yet unique, it stands possibly for that fiction of the self which each person blindly assumes to exist in order to see himself as a living, active entity at all. And yet here it is displaced, outside the self, a threatening admonitory presence. It is impossible to literalise the dark tower, and yet the suggestion

315

of the text is that it *has* been literalised, as goal, as phallic power. It has organised the knight's experience as continual self-testing and the quest for objectives, even though it drives him to disintegration. For this is not simply an existential poem. It registers psychological violence, but it is the violence created by a world of masculine values, of linear progress, of the goal which 'proves' identity. No women enter the poem except through hints of adultery which may as well suggest homosexual relations. Shaping its hatred and anxiety is another coercive myth, the fiction of male power. The blast on the horn is an act of defiant fear and celebration, celebration that a unifying power has been provisionally discovered, fear that such a dominance may collapse. The dominant figure of 'Childe Roland' is fighting, warfare, aggression, death. One remembers the Grotesque fascination with the horror of death and its inability to comprehend it. This is surely Browning's prophetic Crimean-war poem. It was actually written in 1852. Through the violent terror of the restricted and distorted vision of masculine values it makes its critique indirectly, considering the destructive effect of the coercive ideology of heroism, the black mythos which was to cause such carnage in the Crimean war. The inexplicable caged cats and poisoned toads become less the product of sadistic imaginings than a prescient understanding of the significance and implications of the martial beliefs which sent men into 'the valley of Death', as Tennyson called it, in 'The Charge of the Light Brigade', written to mark a military blunder two years later.

After *Men and Women* Browning's work came increasingly to be preoccupied with the nature of the fiction and imaginative constructs. In *Men and Women* ideological forms of thought and modes of feeling are his primary materials and the epistemological problems of the fiction follow from them. In *Dramatis Personae* (1864) these priorities seem to be reversed. The pure palace of sound in 'Abt Vogler', the travesty of Romantic vision in 'Mr Sludge, "The Medium"', the difficulties of textual transmission in 'A Death in the Desert' and the elementary cognitive processes of what we define as 'primitive' consciousness in 'Caliban upon Setebos', all these poems begin with abstract problems dramatised through an individual consciousness rather than releasing them through particularities. They are fine poems, but a tendency to theoretical dryness marks them. With *The Ring and the Book* (1868), however, Browning returned to the intensity and concentration of the 1855 volume. The story of a violent sexual murder committed by a run-down seventeenth-century Italian aristocrat is told and retold as different people interpret the same event, and often recounted more than once within each book. No version of the story, however, is ever an exact repetition, whether it is told by the murderer, the victim, factions of the community or the lawyers in the case.

Why did this case call forth all Browning's virtuosity? With this poem Browning returned to his earliest formative moments: the sources of the

Benthamite fiction are the *legal* fiction and the endless work of redefinition it demands. He also returned to the non-conformity of his youth, for *The Ring and the Book*, as the Pope's monologue recognises, interprets the moment of the trial as a test case for individual conscience against authority, both political and ecclesiastical authority.[33] We are back with the issues of *Strafford* in a new seventeenth-century context. Browning found the source material for the poem in 1860 and returned to England in 1861. It was the year John Stuart Mill, Browning's old liberal antagonist of the 1830s, published his *Representative Government*. This work was part of the intense debate on democracy, on what representation represented, which led up to and followed the Reform Bill of 1867. Bagehot's *The English Constitution* (1867) and Arnold's *Culture and Anarchy* (1869, but published in *The Cornhill* in 1867–8) were contributions to that debate. *The Ring and the Book* must be seen as Browning's contribution to the debate on representation. The nature of language becomes crucial again. The Grotesque vision again distorts to investigate the anti-aristocratic, pro-aristocratic and 'neutral' positions of the popular voice, the exploitation of privilege in the voices of the lawyers, the Pope's attempt to use power judiciously. The poem uncannily parallels the categories of barbarian, philistine and the populace in *Culture and Anarchy*, and we hear of the crowds surging forwards past the railings of the church to get a sight of the dead protagonists very much as a nineteenth-century English crowd surged through the railings of Hyde Park at the time of agitation for reform. The poem is an exhaustive reading of the implications of *vox populi* and the different forms representation can take. All these are given a voice. If *vox populi* is not *vox dei* it is not, as Bagehot called it, *vox diaboli* either.[34] That is the prerogative of Guido, the decayed aristocrat who has married and murdered to save his family fortunes. *The Ring and the Book* is one of Browning's fullest vindications of the radical vision of the Grotesque.

12

'A MUSIC OF THINE OWN'

Women's poetry – an
expressive tradition?

PRECURSORS

The altar, 'tis of death! for there are laid
The sacrifice of all youth's sweetest hopes.
It is a dreadful thing for woman's lip
To swear the heart away; yet know that heart
Annuls the vow while speaking, and shrinks back
From the dark future which it dares not face.
The service read above the open grave
Is far less terrible than that which seals
The vow that binds the victim, not the will:
For in the grave is rest.
                    (Letitia Landon [L.E.L.])[1]

Swept into limbo is the host
    Of heavenly angels, row on row;
The Father, Son, and Holy Ghost,
    Pale and defeated, rise and go.
The great Jehovah is laid low,
    Vanished his burning bush and rod –
        Say, are we doomed to deeper woe?
        Shall marriage go the way of God?

Monogamous, still at our post,
    Reluctantly we undergo
Domestic round of boiled and roast,
    Yet deem the whole proceeding slow.
Daily the secret murmurs grow;
    We are no more content to plod
Along the beaten paths – and so
    Marriage must go the way of God.

Soon, before all men, each shall toast
    The seven strings unto his bow,

Like beacon fires along the coast,
  The flames of love shall glance and glow.
Nor let nor hindrance man shall know,
  From natal bath to funeral sod;
Perennial shall his pleasures flow
  When marriage goes the way of God.

Grant, in a million years at most,
  Folk shall be neither pairs nor odd –
Alas! we shan't be there to boast
  'Marriage has gone the way of God!'
                                        (Amy Levy, 1915)[2]

It is not difficult to find, from the beginning to the end of the nineteenth century, poems of protest such as those by Letitia Landon, writing early in the century, and Amy Levy, writing towards the end, in which an overt sexual politics addresses the institutions and customs which burden women, including, in Levy's case, the taboo against lesbianism. There is Elizabeth Barrett Browning's outburst against the trivial education which trains women for marriage in *Aurora Leigh* (1856), and which conditions them into acceptability 'As long as they keep quiet by the fire/And never say "no" when the world says "ay" ', a statement which perhaps adds another kind of complexity to Robert Browning's 'By the Fire-side' (1855).[3] There is Christina Rossetti's passionate wish to be a 'man',[4] and as one moves later into the century there are, if possible, fiercer expressions of protest in the work of poets such as Augusta Webster and Mathilde Blind. And yet the poems by Landon and Levy are as interesting for their differences as for their common theme. For Landon marriage is a terminal moment which requires the language of sacrifice and victim. For Levy, the end of marriage and the 'law' of God still leaves a patriarchy intact, for it is men who benefit from promiscuity, not women, and the narrow coercions of heterosexual pairing continue. Ironically, a world without marriage still goes 'The way of God' by perpetuating His patriarchal ways informally.

Yet it is too easy to describe the work of these very different women as a women's tradition based on a full frontal attack on oppression. Though such an attack undoubtedly often existed, a concentration on moments of overt protest can extract the content of a direct polemic about women's condition in a way which retrieves the protest, but not the poem. It is sometimes tempting to extrapolate such material from the poems (because they supply it in such abundance), personalising, psychologising or literalising by translating this material back into what is known or constructed as socioeconomic patriarchal history in a univocal way, so that all poems become poems about women's oppression. In this way the nature of the particular language and form of individual poems becomes obliterated by the concentration on a single theme.

319

Similarly, the same kind of difficulty attends the construction of a women's tradition according to a unique modality of feminine experience. For this would be to accept the distinction between two kinds of gender-based experience, male and female, and leaves uninvestigated a conventional, affective account of the feminine as a nature which occupies a distinct sphere of feeling, sensitivity and emotion quite apart from the sphere of thought and action occupied by men. This *was* a distinction frequently made by women poets themselves and by male critics in the nineteenth century, but it is necessary to be wary of it because, while it gave women's writing a very secure place in literary culture, it amounts to a kind of restrictive practice, confining the writing of women to a particular mode or genre. W. M. Rossetti, for instance, had this to say in his Preface to his edition of the poems of Felicia Hemans:

> Her sources of inspiration being genuine, and the tone of her mind being feminine in an intense degree, the product has no lack of sincerity: and yet it leaves a certain artificial impression, rather perhaps through a cloying flow of 'right-minded' perceptions of moral and material beauty than through any other defect. 'Balmy' it may be: but the atmosphere of her verse is by no means bracing. One might sum up the weak points in Mrs Hemans's poetry by saying that it is not only 'feminine' poetry (which under the circumstances can be no imputation, rather an encomium) but also 'female' poetry: besides exhibiting the fineness and charm of womanhood, it has the monotone of mere sex. Mrs Hemans has that love of good and horror of evil which characterize a scrupulous female mind; and which we may most rightly praise without concluding that they favour poetical robustness, or even perfection in literary form. She is a leader in that very modern phalanx of poets who persistently coordinate the impulse of sentiment with the guiding power of morals or religion. Everything must convey its 'lesson', and is indeed set forth for the sake of its lesson: but must at the same time have the emotional gush of a spontaneous sentiment.[5]

'Cloying', 'feminine', 'female', 'sentiment', 'lesson', 'emotional gush': not all this vocabulary is offered in a critical spirit, though it betrays uneasiness, but even the most cursory examination of the language here suggests the qualities attributed to women's poetry – conventional piety, didactic feeling, emotions, sentiment. Coventry Patmore parodies women's religious verse in *The Angel in the House* in a way which attributes the same qualities to their work. Honoria's pious sister entrusts a poem to the hero:

> Day after day, until today.
> Imaged the others gone before,

The same dull task, the weary way,
　　The weakness pardon'd o'er and o'er.

The thwarted thirst, too faintly felt,
　　For joy's well nigh forgotten life,
The restless heart, which, when I knelt,
　　Made of my worship barren strife.

Ah, whence today's so sweet release,
　　This clearance light of all my care,
This conscience free, this fertile peace,
　　These softly folded wings of prayer,

This calm and more than conquering love,
　　With which nought evil dares to cope,
This joy that lifts no glance above,
　　For faith too sure, too sweet for hope?

O, happy time, too happy change,
　　It will not live, though fondly nurst!
Full soon the sun will seem as strange
　　As now the cloud which seems dispersed.[6]

Since the hero is courting one of three sisters, this is possibly a cruel parody of one of Anne Brontë's poems, but the conventions of women's writing were sufficiently established for it to be a parody of the work of Letitia Landon (in some moods), Adelaide Anne Procter or Christina Rossetti. What is interesting about it is that it suggests that there *were* recognised conventions established for women's verse by this time in the century (1854). Interestingly, Patmore's carefully regular quatrains pick up a *limited* assent to the sense of limit in neutrally simple religious and psychological language, a self-admonitory withdrawal from protest and a pious but none too easy recognition of the difficulties of transcending limit. His parody responds to pessimism rather than to piety, and even at the level of satire negotiates with more complex elements than the self-abnegation attributed to it by Patmore's hero.

It is probably no exaggeration to say that an account of women's writing as occupying a particular sphere of influence, and as working inside defined moral and religious conventions, helped to make women's poetry and the 'poetess' (as the Victorians termed the woman poet) respected in the nineteenth century as they never have been since. In a survey of poetry early in the century in *Blackwood's Magazine* John Wilson ('Christopher North') wrote enthusiastically of women poets, and a respectful study of British women poets appeared in 1848, *The Female Poets of Great Britain*, selected and edited by Frederic Rowton. At the end of the century Eric Robertson published his *English Poetesses* (1883). Though Robertson was

321

less sympathetic than Rowton to women's poetry, believing that it would never equal the poetry of men, it is clear that the category of the 'poetess' was well established. Men assiduously edited women's work. Laman Blanchard edited Letitia Landon's *Life and Literary Remains* in 1841. W. M. Rossetti edited not only the work of his sister and Mrs Hemans but also Augusta Webster's *Mother and Daughter* sonnet sequence after her death (1895). Arthur Symons edited Mathilde Blind's works in 1900, with a memoir by Richard Garnett. It seems that men both enabled and controlled women's poetic production in a way that was often complex, and which requires more sustained discussion than can be given here. After a literary scandal about her association with a patron (probably William Maginn), Letitia Landon, in her early twenties, described her complete dependence on male help for the business of publication in moving terms.

> Your own literary pursuits must have taught you how little, in them, a young woman can do without assistance. Place yourself in my situation. Could you have hunted London for a publisher, endured all the alternate hot and cold water thrown on your exertions; bargained for what sum they might be pleased to give; and, after all, canvassed, examined, nay quarrelled over accounts the most intricate in the world? And again, after success had procured money, what was I to do with it? Though ignorant of business I must know I could not lock it up in a box.[7]

Like Mrs Hemans, Letitia Landon relied on her earnings for the support of her family, and so her dependence on men to gain access to the publishing world was of great importance to her.

That middle-class women were hosted by men into the literary world through editions of their work may be one explanation for our lack of knowledge of working-class women poets, who were not edited in this way. Contrary to common understanding there were working-class women poets, and they are still being discovered.[8] Those we know of tend to have survived because they supported conventional morals, such as the anonymous millgirl who wrote eloquently on the Preston lockout in 1862 but connected working-class well-being with temperance. Bamford praised Ann Hawkshaw but she seems to have been an educated poet with strong working-class connections who produced orthodox-seeming work with unusual subtexts. Her *Dionysius the Areopagite* (1842), for instance, is ostensibly about Christian conversion. Quite apart from her vision of an egalitarian heaven, the story is primarily concerned with a relationship between two women. She was an impressively strong and independent writer who wrote a series of sonnets on British history with another subtext concerned with subjugation. Her shorter poems, 'Why am I a slave?' and 'The Mother to Her Starving Child', are impressive. The slave cannot understand his exclusion from 'the white man's home': 'Who had a right to bind these limbs/And make a slave of me?' The mother is forced to wish her child dead rather than see it starve – and then to go mad with grief. The pun on the 'relief' of madness is sombre, with the ironic social meaning of 'poor relief' shadowing the psychological term.[9] Her work is exceptional. The pastoral didacticism of Louisa Horsfield, a contemporary, contrasts with it. Horsfield retrieves the natural world from the social sins of drunkenness, truancy and immorality in a more conventional way.[10] Ellen Johnston, addressing occasional poems to local bodies and factory workers, moves from awkward heroic poetry to simple ballad and cheerful dialect verse (for instance, in 'The Working Man'). Some of her love poems, particularly 'The Maniac of the Green Wood', are moving, but her work discloses the difficulties of discovering a language in which to address both a total community and a 'literary' audience.[11] Poetry by working-class women could be as didactic as that of middle-class women, if not more so.

If, then, a middle-class women's tradition is constructed by reference to the Victorian notion of what was specifically feminine in poetry, it is likely to be formed not only out of what were predominantly male categories of the female but also out of categories which were regarded as self-evident and unproblematical. This does not enable one to take the analysis of women's poetry in the nineteenth century very far. On the other hand, it is undoubtedly the case that women wrote with a sense of belonging to a particular group defined by their sexuality, and that this sense comprehends political differences and very different kinds of poetic language. Letitia Landon recognised this when she wrote, in her 'Stanzas on the Death of Mrs Hemans', that the poet had made 'A music of thine own'.[12] So it is possible, in spite of the reservations and precautionary remarks expressed above, to consider women poets in terms of a 'music' of their own.

What was the 'music' of the Victorian woman poet? It can be listened to, first, by seeing what the poetry of Letitia Landon and Mrs Hemans could have meant to later writers, for these were the poets to which a number of them looked back as precursors. Even when there seems no direct link between these earlier and later writers it does seem as if they worked within a recognisable tradition understood by them to belong to women. Secondly, this music can be listened to through the dissonances women's poetry created by making problematical the affective conventions and feelings associated with a feminine modality of experience even when, and perhaps particularly when, poets worked within these conventions. Victorian expressive theory later in the century, one of the dominant aesthetic positions of the period, created a discourse which could accommodate a poetics of the feminine. But women poets relate to it in an ambiguous way and interrogate it even while they negotiate and assent to expressive theory. It was this assimilation of an aesthetic of the feminine which enabled the woman poet to revolutionise it from within, by using it to explore the way a female subject comes into being. The doubleness of women's poetry comes from its ostensible adoption of an affective mode, often simple, often pious, often conventional. But those conventions are subjected to investigation, questioned, or used for unexpected purposes. The simpler the surface of the poem, the more likely it is that a second and more difficult poem will exist beneath it.

Letitia Landon, already a prolifically successful poet publishing in periodicals and popular album books, published her first volume of poetry in 1824, *The Improvisatrice*. It was, she wrote,

> an attempt to illustrate that species of inspiration common in Italy, where the mind is warmed from earliest childhood by all that is beautiful in Nature and glorious in Art. The character depicted is entirely Italian, a young female with all the loveliness, vivid feeling, and genius of her own impassioned land. She is supposed to relate her own history; with which are intermixed the tales and episodes which various circumstances call forth.[13]

The Troubadour: Poetical Sketches of Modern Pictures; and Historical Sketches (1825) followed, and her last volume, reiterating the Italian theme, was entitled *The Venetian Bracelet* (1829). The uncollected 'Subjects for Pictures' begins characteristically with a poem on Petrarch and Laura. The movement to Italy is taken up by Elizabeth Barrett Browning in *Aurora Leigh* (1856), and again by Christina Rossetti who in her extraordinary preface to *Monna Innominata*, as will be seen, considers the status of the Petrarchan tradition in relation to modern poetry by women. But perhaps the movement to Italy is less important in itself than the association of women's poetry with an 'impassioned land' or emotional space *outside* the definitions and circumscriptions of the poet's specific culture and nationality. As a child Letitia Landon invented a fantasy country located in Africa (it is the tragic irony of her career that she died there), very much as the Brontës were to do when they constructed Gondal and Angria (Angria was located in Africa), the imaginary lands from which so much of their poetry sprang. Adelaide Anne Procter's narrative poems move to Provence, Switzerland and Belgium. George Eliot's *The Spanish Gypsy* (1868) sends the heroine of the poem from the conflict between Moors and Spaniards to consolidate a Gipsy race in Africa. This need to move beyond cultural boundaries manifests itself in the work of the earlier poets as a form of historical and cultural syncretism which both juxtaposes different cultures and reshapes relationships between them. *The Improvisatrice* unfolds narratives within itself of Moorish and Christian conflict, and of Hindu suttee, for instance, which are juxtaposed. Felicia Hemans brings together British, French, Indian, German, American and Greek narratives from different historical periods in her *Records of Woman* (1828), which ends, in startling contrast to the historicised records, with an elegy on a recently dead poetess, Mary Tighe, taken as a point of reference by Landon in her elegy for Mrs Hemans. The dedication is made in a footnote, however, and the very possibility of a 'record' of woman is thus questioned.

This insistent figuring of movement across and between cultural boundaries, with its emphasis on travel, could be seen as a search for the exotic, an escape from restrictions into the 'other' of bourgeois society. Allied, as it so frequently is, with a metaphor of the prison, or of slavery, it could be seen as an attempt to transcend restrictions in fantasy, or an effort to discover a universal womanhood which transcends cultural differences. But it is rather to be associated with an attempt to discover ways of testing out the account of the feminine experienced in western culture by going outside its prescriptions. The flight across the boundary is often associated with the examination of extreme situations – of imprisonment, suffering, or captivity and slavery – and with an overdetermined emphasis on race and national culture, as if an enquiry is being conducted into the ways in which the feminine can be constituted. Mrs Hemans's elegy appears to emancipate its subject from cultural and historical determinations, but it suggests that we can only think of the poetess in this way when she is dead, and even that is problematical. The elegy has an uncanny aspect of contextlessness which makes it oddly surprising after the very specific 'records' which have preceded it.

The emphasis on the woman as traveller through the imagination can be associated with another aspect of Letitia Landon's account of the *Improvisatrice*. The poem is supposedly the utterance of a persona: it is a mask, a role-playing, a dramatic monologue; it is not to be identified with herself or her own feminine subjectivity. The simplest explanation for this is that, given the difficulties of acceptance experienced by women writers, the dramatic form is used as a disguise, a protection against self-exposure and the exposure of feminine subjectivity. But, given the insistence on speaking in another *woman*'s voice, from Mrs Hemans to Augusta Webster and Amy Levy (these last two wrote consciously as dramatic monologuists), it is worth considering further as a phenomenon. The frequent adoption of a dramatised voice by male poets in the Victorian period is, of course, to be connected with dramatic theories of poetry. But Landon's and Hemans's work predates these theories (though not, admittedly, the work of Walter Savage Landor, who might be said to have initiated the dramatic monologue if we are content to think of this as a tradition established by male writers), and it seems that such a mask is peculiarly necessary for women writers. The adoption of the mask appears to involve a displacement of feminine subjectivity, almost a travestying of femininity, in order that it can be made an object of investigation. It is interesting, for instance, that one of Charlotte Brontë's earliest known poems is a monologue by the wife of Pontius Pilate, and that Augusta Webster also wrote a miniature drama between Pilate and his wife, in which the woman's role and moral position is sharply distinguished from association with the husband, as if both are testing out the extent to which it is the woman's function to identify unquestioningly with the husband (and, of course, with orthodox Christianity).[14] A number of poems by women testifying to a refusal to be regarded as an object have been described by feminist critics, but by using a mask a woman writer is in control of her objectification and at the same time anticipates the strategy of objectifying women by being beforehand with it and circumventing masculine representations.[15] This is the theme of Christina Rossetti's poem about masking, 'Winter: My Secret'. It should come as no surprise, then, that it was the women poets who 'invented' the dramatic monologue.

The projection of self into roles is not, as will be seen, really opposed to the axioms of expressive theory which assumes the projection of feeling and emotion onto or into an object, and thus it is not strange to find Letitia Landon speaking of the search for an 'impassioned land', a space for the expression of emotion. Brought up on Hume, she was fascinated by the nature of sensation (often isolating moments of sensation in a narrative), and with the pulsation of sympathy. She uses a metaphor of the responsively vibrating string or chord of feeling which became so common that it could perhaps hardly be said to originate with Hume, but she would certainly have found it in his work, and it recurs in her poetry with an unusual intensity. Allowing as it does of subliminal sexual meaning, it is a thoroughly feminised metaphor for her. In her elegy on Mrs Hemans, for instance, she wrote, 'Wound to a pitch too exquisite,/The soul's fine chords are wrung;/With misery and melody/They are too highly strung'. Such intense vibrations, of course, can kill, as the 'chord' becomes the result of a 'cord' or tightened string which ends sound or strangles even while it produces it. This metaphor was to resonate in women's poetry. Closely allied with it and partly deriving from it is another characteristic figure, the air. An air is a song and by association it is that which is breathed out, exhaled or expressed as breath, an expiration; and by further association it can be that which is breathed in, literally an 'influence', a flowing in, the air of the environment which sustains life; inspiration, a breathing in. All these meanings are present in the elegy, as perfume, breezes, breath or sighs, where they are figured as a responsive, finely organised feminine creativity, receptive to external influence, returning back to the world as music that has flowed in, an exhalation or breath of sound. It is the breath of the body and the breath as spirit. 'So pure, so sweet thy life has been,/So filling earth and air/with odours and with loveliness . . . And yet thy song is sorrowful,/Its beauty is not bloom;/The hopes of which it breathes, are hopes/That look beyond the tomb'.[16] Breath can dissipate, a fear peculiarly close to the Victorian woman poet. Expressive theory, as will be seen, tended to endorse and consolidate this figure.

326

The body imprisons breath but involuntarily releases it: this is an apt figure for the release of feeling which cannot find external form.

Letitia Landon and Felicia Hemans each explore the multiplicity of roles and projections which they make available to themselves in different ways, and each takes the affective moment in different directions. A marked feature of Landon's work is the use of tenses in narrative, particularly the historic past, and the present tense used in a succession of discrete phrases to denote successive actions in the past. It is used in such a way that an action is registered, not *as* it happens but when it is either just over or just about to happen. Effects often precede causes. Seen in this way the agent is oddly detached from actions in the slight hiatus when actions are seen but not the agent's acting of them. Such a procedure makes uncertain how far the woman is in responsible control of cause and effect – she seems to *suffer* rather than to act. The woman herself seems to be displaced from action into the psychic experience existing in the gap between actions, and the whole weight of these lyrical narratives is thrown on the temporal space of the affective moment, the emotional space occurring just before or just after something has happened. In 'The Indian Bride', for instance, the girl's prenuptial journey alone on the Ganges is presented in moments which are either over or which precede their causes: 'She has lighted her lamp. . . . The maiden is weeping. Her lamp has decayed'.[17] The reunion with the lover follows the same syntactic pattern: 'Hark to the ring of the cymeter! . . . The warfare is over, the battle is won. . . . And Zaide hath forgotten in Azim's arms/All her so false lamp's falser alarms'. But the lamp is and is not 'false'. The bridegroom dies and she goes deterministically to her death: 'A prayer is muttered, a blessing said, –/Her torch is raised! – she is by the dead./She has fired the pile'.[18] The tenses both obliterate and sharply question, through this strategy of detachment, by whose agency the girl goes to her death, her own, or the mores of cultural ritual. Before this the narrator has analysed the moment of acute superstitious fear when the girl is on the Ganges without light in tenses which blur the distinction between what does happen and what will happen: 'How the pulses will beat, and the cheek will be dy'd'.[19] This becomes not only a description of the girl's immediate emotional present but also a *prediction* of the future. The affective moment is in the right and the wrong place, describing the girl's immediate fears, proleptically describing the emotions of her death. But the ambiguous status of the tenses proffering the moment of feeling suggests that the girl, or the lamp, was right after all. The irrational affective moment could be trusted, and retrospectively it expands to include her death. The tenses here foreground and investigate a world of intense sensation and emotion and implicitly ask what its place in experience is.

Landon wrote many poems which pictured pictures, freezing women in a static but intense moment just before or just after an event (usually an

327

event of communal significance) has occurred. They become objects whose life is in suspension, waiting for a critical event to occur either through their own or someone else's agency, or else waiting choicelessly. But whether dependent or independent, it is as if emotion and sensation rush in to fill the vacuum of subjectivity. Whether feeling is precipitated by action or whether action is precipitated by feeling seems to be the question such poems raise. Whether consciousness is determined by feeling or action, and what it is when there is no action to be taken at all, and where choice is limited by cultural prescription, is at issue. 'Subjects for Pictures', for instance, considers the woman as subject, often subordinate to men, in innumerable variations on the theme of choice, alternating enclosed environments with open landscapes, moving from history to history, culture to culture, ritual to ritual, myth to myth, marriage, death, murder, revival. These are all studies in the dislocation between consciousness and action, where the subject is placed remorselessly in fixed locations, immobilised by ritual or vigil. In what way the moment of feeling relates to or is determined by the rituals of a culture is a problem which fascinates Landon.

Whether Letitia Landon's figures belong to cultural rituals or place themselves in a transgressive relation to them they are almost always at the mercy of passion. Accused of an excessive preoccupation with love, Landon defended herself by arguing for what is effectively a politics of the affective state: 'A highly cultivated state of society must ever have for concomitant evils, that selfishness, the result of indolent indulgence, and that heartlessness attendant on refinement, which too often hardens while it polishes'.[20] The choice of love as a theme can 'soften' and 'touch' and 'elevate'. 'I can only say, that for a woman, whose influence and whose sphere must be in the affections, what subject can be more fitting than one which it is her peculiar province to refine, to spiritualise, and exalt? . . . making an almost religion of its truth . . . woman, actuated by an attachment as intense as it is true, as pure as it is deep', is more 'admirable' as a heroine. For as she is in art, so she is 'in actual life'.[21] If Landon appears to be completely accepting the sentimental terms in which women were seen, she is turning them to moral and social account and arguing that women's discourse can soften what would now be called the phallocentric hardness and imaginative deficiencies of an overcivilised culture. It is as if she has taken over the melting softness of Burke's category of the 'beautiful', which he saw as an overrefined and 'feminine' principle in contradistinction to the strenuous labour of the 'sublime', and reappropriated it as a moral category which can dissolve overcivilised hardness. Burke associated beauty with nostalgia for a condition which we have 'irretrievably lost'.[22] In particular its nature is questioned and explored when it hovers over that last situation occasioning the last rituals of a culture, death.

Her own early death, which seems to have been the result of an accidental overdose of poison, self-administered to cure a palsy, occasioning scandal and suspicion as her life had done, made her the Keats (or perhaps the Sylvia Plath) of women's poetry. Witty, exuberant and unconventional, and like Mrs Hemans a vigorous and energetic intellectual (just before she died she wrote to ask her brother to send to Africa ' "Thiers's History of the Revolution", in French, and all George Sand's works . . . send me also Lamb's works'),[23] she was seen as a seminal figure by later writers.

Rather than exploring what cultural ritual does to the feminine subject, Mrs Hemans figures the flight beyond it, and the condition of extremity and disintegration which occurs when constraints press upon consciousness. Her method is inward and psychological where Landon's is external and classical, but it is just as analytical, turning the expressive moment towards investigation and critique. The heroic rebel and the conformist stand in dialectical relationship to one another in her work, each in dialogue with the other as each is pushed to extremity. The archetypes of her work are represented in the first section of *Records of Woman*, 'Arabella Stuart', and 'Casabianca', a short poem about an episode occurring in the battle of the Nile. 'Arabella Stuart' is a monologue spoken in imprisonment by a woman whose disintegrating mind struggles, and fails, to make the past coherent. The meaning of her history collapses. It is this, as much as the endurance of immediate confinement, which dissolves her reason (though an implicit question here is what 'reason' means). Hers was a political imprisonment (she died in captivity), made at the instigation of James I after a secret marriage and an attempted flight to France. Arabella does not know what has happened to her husband, or whether he has deserted her. The monologue opens with a memory.

> 'Twas but a dream! I saw the stag leap free,
>   Under the boughs where early birds were singing;
> I stood o'ershadowed by the greenwood tree,
>   And heard, it seemed, a sudden bugle ringing
> Far through a royal forest. Then the fawn
> Shot, like a gleam of light, from grassy lawn
> To secret covert; and the smooth turf shook,
> And lilies quivered by the glade's lone brook,
> And young leaves trembled, as, in fleet career,
> A princely band, with horn, and hound, and spear,
> Like a rich masque swept forth. I saw the dance
> Of their white plumes, that bore a silvery glance
> Into the deep wood's heart; and all passed by
> Save one – I met the smile of *one* clear eye,
> Flashing out joy to mine. Yes, *thou* wert there,
> Seymour![24]

329

A superficial glance at this text will immediately register what appears to be a slightly mannered Keatsian diction followed by the faintly absurd address to Seymour. 'Yes, *thou* wert there'. But women's poetry deliberately risked absurdity, as Christina Rossetti was later to see. In the extremity of the memory it is precisely important that the lover was *there*, as he is *not* in the present moment of the voice speaking from prison. The diction is used to render the vestigial, uncertain and discontinuous retrieval by memory of an event which even then may have been a dream and 'seemed' (there is a double 'seeming', the event and the memory of it) like a masque. The movement of the eye and of light is uncertain, the gaze fleeting, as the mere insignia of the helmet plumes 'glance' into the wood, with a superficial lightness whose pun on glance/gaze casts doubt on the clear eye which gazes at the woman. And if Seymour was not 'there', it is not clear 'where' the woman is either, as her gaze is constantly displaced from stag to fawn to quivering lilies (aroused *and* fearful sexuality), to huntsmen, plumes and lover. Though stag and fawn stand as conventionalised proleptic figures of the hunted woman's condition later in her story (the syntax allows that both stag and woman are 'Under the boughs'), she is not quite identified with either, or symbolically split between both, as they escape to different hiding places. This split condition is a function of her imprisoned consciousness, but it appears to be just as much a condition of her freedom: she stood isolated, 'o'ershadowed' by the tree, subject and metaphorically imprisoned even when her isolation seemed to make possible the rebellious independence of the secret love affair and marriage. These are the bitter insights disclosed by a fracturing consciousness whose mind and history disintegrate simultaneously. The bitterness, indeed, rests precisely on an awaresnss that the rebellion was in fact in conformity with a romantic paradigm which failed to work.

Like the woman in 'Arabella Stuart' who 'stood' transfixed under the greenwood tree, the boy in 'Casabianca' 'stood' on the burning deck, and in both cases the word seems to denote positioning outside the control of the character. The boy is subject to commands, standing ground and withstanding the assault of battle in absolute obedience to the father's orders, responding unquestioningly to the law of the father. Ostensibly this is a tale of the heroism of simple obedience of son to father. But in the oedipal fiasco the heroism of absolute obedience is misplaced, for the dead father, beneath the deck, like the unconscious, is 'Unconscious of his son', and 'His voice no longer heard'. Consummately, Hemans transposes the terror of a condition of not knowing and hearing to the father, marking the tragic irony of the son's situation, for it is he who rather 'no longer heard' his father's voice, but continues to obey that voice from the past when it no longer sounds in the present. But at a deeper level, the law of the father is founded on its imperviousness to the son's voice, begging for a relaxation of its commands. In the culminating destruction we are enjoined to 'Ask of the winds' (like the boy to his father) which 'strewed the sea' with 'fragments', what became of the son, who is burned and blown to pieces through the act of blind obedience. The voice of the 'natural' elements may, or may not, perhaps, operate with analogous laws as fierce as those of patriarchal imperatives (the voices of the father and the wind are set questioningly against one another), but the natural certainly wreaks as much havoc as the human law, whether they can be differentiated from one another or not. For a frightening moment the 'fragments' seem parts of the boy's body, resolve themselves into mast, helm and pennon 'That well had borne their part', in the final stanza, and then as frighteningly, with all the referential hazardousness of metaphor, become metonymic hints of fragmented phallic parts. The absoluteness of the patriarchal imperative is absolutely ravaging in its violence. There is a kind of exultation in this violent elegy about the way phallic law destroys itself: at the same time the boy's 'heart', both his courage and the centre of his being, the identity bound up with the patriarchal imperatives of heroism, has 'perished'. The remorselessness which separates out 'part' and 'heart' and rhymes them to suggest the way masculine identity is founded, also recognises that this is a law to the death, killing a child on a burning deck. The unmentioned element in this masculine tragedy is the mother, but, with its constant reminder that this is the death of a child (he was 13), victim of the crucial Napoleonic battle of the Nile, the voice of the poem is gendered as female and thus brings war and sexual politics together. It is at once a deeply affective lament and a strangely Medaean lyric of castigation – and castration – which takes its revenge on war even as it sees that war takes revenge on itself.

Casabianca

The boy stood on the burning deck
   Whence all but he had fled;
The flame that lit the battle's wreck
   Shone round him o'er the dead.

Yet beautiful and bright he stood,
   As born to rule the storm –
A creature of heroic blood,
   A proud, though child-like form.

The flames rolled on – he would not go
   Without his father's word;
That father, faint in death below,
   His voice no longer heard.

He called aloud: – 'Say, father, say
   If yet my task is done!'

331

He knew not that the chieftain lay
  Unconscious of his son.

'Speak, father!' once again he cried,
  'If I may yet be gone!'
And but the booming shots replied,
  And fast the flames rolled on.

Upon his brow he felt their breath,
  And in his waving hair,
And looked from that lone post of death
  In still yet brave despair;

And shouted but once more aloud,
  'My father! must I stay?'
While o'er him fast, through sail and shroud,
  The wreathing fires made way.

They wrapt the ship in splendour wild,
  They caught the flag on high,
And streamed above the gallant child
  Like banners in the sky.

There came a burst of thundersound –
  The boy – oh! where was he?
Ask of the winds that far around
  With fragments strewed the sea! –

With mast, and helm, and pennon fair,
  That well had borne their part;
But the noblest thing which perished there
  Was that young faithful heart![25]

THE POETICS OF EXPRESSION

Hemans wrote overtly of politics, of Greece, emigration, the Pilgrim Fathers
(the first 'trade unionists'), and declared a Byronic response to liberty.
But the politics of women's poetry in this century cannot necessarily be
associated with the uncovering of particular political positions but rather
with a set of strategies or negotiations with conventions and constraints.
It is remarkable how resourcefully the three Brontës, each of them highly
individual writers (though Anne and Charlotte at least, politically conservative), follow Mrs Hemans in exploring consciousness under duress,
imprisoned within limit, or how Anne Adelaide Procter (to be associated
with radical thinking in the mid-century) follows Letitia Landon in exploring the alien rituals of another culture in her tales, and the demands of
either moral or affective conventions in her shorter lyrics. It is not necessary

to assume a direct relationship between these poets, though in some cases that can be ascertained, to see that they share common strategies. They also share a capacity to produce a poem with a simple moral or emotional surface which actually probes more complex questions than its simplicity suggests. Three poems by the Brontës and a group of poems by Adelaide Anne Procter indicate how Victorian women poets could exploit the legacy left by late Romantic writers such as Letitia Landon and Felicia Hemans, in particular the poem of the affective moment and its relation to moral convention and religious and cultural constraint. This will suggest the basis on which a women's tradition can be constructed – necessarily briefly in a chapter of this length – and provide an introduction to the way in which expressive theory could be allied with a feminine poetics.

Anne Brontë, a poet of great subtlety and far wider range than is often thought, negotiated the sobriety of the religious and didactic lyric to suggest precisely where its conventions are most painful and intransigent by *not* breaking these conventions, but by simply following through their logic. In this way a poem on the inevitability of suffering can end with a challenge to God either to provide the strength to endure or to release the sufferer through death ('If this be all'). 'Song' ('We know where deepest lies the snow'), a poem on the inevitability of oppression even when master and slave, hunters and hunted, reverse their positions and displace one another, chooses the trembling life of the hare rather than the cruelty of the hounds, and ends almost triumphantly by asserting the knowledge that only oppression can bring. Intransigently, it refuses the knowledge brought by power. But it is in a more overtly conventional poem such as 'The Arbour' that her gift for turning an orthodox position can be seen. It is a pastoral poem both of the affective moment and the moral lesson. It depends on the discovery of a deceptive perceptual and psychological experience which is withheld from the understanding of the reader in the same way that the discovery of the writer's mistake is delayed until it is recognised. The security, protection and fecundity of an arbour, with its 'thickly clustering' trees, 'green and glossy leaves', sunshine and blue sky, prompts a moment of release into emotion and reverie, in which the past becomes imbued with autumnal pleasure and the future invested with the fulfilment of summer: memory and desire are devoid of pain. But a perceptual trick or misprision has occurred; what has seemed 'summer's very breath' occurs when 'snow is on the ground'; 'How can I think of scenes like these?'

> 'Tis but the *frost* that clears the air,
> And gives the sky that lovely blue;
> They're smiling in a *winter's* sun,
> Those evergreens of sombre hue.
>
> And winter's chill is on my heart –
> How can I dream of future bliss?

333

How can my spirit soar away
Confined by such a chain as this?[26]

The conclusion reproaches the speaker for factitious sentiment, which attaches feeling to conventional metaphors of the seasons and provides an escape into fantasy from the demands of the chill winter present. Nevertheless it is an interrogative conclusion: 'How can. . . . How can . . .' not only implies the reproach, how could I?, but also asks the question, how is it possible?; it may well be that it is the moral reproach which is profoundly conventional and narrow, refusing the possibility of imaginative transformation and accepting the orthodox symbolism of winter as constraint, restriction and dearth too facilely. For the frost and the winter's sun *were* transforming. Shifting slightly the context of the feminine metaphor of breath and breathing, Anne Brontë allows that the 'whispering' of boughs 'through the air' (8) may not have been 'summer's very breath' (17), but they nevertheless nourished the body and soul, enabling the ear to 'drink[s] in' sound, and the soul to 'fly away', a statement repeated and modulated in the last stanza when the 'spirit', another form of breath, can 'soar away'. The confinement of the frosty arbour – 'Confined by such a chain as this' – is seen in two ways by the end of the poem. The wintry enclosure is a material imprisonment, holding the soul in thrall. On the other hand it is a paradoxical context of rebirth, in which the soul can soar precisely because it is chained to the material world whose wintry 'evergreens' may be more reliable auguries than the transient leaves of summer. In this context the words 'confined' and 'chain' strangely dislodge the connotation of imprisonment and take on the generative implications of the womb and the birth cord in another feminine pun on the cord which tethers and the chord from which the breath or air of life and of music is created. This seemingly docile poem is a sustained pun on the sense of confinement as imprisonment and confinement as gestation in the womb, one sterile, the other creative.

Confinement is the structural figure in both Charlotte Brontë's 'The Lonely Lady' and in Emily Brontë's 'Enough of Thought, Philosopher', though they work respectively through psychologised experience and symbol. Charlotte Brontë's poem is ostensibly a study in 'Mariana'-like hysteria and unreciprocated sexual desire. Confined and alone, insomniac, weary with the women's tasks of lace-making and music-making, the tension of the lady's feeling is expressed through the 'quivering strings' of the harp she abandons. The intensity of her emotion meets no recognition, and, in a brilliant verbal displacement, this condition is externalised in the sounds of the clock which mechanically records time and listens to itself doing so, and to the *cessation* of its own responses which vibrate – the characteristic feminine metaphor appears again – to nothing: 'the clock with silver chime did say/The number of the hour, and all in peace/

Listened to hear its own vibration cease' (6–8).[27] The setting sun casts a lurid, blood-red crimson blush on the lady's face, and until the last stanza this appears to be the psychological counterpart of violent feeling which can only return upon itself. In the last stanza an army in battle, too, 'leagues away' (40), sees the sunset, 'The last ray tinged with blood' (45), and the way in which the light gives all the features of the landscape the semblance of gore, just as it had to the features of the lady's face. But the sunset is no longer simply the extension of hysterical feminine sexuality. The syntax of the last stanza affirms that the literal burning of the battle is the cause of the bloody light. The lady's hysteria is accounted for by her anxiety and ignorance as to the state of the battle. And yet there is no simple distinction here between feminine emotion and masculine violence. Feminine sexuality becomes horribly dependent upon and implicated in male aggression and warfare. It is the battle, certainly, which makes the sunset not a symbolic but a literal portent of disaster, and it is the raging battle which has caused the lady's isolation: yet she is committed to a vicarious experience of it in which hysteria and warfare have an uncanny affinity. The metaphor gives them a blood relationship.

Emily Brontë's poem rages too, but again simple opposition is deceptive, and a poem which appears to be caught in a familiar dilemma, a 'cruel strife' between 'vanquished Good' and 'victorious ill', actually breaks the restrictions of this confining oppositional and binary terminology altogether. 'The Philosopher' is a monologue which includes a dialogue within itself, and this makes problematic the 'identity' which the poem longs to lose.[28] 'O for the time when I shall sleep/Without identity' (stanza 2). Identity means both that which is in unity with itself and without difference and that which is uniquely different and the founder of difference. The Philosopher who speaks these lines is an aspect of the speaker's self, and the 'I' which resounds through the poem splits and fragments into separate experiences and definitions. The Philosopher describes a vision of a 'Spirit' in contradistinction to the listening 'man' or speaker, and the 'man' or speaker replies by addressing the Philosopher as 'seer', assimilating him to spirit and juxtaposing the two terms – 'And even for that spirit, seer,/ I've watched and sought my lifetime long' (stanza 5). 'Man' appears to comprehend seer, philosopher and spirit just as philosopher comprehends seer, spirit and man. Thus the speaker's earlier statement (stanza 3) that 'Three gods, within this little frame,/Are warring, night and day' becomes easier to understand. And similarly, the second stanza's fierce assertion that the stark Manichean opposition between heaven and hell are categories whose simple dualism cannot contain the energies of desire or will is related to this. But the identity is violently at war, it seems, precisely because a universe founded on rigid categories of binary difference constantly excludes the third term. The narrator him or herself is also committed to the epistemology of opposition, so habitual is it, seeking the 'spirit',

335

or breath, in 'heaven, hell, earth and air', and thus, not surprisingly, 'always wrong' (stanza 5). In the same way the narrator has earlier brought 'spirit' and 'man' into relationship but excluded 'woman', the unmentioned term of the poem. The vision of the spirit, on the contrary, offers a revelation of another universe, a world of 'three rivers' 'Of equal depth, and equal flow'. The rigid antitheses are broken. These are rivers of gold, blood and sapphire, retaining prismatic difference but transformed from their black confluence to the unifying whiteness of light by the spirit's agency. The specific symbolism of these rivers, reaching back to *Revelation*, matters less, perhaps, than their triple nature, their capacity to include the third term. Gold, sapphire and blood could signify Father, Son and ungendered Holy Ghost, or spirit, matter and the human, or divine, satanic and human, or androgyne, male and female. What matters is that the violence of a universe constituted through rigid categories of difference, whether spiritual, moral or sexual, needs to be 'lost'. The spirit, which is also comprehended in 'this living breath' (stanza 5) of the narrator and by the 'air' of earth is otherwise murderous and destructive. There seems to be an attempt to remove the 'spirit' and 'this living breath' from the categories of gender and a refusal to consent to the 'feminine' associations of this figure. On the other hand, the powerful energies of Emily Brontë's poetry, which push the hymn-like form of her stanzas towards violence, tend to reaffirm terrible alternatives despite the move to the third term – heaven or hell, spirit or man, male or female, a gendered or an ungendered world: the negations sound with the force of affirmation, and the affirmations with the force of negations.

Adelaide Anne Procter, writing between the mid-1840s and the 1860s, takes up the figures and forms associated with the thematising of feminine issues and virtually typifies the woman poet's interests at this time. Like Mrs Hemans before her and like her contemporaries, Dora Greenwell and Elizabeth Barrett Browning, she wrote of political matters, particularly on the oppression and the suffering of the poor (for instance, 'The Cradle Song of the Poor', 'The Homeless Poor') and on the complexities of the master–slave relationship (for instance 'King and Slave'). She also wrote some magnificently humane lyrics on the Crimean war, refusing superficial heroism and narrow patriotism ('The Lesson of the war', 'The Two Spirits'). Like Letitia Landon, she worked with the external narrative poem and with the didactic lyric. Her narrative poems, dealing with the movement beyond the boundary, with escape, with ex-patriotism and return, are deeply preoccupied with displacement, and through this with the woman's 'place' or displacement in a culture. As so often with women writers, the more conventional the didactic lyric, the more accepting of its conventions the writer is, the more it can be used as a way of looking at conformity from within. Writing with a boldly simple directness and immediacy, Adelaide Anne Procter developed increasing strength here. A series of lyrics redefine the emotional space of sexual love arrestingly, by a conventional refusal of the role of exclusively sexual passion in a love relationship with a man in a way which outflanks conventionality. Neither 'A Parting' nor 'A Woman's Answer' retreats to celibacy or virginity as an alternative to marriage. 'Parting' thanks the man who has rejected the woman's passion and, half ironically, half seriously, expresses gratefulness for a 'terrible awaking'. The poem conventionally redirects desire towards divine love; but that desire is explicitly affirmed as the intense power of sexual love, 'all too great to live except above'.[29] It is neither sublimated nor repressed. 'A Woman's Answer' professes to promiscuity by redefining love as intense libidinal passion in many spheres – for knowledge, the natural world, art, books (*Aurora Leigh* in particular) – and not simply the sphere of sexual love. 'Envy', a terse, abruptly economical lyric, is another poem which expresses a conventional moral position, but dramatically turns the commonplace. The speaker is envious of envy, always losing to him: 'He was the first always: Fortune/Shone bright in his face./I fought for years; with no effort/He conquered the place'. Envy wins the competition every time, and even dies first: 'God help me!/While he is at rest,/I am cursed still to live; – even/Death loved him best'.[30] The startling combat with envy comes about because it is both a traditional Christian allegorical combat *against* envy, an attempt to defeat a moral and psychological condition, and a representation of envy itself, a jealous fight *with* envy for possession of all that we envy – success, mastery, recognition – on envy's own terms. This constantly reproduces jealousy even when it is seemingly 'conquered'. Even the death of jealousy is something to be jealous of. Envy, the successful combatant, is gendered as 'him'; the speaker is a shadowy other, the bleeding subject of loss, the one 'without', even to the extent of being without a coffin. Ironically Envy engenders envy, and the *speaker* is actually forced to become the personification of envy. The submerged phallic symbolism here testifies savagely to the dominance of male power and to the *anger* of loss.

Adelaide Anne Procter began her writing career by publishing in *Household Words* and *All the Year Round*, journals which were associated with popular radicalism, and was converted to Roman Catholicism in 1851. Tractarian or Anglo-Catholic aesthetics, enunciated through Keble in particular, paid special attention to developing an expressive theory of poetry as the vehicle of hidden emotion, and that may be why Procter's poetry takes up the feminised expressive figures of the musical vibration as the epitome of feeling, and breath or breathing, air and spirit, as the representation of the imprisoned life of emotion needing to escape or to take form. Her poems of displacement, and the exploration of the 'place' of women in several senses, particularly 'A Tomb in Ghent', provide a context for the exploration of expressive feeling and its relation to the feminine and lead to a fuller consideration of the importance of expressive aesthetics to

337

women's poetry. This is required especially for the work of Dora Greenwell, Christina Rossetti and Jean Ingelow, who seem to have been consciously aware of this theory as a problematic model of the feminine.

The longer narrative poems frequently use travel and change of place to examine the degree to which institutions are capable of flexibility. In 'Homeward Bound', a long-lost sailor, anticipating Tennyson's *Enoch Arden* (1864), returns to find his wife with another man and his child and refuses to claim her back rather than endanger her happiness or reputation. A mother transposed from one environment to another sacrifices her child to a second marriage in 'The Sailor Boy', a motif of the second marriage also explored in 'A New Mother'. In 'A Legend of Provence', a novice elopes with a wounded knight but returns to her place when marriage fails. An exiled Tyrolean girl returns to her country from Switzerland to warn of the Swiss intention to attack Austria in 'A Legend of Bregenz'. The return to roots, the testing out of the limits of the shaping and determining agencies in a culture, these seem to be at the heart of the narrative poems.

'A Tomb in Ghent' charts the commitment to a new culture by a skilled mechanic who has emigrated to Belgium, and an enforced withdrawal from it by his granddaughter, who returns to England when her father dies, attempting to find a place, to be assimilated into what is now an alien culture. This unsolved dilemma forms the frame to the story of her parents who achieve, it seems, a kind of self-expression, communication and mutuality unknown either to their parents or their children. The tale is prefaced by the legend of the dragon given to Bruges but stolen by Ghent. The story goes that the dragon will one day spread its wings and return to Palestine, where the Crusaders stole it. The legend within the legend achieves a number of purposes: exactly where the dragon belongs, and to whom, is problematical; it is displaced, like the characters, and implicitly questions the idea of the nation and the boundary. Its status as military trophy also question the martial values and gender-bound rituals of war. The exiled son abrogates conventional roles and releases his own being through music, eventually playing the organ in the great cathedral. Music in this poem replaces the flight of the dragon and its aggression with the feminised flight of sound, analogy for the language of the spirit, a flight parallel but antithetical to that of the totem of war. Waves of sound break 'at heaven's door' bearing 'the great desire' of spiritual feeling on 'eagle wings'.[31] The expressive figuring of the feminine is associated with a male experience, but in fact this expression is enabled or inspired by the statue at the 'White Maiden's Tomb'. The player can make the organ 'answer' and 'thrill with master-power the breathless throng' – give the congregation breath or inspiration – because he in turn is handed passion through the 'expectant' statue who 'holds her breath' with parted lips, and through the wife who is an image of the statue. Again the figure is many-sided in its implications.[32] There is a frank assimilation of mystical and musical experience to sexuality: on the one hand male creativity emerges out of female silence and becomes its gift; on the other hand the gift is returned to the woman as song, and the daughter is endowed with the power of expressive singing. Music, or the 'air', literally circulates in and between the group and the congregation, cancelling the fixities of gender and social division and releasing the stony categories from their rigidity. Momentarily, in an alien country and in the safe space of the cathedral, expressive song reconfigures relationships – but only in a place of safety untouched by national boundaries rather than transcending them.

But there are a number of poems – some of her finest – in which Adelaide Anne Procter writes with anxiety about the nature of expression. 'A Lost Chord' is the perfect harmony which eludes discovery; 'Hush!' turns on the deathly silence which displaces the sounds envisaged by the internal imagination; 'Unexpressed' speaks of the failure of articulation and the ephemeral nature of language, which dissipates and recedes 'Like sighings of illimitable forests,/And waves of an unfathomable sea'.[33] In 'Words', language is so fragile – 'the rose-leaf that we tread on/Will outlive a word' – and yet so powerful that it can transform the course of a life.[34] Nevertheless words can remain imprisoned in the self, and though each has its own 'spirit' or breath it is externalised only as *echo*, as representation without substance, dissociated from its hidden originary experience, the shadow of a sound, inveterately secondary. Thus the expressive moment is by no means unproblematical. The figure of overflow is warily explored by contemporaries such as Greenwell and Barrett Browning and by the slightly later poets, Rossetti and Ingelow. To see how these poets negotiate the dominant poetics of expression and deal with its ambiguities it is necessary to look more closely at the expressive aesthetic, and to recapitulate some points made in other chapters. The incipient sexual implications of the recurrent figurings of feminine discourse, the receptive vibration of the musical chord in sympathy, the exhalation or release of feeling which moves ambiguously between the body and the spirit, are present in the metaphors of expressive aesthetics, but they are given both a negative or pathological and a positive or 'healthy' signification, a hysterical and a wholesome aspect, often implicitly gendered respectively as 'feminine' and 'masculine'. Expressive theory becomes morbid either when the overflow of feeling is in excess or when it is unable to flow at all, and repressed into a secret underground life. For expressive theory is above all an aesthetics of the *secret*, the hidden experience, because the feeling which is prior to language gives language a secondary status and is often written of as if it cannot take linguistic form at all. The politics of women's poetry emerges in its transactions with this orthodoxy and, strangely, the hermeneutic problem of discerning a feminine discourse in the structure and language of a poem can be approached by addressing a theory which often tries to do without an account of language. This account of the poetics of expression is

339

illuminated by the terms of Dora Greenwell's essay, 'Our single women', where the negative aspects of expressive aesthetics belong to the language which gives an account of the feminine.[35] The essay enables one to see how Greenwell, Barrett Browning, Rossetti and Ingelow deal with the structural implications of expressive metaphors in relation to gender, and how far later poets, Mathilde Blind, Augusta Webster and Amy Levy, were able to depart from the expressive model.

Victorian expressive theory is affective and of the emotions. It is concerned with feeling. It psychologised, subjectivised and often moralised the firm epistemological base of Romantic theory, though its warrant was in Wordsworth's spontaneous *overflow* of feeling. The idea of overflow, of projection and expression, a movement of feeling out of the self, develops metaphorically from a cognitive account of consciousness, in which mediation between subject and object was the constitutive structure of mind, and the idealist implication that the subject constructs the other as a category of mind. This can be shifted to describe projection, empathy, a moving out of the self in which the barriers and limits of selfhood are broken, a liberation of feeling almost like love, and certainly like breathing, which finds or invents forms and images to which it is attached. Expansion, movement outwards, the breaking of barriers, is the essence of poetry and the essence of *healthy* poetry. To Sydney Dobell, as we have seen, the function of poetry is to express a mind: 'To express is to carry out'; 'to express a mind is to carry out that mind *into some equivalent*'.[36] For Arthur Hallam the movement outwards into 'energetic love for the beautiful' was a moral activity because it educated the self in a liberation from the bonds of the ego. He praised, in Tennyson's work, 'his power of embodying himself in ideal characters, or rather moods of character', so that the

> circumstances of the narration seem to have a natural correspondence with the predominant feeling, and, as it were, to be evolved from it by assimilative force . . . his vivid, picturesque delineation of objects, and the peculiar skill with which he holds all of them *fused*, to borrow a metaphor from science, in a medium of strong emotion.[37]

There is a perfect chemistry here in which empathy is called forth by objects while correspondingly subjective life moves beyond the self to fuse objects in feeling. There is also a perfect reciprocity because emotion does not master objects, and neither do objects take priority over feeling. But it is not altogether clear whether feeling is simply displaced or represented and verbalised in some way, and for some critics there is an almost inevitable hiatus between the movement of feeling and the form in which it is embodied. In 1842 G. H. Lewes quoted with approval John Stuart Mill's account of poetry from the *Monthly Repository* of 1833, where Mill assumed a disjunction between emotion and its form of expression. Poetry 'is the delineation of the deeper and more secret workings of human

340

emotions'. It is 'feeling confirming itself to itself in moments of solitude and embodying itself in symbols which are the nearest possible representations of the feeling'.[38] The assumption is that ideally there should be a perfect match between feeling and symbol but that the correspondence is necessarily impossible and imperfect. Emotion remains secret, inaccessible, hidden. There is always a barrier to its expression. Lewes more confidently seizes on those aspects of Hegel's thinking (whose work he was reviewing) which enable him to speak of the representative medium which allows those emotions 'which fill and expand the heart' to be expressed. He quotes Hegel on mourning and the need to be 'relieved' by seeing grief in 'external form'. Tears, of course, are the model of the expressive moment, the visible, literal expression of the 'oppressed heart'.[39] He reads Hegel unashamedly as an expressive theorist but he also acknowledges that expression is bound up with repression. He thinks of Greek art, for instance, with Goethe, as a volcano burning beneath a covering of ice. Once the representation of emotion fails to be adequate to it the representation itself becomes a barrier. And this is where expressive poetics moves to the pathological. Keble's sense that the secret and hidden currents of feeling resist expression to the point of driving the poet mad, even though he had theological reasons for endorsing their repression, is not an extravagant form of expressive theory. Feeling for him is always pressing for a release which cannot be granted. One might say that the poet becomes hysterical in these circumstances, like a woman.

> What must they do? They are ashamed and reluctant to speak out, yet, if silent, they can scarcely keep their mental balance; some are said even to have become insane.[40]

The problem is accentuated for Tractarian aesthetics by the theological necessity of a due 'reserve', a refusal to bring forth an excess of feeling and an assent to hidden meaning. Keble's theory of symbol speaks of the *concealing* as well as the *revealing* nature of symbol. Christian meaning should not be carelessly *exposed* to misprision (and to democratic reading).

So there are two related aspects of Victorian accounts of expressive projection. First, if the mind cannot be 'carried out' into an equivalent of itself and find a form in representation, there will be a disjunction between the secret feelings of the mind and the form of the representation. The representation then becomes the barrier feeling is designed to break. Secondly, since the representational symbol is both the *means* of expression and the *form* of its repression, *ex*pression and *re*pression, although in conflict with one another, become interdependent. They constitute one another, so that expression is predicated upon repression. The overflow of secret and hidden feeling creates the barriers which bind and limit it, while the limits enable the overflow of feeling. This is not willingly acknowledged by the writers I have mentioned, but it follows from their thinking. Indeed, it is

341

their willingness to construct an opposition between expression and repression rather than to allow the structural interdependence their theory implies, which accounts for the uneasiness and frustration of their thought and its ambiguities. People have noticed the superficial resemblance of this theory to Freud's account of repression, but it is radically different because it assumes a consciously *known* experience which is inexpressible because the verbal forms of language are inadequate, ineffable. Freud, on the contrary, assumed that representation is part of a symbolic structure of displacement which is a manifestation of the *unknowable* unconscious. Thus he places emphasis on the importance of the material sign or symbol where Victorian expressive theory does not. Expressive theory does have something in common, however, with Julia Kristeva's account of the opposition of the semiotic and symbolic in language. Syntax operates as a symbolic law of the paternal function in exercising grammatical and social constraints, while the instinctual drives of the semiotic and the primal processes of condensation and displacement refuse to be accommodated by the symbolic and subvert and dissolve it.[41] Kristeva is worth mentioning because she provides a way of thinking of expressive theory in terms of language. On the other hand, it is the assumption of expressive theory that language fails to embody or symbolise primal feeling which precisely defines its difficulties. It cannot account for language. For Kristeva both the semiotic and the symbolic do have linguistic form.

It is interesting that in her remarkable essay on single women (first published in the *North British Review*, 1860) Dora Greenwell, who had sympathies towards Quakerism rather than to Tractarianism, adopts the language of secrecy when she is speaking of women but, in a surprising move, compares the withholding and suppression required of women in social life with the expressive openness of their art. In poetry the female subjectivity is to be defined by its capacity to create through writing a self which is commensurate with the 'secret' identity concealed in social dealings. And yet, paradoxically, this self is constituted by secrecy, and thus the poem is an expression of feminine subjectivity through its very capacity to conceal as well as to reveal: the secret is an open secret – and a closed one.

> It is surely singular that woman, bound, as she is, no less by the laws of society than by the immutable instincts of her nature, to a certain suppression of all that relates to personal feeling, should attain, in print, to the fearless, uncompromising sincerity she misses in real life; so that in the poem, above all in the novel – . . . a living soul, a living voice, should seem to greet us; a voice so sad, so truthful, so earnest, that we have felt as if some intimate secret were at once communicated and withheld, – an Open Secret, free to all

who could find its key – the secret of a woman's heart, with all its needs, its struggles, and its aspirations.[42]

The theological language of the open secret of the Gospel is directly, and with extraordinary boldness, related to women's experience, so that through this language women become the prime bearers of the Christian message (we shall see that in the same way Barrett Browning identifies the fallen woman with Christ). In terms reminiscent of Letitia Landon's justification of and apologia for the introduction of the affective into the hardness of phallocentric society, Dora Greenwell defends the introduction of feminine sensitivity into art and into life, but with the difference that modern life makes it increasingly difficult to give that feminine subjectivity *expression*, thwarting and obstructing it so that there is a disjunction, just as in expressive theory itself, between internal experience and external form.

> The conditions of life grow continually less and less severe, yet more and more complicated: the springs of thought, of love, lie deeper. Conscience grows more exacting, responsibilities wider. Women's whole being is more sensitive. It may now, perhaps, be harder for her than it has ever yet been to make her wishes and her fate agree – '*to bring her external existence into harmony with her inner life*' [my emphasis].[43]

The affective and expressive vocabulary continues throughout the essay: Dora Greenwell asks for '*a more perfect freedom and expansion* in that which is already their [women's] own' (my emphasis).[44] She quotes Mrs Jameson on the particular nature of the 'feminine and religious element' in women's identity, and argues for the superior capacities of sympathy in women, the expressive capacity to project themselves into different psychological conditions – 'In such a task, the complicated play of sympathies ever at work within her – the dramatic faculty by means of which she so readily makes the feelings of others her own – find full expression. To her, *sympathy is power*, because to her it is knowledge'.[45]

The essay challenges Mill on the subjection of women a number of times, claiming that women accept subordination, and adopts a flagrantly essentialist account of feminine consciousness. Women are innately passive, responsive and nurturing rather than original and creative.

> In imaginative strength she has been proved deficient; she unfolds no new heaven, she breaks into no new world. She discovers, invents, creates nothing. In her whole nature we trace a passivity, a tendency to work upon that which she received, to quicken, to foster, to develop.[46]

Intellect becomes as one-sided as feeling in women: no woman remains single from choice; the true oneness of men and women in love is – the sense of loss combined with the phallic language is poignant here – 'like the healing of some deep original wound'.[47] And yet neither the essentialist conformism nor the poignancy should be allowed to obliterate the boldness of this essay. Dora Greenwell certainly wanted the 'power' granted by imaginative sympathy for women. Though she saw that it would be necessary to appeal to the agency of men to enable women to use their energies in productive work, she attacked the conservatism and conventionality of contemporary accounts of women, and what she advocated is striking. Though she concentrated on nursing, she wanted women to be able to work together in groups, in collaborative projects (she advocated a museum of women's arts): she wanted women to be able to enter the ministry of the church with a clear and defined and officially recognised status, participating in 'aggressive' moral reform, and she believed that in undertaking unpaid work among the poor, female labour could democratise society and erase class difference; she praised the moral qualities of working-class women. A 'certain mingling of classes on one ground' could take place.[48] In working in hospitals and with fallen women, middle-class women could assuage differences because they were egalitarian in their sympathies and did not '*come down*' to the poor.[49]

The mixture of the conventional and the unconventional in this essay is surprising and often unpredictable; it consents to a passive account of women and simultaneously subverts it, seeing the expressive model of femininity as one of struggle and limit. Rather like her own double poems, the essay is both conservative and subversive. If she could assert the virtues of passivity she could also castigate and question the 'self-complacent idolatry of the safe and mediocre, in the fullness of which we once heard a lady thank Heaven that her daughters were not geniuses. True apotheosis of the commonplace!'[50] The truth is that expressive accounts of consciousness sanctioned both the 'aggressive' movement of self outwards (here made safe by being associated with the church) and the hidden, secret life of feeling, expression and repression, energising movement and hysteria, concealment and revelation, silence and speech. Thus the woman poet's negotiation of the aesthetics of secrecy and its contradictions is highly complex, and always deeply concerned with struggle and limit, transgression and boundary, silence and language.

Christina Rossetti took up this theme directly in relation to poetry in another extraordinary documenting of the cultural dilemma of women, her Preface to a fairly late poem, *Monna Innominata*. In this brief discussion, and with characteristically 'secret' obliquity and indirection, she claimed, like Greenwell, expressive rights for the unmarried woman in poetry. She claimed, not only the freedom of the unmarried woman to express her sexuality, but also the freedom to be absurd, undignified, if feminine sexuality necessitated this.

She calls Elizabeth Barrett Browning 'the Great Poetess of our own day and nation' and yet implicitly offers a critique of her position.[51] Beatrice and Laura, she writes, dismissing a whole mythology of women, may have been immortalised by Dante and Petrarch, but they come down to us 'scant of attractiveness'. The reason is that they and the 'unnamed ladies' who preceded them were the objects of sexual love and religious feeling but could not express it themselves. They come down to us as remote and unpassionate beings. In the same breath she makes a characteristically oblique and ambitious historical statement: 'in that land and that period which gave birth to Catholics, to Albigenses, and to Troubadours', Renaissance Italy, in other words, were generated the forms of thought and feeling and the religious and sexual conflicts which have conditioned the nineteenth-century culture evolving from them. In both periods it was impossible for a lady to 'have spoken for herself'. Elizabeth Barrett Browning, the 'Great Poetess' of her period might, she continues, have achieved another kind of art than the 'Portuguese Sonnets' 'had she only been unhappy instead of happy'. The mysterious indirectness here (for 'Sonnets from the Portuguese' is hardly a happy poem) is to be understood by remembering that in Victorian terminology to be 'happy' was to be married. And when the euphemistic terms are reversed, to be 'unhappy' is to be a spinster. Spinsters are not free to write of sexual love or passion as the 'happy' married woman is. The claims are striking. Elizabeth Barrett Browning might have been a different and perhaps a greater poet if she had remained single. Correspondingly, the unmarried woman has something important (perhaps more important?) to say about sexual feeling, but is blocked by convention from saying it. No wonder such spinster poetry might be 'less dignified', if just as honourable, than that written *to* her. She would be writing of the 'barrier', implicitly both hymenal and societal in this prose, between women and men, between herself and the object of her passion, sexual or divine. The barrier 'might be one held sacred': she would be writing of taboo subjects, unfulfilled feminine desire and rejection.[52]

The 'barrier' as the topic of expressive theory is explored, necessarily indirectly, by Rossetti, Greenwell and Ingelow. These poets worked inside the religious lyric and the love lyric and radically redefined them by exploring their limits. How they do this, and how they not only metaphorise but establish the barrier as a structural principle of their poems, is perhaps more fundamental to the nature of Victorian women's poetry than any of the direct accounts of women's experience to be found in their poems.

Of course, overt polemic about women can be found in the work of these poets, but these are less fundamental than their indirections. Certainly Christina Rossetti's work yields enough, at the level of direct statement, about sexual, social and economic matters for one to be sure that she thought of herself as a 'woman' writer and indeed saw that she was marginalised as one by the very nature of her situation. She contributed to *The Germ* but her sex naturally excluded her formally from the Pre-Raphaelite *Brother*hood.

The P.R.B.

The two Rossettis (brothers they)
And Holman Hunt and John Millais
With Stephens chivalrous and bland,
And Woolner in a distant land –
In these six men I awestruck see
Embodied the great P.R.B.
D. G. Rossetti offered two
Good pictures to the public view;
Unnumbered ones great John Millais,
And Holman more than I can say.
William Rossetti, calm and solemn,
Cuts up his brethren by the column.[53]

This poem, dated 19 September 1853, might have been even tarter if she had known that William was to cut up his sister by the column when he edited her poems in 1904.

Illegitimacy, fallen women, the fierce legal bond of marriage, the sexual fate of the woman who waits, while the male is given social licence to experiment, the experience of exclusion, all this is to be found particularly in Christina Rossetti's earlier work. Her poems constantly define the lyric writer as shut out, outside, at the margin. 'Shut Out' is the title of a poem which makes the condition of exclusion paradoxically that of being shut in. 'At Home' is a poem about being not at home in this woman's place, ironising the visiting-card title – 'When I was dead my spirit turned/To see the much frequented house'. 'The Iniquity of the Fathers upon the Children' (1866) clearly emerges from her well-known interest in fallen women: ballads about prohibition, possession, rivalry, the rigour of the law, bonds and legal forms ('Love from the North', 'Cousin Kate', 'Noble Sisters', 'Maude Clare') testify to her awareness of the social and economic circumstances of women. She is fierce about the dependency of marriage in 'Triad' for instance. There three kinds of passion are envisaged. The last, institutionalised sexuality in marriage, is enervated and passive – 'One droned in sweetness like a fattened bee'. And yet Rossetti's generalised lyric seems almost created to resist and circumvent such analyses. The seeming sourcelessness and contextlessness of lyric, its impersonal reserve, its *secrecy*, is the form Rossetti chose. On the other hand, the intransigently enigmatic, by declaring itself as such, allows itself an extraordinary openness. Reserve and intensity, constraint and exposure, belong together because, as Dora

Greenwell recognised, reserve is necessarily built upon its opposite. Once you have let it be known you have a secret you allow that there is something to give away.

Part of the secret of *Goblin Market*, the title poem of Christina Rossetti's first volume, is the questioning feminine discourse it masks. Two girls, ambiguously children and adolescents, seemingly autonomous and without parents, crouch as if nesting in the rushes as they hear the goblin's cry, 'Come buy'. Distorted, half-animal creatures, resembling cats, rats, wombats and snails, offer a collection of fruits (which violate all seasonal patterns) for sale in a jingle of plenitude, 'All ripe together'. The poem has the unplaced contextlessness of a fairy tale. Arthur Symons called it 'the perfect realisation of those happy and fantastic aspects of the supernatural which we call fairy land'. It was to him 'naive and childlike', but he added that it was also 'fantastic and bewildering' in its 'faery' atmosphere (this archaic spelling often indicates discomfort in Victorian writers).[54] The consummate metrical virtuosity of the jingle sophisticatedly deflects the poem into the 'naive' aural and oral tradition, a literary way of masking the literary, perhaps (and there is something of an astringent, sharpened almost ironised Keats here), but one which does propose that the tracks of the poem are in some way covered. It proposes to the reader precisely a deferral of placing. It is 'bewildering'.

> Morning and evening
> Maids heard the goblins cry:
> 'Come buy our orchard fruits,
> Come buy, come buy:
> Apples and quinces,
> Lemons and oranges,
> Plump unpecked cherries,
> Melons and raspberries,
> Bloom-down-cheeked peaches,
> Swart-headed mulberries,
> Wild free-born cranberries,
> Crab-apples, dewberries,
> Pine-apples, blackberries,
> Apricots, strawberries; –
> All ripe together
> In summer weather, –
> Morns that pass by,
> Fair eves that fly;
> Come buy, come buy:
> Our grapes fresh from the vine,
> Pomegranates full and fine,
> Dates and sharp bullaces,

> Rare pears and greengages,
> Damsons and bilberries,
> Taste them and try'.[55]

This is a deeply, insatiably oral poem in another way. The words 'fill the mouth' as the goblins' figs do, with a materiality which is taken up in the 'tingling cheeks' of the listening girls. And when Laura is forced not to take but to *buy* the fruit by giving up part of herself (a lock of her hair is exchanged instead of money), she 'sucks' it.

> She sucked and sucked and sucked the more
> Fruits which that unknown orchard bore;
> She sucked until her lips were sore.[56]

It is tempting to literalise the sexuality of such lines, but it is important to be sceptical about doing so. What can be said is that the poem is not, in Rossetti's words, 'dignified'. Laura's orgiastic sucking, the passionate fury of her loss when she can have the fruit no more ('she gnashed her teeth for baulked desire and wept' (267)), the assault of the goblins upon Lizzie, who resists the fruit which they smear and crush upon her face, Laura's eager kissing of her sister to regain the juice of the fruit, such passages are not only not 'dignified' but transgress and outrage in their violence and agony.

> Kicked and knocked her,
> Mauled and mocked her,
> Lizzie uttered not a word;
> Would not open lip from lip
> Lest they should cram a mouthful in:
> But laughed in heart to feel the drip
> Of juice that syrupped all her face,
> And lodged in dimples of her chin,
> And streaked her neck which quaked like curd.[57]

But what can be made of this narrative? Laura never sees or hears the goblins again. Pining and starvation follow fierce agony and rage, that most poignant condition. Lizzie, seeing that Laura is near to death from deprivation, searches for the goblins. Wiser than Laura, she has her silver penny in her pocket. Something happens to her: 'And for *the first time in her life*/Began to listen and to look' (327–8) (my emphasis). Once she finds the goblins she bargains in order to be able to carry the fruit to Laura but they, refusing to accede to the take-away principle, attack her, grind the fruit against her face, literally expressing the juice, and smear her with it. Laughing with glee, her silver penny still intact, she returns dripping to Laura, who expects to see her 'goblin-ridden'. Laura licks the fruit from her face, and this secondary experience induces paroxysms of pain. But she recovers. The poem ends almost perfunctorily, celebrating the love of sisters and declaring that the tale is handed onto the children when the sisters marry.

Payment for forbidden fruit, prohibition, taboo, punishment, the consumption of what is itself dangerously consuming, the harsh moral exclusion of the erotic, all these are in play here. The difficulty is to place them. Some critics have literalised the poem in terms of masturbation: menstruation and faeces would do as well because the images are so enigmatically precise that they are open-endedly generalisable. Some critics see a lesbian passion between the two girls: some have seen fantasies of the colonial other at work in their response to the goblins; some have been tempted to see Laura and Lizzie in conflict and moral opposition to one another, in a cautionary tale of freedom and repression. All these readings are possible. But why the strange collusion in which Lizzie displaces the pulped fruit for Laura's consumption, a 'sacrifice' which leaves her not merely untouched but gleeful and energised? Why the recovery in which light dances in Laura's eyes? Is the fate of Jeannie, who went to her death before marriage on encountering the goblins, an attempt to reinforce the harsh moral intransigence of a cautionary tale or an indication that it is not an analogue for the central episode? The harshness of the poem is not so much in its sense of retribution as the cruel way in which the fruit is offered as a saleable commodity and arbitrarily withdrawn. It has to be bargained for, but it belongs to a mystified economy to which both girls are inalienably subject. You exchange or sell something for it but the exchange is unequal. The fruit is *made* into temptation according to arbitrary laws. Some of these questions can be clarified by recourse to the aesthetics of expressive theory.

How does expressive theory return upon *Goblin Market*? Boldly and dramatically Christina Rossetti transfers the structure of aesthetic thought, with all its uneasiness and ambiguities, directly to the sexual and erotic conflict bound up in the forbidden fruit. Sexual and moral conflict is metaphorically incipient in expressive theory but Rossetti exposes this through the context of the goblins' temptation. Laura is like one of Keble's poets. She will go mad or die unless she can carry out her desires and consume the fruit once more. The dissipation of her energies when they have no means of expression and find no meaningful object in formerly happy tasks is extreme. In anorexic grief,

> She no more swept the house,
> Tended the fowls or cows,
> Fetched honey, kneaded cakes of wheat,
> Brought water from the brook:
> But sat down listless in the chimney-nook
> And would not eat.[58]

349

act of Breaking rules

Desire without an object, which has been summarily and cruelly removed, cannot move out of the self. To go back to the aesthetic terms, feeling can find no equivalent for itself, no form or object to invest or 'fuse' with emotion. The object isn't there. It isn't there because it is mysteriously forbidden. Either to have the object or to represent it is a transgression. So feeling thrusts against barriers or expends itself on nothing. Laura's representations of her experience to Lizzie ('You cannot think what figs/ My teeth have met in') only make her more desperately aware both of her loss and of the disjunction between her symbolic expression and the experience itself. 'She dreamed of melons, as a traveller sees/False waves in desert drouth . . . /And burns the thirstier in the sandful breeze'.[59] The symbolic representation turns out to be illusory, the false equivalence of a dream.

One way of reading Lizzie's anxious ethical care for Laura, her sense of the rules, her escape from the consequences of the goblin fruit, is to see it in neat moral opposition to Laura's experience. The answer to Laura's suffering is a punitive medicinal exorcism, in which pleasure turns to pain, effecting Laura's moral transformation and reincorporation into social life. Part of the complexity of the poem arises because this is one feminine discourse allowed by the work – the agony of repression, denial and sacrifice. But it is at this point that the questions which have been asked make their claims. And the ambiguities of expressive theory help here. If expression is predicated upon repression, if they are interdependent as much as in antithesis, the structure of the poem shifts. The interdependence of Laura and Lizzie becomes a possibility. It is not a question of choosing either Laura or Lizzie, freedom or prohibition. Laura and Lizzie are doubles of one another. Rossetti has seized on the interdependence of the overflow of feeling and the barrier. Each reciprocally enables and disables the other. It is only through Lizzie's resistance that Laura is able to gain access to the (significantly) expressed fruit. It is only through Laura's longing that Lizzie finds herself resisting the goblins. Laura is liberated by repeating the tasting of the fruit but it is only through a process of displacement that the fruit can be regained. As if to endorse this doubling, Lizzie's resistance to and Laura's assimilation of the fruit are represented by the same traditional images of virginity under attack. Lizzie resists like a lily or a stone assaulted by the surging currents of the sea, or a town under attack, 'Made to tug her standard down' (421), and the breaching current of feeling becomes the force of aggression. Laura is *carried* by the force of her experience, 'Like a caged thing freed', 'like a flying flag when armies run' (505, 506). Like a town in an earthquake, a mast or a tree in a tempest, she is overwhelmed.

The passages have the metaphor of current, surge, overflow, which is constantly present in Victorian poetics to describe the force of expressive feeling. The condition of Laura's freedom seems to be an *assent* to being

350

overwhelmed by the power of the fruit rather than a resistance to it, a reversal of what one would expect of a 'moral' reading of the poem. For if we pursue the metaphor, the barriers of virginity are breached. And yet the situation is paradoxical. Her freedom is in proportion to, and depends upon, her resistance to it. On fire, 'she loathed the feast' (495) and 'Gorged on bitterness without a name' (510). The energy of resistance is the condition of the energies of expression. They partake of one another so that expression *is* 'mortal strife' (513). Laura's liberation does not rest on the elimination of constraint but on a consent to its power.

The poem is deeply ambiguous here, reproducing the ambiguities at work in the poetics of expression, for one reading of this passage reasserts the simple opposition between free unbound sexuality and bitter constraint. It slips into conventional ethics. The fruit becomes a medicinal punishment, a 'fiery antidote' (559), as it is later called, which purges Laura of her poisons and restores her innocence. 'Laura awoke as from a dream,/ Laughed in the innocent old way' (537–8). She is made ready to accept the institutionalised conventions of marriage and passes on her 'fears' to her children. Certainly this is one feminine discourse in the poem, an acceptance of patriarchy and the rigour of repression. But there is another working against the simplicities of the first. If we accept the structural dependence of expression and repression upon one another, Laura's recovery of energy – her grey hair disappears, her locks gleam and light dances in her eyes – becomes a function of her acceptance of the full power of sexuality. It is not a second fall but a *new* second innocence. The words 'gorged on bitterness' recall Milton's Eve, who 'greedily engorg'd' the apple from the tree of knowledge of good and evil. And yet in a bold rereading of Milton, Laura's second taking of the fruit is not a fall but a recovery and consolidates the power of the fruit. Sexuality is neither freedom nor constraint, but both. As such its energies are ambiguous – 'sweeter than honey from the rock' (129) and 'wormwood' (494) to the tongue. That is why the power of the fruit is 'without a name'. No single representation of it can be adequate or, indeed, it *can't* be represented. Rossetti's representation of sexuality is not in the names or images she finds but in the structure of the whole poem with its repeated tasting. It is important to the intransigence of the poem that Laura does not *do* anything with her acceptance. It simply enables her to stay alive. She is absorbed into the female patterns of marriage, 'beset with fears' (547) for her children, for what is celebrated in *Goblin Market* is also to be feared. And, to become a Victorian parent is to be dogged by fear of sexuality. The syntax of the first jingle allows that to buy the fruit is also to buy 'Morns that pass by,/ Fair eves that fly', loss and fulfilment, delight and fear. Sexuality itself is defined by, locked into, the institutions in which it has its being. It is governed by money and a principle of exchange. It is construed as temptation.

Goblin Market is Christina Rossetti's most remarkable long poem. She was also a writer of consummate lyrics. What can be called the feminine discourse which responds to the aesthetics of expression and repression, overflow and barrier, in *Goblin Market*, is also at work in her short poems. Her lyrics of love or devotion are written with a curious intensity and authority and the traditional forms she chooses, pastoral, song, incantation, riddle, allegory, ballad, make them into quintessences of themselves. They are offered as if – Symons' word is right here – they are 'naive' forms of known conventional lyric. They have at first sight a crystal ingenuous openness, inviting the simple reading. Yet in them a rigorous reserve and economy is under pressure. The 'naive' lyric becomes a way of being secret. The theological concept of reserve, of keeping back, which is openly accepted by Keble as a poetic principle seems to be a principle of these lyrics, and yet they disclose the struggle and difficulty Greenwell described as the founding moment of feminine consciousness. They come to be *about* reserve, the struggle to express and not to express, to resist and not to resist. All her work is adamantly locked in repetition. Doubling of words, phrases, patterned iteration and duplication, create the spareness of her lyrics. Repetition works as a barrier. It is a way of setting up a pattern, resisting or confirming it. The shifting and deflecting which goes on in and through the process of repetition indicates a play in and *with* limit, which is set up, violated, transgressed, confirmed. The formal constraint, as with rhyme, enables a play with regularity and irregularity. Her early games of bout rimés (the Rossetti family game, an exercise which is described interestingly in *Maude*, Christina Rossetti's adolescent tale of religious hypochondria) were fundamental to her poetry.[60] Refrain is another way of defining and redefining barriers, because it falls inside and outside the poem simultaneously. These strategies of restriction achieve startling shifts and realignments, just as Rossetti's conventional language produces arresting collocations – 'bloodless lily', 'fattening rain', 'chill-veined snowdrop'. Through them her lyrics experiment with boundaries and the transgression of boundaries in such a way that a seemingly conventional lyric moves into a questioning of convention. Conventions are arbitrary in themselves and the poetry becomes a questioning of the arbitrary.

Christina Rossetti's response to the aesthetics of overflow is not unique, though it is explored in a uniquely original way. It is shared by the other poets I have mentioned, Greenwell and Ingelow, who are compulsively concerned in form and content with the implications of expressive thought. It is useful to put some of their work against hers. An early poem bears a striking resemblance to Dora Greenwell's *Qui sait Aimer, sait Mourir*.

> 'I burn myself away!'
> So spake the Rose and smiled; 'within my cup

All day the sunbeams fall in flame, all day
    They drink my sweetness up!'

'I sigh my soul away!'
The Lily said; 'all night the moonbeams pale
Steal round and round me, whispering in their play
    An all too tender tale!'

'I give my soul away!'
The violet said; 'the West wind wanders on,
The North wind comes; I know not what they say,
    And yet my soul is gone!'

Oh Poet, burn away
Thy fervent soul! fond Lover at the feet
Of her thou lovest, sigh! dear Christian, pray,
    And let the world be sweet!
                        (Dora Greenwell)[61]

She sat and sang alway
    By the green margin of a stream,
Watching the fishes leap and play
    Beneath the glad sunbeam.

I sat and wept away
    Beneath the moon's most shadowy beam,
Watching the blossoms of the May
    Weep leaves into the stream.

I wept for memory;
    She sang for hope that is so fair:
My tears were swallowed by the sea;
    Her songs died on the air.
                (Christina Rossetti, 'Song')[62]

In Greenwell's poem the Rose, the Lily and the Violet, conventional symbols of erotic love, are given speech, as if the role of the 'unnamed ladies' mentioned in Rossetti's Preface is reversed. They are no longer objects but agents. They are explicitly compared to the poet who, like them, breaks the limit of selfhood, burning, and to the male lover, sighing. The sigh, the exhalation, is an appropriate image for that moving of being beyond itself and indeed takes up the poet's projection of self which is often described as the empathy of love in Victorian criticism. Rose, Lily and Violet, however, are consumed or dissipated in the expressive act. The male lover has an object. As if aware of its dangerous implications, the poem ends as Christian prayer in which the overflow of feeling has a transcendental object. Rossetti's poem, characteristically condensed and terse, is based not upon a triad but an antithesis – 'She sat and sang alway. . . . I sat and wept away'. With near repetition 'away' shifts from an intensifier to reflexive – I wept myself away. Expressive feeling momentarily finds a correspondent image in the world as the May blossoms 'weep leaves into the stream' but the representation cannot contain the overflow of feeling which is dispersed in an unresponding universe. Antithesis is superseded by a new parallelism. Both tears and songs dissipate, swallowed by the sea, dying on the air. Because it can find no equivalent or limiting form the expressive act is a death. There is no Christian resolution.

Goblin Market and Other Poems was published in 1862. Dora Greenwell, already an established poet, published another volume of *Poems* in 1867. These later poems in particular return repeatedly to a language of burning and blushing, exposure, overflow, sighs, breathing exhalation, and to a structure in which hidden and secret feeling kills and is killed if it finds no expression but expires in the expressive act. 'A Song' is a virtual pun on the idea of expiration, the sigh, a death. A cloud can neither condense 'To fall in kindly rain', nor project its colours onto the world. It exists merely as that which 'sighed': 'What could it do but die?'[63] The golden heart of the rose 'o'er flows' and decays in 'Amid change unchanging'. In 'One Flower' the blush, the tear, the smile, the sigh, achieve a transitory moment of expression, breaking out of limit but dying in the act. 'Thy soul has burst its sheath,/Oh, is it love or death,/Sweet flower, that thou hast won?'[64] 'A Picture' plays with expression both as a physical embodiment in eye, cheek, smile and lips and expression as an unbodily, fleeting manifestation of hidden and intangible spiritual being: 'And on her lips that, like an opening rose,/Seemed parting some sweet secret to disclose'.[65] The pun on 'disclose' makes expression both released and withheld. The physical form is both the means of expression and its obstruction. This is a love poem to a woman by a woman. Or, more complexly, perhaps, by a woman envisaging a love poem by a man. In 'Reserve', the problem is dealt with directly, as the speaker longs to gain access to 'thy Being's overflow' and liberate the 'deeper' 'tide/Of feeling' from 'the bar' of constraint. 'Bar' is a pun on both barrier and music, as if the representation of feeling becomes its barrier in a way characteristic of expressive theory.[66] The virtuosic 'A Scherzo' is about the overprotected and yet constricted heart which longs to escape 'Anywhere, anywhere, out of this room!'[67] It is not surprising that Dora Greenwell's remarkably detailed and humane essay 'On the education of the Imbecile', published in the *North British Review* in 1868, sees idiocy as potential feeling and intelligence which has been blocked.[68] Idiots *are* educable and capable of love and mental effort, even though it is as if 'a secret finger had been laid upon some hitherto unsuspected *stop* in the great organ'. 'Fast-bound', 'bondage', 'captivity', 'clogged', are the words she uses to describe their condition. She compares the idiot to the maniac, 'who has at least *lived*'.[69] The idiot, blocked from expression, has something in common with women, though she does not say so. It shares the same experience of constraint.

If Dora Greenwell's work is concerned with expression obstructed or dissipated in the act, Jean Ingelow, also publishing in this decade (*Poems*, 1863), deals with expressive metaphor as passionate overflow, flood, outpouring. 'The High Tide on the Coast of Lincolnshire', a narrative historical ballad of disastrous flood, is emblematic of her work. The river Lindis breaks its banks as the result of a huge, unforeseen tidal wave, sweeping away Elizabeth, the cowherd's wife, and her two children.

> Then bankes came downe with ruin and rout –
> Then beaten foam flew round about –
> Then all the mighty floods were out.[70]

Water, or light, forcing a passage outwards, but hurrying towards extinction and destruction, flows through her poems. The 'Star's Monument' turns on the eclipse of a star which had fulfilled its existence simply by giving out light. Passion and outpouring, however transient, is celebrated as meaningful.[71] In 'Requiescat in Pace!', sunset, uncannily flushing landscape and sky, is an image of the expenditure of Christ's life in the Passion, a transformation of matter by spirit. This is a metaphor of flow and *influence*, feeling justified in and by itself. Its language of light and flush owes much to Tennyson and the rhythms of *Maud*.

> Below me lay the wide sea, the scarlet sun was stooping,
>   And he dyed the wasted water, as with a scarlet dye;
> And he dyed the lighthouse towers, every bird with white wing
>   swooping,
>   Took his colours, and the cliffs did, and the yawning sky.
>
> Over grass came that strange flush, and over ling and heather,
>   Over flocks of sheep and lambs, and over Cromer town;
> And each filmy cloudlet crossing drifted like a scarlet feather
>   Torn from folded wings of clouds, while he settled down.
>
> When I looked, I dared not sigh: – in the light of God's splendour,
>   With his daily blue and gold, who am I? What am I?
> But that passion and outpouring seeming an awful sign and tender,
>   Like the blood of the Redeemer, shown on earth and sky.[72]

Interestingly, God's expressive act supersedes and extinguishes the writer's: 'I dared not sigh'. It provokes the question 'who am I? What am I?' Both Greenwell and Ingelow present the female subject in extinction, as obliterated. Uncontained by it, unable to find representation, or without an object, overflow and flood are self-extinguishing. These poets appropriate the dominant aesthetic of expression, take over its metaphor and linguistic forms and work within it, but they explore its impossibilities.

Dora Greenwell's *Poems* (1867) are dedicated to Elizabeth Barrett Browning, and some of the poems in that volume are clearly influenced by her. 'A Song to Call to Remembrance', subtitled 'A Plea for the Coventry Ribbon Weavers', engages in direct political writing: 'When anxious fathers have no work, the children dare not play'. It is an indication of Elizabeth Barrett Browning's independence that *Aurora Leigh* does not negotiate with the terms of expressive theory. Expressive metaphor, the flow of milk and love, for instance, is present in *Aurora Leigh*, but without the tensions it has in the work of Greenwell and Ingelow. The terms of expressive theory are more nearly present in 'Sonnets from the Portuguese', and there, in the hesitating affirmations of these poems, Elizabeth Barrett Browning is interested in a dialectic of subject and object which attempts to represent the struggle for identity in passion between two people and the struggle for *language*. 'Sonnets from the Portuguese' is about idolatry, dependency, the temptation to disappear before the object of adulation. It is ambitious because it attempts to discover a language to represent and go beyond the structure of an unwilling master–slave relationship. It is a language of dissolving categories which attempt to coalesce into new forms. Though its language is very different, its preoccupation is the same as those of Greenwell and Ingelow, the dissolving of selfhood.

The aim of 'Sonnets' is to redefine 'the whole/Of life in a new rhythm', as Elizabeth Barrett Browning puts it in Sonnet VII, and the sliding cadences, the deliberate elisions and metrical freedoms which break away from the established regularities of the sonnet form are clearly intentional.[73] The late caesuras and enjambement declare an attempt to dissolve the customary forms and restrictions. Language goes into a flux, as if enacting the dissolution of categories. In XV, for instance, an adjective acts with a double function, as both adjective and noun – 'Love's *divine*' (6), shut 'in a *crystalline*' (7). The effect is of expansion, a going beyond the limit of definition. In the same way the lover's gaze attempts not to be 'shut . . . in' or subordinated by the gaze of the other, but to look away and move beyond the definition of the other's sight – 'As one who sits and gazes from above,/Over the rivers to the bitter sea' (13–14). But to gaze 'from above' is simply to invert the relationship and this seems only to circumvent the 'rivers' of feeling by looking beyond them to death and the 'oblivion' (12) of the 'bitter sea'. The sonnets chart the struggle of the feminine subject to take up a new position which is free of dependency. They struggle with their own dissolve as they try to break into new areas of being. The door and the threshold, that peculiarly Victorian image of barrier, of lines crossed and partition established, determined space, are the incipient images of these sonnets. In Sonnet IV the expressive model is reversed as the poet experiences the overwhelming power of the other as *influence*, a breaking in, a shattering of the doors of the self – 'My cricket chirps against thy mandolin' (11). The 'voice within' (13) can only be retrieved in solitude and paradoxical silence. The male poet's expression is music falling 'In folds of golden fullness at my door' (8). Music material- ises as the folds of a curtain and dematerialises as space, 'folds . . . of fullness'. Colour, texture, space, the reconfiguring of categories, denotes new dimensions and possibilities. Elizabeth Barrett Browning is attempting to reconfigure the expressive act as music so that it finds not a represen- tation, for non-referential music cannot be that, but releases itself from contradiction by going beyond the barrier of equivalences and inventing new forms and experiences independent of them. So *Sonnets* moves towards language as a self-referring or self-creating act. This is one way out of the impasse of expressive theory. The poem does not always measure up to its ambitions but it is a fertile experiment.

Christina Rossetti does not write with the heat and prolixity which the expressive lyric seems to imply for her contemporaries. Her lyrics do negotiate with the terms of expressive theory but not in terms of the *obstruction* to expression to be seen in the work of so many women poets of this time. The insight of *Goblin Market*, that overflow and resistance, expression and repression, create one another, leads her to exploit the barrier ambiguously. It restricts and creates possibility. It invites and refuses transgression. This may be why in her hands the 'conventional' religious lyric is more unorthodox than any other religious poetry by women at this time.

The cool discipline with which the struggle for the smallest space goes on, the nakedness and reserve, passion and restraint, the aggression and rigour of so much of Rossetti's work, creates both the moments of lyric exhilaration and the resilient and savage wit in her poems. In 'A Birthday' – 'My heart is like a singing bird' – the release of exuberant passion is celebrated characteristically with a ritual of artifice. In 'My Dream' a lascivious and bloated crocodile works destruction, crunching and sucking his victims, until it is time for it to conform to convention: his tumescent size diminishes; 'The prudent crocodile rose on his feet/And shed appropri- ate tears and wrung his hands' (47–8). In 'Eve' 'Huge camels knelt/As if in deprecation' (60–1) of her grief. Only the serpent grins, truthful to a world of nature in which animals and human beings cannot exist in mutual sympathy.

'Winter: My Secret' is a poem in which the wit and lyric energy of Rossetti's work come together. It is a poem about secrecy and reserve, prohibition, taboo, revealing and concealing, and is almost a summa of her work. Provocative and flirtatious and yet deeply reticent, it turns on the refusal of expression. It is about and is itself a barrier.

357

I tell my secret? No indeed, not I:
Perhaps some day, who knows?
But not today; it froze, and blows, and snows,
And you're too curious: fie!
You want to hear it? well:
Only, my secret's mine, and I won't tell.

Or, after all, perhaps there's none:
Suppose there is no secret after all,
But only just my fun.
Today's a nipping day, a biting day;
In which one wants a shawl,
A veil, a cloak, and other wraps:
I cannot ope to every one who taps,
And let the draughts come whistling thro' my hall;
Come bounding and surrounding me,
Come buffeting, astounding me,
Nipping and clipping thro' my wraps and all.
I wear my mask for warmth: who ever shows
His nose to Russian snows
To be pecked at by every wind that blows?
You would not peck? I thank you for good will,
Believe, but leave that truth untested still.

Spring's an expansive time: yet I don't trust
March with its peck of dust,
Nor April with its rainbow-crowned brief showers,
Nor even May, whose flowers
One frost may wither thro' the sunless hours.
Perhaps some languid summer day,
When drowsy birds sing less and less,
And golden fruit is ripening to excess,
If there's not too much sun nor too much cloud,
And the warm wind is neither still nor loud,
Perhaps my secret I may say,
Or you may guess.[74]

The poem plays with withdrawal and expression, guardedness and openness; 'I tell my secret? . . . Suppose there is no secret after all . . . Perhaps
my secret I may say,/Or you may guess'. Through the movement of
flirtation the ironies work. It might be that the 'secret' of sexuality has no
content. The 'secret' could be the writer's 'winter', her frigidity or virginity,
just as easily as it could be the 'golden fruit' of fulfilment. The secret,
guarded as it is by the two 'I's which lock the first line at both ends, is
at once part of the privacy and silence of identity, the 'I', and yet comes

into being as the creation of curiosity from outside – 'you're too curious'. The decision not to 'tell' would be a violation of self, 'not I', and yet that 'not I' defines the self, since the refusal to tell betrays the existence of the secret. The habitual Rossetti image of being locked in becomes voluntary and involuntary in the second section as a half-self-mocking, spinsterish retreat is effected with witty self-protection. The shawl, veil, cloak, wraps, against the 'nipping day' are resistance to assault and to restriction. For the 'astounding' breezes are, as the punning internal rhyme asserts, energetically 'bounding', *binding* and wounding. The 'peck' is of course a bite and a kiss. The defence becomes a kind of collusion, mutually created by the speaker and curious questioner, as the retreat responds to the energetic but damaging assault, the assault to the retreat. The secret itself, perhaps, is created out of this double movement. 'I wear my mask for warmth'. A mask, that vulnerable barrier, is a covering and a protection. It conceals and deceives, but a mask can also be a representation. It constitutes at once barrier and exposure, concealing and revealing. It is both forced upon the wearer and entices the onlooker. It is worn, a curiously moving justification for such minimal covering, for 'warmth', for protection, but also to *generate* warmth, a word inevitably with erotic resonance here. The mask comes to represent a signifying process whose form and mode of existence is stratagem, ambiguity, delay, displacement, which depends upon leaving a resolution 'untested'. The vulnerable response to the erotic and aggressive energy of curiosity is itself erotic and aggressive, but the arousal of energy can never be tested with closure or revelation. Expression of sexuality, the secret, actually depends on maintaining the teasing barrier to itself. With extraordinary lyric wit the poem acts out the manoeuvres, the reciprocal collusions, between vulnerability and aggression which are created not only by but for the speaker.

A poem about telling a secret becomes a poem about the conditions under which the sexuality of the speaking subject is created and bound. Again, there is that sense, familiar to a Rossetti poem, of simultaneous restriction and liberation as the poem searches for a space by proposing a time of impossible plenitude and equilibrium – 'If there's not too much sun nor too much cloud' – as the conditions of 'telling'. But, the implication is, the times never will be auspicious, and perhaps precisely because in such golden fullness the secret would disappear and would not be necessary. The poem returns to the conditional movement of provocation – 'Or you may guess'. You may guess, or you may go on guessing.

'Winter Rain' is characteristic of the unique movement of her lyrics. These are complex poems because they work with the ambiguous structure of expressive aesthetic as much as with its terms and content. This poem begins with the receptivity of landscape to the fall of rain, internal and external seemingly perfectly matched. Rain absorbed into the earth embodies that world of *in-fluence*, a world of flow and permeable physical being

359

which enables the earth and the body to be nourished. A crystal pastoral convention, rigorous and self-effacing, posits a world of sexual and erotic activity.

Every valley drinks,
    Every dell and hollow:
Where the kind rain sinks and sinks,
    Green of Spring will follow.

Yet a lapse of weeks
    Buds will burst their edges,
Strip their wool-coats, glue-coats, streaks,
    In the woods and hedges;

Weave a bower of love
    For birds to meet each other,
Weave a canopy above
    Nest and egg and mother.

But for fattening rain
    We should have no flowers,
Never a bud or leaf again
    But for soaking showers;

Never a mated bird
    In the rocking tree-tops,
Never indeed a flock or herd
    To graze upon the lea-crops.

Lambs so woolly white,
    Sheep the sun-bright leas on,
They could have no grass to bite
    But for rain in season.

We should find no moss
    In the shadiest places,
Find no waving meadow grass
    Pied with broad-eyed daisies:

But miles of barren sand,
    With never a son or daughter,
Not a lily on the land,
    Or lily on the water.[75]

Sparely, through the repetition of 'sinks', with its correspondence in the rhyme-word 'drinks', the first stanza establishes the gentle reciprocity between the irrigating overflow of rain and the world it penetrates, a world of inlet and receptive concavity – 'Every dell and hollow'. Rain belongs

360

to a natural temporal and causal sequence in which buds break and birds mate and breed, love grows securely in a world of happy sexuality. But already something sinister is at work: the insistent repetition of 'sinks' hints that the rain sinks *away*, and figures dearth and drought. After stanza 3 the last four stanzas set up an intricate series of syntactic obstacles and parallelism. The power of rain is denoted through negatives: 'But for fattening rain/We should have no flowers'. 'But for . . . no . . . /Never . . ./ But for'. The sequence of negation is intricately varied. 'Never . . . / Never . . . no . . . /But for . . . no . . . no . . . /But . . . /Not'. The fertilising, impregnating property of rain is conjured by its negation until the teleological necessity of its regular recurrence becomes infinitely precarious, called into question – 'But for rain *in season*'. Rain out of season, or no rain at all, are the possibilities which come into play through the negatives. The lyric ends with the remorseless logic of its denials. Desert, sterility, a world without procreation, 'Not a lily on the land,/Or lily on the water', these are real possibilities. The significance of 'fattening' rain comes retrospectively to the fore. Famine and drought and the end of generations are implied in the terse refusal of reproduction. This would be a world without sexual difference – never 'a son or daughter', parents and children, and the power relations they imply. The final mirror lines set up a parallelism between land and water but simultaneously deny it. If there were no rain there would be no matching correspondence between land and water because there would be no water for the lily to grow in. Indeed, the subjunctive makes these verbal phantasms, constructions of language in disjunction from experience, the nightmare of expressive poetics. The abolition and refusal of antithesis here is a sweeping refusal even to accept the neat ordering of opposites and equivalences. The lily, emblem of virginity, would not grow. Virginity only has meaning if it is defined by its opposite, if it is something to be violated, but it becomes a useless concept, an idea without meaning, when the conditions required for its existence are annihilated. The consonance becomes disequilibrium, just as the confirmation through negation becomes a negation of confirmation. The very means of syntax by which the poem is ordered become the agents of disruption. The rain, perhaps, 'sinks and sinks' away forever. Christina Rossetti is able to transgress conventional pastoral optimism and confront the possibility of an unteleological world by using pastoral convention. Convention and transgression create one another, just as a meaningful, ordered, causal world is built upon the repression of disorder and unmeaning. The inexorable coolness of the logic moves in step with the delight in fecundity, so that they exert pressure on one another. Distantly there is the suggestion that if language and nature exist in contradiction with one another, it may be that there is the possibility of remaking the world in a way more consonant, in which culture and nature do not exist in disjunction. But the idea *is* distant.

361

'Up-hill' is another poem where the simplest language erects difficulties. It is a question and answer poem and resembles those of Herbert, whose poems Christina Rossetti loved. It has found its way into hymnals, an almost inevitable guarantee of, perhaps, overly simple reading.

> Does the road wind up-hill all the way?
>> Yes, to the very end.
> Will the day's journey take the whole long day?
>> From morn to night, my friend.
>
> But is there for the night a resting-place?
>> A roof for when the slow dark hours begin.
> May not the darkness hide it from my face?
>> You cannot miss that inn.
>
> Shall I meet other wayfarers at night?
>> Those who have gone before.
> Then must I knock, or call when just in sight?
>> They will not keep you standing at that door.
>
> Shall I find comfort, travel-sore and weak?
>> Of labour you shall find the sum.
> Will there be beds for me and all who seek?
>> Yea, beds for all who come.[76]

The Christian journey of aspiration and fulfilment is endorsed by the affirmative answers to the pilgrim's questions. But as the poem proceeds the answers become less and less reciprocal and more intransigently negative and deterministic as it is clear that the questioner is unwilling to journey uphill and wants different answers to the questions. The answerer can reply as he (or she) does because the answers literalise and strip the metaphor from the questioner's formulations. The journey will take the whole long day if it is thought of as life itself. There will be a resting place at night which cannot be missed because death is inevitable. The barrier of death is not subject to the will of the dying because it is one which all pass. Whether comfort is found cannot be decided, but death is literally the consummation of labour. There are 'beds for all who come' because death is the inevitable 'resting-place'. The answer, in fact, is almost the same every time, though the questions are different. To the increasing panic of the questioner and the need for comfort the voice offers resistance. What it says can be read off as comfort, but the comfort is at the same time derived from the determined inevitability of death. The intransigence of Christian myth – and a very un-Christian severity – are here simultaneously recognised and accepted beneath the consoling metaphor. No one would wish to question the intensity of Christina Rossetti's belief, but this is a poem of suffering. Death is both the ultimate consolation and the ultimate finality. Because it is the end or goal and final judgement of 'labour', death nullifies both work *and* the giving of birth (the pun allows both) because they become instrumental processes seen merely in terms of their 'economic' *worth*, things which must be assessed, or added up as a sum is added up. There is a kind of dogged, trudging exhaustion about the poem, because the process of life is seen so rigorously in terms of its termination, the final barrier against which the speaker knocks. If we are released into death we are not released from it. And the obstruction of death makes life itself into a barrier, a road to be traversed, a hill to be climbed, as the poem works out the terrible implications of Christian allegory. The barrier is also the barrier of language. The representation of the voice as comforter is inadequate, not only because it hovers ambiguously between metaphor and the literal, but because it repeats the same statement, death is death, in a tautology which is incapable of saying other than that death is an ending. Where so much Victorian poetry moves to the transcendental object, this poem refuses it as unknowable and unrepresentable. The expressive needs of the questioner are turned back upon themselves as questions are given answers in their own terms, and yet the needs arise from the obstacles they create. The terminal answer produces terrible frustrations at the same time as it implies the necessity of beginning all over again. The answers seem the statements of a split God, who consoles maternally and at the same time offers the 'non' of the father as law. Are these the irreconcilable statements of an androgynous God or the double movement of divine judgement and mercy?

The brevity of Christina Rossetti's poems is an experiment with limits. They look for space in the tragic impasse itself and where they find it the liberation is often a loss.

> Two doves upon the selfsame branch,
>> Two lilies on a single stem,
> Two butterflies upon one flower:–
>> Oh happy they who look on them.

> Who look upon them hand in hand
>> Flushed in the rosy summer light;
> Who look upon them hand in hand
>> And never give a thought to night.[77]

The pairing of doves, lilies, butterflies, in the first stanza is reciprocally paired with those who 'look upon them'. And since those who look upon them, the syntax allows, are 'hand in hand' as the paired flowers might be said to be, the symmetry of the perceived is matched by the perceivers. It is a world of doubles and redoubled equivalences which is suddenly and sharply broken in the final line. 'And never give a thought to night'. Night is the unincluded element, falling outside the poised limits established

between and by watchers and watched, making them vulnerable but defining them. The couples are locked inside their boundaries, but unaware of
that or of their vulnerability. Another brief poem which uses a single line
to redefine limits – this time a refrain – is 'Mirage', where 'For a dream's
sake' follows each of the three stanzas.

> The hope I dreamed of was a dream,
>   Was but a dream; and now I wake
> Exceeding comfortless, and worn, and old,
>   For a dream's sake.
>
> I hang my harp upon a tree,
>   A weeping willow in a lake;
> I hang my silenced harp there, wrung and snapt
>   For a dream's sake.
>
> Lie still, lie still, my breaking heart;
>   My silent heart, lie still and break:
> Life, and the world, and mine own self, are changed
>   For a dream's sake.[78]

To *dream* of a dream, as the reiteration insists, is to make hope into a
double illusion and yet the waking, 'worn and old', is material, and the
direct consequence of the dream. The usual antithesis between illusion and
reality cannot be sustained because the conditions of waking life have
actually been created by a dream, a representation. It is a characteristic
making and breaking of opposition. The speaker is worn and old *because*
of a dream. Hope is no longer at the double distance from waking life
created by the first two lines, because the dream of it has become a
material condition and worn and aged the speaker's physical being. The
refrain line is not isolated form the stanza but runs on in continuity with
it just as the dream does not stand over and against experience. With the
second stanza the refrain words take up another meaning because of the
ambiguous possessive, 'dream's', and the dream becomes the dominant
agent, possessing, working its purpose and displacing the speaking subject
who is forced into silence, harp (or song) twisted and snapped. The
depredation of the dream continues as 'snapt' is passed on to the breaking
heart of the last stanza, and the words silenced/silence link harp and heart
together, the traditional images for song and passion. 'Life, and the world,
and mine own self', both subject and object, self and other, are changed
because they possessed a dream, and because, as the ambiguous possessive
asserts, a dream possessed them. Paradoxically the dream can only become
the possessor (rather than the possession) of the dreamer once the damaging antithesis between life and dream has been made. Once it has been
established as a separate entity the dream can become autonomous and
ravage the dreamer, breaking down the barriers set up to create it. The

'breaking' heart, breaking still in the painful present, and addressed by the speaker in the possessive as an aspect of her selfhood – '*my* breaking heart' – is breaking with other boundaries and delimitations. There is a painful sense of the destabilising of finite categories as 'life', 'the world' and 'mine own self' are jostled for definition against one another, and as all of them are declared to be 'changed' in relation to *one another*. Are 'life' and 'world' synonymous or separable categories? What relation does each, either paired or separately, bear to 'mine own self'? If self and world are paired according to the customary subject/object dualism then 'life' is an extraneous element. If life and world are paired, then the 'self' becomes the excluded element. Whicheve set of relations is given priority, an uneasy disequilibrium takes place in which the speaking subject seems to be being redefined as it speaks. Utterance itself appears to be both cause and effect of 'change'. The 'dream's sake' has changed the totality of experience, which must include itself, and, with Christina Rossetti's inexorable logic, is also changing the processes of verbalisation as they attempt to render and define changed relationships. The repeated closure of the refrain both opens and re-establishes the tragic impasse. An extraordinary energy and tension is generated as the lyric manoeuvres within and with its own confinements.

In both love and religious lyric the response to limit is deeply ambiguous. The space for manoeuvre is accepted as limited, even though the play of energy arises from restriction. Often the barrier can only be suffered by an act of deferral. 'Twice' moves from the acknowledged suffering of sexual love to the acknowledged suffering of divine love. Degrees of freedom are denoted by a shift in pronouns. In both cases 'I', the speaking subject, is subservient to 'you', the lover, or 'Thou', God. '*I* took my heart in my hand [1] . . . /*You* took my heart in your hand [9] . . . /As you set it down it broke [17]'. The heart shatters like a vessel (the poems repeatedly use the conventional image of the breaking heart as the disintegrating confines of an identity which fragments), but in the second case the identity of the self as agent is retrieved. 'I took my heart in my hand [25] . . . /Yea hold it in Thy hold [39] . . . /*I take* my heart in my hand [41]' (my emphasis). The change of tense acknowledges the authority of the self and a release from passivity through submission. The poem ends with a fierce and almost aggressive assent to a circumscribed autonomy. 'I shall not die, but live [42] . . . /All that I am I give,/Smile thou and I shall sing,/But shall not question much [46–8]'. Expressive authority is redeemed, as the narrator can at last speak or 'sing' and refuses to be silenced. But the poem questions despite its assertion to that contrary. Does that 'shall' denote a postponed future or the present? Or both? Maybe the silenced feminine voice can only sing in heaven.

Frequently, however, there is deferral alone, in which the self remains locked in, or locked out of, experience, as in 'Memory' or the finality of

365

'Despised and Rejected'. In both the speaker is incarcerated. 'I have a room whereinto no one enters . . . think how it will be in Paradise/When we're together' (21, 35–6) ('Memory'): 'I will make fast my door/That hollow friends may trouble me no more' (6–7) ('Despised and Rejected'). This poem questions whether or not passivity and rejection belong together as a dialectic so that Christ and self mutually reject one another. Christ is *made* passive, a sufferer, through the passivity of the self. These poems do, in fact, 'question much'. 'Another Spring' questions whether the act of deferral is in reality a retrieval. It is a *carpe diem* poem which recognises the irony of an assent to experience which is built on the conditional – 'If I might see another Spring/I'd not plant summer flowers and wait' (1–2). The first stanza is reckless in its desire for immediate satisfaction: 'any-thing/To blow at once, not late' (7–8). Blow, of course, means to blossom and to die. And the poem ends in bitterness, blocked again.

> If I might see another Spring –
>   Oh stinging comment on my past
> That all my past results in 'if' –
>   If I might see another Spring
> I'd laugh today, today is brief;
> I would not wait for anything:
> I'd use today that cannot last,
>   Be glad today and sing.[79]

Deferral negates the past which is seen as perpetual postponement. It also negates present and future. The syntax of the last four lines is ambiguous. The 'today' is a deferred present, or an actual present but both are perpetually conditional, for to 'use today' means to destroy the present which cannot last, and the future which therefore cannot be, in one act of appropriation. And so it is impossible to 'Be glad today and sing'. The expressive movement is closed down. The reiterated impossibility of experi-ence 'today' closes in with repetition, a conditional world in which the only freedom is to defer. As with so many of the lyrics the poem balances with dangerous energy between affirmative release and the bleak accept-ance of limit which enables it to exist. 'Be glad today' is a virtual impera-tive, denying and accepting. Be glad today because you can only be glad tomorrow. The margin of escape is the margin of restriction.

It is in Christina Rossetti's earlier poetry that her most powerful energies are at play. Her later work seems to reassert the barrier as limit without the liberating aspects it has for her earlier work. Later poems stress the opposition between expression and repression rather than their interdepen-dence. Interestingly, she did literally turn to play by writing children's poems in later life. These are fascinating, for childhood is one of the times when a play with limit is permissible. (Perhaps that is why so many Victorian women turned to children's literature.) In them she plays with the child's interest in fundamental metaphysical questions: 'Who has seen the Wind?' is a poem about a cognitive puzzle (the wind's presence is only perceptible through its effect on physical things), with riddles, jokes, puns and puzzles, which question the categories of things. A colour poem breaks its elaborate series and ends not with an adjective but a noun ('Just an orange!'). A poem on card-houses subversively joins with the child to shake the construction down ('That's the fun!'). But it is interesting that the subversive should be confined to an area where it does not seem quite to matter, the world of infants.

In her religious writing she turned more and more to a longing for the end of unrest. In *Seek and Find* she writes on a text which has affinities with 'Winter Rain' – 'and there was no more sea' (Revelation 31:1) but the tensions between expression and repression seem to have disappeared. If the heart sinks at the idea of the overwhelming sea, she writes, there are deep compensations:

> Troubled restless waters we shall lose with all their defilement (Is. lvii. 20), and with waves that toss and break themselves against a boundary they cannot overpass (Jer. v. 22), and with the moan of a still-recurrent ebb, 'The sea is not full' (Eccles. i. 7). We feel at once that the sea as we know it, a very embodiment of unrest, of spurning at limits, of advance only to recede, that such a sea teaches us nothing concerning that rest which remaineth to the people of God (Heb. iv. 9).[80]

'He bindeth the flood from overflowing (Job xxviii. 11)', she quotes. It is disturbing to see that the later work increasingly asks for the binding of the flood. The feminine subject brought into being in the earlier work through a perpetual experiment with the condition of bondage and restriction, through experiment with the transgression of limit, no longer challenges orthodoxy, is no longer 'spurning at limits', is no longer undignified.

THE POETICS OF MYTH AND MASK

Strangely enough, the impersonal self-exposure which occurs through the negotiations with expressive structures in the earlier work becomes, as in 'Winter: My Secret', a form of mask for Rossetti in later work. Poets such as Augusta Webster and Amy Levy, writing later in the century, also adopted the mask of the dramatic monologue. But some poets wrote, as Elizabeth Barrett Browning said of herself in *Aurora Leigh*, 'without mask'. Nevertheless, the persona of Aurora is very much a mask: what is not masked are propositions about women and aesthetics and women and society.

By the end of the century one finds women's work dividing (though this is a very rough distinction) between the poem written with and without a mask.

We can group the 'unmasked' Elizabeth Barrett Browning's work together with that of George Eliot and Mathilde Blind (who wrote on George Eliot), in contradistinction to those who used the 'mask' of dramatic monologue, but this is a very approximate division. At any rate, it is a distinction which preoccupied some writers, particularly Webster. And, as the powerfully held religious beliefs of women writers became less predominant, the extent to which women could create, or recreate, new myths for their culture becomes a pressing concern later in the century.

No less than Christina Rossetti, however, women experimenting with mask or with myth call upon the resources of the double poem – the expressive 'I' speaking in parallel with another poem emerging out of the same words which contradicts and questions the limits of that subjectivity. Perhaps because women in the nineteenth century were confronted with contradictory experience they use the double poem persistently.

Nearly a decade before the publication of *Aurora Leigh* (1856), Elizabeth Barrett Browning had pondered on the possibility of using Christianity as myth in a way that would have been unthinkable to Christina Rossetti. In *Aurora Leigh* she achieves the double feat of writing 'without mask' and of rewriting Christian myth. Many of these unmasked opinions are liberatingly and energetically expressed – for instance, the attack on the triviality of women's education, the aesthetics of the contemporary city poet – but some are disturbingly reactionary. Aurora Leigh's hatred of her cousin Romney's philanthropy and Christian Socialism, which she sees as abstract and coldly theoretical, derived from an unimaginative perusal of Blue Books which 'Lives by diagrams' and 'mere statistics', is hard to accept.[81] There is some sign that Aurora modifies her view. Romney's house is ultimately burned down by the mob to whom he has extended philanthropic care, and this appears to vindicate Aurora's beliefs, her disgust for the 'people' and her sense that they are degraded almost beyond redemption. On the other hand, at the end of this verse novel Romney is blinded by the fire – rather like Rochester in *Jane Eyre* – defeated by the subversive mob he has himself nurtured in his political idealism, as Rochester is symbolically defeated by the incendiary sexuality of his repressed first wife. This nemesis is surely a comment on the resolution of Charlotte Brontë's novel, for it is presented in political and social terms rather than in a private, sexual context. Aurora Leigh does not become the domestic nurse of her blinded companion as Jane Eyre does, but rather his social vision of a new economy and freedom is fused with Aurora's imaginative energy and transformed by it. It becomes a radicalism suffused with the affective life of poetic insight, a vision rather than a theory.

The movement away from Aurora's conservative dogmatism is circuitous, and complicated by the fact that until the third book Aurora does not write in the present but is describing her past prejudices. Aurora is altered, not by a change of theory so much as a transformation of her imaginative perception of the poor through her relationship with Marion Erle, the destitute girl whom Romney wishes to make his wife through an abstract sense of duty (and because Aurora has rejected him). Aurora discovers Marion Erle in Italy with a child after she has been lured away from Romney and raped. Through Marion the Christian myth is transformed, for Marion takes on not only the attributes of Mary as mother with child but also the attributes of Christ, who is through her persistently gendered as a woman. Romney responds to the story of her sufferings as if they are the 'wounds of Christ' (3, 1260). After the rape, in a hideous parody of the crucifixion and resurrection, Marion thinks of herself as abandoned and cast into the pit, 'cheek to cheek/With him who stinks since Friday'. 'But suppose;/To go down with one's soul into the grave, . . . And wake up with corruption' (6, 1198–9, 1201). The suffering female Christ awakes to a vision of physical and moral corruption, an untransformed world – 'man's violence,/Not man's seduction, made me what I am'. In her subsequent wanderings the superstitious peasants put a heavy image of Mary round her neck – 'A woman has been strangled with less weight' (6, 1258). But paradoxically it is Marion who incarnates a new feminine and demystified form of the Christian myth even when she rejects its forms as obsolete and untruthful.

Aurora and Marion are united in a truly democratic way which transcends class through their capacity for imaginative passion and outgoing love, particularly the love of children, for the poem is an intense defence of the expressive, emotional, affective life allied with passionate intelligence. This is a far from adequate analysis of class relations (a much more successful attempt at the analysis of oppression occurs in the short poem, 'The Runaway Slave at Pilgrim's Point') but the attempt to defend the affective is by no means unsophisticated. In this it reaches back to one of its precursors, Letitia Landon. Like her work also, it uses the representation of women in painting as a form of commentary. The economic dependence of women, which oppresses both Aurora and Marion in different ways, is registered through the recurrent use of the myth of Danae's rape by Jove as it is represented in painting. In order to seduce Danae Jove turned into a shower of gold. This becomes a seering modern myth disclosing the way in which sexual relations for women – and men – are degraded by the commercial necessities to which they are bound. The ways in which women are mythologised and transfixed in painting by men exert a strong fascination in this poem. As a child Aurora gazes at a picture of her mother in which she sees the artist has represented her ambiguously but in conventionalised roles as Psyche, Medusa, Mary, Lamia (1, 128–68). Aurora's assertive voice, its overconfident bourgeois arrogance (so hard to dissociate from Barrett Browning's voice), is partly there as an attempt to subvert the conventional role of gentle femininity. For just as Marion can be both Christ and Mary, so Aurora speaks of the 'man' in herself. 'Since when was genius found respectable?' she enquires (Book 6) aggressively. Dora Greenwell speaks of the spinster's 'crustiness and angularity' as a fierce defence against the conventional demands on her to be self-abnegating and ever at the service of others. Something of this angularity is in *Aurora Leigh*. Expressive theory allows of both the affective, and the aggressive, as we have seen. *Aurora Leigh* sanctions both.

It might seem that the poetry of George Eliot, who did not willingly associate herself with the 'feminine' tradition, and who repudiated 'silly novels' by lady novelists, would lie outside the concerns of the poets discussed here. Her use of an apparently 'masculine' form, the narrative-dramatic epic, in *The Spanish Gypsy* (1868), possibly suggests a lack of interest in the themes which bound women poets together. But just as Elizabeth Barrett Browning attempted to write the first verse novel by a woman, George Eliot attempted to write the first humanist epic by a woman. Even though her verse is laborious and slow-moving, it would be important simply on this account (and arguably it was an important influence on later writers such as Mathilde Blind). But in fact questions of the status of women's experience actually dominate George Eliot's poetry, perhaps more than they figure in her prose: both in the Tennysonian idyll of 'Agatha' and the Browningesque drama of 'Armgart' (about the artistic difficulties and conflicts of a woman singer and the daemonic nature of creativity) a concern with women is central to the poem.

The massive *The Spanish Gypsy*, to which George Eliot was deeply committed, is the narrative of a sort of female Daniel Deronda. Fedalma, an orphan brought up in the court of Don Silva at the time when the conflict between the Moors and the Spaniards was at its height, renounces marriage to him because her father, Zarca, reveals that she is of Gipsy origin and persuades her to take up the mission of leading the Gipsy race to unity in Africa. At the heart of the poem is a question about the extent to which women are capable of producing a powerfully imaginative national myth about unity and cohesion, a matriarchal myth. But, importantly, the experiment fails, fails essentially because of racial strife, but also because racial *categories* distort and corrupt. *The Spanish Gypsy* considers an ugly racism founded on distinctions which are *artificial* and constructed. This was the time when Christianity was establishing its own and western hegemony concurrently. God rules by armies, the narrator says ironically; Christianity is founded on the stamping out of difference and the establishing of 'pure' theological and racial categories. The poem abounds in what Christianity defines as hybrids – Spanish Jews 'converted' to Christianity, Moslem Gipsies. Fedalma, a Gipsy, brought up in the racial purity of the Spanish court *as* a Spaniard is another such hybrid. As outsiders even to non-occidental ethnicity Gipsies are seen by one Spanish Christian, Blasco, as a resource of 'draught cattle' and 'slaves'. Church authority condemns Fedalma's 'infidel' blood, and her marriage to the Don would be 'union of light with darkness', a fatal mixing of 'pure' opposites.[82] But Fedalma is patently a hybrid. The Christian and *masculine* myth of racial 'unity' is thus full of impossibilities and contradictions.

The poem's concern with myth-making and with remaking a humanist myth relates it backwards to *Aurora Leigh* and forwards to the work of Mathilde Blind, who was also deeply concerned with constructing new myths. The Gipsy race disperses in scattered bands to 'propagate forgetful-ness' (361), a cultural amnesia dreaded by George Eliot, and the woman fails in the work of integration. Perhaps the reason for this failure is to be found in the later, highly enigmatic and strangely sardonic poem about myth, *The Legend of Jubal* (1870). Jubal becomes a legendary figure who can sustain generations of wandering. When he returns to his country he finds to his delight that he has become the subject of national myth, hymned and celebrated in heroic poetry on national occasions. He makes himself known to the singing procession, convinced that they will welcome the magical return of their legendary hero. But he is kicked and mauled and treated with derision and regarded as a mad imposter. For he has actually mistaken the nature of myth: as Strauss (whose life of Jesus George Eliot translated) had emphasised, myth is not about a 'real' figure but precisely an idealised legendary one; for it is not *true*. It is constantly remade and renewed as an imaginative account of history, a fictional memory, which answers to the needs and demands of the present and the future. Myth is both the condition for and the fulfilment of imaginative life and constitutes social reality. In *The Spanish Gypsy* the weight of symbol-making is placed on the woman. Fedalma fails as a prophet (George Eliot is more honest about the fragility of her idealist accounts of race than is often thought), perhaps because the vision itself is not adequate to the realities of the situation. It was after all imposed upon her by her father who is also a 'Spanish Gypsy', and the question of what race *is* is raised by the double name of the title of the poem: is it possible to be both a Spaniard and a Gipsy, and what difference does it make if this paradoxical identity belongs to a man or to a woman?

George Eliot seems to have used poetry both to consider consolations which were simpler than those of her novels and to explore a devastating scepticism which was often harsher than her novels intimate. A late poem, for instance, suggests that what we assume to be our solid subjectivity 'melts to molecules', and that the object we relate to is merely a Pater-like 'Phantasmal flux of moments' ('I grant you ample leave', 1874). Differences of gender and race, it follows, may also be 'Phantasmal'. The self is made by culture, memory and myth, the memory of myth and the myth of memory.[83] It may be this conviction whch made George Eliot adopt the overdetermined 'feminine' figures of music, pulsation and the dilated, breathing spirit, so often given an inward and sexual connotation in women's poetry, but transpose it from being a figure for the privacy of feminine subjectivity to a representation for a common cultural and racial identity. Breath, air, is mystic essence and material being, simultaneously. Cultural identity is something we breathe in necessarily with the air of the environment. And it may be the 'strain' of music which determines the racial 'strain' of community, rather than the other way round. The transmission and circulation of memory through art and music is the essence of culture as the shared throb of feeling and creation. Music is a monologue of emotion, Feuerbach said, and as his translator George Eliot would have known, he saw communal prayer anthropologically as the expression of 'political community'. As Fedalma dances in the market place the musicians sing songs that seem 'emergent memories' (66) and the singer, Juan, is later described as possessing a life 'breathed in him by other men' (127). The interrelated metaphors of air and music are tested, explored and questioned as an image of cultural cohesion and continuity. Ultimately they fail to sustain themselves, but it is important that George Eliot chose to privilege and extend the affective feminine terminology of expressive poetics in her attempt to explore the myth of a new matriarchy. The 'feminine principle', Feuerbach said, tends to be repressed in Protestant religion, though as such it is the vital principle of all religious experience. *The Spanish Gypsy* is an attempt to see how the feminine principle might be the source of a new humanist myth, even though it explores its breakdown.[84]

The women poets who established themselves in the last quarter of the century develop the now powerful tradition available to them in different ways. Mathilde Blind, following Elizabeth Barrett Browning and George Eliot, wrote 'without mask', exploring the possibility of a new myth and writing directly of political matters. Augusta Webster and Amy Levy adopted the dramatic monologue as a way of making a 'masked' critique, though Augusta Webster also wrote a series of sonnets to her daughter, *Mother and Daughter*, published posthumously (1895), which look back to 'Sonnets from the Portuguese'. Though women still wrote of confinement and imprisonment, identified frankly with oppression and slavery and demonstrated concern, like Christina Rossetti and Elizabeth Barrett Browning, with prostitution and the treatment of 'fallen' women, the recurrent figure of music, the vibrating string of sympathy and the cognate respiratory image of breath and air which was associated with expressive poetics, became less overdetermined at this time. It is certainly to be found (for instance, in the work of Alice Meynell, whose work was published to the very end of the century, though her first volume was published in 1875), but it is less in evidence as a central figure.

Perhaps one reason for the absence of the figures of music and air is that they had already done their work as coded images for the special intensity of the affective condition. At this stage it did not seem so necessary for women to exploit the ambiguity of expressive poetics, which sanctions both a conservative 'suppression', as Dora Greenwell called it, of intense feeling – the *more* intense and vibrating because of its secrecy – and the 'aggressive' (another Greenwell term) overflow of feeling and self-projection. The expressive rather than the suppressive aspect of expressive theory allows of dramatic projection and representation which paradoxically make possible, *because* they are distanced as drama, a far more *overt* critique (though not necessarily any less bold) of the cultural construction of the feminine subject than the powerfully coded, secret and indirect manoeuvres with affective experience which go on when the female poet speaks 'without mask', or, more accurately, with a different kind of mask, in the earlier period. Augusta Webster, whose *A Woman Sold, and Other Poems* (1867) indicates the more open kinds of statement available to women at this time, discussed the question of dramatic poetry in an article, 'Poets and personal pronouns', and her discussion suggests how liberating the explicit dramatic mode could be.

She argues that all poetry is dramatic, as many Victorian critics before her had done, but takes great pains to show that poetry is the construction of experience, known and unknown, rather than the expression of it. To write of a murderer or of a modest girl it is not necessary to *be* either: 'The poet creates as the sculptor does; he need not make the stone as well as the statue'.[85] She suggests the introduction of a typographical mark, the lower-case 'i', as an indicator denoting the impersonal, dramatic 'I' rather than a personal subjectivity. The poet is not 'his own lay figure', making a 'presentment of himself'.[86] Even confessional poets such as Byron create what is 'less a portrait of him than he of them; he made them and then imitated them'.[87] A poet does not undertake 'a revealing of him but of themselves to others'.[88]

What is interesting about this sharp and acerbic essay, however, is its designation of the poet in terms of the generic 'he'; it seems that the category of the poetess is less secure at the end of the century than it was at the beginning. Also, Augusta Webster introduces the expressive account of poetry as overflow concurrently with her analysis of it as construction: writing is a poet's sixth sense; he sings 'because he must' (a quotation from *In Memoriam*), and to deprive him of expressive power is virtually to kill him. Her own powerful work, deceptively plain in language and immediately accessible in its diction, declares itself as a dramatisation of a series of feminine consciousnesses and an analysis of their cultural determinations. By the time of the publication of *Portraits* (1870), she had matured as a writer of dramatic monologues, and poems such as 'The Castaway' and 'The Happiest Girl in the World' or 'Faded' are striking not simply for their content – the internal monologue of a high-class prostitute, of a girl about to be married whose carefully constructed bourgeois 'innocence' leaves her unable to determine whether she loves her patriarchal fiancé or not, the speech of a middle-class spinster who is growing old – but because of their consummate dramatic treatment.

Perhaps the sinisterly naive innocence of 'The Happiest Girl in the World' indicates Webster's strengths at their most powerful: its irony does not prevent an understanding of the pathos of the speaker's situation. She convinces herself by the end of the monologue that she 'loves' her husband to be, though strangely she cannot determine the moment when this love began ('And did I love him from the day we met?') and cannot understand why the experiences of sexual passion, whose coded signs she has read in books, are absent. Love does not seem to be 'That subtle pain of exquisite excess,/That momentary infinite sharp joy,/I know by books but cannot teach my heart'. 'And oh, if love be fire, what love is mine/That is but like the pale subservient moon . . . ?'[89] There is a double irony here, for the language being used *is* the language of romantic fiction, but at the same time that superficial language warns of the absence of what is important, and Webster demonstrates the thinness of the culture's language of sexuality. The naive speaker schools herself to passivity and submission, with a sad mixture of pathos and realism, in a series of disturbing attempts to accommodate to a coercive set of contradictory roles: she will be 'friend', 'child', 'servant', 'mistress' and 'wife' (in that order) to her husband.[90] She is still uneasy that the idea of maternity seems to bring no instinctive pleasure of anticipation, as she has been taught, and again the poem makes a double critique: the speaker is unable to admit to her lack of maternal feeling because the cultural pressure silences her – and she has also been too infantilised in preparation for being a child wife to be able to have maternal feelings.

Augusta Webster works through intensely analytical psychological exploration which discloses contradictions in the construction of feminine subjectivity. She is fascinated by those areas where we have no language, or where language cannot exist in any richness, because of social constraints. It is interesting to compare her in this respect with Amy Levy. Both poets wrote monologues spoken by prostitutes or women who had sexually transgressed and both wrote 'classical' poems spoken by Medea. Augusta Webster's 'A Castaway' dwells on the silences of conventional morality, which the speaker expresses boldly while suppressing her unspoken fears of loneliness and death.[91] Amy Levy's 'Magdalen', the words of a girl spoken in hospital (where she has come, we deduce, from the Pastor's iterated 'sin', after her labour and possible attempt at suicide), is more concerned with the psychological damage of seduction and betrayal. The girl can 'endure' all the hardship of social rejection and destitution but not the rejection of the 'lover', who seems to have cared for her but has rejected her all the same: 'It is so strange to think on still –/The you, that you should do me ill!'[92] The wish to accept negation and the annihilation of death rather than make further demands on him is intense, but intensely disturbing as the girl takes responsibility for the situation entirely upon herself, relieving him of all 'part' or 'lot' in her – even though that 'part' may be a child. The same destructive impulse of the rejected is explored in the chilling drama of 'Medea'. Augusta Webster's 'Medea in Athens' explores Medea as a paradigm of the non-feminine woman who can hate and kill her own children, but Amy Levy takes this extremity much further, in the fury and anguish of the woman who is dispossessed and denied. Her Medea is the subject of racial hatred and alienation as well as of the cruelty of Jason.[93] She reaches the same violence in 'Xantippe', where Sophocles' wife rages against her status as slave.[94] The nineteenth century's refusal of lesbian identity may be the cause of this violent frustration, as it was possibly the cause of her suicide. For both women poets it seems necessary to rationalise and justify feminine violence, and rewrite the myth of Medea as the type of female destructiveness. It is an indication both of the transformation and the continuity of the feminine tradition of the nineteenth century that the concealed Medean violence of Mrs Hemans's 'Casabianca' is now overtly explored and analysed.

The work of Mathilde Blind shares the intensity, and sometimes the violence, of Levy, but in the context not of rewriting classical myth but the attempt to create new evolutionary and humanist myths. This is what allies her with George Eliot. Like Letitia Landon she ransacked different cultures for material (for instance, in *Birds of Passage: Songs of the Orient and Occident*, 1895), and her first long poem, *The Prophecy of St Oran* (1882), is an attack on specifically Christian myth. And she seems to have seen, in *The Ascent of Man* (1889), evolutionary ideas as the key to reconfiguring a new myth of creativity and gender. A delicate lyric, 'On a Torso of Cupid', suggests how earlier myths of sexuality and passion have to wait for redefinition. The speaker finds a headless Cupid lying dismembered 'in the daisied sod'. The stone torso is almost covered by 'embracing' leaves, 'Clothing the nakedness,/Clothing the marble of/This poor, dismembered love'. Without hands, feet or mouth, the maimed torso, however, causes no Medean rejoicing, as the stone is overlaid by the fecundity of April. On the contrary, he is a 'helpless god of old', and rather than making a facile point about the displacement of castrated classical stone love with 'natural' love, the lyric suggests that the broken god should 'bide' for as long as it can 'feel', looking forward to a new relationship among nature, culture and gender and refusing to make reductive definitions of any category.[95] There is a delicate, but not inflexible, chiming of masculine and feminine rhymes, as if a new response to the fierceness of oedipal sacrifice is being made.

Mathilde Blind's faith in evolutionary fecundity should not be seen as a simple, optimistic myth of generation, although *The Ascent of Man* suggests

375

elements of meliorism reminiscent of George Eliot. It is put in context by an earlier poem, *The Heather on Fire* (1886), which deals with the destruction of a population, a kind of class genocide, when the crofting population of the Highlands was hounded and burned out of its dwellings in the early 1830s to create game land and to assert the power of aristocratic property. A whole community was destroyed, often by its own members acting as agents of the owner, with untold cruelty and ferocity. It is a gripping narrative, charting the way in which a young couple with dependent parents (the grandfather likes to tell stories of his heroism against the French in the Napoleonic wars) and children are flushed out of their crofters' huts and burned out like animals, progressively moved on until they are hounded from the graveyard where they are burying their dead, and ultimately die at sea in their fishing-boat. The disarray of a community in this holocaust is graphically described. When news of the evictions spreads 'unkempt wives anomalously dressed/With querulous infants huddled to the breast' attempt to warn other families. Clothes, bedding, chairs, hoes, herring nets, are thrown indiscriminately out of huts, as the factor orders his men to 'clear away/This stinking rubbish heap' (III. 38) and the grandmother is burned to death.[96] The vulnerability of this family is increased because the factor is paying off an old score – Mary had refused his approaches before she married. The suffering would be unbelievable without the constant reminder of the power of a brutal civilian army of servants carrying out orders from above against the poor and powerless.

> And through the rolling smoke a troop of men
> Tramped swiftly nearer from the upper glen;
> Fierce, sullen, black with soot, some carrying picks,
> Axes, and crowbars, others armed with sticks,
> Or shouldering piles of faggots.[97]
>
> (III. 24)

The Ascent of Man is another attempt to understand violence, the violence of creation and civilisation, which are not read in opposition to one another but as related phenomena. The poem searches for a new language, not entirely successfully, to suggest a plastic transformation and possibility in matter, a vocabulary of movement and coalescing vitality. Throughout, the question of what can be redeemed from blind violence is central. Never satisfactorily answered, the question is asked in different contexts and different ways. Mathilde Blind may have been the first nineteenth-century woman poet to describe the birth of a child, where for a moment violence is productive.

> A life hath been upheaved with struggle and pain;
> Safe in her arms a mother holds again

376

That dearest miracle a new-born child.
To moans of anguish terrible and wild –
As shrieks that night-wind through an ill-shut pane –
Pure heaven succeeds; and after fiery strain
Victorious woman smiles serenely mild.[98]

It is perhaps appropriate to end this necessarily abbreviated account of a gendered tradition in women's poetry of the nineteenth century with Mathilde Blind, for she represents what this tradition could do at its best: it could bring the resources of the affective state to social and political analysis and speculate on the constraints of the definition of feminine subjectivity in an almost innumerable variety of contexts, indirectly and directly. To some extent the uncertain status of women released the woman poet from an identification with bourgeois assumptions, but these assumptions are attacked both from within, in the earlier part of the century, and without, in the later nineteenth century. In particular the expressive aesthetic theory which also stands as a paradigm of the feminine raises the question of language and representation in a fundamental way, which meant that the woman poet was virtually obliged to consider the conventions of language and their implications, and forced to reinvent it.

Part III

ANOTHER CULTURE?
ANOTHER POETICS?

INTRODUCTION

THE 1860s AND AFTER
Aesthetics, language, power
and high finance

His gift is shown by the way in which he accepts such a character, throws it into some situation, or apprehends it in some delicate pause of life, in which for a moment it becomes ideal. In the poem entitled *Le Byron de nos jours*, in his *Dramatis Personae* we have a single moment of passion thrown into relief after this exquisite fashion. Those two jaded Parisians are not intrinsically interesting; they begin only to interest us when they are thrown into a choice situation. But to discriminate that moment, to make it appreciable by us, that we may 'find' it, what a cobweb of allusions, what double and treble reflexions of the mind upon itself, what an artificial light, is constructed and broken over the chosen situation; on how fine a needle's point that little world of passion is balanced! . . . Men and women, again, in the hurry of life, often wear the sharp impress of one absorbing motive, from which it is said death sets their features free. All such instances may be ranged under the *grotesque*; and the Hellenic ideal has nothing in common with the grotesque.

(Walter Pater on Browning)[1]

Racy Saxon monosyllables, close to us as touch and sight, he will intermix readily with those long, savoursome, Latin words, rich in 'second intention.' In this late day certainly, no critical process can be conducted reasonably without eclecticism. Of such eclecticism we have a justifying example in one of the first poets of our time. How illustrative of monosyllabic effect, of sonorous Latin, of the phraseology of science, of metaphysic, of colloquialism even, are the writings of Tennyson; yet with what a fine, fastidious scholarship throughout!

(Walter Pater on Tennyson)[2]

Pater's urbane, patrician paganism places Browning and Tennyson, in 1867 and 1888 respectively, as established poets, but as poets of an older generation. However powerful, Browning's 'grotesque' has nothing to do with the Hellenism of the 1860s: however scholarly, Tennyson's language has nothing to do with the accounts of style prevalent by the 1880s, nothing to do with the art which aspires to the condition of music, with that world of pure form which organises the flood of random sounds, colours, incidents from the world without into a structure where form and content are interchangeable and where there is 'but one', unique word only commensurate with the artist's understanding of what it is he wants to say.[3] They are both tactfully classified as important but obsolete figures, one writing in the Grotesque manner and one the poet of the pure Type which has been forced to become eclectic and ornate, recognisable as Bagehot's categories for these poets. Democratic and conservative poet alike are politely seen as obsolete. Tennyson's Arthurian *Idylls of the King*, which appeared over the years 1859 to 1885, represents a society encumbered with custom and habit, struggling with a damaging mind/body split which determines its culture and forms of thought; it is by no means irrelevant to the situation of the late nineteenth century, but goes unnoticed by Pater. That Browning confronted Hellenism in poems such as *Balaustion's Adventure* (1871), *Aristophanes' Apology* (1875) and *The Agamemnon of Aeschylus* (1877), and continued to meditate on questions of sexuality, politics and volition in poems such as *Fifine at the Fair* (1872) and *Red Cotton Night-Cap Country* (1873), is not seen, either by Pater or the younger poets writing in the 1860s, to be immediately relevant to their work or concerns, however much they may have respected the older writers. Indeed, the work of Tennyson and Browning in the latter part of the century could be seen as a reaction to that of younger poets, which suggests that they were no longer originating debate, and that the centre of interest lay elsewhere. Their work was displaced by different problems. Just as Darwin's work had discredited the Type, they are seen as part of an older formation.

It is this which has led to the assumption that the so-called aesthetic movement initiated by the Pre-Raphaelites and theorised by Pater constitutes an epistemological break, though it was hardly as unified and cohesive as it seems in retrospect. A simplified picture presupposes that an art-for-art's-sake movement supersedes the moral and cultural preoccupations of an earlier generation and runs its course, moving through the 'decadent' poets and culminating in symbolist aesthetics as they are represented in the work of Arthur Symons. Symons's *The Symbolist Movement in Literature* (1899), so this picture suggests, conveniently appearing in the year before Freud published the *Interpretation of Dreams*, completed the work begun by Pater in *The Renaissance* (1873), a volume which gathered work which had appeared in the late 1860s.

> It is all an attempt to spiritualise literature, to evade the old bondage of rhetoric, the old bondage of exteriority. Description is banished that beautiful things may be evoked, magically; the regular beat of verse is broken in order that words may fly, upon subtler wings. Mystery is no longer feared, as the great mystery in whose midst we

are islanded was feared by those to whom that unknown sea was only a great void. We are coming closer to nature, as we seem to shrink from it with something of horror, disdaining to catalogue the trees of the forest. And as we brush aside the accidents of daily life, in which men and women imagine that they are alone touching reality, we come closer to humanity, to everything in humanity that may have begun before the world and may outlast it.

Here, then, in this revolt against exteriority, against rhetoric, against a materialistic tradition; in this endeavour to disengage the ultimate essence, the soul, of whatever exists and can be realised by the consciousness; in this dutiful waiting upon every symbol by which the soul of things can be made visible; literature, bowed down by so many burdens, may at last attain liberty, and its authentic speech. In attaining this liberty, it accepts a heavier burden: for in speaking to us so intimately, so solemnly, as only religion had hitherto spoken to us, it becomes itself a kind of religion, with all the duties and responsibilities of the sacred ritual.[4]

Arthur Symons died in 1945. His famous Introduction to his study of French symbolist poetry, often claimed as one of the first documents of modernism, was a formative work for early twentieth century poets. It made the work of the nineteenth century seem the product of a shallow, positivist culture. Nineteenth-century poetry seemed to belong to a literal-minded rationalism and materialism – contemporary philosophy or social criticism in descriptive verse, where the understanding of the self-reflexive power of language and the epiphany of the image or symbol which condensed a plurality of implication in an instant of time, the image where thought is a sensation, was unknown. To paraphrase Arnold's famous 1853 Preface, in Symons the self-referential poem has commenced; modern problems have presented themselves; we hear already the confidence, we witness the authority, of T. S. Eliot and of Pound. Symons's own poetry presents experience as a series of impressions whose referent seems almost on the point of disappearing. That juxtaposition of entities without copula which is one of the forms of modernism is approached in his work.

But the undoubted importance of Symons's reading of French poetry to early modernism has meant that a selective reading of the poetry written in English in the latter part of the nineteenth century took place. It was judged in relation to the ways it could or could not be assimilated to the symbolist or post-symbolist paradigm. T. S. Eliot's essay on Swinburne is a case in point.[5] All that could be seen as aspiring to the condition of modernism was retrospectively amalgamated into the aesthetic movement, beginning with Pater's formalism: or poets such as Hopkins and Thomson were seen as lone precursors. Such a reading was facilitated by the accident of nationality; as Americans, Eliot and Pound were either unfamiliar with or uninterested in the political affiliations of particular writers – the Victorian poets for them were all more or less homogenised manifestations of nineteenth-century positivism.

Pater's work is certainly significant for this period, but the work of the poets is by no means in parallel with his. Swinburne the republican, Hopkins the conservative Catholic, Rossetti the High-Church reformer, Meredith the Lutheran-trained democrat and Thomson the freethinker (all these descriptions are oversimplifications even when they serve to differentiate these poets, but they do emphasise ideological positions) polarise round a set of problems to which Pater's work is testimony, rather than reproducing it. It is tempting to see Pater and the poets as inheritors of the true *paysage intérieur* suggested by Arthur Hallam's poetry of sensation, beginning at last the work of expunging 'whatever is mixed up with art, and appears under its semblance' three decades after Hallam's confident pronouncement: but there are great differences between Hallam's energising conservative anarchy and Pater's atomism in spite of their mutual interest in Epicurean thought.[6]

It is true that with Pater the post-teleological world is newly configured, as belief is thoroughly historicised and anthropologised, irradiated with the light (one of his favourite words) of a suavely tender but intransigent scepticism. With Pater gothic architecture and Ruskin's art of resistance embodied in the Grotesque are firmly displaced by the rational freedom of classical Greek sculpture. Labour *on* the world is displaced into the recurrent self-making which is made and unmade with each perception. In the post-technological world, where, as Carlyle observed, nothing is done directly, what was problematic for earlier poets is annulled in the aesthetic labour of the direct mediation of sensation by consciousness. *Pure temporality* rather than the pressure of history is the condition of Pater's world, despite his willingness to theorise cultural phases as evolutionary flow and transition on a Darwinian and consciously Hegelian model. Indeed, it is a concern with time which enables him to reincorporate Kant into his thinking with a deft eclecticism which is characteristic of him.[7] Because he was acutely aware of the difficulty of representing sensation in language, introducing and cancelling dualism by assuming the indivisibility of form and content, closing and opening the gap between representation and the content of representation, *words* become the focus of his aesthetic.[8] *Style* is language for Pater, whereas for Arnold it is form.

Language becomes the site of renewed ideological conflict. Whether poets hold to the irreducible materiality of the word and its precision of content, as Pater did, or whether they conceive language in terms of incessant flow and transformation, whether they were materialists or idealists, questions of law, family, gender and time, the dominant preoccupations of this period, are worked out, explicitly or implicitly, through the nature of language. As will be seen, there were a number of accounts of language available to poets. Darwin's thought, making the 'unity of Type' consequent on the 'law' of the 'Conditions of Existence' rather than being prior to them, and thus making problematic the definition of a generic 'family', and consequently a 'family' grouping of languages and the categories within them, put pressure on accounts of language from one direction. Carlyle's old analogy between language and money as forms of substitution developed unsettling implications in the 1860s, when the structure of credit rested on more and more indirect forms of substitution and financial speculation grew inordinate, and this put pressure on accounts of language from another direction. For the substitutive function of money, and by inference of language, became increasingly problematic. Hyndman, writing at the end of this period, saw the crash of the firm of Overend, Gurney and Co. in 1866 as the central crisis of this decade.[9] As a result of these multiple pressures, the double poem begins to disappear. The *ambiguity* of the discrete word or phrase supersedes it. The double poem turns on the utterance of a subjectivity which is reversed into the dramatic objectivity of phenomena for investigation, and depends, however precariously, on an epistemology which guarantees a vital interaction between subject and object and the play of language between these two fields, so that the relationship is given a new content. In Pater's work, on the other hand, a form of nominalism produces the symbol with a disappearing referent, a sign whose meaning is behind or *beyond* the word. Meaning does not lie between words and world but beyond them.

What has been retrospectively theorised as an epistemological break by modernism can be seen as a time of polarisation and extremity which produced some unexpected alignments and strategies and new configurations. In the late 1850s Morris had combined the poetry of sensation with the radical strategies of Grotesque art and redefined the conservative implications of the language of sensation. In the 1860s Swinburne co-opts the poetry of sensation, free from the restraints of the Type, in the service of a republican poetics. The anti-democratic Hopkins reworks the idiosyncrasy of the Grotesque, and claims it for a new theory of language associated with Catholic teleology. Meredith normalises the Grotesque element in psychological and social critique while Dante Gabriel Rossetti moves between realism and a democratised high Tractarian symbol, and the atheist Thomson continues the secularisation of the symbol which Pater's work had begun.

At the time they were writing, however, the work of Morris, Swinburne, Rossetti and Meredith was seen strictly in terms of *moral* categories. They were designated as 'The Fleshly School of Poetry' (1871) by Robert Buchanan in an attack which skewed the debate on their work and still continues to mislead. It is arguable that his critique was a massive didactic and *moral* diversion which obscured the serious issues their poetry raises. He adopted one of the tactics of reactionary rage, describing as *immoral* what is *politically* complex and unsettling. What alarmed Buchanan was that Swinburne's poetry in particular was becoming increasingly popular (while his own moral and 'popular' ballads of the London poor (*London Poems*, 1866–70) were ignored).

> [B]ut it unfortunately happens in the present case that the fleshly school of verse-writers are, so to speak, public offenders, because they are diligently spreading the seeds of disease broadcast wherever they are read and understood. Their complaint too is catching, and carries off many young persons.[10]

Buchanan's complaint is simple: these poets are prurient, erotic poets exposing their morbid and self-indulgent sexuality and preaching an adolescent transgressiveness which is ultimately trivial because it is out to sensationalise and shock.

> Strange to say, moreover, no one accused Mr Rossetti of naughtiness. What had been heinous in Mr Swinburne was majestic exquisiteness in Mr Rossetti. Yet we question if there is anything unfortunate in 'Poems and Ballads' quite so questionable on the score of thorough nastiness as many pieces in Mr Rossetti's collection. Mr Swinburne was wilder, more outrageous, more blasphemous, and his subjects were more atrocious in themselves; yet the hysterical tone slew the animalism, the furiousness of either lowered the sensation; the first feeling of disgust in such themes as 'Laus Veneris' and 'Anactoria', faded away with comic amazement. It was only a little mad boy letting off squibs, not a great strong man who might be really dangerous to society. 'I *will* be naughty!' screamed the little boy.[11]

Effeminacy, schoolboy snickers and tumidly ineffectual blasphemy, these defensive attempts to emasculate and trivialise the poetry suggest that the offensiveness of these poets is radically threatening, and genuinely 'dangerous to society'. Dangerous because of the clear imputation of homosexuality, dangerous because of political radicalism.

What were they doing? Both Swinburne and Rossetti offered accounts of their poetry which were deeply serious, and they present one of those rare occasions when a poet's explanation of his work is genuinely illuminating. Rossetti showed by careful attention to context that systematic misreading of 'The House of Life' damaged its dramatic nature; such misprision imputed physical description to what was in fact a psychological symbol associated with the narcissistic image of water, and not a 'bubble-and-squeak notion of an actual kiss'.[12] This kind of reading, he said, refused to confront the exploration of disturbing areas of sexuality. Swinburne described 'Laus Veneris' in terms of the paradox of sexuality which is unsatisfied by both Venus and Christ but tragically caught in the antithesis they constitute. Pater-like, he recalled the Hellenic statue of Hermaphroditus to defend his poem of that name, arguing that it portrayed a perfect but impossible androgynous moment, 'the union of sexes in one body of perfect beauty'.[13] The attempt to unsettle restricted accounts of gender is seen not as an end in itself but as part of a serious enquiry into the conventions and categories which have shaped thought and institutions in the nineteenth century. Here is a defence of critique in art very much like Hallam's in that it refuses to limit itself to the *'usual'* themes.

And yet Swinburne's work sold well, as Buchanan saw. He was not the coterie poet envisaged by Hallam. Nor is he subversive by subterfuge, as Hallam had understood the poetry of sensation to be. The same goes for Rossetti and Meredith. They sold *because* they were shocking. For there is a certain disingenuousness in their apologia despite the obvious seriousness and sense of complexity. Part of the strategy of their writing was to question by shock. The problem of shock is the difficulty of sustaining it, as even Tennyson had found in *Maud* and in 'Vivien' (*Idylls*, 1859), the precursor poems Buchanan rightly pointed to as an important influence. The difficulty of going beyond Tennyson sometimes leads to that *didactically* self-conscious shockingness which can intervene coercively, particularly in Swinburne's work. Tennyson's alignment with conservative poetry protected him from the kind of assault received by the 'fleshly' poets. They on the other hand declared their subversiveness by their public celebration of Shelley, the poet most associated with revolutionary thought in the nineteenth century, and discussed so unfavourably by Arnold and by Bagehot.[14] Their adherence to Blake was another indication of unconventionality, not to speak of Baudelaire and de Sade. But it is important to distinguish the superficial from the searching in these poets' work. When Rossetti and Swinburne seized upon Edward Fitzgerald's *Rubaiyat of Omar Khayyam* (first published in 1859 but revised in three subsequent editions), they were responding to a new sensuousness and scepticism which makes the Persian Omar's 'Epicurean Audacity of Thought and Speech' an important cultural document. Unlike the high seriousness with which Arnold regarded his Persian sources, Fitzgerald could 'vamp' Omar up, as he put it, with a curious mixture of slang – 'Ah, take the Cash in hand and waive the rest' (1859, stanza 12) – and easy sensuousness – 'the Nightingale cries to the Rose/That yellow cheek of hers to incarnadine' (stanza 6).[15] Omar's cheerful nihilism, his oppositions between temple and tavern, thought and sexuality – Fitzgerald writes as if he is dealing with an Empedocles who has suddenly turned hedonist – is pleasingly rendered. Its goal-refusing, anti-economic view of life is refreshing. It says much for the restrictions of Victorian society if this could be read as a serious invitation to transgression. But its mildness renders it acceptable. To place its superficiality beside the work of the poets of the 1860s suggests that it is possible to distinguish what is serious in their work, even though seriousness is a quality Swinburne at least wished to subvert.

Before considering the work of the poets of the 1860s and 1870s it is necessary to look in more detail at the implications of Pater's work for their poetry, and at the accounts of language available to them. The term 'Pre-Raphaelite poetry' is often used as a loose category for three of these poets (Rossetti, Swinburne and Meredith lodged together for a time) but it is misleading because it yokes together very different kinds of writing, and leaves Hopkins (who was actually deeply interested in Pre-Raphaelite painting) out of account. I prefer to see all these writers, including Thomson, as writers of the 1860s and 1870s, all of them redefining the nature of poetry.

The last chapter of *The Renaissance*, on the 'passionate intellectual life' of Winckelmann, the eighteenth-century German who opened up the modern study of Greek sculpture, 'the happy light of the antique', is a virtual precis of Hegel's *Aesthetics* (known since the early 1840s in England and enthusiastically if incoherently reviewed by G. H. Lewes).[16] At the same time it is a repudiation of Ruskin's Grotesque. Architecture in comparison with sculpture is a low art. The central ideas of medieval Christian art move to the inexpressible and are inadequate to the matter they clothe; such art would have shrunk from the notion that what the eye apprehended was all (he is taking on *Modern Painters* and *Stones of Venice* here). By contrast Greek sculpture, as Hegel realised, represents thought adequate to its matter where form and idea are perfectly commensurate and the mind is not independent of flesh: 'The mind begins and ends with the finite image'. The pure, abstract, unified Type is eased away from religion and in the male world of 'moral sexlessness' exists in unashamed 'immersion in the sensuous'. Thus Tractarian symbol is relocated in the *pagan* spirit, and its hidden meaning brought into the light. Throughout *The Renaissance*, Pater uses the idea of the symbol, with its multiple analogy and correspondence, to express the nature of Renaissance thought (see 'Pico della Mirandola') as well as of the Greek spirit, though the symbol takes on an increasing 'vagueness' ('Leonardo da Vinci') as modern ideas arise. Likewise, rituals are less religious than anthropological forms, and become aesthetic ends in themselves. An aristocracy of the 'aesthetic' develops as beauty 'becomes a distinction, like genius or noble place' (later, in the essay on 'Style', he was to say that the appreciation of style belongs to a small group of scholars).[17]

Pater added three things to this Hegelian historicism. First, he clothed it in the Schillerian language of living form. Intense, fervent, sharp, enthusiasm, excitement, delight, blitheness, sensuous form, pure form, penetrate, penetrative, restraint, unity, are key words in the nervously subtle arpeggios of his prose. Secondly, he pushes pure form towards formalism by saying that all art aspires to the condition of music as form becomes an end in itself and penetrates 'every part of the matter' ('The school of Giorgione').[18] Lastly he brings to his discussion a strangely ambiguous account of women. Epitomised by Leonardo da Vinci's *Medusa*, 'the head of a corpse' bringing 'violent death', and in women who are the daughters of Herodias, and in *La Giaconda*, 'the symbol of the modern idea', a face showing 'the soul with all its maladies', the feminine is pathologised.[19] Women are associated with primordial cyclical time, with death, necrophilia, and with transgressive knowledge. They fascinate and repel.

We can begin to find a context for the famous 'For art comes to you proposing frankly to give nothing but the highest quality to your moments as they pass, and simply for those moments' sake'.[20] It is noticeable that Pater considers sculpture as pure form emancipated from background and context – its detachment and contextlessness fascinates him despite his tendency to historicise phases and movements into epochs. The way to recreate the integrity of the Greek spirit in the complexities of the modern world is to *internalise* its detachment as a unified psychological moment in the process of self-culture with a 'passionate coldness'. The Greek ideal of freedom can be regained and disengaged from 'this entanglement, this network of law'. These are the laws not of society but of physics, where there is no inside or outside, subject or object, but a network of forces 'penetrating us'. Consciousness is a node, 'renewed from moment to moment' in the perpetual waste and repair of physical tissue. Language invests objects with solidity but in reality they are groups of unstable and evanescent impressions, 'colour, odour, texture' in 'perpetual flight'. Yet if we hold to the integrity of each discrete moment the law of time can be both accepted and defeated because time is infinitely divisible: and theoretically we can enable it to 'appreciate' an infinity of experience *within* any moment. By investing in time self-culture can 'feel itself alive', counting out the energy of an infinity of 'pulses', and escape the frost of habit even while it sees itself vanishing away.[21] Arguably, despite the formidable pressure exerted by evolutionary ideas, it was the atomism of physics which preoccupied intellectuals late in the century: the world of physics shows one to be 'sift' in an hourglass (Hopkins) or turns experience into 'a glass that ran' (Swinburne).

Logically in the world which is at the mercy of a series of impressions the only freedom that is possible is the freedom to make *form* or the freedom to shape language. We have to work with *general* notions, but those have to be given individuality through the linguistic sign. Pater was interested in the work of H. L. Mansel, who located agency and choice solely in the act of representation. Presentative or intuitive consciousness is of individual impressions or conditions, Mansel said. Representational consciousness conceptualises: the presence of an object is

> the result of a representative act on the part of the subject. In the former [presentative] case, the presence of the object is involuntary;

in the latter [representative] it is voluntary. In both, the presentative and representative faculties are in combination, for this is the condition of all complete consciousness; but in the former case the object is *given to*, in the latter it is *given by*, the conscious act.[22]

Form and *matter* denote the double elements of consciousness; whereas matter is given *to* mind, the form is given *by* mind. Pater's possessive response to the moment is recognisable in Manser's formulation of the consciousness which works on its materials: 'I can become conscious of them only by recognising them as *mine*'. '*I know*, or *I know that I know*':[23] this double process actually constitutes the supreme act of freedom, which is located in the act of consciousness itself. Will and volition exist as an act of consciousness, of *knowing* that one can give form to experience. We can have no knowledge of an 'abstract self', only 'successive states of consciousness'. Thus 'the consciousness of myself having power over my own determinations is illusory'.[24] Freedom is simply a psychological condition in which we can decide to choose.

But the representative consciousness derives its content only from the intuitive faculty and presented phenomena, and is involved in a circular process whereby to have meaning it has to construct an image, 'which image represents the original figure from which the notion was derived', because no general representation can exist independent of particulars.[25] So the ultimate objects of consciousness are always discrete *individual phenomena* and *clearness* and *distinctness* must be the essential attributes of consciousness for perception to take place at all. The materials of consciousness resolve themselves into an infinitely divisible series of independent objects. A single leaf, a tree, a forest, are not categories in a progressive process of linked relations but discrete entities, just as a chain can be resolved into each one of its links in isolation from one another, Mansel argues in his first chapter. By inference Pater's God is not Arthur Hallam's God of passionate warmth who longs for union with his objects, but a God of passionate coldness who knows that he is alive when he understands the atomised phenomena of consciousness to be *his*, and can shape the evanescent materials of human life as aesthetic form. He is always in danger of petrifaction unless he can do this and bring decaying sense into life.

Mansel's refinement of Kant's account of representation or *Vorstellung* into two aspects, an immediate and a reflexive act, has implications of a curious kind for language, and opens up problems less immediately obvious in Pater's work. On the one hand experience must be fixed in a representative sign which is only given content by the singularity of phenomenal experience. On the other hand it is at a *distance* from what it represents: the sign represents the general notion which represents the image which represents the object of intuition. We cannot think, or even perhaps experi-

390

ence, without language, but language is substitutive in a way which does not guarantee 'the original signification' because it is abstract.

To this it may be added, that the notion, as represented in language, is but the substitute for the notion embodied in intuition, and derives all the conditions of its validity from the possibility of the latter; for language, though indispensable as an instrument of thought, lends itself with equal facility to every combination, and thus furnishes no criterion by which we can judge between sense and nonsense – between the conceivable and the inconceivable. *A round square* or *a bilinear figure*, is, as a form of speech, quite as possible as *a straight line* or *an equilateral triangle*. The mere juxtaposition of the words does not indicate the possibility or impossibility of the corresponding conception, until we attempt to construct, by intuition, an individual object in accordance with it. Language, like algebra, furnishes a system of signs, which we are able to employ in various relations without at the moment being conscious of the original signification assigned to each. Like the bank-note, it is the representative of value without having an intrinsic value of its own, and, like the bank-note, its real worth depends on the possibility of its being at any time changed for the current coin of the realm. But, as in practice the note is treated as if it were the money which it represents.[26]

The implications of such an account of language resonate among the work of all the poets discussed here. And perhaps its disruptive implications are best to be seen in nonsense poetry. Lewis Carroll's nonsense depends on a play with structure which goes beyond pun or ambiguity. The language which 'lends itself with equal facility to every combination' and which does not distinguish between the conceivable and the inconceivable, can be seen in the way categories are dislodged – a grin without a face (*Alice in Wonderland*) – and particularly in the way a conventional syntax will sustain a sense without a meaningful referent, or organise words which have no known referent but which belong to a 'grammatical' structure. The substitution of 'bat' for 'star' in the parody of the nursery rhyme 'Twinkle, twinkle, little star' and 'tea-tray' for 'diamond' also dislodges the meaning of the words *with* referents – 'Twinkle, twinkle' starts to 'mean' something else.[27] Alice's discourse with Humpty Dumpty in *Through the Looking Glass* turns on the liberties it is possible to take with language. Proper names are turned into general categories and words with universal meanings have only a private, individual significance. The logic of this reversal is carried through in the discussion of the Jabberwocky poem – ''Twas brillig and the slithy toves/Did gyre and gimble in the wabe'.[28] Verbs, conjunctions and articles remain, but nouns, adjectives and some verbs have to have a meaning negotiated word by word: 'adjectives you can do anything with'. Each word is brought back to an 'original' meaning

391

derived idiosyncratically from experience, although some words are simply defined through other words: 'slithy' means 'lithe and slimy', though it could presumably be a portmanteau word founded on slit, or slim or filthy. The anarchy of language opens out when Alice objects to private signification and polyvalent sense, asking whether you '*can* make words mean so many different things'. Humpty Dumpty has said that a word means 'just what I choose it to mean – neither more nor less', and answers this objection simply by saying that meaning ultimately depends on who is master. ' "The question is," said Humpty Dumpty, "which is to be master – that's all" '.[29] Meaning, in fact, can be *imposed* by the powerful. The control of language is in the hands of those strong enough to have their way, so that cultural meaning operates through a kind of linguistic terrorism. Perhaps nonsense poetry is an anarchic response to this frightening power. It is interesting in this context to see Edward Lear's work moving from the limerick in 1846 to a play with proper nouns in later work – the Jumblies, the Quangle Wangle Quee, the Pobble – often in weird family and community contexts, and to an unsettling post-Darwinian sport with the private naming of categories for botanical species. Nonsense poetry asserts the uncontrollable nature of language in defiance of powerful social law. Like Pater's self-culture it escapes the 'network' of the law – but only by imposing its own.

An anxiety about language and law, its tendency to nonsense, and the escaping referent dominates the work of Hopkins and Swinburne in particular as in different ways they work out the problem of who is 'master' in language-making. To complete this context for the poetry of the later part of the century it is necessary to return briefly to Mansel, and to consider as well the significance of the work of Max Müller.

Humpty Dumpty tells Alice that words come to be paid at the end of the week. Mansel, as we have seen, takes up the same economic metaphor at the end of his discussion of the sense and nonsense that language can create. 'Like the bank-note, it is the representative of value without having an intrinsic value of its own. . . . But, . . . in practice the note is treated as if it were the money which it represents'.[30] The financial metaphor is a contributory cause to the anxiety about language in its function of substitution. The more so because this metaphor was experienced as a literal problem in the financial speculation of the 1860s, and the economic situation was certainly seen by commentators as different as Bagehot and Hyndman as a situation in which the substitutive nature of credit had got out of control. In his *The Commercial Crises of the Nineteenth Century* (1892) Hyndman saw the crisis of 1866 as the first purely financial crisis of the century, rather than a crisis of labour or supply and demand. The excessive speculation of Overend, Gurney and Co., the firm whose collapse he took as a paradigm of the economy, could continue while people treated the note 'as if it were the money which it represents', in Mansel's words. But when the firm 'suddenly stopped payment' on 10 May 1866 panic swept the country, endangering the whole structure of credit. Hyndman blames this partly on the immense sums available for capital investment (railways raised £70,000,000 capital in a few years) which made for wild speculation, but partly also on the immensely complex and indirect nature of the banking system which had grown up since the Napoleonic wars. The lending system was devolved through a series of subsidiary discount houses and as they themselves began to participate in speculation, share issue and the risk of development enterprises, the pattern of interdependence became so complex and remote from the sources of funding that 'nobody knew what might be the end of their break-down'.

> At the same time with these great joint-stock banks there grew up a whole series of discount houses and bill-brokers, in addition to the large mercantile and accepting houses whose bills had to be dealt with. It was and is the business of these establishments to deal specially in bills . . . at a very small profit with the great joint-stock banks. It is in no sense the business either of the banks or of the discount houses or of the bill-brokers, to foster trade or to develop new enterprises. They, in theory, deal only with the results of improved industrial conditions and the increased trade which springs from them. But in practice, as we have seen, the facilities given in times of inflation and high prices have the effect of enhancing both the one and the other. In some cases, means were found to start new enterprises by these financial firms themselves, and the circle of finance was thus not merely indirectly but directly involved in the risks of promotion.[31]

'The circle of finance': a caucus race with no end and no beginning ultimately casts doubt on whether the representative value of money has an intrinsic value which can be realised and on who is 'master' of its meaning. Money and language might both have an imaginary value, might both be a form of nonsense. In this context of insecurity where the 'possibility or impossibility of the corresponding conception' is not guaranteed, Pater's attempt to make form and content indivisible while yet multiplying the value of the infinitely divisible moment, Hopkins' attempt to individuate words with the primal perception from which they are derived, and Swinburne's anxiety over the ever vanishing referent of words takes on a sharp urgency, as each writer reacts to the problem in different ways. The worry about language is an economic worry, and vice versa.

Max Müller's *Lectures on the Science of Language*, which were derived from a lecture course given at the Royal Institution in 1861, add a further dimension to the language question. The use of analogies from geology was becoming common in many fields of discourse (for instance, in *Essays and Reviews* (1861), in the context of theology, where Jowett invoked geological imagery[32]), and Müller was no exception. But his dominant model of language was taken from Darwin's *Origin of Species* (1859). Where Lyell's work had been informed by accounts of language earlier in the century, emphasising the permanent Type, Müller reconceptualised language through Darwin – not always with great subtlety, but with a boldness and brio which conveyed something of Darwin's own wonder ('staggered' is a word Darwin uses with extraordinary effect) at the complexity of biological adaptation. Darwin's hypothesis breaks down the distinction between species and variety by demonstrating the ways in which species adapt and differentiate and survive according to the conditions of particular environments in a series of irreversible changes. He proposes, of course, the 'origin' of man not as a created being but as a developed species. His theory offers at once the operation of impersonal law (and sometimes impersonal chance) and a universe of extraordinary plenitude. The 'struggle for survival', a phrase Müller uses several times to describe the development of language, is perhaps the most obvious and striking paradigm for language. But just as important is the way in which Darwin's theory charged common terminology with new meaning and disturbing possibilities. Law, polity, community, parent, family, home, stock, reproduction, competition, female (males compete for females in the process of natural selection), territory, immigration, parasite, slave: all these terms, some used partly as metaphor and some in new and very specific contexts (slaves are an indispensable part of some ant communities), take on further meaning after Darwin.[33] Müller uses many of them dramatically. In his work the notion of the Typing of language is displaced by other concepts. Many of the ideas he explored had been available to linguists for some time, but he produced a striking work of synthesis.

What Müller attempted was a natural history of language. His world of language is one of fantastic plenitude and variation in constant change and unrestrained growth, diversifying, regenerating, hybridising. The study of language is a science precisely because language is outside the *control* of man even though it is humanly made.[34] The study of language raises the question of necessity and free will: linguistic change has a historical form, but it is a natural growth, and though man is a language-maker he cannot affect its laws by either producing them or preventing them, for they are independent of his will.[35] A language can change in two or three generations or less, dialects can proliferate and die. 'Language exists in man, it lives in being spoken, it dies with each word that is pronounced'.[36] Linguistic change is checked and arrested in developed nations and cultures with a complex civil organisation, but language does not develop by mutual social agreement any more than it grows by organic necessity, containing its future within itself. It is subject to the law of adaptation and selection. The roots which belong to the primeval beginnings of language and which represent both general categories *and* metaphorical ideas (for Müller there is no contradiction here) once existed in unrestrained growth, but the process of selection reduced their superfluity; 'Hence the superabundance of synonyms in ancient dialects, and hence that struggle for life carried on among these words, which led to the destruction of the less strong, the less happy, the less fertile words, and ended in the triumph of one, as the recognised and proper name for every object in every language'.[37] The term 'proper' here looks to *Alice Through the Looking Glass* and the concern with what 'proper' names really are.

Much of this thinking is crude, but Müller's lectures make two important moves. In the first place, he rejects the idea of an authoritative language, noting that the distinction between 'barbarian' and civilised language cannot be maintained, and that indeed the study of language could not commence without the Christian concept of brotherhood. Connected with this is his insistence on the supreme importance of *dialect*. The plenitude of dialect throughout the world in hundreds of clans, tribes and countries, African, Indian, Persian, Tartar, is a constantly renewing and revolutionary force. Müller speaks constantly of the ever changing 'stream' or flux of language. The unbounded resources of dialects prevent the stagnation of language and break the ice of its polished surface, refusing restriction and limit. Dialects feed the living language democratically and support the dynastic literary forms of civilised communities: the 'lower and popular strata of speech from which these dynasties originally sprang, and by which alone they are supported'.[38] Thus a purist approach to language is impossible and standards of 'correctness' are manifestly artificial. Children, forming constructions such as 'badder' and 'baddest' are in their own way as 'correct' as any purist.[39]

Secondly, by maintaining that languages can be classified according to a Darwinian unity of descent and genealogy, springing from definable 'families' whose morphological structure is distinct, such as the Aryan and Semitic groups (Müller was the first writer to describe 'the original common Aryan type' and to use the name 'Aryan'), Müller both reinforces and loosens what the category of race and the family can stand for. The comparative grammar of Grimm and Bopp had shown that the morphological structure of language groups can never be changed or altered by admixture with the forms of another 'family' (Darwin had called morphology the 'soul' of natural science).[40] On the other hand, what was comprehended in the 'family' was broadened and extended so widely that new juxtapositions and affinities could be perceived: 'the grammatical articulation of Sanskrit, Zend, Greek, Roman, Celtic, Teutonic, and Slavonic, was produced once and for all. . . . [A]pparent differences . . . must be explained by laws . . . which modified the original common Aryan type, and changed it into so many national languages'.[41] Language thus transcends national formations just as it transcends class. We can show by means of comparative grammar alone, without written records of any kind, that the language of a ploughboy reveals its own history.[42] We can also see that the sepoy and the English soldier are united, and both alike share the characteristic that no new root has been added to their language after the Teutonic and Indic branches separated.[43] The constant sifting and refining of language produces differentiation and simplification, refusing superfluity and homonym to such an extent that the 'caprice' of an individual poet cannot produce new words, even though languages begin in a staggering plenitude, to use Darwin's word.[44] For all languages regulate themselves according to morphological laws. In contradistinction to a 'financial' account of language in terms of mastery, Müller asserts deterministic law.

Müller the populariser made sure that there was something for everybody. His insistence that civilised languages polish and refine and refuse superfluity would please the Pater who, in the essay on style, sought for the exact, precise word and repudiated excess. On the other hand, the radical unsettling of categories, the generation of a flow and stream of language which seeks to break barriers of definition and to prevent the freezing of words (that arrest of form and meaning which Müller saw in civilised languages), is clearly important in the work of the republican Swinburne. Hopkins' fascination with dialect and the language of children, his attempt to reanimate primitive forms and return to the essential roots of language, owes much to those conceptualisations and categories of Müller which move in an opposite and conservative direction.[45] Both Hopkins and Swinburne are preoccupied with living speech rather than the written word, with the oral and aural sound. Swinburne, like Hallam thirty years before, sought out the oral tradition of the Border ballads. *Poems and Ballads* (1866) is an attempt to appropriate and transform the popular ballad for new radical political purposes against its conservative use (W. E. Aytoun, for instance, had written middle-class ballads and Alfred Austin tried his hand at them). The boom and thunder of Swinburne's aural poetry is very different from the speech-based writing of Hopkins, who thoroughly disliked its flow of sound, but in their refusal of the purism of conventional written language they were alike. Meredith and Thomson are less obviously responsive to Müller's accounts of language. But Meredith's sense that the language of 'John Bull' required deconstruction, and Thomson's vocabulary of class warfare and satirical lampoon, particularly in the work before *The City of Dreadful Night*, belong to a changing understanding of what language can be and do. And all the poets of this time were preoccupied in different ways with the problem of language and power.

The Aryan language, as Müller put it, 'obtained a mastery' (211) in the struggle for life. The poets of this period, whether it is Hopkins' 'mastering me God', Swinburne's preoccupation with subjugation and slavery, Meredith's understanding of sexual power struggle, Thomson's troubled sense of class, participate in a complex discourse of mastery. This discourse was complex for a number of reasons. We have seen that Müller's understanding of linguistic mastery moves in two directions. On the one hand, his theories sanctioned a 'republican' attack on rigid hierarchy through the constant challenge of dialect from below. On the other hand the incessant struggle for mastery legitimated power relations conceived as the unceasing movement of competition for domination. Müller thought of these patterns immediately in terms of class relations, but his ideas also have a far wider significance. Colonial power, its meaning and authority, is also at stake in his work. His 'Aryan' category, as we have seen, like Darwin's classifications, both breaks down and reinforces the idea of 'family': it gives family both the substantiveness of a primary, originary and indivisible social unit *and*, in contradiction to this, makes family a transnational category, with far more widespread, distant and *diffused* affiliations and connections than could have been conceived before the reconceptualisation of language in terms of Indo-European and other groups.

Exactly the same thing happens with the idea of nation. This, on analogy with family, is both consolidated and dissolved as a unit. The consolidation of nation and the national language enables the exploitation and mastery of the colonial other to be sanctioned by actually creating the dichotomy of nation and colonial other. On the other hand, those deep linguistic affiliations and connections which unite the Indian sepoy and the British soldier on Indian territory, confuse these confident demarcations, undermine the hegemony of nation and provide no justification for power relationships between European state and colonial other. Just as economic relations appeared to be increasingly complex, so racial categories and ethnic formations are more uncertain, and less distinct, than they might appear. Hence enormous anxiety surrounds the idea of power and domination throughout the latter part of the century.

Social Darwinists such as Herbert Spencer tend to concentrate on the complex pattern of adaptation and survival in the social organism and have perhaps led us to a reading of this period which understates the element of struggle which can be metaphorised from both Darwin's and Müller's work.[46] Social Darwinism emphasises the orderliness and efficiency of the survival of the fittest. In poetry, on the other hand, power, the discourse of the master–slave dialectic, emerges with a new and startling nakedness. The categories of master and slave dissolve and reconfigure in a number of discourses across a number of areas, but what is striking is the frankness with which the question of mastery is everywhere addressed. J. S. Mill, for instance, for whom the intersecting of concentric ideological circles later in the century produced some strangely contradictory positions, can stand as an example. Writing on representative government, he was directly concerned with the distribution of power in different forms of government, and ranged over barbarian and classical polities to consider despotism and popular government. He struggled with the paradox that

397

majority rule is not necessarily *representative* rule because minorities can always be effectively disenfranchised, though 'man for man they would be as fully represented as the majority'.[47]

He was also ruthlessly concerned to exclude working-class representation, however much his liberalism disguises this. His discussion is, indeed, deeply undemocratic. The Reform Bill of 1867, by failing to create a democracy, intensified these problems rather than solving them, and that is why, unlike the Reform Bill of 1832, it was not a historical watershed. Arnold, for instance, returned to the question of democracy in 1861 and his concern with popular education throughout the 1860s is an aspect of the same debate. Another indication of the opening rather than closing of debate and its extension to new areas is Mill's publication of *The Subjection of Women* in 1869, where he unequivocally compared the status of women to that of slaves. It is typical of the anxieties and confusions of the period that he was more willing to enfranchise women than the working class. And slaves, of course, existed. To think of women as slaves was not to relate to the distant classical past but to the immediate present and to align women with colonial exploitation. The atrocities of Governor Eyre in Jamaica which came to light in the 1860s (Mill took a powerful part in attacking this scandal) were sufficient reminder of the violence of colonial relations.[48] There is a deep uneasiness about the legitimacy of power both at home and abroad. The work of Engels on the structure of the family, strangely converging with the liberal Mill, is another instance of the way in which institutions and social structure were under the pressure of investigation at this time.[49]

This concern with power results in an almost obsessive interest in the master–slave dialectic in the last part of the nineteenth century. The poets tended to write in terms of paradigms of power and explored despotic structure through analogy with ancient or mythic societies rather than writing directly of the political abuse of class oppression and colonialism. But both are a disguised or incipient presence. It is interesting that the reading of Hegel shifted its emphasis towards the master–slave relationship later in the century. G. H. Lewes, as has been seen, began a reading of Hegel by celebrating the *Aesthetics* in a review of 1842. In 1857 his *Biographical History of Philosophy* devoted twenty pages to Hegel (600–20), but made a first attempt to deal with the *Phenomenology*, where the master–slave dialectic is elaborated. In the two-volume fourth edition of his *History of Philosophy* in 1871, the Hegel chapter was expanded to eighty pages. He himself admitted that he dealt clumsily with the *Phenomenology* but it is nevertheless central to his argument. He skirted the master–slave dialectic, and perhaps this occluding of the notion of conflict, which is fundamental to Hegel's understanding of self-consciousness, is a sign of its haunting importance to this time. Lewes later said that the chapter would have been improved if he had tackled the constitutive problem of self-consciousness at the start of it, recognising its deficiencies.[50] His companion, George Eliot, certainly understood the significance of the master–slave dialectic, for *Middlemarch* (1872) contains a brilliant precis of it in chapter 11, which considers sociological models of culture. The 'double change' of 'self and beholder' which the inhabitants of Middlemarch both experience and witness is a condensed and abbreviated allusion to the negotiations of power which Hegel locates in self-consciousness.[51] It would be quite wrong to suggest that a general acceptance of the structure of the master–slave relationship took place at this time. The troubled and uneasy handling of the theme of power in the texts themselves is witness to this. It is precisely that the concept of mastery becomes problematic across a number of discourses which makes it important. There is no simple cause-and-effect relation among Darwin, Humpty Dumpty, Müller and Swinburne. But what one can say is that mastery and its cognate terms were unsettled and unsettling questions. England, it has to be remembered, was no more a democracy in 1867 than it was in 1832, and the increasing anxieties about the legitimacy of hierarchical power which continued until the end of the century and beyond, are symptomatic of a society under strain.

What of the poets who witnessed the master–slave dialectic not as middle-class intellectuals but as working-class writers? In this period, and to the end of the century, we see the poetry of the self-taught artisan giving way to the music-hall song and the variety act. 'I don't call myself a poet, I call myself a song-writer', the Tynesider, Joe Wilson, said, when his work was praised.[52] Protest and challenge tend to be displaced by songs which represent the domestic conditions of working-class life comically, from Wilson's song about nursing the baby while the wife is out ('Cum Geordy, haud the bairn') to Gus Elen's frankly ironic and intensely urban song about the magnificent 'pastoral' views potentially available to the working classes living near gas works and dust holes, 'If it wasn't for the 'ouses in between'.[53] Women performers became as successful as men: Marie Lloyd's performance of Fred W. Leigh's 'My Old Man said, "Follow the Van"', a song which presupposes an unstable world of social mobility in which the 'home' is 'packed in' a cart, was widely known; Lottie Collins's 'Ta-ra-ra Boom-de-ay' registers the changing sexual mores which enabled women performers to come into prominence.[54]

Dan Leno's satires on unemployment and the stereotyping of working men are an exception to the mediation of political feeling through domestic songs. His hudibrastic rhymes – 'working classes' pairs with the ending, 'Tryin' to improve 'em such a bootless farce is' – and bitterly comic attacks on the lazy phrases which justify exploitation and conceal ideological positions are unusually open for this time.[55] But the more usual trajectory of working-class writing is represented in the poems of the earlier poet, his namesake, J. B. Leno. J. B. Leno's poems became increasingly nostalgic and backward-looking. His *Kimberton, A Story of Village Life* (1875–6), a celebration of the idyll of an agricultural village of a generation or so back in Buckinghamshire, appeared with advertisements for an act described as 'Smock-Frock entertainment'. Earlier forms of popular entertainment such as the fair are celebrated, and the integration of community. Though the sufferings and tragedy of labour are portrayed in poems such as 'Poor Bill', as well as the rigidity of the class system ('The Old and New Parson'), political analysis is absent and sentimental recollection takes its place. Leno's essential conservatism is apparent in his tract on 'Female Labour', in which he argues that working-class women should emigrate in search of husbands rather than compete with men on the home labour market, displacing them from traditional male jobs by providing cheap labour. Though one of the best poems in *Kimberton* is about the female field-labourer, midwife and woman of all trades, 'Bet Graham', he is emphatic that 'Female Labour in trades' is unacceptable to him.[56]

There was one voice, a throwback to the past rather than a new poetic style, which sounded powerfully in the 1860s. Joseph Skipsey's ballads and narrative poems continued the tradition of popular urban and industrial broadside writing but used its conventions with an energy, terse strength and lyrical economy which are unprecedented. Working in a North Shields coal mine from the age of 7, teaching himself to read underground, he wrote with Blake-like, uncompromising power, of the contrast between the 'sheen' of starlight above and the 'gloom' of the mine below the earth ('The Stars are twinkling'). In two stanzas, simultaneously grimly laconic and tender, he described the consuming labour which could deprive his children of a father through the very work undertaken to enable them to eat (' "Get Up!" '). His masterpiece is 'The Hartley Calamity', describing a pit disaster in which 200 men were trapped underground and poisoned by gas fumes. A shorter poem, 'Mother wept', could well stand as a prologue to this extraordinarily understated narrative poem. A young boy rejoices in his impending departure from home to work in the pit, eliciting a range of feelings – congratulations, envy, advice. The last stanza expands on the first line, 'Mother wept, and father sighed'.

> 'May he,' many a gossip cried,
> 'Be from peril kept;'
> Father hid his face and sighed,
> Mother turned and wept.[57]

The added verbs signify the parents' attempt to protect the child from their own knowledge of possible disaster, an attempt to contain a prophetic grief scarcely recognised even by themselves.

Dreaded knowledge and the silent, though shared understanding of their predicament by the miners is the theme of 'The Hartley Calamity'. ' "Are we then entombed?" they *seem* to ask' (stanza 9) (my emphasis), before the blocking of the shaft is verified. It is a heroic poem. Intense communal activity engaged on to release the trapped passage is superseded by an equally powerful fight, equally involving shared activity and mutual help, to resist the passivity of sleep induced by the poisoned gas. Son begs father to remain with him while he succumbs to sleep: father attempts to watch by son while succumbing to sleep himself – 'My eyelids are together glued,/ And I – and I – must sleep'.[58] The universal quiet of sleep, both a literal condition and a euphemism for death, eventually fills the mine. The tragic move from resistance to passivity is a paradigm not only of the essential nature of a pit disaster, but also of the political and emotional condition of oppressed labour – silence underground, incarceration and burial from which the political repressed can never return. Only, indeed, by telling and retelling this story, as Skipsey did at many recitals, can its allegory of silencing be redeemed.

Skipsey's is one of the last flowerings of working-class poetry in the century. Nothing quite so powerful appears after him. It is interesting that middle-class poets increasingly speak for the class below them, often appropriating the forms of earlier working-class poetry, whether it is Swinburne's ballads to freedom, Hopkins' fascination with figures such as Harry Ploughman and the dialect of the poor, Meredith's representation of Crimean-war veterans or Thomson's furious analysis of oppression. Eloquent as these often are, sometimes stealing the very rhythm of working-class poetry in order to represent the oppressed by proxy, such writing strangely consolidates Skipsey's allegory of doomed resistance. A poetry of the people was no easier to solve in the 1860s and after than it was when Fox first defined the problem in the 1830s. No wonder that, with the economic problems of class and colonialism becoming ever more complex, an uneasy fascination with power relations marks the latter part of the century.

13

SWINBURNE: AGONISTIC REPUBLICAN

The poetry of sensation as democratic critique

I once jokingly asked him 'what is the most original and unrealisable thing you would like to experience at the moment?' 'I'll tell you,' Swinburne replied, 'to ravish Saint Geneviève during her most ardent ecstasy of prayer – but in addition, with her secret consent!'

(Turgenev on Swinburne)[1]

I did not follow Dr Sandwith in quoting the loathsome detail about the 'whips made of piano-wire' being 'first tried on the backs of women' and showing 'that their skins were easier cut (sic) than those of males', for very shame and physical nausea.

(Swinburne on the atrocities of Governor Eyre of Jamaica, described
by Sandwith in the Fortnightly Review, July 1871)[2]

The two quotations juxtaposed above are indicative of the Swinburne problem. Complicated here by a slightly ironised sado-masochism and a self-conscious understanding of its own desire to shock, a de Sadean pleasure in the transgressive and orgiastic excitements of violation signals that subversive 'naughtiness' which enabled Buchanan to trivialise Swinburne's poetry so effectively. On the other hand, when faced with the 'real thing', with Governor Eyre's barbaric violence perpetrated on Black rebels in Jamaica, one of the most sickening examples of colonial violence in the 1860s, Swinburne was revolted. Like other intellectuals he read accounts of the atrocities with disgust. It is moral seriousness of this kind which prompted him to make claims for the essential morality and seriousness of his own poetry. And yet, the transgressive poet such as Swinburne undoubtedly is *needs* to shock – and to go on shocking. He cannot allow his work to be normalised or assimilated to conventional paradigms. What we know of the life – the flagellations at St John's Wood, the de Sadean cottage, La Chaumière de Dolmance, in Normandy – tends to put Swinburne in a pathological context and to consolidate that sense of the superficially and irrelevantly shocking which Buchanan fostered. By being categorised as 'abnormal' erotic experiments the biting kisses and stinging cruelties of Swinburne's texts can be dismissed. The poetics of algolagniac fantasy might seem to be literally on a hiding to nothing.

But Swinburne is an important figure, a premodernist central to the latter part of the nineteenth century, if only because his psychological experience gave him insights into nineteenth-century bourgeois culture which were to be relevant to poetry through the decadence of the *fin de siècle* and into early modernism. A way to begin taking his work seriously without normalising it is to think of him as the uncanny twin or perverse double of Gerard Manley Hopkins. Hopkins's irritable awareness and repudiation of Swinburne's excesses suggest that he saw him as a shadowy self. Swinburne the agonistic republican, Hopkins the agonistic reactionary, share a set of problems – ontological, sexual, linguistic, political – which are mutually illuminating. Both are deeply theological writers, one through transgressive blasphemy and the other through Catholic sacramentalism. Swinburne's fantasy, though neither poet could have known it, of the willing rape of St Geneviève is a parody of the central trope of *The Wreck of the Deutschland*, the moment of the nun's union with Christ, who is asked to 'come quickly'. Both are aware of the taboos of gender and the censorship of homoerotic feeling, Hopkins with uneasy strain, Swinburne with a triumphant bravura which denaturalised gender distinctions. If Hopkins dreaded the philosophy of flux, which, like the sea in *The Wreck*, dissolved kinship structures, unfathering and unchilding, Swinburne celebrated the equal and opposite dissolution of incest and the confusion of kinship categories. Though Hopkins passionately explored and constructed a notion of 'Englishness' and Swinburne deconstructed Englishness and sought for a non-Eurocentric reading of culture, both looked beyond the immediate national, institutional and ideological boundaries of the British Isles, Hopkins because of the international nature of Catholicism and Swinburne because of the internationalism of his politics and aesthetics. Both were obsessed with power and the law, the 'mastering me/God', but Hopkins sought to maintain their authority (sunsets and oak trees have a law, an inscape) and Swinburne sought to dissolve their tyranny. Both were thoroughly aware of the connection between language and law: for Hopkins in *The Wreck* words 'lash' subjects into devotion; for Swinburne in *Atalanta in Calydon* words kill.[3] Both knew Pater, and seemed to have internalised his theory of style in different ways.

What brings both poets into a fully dialectical relation to one another is a quality that can only be termed *hysteria* in language. In an odd crossing over of customary functions, Swinburne adopts the conservative poetry of sensation for a radical politics and Hopkins appropriates the radical Grotesque for a poetry of conservatism, but both are hypersensitively aware of the breakdown of language which they express in terms of the collapse of form and content, the breaking apart of sign and referent. Both are left with a fevered sense of the brute materiality of language: for Hopkins this means a world bereft of the organising spiritual form incarnate in matter, the materialism which rejects godhead; for Swinburne this means exactly the reverse – the non-transcendent world of brutal Christian materialism which leaves us with the literal sign and that only. Swinburne through the bringing together of spirit and matter in the symbol, Hopkins through the copula, the verb 'to be' which brings difference into relation by bringing metaphor into being, attempt to assuage this fracture, but both remain with the sense of living in a closed system, a linguistic world without relationships beyond itself.

'Forgive us our virtues', Swinburne prayed in 'Dolores', and the chorus of *Atalanta* points to 'The supreme evil, God'.[4] Such transgressive statements are a way of overcoming the violence of a Christian God who, in introducing the soul/body distinction as an inherent part of experience, saw to it that the oppression of the material, with its corollary of desire, would be a permanent condition. Swinburne assembled the curious trinity of Blake, Baudelaire and de Sade to find a way out of the Christian discourse. Arguably, his way out of Christian discourse is Hopkins's way in. The discourse of one of Swinburne's masters, de Sade, bears an odd structural similarity to the discourse of Ignatius Loyola, the founder of the Jesuits, and whose *Exercises* are central to this order, to which Hopkins belonged. Roland Barthes has looked extensively at this parallel between the closed groups of the Sadean Société des Amis du Crime and the Society of Jesus. Its details need not concern us; but the affinity enables one to understand how the two poets approached language.[5]

The Sadean and Jesuit societies share the condition of the enclosed retreat, hierarchical instruction, the organised theatrical scene of enactment, the existence of two classes only in a power relationship of subservience (torturer/victim: instructor/exercitant); but above all they share the same inverse but parallel relationship between the sign and the body. The object of de Sadean ritual, on which identity rests, is an ultimate physical literalism, orgasm, ejaculation. The object of the Jesuit training of the sensory imagination is the conjuring of the body of Christ and its suffering in all its literalness. Both 'systems' terminate in a condition which is simultaneously material body and empty sign. Once the Sadean, as Harold Bloom has pointed out, has literalised the body and its sensations there can be no troping, no signification beyond its materiality.[6] He is confronted with death. Once the body of Christ has entered the imagination it is an empty sign, a sign *of* emptiness and absence, indeed, unless it can be reinvested with spiritual meaning. The frightful limit of the literal, by one poet attributed to a godless universe, by the other to the violence of the Christian god, is what provokes such linguistic violence in both. In both this becomes a social critique, for the literal, material body, devoid of social or personal meaning, is the ultimate nightmare of the bourgeois world. It is a nightmare the bourgeois economic system has itself created:

when commodity escapes from the system of exchange with its network of signification and value it is confronted as pure, brute materiality.

Both poets use a feverish vocabulary of 'flushing' matter with form. For Hopkins the 'flesh-burst' (*The Wreck of the Deutschland*) of a sloe in the mouth flushes the body with meaning and he asks in desperation for the material signs of Christ's wounds to yield a significance. 'When the sense in the spirit reposes,/Thou shalt quicken the soul through the blood', so the speaker of Swinburne's 'Dolores' abjures in frantic spondees. Swinburne's work is dominated by the materiality of the oral sensation and its failure to create a 'mark' or figure which survives the immediacy of experience: 'Below her bosom, where a crushed grape stains/The white and blue, there my lips caught and clove/An hour since, and what mark of me remains?' ('Laus Veneris').[7]

While Hopkins's model of the possible immanence of spiritual meaning and signification in sense is Eucharistic and based on the Incarnation, in which spirit, as Carlyle put it, plays 'into the small prose domain of sense', Swinburne's model inverts this paradigm. It is a reverse Eucharist, Incarnation in reverse, as the material body has to be forced towards a transcendence beyond. His symbolist theory is expressed in mystical and theological terms as the inherence of meaning and sign, but for him as for Symons and Pater, meaning is *beyond*, outside. Rossetti's poems possess a 'sweet and sovereign unity of perfect spirit and sense, of fleshly form and intellectual fire': Baudelaire's writing is invested with a 'mystical moral', a 'rich symbolic manner'.[8] But though the Baudelairean symbol may represent correspondences, things and spirit do not cohere. There is always a 'divorce between all aspiration and its results', a 'divorce of will from deed', which is founded on the divorce between the palpable sign and its signification.[9] Thus words, the things of sense, have to yearn after an unreachable and unknown beyond which transcends their limits. The material sign, since linguistic and literal violence are virtually identical, is flayed, stung and trammelled into transcendence. Words have to transgress their limits and move beyond the boundaries constituted for them. Swinburne's habit of doubling a word with an alliterative synonym, and doubling that synonymous double with a synonymous alliterative phrase, is a way of dissolving the boundaries of language by coalescing distinctions of sound and meaning. The synonym chain produces an endless chain of substitution in which doubled words and phrases blur and exchange semantic and aural attributes with libidinal energy, impelled by an insistent and self-perpetuating metrical form which has the physical shock-effect of the regular waves of the sea, a repeated image of transcendence in Swinburne's work.

Swinburne's insistent, tautologous, substitutive chains create a parallelism which is the inverse of Hopkinsian parallelism. Hopkins's language works through the containment of metaphor, not the dispersal of substitution: his language operates through trope, not through synonym. His is the language of law, not the language of transgression. His fiercely totalising metaphor offers to inscape and organise relationships, fusing them in a simultaneous moment of systematic identity and difference. Swinburne, on the other hand, disorganises and unfixes relationships of similarity and difference, which only belong together in the contiguity of mere temporal sequence, manifesting the chromatic philosophy of flux so ideologically repugnant to Hopkins.

But extremes meet, and both poets create closed systems, poetic languages which arise from the empty material sign, the sign without a referent. We can pathologise this linguistic hysteria. Indeed, such language has been seen as a manifestation of a late-nineteenth-century crisis of masculinity, in which the signification of the phallus (for Freud that simultaneously literal and figurative entity) and the nature of gender roles were unsettled by a culture which gave rise to algolagniac fantasy. Hysteria is a displacement, however, and it is instructive to consider what structural relationship this language has to other discourses in the culture. This can lead one to the wider politics of gender in Swinburne's language as well as to its pathology. For the logic of violence on which it is founded has, as Swinburne himself insisted, a political as well as a psychological aspect.

Language change, Müller said, is arrested and checked in civilised societies with a high degree of social control and developed organisation. The disappearance of synonym and the triumph of the 'one' *proper* name is a condition of civilisation, and it is only dialect which prevents linguistic stagnation and breaks the rigid surface of conventional language. Hopkins chose the 'folk' democracy of dialect (less dangerous than a language of class because less divisive) to explode rigid forms: Swinburne chose the squandering of synonym to rupture the surface of polite language. It is as if his language reproduces Müller's natural history of language, manifesting that plenitude, change, diversification and hybridisation which are the condition of dynamic change and unchecked growth. Müller emphasised that the paradox of language is that though we make it we are subject to its laws. That is why it raised for him questions of determinism and free will. Swinburne's poetry effectively raises the same problems by creating a language which may be determined but which is nevertheless out of control in the sense that it is *outside the law*, or outside humanly made laws. It is both anarchic and *subject*.

This anarchic language of excess, in its emphasis on sound rather than sense, can end up as a form of nonsense language. Mansel, as has been seen, had also emphasised the possibility of language's being out of control, but in a different context than the one Müller describes; his is a context of economy and finance rather than one of law. For him the uncontrollable nature of language stems from its capacity both to *say* what does not and cannot occur in reality (such as the round square), thus escaping from referentiality, and to be treated mistakenly as if it *were* what it represents. Just as the bank note can be treated as though it were the money it represents, so words, essentially substitutive in character, can be treated as if they are what they represent. The fallacy of such an economy of language is obvious, but the infinitely substitutive nature of the sign can also be exploited to make language behave as if it falls outside the economy of closure and referentiality altogether. In its capacity to postpone and substitute, language can flout the point at which sign and reference come together indefinitely. The empty material sign can be perpetuated as if autonomously, possessing its own independent life quite outside a restricted system of meaning. Such poetic discourse avoids being treated as if it *were* what it represents by taking flight into transgressive chains of nominalist language.

This alternative economy of language frees itself, or attempts to free itself, from the taboos of both Christian and bourgeois materialism. Swinburne recognised in Blake's dualistic God of crime and punishment, profit and loss, a God of the law who could only be flouted by desecration and transgression, a God whose blasphemies could only be counteracted by an equivalent outrage. The de Sadean hero establishes his autonomy by criminalising himself, refusing to submit in passivity to the weakness of evil. The Baudelairean dandy exempts his life from bourgeois morality to live through the aesthetic in contradistinction to the laws of nature: 'The art of poetry has absolutely nothing to do with didactic matter at all', Swinburne wrote in his review of *Les Fleurs du Mal* in 1862.[10] Such poetics of excess place value on the wasteful, exorbitant expenditure of energy in violation and transgression. To break through ethical, psychological and sexual categories in desire and lust, madness, violence, incest, is to assert a plenitude which recognises no limit and begins to assuage that furious dependence on the literal by which the poet is bound. It is also to assert a new celebration of virtue and vice which refuses to pathologise violence (as, for instance, the violence of the hero's madness in Tennyson's *Maud* is pathologised), but brings it into the light as a part of nature, part of a dialectic of being rather than an aberration. It is significant that the categories Swinburne most exults in defying are those of gender, kinship and the family, categories which belong to the deepest anxieties of Victorian culture at this time, and which must also be associated with the categories of class and race. Müller's genealogies of the descent of language had, as we have seen, both restricted and expanded what the category of family and race could stand for. It is Althaea's incestuous love for her brothers, and her recognition that they can occupy the same place as her son in her affections, which brings about the tragedy of *Atalanta in Calydon*: Dolores, in the poem of that name, is sister, spouse and mother simultaneously (stanza 19).

The poetics of excess lends itself to the 'anthropological' analysis of

407

ritual or sacramental violence in response to prohibition. It constitutes what Derrida calls the 'general economy' of waste and expenditure in contrast to the restricted economy of recuperative bourgeois morality and psychology, in which no area of experience is allowed to become ethically or emotionally unfunctional but is reincorporated for use.[11] The problem, however, is that the inevitable cycle of transgressive desire, an insatiable breaking of limit and prohibition, has to set up new boundaries to transgress if it is not to consume itself. Delight consumes desire, and desire outruns delight, the fourteenth stanza of *Dolores* asserts. Distinctions collapse into tautology as boundaries are pushed outwards. The paradoxical trap of this centripetal poetry is that the needs of violation become oddly dependent on limit and law to sustain themselves. Moreover, the poetics of expenditure and superfluity which is energised by the treadmill of sadomasochism with its boom and batter of sound (a 'fuzz' of sound, Browning called it) begins to mimic another 'economic' structure which is dangerously close to the bourgeois world Swinburne repudiated. The ungrounded chains of linguistic substitution begin to mimic the inflationary production of those chains of indirectly devolved credit which, as we have seen, characterised the finance of the 1860s. Like the infinitely substitutive nature of credit, Swinburne's language becomes a form of speculation, a caucus race or circle of finance without end, actually participating in the overproduction of credit. It is fascinating that he is fond of devolved linguistic structures depending on the 'of' adjunct (such as the line which ends a chorus in *Atalanta in Calydon*, 'Filled full of the foam of the river'). The complexities of capital in this period, as Hyndman saw, rest on the production of substitutive credit which can be sustained if we forget that it is not the money it stands for. Speculation sets up a deliberate and provocative play between the empty sign and the literal content, occulting one through the other; sometimes conjuring the material, literal substance through the empty sign, sometimes replacing content with the sign, which is made to take on a materiality of its own. In its rage with the literal, Swinburne's language is caught in the provocations of bourgeois capital. We might say that if the terminology of pathology is to be used it is the pathology of capital as much as a psychosexual condition which underlies his language. And that pathology, ever breaking limits, powered by the need for continual expansion, is a veritable paradigm of the 'masculine' colonial moment, just as it is a paradigm of overproduction.

Two further problems arise from the nature of Swinburne's language. In a system where both money and language can work free of referentiality, they require regulation, and value and meaning depend, as Humpty Dumpty remarks, on who is 'master'. The regulation of meaning as an act of violence is never far from Swinburne's work, and belongs to the anxiety of mastery everywhere in his poetry. But the substitutive nature of credit also gets out of control: panic ensues when confidence in the form–content relation of credit collapses. Swinburne is the poet of panic and stampede. The first chorus of *Atalanta in Calydon* portrays panic flight and pursuit. Pan and Bacchus, Pater-like in their refined sensuality but Swinburnian in their violence, pursue 'the maiden hid' while intervening leaves oscillate between exposing and occluding the object of desire – a pattern of the structure of the poet's language and its teasing relationship with the literal.

Swinburne, as we have seen, insisted on the political seriousness of his poetry, and that it constituted not only expression but cultural critique. The linguistic structures which are disclosed in his poetry suggest the complexity and contradictions in which he was involved. The test of their seriousness must be the intensity with which they negotiate such complexities. It is easy to forget the directly political and fiercely anti-reactionary poems in *Poems and Ballads* (1866; there were even more in 1878), but they do form a context for the work which is often read in isolation from them – 'Laus Veneris', for instance, or 'Dolores'. We forget them because it was in the interests of conservative readings such as Buchanan's to trivialise them by omission. Swinburne was master of the lyrical ballad of blasphemy and execration, execration of kings and priests, and could produce a declamatory lyricism which was both public and popular. 'A Song in Time of Order' (*Poems and Ballads*, 155–7) presents itself as a robust sea shanty of republican exile: 'Let the kings keep the earth for their share!/We have done with the sharers of land'. It is a response to the events of 1852, when Napoleon III was made emperor, as France finally reneged on revolutionary politics. European alliances were reconfigured as Britain, France and Austria made pro-Turkish alignments in readiness for the Crimean war: 'We shall see Buonaparte the bastard/Kick heels with his throat in a rope'. The language is accurate – Bonaparte is a bastard because of his politically illegitimate claims. More fundamentally, the poem rests on an impossibility, and declares that it does: when you have taken to the sea in exile there is nowhere to go. The fallacy of emigration is pointed up in the penultimate stanza. For there is no escape. The world bears the burdens of oppression 'From Cayenne to the Austrian whips'. Napoleon made Cayenne in French Guiana a convict settlement in 1852. European colonial oppression and violence is everywhere and has 'tied the world in a tether'. Not only are the kingdoms of Europe 'less by three', as the refrain asserts ('The Kingdoms are less by three'), but there is *no* land capable of being settled by republicans. European power is predicated on violence. The 'Austrian whips' are no fantasy: the reactionary regime had reintroduced corporal punishment by police orders as part of a policy to quell revolutionary activity.

It was with *Poems and Ballads* that the outrage against Swinburne began. *Atalanta in Calydon* (1865) did not provoke such feeling, assimilated as it was to neoclassical pastiche such as Matthew Arnold's *Merope* (1857). Yet Swinburne did not attempt to disguise its, to him, subversive nature.

Thanking Lord Houghton for recognising the poem's 'Antitheism' in a not altogether favourable review, he wrote, 'I should have bowed to the judicial sentence if instead of "Byron with a difference" you had said "De Sade with a difference". The poet, thinker, and man of the world from whom the theology of my poem was derived was a greater than Byron. *He* indeed, fatalist or not, saw to the bottom of gods and men'.[12] These are claims for both de Sade and the poem which might well astonish. But this de Sadean drama, arguably one of Swinburne's most impressive poems, can help to place the notorious poems of *Poems and Ballads* ('Laus Veneris', 'Dolores'). The multiple tensions of drama – and we remember that early radicals saw drama as *the* democratic form – can clarify the expressive, seemingly monologic lyrics of the following year.

What, then, is this de Sadean drama 'with a difference'? And what is 'the difference' between poet and pornographer? For one thing, the play possesses a chastity and control of diction which Swinburne never quite reached again, a paradoxical control of violence which is equalled by the static, immobilised nature of the drama in a tragedy centrally concerned with what constitutes absolute freedom of action. The myth which is its basis clearly attracted Swinburne because of its punning relation to his own name. Meleager suffers a strange death by remote control when his mother, Althaea, sets alight once more the brand whose burning, the fates have decreed, will bring his life to an end. She is motivated by revenge: Meleager has killed her brothers in a dispute over the spoils from the wild boar (or swine) which Artemis has set upon the land of Calydon. Despite the title, Atalanta's function in the drama is marginal. She makes the first strike at the boar and is offered the spoils which create such discord. She is an alien whose intervention in Calydon helps to create the tragic cycle and is a type of the powerful woman (Althaea, Artemis) who is overdetermined in the play. And perhaps it is precisely because a question mark hangs over the extent to which her actions are a *causal* feature of the play that she is named in the title. Both women, Atalanta and Althaea, are in fact subject to the existence of *tokens*, the burning brand, the spoils of the boar, which, once they enter the structures of society in the institutions of the family and of war, assume a potency and turn out to possess a capacity for setting destruction in motion almost irrespective of the individuals who surround them. They are, ironically, empty signs which nevertheless destroy by virtue of the place they are assigned in a culture. This is why they are seen as and act as fate. And of course, 'fate' depends crucially on gender and the given structure of family relations. Althaea's tragic error is to ignore this and to assume total individual responsibility for revenging the murder of her brothers and to assert total freedom in revenge.

The logic of total freedom turns out to be the logic of violence. Revenge is a form of substitutive transaction in which one *body* is substituted for another, the ultimate manifestation of sterile materiality. It is an enactment of the Sadean fantasy of the completely free agent. Total freedom depends on total possession of the other (here the mother of her son), but total possession logically leads to the power to kill. Such freedom depends on the making of the other into an object. Yet once the other has been objectified and destroyed, it becomes apparent that the identity of the agent actually depends on that of the victim. The mother's body and the son's body, Althaea and Meleager, are incestuously dependent on one another. This syllogism of Sadean violence is evoked to consider the structure of violence in the family, the unit of society which seems most 'natural' even though it may be the most artificial of groups. The insatiable and devouring woman, the *mother* who destroys, is the type of the remorseless, castrating female figure in Swinburne's poetry, for the woman can both destroy and *be* destroyed in a way that the father-figure, epitome of the law, cannot. Althaea's will to control, to be fate, is set contrapuntally against the chorus, who warn of the deterministic universe outside her control. Abdicating from agency, they speak an agent-less, autoverbalising language, which, by the end of the play, has taken them over.

The 'theology' of de Sade sounds most obviously in the chorus, which celebrates the inexorable and 'rational' law of the strong and the principle of cruelty and destruction in a nature indifferent or positively hostile to man – 'Yea, with thine hate, O God, thou hast covered us'. God's hate (he is like Blake's covering angel) operates through the natural violence of sexuality. This is why it can destroy without a sword, and why it converts all things back into the 'ashes' of matter.

> Intolerable, not clad with death or life,
>   Insatiable, not known of night or day,
> The lord of love and loathing and of strife
>   Who gives a star and takes a sun away;
> Who shapes the soul and makes her a barren wife
>   To the earthly body and grievous growth of clay;
> Who turns the large limbs to a little flame
>   And binds the great sea with a little sand;
> Who makes desire, and slays desire with shame;
>   Who shakes the heaven as ashes in his hand;
> Who, seeing the light and shadow for the same,
>   Bids day waste night as fire devours a brand,
> Smites without sword, and scourges without rod;
>   The supreme evil, God.[13]

Man, de Sade says, noted by Simone de Beauvoir in what is still an important essay, is 'the froth, the vapor which rises from the rarefied liquid in a heated vessel. . . . It owes nothing to the element and the element owes nothing to it'.[14] 'Man' is virtually the dispersal of semen in a kind of negative sublime. 'And the high gods took in hand . . . froth and drift of the sea'; 'For an evil blossom was born/Of sea-foam and the frothing of blood'.[15] A spume of Sade's imagery plays in the poem.

'Thou shouldst die. . . . With the brilliance of battle . . . the splendour of spears';[16] OEneus laments that his son did not die in action. Meleager is a passive figure, despite his own zest for the male pursuits of war and action, and despite his parents' insistence on the importance of the male role. Althaea's attempt to control her son's sexuality presages her actions later in the play, as she attempts to deflect him from Atalanta and towards the destruction of the boar. The apotheosis of the will to control is the parents' desire to see the child as its possession. Meleager, consumed by fire, is consumed by the mother because she lives a vicarious life through him – a form of incest. Althaea, constructing her freedom as her son's fate, is the true centre of the play. In the one true *choice* of the play, she imitates the deterministic cruelty of the universe by being fate. 'Fate's are we,/Yet Fate is ours a breathing-space; yea, mine,/Fate is made mine for ever; he is my son,/My bedfellow, my brother'.[17] The de Sadean character validates the freedom of his being in action. He makes himself a criminal, we have seen, in order to avoid *being* evil. For by imitating the outrage of nature with outrage, he will not collude with it in passivity; his object is to force passivity upon his victim. He finds the sensation of freedom and sovereignty in physical sensation itself. Althaea confirms herself as agent through consuming sensation, by burning. As the brand wastes Meleager she experiences its flames. The victim's suffering creates her identity even though it leads to her own destruction. This is the more scandalous because here the Sadean hero is a woman. Althaea insists that Meleager is her 'own' possession and therefore 'mine own wound through mine own flesh'.[18] The torture of her possession confirms her self-hood. The violation of Meleager is expressed as an incestuous rape ('That is my son, my flesh').[19] Both fate and child are son, bedfellow, brother. The child is the mother's fate, inevitably entering into relationships of power. And like the Sadean actants in the drama of sexual power, roles and positions can be changed, varied, interchanged. The mother can take on the 'male' power role. Pre-established ties of mother–son kinship are artificial and conventional; there are no a priori values which establish it. The mother–son relationship is not a 'natural' construct and can just as well be replaced by another. In the same way Althaea *decides* to give priority to her brothers over her son and asserts her sovereignty.

The text questions the 'naturalness' of institutionalised family relationships through Althaea's experience of herself as an agent completely free in action. The first chorus questions *these* questions. It has a double movement, evoking the violence of sexual pursuit and transgression, and yet setting up an opposing drive of inhibition, constraint, hierarchical order. Pleasure principle and death wish vie in its rhythms as it sets up a movement of drive and impediment, libidinal energy and limit. It begins and ends like speeded-up Shelley.

> When the hounds of spring are on winter's traces,. . . .
> The wolf that follows, the fawn that flies.

Spring, hounding out the tracks of winter, pursues a disappearing object, known only by its traces or posthumous signs. On the other hand, the sense of winter's traces as a yoke or constraint in which spring is inevitably leashed to the power of winter, not driving but drawn, reverses the sequence of priority. Spring is arrested, though violently kicking over the traces, transgressing limits. The same reversal or struggle with precedence is present in the allusions to the predominance of one *generation* over another.

> And the brown bright nightingale amorous
> Is half assuaged for Itylus,
> For the Thracian ships and the foreign faces,
> The tongueless vigil, and all the pain.[20]

Itylus was killed to redress the rape of a mother's sister as Meleager is to be killed to redress the death of a mother's brothers – spring caught in winter's traces. Though another counteracting myth is evoked in 'all the pain', with its reference to Milton's 'all *that* pain', powerful Ceres redeeming her daughter from the underworld, it is still one in which a mother is the powerful actant. The chorus is committed to an imagery of a constraining past. Grasses 'trammel', ivy 'catches and cleaves'. And yet if limit can be transgressed action is either thwarted by new boundaries or dissipated and dissolved. The sense of transgression in either case turns out to be illusory. The insistent repetition of the chorus ('lover and lover', 'blossom by blossom' (stanza 4)), and the way in which Swinburne pairs words which are driven towards the condition of homonym ('rains and ruins' (stanza 4)), so that the bounds between words are weakened or their 'traces' broken, move to the elimination of difference and limit into tautology. Language is in a state of dissolve in which one thing can equally well be another. The fetishising concentration on feet/foot (see stanzas 2, 5 and 6) creates a metonymic universe of parts. But since literal and figural are, as it were, on an equal 'footing', distinction collapses.

> Bind on thy sandals, O thou most fleet,
> Over the splendour and speed of thy *feet*;
> For the faint east quickens, the wan west shivers,
> Round the *feet* of the day and the *feet* of the night. (my emphasis)[21]

The same dissolve occurs in the action. Althaea, 'insatiate and intolerant' (80), committing an action above the law, pre-empting the work of nature by being the 'source' and 'end' of her son, experiences supreme self-affirmation in freedom without 'constraints' or 'compelling'. Since her son is her possession she is committing an action upon herself – 'doing right upon myself'. The Sadean character is concerned with his own sovereignty. The other merely confirms his self-identity. The verbs of doing do not take objects.

> For none constrains nor shall rebuke; being done,
> What none compelled me doing; thus these things fare.[22]

For the Sadean character vice is rational because it ends in sensation, orgasm, ejaculation (Simone de Beauvoir describes the Sadean reality principle as orgasm – nature – Reason). Althaea can kill her son in his absence and experience a rapture of selfhood just as the Sadean character reaches orgasm by hearing the cries of tortured victims in another room. Meleager's absolutely alienated death, without *contact*, achieved without sword or rod, is a measure of alienation within the family. The mother can kill because she has violently inscribed her power on the child who is destroyed by it even when she is absent. But the mother as free, emancipated agent nevertheless discovers dependence on an object as his sexuality becomes hers. 'I am swollen with subsiding of his veins,/I am flooded with his ebbing'. Meleager's death is her life. 'What have we *made* each other?' (my emphasis). Sade's freedom turns out to be the opposite of itself – 'I am severed from myself'.[23] Althaea becomes victim as the power relationship reverses. The solution is either death, which Althaea chooses, or a perpetual repetition of the act of transgression, to maintain the sensation of action, the necessity of transcending limits which are pushed ever further beyond reach. For if freedom is constituted by transgression the agent is committed to recreate the receding boundary of limit continually, postponing both the point of dissolve and the point of finitude, for both are death. '*Being* done . . . me *doing*'. The participles here postpone the perfective moment of the act, which would assert the agent's dependence on and relationship with another and declare that his/her being is constituted by other than him/herself. The circle of repetition, tautology, is the only thing which guarantees freedom and yet it is a freedom in which one is *caught*. The more Althaea asserts freedom in power and violence, the more she lives outside the law, the more she is constrained. It is as if she exemplifies the central problem of Swinburne's poetry, the slippage from a poetics of excess and transgression into a circular 'economy', driven by perpetual repetition, the overproduction of the same substitutes for the same thing.

The only escape from the circularity of language is silence, 'my name is gone' (81), Althaea says, and takes a vow of silence forever. The frustrations of language are central to the poem. 'Who hath given man speech?' the central atheistical chorus of *Atalanta* begins.

> Who hath given man speech? or who hath set therein
> A thorn for peril and a snare for sin?
> For in the word his life is and his breath,
>   And in the word his death,
> That madness and the infatuate heart may breed
>   From the word's womb the deed
> And life bring one thing forth ere all pass by,
> Even one thing which is ours and cannot die –
> Death.

Why is both life and death in the word? The chorus returns to reiterate this at its close.

> But ye, keep ye on earth
> Your lips from over-speech,
> Loud words and longing are so little worth;
>   And the end is hard to reach.
> For silence after grievous things is good, . . .
>   For words divide and rend;
>   But silence is most noble till the end.[24]

This seems a strange statement to make in view of the 'over-speech' of Swinburne's verse, the noise, the thunder, the clamour, that it conjures, the sheer sound to which it aspires. But the 'word' contains opposites: 'in the word his life is', 'in the word his death'. The word is life because with its capacity for constant movement and substitution it is perpetually capable of figural expansion. While it transgresses limits, and moves beyond the constituted boundaries of language, it repeatedly postpones limit, keeping language open, refusing closure, as in the libidinal drive of Swinburne's metaleptic series. The aim of the series is to stop words from ending by pushing back limits, to stop them dividing and rending, by refusing them delimitation, circumscriptions, bounds. But words are death (not only because they lead to destructive action) because they are 'deeds', and they *do* close on a signified. Words produce termination because in bringing discourse into being they must finalise meaning. The ever open figural chain is 'destroyed' by the literal, perfective deed of language. The closing on the signified becomes an act of law by which the onward surge of transgression is halted. The alternative to silence or the abnegation of poetry altogether is the 'fuzz' of material sound, the sustaining of a series of signifiers deprived as far as possible of the process of signification, the desire for language not to signify, the assent to the tautologous.

The metaleptic chain is Swinburne's habitual trope. It lends itself both to an inexorable continuity of substitution and to disorganisation simply because the substitutions are not exchanges so much as arbitrary replacements of one thing by another.

415

> Before the beginning of years
>> There came to the making of man
> Time, with a gift of tears;
>> Grief, with a glass that ran;
> Pleasure, with pain for leaven;
>> Summer, with flowers that fell;
> Remembrance fallen from heaven,
>> And madness risen from hell;
> Strength without hands to smite;
>> Love that endures for a breath:
> Night, the shadow of light,
>> And life, the shadow of death.[25]

By definition the beginning of years is the origin of temporality and yet time is anterior to the beginning of years here. If life is the shadow, the secondary copy of death, and death, the product of the temporal, predates the beginning of temporality, then there is no beginning, no primal condition, and no ending, but a continual repetition. The attributes of time, grief, pleasure, summer, remembrance are reversible and circular. Time's gift of tears is grief's glass that ran. Remembrance fallen from heaven is summer's flowers that fell, for remembrance depends upon the fall into temporality and yet lives on the ending of things. Remembrance's fall from heaven is the rise of madness from hell, for the mixing and interpenetration of categories and attributes which is remembrance is a confusion in which things surrender their limits, the point of dissolve, energy without power – 'strength without hands to smite'. The passage works through a chain of metalepsis, a chain of substitution which is itself used figuratively. Logically there is no terminal point to this process, in which one attribute is handed on to another, and in this strophe death, the end, predates the beginning. The unending figural process both declares the possibility of the transgression of limits, and yet, by its continuous figural activity, postpones the moment of terminus and limit, pushing it beyond reach with every new occurrence of substitution and enabling continual repetition of the process.

The 'difference' between his poem and de Sade which Swinburne insisted upon is important in a reading of the poem. It is a critique of bourgeois institutions and categories of gender according to Sadean paradigms which makes these things scandalous. Scandalous, but more than that, full of tragic suffering. Swinburne puts in what de Sade leaves out, the impossibility and horror of the Sadean world, precursor of the Victorian world. Algolagniac experience also finds a place for women, which de Sade does not. It would be precipitate to see in Swinburne's fascinated horror of feminine power and the mother's body an uncomplicated misogynistic violence. If the linked bodies of mother and son are the occasion for torture they are also portrayed in pitiable suffering. Althaea is not quite Pater's sinisterly powerful woman.

Atalanta in Calydon is a microcosm of Swinburne's poetry and that is why it is important to dwell on it. Arguably he produced nothing new after this but continued to reinvent further replicas of *Atalanta*. If we see the language of *Atalanta* as the language of capital, a psychocultural description of this language becomes possible. One can either continually reinvent transgression and aberrancy or find a way of flogging words into transcendence. The search for the aberrant logically produces the endless poem, while the search for transcendence, for that 'harmony' of religious symbol aestheticised, where 'spirit and sense' are fused in 'splendour of sounds and glory of colours', logically produces *only* sound. These two impossibilities, and the contradiction between the aberrant and the transcendent produce the thematics of Swinburne's later writing.

The later writing, founded on impossibility, discloses the furious carnal desperation and the – not quite convincing – blasphemy of *Poems and Ballads*. Swinburne liked to think of himself as an English Baudelaire, responding to the poetry of 'strange disease and sin', 'lurid beauty' and 'dangerous hot-house scents'.[26] But his work lacks the concentration and intensity of *Les Fleurs du Mal*. And perhaps the problem of the poetry of blasphemy in Victorian England was that its muddled humanistic and ethical society managed to produce outrages, like that of Eyre, which exceeded Swinburne's own. Nevertheless, his agonistic violence probes more deeply than the work of his successors in the aesthetic movement and the decadence whose language he shaped – Lionel Johnson, Ernest Dowson, Oscar Wilde. Only Wilde, whose first-hand experience of institutional violence made him see that bourgeois society was bizarrely symbiotic with the violence it condemned, can equal the shock of Swinburne's poetry, and it is the shock of moral anguish rather than blasphemy. Here the dancing feet of the hanged man in *The Ballad of Reading Gaol* are juxtaposed with the society ball.

> It is sweet to dance to violins
>   When Love and Life are fair:
> To dance to flutes, to dance to lutes
>   Is delicate and rare:
> But it is not sweet with nimble feet
> To dance upon the air![27]

Though Swinburne claimed for his poetry of excess the dignity of moral analysis, seeing the poetry of outrage as a moral need, he never *moralised* its nature or gave expression to moral feeling. Its ethical importance for him was in its analysis of contradiction. His transgression is impervious to conventional morality. That is its point. But both Lionel Johnson and Ernest Dowson, the one more timorously morbid and the other more

417

timorously sentimental, forgot Swinburne's dictum that the didactic does not belong to poetry. Dowson infuses the sense of self-debasement with nostalgia in 'Non sum qualis eram bonas sub regno Cynarae' (1896). The 'bought red lips' and loss of selfhood in ecstatic vice do not repress the sickness of 'an old passion'. The refrain, 'I have been faithful to thee, Cynara! in my fashion', buys off immorality with guilt.[28] Johnson's 'The Dark Angel' (1893), a far stronger poem, normalises Swinburnian transgression with despair, reintroducing the Christian dualism of good and evil which Swinburne sought to dissolve:

> Dark Angel, with thine aching lust!
> Of two defeats, of two despairs:
> Less dread, a change to drifting dust,
> Than thine eternity of cares.[29]

More prolix (for the Swinburnian poem cannot end), the affirmation through negation less concentrated, *Poems and Ballads* nevertheless makes some important experiments. The realignment, the recalibration so to speak, of vice and virtue, freedom and oppression, male and female, homosexual, heterosexual, and the questioning of these oppositions, was a unique project in the poetry of the late 1860s and 1870s.

Despite the expressive prolixity of the poetry of sensation, the poems possess a genuine dialectic. Swinburne himself, as we have seen, pointed to the structural problem being explored in 'Laus Veneris', the movement between the two equally unsatisfying poles of Eros and Christ. He could also have pointed to another equally important and paradoxical opposition in 'Dolores'. This poem realigns the Christian opposites of erotic experience and Christian war so that war is deeply sexualised. The sadistic passions around the worship and fetishisation of the woman as pain and cruelty expose the aggression behind Mariolatry. In all forms of goddess cult, and the apotheosis of the feminine, gladiators 'grow pale for thy pleasure' (stanza 31), as society is mutilated by its own masochism. In 'Laus Veneris' the same equation is made.

> Ah, with blind lips I felt for you, and found
> About my neck your hands and hair enwound,
>   The hands that stifle and the hair that stings,
> I felt them fasten, sharply without sound.
>
> Yea, for my sin I had great store of bliss
> Rise up, make answer for me, let thy kiss
>   Seal my lips hard from speaking of my sin,
> Lest one go mad to hear how sweet it is.[30]

As in *Atalanta*, the real political centre of *Poems and Ballads* is in the poetry of *desire*, the consuming, exhausting desire, which needs to be ever stimulated and ever expanded. It is kind of sexual hegemony, ever seeking new objects, ever striving to maintain and energise itself. As such it points to the exhaustion which haunts hegemonic power and its strain.

The Sapphic song, 'Anactoria', 'The Triumph of Time' and 'Dolores' all deal with the paradox that the more immediate and violent sensation is, the more the need to sustain it, the more it recedes into memory and desire, the less the unity of 'body and soul'. Sappho's passion is only vindicated because it will become memories and metaphors. The music of 'The Triumph of Time' comes 'face to face with its own desire' rather than the object. In 'Dolores' the association of femininity and pain produces further fantasies of pain. The bloody kisses, the shudder and smart of sensation which seem to exchange 'the lilies and languors of virtue' for the 'raptures and roses of vice' actually pale as the self has to *imagine* some 'new sin' or 'dream of impossible wrongs'. Sensation crosses over to its opposite, the empty contentless dream. The blasphemies here do not reaffirm what they negate but indicate an absence, a gap. Violence and emptiness are part of a dialectical movement. This insight into the structure of violence is commensurate with the exhaustion one feels near to the surface of the poetry despite, or perhaps because of, its intensity. It fears sterility. In 'Hermaphroditus' the wavering transpositions of gender produced one poem unusually subdued and subtle for Swinburne. It is concerned not so much with transgression but with the dialectical interdependence of the sexes, which might be dissolved by sterile androgyny.

> Turning the fruitful feud of hers and his
> To the waste wedlock of a sterile kiss[31]

The subdued emptiness and exhaustion of 'The Garden of Proserpine' suggest the cost of blasphemy against a society which did not seem to hold affirmation strongly enough to enable blasphemy to be effective, a society where there were conventions and constraints, but not beliefs. The effort of blasphemy exhausts Swinburne's poetry, not, ultimately, because transgression is exhausting, but because the excess of the poetry is forever in *competition* with the excesses of an economic and political system which can always outdo the poet in its violence. The effort of maintaining a position which does not collude with this violence, the energy required to prevent the verse from collapsing back into exactly the same terms as the system it attempts to subvert; this almost single-handed effort on Swinburne's part produced a strain only rivalled in the work of Hopkins.

14

HOPKINS: AGONISTIC REACTIONARY

The Grotesque as conservative form

There would be no bridge, no stem of stress between us and things to bear us out and carry the mind over: without stress we might not and could not say/Blood is red/but only/This blood is red/or/The last blood I saw was red/not even that, for in later language not only universals would not be true but the copula would break down even in particular judgments.

(Hopkins, 'Parmenides', *Journal and Papers*, 9 February 1868)[1]

These journal notes, typically condensed and elliptical, suggest how Hopkins, Catholic convert and anti-democrat, was both a revolutionary and a reactionary poet. To begin with these complexities is to see the paradoxes of his mind at work. Highly theoretical, yet developing an idiosyncratic and self-made vocabulary which is concrete and substantive, this passage moves rapidly from epistemology to language. Hopkins is wrestling with a perennial nineteenth-century problem, the relationship between subject and object and the representation of this relationship, or, as he puts it, the relationship between 'us and things'. But the innovative move is that this is expressed in terms of *linguistic* relations. His is an ontology of grammar. The relationship of representation to things is expressed in terms of the word, the relationships of subject and object in terms of syntax. He was the first poet to develop a poetics out of a theory of the structure of language, and strangely, this rigorously modernist procedure – structuralism before its time – came about because he was the last poet to hold a strictly theological account of the logos, the authority of the Word made flesh through the incarnation of Christ. The strain of holding these two things together, and of making them compatible, marks the passionate torsions and desperate ecstasies of his work.

The notes on Parmenides of 1868, a fragment from various writings on language at that time, are implicitly an attempt to solve some of the problems Hopkins had recently met as an undergraduate at Oxford, where he had been taught both by Walter Pater and by the Hegelian, T. H.

Green.[2] He was profoundly unsympathetic to the cold, detached (but avid) seeking for the Epicurean moment in Pater's thought. It represented for him the disintegration of an unstable 'philosophy of continuity or flux' which he identified as peculiarly modern.[3] It signified for him the dispersal of the relationship between subject and object, the eradication of the 'fixed points' which guaranteed an ordered and politically and socially hierarchical world and the eradication of memory, the faculty which constitutes the subject's identity and ensures its continuity. For him Pater's belief that the infinitely divisible moment could be experienced as an evanescent fusion of form and content actually ensured the collapse of that unity by conceiving it in terms of dualism. The philosophy of flux, moreover, had political implications for him. Its understanding of atomism was essentially materialist, and it produced not only the refined élitist purism which values the moment of sensation as a form of aristocratic aesthetic distinction, but also the drift towards democracy. For democracy, obliterating the uniqueness of individuals by *quantifying* them as equal units in a calculus of the greatest happiness of the greatest number, was the ideological form of the philosophy of flux.

In modern culture, personal morality, he wrote in 1867, has come to seem not 'the same as political morality, and the failure of insight of which this fallacy is an instance [the separation of personal and political morality] is being made by the Empirical and Utilitarian schools to overrun the whole field of thought'.[4] A rational account of happiness is merely a materialist account of comfort and amusement for the masses and leads directly to cultural decadence. He instanced the spread of huge public shows – circuses and theatres and pleasure gardens – as an example of the declining political morality of the Roman empire comparable with that of the British empire. Hopkins's politics were naive – the fear of being 'overrun' by democratic ideas is a deeply emotional one – but they are an important and often overlooked formative element in his poetics. He wrote with repugnance of Swinburne's obsession with flesh and flowers, democracy and damnation, though he admired his 'astonishing' genius.[5] For him Swinburne would have been what he called a 'chromatic' figure both ideologically and linguistically. This musical metaphor designated undifferentiated flux, as opposed to the sharp distinctions of the 'diatonic' scale in Hopkins' unique aesthetic terminology. Swinburne's capacity to generate a poetry of aural sound, where repetition merges each lexical item with the next, and fends off the process of signification almost indefinitely, would be a materialist poetry of meaningless relationship for Hopkins, where the language of flux would be inseparable from a politics of flux. It is interesting that Hopkins's 'Ad Mariam' imitates the structure of the choruses in Swinburne's *Atalanta*, contradicting the nihilistic hymn to Aphrodite by exchanging her for Mary. This suggests a Hopkins protecting himself against Swinburne.

421

For Hopkins much hangs on the condensed exegesis of Parmenides. How is the flux of impressions to be stabilised? And how is a world of permanent relationships and categories to be guaranteed? 'The copula would break down even in particular judgments': at issue is the breakdown of syntax. The fundamental importance of the verb 'to be', which allows us to say that 'things and us' *are*, to establish relationships and connections and to predicate the world of being, is at stake in the philosophy of flux and atomisation.

Though Hopkins associated the epistemology of flux with democracy, Darwinian evolutionary ideas and Hegelian accounts of process, the thought of the Oxford Hegelian, T. H. Green, as will later be seen in more detail, is behind the notes on Parmenides. Green mounted a systematic attack on the contradictions of Hume's philosophy of mind, from which Pater's thought is derived, and Hopkins shared with him the project of arresting the ever vanishing flight of impressions, but he invented a terminology all his own. If we conceive of mind as a flux of impressions, it would only be possible to experience a life of discrete and particular instances: 'this blood is red', a new naming with each instance of seeing blood, would have to occur, for it would be impossible to generalise the colour red as a universal attribute of blood – 'Blood is red'. As he writes – and the writing process actually demonstrates the collapse of perception – Hopkins corrects himself, realising that it would not even be possible to say that 'the last blood I saw was red' because there would be no means of relating one instance of seeing blood to a previous instance, and thus logically there would not only be no means of conceptualising colour but also the concept 'blood' as a universal category would collapse. If we could not say 'blood *is*', then language collapses too. The pressure of Hopkins' intellectual excitement is a manifestation of the solution he sees to this problem, 'stress'. 'The truth in thought is Being, stress, and each word is one way of acknowledging Being'.

Stress, Being, gives the subject a predicate. Stress provides the leap between past and present, self and world, by carrying over the force of perception in memory. Stress provides the connectedness which flux dissolves. Stress retrieves each item of perception and each object of perception from a unique self-contained totality and separateness. 'Being cannot break off Being from its hold on Being', he wrote, in the same essay on Parmenides. Being is not discontinuous, Hopkins is saying, but Being grasps Being with Being. Why is the word 'stress' so important to him? Stress implies physical pressure and force. At the same time it cannot be materialised. It thus brings together and fuses the material and the non-material, spirit and sense, form and matter, and it brings them together *dynamically*. Like a charge of electricity (Hopkins was to write of the world being 'charged' with the grandeur of God) stress is at once and instantaneously the bridge we leap across and the leap itself. That is why it 'bears us out', simultaneously *carries* us and constitutes and confirms us. The purposive current rather than the discontinuous flux has other associations. It is related to aesthetic form, for it also means stress as accent, metre, the formative emphasis of rhythm. (Hence, perhaps, Hopkins's enduring fascination with metrical experiment.) Not only do metre and rhythm through repetition create pattern, relationship, parallelism, but the stress of an accent is not something that can be abstracted from the words it gives form to. The word and the stress cannot exist independently of one another. Later, typically taking risks with the Heraclitean idea, Hopkins said that metre was a channel through which different words flow. A channel both carries water and is made by it. Stress also bears another meaning which is inherent in Hopkins's work: stress as anxiety, as strain, as desire, as the sense of lack. For Hopkins's solution to the gap between 'us and things' acknowledges the breaks and discontinuities he sought to assuage. It is founded on an isolated subjectivity and an isolated world and thus every solution to the problem reintroduces it. The copula is always threatening to break down in his poetry.

Hopkins seemed to need to choose the most difficult cases with which to refute the philosophy of flux. Where Pater had seen all art as aspiring to music, Hopkins did not replace the metaphor, but attempted to wrest it from undifferentiated experience by enunciating his distinction between the chromatic and the diatonic. Similarly, he replaced Pater's solution to dualism with a solution to dualism all his own. Disliking the idealism of Hegelianism, and its to him Heraclitean propensities, he nevertheless made use of the Hegelian thinking of Green. In his diaries and notebooks he meditates continually on that most difficult of all attributes to describe and define – colour, and particularly the colour of skies. It is as if the colour of skies is a test case against that melting and merging evanescence which cannot guarantee us *shared* stable categories and thus consciousness and Being.

> The blue of the sky was very good. A web of the thinnest lacy cloud near the sun had films of colour chiefly rose (pale) and greenish blue in broad bars caught on its tissue.[6]

Here the colour is part of the structure of clouds, the structure indivisible from colour. The broad bars of rose and greenish blue are 'caught' in the cloud's tissue, and tissue here is something woven as a texture and something like the tissue of skin. It is interesting that Hume's understanding of colour is contested by T. H. Green, and his argument here is an exemplum of his way of showing that Hume's epistemology of 'decaying sense' (adapted from Hobbes) collapses through its inner contradictions. How can qualities of an object, such as colour, he asks, be perceived, when 'objects' for Hume are only a succession of disappearing impressions? Hume has to argue that qualities such as smell, taste and colour are contemporaneous with the impression of the object. Yet on his own showing a 'total impression' is impossible: 'How can feelings successive to each other be yet co-existent qualities?' If they are successive, as Hume's logic compels him to argue, then perception breaks down, for 'Must not the two feelings [of the object and its colour] be successive, however closely successive, so that the one which is object will have disappeared before the other, which is to be its quality, will have occurred?'[7] Such a fragmentation is impossible. The copula, as Hopkins put it, would break down. The connection between object and attributes turns out to have vanished.

Green insists that without the synthesis of the total impression the element of comparison essential to perception would vanish:[8] memory, which is 'wholly different' from the return of perishing feelings, as Hume would have it, would be impossible. Memory does not depend on 'a world whose existence' simply depends 'on its being remembered'.[9] The presence of a thinking subject and a world which is 'one throughout its changes' (God, Hopkins was to write in 'Pied Beauty', is 'past change') and the necessity of a 'conceiving, as distinct from a feeling, subject' arises from the fact that an object exists in a 'system of its relations' and not as a sequence of impressions.[10] For relations have a permanent, *structural* and morphological existence. We can presuppose a structure from its parts, carry over or predicate a whole, produce, effectively, a coherent syntax. And this requires an assent to the permanence of the 'combining and comparing thought which alone constitutes it'.[11] It is in this non-reversible process (for we cannot infer its attributes from a whole) that Green sees both God and the soul. A personal God or a personal identity is irrelevant to him. That which can evolve out of itself the syntax which constitutes an interdependent set of permanent relations is 'eternal, self-determined, and thinks'.[12] We might call this 'stress'. Both for Green and for Hopkins God is very nearly grammar, or at least a grammarian. In a very real sense Hopkins would have concurred with Nietzsche's aphorism that to get rid of grammar would be to get rid of God, except that he hoped this was impossible. Here there is some continuity between his work and that of Tennyson.

Hopkins's early poems in particular aspire to a holistic grammar which synthesises discrete elements into a whole, a series of little wholes which form a system of relations with one another. These are not the atomised units, the discrete links in a chain, which for Mansel constituted experience. 'Pied Beauty' is organised round the copula, the verb 'to be': 'Glory be to God for dappled things'.[13] Glory is both something offered to God and something God *is*. The fecund list of dappled things which stem appositionally out of the particle 'for' – 'For skies', 'For rose-moles' – are particular attributes both of the glory offered to Him and of God Himself. The last four lines of the poem, which begin a new sentence, appear to be similarly appositional attributes. But they are actually gathered up as the predicate of the God who 'fathers-forth' in the last line, and the subject, God, ends the poem. God is presupposed from the predicate which precedes the main verb, from His parts and attributes. The predicate *is* His 'beauty'. Not merely the variety of dappled things is to be derived from God but a structure which constitutes beauty itself.

> Glory be to God for dappled things –
>> For skies of couple-colour as a brinded cow;
>>> For rose-moles all in stipple upon trout that swim;
>> Fresh-firecoal chestnut-falls; finches' wings;
>>> Landscape plotted and pieced – fold, fallow, and plough;
>>> And áll trádes, their gear and tackle and trim.
>
> All things counter, original, spare, strange;
>> Whatever is fickle, freckled (who knows how?)
>> With swift, slow; sweet, sour; adazzle, dim;
> He fathers-forth whose beauty is past change:
>>>>> Praise him.

But there is more to be said about 'Pied Beauty'. It would be misleading to see a complete consonance between Hopkins and Green reflected unproblematically in the poem. For one thing, Hopkins's God *is* a personal God, and he was deeply concerned with personal identity. His world of 'fixed points' and categories is not only a world of structure but also a world of hierarchy. His 'mastering me/God' is the ultimate authority for structure and unity just as He is the ultimate authority for language and 'fathers-forth' His power with a masculine energy which can be disturbingly violent. 'The Mastery of the thing' in 'The Windhover' is a dangerous and violent mastery, particularly as Hopkins's 'fixed points' must mean the fixity of gender and gender roles. Indeed, in constructing a wholly new poetic language and a wholly new poetics which grounds experience in language, Hopkins drew eclectically and exuberantly on a number of ideas and explored possibilities which were potentially if not actually contradictory. The earlier poems result from a synthesis of different accounts of language and just hold these together, though not without strain. The possibilities he saw in Müller, Duns Scotus and Ruskin jostle in his journals. Moreover, at about the time he wrote on Parmenides he explored an account of language in some succinct *Notes* (1868) which contain in fact two different and opposing accounts of the word. Just reconciled in the earlier work, these disparate possibilities fracture the later poems, particularly the sonnets which have come to be called the terrible sonnets. These later poems will be considered shortly. Meanwhile the plenitude of Hopkins's theoretical and poetic experiments can be further disclosed by returning to 'Pied Beauty'.

Always alert to the structure which constitutes beauty itself, Hopkins's journals record the 'laws' by which the puckering of the surface of milk as it comes to the boil finds its shape, the geometrical form embodied in the 'great elliptic-curve oaks' (*Journals*, 23) (the curve *is* elliptic and *is* a curve indivisibly, the compound asserts), or the architectural 'horizontal ribs' of clouds, the evanescent arrested by form, with an intensity which is of the same nature in 'Pied Beauty'. The poem attempts to leap the gap between unlike things, establishing relationship while expressing and preserving difference. Rhyme, metre and above all parallelism, are ways of establishing that structure which can be *anticipated* and confirmed by reference to a part. In the early dialogue on Beauty parallelism is not simply pattern but a way of expressing an infinite series of relationships of similarity and dissimilarity (as it is in the essay on poetic diction, 1865), as what Coleridge would have termed 'multeity in unity' is defined in formal terms. In the plenitude of 'dappled things' in 'Pied Beauty', despite the insistent parallelism of alliteration and rhyme, the world seems to be breaking down into a discontinuous, dappled series of discrete objects and attributes without a principle of unity. It is 'spare' (unique, like something left over, the exception), 'fickle' (inconsistent) and 'freckled', full of variety. And yet it is a world unified 'past change' because it is precisely the dissimilarity, dappledness, stippledness, piecedness, precisely a relationship of difference, which is the source of relationship. It 'couples' things, not by consisting of mere variety and contrast but by *constituting* relationships. 'Couple-colour', significantly leaping the gap between noun and adjective by being compounded and almost allowing 'couple' to act as a verb, means not only *two colours*, disjunct parts side by side, but *coupled or coupling colour*, acting as copula, establishing Being or stress, and moving to that structure which we can conceptualise through difference.

So far the poem seems unthreatened by problems. Perhaps a hint of trouble can be seen in the fact that this celebration of difference can operate best through the pastoral or the rural. The 'trades' with their differentiated skills are apparently rural trades, that world which Hopkins himself admitted was becoming obsolete and forgotten: it is 'spare', left over, the exception. The knowledge which presupposes the whole from the parts rather than simply aggregating parts, he said in his essay on political morality, is the now obsolete knowledge belonging to the 'science' of shepherds and graziers and hunters, 'when they gave names to the success-ive years of the stag – brocket, pricket, and the rest'.[14] The poem arrests us in a lost history and social order to demonstrate the lost understanding of relation through difference, a history where individuals were defined through their uniqueness, and the uniqueness of their language, and not in terms of an aggregation of parts. It seems that we *need* an undemocratic social order to understand true uniqueness and true form and the unique-ness of language. It also suggests that 'couple-colour', the compound acting as a verb or copula, with its intimation of sexual union and copulation, a

426

world coupling in an infinite series of ordered marital unions, can only occur in a world of fixed gender relations. The strictness of this position is particularly striking when one remembers Hopkins's own sexual longing for his male friends.

The problem with this stress on uniqueness, however, is that it can resolve back into atomism again, and does not necessarily guarantee that all experience can be subsumed under a unifying structure. For dapple and stipple *are* discontinuous and there is no immediate reason why the rose-moles on the swimming trout and the 'Fresh-firecoal chestnut-falls' should be subsumed under one category. Words and things, Hopkins thought, have an 'inscape', an in-shape, an inherently individuating form which can itself be inscaped. In the thinking of Duns Scotus, the logos, the Word made flesh through the authority of the Incarnation, is penetrated by the unique form which gives it its identity and individuality. Form penetrates matter enabling what Scotus thought of as the 'thisness' of things and repudiating a world which is simply a mass of phenomena and heterogeneous difference. But there are ways in which 'inscape' works directly against 'stress', and not with it. Hopkins's exploration of language in his notes of 1868 concentrate on the individuating nature of the word, a discrete item or sign. He was anxious to avoid dualism and concluded that the 'deeper the form penetrates, [the more] the prepossession [the unique particularising attribute] flushes the matter'.[15] 'Flushes', part-colour part-motion (a colour-word recuperated from Hume for a non-Humean epistemology), integrally fused with what it colours, is typical of his aesthetic nomenclature, a concrete, individuating and non-abstract term. But the more the unmediated unity and uniqueness of the word are emphasised the more it resists incorporation into a larger synthesis, the more it becomes 'spare'.

Hopkins seems to yearn for a primitive condition which he knows to be fallacious – that words might be so individuated and concrete that they will be closely related to the things they represent in almost unmediated unity with them. If they cannot do this they will possess the quality of the things themselves, having a physicality, substantiveness and materiality which almost turns them into solids. Hopkins's early preference for an onomatopoetic account of language in which the sounds of words participate in the things which originate them is related to this desire.[16] The notes on language recognise that the unique attributes and associations of a word, which he calls a 'prepossession', or form, because in his view connotation actually gives a word its individuating structure, not its abstract meaning, might actually be thought of as a 'soul'. But he abandons this idea, though with regret, because 'all names but proper names are general while the soul is individual'.[17] Language deals in categories and universals, which means that it would be impossible – and mad – to have a unique word for every thing or concept in the world.

427

Even though he abandoned it, we can see how this atavistic strain in Hopkins's thought shapes both his theory and his poetry and makes it linguistically a throng of highly individuated particularities, straining against the cohesive predications which achieve structural wholeness. He searches for the least abstract and most physically immediate word so that it becomes solidified into sensuous being, behaving as what it designates: 'spare' for exceptional, 'fickle' for inconsistent, wayward. Each compound is a little totality, a self-contained, newly individuated prepossessional structure which drives away syntax and process and arrests each new verbal unit in an unmediated and non-transitional form, dynamic but curiously immobilised. 'Rose-moles', for instance, are not moles like roses or even rose-coloured moles, but moles fused or 'flushed' with the colour of the rose, participating in its attributes and thus creating a wholly new prepossession. Indeed, they are 'Having-rose' or 'having-risen' moles, moles which have become a growth on the surface of skin in the form of a rosette. They have flowered, and are all these things indivisibly – colour, action, form, shape.

It is striking that the formations in this poem resemble Hopkins's *Journal* by evolving lists of related series of words, words, he thought, related by their roots. Rose-moles could be part of a series rose, arose, rosette. 'Fickle, freckled' resembles the ingenious series 'Flick, fillip, flip, fleck, flake'.[18] From each word Hopkins attempts to extract a metaphorical meaning bound intrinsically to the morphological root of the word but unique to every form or variation of it, inscaping the different forms of the root. It is the relation of metaphor to morphological form which could theoretically ground the prolific individuation of Hopkins's vocabulary in permanent form, and solve the problem of structure. Müller had said that the roots of words generate metaphorical and abstract meanings alike, but Hopkins's fascination with roots is much more a fascination with the particularities of metaphor, than with morphology. Metaphor drives together disparate categories and creates new meaning by affirming an absolute equation and identity through the copula – rose is mole, mole is rose. A new *internal* and simultaneous structure of relationship is created intrinsic to each verbal unit, but this tends to emphasise particularity and its very simultaneity tends to isolate each metaphorical cluster from another.

What Hopkins took from Müller in fact tends to loosen language's hold on structural relations. It was the sense of plenitude and superfluity in language, of ever-created meanings which constantly broke the smooth uniformity of civilised, polished, language, the language Pater respected. Though Hopkins would have rejected Müller's belief that dialect is democratic, thrusting up revolutionary change from below, he would have respected Müller's belief in the 'brotherhood' created by linguistic roots and the energy and vitality which prevents language from atrophying. He would have respected, too, Müller's understanding that living language is

428

the language of speech rather than the conventional written language, for living speech in its immediacy and uniqueness comes closest to the inscape of the word and its concrete being. Hence Müller's lack of sympathy for purism and correctness is something for which he also felt affinity. The primitive metaphorical language of the child and its instinctive feeling for new orderings of language in speech ('bad', 'baddest', Müller pointed out, is actually the more 'correct' form however idiosyncratic) are reflected in his own usage. He was fascinated by *difference*: his journals record some notes on the language of the tribes around Lake Nyanza, for instance, and a language system based on euphony.[19] The series 'Swift, slow; sweet, sour; adazzle, dim' may not be nouns, adjectives or adverbs, but they are consistent within themselves and, by sinking the adjectival form into the noun, create that living concreteness in uniqueness which Hopkins valued so highly. The spoken word guarantees a presence, an immediacy of utterance which minimises the gap between speaker and listener and foregrounds the specificity of every statement. When using 'current language heightened' he aims not for a mimesis of speech but for an inscape of its improvised, living structure. Exclamations, imperatives and interrogatives break into his condensed and often incomplete sentences. The sudden interruptions and changes between sentence types, the paratactic, coordinative grammar, the elliptical compression and embedding of clauses, are all ways of creating the structure of living speech and from which we can infer a syntactic order from the unfinished grammatical forms. The disparate and often incompatible dialect – slang, archaism, neologising compounds – which coexist in his work are for him permissible because they are all ways of producing, in their arresting oddness, the distinctiveness of inscaped speech. They also manifest the synchronic nature of speech, which holds within itself a huge range of forms and expressions belonging to different historical moments.

Hopkins knew that it is the vice of distinctiveness to become queer, or 'odd', his most frequent expression in the long argument with Bridges about the obscurity of his poems.[20] Though what is queer carries its unique inscape its very uniqueness prevents it from being inscaped or stressed into a larger relation. It is almost as if Hopkins challenges Müller's understanding that the 'caprice' of a poet alone cannot invent new words and forms by offering up the caprices of his neologism and new constructions as a form of that unique agency in language-making which Müller deemed impossible, asserting the power of the individual subject to create. Oddly enough it is this which makes his own poetic language come near to the very aspects of language which he rejected so strongly. For when distinctiveness becomes queer it disengages itself not only from structure but also, as Mansel recognised, from its links with a corresponding conception. It establishes its anarchic and self-referential forms which lose contact with existing things in the world. Not only does Hopkins's language come to the verge of collapsing into discrete entities: it also risks nonsense by inventing metaphorical forms so tenuously related to an originary meaning that they push comprehension to the limit. 'Spare' and 'fickle' would be examples from 'Pied Beauty', for they cannot easily exclude their conventional associations (economical, unfaithful), and the effort to create new ones is almost an act of will. Paradoxically, one is back with Humpty Dumpty's assertion: it all depends who's master-poet. In Hopkins's work the language celebrating God's mastery often cuts across a cultural agreement about meaning.

The curiously coercive nature of Hopkins's vocabulary discloses the paradox of his revolutionary language – or perhaps one should say, the paradox of his conservative language. His desire to individuate words (to dispense with synonym in Müller's terms) and to form the exact, the 'proper' meaning, so that the word is as close as possible to the thing it represents, actually has the consequence of dislodging the referent. Theoretically the exact inscaping of words solves the problem of freedom and necessity raised by both Müller and Green by individuating a word's uniqueness at the same time as demonstrating the necessity of a particular form. But in practice the attempt to treat the word as if it were the thing it represents has the effect of detaching it from reference as the idiosyncratic substitution (for instance, 'spare' for 'exceptional') is made. It is as if the substitutive nature of language intervenes at the very moment when the word appears to be in identity with the thing – the blank banknote or abstract algebraic sign, which is Mansel's metaphor for the arbitrary signification of language and its unfixed value, asserts itself. And so the 'fixed points' of Hopkins's language enter an ungrounded economy of signification in spite of his attempt to refuse this abstraction and flux. The word/thing relationship, a kind of use value of language, actually creates the conditions of ungrounded exchange value and 'flux' of meaning.

The notes on language actually recognise this possibility, for the second account of language explored in them is that of the arbitrary sign. In this account of language the concept is not intrinsically related to the sound of the word, and the sign is not intrinsically related to the thing.

As the notes proceed the first account of language is implicitly abandoned and replaced by an account of the sign as an auditory unit indissolubly linked to a 'conception'. Only one thing 'in propriety is the word', its 'vocal expression' (that is, aural sound), and its 'definition' (that is, the concept called up by the sound).[21] It is this that has made people think of Hopkins as the precursor of Saussurean linguistics. More immediately the consequences for Hopkins are that he was torn between a primitive account of language asserting the primordial relation between word and thing, the prepossession inscaping the word, and one which asserts the independence of the sign and the chasm of irredeemable difference between language and things in the extra-linguistic world. Here the inscape lies in the particularities of sound which call for the concept – 'a word to oneself, an inchoate word', as he puts it.[22] Thus the cry about the nun's utterance in stanza 25 of *The Wreck of the Deutschland*, 'What did she mean?', is no rhetorical question, but raises different problems and different kinds of interpretation according to the account of language being accepted. The first directs attention to the subject of her utterance, the second, much more troubling, to the problematical nature of meaning itself. The earlier poems rest implicitly on the first account of language, but after *The Wreck of the Deutschland* and in the later terrible sonnets, it is the arbitrary nature of language which preoccupies Hopkins.

'Hurrahing in the Harvest' is a poem which manages to hold together disparate accounts of language by invoking 'stress', to redress the potential 'queer'-ness of inscape. It has two projects, to leap the gap between us and things and to leap the gap between us and God, to 'glean our Saviour'. To 'glean' God, to understand Him in gestalt-like synthesis by gathering parts as we gather the leavings after harvest, and to find evidence of Him precisely in the physical remains of the material world, turns out to be identical with bridging, or eliminating, the gap between us and things. Hence the self or heart 'hurls for him', reflexively throws itself towards or aims itself at God. In the repetition 'hurls' moves from an intransitive to a transitive moment – hurls 'earth' (matter, *incarnate* with 'heart' or spirit) and, indeed, appears to sweep God off his feet in the violent power of love. Words such as 'glean' and 'hurl' are typical of the concrete inscaping of metaphor and the kinaesthetic movement created by the copula.

For this poem is a consummation, a mutual identifying of God and self or 'heart': its three sections construct a bridge in which the middle quatrain becomes the 'stem of stress' fusing 'us and things, us and God'.

> Summer ends now; now, barbarous in beauty, the stooks rise
> Around; up above, what wind-walks! what lovely behaviour
> Of silk-sack clouds! has wilder, wilful-wavier
> Meal-drift moulded ever and melted across skies?
>
> I walk, I lift up, I lift up heart, eyes,
> Down all that glory in the heavens to glean our Saviour;
> And, éyes, heárt, what looks, what lips yet gave you a
> Rapturous love's greeting of realer, of rounder replies?
>
> And the azurous hung hills are his world-wielding shoulder
> Majestic – as a stallion stalwart, very-violet-sweet! –
> These things, these things were here and but the beholder
> Wanting; which two when they once meet,
> The heart rears wings bold and bolder
> And hurls for him, O half hurls earth for him off under his feet.

The presence of 'fixed points' makes the necessity of 'Saltus' or leaps between one thing and another correspondingly more pressing. But the existence of fixity paradoxically endangers the possibility of saying 'it is' and threatens the breakdown of the copula. To leap the gap, to 'greet' or to 'catch' (both favourite verbs) experience in a moment of totality and unity, is the intense preoccupation of his earlier poems. 'Summer ends now; now'. The poem begins with an almost predicate-less sentence, an act of termination. Yet the predicate is 'now', and the rest of the poem is governed by 'now' and is a virtual attribute of that 'now' as 'now' cancels termination and turns out to be a moment of union which is paradoxically extensive. Parallelism asserts both the separateness and the relationship of earth and heaven. The barbarous stooks are metaphorically 'bearded', but are also primal, primitive, *fierce*, intense. This is another word in which the prepossession, the attributes of 'barbarian' and the sensuous reality of 'bearded', come together to form almost a new adjective when governing 'stooks'. They parallel the almost anarchic clouds – 'wilder, wilful-wavier'. The clouds are 'silk-sack', not 'silk-sacked', a form which would distance and generalise the adjective by withdrawing it from its affinity with the particular substantive noun, and 'silk' and 'sack' are locked together as a pair in which they are both adjectives and both nouns, neither taking precedence over the other. Both words suggest not only a billowing shape but textures, structures. 'I walk, I lift up, I lift up heart, eyes . . . to glean our Saviour'. The self bridges earth and sky and is rewarded by 'greeting' and 'replies', a reciprocal movement. Nevertheless, almost until the last two lines, the poem is full of unfinished constructions and self-contained activity. I have already noticed the vestigial predicate of the first sentence. Similarly stooks 'rise/Around' without an object. The 'meal-drift' of the clouds is 'moulded . . . across' skies and 'melted across' skies, moulding itself and dispersing itself, not acting on the sky. The open comparatives, 'wilder, wilful-wavier', 'realer, of rounder replies', seem to want a closure which is only achieved in the penultimate line – 'bold and bolder'. Things want objects. The 'beholder/Wanting' is a double form. Things need a beholder, but the beholder is also 'Wanting', in a condition of lack, wanting 'things'. The effort of false starts towards a predicate occurs in 'I lift up, I lift up heart', 'These things, these things were'. The project of the poem is a pun on the second line, 'A round'. It needs to create a circle, a 'rounder' relationship which holds the stress of perceiver and perceived. In order to do this it needs to look not only up but 'Down all that glory in the heavens' to understand the parallelism *between* earth and sky. It finally achieves this 'round' with the metaphor of Pegasus in the sestet. The hills hung with azure (sur*rounded* with heaven) are a world-wielding shoulder. The *earth* and heaven are fused. Hills thus support heaven and are interpenetrated by it – 'very-violet-sweet'. Stallion and 'stalwart' partake of each other's sounds and there is a strange clash of qualities in 'very-violet-sweet' which registers the almost impossible very – *violent* – sweet conjoining of things. The parallelism is completed as the heart 'rears wings' like Pegasus and 'meets' in one identity with the Saviour and His attributes, of which he is himself part. Such meeting for Hopkins is always difficult, almost desperate, an 'achieve of' as he puts it in 'The Windhover', an effort, a 'stress' in the sense of strain, as he struggles to leap the unmediated gap between 'things and us'. But the poem is held together because it is an inscape on the inscape of morphological root and metaphor. Like the corn, God is rooted in heaven and earth and guarantees the form and uniqueness of sky and earth and their relationship. He becomes the copula, moulding the furrows of sky and earth. Thus roots and metaphors unite in primitive form and immediacy – 'barbarous' 'gleans' or gathers multiple meaning out of the root 'barb' and words do not fall apart from things, and signs do not detach themselves from referents. God flushes earth and sky with the prepossession or attributes of gathered corn – 'meal-drift' clouds and bearded barley in the earth. A perfect union with God is possible. It is a union made possible, however, by the governing metaphor of rural labour and an archaic, agrarian economy.

One might feel that *The Wreck of the Deutschland* is the consummate example of such union. It celebrates the call of the nun in the sinking ship, who 'rears' herself like the Pegasus heart in 'Hurrahing in the Harvest'. She calls 'O Christ, Christ, come quickly' and experiences, it seems, a direct vision of Christ or union with Him. But Hopkins asks, 'What did she mean?' (stanza 25) and the syntax of the poem breaks down in stanza 28. 'But how shall I . . . make me room there:/Reach me a . . .'. Hopkins's language is nowhere so bold, so innovative and so confident, and yet the poem seems to falter. The first ten stanzas, in which Hopkins meditates on the personal relationship with Christ and the significance of the Incarnation, are very successful. They are actually the *result* of his response to the wreck but are placed prior to the narrative in an effort to withstand the flux of the storm before it is described, to prevent it from dissolving value and significance. It is an effort to transfer the model of a redeeming personal union with Christ to the fate of the 'two hundred souls' lost in the wreck who are redeemed by the nun's utterance. But the model cannot bear the 'stress' of this effort.

'Thou mastering me/God!' God in this verbless sentence is a mastering me God, a God who includes all objects within Himself. He is subject and predicate. The Incarnation, which Hopkins celebrates in language of a virtuosity he hardly reached again, is the guarantee of this inclusion. It enables man to take God into himself just as God takes man into Himself. The language here is oral, sexual, orgasmic. It is only in union with God through the Incarnation that Hopkins's troubled homosexual passions could find release, perhaps because it is a union which transcends gender (stanza 8).

How a lush-kept-plush-capped sloe
Will, mouthed to flesh-burst,
Gush! – flush the man, the being with it, sour or sweet
Brim, in a flash, full!

Taste, always Hopkins's sense for the most immediate experience of identity, makes taster and thing tasted inseparable. The resistant sloe, its self-identity, 'kept' single by its 'capped' defensive skin will 'flush' the man, organically penetrating his being. The 'flesh-burst' is its breaking open of separateness and also the mouth of the man himself in sensuous union with what he takes into himself. 'Lush', 'plush', 'gush', 'flush', 'flash': the series enables physical properties to move towards verbs and verbs to assimilate one another so that flushing flashes and flashing flushes. Flesh and flush provide another linked pairing. The whole stanza is interesting. Such words, Hopkins says, are 'best' or 'worst' because they describe the Incarnation and Passion which is both joy and horror. Best and worst because they incarnate meaning and yet may be inadequate or disjoined from reference. Certainly words are *functional* here. We 'lash' with them, they are instrumental in moving people to faith. Men go to Calvary, with a volition which is not questioned, such is the energy of language; 'Never ask if *meaning* it, wanting it, warned of it' (my emphasis). It is almost as if the *sound* of words rather than their 'prepossession' or 'definition' compels obedience. Paradoxically the generalised orgasmic language of 'flesh-burst', allied to a sense of the violence of language and its coercive power to command obedience, is conveyed through the Swinburnian strategy of making sound work so that it becomes autonomous and detached from meaning. Sound becomes an algolagniac, sadistic lash with which to coerce the faithful to God's will. Hopkins himself said that *The Wreck* had affinities with Swinburne's work because of its 'logoaedic' rhythm, but there are other and more disturbing similarities.[23] The project of the poem is the attempt to justify the 'lash' of language by restoring and giving meaning to 'unshapeable' sound, just as it attempts to give meaning to the flux of the sea. These are related and parallel concerns. The poem is an attempt to bring all experience under the ordering telos of a meaning which will finally preclude questioning, a telos which will fix language and experience forever.

For *meaning* becomes crucial in the following narrative section: the sea is the agent of flux and the undoing of intrinsic value and relationship: it is 'widow-making unchilding unfathering' (stanza 13); it is 'sloggering' (stanza 19); the dialect word expresses the brute, mindlessly repeated material action of waves and their tendency to undifferentiated flux, the resistant element of pure physical matter. It is meaningless flux, and 'dandled the to and fro' (stanza 16), playing with a ceaseless backwards and forwards motion which arbitrarily catches up victims. The cry of the nun redeems this. 'What did she mean?' (stanza 25). This means not only what did she mean or intend, to what was she referring, but what is the meaning of the nun's cry, *how* does she mean? Hopkins insists not only that she experienced a direct vision or union with Christ (*what* she meant) but also that she 'read' the 'unshapeable shock might' (stanza 29) (*how* she meant). Her cry inscapes the wreck, flushing matter with meaning in the logos, giving the unshapeable flux of time-bound sea, a unique shape.

> Wording it how but by him that present and past,
> Heaven and earth are word of, worded by?
>
> (stanza 29)

Her words signify Christ. Time, present and past, matter and spirit, heaven and earth express Christ: they are his 'words' or utterances which comprehend and unify opposites and Christ is reciprocally 'worded by', given meaning, by temporality, spirit, matter, in the Incarnation. Words and things are in reciprocal identity with one another and partake of one another. 'Word, that heard and kept thee and uttered thee outright', Hopkins writes in stanza 30. The word of the nun uttered, gave being to the outright presence of Christ without mediation, or 'stain', just as the immaculate conception 'uttered' Christ.

Perhaps the word 'kept' indicates the uneasiness of the solution. It means gestation, but also retain, hold on to. And words do have difficulty in holding onto, possessing, what they designate in this poem. The poet himself almost breaks down in the effort to read the nun's reading. In the fallen world of the wreck interpreting, counting, seems to take place without significance, as the repeated verbs 'tell', 'tell', 'told' suggest in the early part of the narrative (12, 16, 17). 'They could tell him for hours', Hopkins writes of the drowned man who is 'dandled' in the to-and-fro flux of the sea. Telling is the mere registering of discrete signs. Telling is mere computation and aggregation, the activity of that terrible world of ungrounded economic activity which threatens Hopkins's world. The wounds of Christ on Calvary are described in an almost hysterical series of alternative words for mark or sign as if to prevent them precisely from being discrete signs – cipher, mark, word, stigma, cinquefoil, token, lettering. The 'mark' is of man's 'make' – wound, word, stigma, token, are the creation of fallen man, only given meaning by being 'scored' on and thus *physically* part of Christ's body, bespoken by Christ as he was bespoken by man in the Crucifixion (stanza 22). Bespoken suggests the immediacy of speech as well as the sense of being reserved, or preordained; it also suggests distance – to betoken. That words might open up a gap between themselves and things and become empty signs is one of the fears of *The Wreck of the Deutschland*. The second account of language in the 1868 notes haunts the poem. The frantic, hysterical attempt to fix meaning is the very cause of its dissolution. Perhaps signs will not even call up concepts. The distance of writing from speech is a distance it tries to keep at bay by the most elaborate insistence of its sounds. However, the elaborateness, the 'oddity' of the words as the poet attempts to inscape their being becomes itself an independent entity – 'a word to oneself, an inchoate word'. There is violence and a curious fancifulness of language in this poem, particularly when the storm is metaphorically transformed into a paradisal martyrdom – 'Storm flakes were scroll-leaved flowers, lily showers – sweet heaven was astrew in them' (stanza 21). That words might be inchoate as the night is unshapeable is a threat to the poet, perhaps, though it is also evidence of a saving honesty. The model of an essentially individual relationship with God cannot be transposed to organise the unshapeable shock of the storm. The nun's act of self-confirmation in God isolates her from the drowned passengers of the wreck. The unique supremacy of selfhood in private communion with God and nature does not provide a sufficiently radical analysis of relationship to make a 'reading' of the wreck possible.

The poem's troubled sexuality is perhaps an index to its problems. Earlier poems generalise sexuality and Eros as stress, rejoicing in the leaping of the gap between beings, even while these are gendered as the same sex, and the desire for union is a generalised desire. The nun, however, accepting God's mastery, 'keeping' Christ in gestation and experiencing union without 'stain', is emphatically placed as feminine: the sea, paradoxically, has not 'unmothered' her in her virginity. Yet, in the traditional ecclesiastical pun on erection and resurrection, she 'rears' herself towards Christ, and becomes androgynous in taking on His qualities, so that the Christ who is asked to 'come', reciprocally takes on hers. Hopkins is staggered at the revolutionary meaning of this reading (a male *and female* God) and the breakdown or gap in syntax at this point of the poem indicates that aporia, and the temerity of this idea. But, as in the dream work, this is a *signifying* gap: it 'means', signifying the constitutive 'gap' of feminine sexuality and the gap of sexual difference, which would dissolve if the 'saltus' or leap of union between nun and Christ were fully achieved. There would be a dissolution of traditional meaning and perhaps of meaning itself. The pun on the meaning of 'wreck' – to *regard, take notice* (or 'read' for meaning) or to *destroy* – is cruelly preserved in the poem, as Hopkins's solutions to the dissolution of meaning actually recreate it.

'And my lament/Is cries countless, cries like dead letters sent,/To dearest him that lives alas! away' ('I wake and feel the fell of dark', sonnet no. 67): 'Man, how fast his firedint, his mark on mind, is gone!' ('That Nature is a Heraclitean Fire', no. 72). That 'marks', either God's or man's, might be obliterated, that language might be at an increasing distance from its object, is one of the preoccupations of the terrible sonnets of Hopkins's later period. The stem of stress between things and us is severed as the poet finds himself existing as an estranged being. The language acts out an enclosure in consciousness, the consciousness of the isolated subject, a consciousness, moreover, which can only duplicate itself in a reflective disjunction from the world and God. All Hopkins has is Mansel's 'I know' and 'I know that I know', Pater's credo, but for him this psychological condition is not the condition of freedom but of imprisonment.

> My own heart let me more have pity on; let
> Me live to my sad self hereafter kind,
> Charitable; not live this tormented mind
> With this tormented mind tormenting yet.
>
> I cast for comfort I can no more get
> By groping round my comfortless,
>
> (no. 69)

The syntax creates a divided consciousness in which 'my own heart' is both the subject of an apostrophe and its own object: 'me' is distinguished as another self from the heart, and a further 'sad self'. The 'mind' reduplicates itself as a series, continually reversing the 'tormented' and 'tormenting' position of subject and object. Comfort is something cast and groped for and yet the self is caught in a condition, 'comfortless', which has no substantive definition but doubles back on itself, postponing the completion of a predicate, and can only be described in terms of an adjunct striving to be its own definition.

As in 'That Nature is a Heraclitean Fire', this poem moves to joke, into ironising the adjunctive and disjunctive consciousness: 'Sons, self; come, poor Jackself'; 'This jack, joke, poor Potsherd' ('That Nature is a Heraclitean Fire'). At the same time, the language becomes increasingly strained, fancifully grotesque in its effort to express the return to a world in which God and man belong together. The splitting of 'whose smile/'s not wrung', the invention of 'Betweenpie mountains' (no. 69) to express the leap of God's smile over gaps and distance, and the analogous presence of the sky, making the discrete distance of the space between mountain peaks unify the landscape by producing a 'pied' contrast of air and matter, are devices which certainly produce that oddness of which Hopkins was aware. It is an oddness which, if we follow through the meaning of 'spare' as 'left over' in 'Pied Beauty', moves to the oddness of being left out, a singularity which is isolated and self-referring. Hopkins himself talks of his later work as 'fever fussy', seeing 'life's masque' mirrored in distorted forms in the bowl of a spoon (no. 75).[24]

Here he is inadvertently almost at one with Ruskin and his account of the decadent form of the Grotesque in *The Stones of Venice* (vol. III, chapter 3, paragraphs 59–60). Ruskin talks of the 'fantastic', even playful or 'sportive' distortion of vision in the decline of gothic art which signifies complete cultural breakdown, and offers an explanation of this in terms of the incapacity of consciousness to produce, at this historical moment, symbols which mediate truth in its wholeness. The 'terrible grotesque', we have seen, is like a 'disturbed dream' (paragraphs 59–60). 'Now, so far as the truth is seen by the imagination in its wholeness and quietness, the vision is sublime; but so far as it is narrowed and broken by the inconsistencies of the human capacity, it becomes grotesque' (paragraph 62).[25] For Ruskin the caprice and caricature of late Renaissance art, whether sickness or health, or the holy terror of death, inspires it, take on a kind of independent life. This distinction between the wholeness of the sign and the autonomy and self-referring nature of Grotesque signification is analogous to Hopkins's two accounts of language as total identity of word and thing and as independent entity. Ruskin calls the third volume of *The Stones of Venice*, 'The Fall'. This latter-day cultural Fall is the experience of break and discontinuity with both the world and God and consequently of language. An isolated modern subjectivity emerges, a 'fall' Paul de Man associates with a post-Romantic irony which demystifies transcendent and theological accounts of the world.[26] Hopkins, stranded on his 'cliffs of fall', is unable to leap from them to God. It is ironic that Hopkins's language should be so clearly akin to what Ruskin thought of as a fallen decadent language of the Grotesque which had lost that urge to resistance and critique embodied in primal gothic form. Hopkins's own reading of Ruskin and his own fascination with gothic architecture (which he explored enthusiastically in his early days) were directed towards reading the Grotesque in a conservative (and often masculine) way. With him the category of the Grotesque is appropriated for a non-radical, and anti-radical, archaic and reactionary project. His passionate sense of the chivalric saw in the Grotesque the representations of a living culture and social order which, though hierarchical, yet enabled each individual his own uniqueness in the hierarchy. The fecundity and variety of the gothic appeared to express the virility of the will to individuation in a unified culture, just as the native thew and sinew of the English language was founded on a rugged individuality forged through historical and philological continuity. His interest in William Barnes's experiments with dialect poetry arise from this fascination with an authentic Englishness. Purism and antiquarianism converge with experiment and eccentricity in an odd way.[27]

It is strange indeed that the linguistic caprice of the later work should find its critique in Ruskin's description of the decadence of the Grotesque, where the sign seems no longer adequate to its referent, where gaps open up, calling attention to the consciousness of the isolated subject which lives in discontinuity with the world and with itself, seeing itself as an alienated empirical subject. This very estrangement of the modern condition was the state Hopkins struggled so hard against, and against which, entirely alone, he expended such prodigious intellectual and imaginative energy in an attempt to construct a system which might resist it. The 'stress' of this system was conservative, looking forward as it does to fascist accounts of language such as we see in Heidegger, but it can also be inscaped as revolutionary in its innovation and experiment.[28] In an astonishing letter to Robert Bridges he declared himself a communist. Strangely, political extremes meet in his work. Its agonising stress and strain is symptomatic of this.[29]

15

MEREDITH AND OTHERS
Hard, gem-like dissidence

When Meredith began to seek a literary career in London in 1849 he sought out Richard Hengist Horne, who was still writing in the cause of popular poetry.[1] Horne's last poem, *The Poor Artist*, was published in 1850: his *A New Spirit of the Age* (1844) was modelled on Hazlitt's *Spirit of the Age*, the Unitarian writer whom the *Monthly Repository* had seen as creating some of the central terms of its critical debate. Horne put him in touch with Dickens' *Household Words*, and his first poems were published there. Horne probably also introduced him to the liberal/radical intellectual journal, *The Leader*, founded by Thornton Hunt and G. H. Lewes (its contributors included the exiled Mazzini and Harriet Martineau). A quotation from Horne's *Orion* is an epigraph to Meredith's *Poems* (1851).[2] Always edgy about his background, and writing with a restlessly paradoxical and quizzical detachment, Meredith is difficult to place politically. It would be an exaggeration to say that Horne played the part of 'literary God-father', as Browning described Fox's relation to himself, but, an early supporter of Hungarian and Italian republicanism, Meredith continued to be in touch with liberal thought, and indeed, with his responsiveness to the Russian revolution of 1905, bridged humanitarian liberal nationalism and revolutionary thought. Always an iconoclastic, dissident voice, it is yet hard to place him in sexual politics as much as in radical politics, because of his deconstructive sharpness and ironised equivocation. He read Mill's *On the Subjection of Women* (1869) at a sitting and wrote the equivocal 'A Ballad of Fair Ladies in Revolt' (published in the *Fortnightly Review*, 1876) in response to it.[3] Like Browning in later life, he was happy to move in aristocratic circles, but his friends numbered among them H. M. Hyndman, the socialist who popularised Marxist ideas, and James Thomson and his atheist circle. The man of whom Hardy said that Westminster Abbey would need 'a heathen annexe' for him when he died had an ambiguous attitude to class and to women (he disliked the suffragettes though some were his friends),[4] but he continued to write poems about war and revolution and anti-imperialism to the end of his life. But the very intensity of his awareness of these issues enabled him to approach them with an extraordinary lucidity. It enabled him to capture the high ground of a kind of aristocratic radical deconstruction which makes a remorseless critique of institutions, particularly the institution of marriage.

Meredith's first attempts to earn a living by writing were made through his poetry, though it is as a novelist and as the writer of a single narrative poem constructed in terse, sixteen-line internal monologues, *Modern Love* (1862), that he is now best known. From 1851 to 1901, however, he published seven full volumes of verse and a number of uncollected poems. Several significant poems were published in the *Modern Love* volume, but the dominance of the title poem in Meredith's reputation has obscured them, and arguably it has paradoxically obscured the way in which *Modern Love* itself might be read. The poem's anguished awareness of psychological complexity in sexual relations, the way in which it veers between misogyny and a strikingly sensitive response to feminine sexuality, enables it to be read solely as a realistic dramatisation of a psychological condition – Browning's monologues without the Grotesque element of cultural critique and philosophical intervention. Read in the context of Meredith's other poems, however, different aspects of it emerge, and suggest that the poem can be read not only as psychological expression but as *comedy*, comedy in the sense understood by Meredith's later essay, 'On the idea of comedy and the uses of the comic spirit', delivered as a lecture in 1877. A reading of this essay together with the poem sharpens one's sense of what is at issue in *Modern Love* and other less well-known poems.

The essay on comedy helps to illuminate what can be described as the 'mask' of Meredith's poetic language. There are times when his work reads as an exemplary illustration of Pater's remarks on style. Pater's language-making atomist, seizing the moment of sense and intuition by imposing form on the materials of perception, exacting an intensity of precision from the Flaubertian *mot juste*, refusing superfluity and refining Latinate vocabulary to an exactitude of meaning, seems often to be at work in Meredith's texts. However, for Pater the sense that language might enable the production of terms without corresponding realities, of sense without reference, made him insist sharply, almost voraciously, on the art which aspires to the indivisibility of form and content. But Meredith's language, on the contrary, recognises the divisibility of form and content and virtually inverts Pater's presuppositions by ruthlessly manipulating terms to expose the gap between words and experience. Language becomes a mask which is always slipping to disclose the non-correspondence between words and the non-linguistic world. An example is his habitual and self-consciously demythologised handling of personification, where attributes and qualities are given a sharp and momentary existence as substantive entities – Pity, Love, Nature, Time, Shame, Pride, Pain, to name a few of the personified spirits and characters which sweep through *Modern Love* – but whose life is then withdrawn so that they return to abstraction and become fictions, mere artificial postulates which are purely formal. Far from being the Benthamite fictions which we have to treat as 'real', a deconstructive movement demonstrates them to be unreal and formal. For Meredith this is one of the devastatingly detached procedures of comedy, which pulls out the carpet of uninvestigated assumption about reality from under the feet of those who rest on it. It is a form of ironic tripping up which demonstrates the intransigence of the non-linguistic world – but through language itself.[5]

Meredith produced few sustained, general discussions of poetry and never defined an aesthetic position fully except in the essay on comedy. He was fond of using an idealist–realist opposition, but tended to dissolve it: 'The greatest idealists sprang from a school of hard realism'.[6] The essay on comedy gives some content to such formulations. It proffers a patrician common sense as the essence of comedy's 'thoughtful laughter' and 'beautiful translucency'. Those who understand the true comic spirit, its 'peculiar oblique beam of light', the laughter of the mind and its 'subtle delicacy', can become 'a citizen of the selected world. . . . Look there for your unchallengeable upper class!' The emphasis on comedy's 'bright and positive, clear Hellenic perception of facts' recalls Pater's celebration of the Hellenic spirit and looks forward to his belief in an aristocracy of the aesthetically initiated.[7] Despite the irony of the allusion to the upper class (for, of course, comedy always challenges) comedy appears to be being presented as a standard: several times Meredith returns to an attack on the 'Grotesque' effects of satire, irony and mere polysyllabic humour. The spirit of comedy is polite. The objects of Grotesque humour are too 'gross' for comedy. Anger, contempt and derision are foreign to it. There are a number of vigorous, Arnoldian attacks on middle-class prejudice and Philistinism.[8]

At first sight the 'Spirit' of comedy described in the last pages of the essay seems like a rational, masculinised counterpart to Pater's descriptions of the feminine face, Meredith's alternative to the Giaconda. There is the same concentration on the eyes and lips, the same hint of transgressive mystery:

> so closely attached to them [the surfaces of life] that it may be taken for a slavish reflex, until its features are studied. It has the sage's brows, and the sunny malice of a faun lurks at the corners of the half-closed lips drawn in an idle wariness of half tension. That slim feasting smile, shaped like the long bow, was once a big round satyr's laugh, that flung up the brows like a fortress lifted by gunpowder. The laugh will come again, but it will be of the order of the smile, finely tempered, showing sunlight of the mind, mental richness rather than noisy enormity.[9]

Pan, the disruptive god of panic, the satyr, is a double creature of libidinal energy and dissidence compounded with the sage. These elements will not be tamed by the sunlight of the mind but coexist with it. And these are not the 'reflex' of life, not imitations of it, but a *construction* out of it, one of Meredith's patently artificial personifications with a formal existence, manipulated to expose false or limited expectations of the real, by being 'unreal' themselves, 'out of proportion, overblown, affected, pretentious, bombastical, hypocritical, pedantic, fantastically delicate'.[10] Comedy is not so much a corrective as a volatile *figure* or representation used as a tool of analysis. Idealised because such figures are hypotheses, lenses testing out experience, they are nevertheless not to be confused with it. We cannot think without language, Manser said, but language does not necessarily correspond with things outside it. The language of comedy and its presuppositions are of the same order.

The strangeness of Meredith's comic spirit accompanying the patrician tone becomes apparent. The comic spirit is sage-like, Pan-like and satyr-like, and yet at other points in the essay comedy is a woman, a *muse*. 'Comedy, we have to admit, was never one of the most honoured of the Muses. She was in her origin, short of slaughter, the loudest expression of the little civilisation of men'.[11] The bisexual nature of comedy accords with other contradictions. The sentimental and irrational nature of middle-class society, with its wealth and leisure, which refuses to look at complexities and difficulties (' "Surely we're not so bad!" . . . "If that is human nature, save us from it!" '[12]), is scourged, but comedy, Meredith says, is itself a bourgeois form. The spirit of comedy is impersonal and polite, but in it the deceptions, hypocrisy and philistine 'barbarism' of 'polite society' are attacked.[13] Comedy idealises but 'strips Folly to the skin', flaying it as Pan flayed Marsyas.[14] Women, indeed, are possibly the one group Meredith keeps free of this confusion. He begins his essay by saying bluntly that comedy cannot exist without a culture which recognises equality between men and women. It never exists where there is a 'state of marked social inequality of the sexes'.[15] At the heart of comedy is the 'battle' between men and women but it refuses a master–slave relationship and acknowledges that 'when they draw together in social life their minds grow liker; just as the philosopher discerns the similarity of boy and girl, until the girl is marched away to the nursery'.[16] This pre-Freudian insight into sexual difference as a cultural construction runs throughout the essay. Meredith takes misogyny and quarrels between man and wife as one of the types of comedy.

Though the pantheon of comedy is strangely restricted to Molière and Menander (Shakespeare and Chaucer are admitted occasionally), it is clear that the essay attempts to redefine what is comprehended in the category of comedy. It is 'a conception of the Comic that refines even to pain'.[17] It exposes contradictions, examining, as it were, the anagnorisis, the reversals, which are to be found in tragedy without the element of peripeteia or discovery. Comedy is inveterately social and thus concerned with ideological critique: it is about people who do not *know* about the contradictions in which they live. I know and I know that I know, Manser said. Comedy deals with people who do not know that they know. And yet it refuses mastery. Its analytical method is prismatic. It refuses the monolithic nature of tragedy by splitting a situation into elements and allowing them to criticise one another. In a comedy the poet is 'laughing at the chorus; and the grand question for contention in dialogue . . . with tremendous pulling on both sides'.[18] Judged by this description, a whole range of texts becomes comic, from one of his own or Thackeray's novels (implicitly Dickens the bourgeois humorist and *joker* is ruled out) to the cool deconstruction of *Essays and Reviews*, published two years before *Modern Love*. Mark Pattison's essay in that volume, for instance, 'Tendencies of religious thought in England 1688–1750', a scourging analysis of the theology of the English church since the Restoration, arguing that the rational doctrines of deism did not produce the social and moral licence of the period, but that *it* produced *them*, would be a typical example of the comic spirit at work.[19]

There is a lot that is troubling about Meredith's essay; its exclusiveness, its attempt to preserve an uninvolved detachment. Though this is possibly to be attributed to the uneasiness of the 'brilliant outsider' in British society, as he called Congreve, perhaps thinking of himself (significantly likening his wit to that heard at school, place of the unerring exposure of social class and insecurity), its stance is disturbing.[20] It is on the one hand thoroughly iconoclastic and on the other patrician in Pater's way. The Derridean technique (before its time) of doubling a problematical question (polite comedy, polite society, middle-class values, bourgeois comedy) rather than setting up oppositions to expose a contradiction is often superbly skilful: the problematical areas of sexuality and class are deftly encountered; but there are times when Meredith reads like a reactionary middle-class Nietzsche on these topics.

The poetry is not free from these problems, but its best moments are moments of the comic spirit, and this is particularly the case of *Modern Love*. The virtuosity and intensity of these internal monologues, bringing together the 'now' of immediate perception and analysis with the 'then' of retrospect (the analysis is both concurrent with events and yet places them in the past so that the poem constantly fuses present and past), lead to a form of narrative in which the speaker is ambiguously 'inside' experiences and events and yet *external* to them, never fully in possession of an analysis yet always seeking the detachment which would enable him to 'know that he knows'. The very incompleteness of his understanding becomes a part of the 'comedy'. The monodrama form has led critics to make an analogy between *Modern Love* and Tennyson's *Maud*, and this would be both correct and misleading. The speaker experiences the death of love between himself and his wife, and her agonised unfaithfulness to him, on the nerves and in the blood with an acute physical hypertension: the movement of a hand's 'light quiver by her head' (I. 2), hair in a mirror, the turning away of eyes, these minute signs and moments of perception come into the poem with an intensity of sensation which can be felt with nervous, kinaesthetic intensity.[21] The world looks 'wicked as some old dull murder spot' (II. 11) at such moments. And yet the language makes a sharp incision into this material in a way Tennyson's does not. It cuts a sequence of experience into sharp, discrete moments which register the sequence of perception and yet this very detachment of experience into parts declares itself almost coldly as highly artificial construction. The first section of the poem moves from the hand's light quiver as the husband reaches over to caress his wife's head to the wife's 'strange low sobs' (I. 3) which shake their bed, and which are called back into her with 'sharp surprise' (I. 4). Thus a double psychological movement on the part of both man and wife is rendered with wonderful precision. The sobs are 'like little gaping snakes,/ Dreadfully venomous to him' (I. 5–6). They shake their common bed, but they are not the sobs of sexual love. The colloquial ease of the cadence is cut across by the melodrama of the analogy. There is no way in which '*strangled*' sobs resemble '*gaping snakes*', for they are already being made 'mute' as he listens. Snakes hiss, but the visual takes precedence over the aural in the image and in what follows: 'She lay/Stone-still' (I. 6–7); and this resolves the almost mixed metaphor, for the wife is a Medusa-figure, and it his *imagining* of her in this way which has led to the conceptualisation behind the metaphor of the snakes. The gap between verbalisation and the experience it interprets is exposed as the constructed figure of Medusa makes her snakes 'dreadfully venomous to *him*'.

> By this he knew she slept with waking eyes:
> That, at his hand's light quiver by her head,
> The strange low sobs that shook their common bed,
> Were called into her with a sharp surprise,
> And strangled mute, like little gaping snakes,
> Dreadfully venomous to him. She lay
> Stone-still, and the long darkness flowed away
> With muffled pulses. Then, as midnight makes
> Her giant heart of Memory and Tears
> Drink the pale drug of silence, and so beat
> Sleep's heavy measure, they from head to feet
> Were moveless, looking through their dead black years,
> By vain regret scrawled over the blank wall.
> Like sculptured effigies they might be seen
> Upon their marriage-tomb, the sword between,
> Each wishing for the sword that severs all.
>
> (I. 1–16)

The wife is a Medusa trying to strangle her own venomous snakes and to take them back into herself, but the pathos of this predicament is not uppermost in his mind as his misery takes precedence over hers. Instead the text sweeps on, incorporating the Medusa-figure in a wider personification. Midnight, personified as a woman, a gigantic and consuming figure, absorbs the drug of silence into her 'giant heart of Memory and Tears', a heart metonymically split into psychological and physiological elements as the 'snakes' of remembrance and grief are lulled by sleep. Both husband and wife are 'Like sculptured effigies' on the tomb of their marriage bed. The all-consuming Medusa image has extended to include them both, but it is as if the man has been taken into the woman's body or made an extension of it as the stone created by the poison of her snake-like tears, and as if she has turned herself to stone by trying to introject her own guilt and remorse. The woman has turned them both to stone. The tomb image is cold and external, and just as the couple are *figures* on a tomb, the image declares itself to *be* a figure which has determined the man's partial understanding of their predicament. It is a figure, indeed, the figure of grief as graffiti-like writing disfiguring their past, which guides interpretation of their condition. Meredith's tendency to use the colder, sculpted form of simile rather than the identifications of metaphor favoured by Hopkins and Swinburne marks the self-consciousness of figure throughout the poem – 'He sickened as at breath of poison-flowers'; 'star with lurid beams, she seemed' (II. 6, 12). Pater's imposition of form on content might be being parodied here, as hypothetical similitude *marks* and *masks* the unlikeliness of the image rather than its correspondence with the woman's state. The image corresponds with the man's *feelings*, perhaps, but not with any condition that can be determined in her.

The male speaker sees his traumatic experience as a tragedy: 'In tragic life, God wot,/No villain need be!' (XLIII. 14–15). And read as an expressive utterance the poem could well be one. The man's acute sensitivity to the signs of betrayal, his analyses of the terrible subtleties of the psychological contradictions he finds himself in, are intense enough. That an unfaithful woman can still be jealous of her husband's infidelity, that a new passion can be undermined by 'The dread that my old love may be alive' (XL. 15), the claustrophobic intensity which narrows perception to register as discrete items the laugh of his wife and another man, then the heel of his new lover just ahead of him on the terrace (XXXVI), then the moon, taking on his emotional condition, rising with 'slow foot', these are precisely rendered. The shock of the wife's suicide after a seeming reconciliation is registered with tragic pathos.

But what makes this a comedy can be seen even in the moments of greatest 'tragic' feeling as the man appropriates the world around him by projecting his feeling onto it, that 'selfish' act involved in the pathetic fallacy which Ruskin deplored. The Medusa image recurs with suspect frequency, fashioned as figure by aggression and sadism. In section XI, for instance, the woman is a deadening influence, without eyes or heart to respond to the contradiction between the day, where the heavens embrace the earth, and their own condition. Indeed, she is figured as actually killing the day and their own love like a child murderer – 'a dead infant, slain by thee' (XI. 16). The fascination with the mystery in the eyes and lips of the woman, always seen as dissociated physical items without relation, dominates the poem in an obsessive way. Like Meredith's language the face is a mask (II) which slips. Its pallor, like the Giaconda, fills the speaker with erotic violence (XXIV) as he feeds upon it for signs of suffering or of betrayal. Glancing references to the mocking Pan implicitly suggest a comic and satirical counter-interpretation of the text. Pan is said to have deserted the 'reed pipes' (VIII. 8) of the lovers; the 'wild beast' in the man is one-sided (IX. 1); the 'mad Past, on which my foot is based' (XII. 12) – the cloven foot of the wild beast? – mocks him as he experiences but does not own the anarchic life of the passions.

For the speaker is not a modern Othello. This is a profoundly social poem, as Meredith required of comedy, and it turns on that 'battle' between men and women and the misogyny which is at the heart of comedy. The speaker frequently sees himself and his wife as actors with masks, acting 'the wedded lie' (XXXV. 16), and in a bitter moment he congratulates her on her performance in a game of forfeits, a performance of which, she says, with equal bitterness, ''Tis hardly worth the money' (XXXV. 15), referring to her financial dependence as well as to the 'rewards' of acting. The 'performance' takes place between themselves, in (ironically) the dressing-room, the bedroom, the enclosed domestic spaces of the bourgeois house and its equally enclosed public spaces, the dinner table where they perform their wit to guests, the terrace, the lawn. But paradoxically, though they act, they cannot speak to one another, and this is what produces the comedy even to 'pain' which for Meredith is the finest aspect of the comic spirit. The battle turns on the refusal of speech: the husband seizes the wife's wrists, and she asks a question without a predicate, the nearest to speech that she can go: ' "You love . . . ? love . . . ? love . . . ?" ' (XLII. 16). He angrily demands the 'name' of the new lover, but to himself: 'what's the name?/The name, the name, the new name thou hast won?' (VI. 11–12). He sees a love letter like one once sent to him, the same words addressed to a different name; he is tortured by the thought that a wife bearing his 'name' is with another man. Naming becomes an obsession as the mask of language both obfuscates and exposes. He cannot say directly, and nor can she, that she will no longer have sexual relations with him. He can only 'read the steel-mirror of her smile'. 'She will not speak. I will not ask'. 'Our chain on silence clanks' (XXXIV. 3). This silence is what the comedy turns on. And the husband takes a sadistic pleasure in refusing speech when it is asked for. In the magnificent

447

melodramatic encounter of section XXXIV, an interview she has requested reduces the wife to silence as the husband reads the newspaper. He finds there, in news of Vesuvius and Niagara, his own images for pent-up emotion: 'The Deluge or else Fire! . . . With commonplace I freeze her, tongue and sense./Niagara or Vesuvius is deferred' (XXXIV. 2, 15–16).

The absence which is language becomes progressively more important as they 'read' each other for signs in other ways, and fantasy festers more intensely as speech is deferred. In the comedy essay Meredith says that those who see life as a comedy, a 'hideous human game', as the husband puts it, actually trivialise comedy.[22] Contempt and derision are alien to the genre. Yet *Modern Love* is a comedy of contempt and derision, as the man attributes the sexuality of the lower classes to beer, generalises about 'women', those who infantilise men as the 'little lap-dog breed' (XXXI. 8) (his mistress), or who masochistically enjoy martyrdom (his wife): 'There is much grace/In women when thus bent on martyrdom' (XLII. 1–2); 'Their sense is with their senses all mixed in,/Destroyed by subtleties these women are!/More brain, O Lord, more brain!' (XLVIII. 1–3).

What becomes at issue between the couple is power, and the reversals of sadism and masochism take place in the gap where language should be, in a Jamesian fashion. The final fierce irony of the comedy is that it ends in tragedy. It is a tragedy of silence but a comedy of language, as the verbalising and imagining which takes place in the silences spin a net of constructions in which both are caught, and take them and the text's reader further and further away from understanding what 'reality' may lie behind its formal artifice. As one reads the poem the analogy with Tennyson's *Maud* is certainly a possible one, but the constant seeking and supplication of Browning's 'Love in a Life', its oppressive enclosures, its mirrors and cornices, the appurtenances of bourgeois life, seem more consonant with *Modern Love*. The prismatic structure of comic form is present in *Modern Love* in a way it is not in Tennyson's poem. The speaker, as has been seen, is both immersed in his experience and attempts to be external to it, as the poem is presented as both psychological experience and simultaneously as objectified narrative and analysis, a choric comment on his own condition. Indeed, throughout the poem it is genuinely ambiguous as to whether the 'sonnets' are spoken in the first or third person, uncertain whether they are being *narrated* or *experienced*. This strategy produces a textual complexity in which it is possible to be 'laughing at the chorus', satirically undermining the analyses, even while the suffering is apparent. The 'grand question' of blame and remorse between the couple is consummately presented as the 'dialogue' which *could* be possible, but which never takes place, there by implication and with a potential existence, but not in fact. The 'tremendous pulling on both sides' is a result of this, for through the husband's exaggerations and self-pity, the acute suffering of both man and wife emerges. The wife, turning things to stone in the husband's fantasy, is herself reduced to one of Medusa's snakes – 'Poor struggling worm' – or to stone, as she faints at the news of a friend's happy engagement.

The extraordinary nature of Meredith's 'comedy' is seen when one places beside it other poems of sexual love appearing within ten years of it, Coventry Patmore's *The Angel in the House* and Dante Gabriel Rossetti's *The House of Life, A Sonnet Sequence*. Patmore's poem, in many ways as overwrought as Meredith's, is the narrative of a happy courtship and marriage, and might be the anti-poem of *Modern Love*, which is about the witch or the Medusa in the house. Patmore's poem, often seen as the ideological paradigm of Victorian domesticity, is not so free from strain as this description suggests, and it is more helpful to read it as a mirror image, the conventional double of Meredith's poem, rather than its antithesis, even though it certainly points up Meredith's iconoclasm. Rossetti's prolix but interesting sequence differs from the work of both poets, and, with its insistent soul/body distinction, the 'Spirit' or ghost in the house, suggests how un-Pre-Raphaelite Meredith is, and indeed throws doubt on the usefulness of the term 'Pre-Raphaelite' as a descriptive category.

Patmore, like almost every poet of the latter part of the century, came under the influence of the Rossetti circle for a time, and this no doubt helped to confirm his belief that the sexual and the spiritual are truly one, but there the resemblance ends. *The Angel in the House*, published over a period from 1854 to 1862, is an extended idyll written in plain and simple quatrains and octosyllabic couplets (when in 'The Victories of Love' the metrical pairing signifies domestic union) in language which is so accessible and uncomplex that it borders on verbal nonentity.[23] It is a conservative conduct book for family life, a manual for husbands rather than for wives, despite its praise of women and the power of women. It has some unusual moments, firmly asserting that male and female are both made in God's image: 'Female and male God made the man;/His image is the whole, not half' (I. Canto 8. iv), and adapting the Lord's Prayer: 'He does not rightly love himself/Who does not love another more' (I. Canto 6. iii), and 'We love, Fool, for the good we do,/Not that which unto us is done!' (I. Canto 6. iv). But though, unconventionally, women are 'Mar'd less than man by mortal fall' (I. Canto 4. i), the special beauty of their knowledge is 'infantine' and they lack the 'patient brain' (I. Canto 5. i). Artless intuition is the essence of their power and superiority to men. But though Patmore may seem to be going in the direction of the early Apostles here (Felix, the narrator, is a member of the Sterling club, half-Puritan and half-cavalier), his text asserts the value of law: chaste men 'live by law, not like the fool,/But like the bard, who freely sings/In strictest bonds of rhyme and rule,/And finds in them, not bonds, but wings' (I. Canto 10. i). If anything, the poem is a corrective to Tennyson. It recalls the parental plighting of children in *Maud*, but brings this into reality; it alludes to the

Crimean war in an interval in which the narrative briefly moves on a decade, but brushes it aside as 'home-destroying' (II. Canto I. i) and returns quickly to domesticity. It alludes to the deeply ambiguous Catullus section of *In Memoriam* and straightens it out. The woman can be 'careless, talkative, and vain' so long as she is 'sweet and womanly!' Significantly, Tennyson's threatening masculine warning, 'If thou wilt have me wise and good', is now associated with the female, and wisdom and goodness are proffered as something which she cannot and need not achieve: 'But what at all times I admire/Is, not that she is wise and good,/But just the thing which I desire' (II. Canto 8. iii). It is essential for men to be 'clean' and to adhere to the external form of polite civility if the marriage relationship is to be familiar, unaffected and free. Patmore returns frequently to the theme that a gentle wife is made by a gentle husband.

But the poem reaches intensity of a kind precisely when it is aware of contraints on the expression of sexual feeling and the narrow sphere of relationships. Meetings on the lawn, at picnics, interrupted conversations, the holding open of a door as the ladies exit after dinner, all these conventions press upon the hero. It is not simply that the excessive pressure of a hand is almost enough to ruin a courtship, or that a glove is invested with intense meaning; but the strain of the effort to fulfil conventional expectations leads to strange excesses. A rose almost 'suffocates' with sexual desire and the lover is like a Tantalus; a man must be pleased by submission to his mastery; he 'fascinates' and 'terrifies' with aggression and power and rewards with tenderness in the section significantly termed 'The Chace' (I. Canto 12. i). Although excesses of mastery and pursuit are repudiated, it is recognised that male anger is a part of sexual play. Extremes occur; the lover wishes that unbearable joy may go no further and actually fears fulfilment, or he experiences a strange blankness when he has 'won' Honoria.

There is an attempt to normalise and domesticate the contradictory experience at the heart of *Modern Love*, but the poem is at its best when it inadvertently strays into that poem's terrain and almost becomes a less trivial work. A revealing moment both mystifies feminine sexuality (hitting upon Freud's uneasy metaphor of woman as the dark continent) and ruthlessly exposes the economic base of sexual relations: 'A woman is a foreign land' with separate 'customs, politics, and tongue'. Women's 'culture' and language can be conquered, ignored – or traded: 'The most for leave to trade apply' (II. Canto 9. ii). In his late work Patmore returned to the theme of sexual love in a series of mature and impressive poems which one critic has called the bereavement odes.[24] They concentrate all the overwrought but dispersed feeling of the earlier long poem into a dozen or so elegies. Shock, accusation, nostalgia, sharpness with an orphaned son ('The Toys'), the paradoxical assuagement of grief and guilt when becoming sexually attracted to a woman like the dead wife ('Tired

450

Memory'), are arrestingly explored. The intensity and frankness of these poems is likely to be remembered when the rest of Patmore is forgotten. Perhaps this is because he is frank, too, about a secret pathology: 'Eurydice' describes a recurrent dream where the dead wife belongs to the dark haunts of city prostitutes, sick in the hell of exploitation and hatred which the poet's fantasy gives to the 'sordid streets and lanes'. This recognition that the protected and 'innocent' life of domesticated middle-class feminine sexuality depends for its privileges upon sexual exploitation is understood also by D. G. Rossetti, though more resiliently and critically, in 'Jenny', a monologue in which a middle-class gentleman ponders callously the seemingly mysterious psyche of the woman whose customer he is and realises, if nothing else, that the purity of his cousin is predicated upon the coins he pays to the prostitute.[25]

In 'Eurydice' the 'unfleshly' post-Tractarian work of Patmore converges oddly with the 'fleshly' Pre-Raphaelite social critique of Rossetti. And just how odd, and how deeply reactionary this is, can be seen from the political odes which intersperse the elegies. In them the wife's death is made symbolic of the death of England, the world of civilised privilege, property and hereditary power killed by the reform bill of 1867, and now given over to the 'Jew', the 'sordid Trader' and the 'orgies of the multitude', or so it is written in the frankly reactionary poem entitled '1867': 'The freedom of the few/That, in our free Land, were indeed the free' has disappeared. A note speaks of the government having 'disfranchised' the middle and upper classes. Patmore is one of the last poets to embrace wholeheartedly the conservative Tractarian account of the material (in his case the *sexual*) world as the vehicle of spiritual meaning, an account which both celebrates the physical world and *dissolves* it into transcendent reality as the physical bounds of 'presence' are obliterated by the meaning beyond them. Such an account of experience allows us to ignore the material conditions of life in favour of a transcendental, symbolic account of them. We have seen how Pater adapted Tractarian symbol as the meaning beyond or behind the phenomenal world on which we impose form. In Patmore's later prose a similar but more theological account of symbol lives on, particularly in *Religio Poetae* (1893) and *The Rod, the Root and the Flower* (1895), and demonstrates the staying power of an indigenous and often deeply reactionary account of symbol which owes nothing to the French symbolists, but which merged with symbolist theory at the end of the century in the work of Arthur Symons.[26] It is, perhaps, Tractarian thinking which is the ancestor of modernist accounts of symbol.

Meredith's 'comic' deconstruction of the formalism of symbol is in complete contrast to the reactionary affiliations of Patmore's aesthetic theory. And this is also the case with Rossetti, who, it has been seen, in contrast with Patmore, discloses in 'The Blessed Damozel' an uneasy fascination with the possibilities of symbol. As so often in Victorian poetry, sexual

451

politics have repercussions in a wider field. *The House of Life* sonnets continue a debate on the meaning of symbolic representation through an intense meditation on sexuality. Many of the sonnets were written in the 1850s. Some were published in *Poems*, in 1870, and the sequence was completed in 1881 when *Ballads and Sonnets* was published. The late publication of Rossetti's work, disinterred dramatically from his wife's grave, but actually *following* the work of poets to some extent inspired by him – for above all things he was one of the most energetic cultural entrepreneurs of the century – both postdates what we call the Pre-Raphaelite movement and gives it a false cohesion.

An apparent cohesion among the so-called Pre-Raphaelite poets is what enabled Buchanan to call the group of poets comprised by Rossetti, Morris, Meredith and Swinburne the 'Fleshly School'. In fact, though the term Pre-Raphaelite may have some importance for the group of painters established in the 1850s, it can only be a very loose designation when it comes to discussion of poetry, and that is why it has been used cautiously as a historical category in this work, and not seen as the organising idea of a dominant group. Strictly speaking, the category would include Hopkins, who was fascinated by Pre-Raphaelite painting, and Patmore, whose very early work, 'The Woodman's Daughter', provided a subject for the painter, Millais. Part Tennysonian idyll and part social critique, as the woodman's daughter, deserted by the squire's son after her seduction, gazes into the pool where her drowned illegitimate child lies, this is a fine poem. But Patmore was not to work in this vein again. Social critique and a concern with vision and the gaze relates some but not all of these poets. Their unlikeness needs to be stressed. There are great differences, for instance, among Meredith's deconstruction of formalism, Swinburne's essentially aural republican rhetoric, Morris's experiments with Grotesque symbol as cultural symptom and Rossetti's appropriation of Tractarian symbol for a radical epistemology and politics. And, properly speaking, Morris belongs to an earlier phase of 'Pre-Raphaelite' writing. The poets of the 1860s can best be understood through their common preoccupation with power relations and language, representation, the sign and the political significance invested in different paradigms of language. *The House of Life* sonnets are no exception. They work through a sexual politics which negotiates an ever changing and elusive relation between body and soul, material sign and transcendent meaning, representation and referent. Always becoming one-sided and always failing to synchronise, the two sides of experience collapse and dissolve. Where Meredith located the relationship of mastery and submission in the psychology of marriage, which allows the male to construct a language for dealing with the institution, but not the woman, Rossetti understands the constant disparity of gender as founded in the master–slave structure of language and symbol itself.

Thus *The House of Life* sonnets are Platonic, but undermine Platonic

452

dualism, not by seeking a union between the ideal and the material or spirit and matter or language and thought, but by exploring the damaging nature of the antithesis itself. Reviewing Rossetti's late work, Pater noticed the obvious Dantesque elements of the sonnets, and the intensity which means that 'Life is a crisis at every moment'.[27] Like Dante, 'he knows no region of spirit which shall not be sensuous also, or material'. The dichotomy between spirit and matter, he said, is a false contrast or antagonism made by the abstract theology of medieval thought: 'In our actual concrete experience, the two trains of phenomena which the words *matter* and *spirit* do but roughly distinguish, play inextricably into each other'.[28] Rossetti was aspiring to an absolute commensurateness of body and soul, language and thought. Thus his 'shadowy world' contains roadways and houses, land and water, light and darkness, fire and flowers. Pater's beautiful discussion (interestingly, he says nothing about 'Jenny'), however, is a more conservative reading of the sonnets than the text can sustain. For it is precisely the difficult and problematic nature of a union between spirit and matter which worries the poems. If body and soul *are* absolutely commensurate they collapse into one another, and sexual difference and language itself collapses because there is no space between the two terms by which they can be understood. And by the same token body and soul, language and thought, can become redundant to one another: for if they are *identical* there is no need of antithetical terms. Meaning can recede from material phenomena in shadowy transcendent autonomy, or material phenomena displace meaning, which endlessly disappears into a ghostly limbo. The sonnets are built on the despair of separation, and yet if division is assuaged, union dissolves the entities it brings together. They become a critique of the consequences of idealism in sexual relations and in language even as they long for it, disclosing a concurrent language of the body and the soul, two languages which are always either diverging or collapsing into one-sidedness or dissolving away. Dante Rossetti exploits what Meredith termed the 'tremendous pulling on both sides' created by these two languages to explore a problem at the heart of relationships – equality in union.

The sonnets are the great conjurors of emptiness in this period. A contentless world, of cold, waste, shadow and annihilation belongs to them. But it is a world where the pressure of physical form *has* been or *might* be. Meaning hovers or dissolves beyond or beneath the material form, or the physical hovers beyond or beneath the state of loss, always incommensurate, always unrealised. 'Without Her' (53) conjures a grey, imageless mirror: 'What of her glass without her?' Such absence is a pool from which the reflection of the moon has withdrawn, a dress without a body, a pillow without the hollow of physical pressure. The woman becomes figured as an empty space which has once *been* filled: 'Of thee what word remains ere speech be still?' The silence where language once was calls forth a need to utter speech which will embody the 'remains' of past presence in memorial words which will restore a lost content, but the language which follows can only register what it is to be 'without her'. Material signs have no 'counterpart'. Nevertheless, the sonnet ends with a material embodiment of a 'counterpart'. 'Where the long cloud, the long wood's counterpart,/ Sheds doubled darkness up the labouring hill'. The long cloud above the landscape is a material, and not a transcendent, form but it replicates its darkness by creating the shadow made by the long wood. Wood, cloud and shadow are indivisible. But with one of those unobtrusive verbal shifts which characterise these poems, the adjective 'long' denotes both the physical limits of material things and the endlessness of the journey towards death and death itself. 'Behind' the word 'long', designating physical limit, is a shadowy abstract meaning made possible by the material sign but escaping its limits as endlessness escapes the finite measurement implied by 'long', and escapes the condition of being 'counterpart'. The affective language of these sonnets – 'Tears, ah me!' – should not prevent an appreciation of their linguistic complexity.

The longing for union makes these intensely *social* poems, despite their concern with absence. The ideal union of 'Secret Parting' (45) in which body and soul come together – 'And as she kissed, her mouth became her soul' – is a union made only to be dissolved. Indeed in this sonnet the physical space inhabited by love exists only in the empty space of memory, which is both protection for love *and* affirms its non-being. In memory neither audible sound nor visual signs can enter: 'Nor spire may rise nor bell be heard therefrom'. A longed-for community materialises from the very absence of social life. Throughout the sequence Rossetti pairs words and duplicates sound in many kinds of insistent alliterative and asonantal combination to register the desired but impossible union of sense and spirit.

In Rossetti's world of only too substantial or insubstantial cloud and wind the poems attempt to restore content to experience. In 'The Morrow's Message' (38) love can 'greet' three times in the present, the past and the future, but only in a world of possibility. 'Severed Selves' (40) is organised round division, 'Two separate divided silences,/Which, brought together, would find loving voice/Two hands . . . Two bosoms . . . Two souls'. The symmetrical pairing is an asymmetrical division and separation, because the body alone, without relationship to another *body* has no meaning: each silence requires speech, each hand touch, before bodies and souls can 'be made the same'. Indeed, speech and touch *are* the new element of 'mutual flame' which make the union of mind and body possible. But though the fact of temporality makes this possible it also guarantees its dissolution. So that the lovers are caught in the empty representations of hope or of memory: 'and only leaves at last,/Faint as shed flowers, the attenuated dream'. The exactness of 'attenuated' gives its full force to this poem; for it means both rarefied or ideal *and* that which is thinned out or slender, thin in *physical* consistency. The sensuous richness of dream loses its consistency with physical separation and representation becomes incommensurate with what it represents. Temporality makes the dream fade, too, and guarantees that language loses its content.

The 'Willowood' sonnets Rossetti defended so eloquently are a consummate figuring of the moment of union sustained in its collapse and yet dissolving through the act which sustains it, the kiss. The paired figures of Love and the poet do not gaze at one another, but their 'mirrored eyes' meet reflected in the water in which their mutual gaze converges. Rossetti uses the water as the only medium in which two people can *see* their gaze. Gradually the abstract figure of Love, an aspect of the poet's self and not himself, capable of conjuring the sound which brings with it commensurate images, loses its abstraction and its male gender and is displaced by the feminine face which rises to the surface (there is a faint, allusive hint of Venus being born from the waves), the poet's self and not himself, Narcissus and not Narcissus. The sonnet magnificently realises the tantalising nature of the material symbol as the image of the face floats like a picture beneath the surface of the water. Pictured as a projection of himself and not himself, it is inaccessible, its meaning floating behind and beneath the physical surface of the water even though the specular image takes form on it and through it. What it means to see 'through' something is at issue here. The poet kisses his own image (we kiss our own lips in the mirror) and not his own image, and that is why the face is drowning, losing its shape and turning grey simultaneously with the kiss. For such a union dissolves the self and the other even as it unites them. The kiss is an effort to overcome separation and history by fusing the dispersed images of the past in physical union, but the lips kiss the flowing waters of the stream, and the dumb and divided figures of history watch the kiss, even as it attempts to annul division. Reflexive memory is simultaneous with immediate experience and indeed it is only through its figuring that immediate experience comes into being. A multiplicity of past selves gazes at the poet gazing, a 'dumb' throng standing 'aloof' like souls from Dante's *Inferno*, the separate trees of the physical landscape marking their dispersal: 'one form by every tree/ . . . for each was I or she,/The shades of those our days which had no tongue' (sonnet 2). The ambiguity of the syntax allows that the forms can be either separate men and women, 'I or she', or the fused selves of the past, I and she, I which has become she, she which has become I. Each 'form' of the syntax, however, implies the other.

Rossetti's poems are often associated with a neurosis which makes the agonistic moment of sexuality in which love and death are one the consuming moment of experience, figuring a Victorian fascination with the sexuality it so uneasily represses. But in comparison with the violent jealousy and anger so adeptly disclosed in *Modern Love*, and with Patmore's self-congratulatory but ultimately savage understanding of sexual relations, these sonnets are extraordinarily free, indeed absolutely free, of the predatory cruelties of a post-Darwinian understanding of sexuality. As family and territory become marked terms for the latter part of the century, the men of Meredith's and Patmore's poems stalk their women through the territory and spaces – lawns, terraces, interiors – arranged for the bourgeois family and its civilised and highly selected class, disrupting in one case, consolidating in the other. Rossetti, on the other hand, sees the predicament of his lovers as mutual and equal – the pronoun 'our' is never very far away from these sonnets – and the lovers are alike in their inequality with one another. In them inequality is a function of the nature of sexuality itself, and of the symbol by which it is mediated. The lyricism of Rossetti's sonnets never ceases to celebrate mutuality even when union is impossible. We know that many of these poems were written throughout the 1850s, before 1862, though Rossetti continued to add to them. Despite their dating it seems possible to read them as more profoundly post-Darwinian poems than those of Meredith and Patmore. The figures of his sequence have no social history: the vestigial presence of the bell and the tower, the mirror and room, denote in a fragile and shadowy way community and social forms which are distant from and external to the internal world of the lovers. The two exist as a residual 'family', whether separate or apart, negotiating experience between themselves. The overwhelming preoccupation is with survival, the survival of mutual identity in the environment of a universe where the conditions of life are elemental and impersonal, always a universe of death. The terrain or territory they 'occupy' (Rossetti's word suggests an intensely vulnerable habitat in the context of his landscapes) is one in constant and endless upheaval, 'Like labour-laden moonclouds' fleeing 'From winds that sweep the winter-bitten wold,–/Like multiform circumfluence manifold/Of night's flood-tide, like terrors that agree/Of hoarse-tongued fire and inarticulate sea' ('Through Death to Love', 41). Rossetti's lovers attempt to confront this world with their mutuality and physical warmth.

Ultimately at issue in these sonnets is the survival of language, not as for Tennyson as a way of preserving the 'Type' but as a human artefact in which speech creates community.[29] Language, however inadequately, represents experience to itself and to the other by making and unmaking difference, the process by which symbol-making is made and which it in turn interprets. In this way experience is rescued from the 'inarticulate sea' because it is literally 'Articulated' even in the universe which identifies the post-Darwinian landscape with the terrain of the *Inferno*. This concern with articulation never left Rossetti. He wrote possibly the last catoptromantic poem of the nineteenth century, 'Rose Mary' (1881), in which a girl, urged on by her mother, speaks what she sees in a magic beryl or divining glass, interpreting the sweep of terrain beyond their castle as her eye moves in an almost cinematic way to detect signs of an ambush for her lover in the landscape. But the mirror deceives her because she has deceived it and her mother, concealing her sexual experience from both, creating misprision like a detached retina. The responsibility for misprision is a complex matter, however, involving sexual taboo and the coercion of another generation. The girl's speech negotiates the hermeneutic and moral complexity of her situation. But she and her mother do not know one thing that the mirror, the source of representation, could never tell them. The lover is ambushed and killed in the mist which was the blind spot detected and not understood by Rose Mary. A letter is discovered by the mother on his body but this shows that he was intending to ride to another woman and not to their castle. The girl smashes the mirror in despair, but what has killed her is not it or speech, but silence, the man's hidden deception, and her own, which does not enter vision or speech, the element beyond or beneath the articulation of language. Written with a narrative tension and simplicity which would make it accessible to a child – the ideal of popular democratic poetry – it is at the same time a poem of almost excruciating complexity. Like all symbols the double name of the girl is both deceptive and true, denoting the rose of sexuality and the purity of Mary – but sexual purity would not have diminished her suffering.

Did Meredith write other poems as important as *Modern Love*? He made an uncertain start in his first volume of 1851, and much in it is best forgotten. The poems might be loosely described as Tennysonian, but they are written even then with a sharpness and cleanness of diction which already suggests that this kind of lyricism was not really his mode. The powerful social element he respected is present in poems such as 'The City by Lamplight' and 'The Sleeping City'. This latter poem, describing the Medusa-made, sculptural calm of the silent city, is much to be preferred to 'The City by Lamplight', a poem on the theme of prostitution lamenting the contrast of purity and vice. Perhaps the volume is of interest by disclosing themes which the subsequent discipline of the novelist enabled him to control with more economy and precision. There is a fascination with the rape of vulnerable women which is disturbing – the other side of the moral posturing of the city poems. 'The Rape of Aurora' and 'Daphne', despite being written with a controlled, externalising, almost classical diction, cannot be redeemed from a self-indulgent eroticism by irony. Pan, voyeur on the rape of Aurora, experiences vicarious pleasure and observes that sexual experience 'Will not do a dove hurt', allowing the metaphor to obscure the fact that she is a woman.

But by the time the 1862 volume appeared, Meredith had matured as a poet. 'Grandfather Bridgman' and 'The Patriot Engineer' have all the sharpness and multi-faceted complexity Meredith required of comedy. 'Grandfather Bridgman' is a fierce, ironic, Crimean-war poem and controls a multiple point of view with considerable virtuosity as the grandfather's

457

patriotic hubris meets its nemesis. He reads a letter from his soldier grandson to his assembled family over a conspicuously hearty dinner, and to the girl, Mary, who rejected the son as suitor, boasting of his exploits. The reading of the letter, interspersed with cross-talk, gossip and dialogue, gives the grandfather the vicarious heroics he hoped for or reads into the description of the Inkermann engagement: ' "We stood in line, and like hedgehogs the Russians rolled under us thick./They frightened me there." – He's no coward. . . . The sight, he swears, was a breakfast' (16); 'it's all on the cards that the Queen/Will ask him to Buckingham Palace, to say what he's done and he's seen./Victoria's fond of her soldiers' (27). But the letter is several weeks old. Tom has been badly wounded since it was written, and has to be nursed to health by Mary. This poem was refused by *Once a Week* in 1861, but Meredith placed it as the first poem in the *Modern Love* volume as if to declare a politics and implicate the subsequent poems in them. It is no accident that the poem is in rhyming hexameters, the metre so often used in *Maud*.

'The Patriot Engineer' is another poem about the naiveté of the ideology of patriotism. The engineer deprecates the Europe of 1848 and its despotism, and expresses a violent xenophobia in his longing to be 'Where freedom's native liquor flows!' Even the Alps are no match for Britain's masculine mountains: 'The mountains Britain boasts are men' (95). The narrator comments sardonically on this excess: 'We glow'd to think how donkeys graze/In England, thrilling at their brays' (127–8). But the comic movement of the poem refuses priority to either side, for it has to be remembered that though Britain may be a country of 'donkeys', it never succumbed to the despotism of 1848 or the revolutionary reaction to it. Nevertheless before a self-congratulatory liberalism can read British history too thoroughly, another political poem, 'The Old Chartist', offers a corrective. These are all poems on the recent past of the previous two decades, but the technique of dramatising ideological misprision refuses a comfortable distance from the events they describe.

'The Old Chartist', the conversation of a returned transportee, combines a passionate love of England – 'I'm for the nation!' – with class scepticism and renewed affirmation of democratic principle, despite his daughter's petty-bourgeois respectability: 'I'm not ashamed: Not beaten's still my boast:/Again I'll rouse the people up to strike./But home's where different politics jar most./Respectability the women like./This form, or that form,–/ The government may be hungry pike,/But don't you mount a Chartist platform!' (stanza 5). The old Chartist's distinction between independent decency and superficial respectability runs through the poem. Chartism had had its day by the time this volume was published, and there is a hint of nostalgia in the poem, but it is firmly outspoken about the impregnable structure of class and power in contemporary society. These incendiary poems are never mentioned in the contemporary discussions of *Modern*

Love as an immoral 'fleshly' poem, but they fire the political significance of the title poem, and could not have gone unnoticed. They provide a context for it. The *Modern Love* volume was a supremely political collection. The agony in the boudoir and transportation to the colonies are set side by side. It is impossible to ignore the juxtaposition.

Another notable poem in this volume is 'Cassandra'. Its hard, terse stanzas of descriptive statement hit with an almost physical power.

> Captive on a foreign shore,
> Far from Ilion's hoary wave,
> Agamemnon's bridal slave
> Speaks futurity no more:
> Death is busy with her grave.

The late Yeats is foreshadowed here, just as he is in 'Jump-to-Glory Jane', a late poem of 1892, which describes the *physical* form religious rhapsody takes, as Jane jumps not only to God but through orthodox social conventions and the religious timidity of the Bishop who so conventionally represents God. The energies of Meredith's poetry always seem to gather when he writes about women, and they continued to do so until his last volume, which begins with 'With the Huntress', another firm, almost classical poem which asserts the power of Artemis to direct the energies of men and *women* 'who each other would devour'. Another late mythological poem, 'The Appeasement of Demeter' (1888), celebrates laughter with a Nietzsche-like intensity even as it preserves the cold artifice of a mythological figure which declares itself as a formal tool for conceptualising a psychological and social proposition about the catharsis of laughter. A late poem on the prodigal-son theme, 'The Empty Purse; A Sermon to our Later Prodigal Son' (1892), a virtual miniature picaresque satirical novel on the wasteful habits of modern young men, concentrates at the point when it describes his dealings with women. Meredith's peculiar lyricism could be called a comic lyricism, refusing empathy even at its greatest intensity. This is particularly the case in a poem he valued highly, 'The Sage Enamoured and the Honest Lady' (1892). Concerned with a situation as complex as *Modern Love*, the passion of an older man for a much younger woman, it maintains a chiselled lyricism and a complex syntax which preserves detachment as abstractions take on an intense and momentary life with a crystal sensuousness: 'Compassion for the man thus noble nerved/The pity for herself she felt in him'. Characteristically, Meredith combines here that capacity to present the immediacy of sensation but to transform it through metaphor into abstraction almost as it is being verbalised: 'the crimson currents ran/From senses up to thoughts'. *Modern Love* is perhaps his most remarkable poem, but it requires the context not only of a politics but of the comic lyricism of the poems on women for its peculiar character to be disclosed. Pater's hard, gem-like classicism is appropriated for genuinely dissident purposes.

16

JAMES THOMSON: ATHEIST, BLASPHEMER AND ANARCHIST

The Grotesque sublime

One of Thomson's earliest published poems was a celebration of Shelley, a visionary poem in Shelley's mode. To declare an interest in Shelley at this time was to align oneself with revolutionary politics and anti-Christian thought, and this Thomson unequivocally did.[1] 'Finding a vast State-church, based upon politico-theology, everywhere in the ascendent', he comments, Shelley sought to defeat the negativity of its ideology.[2] And yet his approving account of Shelley's energising, non-theistic 'Pantheism' adds a corporeal and materialist element which is more characteristic of Thomson than Shelley: he took out the nervous, platonised, spiritualising properties of Shelley's account of the soul and replaced them with Saturnian body. 'Prometheus' is an apotheosis of 'One infinite Soul, self-subsisting, informing all things; one and the same in all masks of man, and beast, and worm, and plant, and slime'.[3] The almost syllogistically worked-out atheistic thought to which Thomson adhered did not in fact admit that matter possessed intelligence. 'Substance', Charles Bradlaugh, Thomson's freethinking associate, wrote in 'A plea for atheism', is not regarded by the atheist as either essentially intelligent or non-intelligent: like the brightness of steel, 'Intelligence is the result of certain conditions of existence. . . . Alter the condition, and the characteristic of the condition no longer exists'.[4] To turn to Thomson's defence of Shelley is actually to find a poem which celebrates a poet working within conceptual and imaginative *limits*; 'I could not understand men [Thomson's Shelley says]; all their hearts/ Had secrets which I could not ever guess'. Then follows a rigorous litany of abuses.

> Their greed for dross upon the daily marts,
> Their pride and fawning in the palaces,
> Their solemn church-attending worldliness,
> Their servile fear of Custom's lawless law
> Filled me with sad perplexity and awe.[5]

When such gods were repudiated as 'hideous monsters' and God was redefined as 'infinite love for all things that exist', Shelley's voice continues,

'I was branded as an Atheist'. When urged to fling 'mutual bonds off and be free:/They paused in their old strife to spurn at me'.

Yet Thomson is the most Shelleyan poet of the nineteenth century despite his reservations, for his project is to construct single-handed a new symbolic language and a wholly new mythological system. It is not the same myth as Shelley's because it is the mythos of atheism. There is nothing utopian about it. But it shares with Shelley's poetry the attempt to break cultural forms and to construct a new imaginative and ideological world, redefining history and consciousness. But this reconstructed modern myth had to be made out of existing forms of thought, images and language, above all Christian language and the cosmology of Dante's *Inferno*. The shock of *The City of Dreadful Night*, published in the freethinking *National Reformer* in 1874, is its use of the traditional language of spiritual experience to overturn it, a language overturned by its own oppressive weight. The extremity of Thomson's experiment places him quite outside any of the radical poetry written in the century, not to speak of the conservative tradition.

High-conservative writing could not have been more unlike Thomson's. It is easy to see how a conservative poet such as Alfred Austin would call forth 'rage' (Thomson's description of his own poem in the Proem to *The City of Dreadful Night*) in a radical writer. A poem such as 'Why England is Conservative' portrays a believing rural England and a feudal peasantry subservient to authority.

> Therefore, chime sweet and safely, village bells,
> And, rustic chancels, woo to reverent prayer,
> And, wise and simple, to the porch repair
> Round which Death, slumbering, dreamlike heaves and swells.
> Let hound and horn in wintry wood and dells
> Make jocund music though the boughs be bare,
> And whistling yokel guide his gleaming share
> Hard by the homes where gentle lordship dwells.
> Therefore sit high enthroned on every hill,
> Authority! and loved in every vale;
> Nor, old Tradition, falter in the tale
> Of lowly valour led by lofty will:
> And, though the throats of envy rage and rail,
> Be fair proud England proud fair England still![6]

This idyllic condition was not perceived to be the case by radical campaigners. In his *The Land, the People, and the Coming Struggle* (1872), Charles Bradlaugh had pointed out the concentration of the land in the hands of fewer and fewer aristocratic property owners since the Georgian period, the exploitation of the poor in wages below a living wage, the exploitation of them as debtors and the huge proportion of rural and urban pauperism

461

in the 1870s.[7] The preservation of game in preference to human life was one of his themes. Austin's language almost inadvertently exposes his awareness of another argument. It would have been necessary indeed for the poor to 'repair' themselves, for more than the winter tree boughs of the estates were 'bare'. Similarly, the rhyming 'share' for ploughshare discloses a fatal ambiguity: the Ploughman's 'Share' or lot was minimal. This poem appeared in *Lyrical Poems* in 1891, five years before Austin became poet laureate. The acute agricultural depression of the 1870s was behind him, but the poem displays an impercipience characteristic of the verse he published so prolifically from 1871 onwards.

The energy of Thomson's poetry, however, arises from something more than an animus against a conservative poetry which was inimical to him. Nor was he simply an urban poet, writing of the city in contradistinction to the rural pastoral and idyll. Other poets had written and would continue to write, culminating in T. S. Eliot's 'Unreal city' in *The Waste Land*, of the estrangement of city experience and urban anomie. Arthur O'Shaughnessy, for instance, wrote of the contrast between country and city in 'A Discord': 'Back to the bloomless city, and athwart/The doleful streets and many a closed-up court/That prisoned here and there a spent noon-ray'.[8] W. E. Henley and John Davidson were later to explore both the horrors and the vitality of the urban world, one in the casualties of the city in poems such as 'Suicide', and the other in demotic renderings of city life, such as 'Thirty Bob a Week'.[9] Such poems, which may seem part of a 'Thomson tradition', only serve to point up the radical difference between Thomson and contemporary or later city poets. Immersed as he was in the alienation of the city, he was not concerned with an account of its physical horror or its psychological estrangement as an end in itself. Rather the city as symbol is symptomatic: it is not the cause of despair but the representations which despair, imprisoned in theological and ideological fallacies, makes for itself. The oppression of the city is literal enough because it is the physical and mental product of a false consciousness which knowingly and unknowingly accepts oppression. The city has a cruel, material, substantive existence in his poem, but for Thomson this is precisely the other side, or complement, of the false utopian dream, such as is embodied in the contrast made in O'Shaughnessy's poem between ideal country and 'real' town. It is thus not the opposite of the utopian dream but its demonised counterpart. The city is at once an incarcerating material environment and a universal metaphysical condition, compounded of London, the biblical landscapes of the Old and New Testaments and the *Inferno*. It has a far more coercive existence than the mere unreality of the nightmare, even when its inhabitants and the narrator himself experience it as nightmare.

By the time Thomson was writing, some aspects of the 'visionary' tradition of Shelleyan writing had become normalised and weakened so that the poet was seen as a dreamer. His poem might almost be an answer to

O'Shaughnessy's 'Ode' of the same year, 1874, 'We are the music makers,/ And we are the dreamers of dreams'. The poet dwells 'a little apart', creating a dream which is brought into being by the 'multitudes' who once scorned it.[10] O'Shaughnessy's idealised city landscapes of past empire might be being fiercely parodied by Thomson: 'Great ruins of an unremembered past,/With others of a few short years ago/More sad, are found within its precincts vast'.[11] Thomson does not write for Christian idealists nor 'sages who foresee a heaven on earth' (Proem). There is no 'secret' in his poem, no hidden symbolic referent, but an open one. His are 'weak words' because they are constructed out of a language which is forced to use the categories of an obsolete metaphysic against itself. *The City of Dreadful Night* is perhaps the last sustained double poem of the century. For it uses the language of hell and of Christian despair to enter fully into that condition, and at the same time withdraws from it to expose it as a mystified mythology which collapses under an antagonistic alternative materialist mythology: 'Mystery is but misery dissolved in thought, the intolerable concrete rendered abstract and vague' ('A Lady of Sorrow', 1862).[12] If it were simply the Christian poem it parodies, consumed with the incommensurateness of symbol, filled with longing and desire, obsessed with death, it would be a Grotesque poem, but the diction exerts such a cold, hard, impersonal, classical control that it is hard to think of it as Grotesque. Though it belongs to that genre in some ways, its intransigent rationalism, insisting on the 'law' from which Pater longed to escape, belongs to the sublime.

The first poem in the sequence, phantasmagoric, yet solid, enervated, yet firmly organised, dissolving, yet precisely realised, establishes the conditions of existence in the city and prefigures the contradictions which subsequently unfold. Visionary materialism is its mode. It can be contextualised in Thomson's earlier materialist rhapsody in prose, 'A Lady of Sorrow', and in Bradlaugh's systematic account of the basis of atheism, but it goes beyond both in its uncompromising intensity. 'The city is of Night; perchance of Death,/But certainly of Night; . . . The sun has never visited that city,/For it dissolveth in the daylight fair'. The second stanza continues as if part of the same syntax: 'Dissolveth like a dream of night away;/Though present in distempered gloom of thought'. The sheer severity of statement, followed by the ruthless negatives of 'Never' – 'The sun has never visited that city' – invokes the traditional symbolism of the dark night of the soul.[13] But this is not presented as metaphor: the sun *partakes* of night, and 'perchance', possibly, of death too. Thomson is invoking the laws of physics, the law of the ever cooling universe and the literal death of the sun. 'As cold comes not, but heat departs; as darkness grows not, but light fades', he wrote in 'A Lady of Sorrow' (50):

this gross multiform mass of matter consuming in the fervency of the

463

one spirit – shall indeed at last be utterly annihilated. The law flames before your eyes in material analogies, the doom stamps itself into your consciousnesses by material symbols. Behold how the nebulous continuity of your sun-system has parted and congealed into separate calcined orbs hollow and centrally candent; and all are dwindling in the millennial cycles, and shall dwindle until the last fire-sustaining atom is exhausted, and remnant there is none of the worlds opaque in the infinite unadulterate empyrean. But now 'in the midst of life you are in death:' not merely *liable* to death, as so shallowly you are wont to interpret the great truth into a truism; but *in* death; you and your transitory phantasmal Universe of matter floating in the midst of the eternal Divine Life which alone is Reality.

The mocking, ecstatic tirade, stealing the language of spiritual rhapsody to portray a materialist universe, insists that the categories of spiritual discourse which describe 'Reality' or essential truth as that which makes the universe of matter 'phantasmal' are fallacious. The city is 'of night' as a result of the laws of physics, for the sun is literally dissolving and fading away in the daylight. But it is also permanently 'of night' because its inhabitants wrongly conceptualise their physical environment as 'phantasmal' in order to make it bearable, and the shadow of the phantasmal does not partake of light. But the sun, fading in the light, also 'dissolveth like a *dream* of night away', though it may be retained as a morbid internal image in the minds and emotions of the city dwellers, in the 'distempered gloom of thought' or in 'the deadly weariness of heart'. The sun can both dissolve in the daylight and dissolve like a dream of night because for the inhabitants the phantasmal nature of the material universe created by Christian myth makes the sun equally as shadowy and phantasmal as night: it becomes an *image* or *dream* of night or shadowy reality in its *representation* as spiritual essence. So logically, as well as literally, 'The sun has never visited that city'. For the internal psychic lives of the inhabitants, the contrast between the sun and the night is merely a symbolic notation which enables them to contrast spiritual 'Reality' or truth with their present state of darkness, and hence it is a sick, distempered and gloomy image of imprisonment.

This 'dream of night', or construction of experience as an opposition between spiritual reality and phantasmal material life, the second stanza continues, is consolidated through repetition: 'But when a dream night after night is brought/Throughout a week, and such weeks few or many/ Recur each year for several years, can any/Discern that dream from real life in aught?' Stanza 3 continues, 'For life is but a dream whose shapes return,/Some frequently, some seldom, some by night/And some by day, some night and day'. When such a dream recurs through nights, weeks and years, the distinction between 'dream' and 'reality' breaks down.

464

Again, the words 'dream' and 'reality' are being used with ironic logic here. The notion of the phantasmal nature of life becomes so coercive by repetition that consciousness has no psychological or *conceptual* means of creating a distinction between its sense of dream and reality, which necessarily collapse into one another when consciousness starts by defining all its experience as shadowy. Life is '*but*' a dream in two senses: it is a purgatory to be lived through, only a shadow, for the Christian; but for the atheist's fierce definition of material experience the idea of dream utterly negates life.

The sequence of night and day – for night and day do come in this city though they are necessarily conceived of as perpetual night – *does* appear to guarantee the Christian's imagery of contrast, but only because he selects or imposes a fixed order on experience by assuming that *recurrence* is a God-given law. In other words, such recurrence is the creation of language and, as will be seen, atheist epistemology put great stress on accounts of the world as an effect of language. The 'law' of recurrence is constructed out of change but ignores or represses the fact of *perpetual* change: 'we learn,/In their recurrence with perpetual changes/A certain seeming order/In their recurrence with recurrent changes' (stanza 3). 'Cause is simply everything without which the effect would not result, and with which it must result. Cause is the means to an end, consummating itself in that end. Cause is the *word* [my emphasis] we use to include all that determines change', Bradlaugh wrote.[14] Change, and not necessarily order, is implied by the recurrence of the 'law' of cause and effect. If the theist attributes recurrence to a predetermined law of God, he is faced with positing a prior existence which, however, could not be infinite because it would be circumscribed with its own laws. Creation would then be impossible. Such a prior existence could not be finite because God is posited as infinite. This logic means that we are thrown back on ceaseless change as a principle of existence. In 'A Lady of Sorrow', Thomson has an incessant march of numberless multitudes moving in procession in synchronic unity, the armies of Troy and of Waterloo moving without historical distinction, because the 'law' of progression is a law of change in which all share at any time, chanting a universal dead, or living, march: 'All must move to live, and their moving/Moves on and on to Death' (24). The order deduced in the poem is a 'certain seeming order': that is, for the Christian, a certain, or indisputably apparent order; for the atheist, an order which only *seems* to be the case. 'Where this ranges/We count things real; such is memory's might' (I. 3). So coercive is memory, with its registering of recurrence as law, that the Christian takes for 'real' order what the atheist sees as the 'reality' of change. The Christian is subject to a 'dream' of the 'real', so the virtuosity of Thomson's paradoxes affirm, with their constant shifting of the ground of the meaning of dream and reality. But this is presented as a ground which the Christian shifts, rather than the narrator, in the manipulation of language made to produce an ordered universe.

Thomson's endless city holds within itself the landscapes of all and any latitudes, the monumental buildings of all and any cultures, 'trackless wilderness' (stanza 5) and civilisation. 'The city is not ruinous, although/ Great ruins of an unremembered past,/With others of a few short years ago/More sad, are found within its precincts vast' (stanza 6). Ruins of the past and present coexist, even though the city is not ruinous. The city does not transcend space and time: it is always being built indifferently, destroyed and rebuilt out of the same material elements; that is the sublimity of the materialist vision. But space and time for the non-materialist are always the objects of the attempt at transcendence. The synchronic climates and histories are there to demonstrate the surreal nightmare of a universe where space and time are transcended, and at the same time they *do* demonstrate that space and time inexorably determine history even when it is 'unremembered', that the savannah and the marsh are alike the particles of matter which have circulated in geological movement and belong to the very stone of which the city is built. Such perpetual movement means that the city is constructed of great geological ruins even when it does not appear to be in ruins. The more recent ruins, 'more sad', are the humanly created ruins of a society which does not notice, or represses, the material squalor and exploitation on which great cities are founded.

'The street lamps burn amidst the baleful glooms' (stanza 7) in the artificial light cast by the intellect's constructions of experience. But as the granite sublimity of the materialist vision moves in these not quite ottava rima stanzas, a question arises: why, in this environment, so spacious and so enclosed, so claustrophobic and so empty, is the city so depopulated, so empty of people? The last part of the poem answers this question. In the benumbing silence of the houses, palaces, rooves, basements, those people who have not fled the city sleep or wander in a stupor of insomniac isolation, faces insensate 'masks of stone', each enclosed in the solipsism of thought. The longing for transcendence is a deeply internal condition, and a religion founded on a repudiation of the body is bound to make human beings unreal to one another and to themselves. The city's inhabitants are oppressed, and oppressed with thought, because theism poses intolerably insoluble problems and contradictions which are consuming. At the beginning of 'A Lady of Sorrow', the narrator lives alone in London with an angel who succeeds in making the millions of its inhabitants utterly unreal and unimportant to him, such is the nature of a *personal* religion: for a personal religion is individualist and the individual's subjectivity is at stake:

And now with her I was to live alone; in the heart of London, yet mysteriously alone. . . . She annihilated from me the huge city and all its inhabitants; they, with their thoughts, passions, labours, struggles, victories, defeats, were nothing to me; I was nothing to them. . . . Scarcely at night, when I went up with her to the solitude of my room, or wandered with her through the deserted thoroughfares and environs, were we more perfectly alone than amidst the noise and glare of the populous day . . . she annihilated so utterly from me the mighty metropolis, whose citizens are counted by millions, that the whole did not even form a dark background for the spiritual scenes and personages her spells continually evoked.[15]

The first step to an insight into the materialist revelation brings with it at least a consciousness of alienation from others, as the 'vast Metropolis' becomes a 'vast Necropolis', in which he wanders as a pariah. So the city *is* populated, but theist anomie nullifies the life of millions to one another.

The wanderers are mature men, rarely women, and 'now and then a child'. Women are not visible in the city because they are so entirely subordinated. But it is the child who provokes the narrator's rage: 'To see a little one from birth defiled,/Or lame or blind, as preordained to languish/Through youthless life, think how it bleeds with anguish/To meet one erring in that homeless wild' (stanza 9). Darwin had revived an interest in Malthus among freethinkers. The spectre of overpopulation haunted them. They saw the cruel indifference to life openly apparent in the factory system and its exploitation as one of the means by which an advanced industrial society limited population as people died of industrial disease. Annie Besant, part of the freethinking group with which Thomson was associated, wrote an eloquent pamphlet on the means by which industrial labour operates population control and advocated birth control as an alternative. 'The too early putting of the children to work is one of the consequences of over-large families'.[16] Malthusian pessimism could be defeated by faith in rational and humane planning. But the oppressed child in the poem suffers a double oppression: it is one of the exploited labour force, mutilated by labour, but it is also spiritually mutilated by the doctrines of theism which teach it to see itself as maimed and sinful. One form of exploitation is a consequence of the other, and the two are indivisible.

That is why the smoke of factories and the visible work of the labouring poor is absent from *The City of Dreadful Night*, for it analyses the ideology which produces these things, not the forms they take. 'Every child is born into the world an Atheist', Charles Bradlaugh wrote, but is socially conditioned by theism.[17] Thomson saw the ceaseless fertility of the world and its prodigal squandering of creation and destruction as the ultimately horrifying and ultimately astounding mystery of pure matter in 'A Lady of Sorrow', and converts post-Malthusian thought into a myth of impersonal creation, constantly squandering its resources, constantly *reproducing* itself.

'Every prodigal aeon squanders broadcast myriads of its lives, and the hours of every cycle are squandered by myriads; yet not one monad, not one moment, to the universe has ever been lost' (24). Since nothing falls outside the material universe, it can never lose, but only change, what composes it. You destroy a gold coin, Bradlaugh said, but not the metal it is made of.[18] For Thomson, ruthlessly reconfiguring the negativity of Malthusian thought and its deep fear of excess, this meant exulting almost wantonly in plenitude, so that the model for human life must be excess and not dearth, sexuality and not restraint. But its inverse appears in the poem's city of dearth, maiming and mutilation, where men turn 'inwardly' mad from mental and physical oppression because they have internalised the postulates of Malthusian dread.

The poem moves to its climax with mordant intensity.

> They leave all hope behind who enter there:
>   One certitude while sane they cannot leave,
> One anodyne for torture and despair;
>   The certitude of Death, which no reprieve
> Can put off long; and which, divinely tender,
> But waits the outstretched hand to promptly render
>   That draught whose slumber nothing can bereave.
>
> (stanza 12)

The atheist reappropriates the motto of Dante's hell. For Dante's *Inferno* hell was a place of despair and punishment and that is why hope is abandoned. For Thomson it is simply a brutal fact that the death which ends consciousness must terminate hope. But more is implied than this: to abandon hope is a prerequisite for atheist thought; theistic hope is the greatest and most corrupting of fallacies, draining life itself of meaning and offering an illusory metaphysical comfort. Whereas for the theist hope is the anodyne, the great ethical and psychological drug, for the atheist death itself is the drug for which we hope if we hope at all, pure and absolute annihilation. Because the theist's hope makes him negate life for the sake of the future, he lives a half-life of death-in-life. The atheist recognises that we begin to die as soon as we live, and life is defined only by its relation to death. Nothing is recuperated in any Hegelian scheme. If we are in despair we can hope only for the end of despair in death. That is the remorseless certitude. In that sense death is, shockingly, an anodyne, and the scheme of this poem comprehends both madness and suicide as a way of escaping despair. Thomson does not invert theism into a rational and optimistic scheme, but by mimicking its language he wins the sombre certitude of an absolute denial of its denials. It is theism which has created despair, and the burden of this poem is the despair inherited by the atheist, who has a double burden, the oppressions of Christianity and the burden of being unable to *assert* his denial.

Hence *The City of Dreadful Night* does not repeat the ecstatic materialist vision of 'A Lady of Sorrow', and actually turns its narrative structure back to front, as will be seen. Nor does it follow Bradlaugh's rational optimism, though these texts can gloss the poem to some extent. Its Nietzschean project is to deconstruct the symbolic language of the western Christian tradition, not destroying these symbols, for 'Some men see truth and express truth best in imagery and symbol' ('A Lady of Sorrow', 3), but demonstrating that their language and imagery can *only* be used to adumbrate a quite different and systematically opposed account of experience. And so Thomson's black epistemological epic rigorously redefines terminology – 'dream', 'real' and 'hope' are examples in the first poem. When the inhabitant of the city becomes aware of subliminal sound in the vast, oppressive silence, it is concealed, muffled and indistinct (III), as of 'hidden life asleep', the throbs of passion and 'Far murmurs, speech of pity and derision', the language of death-in-life, not the true language of death. Bradlaugh argued not simply that theistic terminology is inaccurate and misleading but that Christian antinomies constitute a nonsense language which has no basis in experience. (And so Mansel's idealist propositions turn up in a strange context.) That is why the sounds of the city are incoherent. The atheist project was to change the meaning of the sign and to obliterate its customary distinctions. To the theist's distinction between intelligence and matter, 'The Atheist answers, I do not know what is meant, in the mouth of the Theist, by "matter" '.[19] 'Matter', 'nature', 'substance', 'existence', are words having the same signification in the atheist's vocabulary (i.e. they are not presented in terms of pairs of oppositions). Lewes, says Bradlaugh, uses 'matter' as 'the symbol of all the known properties, statical and dynamical, passive and active, *i.e.* subjectively as feeling and change of feeling; or objectively, as agent and action'; and Mill makes 'nature' 'the sum of all phenomena, together with the causes which produce them, including not only all that happens, but all that is capable of happening'.[20] Since nothing is outside the material universe it is impossible to use a language which posits an opposition between the material and spiritual, matter and intelligence. Words impose categories on the world. 'Can words make foul things fair?' an inhabitant of the city cries in despair, echoing the horror of the witches in *Macbeth*, after listening to the atheist preaching that there is no God. It is an opposition the despairer can use because he is still locked in Christian antinomies.[21] When the narrator of 'A Lady of Sorrow' is led to insight by the Shadow, her terminology is at first both monotonous and confusing, until it is apparent that she is speaking a 'new' language. Her theme is always the same:

> she with her mystic insight seems to call indifferently by any one or more of the names we have thus bestowed – World, Life, Birth,

Death, Time, Eternity, Oblivion, Cosmos, Chaos, Heaven, Hell, Matter, Spirit, Happiness, Misery, Health, Disease, Growth, Decay, Vanity, Reality, Illusion, Truth, God, Fate, All, Nothing; for under all these titles she sees the sole Substance itself always essentially one and the same.[22]

The Shadow is not a *spirit*, but precisely protean matter and shadowy *meaning*.

The monstrous obliteration of difference shocks, but the myth of atheism is rigorous here. The categories of Happiness and Misery, Health and Disease, are not stable and permanent simply because we are aware of the *movement* of experience from one condition to the other. They are not without *momentary* definition but they are without distinction. They require each other to mean anything at all. They are conditions of *transition*, and governed by the principle of change. Time, Eternity and Oblivion are terms without distinction because for the materialist vision they are included in the constant capacity for change in finite matter. *Oblivion* becomes in fact the signal and defining mark of all human experience, the condition without which consciousness could not be. This is not simply the ultimate oblivion of death. 'Can God forget?' Bradlaugh asks.[23] A perfect, omniscient and infinite God can have no new experience because His experience is always already in existence, and because He comprehends objects within Himself He cannot perceive, recollect, forget, compare, reflect or judge. An immutable God can understand neither pleasure nor pain. Thus the thing we most dread, amnesia, forgetting, oblivion, is what must most be celebrated. For without this capacity for amnesia we could have no new knowledge or experience, no sense of time, no awareness of the change from one condition to another. Where Hopkins thought of experience as a chain of marked and permanent difference, and puzzled about the capacity of memory to hold experience together, Thomson thinks of it as differenc*ing*. Only the capacity to forget enables the capacity to remember and differentiate the amorphous movement of change. This is not the willed death-in-life which defers fulfilment to a future heaven, but the positive oblivion which creates the possibility of both experience and language.

The atheist vision constitutes a shadowy parallel to that of the Christian, refuting it through ironic parallelism rather than through direct negation. That is why the narrator of 'A Lady of Sorrow' meets a Shadow as instructor in the third part of the myth. Though Thomson's narrative is a rigorous mythologising of the systematic atheism of the Bradlaugh circle, its symbolic form made it much harder for him to offer the rational, positivist optimism of that group as a solution to oppression, and there is some doubt as to whether he would have wished to do this in any case. Bradlaugh believed that since atheism declares all events to be in accordance with natural laws, men could find practical ways of alleviating ills and evil, based on present and not on future happiness, that poverty is the chief source of crime and disease, and that 'prayers and piety afford no protection against fever'.[24] Atheism is not a cold and negative creed. It repudiates the notion of metaphysical evil. The superstition of punishment in hell never prevented theists from crime and murder. If evil is caused by God He cannot be all good, and if it is not, He is not all-powerful. Religion originated as an explanation of inexplicable power (interestingly, he quotes Thomas Keightley in support of this view). Attempts to dissociate religion from power fail. The deist a posteriori argument from design and analogy – the notorious example of the watch is examined – reasons from effects to a cause, proposing that the universe is designed out of a pre-existing substance by a being of the same substance who is in fact powerless because it is not clear how and whether he commenced designing, and whether he is forced to continue designing: 'if he is always designing what then induced him so to commence?'[25] The phases of the embryo suggest extraordinary inefficiency if we are positing design. From the other end, the theism which simply sees God as an abstract principle of life deprives him of rationality, will, morality.

Such arguments are consummately imaged in 'A Lady of Sorrow' and *The City of Dreadful Night*, but with considerable difference of emphasis. 'A Lady of Sorrow' wrings metaphysical comfort out of a refusal of metaphysical comfort, but *The City of Dreadful Night* begins with this refusal. The prose work has three phases. The speaker comes under the dominion of an Angel, a Siren and a Shadow, who offers the culminating materialist vision. The Angel leads him to the negation of theist experience, the Siren to the excess of restless movement, sexuality and imaginative vision, as the caverns and fecundity of the creative element, water, open out to him. But, like all material things, she decays, and becomes a hag. He cannot understand this, until the Shadow's mythological discourse offers a reading of experience. It is at this point, just before her speech, that the suffering of others becomes horribly real to him:

> gradually the whole outer world – the innumerable armies of woes, sins, fears, despairs, . . . poured in upon and overwhelmed my spirit . . . a waking Nightmare; its inhabitants were no shadows . . . I felt crushing me down the omnipotence of Fate; Fate the Sphynx in the desert of Life, whose enigma is destruction to all who cannot interpret, and a doom more horrible before destruction to him who does interpret; Fate which weaves lives only too real in the loom of destiny so mysterious, uncompassionate of their agonies in the process; Fate, God petrified; the dumb, blind, soulless deification of Matter.[26]

This recognition brings him no nearer sympathy with men, in spite of his awareness of suffering. Then follows the vision of the marching millions of

471

history, singing of change in a darkened universe of mist, moon and stars. This is a Malthusian cycle of creation and destruction raised to the level of agonistic but exultant myth, multitudes 'disappearing into the black, mist-shrouded gulph, while ever-new multitudes appeared emergent on the background of the golden dawn', moving under the surveillance of a veiled image, the principle of life (23). Nature *is* impersonal and indifferent: the principle of love is the dead mother, because love is bound to the cycle of life and decay; the principle of death is the living father because only death exists as a permanent law. The Shadow, a vehicle for the voice of death, her words taken from the mouldering and mouldered volumes of libraries, testifies to the supreme 'beatitude of unconsciousness' as the significant human experience, prefacing her revelation with an anthology of poems to death (Chaucer, Shakespeare, Keats, Emily Brontë). In the squandering economy of matter, hell does not exist: 'better worms winding through that brain than the thoughts which used to possess it' (35). Evil is substantive, circulating as the poison of physical and mental cause and effect in the universe forever, but an ethical God is not. There is no moral economy, no debtors, in the world of matter. 'Why are you so unwilling to acknow-ledge' your affinity with the 'family' of all material existence? Who could recognise in its myriad variants the image of God? the Shadow asks (41, 40). This is not an individual but an absolutely impersonal relationship. The races flourish and die as the coral insects swarm in the sea, blindly building the matter which dies and becomes the land occupied by human culture (the coral reef of Darwin and Lyell becomes incorporated into the myth of matter). The way to live is to replicate this blind excess and to consent to the intensity of the fire which sustains life and the fire which as surely consumes it and which will itself become extinct. You 'have been generous enough to create a God who certainly never created you; you dissect him, every bone, nerve, and tissue . . . in your metaphysical and theological discourses . . . and yet you cannot say why the grass grows' (44).

The City of Dreadful Night omits the vision of refining *material* fire, just as it omits the sun which forms the background to the birth or rebirth of matter. It may have seemed too close to Christian myth in the doubling of its forms, too optimistic, or perhaps even too aesthetic, to be usable: too similar to the sensation-bound intensity of the hard, gem-like flame celebrated by patrician aesthetes such as Pater.

The poem confines itself to the condition prior to the narrator's awaken-ing, allowing the text to imply what is adumbrated in the prose piece. Thus it is an epic of mourning which refuses to mourn. It ends (XXI) with the massive, symbolic figure of Melancholia (based on Dürer's image), whose only 'secret' is the 'bronze sublimity' with which she repudiates metaphysical comfort, redefining Blake's male figure with the compass, as she holds the materials with which a culture builds and protects itself in her hands. In this tenebrae of nescience, she cannot be figured in words, for words are material signs and to figure her would be to understand 'why the grass grows'. She can only be figured as nescience, a terror to the weak, the source of 'iron endurance' to the strong. But she is not the father-figure of death and the law, simply the black creative principle of matter itself. The figure of the law appears in the penultimate poem, where the imperturbable sphinx of time confronts the stone angel which disintegrates from angel to man and to inert stone in three successive cataclysmic moments of history, returning to pure matter while the narrator is lulled to an uneasy sleep of death-in-life as time ends. The inexorable 'river of the suicides', Lethe, flowing in the urban landscape of bridge and dock, precedes this logically (XIX) for time is inescapable except through death, the oblivion which defines life. The despair of the suicide has in it a paradoxical affirmation, because it abandons hope and meets, not eternal punishment, but 'the beatitude of unconsciousness'. Remorselessly turning theistic propositions inside out, the text compares this way out of time to the straits of the wretched, crawling figure of section XVIII, an aged infantilist, who is attempting to return to the original bliss of Eden. Time is irreversible, we cannot 'return' in the post-Darwinian universe: 'What never has been, yet may have its when;/The thing which has been, never is again' (XVIII. 13). The projections of fantasy may possibly be justified by events, but what has been can never recur. The cadences of Wordsworth's 'Peel Castle' are modulated to iron denial. It is fascinating, however, that Thomson sees the principle of creativity as a black, feminine principle, and returns to the non-European sphinx as the source of time. It is characteristic of him to override European accounts of gender and race.

The last four sections suggest how the poem is not a series of expressions of despair but seeks to analyse the totality of despair's nature in a theistic universe. After the first section the poem moves to the majestic negations of the man who seeks to prove the existence of God by analogy and the argument from design, and to the workings of the watch which can only serve to refute him. Following the section on the confused and muffled language of theism, the split self sees love, the principle of death, destroy one part of his being. This destruction is possible because hope has fragmented him into a divided being, a hopeful and thus fearful self: 'As I came through the desert thus it was. . . . But I strode on austere;/No hope could have no fear' (IV. 4). To say of experience simply that 'thus it *was*' demands an impossible heroism, but only true despair is integrating. Consequently section V is a rehearsal for suicide, and section VI turns Dante's 'abandon hope' inside out, as the petitioners *have* to abandon hope, but cannot do so, in order to die. Section VII modulates, with grim humour, to the 'divine' comedy of the grotesque theological speculation and dissection which is the material of hope: 'The phantoms have no reticence at all:/The nudity of flesh will blush through tameless,/The extreme nudity of bone grins shameless'. Section VIII presents a blasphemous speech about the savagely punitive non-indifferent God of Christianity, and section IX portrays the world of oppressed labour guaranteed by such a God, 'strangled by that City's curse'. A funereal Christian 'festival' takes place appropriately in a huge secular mansion in the tenth section. In section XI the repressed energies which are directed to the evasion of death make their appearance in the attempt to transcend through forms of thought and action in a substitute secular paradise – through the construction of rational systems, through wealth and through art. (In the prose piece the aggression of warfare was numbered among these forms of evasion.) These cultural arrangements create intellectual and social hierarchies which are denied to the poor and underprivileged, but since they too encounter death in the return of the repressed, they likewise cannot escape from madness. The twelfth section continues this theme, asking whether the diverse occupations of life can work together for 'the common good'. It is an ironic parallel of section X. The varied forms of secular action, from martial combat to art, to entertainment, to the company of prostitutes, take place in a cathedral, inverting the *religious* ceremonies of section X, which take place in a mansion. Secular or not they are forms of *justification*, and thus feed on damaging hope. Such forms of life ignore the real tasks – fighting 'the powerful tyrants of our land', they are still impotent with Christian or humanist positivism. All, challenged by the 'warder', give some account of themselves which closes off genuine action and closes them *into* an ineffectual world. These include the poet himself, who 'marked the closing of the massive door', inside the 'cathedral' of ineffectual secular action. Now, inside the cathedral, consciousness is consumed with longing to escape (XIII), and is unable to recognise the good tidings (XIV) of the preacher whose creed affirms, 'There is no God'. It is unable to see that the city's 'atmosphere' (XV) is compounded of material life which necessarily fuses *all* physical phenomena even as the poison of life-giving respiration itself circulates through all things. The comfortless speaker of section XVI cries in anguish that the mere social joys and loves of life are all that he possesses, and section XVII affirms the self-consuming world of matter which is indifferent to individuals, as the 'void abyss' refuses to reflect human emotion back to itself in sympathetic reciprocity.

Such an abbreviated account of the poem may indicate its logic but in no way suggests the extraordinarily fierce declamatory rigour of its language, the variety of metre and form which discloses the 'unsecret, dark' cosmology of the city, and the speeches, declamations, dialogues and agonised cries of its inhabitants. As Thomson's anti-humanist challenge to Christian transcendence and Christian humanism proceeds, with its dark satire, black sublimity and intellectual rage, the city becomes more and more populated, more and more full of human life, more and more full of activity and emotion, as if to testify to the potential energies of its oppressed inhabitants. The energy and the visionary negations go *pari passu* with one another. Thomson is often described as a 'pessimist' by those who find his position difficult to bear. His earliest biographer, Bartram Dobell, virtually suppressed reference to his atheism in the cause of getting his poem accepted by readers.[27] The energising and inexhaustible imagery of darkness which portrays the enervation of a politico-theological condition, as he would have called it, is ultimately and necessarily deeply ambiguous, in danger of becoming again what it so remorselessly and grandly mimics – for this is sublime parody in the grand style. More difficult, however, is one's sense that the cruel coercions of oppression reflect back into the work itself by enclosing it in an alternative *system*. The freedom of atheist epistemology becomes frozen. This was Nietzsche's problem, an inescapable one for the deconstructive sublime.

Thomson tried hard to gain recognition by writing more accessible and realistic poems about urban life. His cheerful, tender 'Sunday up the River', an idyll of city holiday, was accepted by *Fraser's Magazine* in 1869, and its simple, robust songs of love and life ('Thank God for Life!' runs one of the refrains) would doubtless have appealed to the muscular Christianity of Charles Kingsley, its editor. Significantly, no further poems were accepted. When *The City of Dreadful Night* was sent to George Eliot, she suggested (class prejudice making her write at her vatic and pompous worst) that Thomson might turn to the celebration of working-class life. Mistakenly she associated him with the poetry of the self-educated working man.[28] Though of lowly birth, Thomson was educated and taught at an army school for some time, so her placing of him was not quite accurate. But perhaps his indefinable status as well as the unacceptability of his ideas explain the incomprehension he met with in the literary establishment. For Thomson belonged to a group politically and ideologically out of the mainstream of cultural life. Though he was no socialist, his views were acceptable mainly to the anarchist group round Bradlaugh with whom he was associated. 'He derided the idea of making a true Republic of a population besotted with religion, paralysed by creeds, cringing to the agents of their servitude, and clinging to the chains that enthrall them', G. W. Foote, the editor of *Satires and Profanities* (1884), wrote, but added: 'Thomson's sympathy with radical and revolutionary causes is not much noticed by Mr Dobell [his first biographer], but it was very strong'.[29] This was a radical and often anarchic sympathy (Bradlaugh debated his opposition to socialism with H. M. Hyndman in 1884), neither utopian nor authoritarian, as socialism seemed to this group to be. It took the form of an intense, satirical, savage indignation in Thomson's prose pieces, which are an essential context for his poetry. When Queen Victoria cut herself off from public life after Albert's death, Thomson satirised the outcry, on the ground that a monarch was dispensable. The Queen may have been drawing money from the state, but she was 'better doing nothing' and actually benefiting the state. Writing in the style of a Royal Commission examining evidence, he wrote,

> If a washerwoman, being stupefied by the death of her husband, neglected her business for more than a week or two, she would certainly lose her custom or employment, and not all the sanctity of conjugal grief (about which reverential journalists gush) would make people go on paying her for doing nothing . . . the Commissioners . . . consider . . . that there can be no proper comparison of a Queen and a washerwoman, and that nobody would think of instituting one, except a brute, a Republican, an Atheist, a Communist, a fiend in human form.[30]

He consistently attacked hypocritical morality and the prurience and timidity of British taste. Writing on the Swinburne controversy, he sympathised with the poet, though he claimed not to have read his work: 'As if there were any great book in existence proper to read aloud to young ladies in drawing-rooms! and as if young ladies in drawing-rooms were the fit and proper judges of any great book!'[31]

But it was his religious views which isolated him most decisively. Commenting on an extraordinary ecclesiastical scandal of 1876, in which a vicar refused to give the sacrament to a member of his congregation because he did not believe in hell, Thomson satirised the intricacies of the case and its evasions, for he was quick to see that the various judgements to which the case was submitted avoided the question of whether hell or the devil existed or not.

> If he [the devil] were to die, or be deposed, it would be necessary to elect another to the vacant dignity. . . . Just as Mr Disraeli lamented the withdrawal of Mr Gladstone, complaining of the embarrassment caused to the Government by having no responsible leader opposed to it, so we can imagine dear God lamenting the absence of a Devil, and declaring that the Christian scheme would not work well without one.

It was the devil which produced 'a balanced constitutional monarchy' rather than an 'Oriental absolute despotism' in theological affairs.[32] He was deliberately blasphemous, looking at the commercial success of Christianity in 'A Fine Old Jewish Firm' (not devoid of anti-semitism, this) and, in 'Christmas Eve in the Upper Circles', portraying God as a licentious man of the world: 'So I, like an old fool, must have my amour; and a pretty intrigue I got into with the prim damsel Mary! . . . (between ourselves, I have never been sure of the paternity)'.[33] He ended 'A Word on Blasphemy' by saying categorically, 'Speaking philosophically, an honest Atheist can no more blaspheme God than an honest Republican can be disloyal to a King, than an unmarried man can be guilty of conjugal infidelity'.[34] Here is another unmasking of the nonsense language which he explored in *The City of Dreadful Night*.

He wrote other materialist myths, 'Vane's Story' (1871) for instance, but nothing in them equals his major poem. 'Vane's Story' is an energetic poem, demonstrating Thomson's extraordinary control of metre, a mixture of fantasy and realism, as Vane goes to a quite ordinary lower-middle-class ball with a visionary companion from hell, his dead lady-love. It contains some of the iron lines characteristic of him – clocks, for instance, are heard 'Slowly chiming far away/The euthanasia of the day' – and the iconoclasm and 'blasphemy' to be found in his prose, but its centre is the simple, energetic and physical joy Vane finds in the dance.[35] The sexual release of the dance parallels the playful release of unrepressed energy in attacks on the morality of what Thomson elsewhere called 'Bumbledom'. Vane talks of the 'sublimated selfishness' of those who gave up goodness for heaven.

> Their alms were loans to poor God lent,
> Interest infinity-per-cent,
> (And God must be hard-up indeed
> If of such loans He stands in need);[36]

The lady sings a 'heathen' Heine love lyric (Thomson wrote a fine critical essay on Heine) to the Sunday-school music of Bishop Heber. Vane fends off the other admiring partners by telling them that the lady speaks a foreign language: 'I've a little knowledge/Of French, – the Working Man's New College', one of them mutters.[37] It is as if Thomson is envisaging a purely unrepressed state here in the real world. But the counterpart of 'Oblivion', the state which annihilates the repressions of the unconscious, soon disappears, and Vane dies not long after his dance of delight.

The poem is like the work of an unsoured Gissing, who has not lost belief in the vitality of people living at the bottom of a class society. 'A Voice from the Nile' is another attempt to write a materialist myth, this time a historical myth, taking the Nile as an image of perpetually self-renewing material life: 'Dark memories haunt me of an infinite past,/Ages and cycles brood above my springs'. The Nile sees fertility and famine, slavery and despotism, exploitation and the supersession of exploitation. It presents a picture of fiercely oppressed labour, of 'hundreds groaning with the stress of toil', starving and dying as they labour.[38] But to the Nile man is only pitiable because transient. Yet, particularly by 1884, when it was posthumously published in volume form, it was hard to mythologise the colonial other in this way, and the poem seems to be straining to make strange and to use the oriental as the materials of myth in a way that was possible to poets only earlier in the century, as, for instance, in Tennyson's

477

'Timbuctoo'. In this context Thomson's myth of impersonal matter and the 'Earth, All-Mother, all beneficent' seems both old-fashioned and curiously lacking in an understanding of the tensions at work in later nineteenth-century colonialism.[39] Thomson must have been aware that a debate on the ethics of imperialism was strongly active. The mythologised lands were becoming known and familiar at this stage, as France and Britain responded to the German industrial challenge by seeking colonial possessions and markets. Rudyard Kipling began publishing in 1886. His work has an inwardness with the uneasiness of imperialism which is quite different from Thomson's myth of impersonality. His ballads, often spoken by jocular sentimentalists unaware of their prejudices and racism, and unaware of the way they themselves are exploited, dramatise the brutalities of a system which Thomson could understand at home, but not abroad.

478

POSTSCRIPT

Browning died in 1889, Tennyson in 1892. Did Victorian poetry die with them? Perhaps the deaths of these colossus-like and prolific writers effectively terminate what we think of as Victorian poetry. They may have seemed old-fashioned and outmoded to younger poets, but they continued to write on questions central to the later part of the century until the end of their writing lives. In *Idylls of the King* Tennyson adumbrated the fatal soul/matter split, the dualism which so preoccupied Swinburne and which presages the new aesthetic of symbolism. Browning, still exceptionally responsive to his culture in the last twenty years of his life, was capable of moving from the exploration of violence and the problems around representation relevant to the 1867 Reform Bill in *The Ring and the Book* (1868) to the brilliant colonial critique, 'Clive', a poem about the damaging and contradictory codes of masculinity and honour in the closed world of Anglo-India, in the second series of *Dramatic Idylls* (1880).

But the deaths of Tennyson and Browning might well seem to complete a phase. While these poets were writing their late work, the conditions of twentieth-century poetry were forming – the increasing marginalisation of the poet, the fragmentation of cultural and literary life into coteries (of which the symptom is the little magazine), the formation of a European and Euro-American avant-garde, the growing aestheticisation of literature strangely concurrent with an increasing exploitation of it as commodity, the growing depoliticisation of poetry through a theory of the symbol which was thought to supersede the positivist and ethical discourses of nineteenth-century poetry, the final breakdown of the idea of a coherent bourgeois audience for literature. The prescient Swinburne anticipated something of this, as he anticipated the bitterness of class conflict and the crisis of imperialism, which 'Conquered and annexed and Englished!' as Browning put it in 'Clive', but was forced at the same time to compete avidly for markets.[1] It is perhaps appropriate to allow Swinburne to speak for the later part of the century: he was a formative poet for later writers, but the history of the 1890s and *fin-de-siècle* poetry seems to belong rather to the history of modernism than to that of Victorian poetry. This is particularly

479

the case in formal terms at least: the high-Victorian double poem, an *expressive* poem and an *analytical* poem in one, gives way to the poetry and poetics of symbol and ambiguity. These are defensive moves to preserve a unique mode of utterance for poetry in the face of a political and technological culture which largely ignored it. They carry to extremes the strategies outlined in Hallam's much earlier account of the poetry of sensation. And in conceding to the situation Hallam predicted – the confinement of poetic production to small groups – they develop a new form of exclusive conservatism. Perhaps the last part of the nineteenth century can be thought of as a final resistance to these conditions as much as an acceptance of them.

Fin-de-siècle poetry, then, is given little space here. But since it is important to beware of a selective reading which cannot wait until Victorian poetry is transmuted into modernism (and modernism, after all, is a highly selective collection of texts, elevated into a movement), it is necessary to look back rather than forward and to ask briefly what happened to those traditions of nineteenth-century poetry which have been effaced or forgotten. And the result might be that twentieth-century poetry will be defined in relation to Victorian poetry rather than Victorian poetry's being seen in terms of a preparation for modernism. What happened, then, to those traditions this study has largely explored? What happened to the poetry of conservatism? What happened to the women's tradition? Where did the radical democratic 'Grotesque' tradition go? A handful of poems must serve to indicate where one might look.

'I will arise and go now, and go to Innisfree': Yeats's 'The Lake Isle of Innisfree' (*The Rose*, 1893) belongs recognisably to the conservative tradition initiated by Hallam and Tennyson. It is the poetry of sensation – emasculated, perhaps, but with the same agenda, the revival of myth to provide a new cultural integration. But there are enormous differences: Yeats's world of fairy is an *alternative* world. It is not the self-conscious, sceptical modern myth of 'sentimental' consciousness which seeks to create new *collective* mythic patterns. Tennyson's myth-making outflanks positivist scientific thinking and scepticism not by excluding them but by subsuming them into the richer imaginative life of sceptical myth and claiming for myth a more profound cultural analysis than could be gained through empirical, post-Enlightenment rationalism. For Yeats myth is a form of oppositional irrationalism. He was interested less in class integration through myth than folk imagination. He criticised Croker's collection, one of Tennyson's fairy source books, by recognising astutely that he came from a class that did not, mainly for political reasons, take the populace seriously. But for him the populace had to be taken seriously because it provided a world of magic, dream and the occult: 'the people of Ireland have created perhaps the most beautiful folk-lore in the world'.[2] Thus, unlike Tennyson, he does not use his mythic poetry to defamiliarise the known or to analyse cultural stress but as a form of escape and withdrawal.

'The Lake Isle of Innisfree' draws on Tennysonian topoi, the Island of Shalott and the hallucinatory 'slow veils of dropping lawn' in 'The Lotos-Eaters' – 'peace comes dropping slow,/Dropping from the veils of morning' (5–6).[3] The world of Innisfree is an inaccessible, private and subjective world, 'in the deep heart's core' (13), the product of alienated urban life and its 'pavements grey' (11). It is an idyll of retreat, a world of self-sustaining isolation – its economy of labour among 'nine bean rows [a magic number]' (3) and bees, is that of private cultivation in which all products can be taken back into the self. It reverses the Tennysonian anxieties of isolation and longs for solitude. This is the poetics of the privileged and aristocratic individual imagination, the cult of aura.[4]

The conservative tradition at the end of the century was at its most robust in the area in which it was weakest at the beginning – the 'popular' ballad. In comparison with the efforts of Monckton Milnes, the poet in the Tennyson circle most anxious to approach the working class directly through ballad, Kipling's skill in *Barrack-Room Ballads* (1892) is remarkable. His is a cunning demotic populism, imitating for the middle class the simple rhythms of the marching song and the music-hall ballad. Whereas John Davidson used the music-hall genre in poems such as 'Thirty Bob a Week' to make a critique of social conditions, Kipling celebrates the resilience of the common soldier in colonial service with a patrician triumphalism. Despite Kipling's ironising of the imperial theme, despite his sharp sense of the oppression and exploitation of military life, these are heroic poems.

> So 'ark an' 'eed, you rookies, which is always grumblin' sore,
> There's worser things than marchin' from Umballa to Cawnpore;
> An' if your 'eels are blistered an' they feels to 'urt like 'ell,
> You drop some tallow in your socks an' that will make 'em well.[5]

The vigour of 'Route Marchin'' depends on its refrain, in which the 'Big Drum' forces the marching pace. Hindustani, the language of the natives, is turned into a form of nonsense language to provide an alliterative drum beat: ' "*Kilo kissywarsti* don't you/*hamsher argyjow*" '. Kipling footnotes the translation as 'Why don't you get on?', and in another footnote to the soldier's boast that he can 'sling the *bat*', he writes disparagingly of the British tommy: 'Language. Thomas's first and firmest conviction is that he is a profound Orientalist and a fluent speaker of Hindustani. As a matter of fact, he depends largely on the sign language'. There is an extraordinary contempt here. This poem *appears* to conjure the situation Müller instanced, demonstrating that language dissolves the conventional hierarchies of race and colour – the British soldier in India and the sepoy are united by the origin of language and the sharing of roots which have

481

not changed over hundreds of years. But in Kipling's poem the British tommy uses the language of the subjugated as a form of play while he himself is reduced to inarticulate signs among the natives, and *slang*, which also requires translation, among his fellow soldiers. He is reduced to linguistic poverty. Kipling is the privileged voyeur of working-class terminology as shared Indo-European *roots* are used, in both these subjugated languages, to urge on *route* marching, and appropriated for authoritarian purposes. Sometimes Kipling expresses the dissident voice of the English soldier: more often he confirms a conservative reading in which the cheerful response of the English soldier to adversity is displayed as a condition which is largely the creation of the colonial imperative. Here Kipling portrays, exploits and glories in a working-class solidarity which consents to an ideology it may not analyse.

It is perhaps easier to see what happened to the poetry of the conservative tradition than to assess the nature of poetry by women at the end of the century, and very hard indeed to determine the existence of a radical poetry. One might take the work of Alice Meynell as a symptomatic example of writing by women. Born in 1847, her earliest volume, *Preludes*, was published in 1875, her last, *Last Poems*, in 1923. Like Christina Rossetti earlier, and like her contemporary, Mary Coleridge, Meynell wrote lyric poetry, producing precise, fastidiously organised verse. Like those of Christina Rossetti, her themes were love and religion (she was a Catholic convert) and her scrupulously finished work was remarkably consistent from the beginning to the end of her life.

Her lyric voice is more passionate and unreserved than that of Christina Rossetti and yet, concurrently with this outflow of expressive feeling, she is preoccupied with silence, with what it is like to be mute. It is as if the poems are determined to celebrate silence and to redeem it from passivity and from the tyranny of *being* silenced. Just as she converts the idea of the mirror image and the narcissistic reflection from passive mimesis into creative transposition and translation (for instance in 'The Love of Narcissus' in *Poems*, 1893), so the exploration of silence attempts to discover a signifying function in the soundless, non-verbal experience.

For instance, in 'To the Beloved', she argues that the pauses of silence create the meaning of utterances – 'Thou art the shape of melodies'. Her poems frequently begin with the problematics of silence – 'Farewell to one now silenced quite' ('Parted'); 'Quiet form of silent nun' ('Soeur Monique') – and end with the possibility of silence as affirmation – 'And make our pause and silence brim' ('Builders of Ruins'); 'And lay the crucifix on this silent heart' ('The Young Neophyte').

Meynell's poems are delicate and searchingly subtle, and yet they do not seem to possess the reach and ambition of work by Augusta Webster, Mathilde Blind and Amy Levy, or of Christina Rossetti before them. It is not simply their smallness of scale, or their thematics of love and religion (for after all, Christina Rossetti wrote in the same mode) that persuades one of the more restricted world of these lyrics. It seems that the preoccupation with silence places the feminine in an empty space, that which is not there, making it seem without a context in which to exist. The disappearances and vanishing points explored in her work presage the eclipse of women's poetry in the twentieth century – or, at least, the steady refusal of women's poetry by modernism.

As the women's suffrage movement got under way, and as women's activities and possible roles became more diversified, it seems that there was a withdrawal of energy from poetry writing of the ambitious scale earlier in the nineteenth century. True, Edith Nesbit was writing such collections as *Ballads and Lyrics of Socialism 1883–1908* (1908), but it is hard to find poets of the stature of earlier writers as the nineteenth century passes into the twentieth. This is a generalisation which would need to be more thoroughly tested, of course, but it seems that, despite the gifts of individual poets such as Charlotte Mew, a major renaissance of women's poetry took place only after the Second World war.

'In Early Spring', an early pastoral poem by Meynell, initiates the preoccupations and anxieties of her whole *oeuvre*.[6] It is a two-part poem representing through its form the divisions of sexual difference, contrasting the different kinds of relationship to the world, and the correspondingly different epistemologies, implied by a female and a male poetics. The feminine speaker is a reader and a watcher of cyclical process – 'A year's procession of the flowers'. A participant in women's time, her knowledge is the knowledge of divination, anticipation and prescience which comes from an understanding of repetition in the natural world. Before seeds unfold and spring birds sing, 'I have it all by heart'. But the female poet has no ownership of this world and no power in it: knowing that 'not a flower or song I ponder is/My own, but memory's', she falls silent in the face of its creativity. She is caught in predictable repetition. The autonomy of the male poet, on the other hand, enables him to intervene in the world, to create new experience and new laws of existence which we cannot 'divine' or predict: 'Sweet earth, we know thy dimmest mysteries,/But he is lord of his'. Superficially the poem is about subordination and the anxiety of influence. However, it is also a poem about the possibilities which come from abnegating power, the very thing the powerful by definition cannot do. The powerless poet can 'know' (the word is repeated four times) in a way that the powerful cannot simply by being able to 'divine' or define two epistemologies rather than one. On the other hand the poem posits the dangers of dominance unequivocally and realistically, and the dangers of a double epistemology, a problem women's poetry contended with well into the twentieth century. And despite its complexity the difficulty of a knowledge only experienced in *silence* is never solved. In Meynell's work the final crisis of expressive theory as it relates to the feminine is being understood and explored. Finding a voice for the hidden, secret experience is, as has been seen, the central preoccupation of women's poetry in the nineteenth century, to which all the boldest responses to expressive theory relate.

Finally, what happened to the radical tradition in poetry? Did the Grotesque, with its intrinsic capacity for critique, die away and disappear as modernist aesthetic and practice, with its curious combination of formal radicalism and reactionary politics, gradually reconfigured Victorian poetics and poetry? If one subscribed to the view that modernism represents an absolute epistemological and cultural break with the Victorian, it is likely that one would not look for the survival of radical writing. On the other hand, if in modernism's strange amnesia about the nineteenth century it is possible to see a repression of the Victorian which betokens its hidden presence despite the ostensibly depoliticised nature of modernist experiment, it is likely that modernist readings and exclusions actually mask the presence of a political poetry. And indeed, this is the case. A misrecognised radical poetry stares us in the face.

Nothing divides poets so much as war. A war comparable in importance to the Crimean war, but much more markedly a modern civilian and colonial war, occurred at the end of Victoria's reign. The Boer war, after a series of prior campaigns, began in earnest in 1899. A tradition of antiwar poetry existed in Britain, from Thomas Hood's 'A Waterloo Ballad', to Alexander Smith's poems on the Crimean war, to A. E. Housman's 'Illic Jacet' (1900) published at the height of the Boer war. Such anti-war poetry sometimes merges with a poetry of humanitarian and later socialist protest which also runs throughout the century. An impressive history of the poetry of the Boer war reminds us of this tradition, which includes the writing of Harriet Martineau, W. H. Mallock and Roden Noel, and is manifested in Ernest Jones's *Battle-Day* (1855), Alasgar Hill's *Poor Law Rhymes* (1871), William Morris's *Chants for Socialists* (1884) and Edward Carpenter's *Towards Democracy* (1883).[7] But a poem rather different from these campaigning verses, though nevertheless a response to war and territorial aggression, published just outside Victoria's reign, can claim to be the last great revolutionary poem of the 'Grotesque' tradition, and possibly the last great double poem to be written. This is Thomas Hardy's *The Dynasts* (1904–8). Hardy had written an extraordinary poem of the Boer war, 'Drummer Hodge' ('They throw in Drummer Hodge, to rest/ Uncoffined – just as found'), but the huge scale of *The Dynasts*, Europe during the rise and fall of Napoleon, not only gives scope for a wider analysis but also fuses critique and formal experiment. The capacity of the rulers of western Europe to perpetrate mass violence on an unprecedented scale, and the willingness of its leaders of whatever ideology to massacre untold numbers of men in order to remain in power, is the almost too starkly simple narrative content of this epic poem. It is not possible to do full justice to this major poem in this Postscript: but something of its achievement can be understood through a brief examination of its 'Grotesque' characteristics. It is often read as a heroic poem, a poem to England's glory. Such a reading is possible, but, typical of the double poem, a dissident analysis is available simply by understanding that the great figures of Wellington and Napoleon are not so much *contrasted* as seen as equivalents of one another.

The element of distortion intrinsic to the Grotesque is present in the title word: a dynast is equally one who is a *member* of a hereditary ruling monarchy and one who *founds* a ruling family. The ruling oligarchies of Europe confront the new-made despot, Napoleon, but though they perceive each other respectively as moribund monarchy and as usurper, their interests are identical, even to Napoleon's desperate need for a son. Not only is the logic of dynasty constant despotism (hegemony must be sustained by an ever more detemined expansion and an ever more rigorous oppression), it is based on a fundamental misrecognition; the right to rule is regarded both as sanctioned by destiny as history and as the product of might (the great-man theory of power) which legitimates itself simply because it is powerful. The English oligarchy claim hereditary right, Napoleon claims the prerogatives of greatness. In fact, all are engaged in turning power into destiny, in masking acts of violence by calling them destiny and seeing them as determined. A distorted, ideological account of history is founded on the idea of destiny. And a progressive distortion occurs because the protagonists attempt to bring destiny about by acting for it. It is a distortion which spreads and perpetuates itself as ideology reinforced by symbol. The bitter irony of the Russian campaign, in which both sides attempt to mythologise their power by rousing their troops to salute the symbol of the crucifix (the Russians) and a portrait of the heir (Napoleon), is an example of this parallelism between the opposing forces of Europe.[8] The remorseless succession of battles, each one more brutally productive of carnage than the last, is the frightful physical consequence of performing destiny, until Wellington and Napoleon, both 46, meet at Waterloo in the climactic moment of the poem.

The two 'heroic' commanders are images of each other, both prepared to sacrifice troops in an almost suicidal way, both refusing reinforcements to subordinates at crucial moments of the battle, both attempting to maintain the mastery of an overview by standing outside the action. This mirror-imaging is the culmination of a careful series of structural parallels: for instance, the abandonment of the Empress Josephine by Napoleon is paralleled with the treatment of Queen Caroline by the Prince Regent; 'mad' King George, pathetically terrified of those who apparently serve him, has his parallel in a mad French soldier, and the common soldiers on each side are portrayed in the same way – brutalised, exploited and quite ignorant of the power relations which have forced them to war. The

French soldiers dressed in petticoats as they flee from Moscow and the winter cold, are as powerless as the British soldiers who drink themselves to stupor with looted wine in France.[9]

Because there is no directive comment, no polemic on the horrors of war and no explicit ideological statement – a convention of Grotesque writing – it would be possible to read this demythologising of the heroic will as a celebration of power, an irony of which this huge double text is grimly aware, as we shall see. But the poem makes it clear that, after a battle in which even the worm underground cannot find shelter in the blood-soaked earth, the post-Waterloo world is left free for Britain to become an imperial power once Napoleon's threat to India and Asia has gone, once he has been removed from Egypt and once the fragile settlement of Turkey between France and Russia has been fatally weakened.[10]

Epics are about power, and power is no less at the heart of the Grotesque tradition of writing. Ruskin said that the Grotesque is both cause and effect of a distorted or failed sublime experience. Whereas the sublime reasserts and recuperates power in the act of self-overcoming, and an ultimate transcendence defeats the sense of limit and negativity confronting consciousness, the Grotesque remains with the sense of break, of limit and powerlessness. At the height of the battle of Waterloo, where in a surreal moment the inner being of physical and psychic chemistry is exposed in pulsating yellow light like a superimposed film image, what is seen is a network of interacting lines of force rather than the individual 'Will' by which all speakers represent purposeful meaning and action in the world. The breakdown of a language of agency and the inadequacy of 'Will' as a representation and symbol of individual power are emphasised through-out the poem as 'Will' becomes a distorting symbol, a Grotesque mis-prision. The Grotesque becomes a critique of the sublime at Waterloo, as the poem shows Wellington caught in the web of interrelation and only 'acting while discovering his intention to act'.[11] Schopenhauerian 'Will' as a retrospective representation is deconstructed here.

The sense of limit (for Ruskin integral to the Grotesque) which leads to the preoccupation with death as the ultimate limit, with violence as a paradoxical form of overcoming and reassertion of power, and with desire as the expression of deep lack and negation, is brilliantly politicised by being transposed to the public arena of European power struggles. It is inner subjective vision *and* the political form of that vision. The dynasts' craving for power and their perpetration of mass killing to achieve it, whether they belong to England or France, are portrayed as forming a peculiarly self-destructive drive as the will to power becomes the other side of a suicidal death wish – the battles of Trafalgar and Tevalera, for instance, are suicidal victories.

For Ruskin the sense of limit and the distortion of vision intrinsic to the Grotesque are both the form and content of nineteenth-century consciousness. They are both experience and its representation, and its representation can become a form of critique. The representation of limit is built into the narrative structure of the poem. The epic has no overview, no total reading of the events it narrates. The shadowy choric commentary of the Overworld is triangulated into the observations of the Spirit of the Pities, the Spirit of the Years and the Spirit Sinister who, to complicate the trinity, is often doubled by a Spirit Ironic who sometimes speaks in satiric jingles like Goethe's Mephistopheles in *Faust*. None of the commentators can see beyond the categories they represent (Pity, for instance, is indiscriminately pitiful) and it is impossible to gain an understanding by aggregating their views because they contradict one another. At the end of the poem Pity, who has learned nothing, expresses the view that ends justify means in a poem which is a virtual parody of Tennyson's ambiguously assertive poems on will, such as the Introduction to *In Memoriam*. But it is contradicted with equally limiting nihilism by the Spirit Ironic, who has earlier commented that the 'antagonistic' interests of the proud and the poor were only momentarily bonded by the threat of Napoleon.[12]

The refusal of an overview is ensured also by the generic discontinuity of the poem. It is a strangely contradictory genre, an epic-drama, a heroic poem about the great *and* a drama, the democratic form of radical writing. It moves through many styles and languages – reportage, epic description, metaphysical chorus, rhetorical blank verse, military-textbook explication, formal prose, demotic speech, dumb show, marching song, satirical jingle, lyric, folk song and music-hall verse. For instance, the popular song, 'Budmouth Dears', gives way to a military march heard from Puebla Heights (Part III, II. ii). A snatch of wild sexual lyric celebrating war by the Casterbridge woman who has been wrapped in a soldier's cloak in a sentry box is juxtaposed with a sober aerial description of the site of the next great battle in Belgium (Part III, V. vi). Despite its overwhelmingly masculine theme, the single masculine vision is denied through the voices of women, from the soldier's wife who faints at Waterloo because the massacre is worse than the pig-killing at home, to the duchess who witnesses Napoleon's sentimental response to the pain of child birth, knowing that a daughter's birth would have provoked a different response – 'He only says that now. In cold blood it would be far otherwise. That's how men are' (Part II, VI. iii).

But perhaps the most brilliant technical innovation of the poem, the feature which makes it a fundamentally experimental text, is the constant change of visual perspective, and particularly a movement in space from far to near and back. A close-up of a musical box beginning to play as it is swept off a table in the violence of the rioting in Goday's house (Part II, II. ii) abruptly changes the perspective of the scene. At Waterloo the Overworld commentary of the Spirits is suddenly displaced by the ascent of the French cavalry and, a sinister and terrible auditory and visual detail, 'the swish of the horses' breasts through the standing corn can be heard'.[13] What Hardy in his 'stage' directions calls 'the point of sight' shifts, moves, expands, foreshortens, pans, constructs montage, changes its angle and reorders space in such a way that the consistency of the gaze and thus its power to create and sustain a single overview are broken. The representation of limit becomes the organising visual strategy of the poem. That there *is* always a narrative gaze comes into prominence and becomes for the reader one of the hermeneutic problems of the Grotesque rather than remaining concealed. The poem is a virtual film script, suggesting that the new Europe requires a different narrative mode, a new form, to register the traumatic transformation of perceptions of space and time – of history, of territory, of national identity and ideology accomplished during the Napoleonic wars. It is possible to read the poem as the 'tragedy' of Napoleon (he is the last human being to speak in the poem and evokes the sympathy of the Spirit of Pity), but the multiple perspectives refuse that stable reading. The reordering of perception fragments and reconstructs, asking for that active, participatory interpretative process which is the hallmark of democratic poetry from the beginning of this period onwards. The cinematic multiple perspectives of Hardy's poem take the multiple perspectives of the dramatic monologue, or collections of the dramatic monologue such as Browning's *The Ring and the Book*, and exploit these in a wholly new way. The dramatic monologue is perhaps the type of the double poem, that mid-nineteenth-century form which offers two simultaneous readings by allowing the expressive utterance of a limited subjectivity to become the material for analysis. It is as if Hardy carries the virtuosity of the dramatic monologue from drama to cinema by superimposing a number of limited and everchanging perspectives on one another. The double poem extends to the multiple poem with its contradictory and self-modifying juxtapositions. The techniques of a Griffiths or an Eisenstein are anticipated and given an existence in language in a truly novel way. And arguably this filmic poem is an attempt to create a new popular form, a genuine successor to the drama on which the *Monthly Repository* writers, including Browning, had pinned their hopes of a democratic art.

The Dynasts is also perhaps the first modernist experiment as well as the last Grotesque poem. Its technique of montage, fragmentation and juxtaposition without copula looks forward to the poetic forms of high modernism. It may even be entitled to be called the only radical modernist poem in existence, whose revolutionary form becomes a political critique as well as a formal experiment. It is certainly interesting to find that the conservative tradition rests with the ballad at this stage, while radical critique in Hardy's case adopts the high-modernist strategy. Some of the reasons for this lie outside the scope of this study and have been explored only in a limited way. The reasons why poetry changed in the twentieth century belong to another discussion. Up to the turn of the century, however, it is possible to trace a conservative and a radical poetry and poetics, each believing that important political and cultural issues are at stake in poetry and in poetic language and form. In Hardy's case a continuity between *The Dynasts* and earlier radical interests is attested by the choice of the Napoleonic wars as a topic for poetry. The demythologising of the Napoleonic wars and particularly of the Tory adulation for 'his Grace of Wellington' was a radical project from the early 1830s on. It is to be seen in the work of William Bridges Adams, R. H. Horne and, later, Thomas Cooper. In 1834 William Bridges Adams wrote a four-part attack on the Tory reading of Shakespeare's *Coriolanus*, which identified Wellington with Coriolanus and his hatred of the plebeians, 'Coriolanus No Aristocrat', in the *Monthly Repository*. He creates another play-prose-poem out of Shakespeare's text to indicate the falsity of the Tory analogy. Wellington was a hireling working for vast sums of money with no sense of 'community', fighting with a starving army and with the aim of maintaining oppressive power. The speech of contemporary British soldiers is interpolated to contrast with the plebeian soldiers of Rome:

> It is true, that, in consequence of being nearly starved in England, we did agree to serve as soldiers . . . yet we find ourselves worse off than your dogs, . . . it is very easy for you to say you'll shoot us if we don't mount that yawning breach of Bajados yonder. . . . The last time we made the attempt, the shot from our own batteries, intended to clear the breach over our heads, killed more of us than the enemy.[14]

Hardy is reticent about Wellington, showing him without comment sanctioning looting, and conducting a military career, with single-minded confidence in his strategy. Adams's more violent reading of Wellington, however, might still be the scenario for Hardy's poem: the analyses of 1834 and 1904 have not changed in their essentials: this study began with the *Monthly Repository;* it is appropriate to conclude with it.

Coriolanus fought in person, in a just war, and ran the same risk with his soldiers. Wellington fought by proxy with officers and soldiers, keeping himself as much as possible out of the 'stroke and flash'; and he fought in an unjust war, to put down an oppressor, it is true, yet not for the benefit of mankind, but only to set up other and more mischievous oppressors in his place.[15]

In Hardy's poem Europe's dynasties 're-robe', as the poem puts it, for the rest of the nineteenth century and arguably for the twentieth century as well: this is the point where this study ends.

NOTES

INTRODUCTION: REREADING VICTORIAN POETRY

1 Michel Foucault makes a critique of continuous 'genetic' history in his foreword to the English edition of *The Order of Things: An Archaeology of the Human Sciences* (1966), London and New York, 1974. 'It was not my intention, on the basis of a particular type of knowledge or body of ideas, to draw up a picture of a period, or to reconstitute the spirit of a century' (x). Such a history ignores 'the implicit philosophies . . . the unformulated thematics . . . the rules of formation' of knowledge which were not always consciously understood by those who were living at the time (xi). 'Archaeology' abandons the notion of 'genesis' and 'progress' and adopts instead a procedure for looking at 'unformulated thematics' which considers 'widely different theories and objects of study' (xi).

2 The Tennyson joke is given to Stephen Daedelus in the 'Proteus' section of *Ulysses* (1922) and Tennyson reappears in 'Circe'. Virginia Woolf's *Orlando: A Biography* (1933) describes the onset of Victorianism as a morbid condition in chapter 5.

3 T. S. Eliot, 'The Metaphysical poets', *Selected Essays*, 3rd edn, London, 1951, 288.

4 Raymond Williams, *Culture and Society, 1780–1950*, London, 1958.

5 The new wave of influential feminist writing on the nineteenth-century novel in the late 1970s is represented by Elaine Showalter, *A Literature of Their Own: British Women Novelists from Bronte to Lessing*, Princeton, N.J., 1977.

6 Illustrative of the preoccupation with Romantic poetry among deconstructionist critics is the collection of essays by Harold Bloom, Paul De Man, Jacques Derrida, Geoffrey Hartman and J. Hillis Miller, *Deconstruction and Criticism*, London, 1979.

7 See 'On some motifs in Baudelaire', *Illuminations* (1955), London, 1973, 157–67.

8 Essay on Shelley (1852), *Robert Browning: The Poems*, John Pettigrew, Thomas J. Collins, eds, 2 vols, New Haven and London, 1981, I, 999–1013: 1001.

9 Substantial biographical work has appeared on Tennyson and Browning. In particular see, for instance, Robert Bernard Martin, *Tennyson, The Unquiet Heart*, London, 1980; William Irvine and Park Honan, *The Book, the Ring, and the Poet*, London, Sydney and Toronto, 1974. John Maynard, *Browning's Youth*, Cambridge, Mass., 1977.

10 Lionel Trilling, *Matthew Arnold*, London, 1939.

11 Foucault, *The Order of Things*, xx. 'Order is, at one and the same time, that which is given in things as their inner law, the hidden network which determines the way they confront one another, and also that which has no existence except by the grid created by a glance, an examination, a language.'

12 Fifteen years after his disparaging comments on Tennyson, T. S. Eliot came

to consider *In Memoriam* as a great poem. He described it as a spiritual diary, a description which is also appropriate to *Four Quartets* and its preoccupation with time. *Selected Essays*, 334. Tennysonian echoes in both *The Waste Land* and *Four Quartets* are numerous but it is the poems of nightmare and madness which seem to press closely on Eliot's work. See, for instance, *The Waste Land*, 377–84, and section LXX of *In Memoriam*; and *Four Quartets*, 'Burnt Norton', II. 1–15, and *Maud*, 102–7, 571–98. The allusion to Shelley's *Prometheus Unbound* in Yeats's 'The Second Coming' is familiar. See *Prometheus Unbound*, I. ii. 625–8. Less frequently remarked is the inversion of the ending of Tennyson's 'The Kraken' in 'The Second Coming'. Tennyson's barely sentient monster dies a violent death on the surface of the sea in apocalyptic upheaval. Yeats's 'rough beast' stumbles towards a violent, apocalyptic birth at the end of his poem.

13 Matthew Arnold's inaugural lecture as Professor of Poetry at Oxford was entitled 'On the modern element in literature' and published in *Macmillan's Magazine*, 1869. George Meredith's *Modern Love* was published in 1862, two years before William Allingham's *Laurence Bloomfield in Ireland, A Modern Poem*, 1864, reissued in 1869 and subtitled *Or, the New Landlord*.

14 Harold Bloom's work on the Victorians and their predecessor poets is mainly collected in *Poetry and Repression*, New Haven and London, 1976.

15 Thomas Carlyle, 'Signs of the times' (1829), *Critical and Miscellaneous Essays*, 6 vols, II, 313–42: 317 (vol. VII, *Thomas Carlyle's Collected Works*, Library Edition, 31 vols, London and New York, 1869–71).

16 'Estranged labour', in Karl Marx, *Early Writings*, trans. Rodney Livingstone, Gregor Burton, Harmondsworth, 1975, 322–34.

17 Carlyle's hostility to 'Codemaking in the abstract' ('Signs of the times', 326), to 'mere political *arrangements*, as itself the sign of a mechanical age' (325), which depersonalises and abstracts human relationships is particularly fierce when he attacks 'external combinations and arrangements for institutions, constitutions' (320). His conviction that the vote is empty of human content, and fundamentally alienating, however, is most clearly to be seen in his description of solutions to the decline of religious belief. 'In like manner, among ourselves, when it is thought that religion is declining, we have only to vote half-a-million's worth of bricks and mortar, and build new churches' (320).

18 *Sartor Resartus: The Life and Opinions of Herr Teufelsdröckh* (1831), *Thomas Carlyle's Collected Works* (Library Edition), 31 vols, 1869–71, I, 38.

19 See particularly *Sartor Resartus*, Book III, ch. 3, 'Symbols'.

20 The failure of Teufelsdröckh's love affair precipitates the crisis of spiritual anguish which dissolves all his certainties. The sceptical treatment of romantic love, regarded as an obsolete mythos (Book II, ch. 5, 'Romance') is characteristic of the complexities of *Sartor Resartus*. It is heavily satirical and grumpily sardonic about *Werther*, Goethe's famous story of love and suicide. On the other hand it celebrates the creative intensity and profundity of passion, which *materially* transforms Teufelsdröckh's experience by transforming his imagination. 'Love is not altogether a Delirium' (139). Love as a consuming egocentric masculine passion actually dissolves the relationship between self and other and this loss initiates a remaking and redefinition of all relationships, undertaken with an intensity which would not have come about without the initial experience of love. In reconstructing a world of creative labour and remaking the mythos, Teufelsdröckh is putting the displaced energies of love to work. Of such are the representations and symbols of a culture made. The perverseness and implicit misogyny of Carlyle's work should not persuade us to ignore his perceptions. *Sartor* struggles sceptically with the harsh limits within which the

individual can change and transform an increasingly complex world. To take the act of love as a paradigm is both a bold and a limiting choice, and this is recognised in the text, which subjects the experience to grotesque parody at the same time as it insists on the motivating energies of passion.

21 Lytton Strachey, *Eminent Victorians*, London, 1918, is the notorious spokesman of this view.

22 I am using rather freely Walter Benjamin's categories from 'The work of art in the age of mechanical reproduction', *Illuminations* (1955), London, 1973, 219–53.

23 Alan Sinfield, *Alfred Tennyson*, Rereading Literature Series, Oxford, 1986.

24 Eve Kosofsky Sedgwick, *Between Men: English Literature and Male Homosocial Desire*, New York, 1985.

25 V. N. Volosinov, *Marxism and the Philosophy of Language*, trans. L. Matejka, I. R. Titanik, Cambridge, Mass., 1986. Volosinov's contention that both written and spoken language participates in a struggle for the sign long precedes, of course, the work of deconstruction, but the possibilities of his work, even though he excluded poetry from the activity of struggle, are only comparatively recently being discovered. In saying that both Volosinov's work and that of Derrida stem from Hegel I am oversimplifying both. Volosinov is a Marxist in contention with linguistics, but his concept of struggle goes back to Hegel's master–slave dialectic. Derrida develops and transforms the premises of Sausserean linguistics, as Volosinov does not, and he dissents from the master–slave dialectic and develops the alternative concept of *différance*. Arguably, however, *différance* as the constant repositioning of relationship arrests a stage of Hegelian thought. The strength of Volosinov is that he finds a way of conceptualising linguistic struggle. See below note 34 on the exclusion of poetry from the struggle for the sign.

26 Herbert S. Tucker Jnr, *Browning's Beginnings: The Art of Disclosure*, Minnesota, 1980.

27 E. D. H. Johnson, *The Alien Vision of Victorian Poetry; Sources of the Poetic Imagination in Tennyson, Browning and Arnold*, Princeton, N.J., 1952.

28 Robert Langbaum, *The Poetry of Experience: The Dramatic Monologue in Modern Literary Tradition*, London, 1957.

29 There is much valuable uncollected work by Morse Peckham, for example, his centenary essay on Browning's *The Ring and The Book*, 'Historiography and *The Ring and The Book*', *Victorian Poetry* 6 (1968), 243–57.

30 G. M. Hopkins believed that the looseness of the language of nineteenth-century poetry reflected the lax relativism of the age, which he describes in some of his earliest writings. 'The probable future of metaphysics', *The Journals and Papers of Gerard Manley Hopkins*, Humphrey House, Graham Strong, eds, London, 1959, 118–21.

31 Arnold's brilliant but limited diagnosis of modernity and its problems appears in the Preface to his *Poems* of 1853, in which he explained his reasons for withdrawing that modern poem, *Empedocles on Etna* (1852), from his volume: 'the dialogue of the mind with itself has commenced; modern problems have presented themselves'. *The Poems of Matthew Arnold* (Longman Annotated English Poets), Kenneth Allott, ed., London, 1965, 591.

32 Nietzsche quotes Schopenhauer's account of lyric critically in *The Birth of Tragedy*: 'It is the subject of the will, i.e. his own volition, which fills the consciousness of the singer, often as a released and satisfied desire (joy), but still oftener as an inhibited desire (grief), always as an affect, a passion, a moved state of mind . . . the stress of desire, which is always restricted and always needy'. *The Birth of Tragedy* (1872), trans. Walter Kaufmann, New York, 1967, 51.

33 Both W. J. Fox and A. H. Hallam conducted sophisticated analyses of Tennyson's early poems in terms of drama. See *Victorian Scrutinies: Reviews of Poetry
1830–70*, Isobel Armstrong, ed., London, 1972, 75–9, 99–101.

34 Mikhail Bakhtin, *The Dialogic Imagination: Four Essays*, ed. Michael Holquist,
trans. Caryl Emerson and Michael Holquist, Austin, Texas, 1981. Bakhtin's
dialogic form is not quite the same thing as Volosinov's struggle for the sign
and I prefer to keep the two names separate rather than viewing them as two
names for the same person. Bakhtin writes of the literary text, whereas Volosinov's interest is in challenging post-Sausserean linguistics. Bakhtin's dialogic
form is oppositional and depends on the reversal of fixed positions, whereas
Volosinov's struggle for the sign is a dynamic on-going process in which contending ideologies constantly redefine the content of the sign. Neither believed
that poetry could generate dialogic structures or that poetic texts could participate in struggle. Manifestly, however, the Victorian double poem generates the
drama of contending principles. I prefer the model of linguistic struggle rather
than dialogism because the nature of language is crucial to Volosinov's thought
(whereas it is not to Bakhtin's) and his model seems particularly appropriate
to *poetic* forms, where the complexity of language is foregrounded. Moreover,
the model of struggle leads to perpetual redefinition in a way which the dialogic
form does not. Volosinov's ideas, however, require far more rigorous development than they can be given in a book of this kind. That is why I have placed
this discussion of Victorian poetry in a general post-Hegelian tradition, to
which, of course, both Marx and Volosinov belong.

35 The Comte de Volney's *The Ruins: or, A Survey of the Restoration of Empires* was
known as *The Ruins of Empire* and was translated in 1795.

36 Friedrich Schiller, *On the Aesthetic Education of Man in a Series of Letters*, trans.
and ed. Elizabeth M. Wilkinson and L. A. Willoughby, Oxford, 1967, Letter
6, paras 3, 6, pp. 31, 33.

37 Carlyle, *Sartor Resartus*, 173.

PART I CONSERVATIVE AND BENTHAMITE
AESTHETICS OF THE AVANT-GARDE:
Tennyson and Browning in the 1830s

1 Two systems of concentric circles

1 William Johnson Fox, *Monthly Repository*, N.S., VI (Jan. 1832), 1–4.

2 Quoted in Peter Allen, *The Cambridge Apostles: The Early Years*, Cambridge, 1978,
100.

3 Ibid., 119.

4 *Mill on Bentham and Coleridge*, F. R. Leavis, ed., London and Toronto, 1950, 40.
I am enormously indebted to the invaluable scholarship of the major study of
the *Monthly Repository* by F. E. Mineka, *The Dissidence of Dissent: The Monthly
Repository 1806–1838*, Chapel Hill, 1944.

5 Leavis, *Mill on Bentham and Coleridge*, 41. It is significant that both the Benthamite group and the Apostles were middle-class gentlemen in paid professional
occupations. The clergy (Dissenting and Anglican respectively) and the new
professions developing either through the expansion of government bureaucracy
or the growth of journalism were choices of occupation in both circles, whatever
the difference of social origin between the groups. W. J. Fox was a minister.
R. H. Horne, who followed him as editor of the *Monthly Repository*, lived through

writing and journalism, contributing to Dickens's *Daily News* and *Household Words*. J. S. Mill was a civil servant. Among the Apostles, John Sterling and R. C. Trench were ordained, John Kemble became editor of the *British and Foreign Review* in 1836 and James Spedding worked in the Colonial Office. Arguably both groups formed a part of the new middle-class hegemony of Victorian England. See Philip Corrigan and Derek A. Sayer, *The Great Arch: English State Formation as Cultural Revolution*, Oxford, 1985, for a larger context for these groups. Though Mill clearly believed in the power and importance of a *fused* Benthamite–Coleridgean group of intellectuals contemporary historians disagree as to its success. See the Introduction to *The Culture of Capital: Art, Power and the Nineteenth Century Middle Class*, Janet Wolff and John Seed, eds, Manchester, 1988, 1–15. Also, in the same work, Simon Gunn, 'The "failure" of the Victorian middle class: a critique', 17–43.

6 Though the terms 'Benthamite' and 'Coleridgean' do, of course, denote broad and fundamental differences between the two groups described by Mill, it is as important to be aware of the debates within the groups as it is to know the differences between them. Some of the disagreements within the Fox group are described in chapter 4 below. There were, similarly, differences between different Apostles. Though Hallam and others were interested in the Saint-Simonians, who believed in a new social order without political change, R. C. Trench complained that their beliefs undermined 'primogeniture, aristocracy, heredity, all that rested on a spiritual relation, . . . must be swept away before the new industrial principle' (Allen, *Cambridge Apostles*, 125). On the other hand, in 1836, John Kemble wrote, subversively, sounding more like Fox than an Apostle, in a letter to W. B. Donne, 'Education must be taken out of the hands of the parsons, till the parsons are educated for their task of educating others. The *clerisy* [a Coleridgean term] of the land must no longer be the parsonry of the land' (Allen, *Cambridge Apostles*, 164). The aspects of the late Coleridge which interested the Tennyson group were his theories of symbol and the anti-Utilitarian organicism of his social and religious thought, as exemplified in *Lay Sermons* (1816, 1817), *Aids to Reflection* (1825) and *Church and State* (1830). The aspects of Benthamite Utilitarianism which most interested the Fox/Browning group were its stance against despotism and its associationist theory of mind together with its philosophical position on the law. 'Philosophical' radicalism was a self-consciously cultivated position. Mill, promoting a *liberal*, reconciliatory reading of Bentham and Coleridge, often plays down the sharp differences between these two seminal figures.

7 W. J. Fox, *Monthly Repository*, N.S., IV (1830), 229. For Tennyson's response to album books, see below chapter 2, p. 43 and n. 6.

8 Thomas Noon Talfourd, *Monthly Repository*, XV (1820), 95. Talfourd's article is entitled, 'On the supposed affinity of the poetical faculties with arbitrary power and superstitious faith': 'But I protest against the principle which gives the cause of power a monopoly of imaginative charms' (96).

9 See, for instance, 'On the intellectual character of Sir Walter Scott', *Monthly Repository*, N.S., VI (1832), 721–8.

10 W. J. Fox, 'The poor and their poetry', *Monthly Repository*, N.S., VI (1832), 189–201: 190.

11 Rev. John James Tayler, 'Some account of the life and writings of Herder', *Monthly Repository*, N.S., VI (1832), 34–42, 86–97, 165–78, 217–33. The *Repository*'s interest in Herder dates from its inception, when Henry Crabb Robinson translated poems and discussed Herder's thought in the first and third volumes.

12 Elliott's first poem, 'Famine in a Slave Ship', to be published in the *Repository*

(N.S., VII [1833], 602) was followed by many more: his work appeared in every volume up to X (1836). Two major poems by R. H. Horne, 'The Age of Steam, a Hudibrastic Poem' and 'A Political Oratorio' (the title relates to William Hone's seditious 'Political litany' [1817]), were published in, respectively, 1834 and 1835. Fox also published the work of Thomas Wade (see below chapter 4, pp. 127–8 and n. 21).

13 W. J. Fox, review of Tennyson's *Poems, Chiefly Lyrical* (1830), in the *Westminster Review*, XIV (1831), 210–24. Reprinted in *Victorian Scrutinies: Reviews of Poetry 1830–70*, Isobel Armstrong, ed., London, 1972, 70–83.

14 'Coleridge and Poetry', *Westminster Review*, XII (1830), 1–31: 3.

15 'On some of the characteristics of modern poetry', *Englishman's Magazine*, I (1831), 616–28. Reprinted in Armstrong, *Victorian Scrutinies*, 84–101: 87.

16 Allen, *Cambridge Apostles*, 123. For the importance of Wordsworth and Coleridge, see ibid., 47–8, 49–50, 77–8 (F. D. Maurice's anti-Utilitarian reading of the poets), 100.

17 Ibid., 103–18. John Sterling, architect of the Spanish mission, was overcome with guilt: 'it is as if the bullets were tearing my own brain' (117).

18 'On some of the characteristics of modern poetry', Armstrong, *Victorian Scrutinies*, 90–2.

19 For an account of Tennyson's reading in mythography, see Isobel Armstrong, 'Tennyson's "The Lady of Shalott": Victorian mythography and the politics of narcissism', *The Sun is God: Painting, Literature and Mythology in the Nineteenth Century*, J. B. Bullen, ed., Oxford, 1989, 49–107: 49, 104–5.

20 Hallam did not directly use the terms 'naive' and 'sentimental' in his review of Tennyson, but the ideas about the belatedness of modern poetry are clearly derived from Schiller's essay. See Friedrich von Schiller, *Naive and Sentimental Poetry and On the Sublime: Two Essays*, trans. and ed. Julius A. Elias, New York, 1966, 105, 108.

21 Thomas Keightley, *The Fairy Mythology*, 2 vols, London, 1828: I, Preface, xi–xii, 1–7. For an extended discussion of Keightley's significance to the Apostles and to Tennyson, see Armstrong, 'Tennyson's "The Lady of Shalott" ', 74–9.

22 See, for instance, reviews of Tennyson's *Poems, Chiefly Lyrical*, 1830, and Browning's *Pauline*, 1833: Armstrong, *Victorian Scrutinies*, 75–7: *Monthly Repository*, N.S., VII (1833), 252–62: 252–4.

23 See 'Coleridge and Poetry', *Westminster Review*, XII (1830), 11. In reading the poetry as drama with its dynamic of conflict Fox can bring out, but need not identify with, Coleridge's changed response to the French Revolution.

24 William Bridges Adams, 'Coriolanus No Aristocrat', *Monthly Repository*, N.S., VIII (1834), 41–54, 129–39, 190–202, 292–9.

25 'Schleiermacher's critical essay on the Gospel of Saint Luke', *Monthly Repository*, N.S., I (1827), 33–48.

26 Allen, *Cambridge Apostles*, 99. Hallam learned German over the academic year 1829–30 (ibid., 142).

27 'Essay on the philosophical writings of Cicero', *The Writings of Arthur Hallam*, T. H. Vail Motter, ed., London and New York, 1943, 142–81: 143, 167.

28 Ibid., 167.

29 'Theodicaea Novissima', ibid., 198–213: 203: 'the doctrine, that this erotic feeling is of origin peculiarly divine, and raises the soul to heights of existence', gives an immediate sexual significance to the phrase, 'God is Love'. God expresses Himself in sexual consummation.

30 William Whewell, *On Astronomy and General Physics considered with Reference to Natural Theology*, Bridgewater Treatise III, London, 1833, 161–2. Notoriously,

Hallam voted 'No' in the Apostles debate, 'Is the existence of an intelligent first Cause deducible from the phenomena of the Universe?' He rejected the orthodoxy of William Paley's *Evidences of Christianity* (1794) at an early stage. Allen, *Cambridge Apostles*, 142.

31 Motter, *Hallam*, 170.

32 Dugald Stewart, *Elements of the Philosophy of Human Mind*, Sir William Hamilton, ed., Edinburgh and London, 1854–60, vol. 4, Part 2, second subdivision, 'Of Articulate Language', 20–2. Stewart devotes considerable discussion to the 'deranged collocation' (46) of ancient and poetic language and the capacity of such transposition to reorder association (40–54). The 'difficulty' that results is discussed by Peter Alan Dale '*Paracelsus* and *Sordello*: Trying the Stuff of Language', *Victorian Poetry*, 18 (1980), 359–69.

33 Fox, *Westminster Review*, XII (1830), 3, refers to an attack on Bentham by the *Edinburgh Review* and a defence of his 'powers of logical deduction and comprehensive analysis' in response to this attack in the *Westminster Review* of April 1829. This describes Bentham's analysis of legal fictions.

34 Many of Jeremy Bentham's writings on fictions and language have been collected by C. K. Ogden, *Bentham's Theory of Fictions*, London, 1932. See particularly, 12–17, 141–50. See also Introduction, cxiii–cxliv, on Bentham and the legal system.

35 Johann Gottfried Herder, 'Essay on the origin of language', *Two Essays on the Origin of Language*, trans. John H. Moran and Alexander Gode, Chicago and London, 1966, 115–19. Herder argues that to distinguish the flood of sensation which is undifferentiated consciousness, a mark must be made by consciousness, and *awareness* of this *as* distinguishing mark must be made simultaneously by the mind. This is why language and self-consciousness must come into being together at one and the same time. As if to control the meaning expressed through sensation and sound, Hallam insisted on precision in writing and remarked on the etymological felicity of archaism as a way of disclosing the history which is also a form of linguistic meaning. Tennyson's language is of that 'compound' kind, registering the history of a culture, which is bound up with philological change. Armstrong, 'Tennyson's "The Lady of Shalott" ', 95, 100. See also Patrick Scott, 'Flowering in a lonely word: Tennyson and the Victorian study of language', *Victorian Poetry*, 18 (1980), 371–81.

36 'A political and social anomaly', *Monthly Repository*, N.S., VI (1832), 637–42.

37 Harriet Martineau contributed an article on 'Female writers on practical divinity', *Monthly Repository*, XVII (1822), 593–6, 746–50. In 1832 W. J. Fox wrote on 'all-comprehensive' suffrage, *Monthly Repository*, N.S., VI (1832), 397. William Bridges Adams, 'On the condition of women in England', N.S., VII (1833), 217–31 (making the point that Mill was to make familiar much later that women were slaves in their present condition [217]), and Mary Leman Grimstone, 'Female education', N.S., IX (1835), 106–12, followed Fox with substantial discussions. Grimstone wrote a poem on the need for working-class women to be educated, 'The poor woman's appeal to her husband', N.S., VIII (1834), 351–2.

38 *Monthly Repository*, N.S., IX (1835), 483.

39 'A Farewell to the South', 1830, ll. 227–30, Motter, *Hallam*, 15. Hallam attributed these powers to poetry, but poetry 'incarnate' in woman, most notably in women such as Dante's Beatrice, is of all forces the most effective.

40 Armstrong, *Victorian Scrutinies*, 94.

41 Michel Foucault, *The Order of Things: An Archaeology of the Human Sciences* (1966), London and New York, 1974, 247. See also 252.

2 Experiments of 1830: Tennyson and the formation of subversive, conservative poetry

1 Quotations from Tennyson's poetry are from *The Poems of Tennyson* (Longman Annotated English Poets), Christopher Ricks, ed., 3 vols, 2nd edn, London, 1987.
2 Ricks, *Poems of Tennyson*, I, 281.
3 William Whewell, *On Astronomy and General Physics considered with Reference to Natural Theology*, Bridgewater Treatises III, London, 1833, 161–2 ('The stability of the solar system').
4 Whewell, *On Astronomy*, 186 ('The nebular hypothesis'). Whewell, of course, was arguing for the inadequacy of these ever regressive enquiries as a basis for an argument of creation from design. In his view such inadequacy forced one towards the argument of divine revelation, a God revealing Himself through miracle and exceptional intervention rather than choosing the 'rational' order of the universe in which to manifest Himself. But his demonstration of regression could just as easily convince one of scepticism.
5 Ibid., 189.
6 *The Letters of Alfred Tennyson*, Cecil Y. Lang and Edgar F. Shannon Jnr, eds, vol. I (1821–50), Oxford, 1982, 146 (to Richard Monckton Milnes, December 1836).
7 John Wilson ('Christopher North'), *Blackwood's Edinburgh Magazine*, XXXI (1832), 721–41. *Victorian Scrutinies: Reviews of Poetry 1830–70*, Isobel Armstrong, ed., London, 1972, 114, 116.
8 *Friendship's Offering: A Literary Album, and Christmas and New Year's Present*, London, 1832. John Clare, 127; Barry Cornwall, 72; Allan Cunningham, 287; Thomas Pringle, 18–44; Caroline Norton, 365.
9 *Friendship's Offering*. Norton, 365; Montgomery, 77–8.
10 Armstrong, *Victorian Scrutinies*, 114.
11 *Minstrelsy of the Scottish Border*, Walter Scott, ed., 3 vols, Kelso, 1802 (I–II), Edinburgh, 1803 (III), III, 297 (John Leyden, 'The Mermaid').
12 Armstrong, *Victorian Scrutinies*, 77.
13 Ibid., 114.
14 Charles Lyell, *The Principles of Geology*, 3 vols, London, 1830–3, I, 82.
15 Scott, *Minstrelsy*, III, 'The Mermaid', 315.
16 Ricks, *Poems of Tennyson*, I, 215, note to l. 16, refers to *Prometheus Unbound*, III. ii. 47.
17 Scott, *Minstrelsy*, III, Preface to 'The Mermaid', 299–301.
18 W. D. Paden, *Tennyson in Egypt: A Study of the Imagery in His Earlier Work*, University of Kansas Publications, Humanistic Studies, 27, Lawrence, 1942, 157.
19 William Blake, *The Marriage of Heaven and Hell* (Oxford Standard Authors), John Sampson, ed., 1913, 252.
20 T. C. Croker, *Fairy Legends and Traditions of Ireland*, 3 vols, 1825–8. Vol. III translates from Grimm.
21 'Written on the Banks of the Tay', *The Writings of Arthur Hallam*, T. H. Vail Motter, ed., London and New York, 1943, 56.
22 Armstong, *Victorian Scrutinies*, 90.
23 'A Farewell to the South' speaks of Dante's 'Startling the nations' (l. 299) (Motter, *Hallam*, 16), and of being inspired by love which can 'shape a nation's spirit' (l. 370) (ibid., 18).
24 'On the Madonna Del Gran Duca, in the Palazzo Pitti' (1830): 'Nothing is law to thee' (ibid., 3).

25 The coded reference to Goethe's Mariana has been pointed out by Ian H. C. Kennedy, 'Alfred Tennyson's *Bildungsgang*: notes on his early reading', *Philosophical Quarterly*, LVII (1978), 82–103: 93–4.

26 Armstrong, *Victorian Scrutinies*, 88.

27 'To the Loved One', Motter, *Hallam*, 93.

28 *Timbuctoo* (1829), 121–4 (ibid., 41), 194 (ibid., 43).

29 Ibid., 98.

30 'Swing, at Cambridge', quoted in Peter Allen, *The Cambridge Apostles: The Early Years*, Cambridge, 1978, 122.

31 Paden, *Tennyson in Egypt*, 155.

32 Scott, *Minstrelsy*, III, Note on 'The Mermaid', 320.

33 Kennedy, 'Tennyson's *Bildungsgang*', 87.

34 Lyell, *Principles of Geology*, I, vii, 116.

35 Ricks, *Poems of Tennyson*, 248, note to ll. 14–15, refers to *The Cloud*, 76.

36 Jonathon Bate writes interestingly on Coleridge's conservative reading of *The Tempest* and Hazlitt's challenge to the notion of Caliban as a Jacobin agitator: 'Shakespeare and the literary police', *London Review of Books*, 29 September 1988, 26–7.

37 Armstrong, *Victorian Scrutinies*, 107.

38 Ibid., 106. Tories expected revolution during 1832, the year of the Reform Bill and of this review.

39 Ibid., 109.

40 Motter, *Hallam*, 170.

41 Armstrong, *Victorian Scrutinies*, 92.

42 Ibid.

43 Ibid., 91.

44 Friedrich Schiller, *On the Aesthetic Education of Man in a Series of Letters*, trans. and ed. Elizabeth M. Wilkinson and L. A. Willoughby, Oxford, 1967, Letter 6, para. 6, pp. 33–5.

45 Armstrong *Victorian Scrutinies*, 85.

46 Ibid., 103.

47 Ibid., 89.

48 Ibid., 90.

49 Motter, *Hallam*, 157.

50 See above, chapter 1, p. 34 and note 28.

51 Armstrong, *Victorian Scrutinies*, 88; Motter, *Hallam*, 154.

52 Thomas Chalmers, *On the Power Wisdom and Goodness of God as manifested in the Adaptation of External Nature to the Moral and Intellectual Constitution of Man*, Bridgewater Treatise I, 1833, vol. I, 142, 146, 148. Chalmers speaks of habit as creating 'stepping stones' to vice or virtue (145), an interesting formulation in relation to the 'stepping stones' on which man rises to higher things in *In Memoriam*, I.

53 Armstrong, *Victorian Scrutinies*, 93.

54 Ibid., 98.

55 Ibid., 94.

56 Ibid., 97.

57 Ibid., 95 (Coleridge), 100 (the nature of the English language).

58 Ibid., 96.

59 Ibid., 96–7.

60 Ibid., 92. There is an important study of Hallam's philosophical position by Eric Griffiths in *Tennyson: Seven Essays*, P. A. W. Collins, ed., London, 1992.

61 John Wilson Croker, *Quarterly Review*, IL (1833), 81–96. For authorship see *The Wellesley Index to Victorian Periodicals*, I, 713.

62 John Wilson Croker, *The Battle of Talavera*, 10th edn, 1816, 52.

63 John Wilson, 'The Magic Mirror', *Works* (12 vols, Edinburgh and London, 1855–8), vol. XII (*The Poetical Works*), 425–32.

64 'Sacred Poetry', *Blackwood's Edinburgh Magazine* XXIV (1828), 917–38. Wilson wrote a number of articles on religious poetry in *Blackwood's* over 1827–8. In them he makes it clear that for him the dominant tradition is and must be religious poetry. How that tradition of English writing may be constructed in terms of a *generalised*, genuinely Christian poetry which falls into neither deism nor sectarianism is the theme of the collection. The essays were first collected in 1842, interestingly establishing a Tory canon in the formative years of Victorian poetry. But to know how widely it was accepted would require more research into readership than has yet been done: it is interesting, however, that the attempt to create a Tory canon was made.

65 John Keble, 'Sacred Poetry', *Occasional Papers and Reviews*, E. B. Pusey, ed., Oxford and London, 1877, 81–107: 87. From a review in the *Quarterly Review*, 1825. The language of Keble's condemnation of radical writing was much stronger in the original review.

66 Leigh Hunt, *The Story of Rimini*, Edinburgh and London, 1816, 70–1.

67 John Wilson, *Recreations of Christopher North*, 2 vols, Edinburgh and London, 1864, II, 54.

68 Wilson, *Recreations*, II, 58.

69 John Wilson, *The Isle of Palms, and Other Poems*, Edinburgh, 1812, canto III, 104.

70 Ibid., canto I, 11.

71 Ibid., canto IV, 141.

72 Wilson, *Recreations*, II, 86.

73 Keble, 'Sacred Poetry', 86.

74 Ibid., 91.

75 Ibid., 96.

76 Ibid., 97.

77 John Keble, *The Christian Year: Thoughts in Verse for the Sundays and Holidays throughout the year*, Oxford, 1827, 56–8.

78 Armstrong, *Victorian Scrutinies*, 84; Wilson, *Recreations*, II, 88–97.

79 Robert Montgomery, *The Omnipresence of the Deity. A Poem*, 1828, 3 (Analysis of Part I).

80 Ibid., Part I, 14; Introduction, 4.

81 Wilson, *Recreations*, II, 88–91. Wilson's quotation from Montgomery's account of the dying sceptic (*Omnipresence*, Part III, 99) has 'scowl'd' for 'quail'd'.

82 Montgomery, *Omnipresence*, Part II, 60–1.

83 Wilson, *Recreations*, II, 92.

84 *In Memoriam*, VI.

3 1832: Critique of the poetry of sensation

1 *The Poems of Tennyson* (Longman Annotated English Poets), Christopher Ricks, ed., 3 vols, 2nd edn, London, 1987, I, 436.

2 Ibid.

3 The tradition of debating Coleridge's poems began in the Cambridge Union in the late 1820s. Peter Allen, *The Cambridge Apostles: The Early Years*, Cambridge, 1978, 47.

4 William Whewell, *On Astronomy and General Physics considered with Reference to Natural Theology*, Bridgewater Treatises III, London, 1833, 182.

5 Hallam on the Greeks, *The Writings of Arthur Hallam*, T. H. Vail Motter, ed., London and New York, 1943, 145–7.

6 *Victorian Scrutinies: Reviews of Poetry 1830–70*, Isobel Armstrong, ed., London, 1972, 123–4.

7 *The Excursion*, Preface of 1814, ll. 63–7, in William Wordsworth, *Poetical Works* (Oxford Standard Authors), Thomas Hutchinson and Ernest de Selincourt, eds, 1936, 590.

8 'On sympathy', Motter, *Hallam*, 133–42: 137, 138.

9 Ibid., 138, 139.

10 'Theodicaea Novissima', ibid., 198–213: 204.

11 Ibid., 205.

12 Ibid., 66. But though 'reasons thrive' on the five senses, knowledge, and nature, 'hath never a bound'.

13 'Lines addressed to Alfred Tennyson' (1830), ibid., 67.

14 Thomas Keightley, *The Fairy Mythology*, 2 vols, London, 1828, I, 7. See also 21; and Preface, xii, for Keightley's belief that popular legends affect 'the feelings of a nation'.

15 Thomas Carlyle, *Sartor Resartus: The Life and Opinions of Herr Teufelsdröckh* (1831), *Thomas Carlyle's Collected Works* (Library Edition), 31 vols, London and New York, 1869–71, I, 65.

16 W. D. Paden, *Tennyson in Egypt: A Study of the Imagery in this Earlier Work*, University of Kansas Publications, Humanistic Studies, 27, Lawrence, 1942, 155.

17 Mrs Gaskell describes the resort to opium by working men (to dull the pain of hunger) in *Mary Barton* (1848).

18 Thomas Carlyle, 'Signs of the times' (1829), *Critical and Miscellaneous Essays*, 6 vols, II, 313–42: 317 (vol. VII, *Thomas Carlyle's Collected Works*, Library Edition, 31 vols, London and New York, 1869–71).

19 Ibid., 322.

20 'Philosophy of Perception: Reid and Brown', *Edinburgh Review*, LII (1830–1), 158–207.

21 J. F. Ferrier's articles on consciousness were published in *Blackwood's Edinburgh Magazine*, XLIII (1838), 187–201, 437–52, 784–91; XLIV (1838), 539–52; XLV (1839), 201–11, 419–30. W. David Shaw first made the connection between Ferrier and Tennyson in his *The Lucid Veil: Poetic Truth in the Victorian Age*, London, 1987, 48–53.

22 *Blackwood's Edinburgh Magazine*, XLV (1839), 204.

23 Ibid., 202.

24 Since sensations are 'enslaving powers of darkness', without being under the control of the will, the paradox is that reliance on sensation leads to a *dearth* of perceptual experience. Ibid., 203.

25 Walter Bagehot's much later (1864) critique of Tennyson as an 'ornate' poet of seductive but superabundant detail which is essentially a defence against uncertainty is an important analysis of this characteristic of Tennyson's work. 'Wordsworth, Tennyson and Browning; or, "Pure, Ornate, and Grotesque art" in English poetry', *National Review*, N.S., I (1864), 27–67.

26 Armstrong, *Victorian Scrutinies*, 18, 23–4.

27 Ibid., 23–5. John Sterling's review of *Poems* (1842), in the *Quarterly Review*, LXX (1842), 385–416, praised the domestic poems for expressing 'the heart of our actual English life' in contrast to the 'phantasms' of the 'mythological romances'

(ibid., 143). Sterling, like some of the reviewers of the *Idylls* in the late 1850s and 1860s, wanted to see Tennyson as the quintessence of a pastoral, domestic, depoliticised Englishness which was, in fact, intensely conservative.

28 *The Letters of Alfred Lord Tennyson*, Cecil Y. Lang and Edgar F. Shannon Jnr, eds, vol. I (1821–50), Oxford, 1982, 134 (2 July 1835).

29 Ibid., 120.

30 Ibid., 120. Tennyson's translations from the Greek of Dionysius of Halicarnassus: the first is a mistranslation, according to Tennyson's editors.

31 *The Works of Sir Henry Taylor*, new edn, vol. I, London, 1883, *Philip Van Artevelde, A Dramatic Romance*, Preface, vii.

32 Allen, *Cambridge Apostles*, 75, identifies F. D. Maurice as the author of a series of 'Sketches of contemporary authors', including Byron, in the *Athenaeum*, 1828.

33 Taylor, *Philip Van Artevelde*, Preface, viii.

34 Ibid., vii.

35 Ibid., viii.

36 Ibid., ix, xi.

37 Ibid., xiii.

38 Ibid., xv.

39 Taylor, *Philip Van Artevelde*, Introduction, xx.

40 Taylor, *Philip Van Artevelde*, Notes, 403.

41 *Philip Van Artevelde*, II. i (*Works*, I, 235). Taylor believed such democratic arguments were answered by James Spedding's *Substance of a Speech against Political Unions, delivered in a Debating Society in the University of Cambridge*, published anonymously in 1832, quoted by Taylor, *Philip Van Artevelde*, Notes, 403–4.

42 Richard Monckton Milnes, *Memorials of a Tour in Some Parts of Greece, Chiefly Poetical*, London, 1834, 83.

43 Ibid., 137.

44 Ibid., 50.

45 Richard Monckton Milnes, *Poetry for the People*, London, 1840, 37.

46 Ibid., 38.

47 Richard Monckton Milnes, *Palm Leaves*, London, 1844, 79–80.

48 Richard Chenevix Trench, *Poems*, New York, 1857, 36–8.

49 Richard Chenevix Trench, *The Story of Justin Martyr and Other Poems*, London, 1835, 76.

50 Trench, 'The Story of Justin Martyr', ibid., 18.

51 Armstrong, *Victorian Scrutinies*, 133.

52 Ibid., 135.

53 Ibid., 146.

54 Ibid., 147.

55 Ibid.

56 John Sterling, 'The Sexton's Daughter', *Poems*, London, 1839, 1–109; VI. i–v (59–60).

4 Experiments in the 1830s: Browning and the Benthamite formation

1 *Monthly Repository*, N.S., VII (1833), 252–62.

2 *Victorian Scrutinies: Reviews of Poetry 1830–70*, Isobel Armstrong, ed., London, 1972, 82.

3 Ibid., 83.

4 *Westminster Review*, XII (1830), 1.

5 *Monthly Repository*, N.S., VII (1833), 252.

6 J. S. Mill on *Pauline*, quoted in *Robert Browning, The Poems*, John Pettigrew and Thomas J. Collins, eds, 2 vols, Harmondsworth, 1981, I, 1022.

7 Ibid.

8 *Monthly Repository*, N.S., VI (1832), 641.

9 'On the condition of women in England', *Monthly Repository*, N.S., VII (1833), 217–31. Women of all classes are *trained* to be slaves, 'a species of prostitution' (218).

10 Harriet Martineau contributed numerous poems, tales, reviews and articles to the journal between 1822 and 1834 (see F. E. Mineka, *The Dissidence of Dissent: The Monthly Repository 1806–1838*, Chapel Hill, 1944, 397, 414–17). In addition to the article on women and divinity already noted she wrote, 'On female education', *Monthly Repository*, XVIII (1823), 77–81. Her interests were wide, ranging from prison reform to associationist psychology and theology. Her work was coloured by her interest in women. See, for example, her two articles, particularly the latter, on witchcraft: 1830, 744–59; 1832, 545–55. See also 'Negro slavery', N.S., IV (1830), 4–9.

11 'On women of no party', *Monthly Repository*, N.S., X (1836), 79, 80.

12 Pettigrew and Collins, *Browning, The Poems*, 1027.

13 'What is poetry?', *Monthly Repository*, N.S., VII (1833), 60–70; 'The two kinds of poetry', ibid., 714–24.

14 *Monthly Repository*, XIV (1819), 403. See Mineka, *The Dissidence of Dissent*, 132, on the advanced principles of biblical criticism developed in the journal.

15 *Monthly Repository*, XIV (1819), 403.

16 'Schleiermacher's critical essay on the Gospel of Saint Luke', *Monthly Repository*, N.S., I (1827), 38.

17 P. B. Shelley, *Alastor: Or, The Spirit of Solitude* (1816), *Poetical Works* (Oxford Standard Authors), Thomas Hutchinson, ed., 1934, ll. 121, 126–8.

18 Compare 'Tintern Abbey', ll. 43–6, in Wordsworth, *Poetical Works* (Oxford Standard Authors), Thomas Hutchinson and Ernest de Selincourt, eds, 1936, 164: 'Until, the breath of this corporeal frame/And even the motion of our human blood/Almost suspended, we are laid asleep/In body, and become a living soul'.

19 The *Wellesley Index to Victorian Periodicals*, III, 569, gives W. J. Fox as author of *Westminster Review*, XII (1830), 1–31. Poetry produces the 'monster' of mechanical personification if the poet is unable to project his own thoughts creatively. The author of the discussion of Bentham, *Westminster Review*, X (1829), 367–93, is not identified.

20 *Westminster Review*, XII (1830), 12, 13.

21 *Monthly Repository*, N.S., VIII (1834), 571.

22 Ibid., 711.

23 'The Copse', *Monthly Repository*, N.S., IX (1835), 91–2: 92.

24 'A Dream', *Monthly Repository*, N.S., VI (1832), 257–9: 259.

25 'How, in such places, varying according to the character of the country, different modes of life, and, finally, states sprang up': 'Religion, under some form or other, is coextensive with, the human race . . . it was transmitted from age to age by means of symbols . . . which in time ceased to be understood even by the priests, and thus a dead form was left in place of a living doctrine', *Monthly Repository*, N.S., VI (1832), 37, 96.

26 'The Vision. A Dramatic Sketch', *Monthly Repository*, N.S., IX (1835), 605–10, 656–64, 610.

27 Ibid., 657, 658, 662.

28 *Monthly Repository*, N.S., VI (1832), 190.

29 Ibid.

30 Ibid., 191.

31 *Monthly Repository*, N.S., VI (1832), 36. The commentary on Herder takes every opportunity to reiterate the importance of a popular literature, without which there *is* no nation. A truly popular literature can tap the language of the feelings which can almost transcend the division of labour and its mutilating effects: 'literature, which addresses itself to the people, must have a popular spirit and character . . . in communities, where there is no *people*, there can be no public and no nation – no language and poetry – that is properly our own and has a living agency in our hearts' (86).

32 *Monthly Repository*, N.S., VI (1832), 193.

33 Ibid., 196.

34 'Sunday. A Poem', *Monthly Repository*, N.S., IX (1835), 623. This poem, published anonymously, was enthusiastically reviewed and favourably compared with the work of Elliott.

35 *Monthly Repository*, N.S., X (1836), 10–14, 90–2, 149–52, 215–18, 286–8. 'Songs for the Bees', stanzas 1, 10.

36 *Monthly Repository*, N.S., IX (1835), 37–44.

37 Ibid., 40, 41.

5 The politics of dramatic form

1 *Monthly Repository*, N.S., VII (1833), 60–70 ('What is poetry?'), 714–24 ('Two kinds of poetry').

2 'What is poetry?', 63.

3 'Two kinds of poetry', 715

4 Ibid., 716. Mill is deeply ambivalent about the two kinds of poetry. Though Wordsworth is never 'ebullient' (718), Shelley lacks 'mental discipline' (719), even though ideally the poet of nature such as Shelley should be superior to the poet of culture in whom thought dominates.

5 'What is poetry?', 65.

6 Ibid.

7 Ibid., 64.

8 J. S. Mill, *On Liberty*, 1859.

9 Quotations of Browning's poetry are from *Robert Browning: The Poems*, John Pettigrew and Thomas J. Collins, eds, 2 vols, Harmondsworth, 1981.

10 *Westminster Review*, XII (1830), 5.

11 A. W. Schlegel, *A Course of Lectures on Dramatic Art and Literature*, trans. John Black, ed. R. H. Horne, 2 vols, 2nd edn, London 1840, xxx.

12 *Monthly Repository*, N.S., VIII (1834), 535.

13 *Westminster Review*, XII (1830), 4. Compare his analysis of Browning's *Pauline* in terms of 'scenery', 'agencies', 'events': *Monthly Repository*, N.S., VII (1833), 254.

14 *Westminster Review*, XII (1830), 5.

15 Schlegel, *Lectures*, 21. In reading unacted drama we are compelled, he writes, to read in a participatory way, 'to supply the representation ourselves' (24).

16 *The Westminster Review*, XII (1830), 5.

17 Ibid. The review begins with a defence of intellect in poetry, claiming Bentham as an imaginative poet, and Milton as thinker. The attributes associated with poetry and prose are deliberately disrupted to demonstrate that these are artificial, culturally made categories.

18 Ibid., 4.

19 Ibid.

20 Browning's introductory essay, dated 1851, to twenty-five letters of Shelley, later discovered to be spurious, was first published in 1852. It was reprinted in 1881. See 'On the poet objective and subjective; On the latter's aim; On Shelley as man and poet', *Browning Society Papers*, F. J. Furnivall, ed., I, 1881, 5–19: 5.

21 'On the poet objective and subjective', 5.

22 Ibid., 6, 5.

23 Ibid., 7, 6.

24 Ibid., 7.

25 Ibid.

26 Ibid.

27 *Bentham's Theory of Fictions*, C. K. Ogden, ed., London, 1932, 12. 'A fictitious entity is an entity to which, though by the grammatical form of the discourse employed in speaking of it, existence by ascribed, yet in truth and reality existence is not meant to be ascribed. Every noun-substantive which is not the name of a real entity, perceptible and inferential, is the name of a fictitious entity' (12).

28 *Westminster Review*, X (1829), 367–393: 387. For the discussion of 'nothingness' in language, see 386. For reference to the elect, 385. The author is at pains to demonstrate Bentham's intense and deeply considered attack on the despotism of the law.

29 Ibid., 391.

30 Ibid., 389–90, 390.

31 Ogden, *Bentham's Theory of Fictions*, 13.

32 Ibid., 12.

33 Ibid., 15.

34 Ibid., 9, 11. Bentham argues that ontological propositions such as God can be derived by inference and thus it is arguable that ultimately they are real entities. But it is also clear that *perceptible* experience alone, which has repercussions in the world of sense and in the immediate materiality of experience, produces the only securely non-fictional terms of existence. See also 44.

35 Ibid., lxviii.

36 Ibid., lii.

37 Browning, 'On the poet objective and subjective', 17.

38 Ibid.

39 *Monthly Repository*, N.S., IX (1835), 484.

40 Ibid.

41 Ibid.

42 Ibid., 485.

43 Ibid.

44 For a discussion of the politics of Browning's plays and their relation to the prose *Life of Strafford*, see Stephen Hawlin, 'The Development of Browning's Religious Sensibility', unpublished D.Phil. thesis, University of Oxford, 1986, 55–69. Hawlin's very interesting chapter on *The Ring and the Book* (255–332) argues for Browning's continued commitment to democratic politics in this poem. He puts the case with moderation, though arguably it could be made rather more strongly, judging by the powerful evidence he supplies.

45 Thomas Noon Talfourd, *Ion; A Tragedy*, 1835, V. iii. 99–100 (privately printed). Talfourd removed the reference to tyranny and substituted 'foreign power' when the play was published.

46 R. H. Horne, *Orion, An Epic Poem – in Three Books*, 1843, prefatory 'Note'. John

Lucas has recently discussed R. H. Horne and the Browning circle as dissidents, arguing that *Strafford* is a republican statement on the imminent death of William IV. See *England and Englishness: Ideas of Nationhood in English Poetry 1688–1900*, London, 1990, 165–9.

47 Horne, *Orion*, 'Note'.

48 Horne, *Orion*, I. iii. 31.

49 Ibid., I. iii. 32–3.

50 Ibid., II. ii. 58.

51 Ibid., III. i. 90. This, the concluding book, sets out the principles of action: 'When thought guides action and men know themselves' (89).

52 For the discourse of civic humanism in the late eighteenth and early nineteenth centuries see John Barrell, *The Political Theory of Painting from Reynolds to Hazlitt*, New Haven and London, 1986, 'Introduction: a republic of taste', 1–68. I am indebted to this chapter for my remarks on the 'classical' aesthetics of civic humanism and the analysis of its breakdown under changing economic conditions.

53 Barrell (ibid., 308–41) ends his book with the decadence of civic humanism in the writing of Robert Haydon and Hazlitt. Talfourd's critique of Hazlitt is one of the moments in the formation of a new discourse of democratic art.

54 In different ways the 'classical' definition of the 'public' was put under strain in the early nineteenth century. See Barrell on Blake, ibid., 253–8.

55 See below, p. 210.

56 Quoted by Martha Vicinus, *The Industrial Muse: A Study of Nineteenth-Century British Working-Class Literature*, London, 1974, 301. The first chapter of this very important study, 'Street ballads and broadsides: the foundations of a class culture', 8–59, discusses the production, dissemination and content of popular broadside songs.

57 Ibid., 298.

58 Ibid., 287–8 (John Grimshaw); 47–8 ('The Factory Bell', anonymous ballad).

59 Ibid., 97. For trade-union songs see 60–93.

60 See *The Poor House Fugitives: Self-taught Poets and Poetry in Victorian Britain*, Brian Maidment, ed., Manchester, 1987, 281–320, for examples of middle-class analysis of working-class poetry by Thomas Carlyle, Robert Southey, George Gilfillan, William Howitt and others. See 305–7 for a discussion of 'Burns and his school' by Charles Kingsley.

61 Ibid., 34, 82, 31.

62 Ibid., 31.

63 Samuel Bamford, 'To the Reader', Preface, *Poems*, Manchester, 1843, vii.

64 'The Union Hymn', *Hours in the Bowers*, Manchester, 1834, 31.

65 In the Preface to *Hours in the Bowers*, Bamford explicitly glosses 'freedom' as 'reform': 'that, in short, he has been confined in a greater number of prisons, for the cause of freedom (by which he means that of reform,) than any other Englishman living'.

66 Preface, *Poems* (1843), iv (for 'the working classes' and 'the labouring class'), viii ('the working man').

67 Ibid., 101.

PART II MID-CENTURY: EUROPEAN REVOLUTION AND CRIMEAN WAR – democratic, liberal, radical and feminine voices

6 Individualism under pressure

1 'A consideration of objections against the Retrenchment Association at Oxford', *The Poems and Prose Remains of Arthur Hugh Clough*, 2 vols, London, 1869, I, 275.

2 *The Letters of Matthew Arnold to Arthur Hugh Clough*, H. F. Lowry, ed., London and New York, 1932, Letter 7 (24 February 1848), 66.

3 'A rather long-winded sketch of my very uneventful life', *William Morris: Selected Writings and Designs*, Asa Briggs, ed., Harmondsworth, 1962, 32. Morris is referring to the eastern crisis of 1877. See p. 80.

4 It must be remembered that the term 'Pre-Raphaelite' is more apposite as an account of painting than of poetry. Morris himself describes his association with D. G. Rossetti, Ford Maddox Brown and Burne-Jones as one formed to improve 'designing'. *Selected Writings*, 30.

5 Arguably the poetry, far from being marginalised, assisted in the centralisation and increasing bureaucratisation and control of the state. See Philip Corrigan and Derek L. Sayer, *The Great Arch*, Oxford, 1985, 119–27.

6 Preface to the first edition of *Poems* (1853), *The Poems of Matthew Arnold* (Longmans Annotated English Poets), Kenneth Allott, ed., London, 1965, 599.

7 *North American Review*, LXXVII (1853), 1–30. Republished in *Poems and Prose Remains*, I, 359–83, as 'Review of some poems by Alexander Smith and Matthew Arnold'.

8 See *Letters to Clough*, 96–7. Richard Monckton Milnes had recently published *Letters and Literary Remains of John Keats*, 2 vols, London, 1848. This caused renewed discussion of Keats and his importance. It was reviewed in *The Times*, 19 September, 3. Milnes had discussed his work with Clough, who was clearly much more interested in Keats than Arnold despite the great differences between his own work and that of the earlier poet.

9 Alexander Smith and Sydney Dobell, *Sonnets on the War*, London, 1855. This impressive joint production does not assign individual authorship to the sonnets. Compare 'Sebastopol' (27) seen as a new Deluge with the rabid patriotism this battle usually elicited: 'We have buried sleep/And Night! The useless sun is in the Deep!'

10 Allott, *Poems of Arnold*, 609.

11 It was William Edmonstoune Aytoun who first brought Bailey's *Festus* (1839), Smith's 'A life-drama' (actually published 1852, but dated as 1853 in *Poems*) and Dobell's *Balder* (1853) together and Charles Kingsley who gave him the epithet, 'Spasmodic', with which to describe them. Aytoun's parody, *Firmillian*, was part of a spoof review of May 1854, in *Blackwood's*, in which he spoke of 'spasmodic throes and writhings': 'My brain is reeling . . . as a drunk mariner/ Who, stumbling o'er the bulwark, makes a clutch/At the wild incongruity of ropes,/And topples into mud'. Quoted by Mark A. Weinstein, *William Edmonstoune Aytoun and the Spasmodic Controversy*, New Haven and London, 1968, 127. Critics associated J. W. Marston's *Gerald* (1842), Tennyson's *Maud* (1855) and Elizabeth Barrett Browning's *Aurora Leigh* (1856) with the Spasmodics. This wide definition of the category 'Spasmodic' must be suspect, because it suggests a hostility to what is new. We must remember that R. H. Horne, Browning and Elizabeth Barrett Browning were all intensely interested in Bailey (Weinstein, *Aytoun*, 74). The almost universal hostility to such writing is best

accounted for by seeing it as a traditional Tory reaction, similar to that of John Wilson, to the new, *and* as a class reaction to the increasing literary ambition of those not from the traditional middle class. A glance at Aytoun's publications suggests his affinity with Wilson. He produced two volumes of ballads, asserting his affiliation with Scotland and conservative values: *Lays of the Scottish Cavaliers and Other Poems*, Edinburgh and London, 1849, and *Ballads of Scotland*, 2 vols, 1858, which went into many editions. His heroic poem, *Bothwell*, Edinburgh, 1856, is clearly intended to be a restrained tragedy of character, unlike the subjective poetry of the Spasmodics.

12 See above, Part I, pp. 60–1.
13 *Poems and Prose Remains*, I, 378.
14 Ibid., 374.
15 Ibid., 361.
16 Allott, *Poems of Arnold*, 591.
17 *Letters to Clough*, Letter 51 (30 November, 1853), 146: Revealingly, Arnold adds, 'This is why, with you, I feel it necessary to stiffen myself – and hold fast my rudder'.
18 Arnold quotes from his own poem (in the letter above, n. 17), 'The Youth of Nature' (51–2).
19 All references to Clough's poems are to *The Poems of Arthur Hugh Clough*, F. L. Mulhauser, ed., 2nd edn, Oxford, 1974.
20 Mulhauser, *Poems of Clough*, 292–3.
21 Allott, *Poems of Arnold*, 243.
22 Mulhauser, *Poems of Clough*, 89.
23 Quoted by Allott, *Poems of Arnold*, 243.
24 Allott, *Poems of Arnold*, 133.
25 Ibid., 104–5.
26 Ibid., 104.
27 Ibid., 112.
28 For Arnold's romantic passion for Mary Claude see Park Honan, *Matthew Arnold: A Life*, London, 1981, 44–67.

7 The radical in crisis: Clough

1 Robindra Kumar Biswas, *Arthur Hugh Clough: Towards a Reconsideration*, Oxford, 1972, 263–86.
2 *The Bothie of Tober-Na-Vuolich*, II, 271, in *The Poems of Arthur Hugh Clough*, F. L. Mulhauser, ed., 2nd edn, Oxford, 1974.
3 *On Translating Homer. Three Lectures given at Oxford*, London, 1861.
4 *The Poems and Prose Remains of Arthur Hugh Clough*, 2 vols, London, 1869, I, 380.
5 *The Poems of Matthew Arnold* (Longmans Annotated English Poets), Kenneth Allott, ed., London, 1965, 398.
6 David Masson, *North British Review*, XIX (Aug. 1853), 338.
7 Post-Romantic 'expressive' theory is not merely a theory of subjective poetry or self-expression. It is founded on the idea of projection of the materials of consciousness into an external embodiment. It is essentially a theory of the objective co-relative in which inner experience finds external form. The model is that of transposition from internal preverbal experience to external expression. See A. H. Warren Jnr, *English Poetic Theory 1825–1865*, Princeton, 1950.
8 Sydney Dobell, another Spasmodic poet, describes expressive theory in his impressively complex lecture on 'The nature of poetry', *Thoughts on Art, Philosophy, and Religion*, London, 1876, 3–65. The poet's problem is to make the

poem a representation of mind: '*a Perfect Poem is the perfect expression of a Perfect Human Mind*' (7). Metaphor is crucial to expressive poetry, which is based on transposition and substitution (of words for the contents of consciousness). 'To express is to carry out. To express a mind is to carry out that mind into some equivalent' (13).

9 'Lecture on the poetry of Wordsworth', *Poems and Prose Remains*, I, 309–25: Clough argues that the Preface to *Lyrical Ballads* may be in 'positive opposition' to Wordsworth's poetic practice (315).

10 Arnold's term, 'Barbarians' for 'Aristocrats' first appeared in *Culture and Anarchy*, London, 1869.

11 The kilt was a politicised garment. There had been an attempt to ban the kilt after 1745, though clan chiefs loyal to the Hanoverian succession continued to wear their tartan. When Scotland was being courted George IV wore a kilt of Royal Stuart tartan (and pink tights) on his state visit to Edinburgh in the early 1820s, thus giving it the status of fancy dress which is described in Clough's poem.

12 'On the formation of classical English: an extract from a lecture on Dryden', *Poems and Prose Remains*, I, 329–33: 332.

13 Ibid., 331.

14 Ibid., 333.

15 Ibid., 332–3.

16 Ibid., 375: undergraduates fritter money away on 'wines, and ices, and waist-coats'.

17 Ibid., 360–1.

18 Ibid., 361.

19 Ibid., 331.

20 *The Letters of Matthew Arnold to Arthur Hugh Clough*, H. F. Lowry, ed., London and New York, 1932, Letter 7 (24 February 1848), 66.

21 Origen was not only the 'founder' of allegorical method but, though influencing early Christian thought 200 years after Christ, was regarded as unorthodox. The point of swearing by him would be to declare oneself unconventional.

22 'A passage upon Oxford studies: extracted from a review of the Oxford University Commissioners' Report, 1852', *Poems and Prose Remains*, I, 403–8: 'Surely there was more in the domain of knowledge than that Latin and Greek which I had been wandering about in for the last ten years. Surely, there were other accomplishments to be mastered, besides the composition of Iambics and Ciceronian prose' (406).

23 A. W. N. Pugin, son of A. C. Pugin who designed the Houses of Parliament, followed up *Contrasts* (1836), which juxtaposed gothic and nineteenth-century buildings to show the inferiority of the latter, with three books in the 1840s: *An Apology for the Revival of Christian Architecture in England*, London, 1843; *The Present State of Ecclesiastical Architecture in England*, London, 1843; *Glossary of Ecclesiastical Ornament and Costume*, London, 1844.

24 'Review of Mr Newman's "The Soul" ', *Poems and Prose Remains*, I, 293–305: see 294–6.

25 John Henry Newman, *Tract Ninety, or Remarks on Certain Passages in the Thirty-Nine Articles* (1841), A. W. Evans, ed., London, 1933, 69, 68.

26 In Martha Vicinus, *The Industrial Muse: A Study of Nineteenth-Century British Working-Class Literature*, London, 1974, 99.

27 Ibid., 302–3.

28 Ibid., 302.

29 Ibid., 103.

NOTES

30 W. J. Linton, influenced in the course of his life by Shelley, Blake and Béranger, developed a remarkable form of secular hymn. This example, in which a positive statement is withdrawn and exposed as a conservative statement, is characteristic. He reprinted the following 'Unenfranchised' hymn in *Prose and Verse written and published in the Course of Fifty Years, 1836–1886*, 20 vols, London, 1886, I, 155–6:

> Who is the Patriot, who is he,
> When slaves are struggling to be free,
> Freedom's best-loved, may claim
> To hear her holiest Oriflamb?
>
> He who joineth hands with Power,
> When the anarch would devour
> Trampled Right insurgent! – He
> Is no friend of Liberty.
>
> He who claimeth kin with Right,
> Perfumed or in ermine dight,
> Knowing not the 'rabble', – He
> Hateth Truth and Liberty.

31 Brian Maidment, *The Poorhouse Fugitives: Self-Taught Poets and Poetry in Victorian Britain*, Manchester, 1987, has some interesting commentary on Chartist poetry. The advantage of his collection is that it places Chartist verse side by side with poems from a very wide range of working-class poets, thus giving a context to it. Something of the scope and importance of working-class writing is indicated, an importance to which I have done no more than gesture.
32 J. B. Leno, *The Aftermath: With Autobiography of the Author*, London, 1892, 68.
33 After *Herne's Oak*, London, 1853, he went on to publish *King Labour's Song Book*, London, 1861; *Drury Lane Lyrics*, London, 1868; *Kimberton, a Story of Village Life*, London, 1875–6. Arguably his work moved from activism to nostalgia. See below, Part III, p. 400.
34 Samuel Bamford, *Poems*, Manchester, 1843, 35.
35 J. C. Prince, *The Poetical Works*, 2 vols, R. A. Douglas Lithgow, ed., Manchester and London, 1880, I, 185.
36 Thomas Cooper, *The Poetical Works*, London, 1877, 283.
37 Maidment, *Poorhouse Fugitives*, 46.
38 J. B. Leno, *Herne's Oak and Other Miscellaneous Poems*, London, 1853, 11.
39 Ibid., 18.
40 Ibid., 14.
41 Ibid., 12.
42 Ibid., 21.
43 Poems such as 'The Fair' and 'The Old and the New Parson', idyllic memory of lost community and gentle satire, are typical of the later work in *Kimberton*. See below, Part III, p. 400.
44 *Herne's Oak*, 9–10.
45 Ibid., 12.
46 *King Labour's Song Book* (II), London, 1861, 15: Trousers sold for 18 shillings 'pass through the hands of three persons, who have each a portion of one shilling'. The shopworker claimed that, deserted by her husband and with a child, 'I was obliged to pledge the trousers, for I could not live upon the money such work affords'.
47 *Herne's Oak*, 20.
48 Ernest Jones, *The Revolt of Hindustan; or, The New World*, London, 1857, 8. The

509

reference is to Bishop Heber's missionary journey to India. His Christianity is associated with the policy – 'We murdered millions to enrich the Jew' (7). Chartism does not rule out racism here.

49 *The Revolt of Hindustan*, 24.
50 Preface to *The Revolt of Hindustan*, describing Jones's 'prison-poem'.
51 *The Battle-Day: and Other Poems*, London, 1855, 82.
52 Ibid., 62.
53 *Ernest Jones – Chartist, Selections from the Writings and Speeches of Ernest Jones*, John Saville, ed., London, 1952, 98 ('On moral and physical force', 1848).
54 *The Battle-Day*, 63.
55 Ibid., 61.
56 Mulhauser, *Poems of Clough*, 623–5.
57 Ibid., 292.
58 Ibid., 218.
59 Ibid., 292.
60 William Allingham, *Laurence Bloomfield in Ireland. A Modern Poem*, London and Cambridge, 1864, 88, 118.
61 In an age sympathetic to poetry, the projections of poetry are able to fuse with its outer forms. In an unsympathetic age poetry becomes disembodied and spiritual, creating 'a world for itself'. Poetry is dramatic because it is founded on a 'mobility' of soul which can create a fusion of internal and external. For an account of de Vere see *Victorian Scrutinies: Reviews of Poetry 1830–70*, Isobel Armstrong, ed., London, 1972, 37–9.

8 The liberal in crisis: Arnold

1 *The Poems of Matthew Arnold* (Longmans Annotated English Poets), Kenneth Allott, ed., London, 1965, 'The Forsaken Merman', 95–100.
2 *Empedocles on Etna*, I. ii. ll. 89–107, ibid., ll. 163–85.
3 *The Letters of Matthew Arnold to Arthur Hugh Clough*, H. F. Lowry, ed., London and New York, 1932, Letter 24 (probably September 1848), 96–7. Arnold rolled up Tennyson with Keats, and 'those d—d Elizabethan poets generally' (97) in his condemnation of Romanticism.
4 Ibid., Letter 30 (March 1849), 105–7: 106.
5 Ibid., Letter 60 (2 October 1868), 160–1.
6 Ibid., Letter 26 (1 March 1849), 101: 'For style is the expression of the nobility of the poet's character'.
7 Ibid., Letter 4 (December 1847), 61.
8 Allott, *Poems of Arnold*, 239.
9 Lowry, *Letters to Clough*, Letter 5 (December 1847), 63; Letter 7 (24 February 1848), 66.
10 Ibid., Letter 8 (1 March 1848), 68.
11 Ibid., Letter 10 (6 March 1848), 72: in England the 'people', Arnold says, would be 'insensible' to Lamartine's social and political rhetoric, just as much as the 'riding class' would be incapable of understanding it. Letter 12 (24 March [probably] 1848), 77: 'I praise a fagot, where-of the several twigs are nought: but a *people*?' This is in the context of distrust of George Sand's politics, a writer he had formerly read with enthusiasm.
12 Ibid., Letter 23, 95.
13 Ibid., Letter 8 (1 March 1848), 69.
14 Ibid., Letter 32 (23 September 1848), 111: despite the desire for retreat, this is an affectionate letter written from Thun, hinting at memories of the object

of the Marguerite poems. 'Parting' is quoted in it (110). See Letter 42 (12 February 1853), 128–31, in which Arnold attempts to formulate a complex response to Clough.

15 Ibid., Letter 9 (4 March 1848), 71.

16 Ibid., Letter 40 (28 October 1852), 124.

17 Ibid., Letter 26 (March 1849), 101.

18 Ibid., Letter 40 (28 October 1852), 124.

19 Ibid., Letter 25 (February 1849), 99.

20 Allott, *Poems of Arnold*, 596, 604.

21 Ibid., 604.

22 See above, n. 14.

23 'Saul', ix. 70–9. David's song is a Callicles-like hymn to joy and the 'wild joys of living' (70). It was first published, unfinished, in 102 lines, in *Dramatic Romances and Lyrics* (1845), and published in its present, much revised form in 1855 in *Men and Women*. The parallels with *Empedocles* are close and suggest a complex relation between the poems, in which *Empedocles* 'replies' to the 'Saul' of 1845 and the 'Saul' of 1855 'replies' to Arnold's poem with a defiant celebration of energy and the pleasures of *mind*.

24 Thomas Cooper, *The Poetical Works*, London, 1877, 60. *The Purgatory of Suicides* (1845), Book II, stanza 34.

25 Cooper, *Purgatory*, Preface to first edition.

26 Cooper, *Purgatory*, Book I, stanza 1.

27 Ibid., X. 17, 18, 251.

28 Ibid., X. 19, 251.

29 Ibid., II. 35, 60.

30 Ibid., II. 38, 60.

31 Ibid., II. 85, 72.

32 E.g. 'Thyrsis' (1868), 'Memorial Verses' (1850), 'Rugby Chapel' (1867), 'Haworth Churchyard' (1855), 'Heine's Grave' (1867), 'A Southern Night' (1861).

33 Allott, *Poems of Arnold*, 302–4.

34 'I am', *The Later Poems of John Clare*, Eric Robinson, David Powell and Margaret Grainger, eds, 2 vols, Oxford, 1984, I, 396–7. 'Dull must that being be', in 'Childe Harold', ibid., I, 62–3.

35 See Philip Dodd on Arnold, 'Englishness and the National Culture', *Englishness: Politics and Culture 1880–1920*, London, 1986, 12–19.

36 'Enclosure', *The Poems of John Clare*, J. W. Tibble, ed., 2 vols, London and New York, 1935, I, 419–20 (written in the period 1821–4).

37 'Dull must that being be', Robinson et al., *Later Poems of Clare*, I, 62–3.

38 See above, Part I, pp. 29–30.

39 Samuel Bamford, *Hours in the Bowers*, Manchester, 1834: 'Eclogue', 52–4. Bamford was imprisoned twice, in 1817 and 1819.

40 Stephen Fawcett, *Wharfedale Lays: Or, Lyrical Poems*, London and Bradford, 1837, 75.

41 Samuel Bamford, *Poems*, Manchester, 1843, vi–vii.

42 *The Village Muse, containing the Complete Poetical Works of Elijah Ridings*, 3rd edn, Macclesfield, 1854.

43 Ibid., 141.

44 Ibid., 145.

45 Ibid., 161, 167.

46 Ibid., 165.

47 Ibid., 320.

48 John Critchley Prince, *The Poetical Works*, R. A. Douglas Lithgow, ed., 2 vols, Manchester and London, 1880, I, 44.

49 Ibid., I, 257–8.

50 Ridings, *The Village Muse*, 168.

51 Prince, *Poetical Works*, I, 105.

52 Ibid., II, 201.

53 Ibid., I, 3.

54 Ibid., I, 9.

55 Ibid., I, 13.

56 Ibid., I, 11 ('Plenty'), 59 (Sonnet 'On receiving the poems of Keats from a friend').

57 Elijah Ridings has a section on the virtues of women in 'The Remembrance'. Samuel Bamford praises the work of Ann Hawkshaw in the Preface to his *Poems* of 1843.

58 Samuel Bamford, *Passages in the Life of a Radical* (1844), *The Autobiography of Samuel Bamford*, 2 vols, W. H. Chaloner, ed., London, 1967, II, 225: Bamford uses this phrase ironically of himself when, newly released from prison and accompanied by his wife, he looks over the countryside and asserts that he can 'see the wind' – or freedom.

59 John Nicholson, *Airedale in Ancient Times*, London, 1825, 26.

60 Ibid., 27.

61 Ibid., 7.

62 Ibid., 2.

63 Ibid., 93–5: 'But his poor heart was most of all subdued/With daughters' pride, and sons' ingratitude'.

64 William Heaton, *The Flowers of Calder Dale*, London and Halifax, 1847, 5, 24.

65 Ibid., 55, 54.

66 Bamford, *Poems*, 1–4. 'Hymn to Spring' is clearly influenced by Shelley's 'Ode to the West Wind'.

67 J. B. Rogerson, *A Voice from the Town and Other Poems*, London and Manchester, 1842, 47, 48.

68 Robert Story, *The Poetical Works*, London, 1857, 299 ('When Freedom'), 270–1 ('Ingleboro' Cave').

69 Ibid., 409.

70 Ibid., 413. Sydney Dobell wrote a very different poem on Sebastopol. Compare also Adelaide Ann Proctor: see below, p. 336.

71 Story, *The Third Napoleon, An Ode Addressed to Alfred Tennyson Esq, Songs of the War*, London, 1854, 19. For Massey's war poems, see below, pp. 271–3.

72 J. B. Leno, *Drury Lane Lyrics*, London, 1868, 231–42.

73 William Heaton, *The Old Soldier . . . and Other Poems*, London and Halifax, 1857, 20.

74 J. C. Prince, *Poetical Works*, II, 181.

75 Assigned to Dobell in *The Poems of Sydney Dobell* (Selected), London and Newcastle-upon-Tyne, 1887, 63.

76 *Correspondence of Arthur Hugh Clough*, F. Mulhauser, ed., 2 vols, Oxford, 1957, II, 491.

77 Ibid., II, 506.

78 *The Letters of Matthew Arnold, 1848–1888*, G. W. E. Russell, ed., London, 1901, I, 46: English officers are 'too beautifully dressed for real service' (6 November 1854): see also his comments on the young uneducated '*nincompoops*' taking commissions in the army (24 August 1854), 42.

9 A new radical aesthetic – the Grotesque as cultural critique: Morris

1 Morris shared accommodation with Rossetti at Red Lion Square from November 1856 until May 1859. See Philip Henderson, *William Morris. His Life, Work and Friends*, Harmondsworth, 1973, 56–78.

2 Letters to *The Times*, 13 May 1851, 30 May 1851, 5 May 1854, 25 May 1854. *The Works of John Ruskin*, E. T. Cook and A. Wedderburn, eds, 39 vols, London, 1903–12, XII, 319–35.

3 Henderson, *William Morris*, 30–1.

4 *The Germ*, January–April 1850, first two numbers January and February. Later renamed *Art and Poetry, being Thoughts towards Nature*, dated respectively March and May 1850. Folded thereafter. *The Oxford and Cambridge Magazine*, 12 monthly nos, January–December 1856.

5 W. Holman Hunt, *Pre-Raphaelitism and the Pre-Raphaelite Brotherhood*, London, 1905, 150. Consider Carol T. Christ, *The Finer Optic: The Aesthetic of Particularity in Victorian Poetry*, London, 1975, 55, as an example of an intelligent critic who attempts to unify the disparate positions of the Pre-Raphaelite Brotherhood under a discussion of detail and accuracy.

6 *The Germ*, facsimile reprint with Introduction by W. M. Rossetti, London, 1901, 16.

7 *The Germ*, 1 (January 1850), 31.

8˙ *The Germ*, facsimile reprint, 1901, 18.

9 *The Germ*, 1 (January 1850), 14.

10 Cook and Wedderburn, *Works of Ruskin*, III, *Modern Painters*, 31–8, 25–32.

11 *The Germ*, 1 (January 1850), 17–18.

12 *The Germ*, 2 (February 1850), 58.

13 *Art and Poetry*, 4 (May 1850), 192.

14 E. S. Dallas, *Poetics: An Essay on Poetry*, London, 1852, reference to Kant, 157; quotation, 291.

15 See above, Part I, pp. 71–4. See also below p. 341.

16 Rev. F. W. Robertson, *Two Lectures on the Influence of Poetry on the Working Classes*, London, 1852, 11, 59.

17 See ‘ "A Joy for Ever"; (and its price in the market), Two lectures on the political economy of art’, in Cook and Wedderburn, *Works of Ruskin*, XVI, 5–176.

18 Walter Pater, *Westminster Review*, N.S., XXXIV (October 1868), 300.

19 Ibid., 300–1.

20 W. Morris, *The Defence of Guenevere and Other Poems* (1858), London, 1896 (1858 reprint), 247.

21 Cook and Wedderburn, *Works of Ruskin*, XI, *The Stones of Venice*, iii, 135–95.

22 Letter to *The Times*, 25 May 1854, in Cook and Wedderburn, *Works of Ruskin*, XII, 334.

23 *The Defence*, 46.

24 Ibid., 26.

25 Ibid., 174–7.

26 Millais based a painting on ‘Mariana’ in 1850. For the Pre-Raphaelite interest in Tennyson see Laura Marcus, ‘Brothers in their anecdotage: Holman Hunt's *Pre-Raphaelitism and the Pre-Raphaelite Brotherhood*’, *Pre-Raphaelitism Reviewed*, Marcia Pointon, ed., Manchester, 1989, 1–21, 15.

27 Cook and Wedderburn, *Works of Ruskin*, X, *The Stones of Venice*, ii, 184: see also XI, *The Stones of Venice*, iii, 178–80, paras. 59–60.

28 A. W. Pugin, *Contrasts, or a Parallel between the Architecture of the 15th & 19th Centuries*, London, 1836, 3:

I will proceed, first, to shew the state of Architecture in this country immediately before the great change of religion; secondly, the fatal effects produced by that change of Architecture; and, thirdly, the present degraded state of Architectural taste, and the utter want of those feelings which alone can restore Architecture to its ancient noble position.

29 Cook and Wedderburn, *Works of Ruskin*, XI, *The Stones of Vencice*, iii, 134.
30 Cook and Wedderburn, *Works of Ruskin*, X, *The Stones of Venice*, ii, 188, 196–201, paras. 9, 17–22.
31 Ibid., 196.
32 Cook and Wedderburn, *Works of Ruskin*, XI, *Stones of Venice*, iii, 154.
33 Ibid., 155.
34 Ibid., 169.
35 Ibid., 173.
36 Ibid., 166, 178.
37 Ibid., 179.
38 Ibid., 185.
39 Ibid., 187.
40 Ibid., 191.
41 Hegel's *Aesthetics* is a text composed by his contemporary H. G. Hotho, from Hegel's notes (and students' notes) for lectures given in Berlin in the 1820s. Hotho's editions were published in 1835 and 1842. The first English translation, *The Introduction to Hegel's Philosophy of Fine Art*, trans. Bernard Bosanquet, was first published in 1886.
42 *The Defence*, 56.
43 Ibid., 4.
44 Walter Pater, *Westminster Review*, N.S., XXXIV (October 1868), 300–12: 305.
45 *The Defence*, 222.
46 Ibid., 169.
47 Ibid., 173.
48 Cook and Wedderburn, *Works of John Ruskin*, V, *Modern Painters*, iii, 410–17, paras. 33–9.
49 *The Defence*, 143.
50 Ibid., 214.
51 Ibid., 225.
52 Ibid., 121.
53 J. H. Newman, *Tract Ninety, or Remarks on Certain Passages in the Thirty-Nine Articles* (1841), A. W. Evans, ed., London, 1933, 69.
54 *The Germ*, 2 (February 1850), 80.
55 Ibid., 83.
56 Ibid.
57 Cook and Wedderburn, *Works of Ruskin*, XVI, 'A Joy for Ever . . . lectures on the political economy of art', 86.
58 *The Defence*, 121.
59 Ibid., 117, 119.
60 Ibid., 121.
61 Ibid., 131.
62 Ibid.
63 Ibid., 115.
64 Ibid., 125.
65 Ibid., 188.
66 Ibid., 193.
67 'A Joy for Ever', 90–1.

68 This chapter has benefited greatly from my reading of Lindsay Smith's unpublished Ph.D. thesis on Ruskin, *The Enigma of Visibility: Theories of Visual Perception in the Work of John Ruskin, William Morris and the Pre-Raphaelites*, University of Southampton, 1989.

10 Tennyson in the 1850s: New experiments in conservative poetry and the Type

1 Charles Lyell, *The Principles of Geology, or, The Modern Changes of the Earth and Its Inhabitants*, London, 1830–3. All references to Lyell in this chapter are to the 7th edition (1847). This, the first single-volume edition of *The Principles*, has been chosen on grounds of availability. Lyell revised his work, often substantially, with every edition, though his thesis remained the same. The Cambridge Apostles (see Part I) seem to have been well acquainted with his ideas at an early stage. My quotation from Lyell is intended to suggest Tennyson's grasp of his thesis rather than that *In Memoriam* is indebted to specific passages.

2 Arthur Hallam, 'On some of the characteristics of modern poetry', *Englishman's Magazine*, I (1831), 616–28. In *Victorian Scrutinies: Reviews of Poetry 1830–70*, Isobel Armstrong, ed., London, 1972, 90.

3 Ibid.

4 As elaborated in Part I, Hallam developed his epistemology in his 'Essay on the philosophical writings of Cicero' and his views on the sexuality of God in 'Theodicaea Novissima'. See *The Writings of Arthur Hallam*, T. H. Vail Motter, ed., London and New York, 1943, 142–81, 198–213, esp. 204–7.

5 William Edmonstoune Aytoun (pseudonym of T. Percy Adams), *Firmilian; or, The Student of Badajoz: A Tragedy*, *Blackwood's Magazine*, LXXV (1854), 550. For the psychological language of the Spasmodic controversy, see Isobel Armstrong, 'The role and treatment of emotion in Victorian criticism of poetry', *Victorian Periodicals Newsletter*, 10 (March 1977), 3–16. See also Mark A. Weinstein, *William Edmonstoune Aytoun and the Spasmodic Controversy*, New Haven, 1968.

6 Henry Maudsley, *The Physiology and Pathology of the Mind* (1867), 2nd edn, London, 1868, 257: 'there is, as it were, a loss of the power of self-control in the individual nerve-cell, an inability to calm self-contained activity, subordinate or coordinate, and its energy is dissipated in an explosive display, which, like the impulsive action of the passionate man, surely denotes an irritable weakness'.

7 'Peace and War: A Dialogue', *Blackwood's Magazine*, LXXVI (1854), 589–98. Author identified by the *Wellesley Index of Victorian Periodicals* as G. C. Swayne. This is a dialogue representing conservative and peace-party (manufacturing and trade interests) views of the war. Hence it is the peace party which is regarded as being feeble-minded. In *Maud* the movement to war is a movement to madness. Ricks (*The Poems of Tennyson* [Longman Annotated English Poets], (Christopher Ricks, ed., 3 vols, 2nd edn, London, 1987), II, 520; n. i refers to Valerie Pitt, *Tennyson Laureate*, London, 1962, 175, who discusses the relation between *Maud* and Carlyle's *Past and Present* (1843), where criminal poisoning in a sick society is described. Also relevant is Kingsley's *Alton Locke* (1850). See also James R. Bennett, 'The historical abuse of literature: *Maud: A Monodrama* and the Crimean war', *English Studies*, 62 (1981), 34–45. I am grateful to Joseph Bristow for directing me to these discussions and for permission to read his unpublished article, 'Tennyson's *Maud* and war'.

8 All references to Tennyson's poems are to Ricks, *Poems of Tennyson*.

9 Sigmund Freud, 'Mourning and Melancholia' in *The Standard Edition of the*

Complete Works of Sigmund Freud, James Strachey and Anna Freud, ed., London, 1953–66, vol. 14, 244. All references to Freud are to this edition.

10 Lyell, *The Principles,* 178.

11 See A. C. Crowley, *The Politics of Discourse,* Basingstoke, 1989, chapter 2, 51–90.

12 R. C. Trench, *On the Study of Words,* London, 1851, 5.

13 Ibid., 23.

14 Ibid., 16–17.

15 Robert Montgomery, *The Omnipresence of the Deity. A Poem,* London, 1828. In this poem the believing mariner is saved from drowning for his equally believing loved one while the atheist dies. The verbal parallels are interesting: 'She blush'd an answer to his wooing tale': 'Clasp'd in his twining arms, her seaman now/Parts the sleek locks that nestle on her brow' (Part 2, 44).

16 *The Letters of Alfred Lord Tennyson,* Cecil Y. Lang and Edgar F. Shannon Jnr. eds, Oxford, 1982, Vol. I (1821–1850), 337.

17 *Language as Living Form in Nineteenth-Century Poetry,* Brighton, Sussex, and New Jersey, 1982, 187–90.

18 George Eliot translated Strauss's *Life of Jesus* in 1846, but the Apostles knew his work in the 1830s. Ludwig Feuerbach, in *The Essence of Christianity* (1841) (translated by George Eliot in 1854), extended his account of Christian myth as the imaginative interpretation of a people by seeing myth as a construct made by the projection of a desire into its object.

19 Lyell, *The Principles,* 746–7.

20 Robert Chambers, *Vestiges of Creation* (1844). Published anonymously, this work argues for the origin of the species in evolutionary terms, but whereas Lyell's argument is about the retrospective construction of uniformitarian change from the ambiguous and discontinuous evidence of geological remains, Chambers is concerned with tracing progressive change from the beginning of creation onwards.

21 Lyell, *The Principles,* 170, 180, 186.

22 See for instance ibid., 172, 174, 182, 187–9.

23 Ibid., 70. Also: 'All geologists . . . must be conscious, therefore, that the inaccessibility of the regions in which these alterations are taking place, compels them to remain in ignorance of a great part of the working of existing causes': 172.

24 Ibid., 70.

25 Ibid., 173.

26 Ibid., 186. Also: 'Organic remains . . . may abandon and revisit many spaces again and again': 187.

27 Ibid., 552.

28 Friedrich Nietzsche, *Twilight of the Idols,* in *Twilight of the Idols and the Anti-Christ,* Harmondsworth, 1987, 38.

29 Lyell, *The Principles,* 190.

30 John Keble, *Tract 89* (1841), in *Tracts for the Times,* London, 1833–41, vol. VI, 65–7, 144.

31 John Milton, *A Mask (Comus), The Poems of John Milton* (Oxford Standard Authors), Helen Darbishire, ed., London, 1958, 470, 1. 476.

32 *In Memoriam,* II. 413; XCV. 46.

33 Freud, 'Civilisation and its discontents', *Complete Works,* vol. 21, 69–71.

34 Lyell: 'But if we may be allowed so far to indulge the imagination, as to suppose a being entirely confined to the nether world – some "dusky melancholy sprite" like Umbriel, who could "flit on sooty pinions to the central earth", but who was never permitted to "sully the fair face of light", and emerge into

the regions of water and of air; and if this being should busy himself in investigating the structure of the globe, he might frame theories the exact converse of those usually adopted by human philosophers' (71).

35 *Anti-Maud*, London, 1855, written by W. C. Bennett.

36 See Brian Maidment, *The Poorhouse Fugitives: Self-taught Poets and Poetry in Victorian Britain*, Manchester, 1987, 55–6, 312–14. A self-taught working man associated with the Christian Socialists, Massey was aware of European socialism and could write powerful lyrics on the redemption of the oppressed working classes, such as 'The Awakening of the People', reprinted by Maidment, who sees Massey as a poet who gained a middle-class audience more easily than some working-class poets. It is interesting that Massey's poems on oppression and celebrations of the war were published virtually concurrently. See also chapter 7 above.

37 'A Battle Charge', *War Waits*, 2nd edn, London, 1855, 38–40: 39. All references to Massey's poems are to this volume.

38 Michel Foucault, *Madness and Civilisation: A History of Insanity in the Age of Reason*, London, 1987, 241–78.

39 Matthew Allen, *Essay on the Classification of the Insane*, London, 1837, 3–4.

40 Foucault, *Madness and Civilisation*, 261: 'It was the man himself, not his projection in a delirium, who was now humiliated'.

41 Allen, *Classification of the Insane*, 20–1.

42 Ibid., 3. See also 27–8 for a similar structure.

43 Foucault, *Madness and Civilisation*, 264.

44 Allen, *Classification of the Insane*, 13; Henry Maudsley, *The Physical Basis of Will*, London, 1880, 11.

45 James Robert Mann, *Tennyson's 'Maud' Vindicated: An Explanatory Essay*, London, 1856, 77. This work considers the poem as a case study of the insane, demonstrating that 'acute eruptive disorder' is preferable to the 'chronic disease' of madness. Though Mann sees the response to the war as in some sense pathological, it produces a catharsis and thus constitutes a 'cure'.

46 Arthur Schopenhauer, *Essay on the Freedom of the Will* (1841), New York, 1960, 40.

47 Maudsley, *Physical Basis of Will*, 27.

48 All the movements of the will are the objects of self-consciousness, which can master actions retrospectively: 'He can *wish* two opposing actions, but *will* only one of them. Only the act reveals to his self-consciousness which of the two he wills': Schopenhauer, *Freedom of the Will*, 17.

49 Freud, 'The theme of the three caskets', *Complete Works*, vol. 12, 301.

50 Henry Maudsley, *On the Method of the Study of Mind: An Introductory Chapter to a Physiology and Pathology of the Mind*, London, 1883, 18.

51 Maudsley, *Physical Basis of Will*, 16.

52 Henry Maudsley, *Body and Will, being an Essay concerning Will in its Metaphysical, Physiological and Pathological Aspects*, London, 1883, 293.

53 Ibid., 302.

54 Ibid., 304.

55 Ibid., 291–2.

11 Browning in the 1850s and after: New experiments in radical poetry and the Grotesque

1 Quoted by Park Honan and William Irvine, *The Book, the Ring, and the Poet, A Biography of Robert Browning*, New York, 1974, 290.

2 Walter Bagehot, *Tinsley's Magazine*, III (January 1869, 665–74, 666: Browning, Bagehot says, is not 'conventional', that is, translated into class terms, not a gentleman (667).

3 'Wordsworth, Tennyson and Browning; or, "Pure, Ornate, and Grotesque Art" in English poetry', *National Review*, N.S, I (1864), 27–67.

4 Ibid., 45.

5 Ibid., 56.

6 Ibid., 66.

7 *The Works of John Ruskin*, 39 vols, E. T. Cook and A. Wedderburn, eds, London, 1903–12 VI, *Modern Painters*, 449.

8 On their visit to London in 1852 the Brownings were on visiting terms with the Ruskins. See Honan and Irvine, *The Book, the Ring*, 299. They seem to have read *Modern Painters* as it was published (I, 1843; II, 1846). Browning admired the first volume of *Modern Painters* but could agree 'only by snatches', Elizabeth Barrett Browning reported. (Cook and Wedderburn, *Works of John Ruskin*, III, xxxviii. See also *The Letters of Elizabeth Barrett Browning*, F. G. Kenyon, ed., London, 1897, I, 384.)

9 *Robert Browning: The Poems*, John Pettigrew and Thomas J. Collins, eds, 2 vols Harmondsworth, 1981, 57.

10 See above, Part I, pp. 149–51.

11 See above, p. 239.

12 Victorian responses to Renaissance painting and Browning's likely knowledge of them are charted by David J. De Laura, 'The context of Browning's painter poems: aesthetics, polemics, histories', *Proceedings of the Modern Languages Association*, 95 (1980), 167–388. A. F. Rio's *The Poetry of Christian Art*, London, 1854, possibly translated by Mrs Jameson, argued for the decadence of Italian art in the fifteenth century, represented by the naturalism of Lippi. Anna Jameson's *The Poetry of Sacred and Legendary Art*, 2 vols, London, 1848, supported this view.

13 For Ruskin's refusal of an ascetic reading of Italian Renaissance painting see Stefan Hawlin's 'The development of Browning's religious sensibility', unpublished D.Phil. thesis, University of Oxford, 1986, 191–3. Joseph Milsand disagreed with Ruskin's analysis of the decadence of the late Renaissance. He saw Renaissance civic thought, politics, art and literature as a phase of human freedom. It was deadening rationality and classicism which killed the imaginative life of the Renaissance. See *L'Ésthetique anglaise: étude sur M. John Ruskin*, Paris, 1864, 58, 156–9. Browning owes more to this liberal view.

14 See above, Part I, p. 152.

15 See above, Part I, p. 153. See also Fox, 114.

16 Karl Marx, 'Economic and philosophical manuscripts', *Early Writings*, Lucio Colletti, ed., Harmondsworth, 1975, 387.

17 Robert Langbaum, *The Poetry of Experience: The Dramatic Monologue in Modern Literary Tradition*, London, 1957. See chapter 2, 75–108.

18 See above, Part I, p. 11.

19 Two among the many theoretical discussions of Browning's poetry are outstanding: Ann Wordsworth, 'Browning's anxious gaze', *Robert Browning: A Collection of Critical Essays*, Harold Bloom and Adrienne Munich, eds, Englewood Cliffs, N.J., 1979, 28–38: (see 31–2, 38), and E. Warwick Slinn, 'Consciousness as writing: deconstruction and reading Victorian poetry', *Victorian Poetry*, 25 (Spring 1987), 67–81. These readings are informed by Lacan and Derrida respectively.

20 Friedrich Nietzsche, *The Birth of Tragedy* (1872), trans. Walter Kaufman, New York, 1967, 51–2.

21 Ludwig Feuerbach, *The Essence of Christianity* (1841), trans. George Eliot (1854), Karl Barth, ed., New York, 1957, 4.

22 Ibid., 2–3.

23 Quoted by De Laura, 'The context of Browning's painter poems', 376.

24 John Ruskin, *Modern Painters*, I (1843), Cook and Wedderburn, *Works of John Ruskin*, III, Part II, 136, 138.

25 Ibid., 141 (Locke), 142, 143.

26 Ibid., 135.

27 Ibid., 143.

28 Arnold's lectures were collected and published in 1865 as *Essays in Criticism* (first series), London, 1865. Most of them belong to the period after 1855, when *Men and Women* was published.

29 Letter of 20 March 1845, *The Letters of Robert Browning and Elizabeth Barrett Browning, 1845–1846*, Elvan Kintner, ed., Cambridge, Mass., 1969, 1, 43.

30 Feuerbach, *The Essence of Christianity*, ch. 13, 'The mystery of faith – the mystery of miracle', 132. Significantly he writes that 'the Spirit of Culture' and that of science is alien to Christianity, 132–3.

31 *Prometheus Unbound*, I. 452–3, *Complete Works of Percy Bysshe Shelley*, Thomas Hutchinson, ed., London, 1934, 218.

32 Harold Bloom repeatedly explores 'Childe Roland' in this way: in *The Ringers in the Tower*, Chicago, 1971, *A Map of Misreading*, New York, 1975, and *Poetry and Repression*, New Haven, 1976.

33 See Hawlin, 'Browning's religious sensibility', ch. 5, in particular 255–88.

34 Walter Bagehot, *The English Constitution* (1867), *Collected Works of Walter Bagehot*, V, Norman St John Stevas, ed., 8 vols, London, 1965–74.

12 'A music of thine own': Women's poetry – an expressive tradition?

1 'The Marriage Vow', *Life and Literary Remains of L.E.L.*, Laman Blanchard, ed., 2 vols, London, 1841, II, 277.

2 Amy Levy, *A Ballad of Religion and Marriage* (one of 12 privately printed pamphlets), 1915 (British Library catalogue).

3 Elizabeth Barrett Browning, *Aurora Leigh and Other Poems*, Cora Kaplan, ed., London, 1978, I, 436–7.

4 'I wish, and I wish I were a man' ('From the Antique', 1854).

5 *The Poetical Works of Felicia Hemans*, William Michael Rossetti, ed., London, 1873, Prefatory Notice, xxvii.

6 *The Angel in the House*, I. ii. 2, 74–5, *The Poems of Coventry Patmore*, Frederick Page, ed., London, 1949.

7 Blanchard, *Life and Literary Remains of L.E.L.*, I, 55.

8 See Julia Swindells, *Victorian Writing and Working Women*, Oxford, 1985. This study retrieves a number of unknown writers.

9 Ann Hawkshaw, *Dionysius the Areopagite*, London and Manchester, 1842: for the egalitarian heaven see *Dionysius*, 97–9; 'The Mother to Her Starving Child', 170–2: 'Why am I a slave?', 191–3. Subsequent volumes were *Poems for My Children*, London and Manchester, 1847; *Sonnets on Anglo-Saxon History*, London, 1854.

10 Louisa Horsfield, *The Cottage Lyre*, 2nd edn, London and Leeds, 1862: 'The Truant', 44–7.

11 Ellen Johnston ('The Factory Girl'), *Autobiography, Poems and Songs*, Glasgow, 1862: 'The Working Man', 79–80; 'The Maniac of the Green Wood', 15–19.

12 Blanchard, *Life and Literary Remains of L.E.L.*, II, 245–8: 246.

13 Letitia Landon, *Poetical Works*, 2 vols, London, 1850, I, xi (Preface to *The Improvisatrice* [1824]).

14 'Pilate's Wife's Dream', *Poems of Charlotte Brontë*, Tom Winnifrith, ed., Oxford, 1984, 3.

15 For a description of objectification see Dolores Rosenblum, 'Christina Rossetti: the inward pose', *Shakespeare's Sisters: Feminist Essays on Women Poets*, Sandra Gilbert and Susan Gubar, eds, Bloomington and London, 1979, 82–98.

16 Blanchard, *Life and Literary Remains of L.E.L.*, II, 246, 245–6.

17 'The Indian Bride', *The Improvisatrice, Poetical Works*, I, 28, 30.

18 Ibid., I, 31.

19 Ibid., I, 29.

20 Preface to *The Venetian Bracelet* (1829), *Poetical Works*, I, xiv.

21 Ibid.

22 Edmund Burke, *A Philosophical Enquiry into the Origin of Our Ideas of the Sublime and the Beautiful*, James T. Boulton, ed., Notre Dame and London, 1958, 51.

23 Blanchard, *Life and Literary Remains of L.E.L.*, I, 205.

24 Rossetti, *Works of Hemans, Records of Woman*, Section I, 'Arabella Stuart', 144.

25 Rossetti, *Works of Hemans*, 'Casabianca', 373–4.

26 *The Poems of Anne Brontë: A New Text and Commentary*, Edward Chitham, ed., Totowa and Basingstoke, 1979, 110–11, 21–8.

27 'The Lovely Lady', Winnifrith, *Poems of Charlotte Brontë*, 202–3.

28 Emily Brontë, 'The Philosopher', *The Complete Poems*, C. W. Hatfield, ed., London, 1923, 5–6.

29 Adelaide Anne Procter, *Legends and Lyrics and Other Poems* (1858), London and New York, 1906, 111–13.

30 Ibid., 151.

31 'A Tomb in Ghent', ibid., 45–52, 47.

32 Ibid., 49, 48.

33 Ibid.: 'A Lost Chord', 159: 'Hush!', 131–2: 'Unexpressed', 137–8.

34 'Words', ibid., 85–6.

35 Dora Greenwell, *Essays*, London and New York, 1866, 1–68.

36 See Part II, chapter 7, note 8.

37 See *Victorian Scrutinies: Reviews of Poetry 1830–70*, Isobel Armstrong, ed., London, 1972, 93.

38 *The British and Foreign Review*, XIII (1842), 1–49. Mill's *Monthly Repository* article is quoted on p. 15.

39 Ibid., 22.

40 *Keble's Lectures on Poetry, 1832–1841*, Edward Kershaw Francis, ed., 2 vols, Oxford, 1912, 1, 20.

41 Julia Kristeva, *Revolution in Poetic Language*, trans. Margaret Waller, London, 1984. See in particular chapter 2.

42 Dora Greenwell, *Essays*, London and New York, 1866, 3–4.

43 Ibid., 4.

44 Ibid., 19.

45 Ibid., 45.

46 Ibid., 27.

47 Ibid., 8.

48 Ibid., 43 ('aggressive action'), 33.

49 Ibid., 59.

50 Ibid., 58.

51 *The Complete Poems of Christina Rossetti*, R. W. Crump, ed., 3 vols, Baton Rouge, 1979–90, II (1986), 198–90.

52 Ibid., II, 86.
53 Ibid., III (1990), 332 (pseudonymous publication).
54 Arthur Symons, 'Christina G. Rossetti 1830–94', *Poets and Poetry of the Nineteenth Century*, A. H. Miles, ed., 11 vols, London, 1905–7, IX, 1–16: 5.
55 *Goblin Market and Other Poems* (1862), Crump, *Poems of Christina Rossetti*, I, 1–25.
56 *Goblin Market*, 134–6.
57 Ibid., 428–36.
58 Ibid., 293–8.
59 Ibid., 173–4, 289, 291–2.
60 *Maude*, William Michael Rossetti, ed., London, 1897, 17.
61 Dora Greenwell, *Poems*, London, 1867, 139–40.
62 Crump, *Poems of Christina Rossetti*, I, 58.
63 Greenwell, *Poems*, 175–6.
64 Ibid., 168 ('Amid Change'), 170–1 ('One Flower'), 171.
65 Ibid., 179–80, 180.
66 Ibid., 195.
67 Ibid., 172–3, 173.
68 'On the education of the Imbecile', reprinted from the *North British Review* (1868), edited for the Royal Albert Idiot Asylum, Lancaster, 1867.
69 Ibid., 8: for the vocabulary of blockage see 11, 37.
70 Jean Ingelow, *Poems*, London, 1863, 'The High Tide', 146–52: 150.
71 'The Star's Monument', 76–104.
72 'Requiescat in Pace', 41–8: 43.
73 Elizabeth Barrett Browning, *'Sonnets from the Portuguese': A Variorum Edition*, Miroslava Wein Dow, ed., New York, 1980, 23, 6–7.
74 Crump, *Poems of Christina Rossetti*, I, 47.
75 Ibid., 30–1.
76 Ibid., 66–7.
77 Ibid., 44.
78 Ibid., 55–6.
79 Ibid., 48.
80 Christina Rossetti, *Seek and Find: A Double Series of Short Studies of the Benedicite*, London and New York, 1879, 108–9.
81 *Aurora Leigh*, I, 525.
82 George Eliot, *The Spanish Gypsy*, London, 1868, 48, 39.
83 Ibid., 57.
84 Ludwig Feuerbach, *The Essence of Christianity* (1841), trans. George Eliot (1854), Karl Barth, ed., New York, 1957, 121, 72.
85 Augusta Webster, *A Housewife's Opinions*, London, 1879, 151. These essays were contributions to *The Examiner*. The volume includes a vigorous suffrage essay, 'Parliamentary franchise for women ratepayers', 275–9.
86 *A Housewife's Opinions*, 153.
87 Ibid., 154.
88 Ibid., 155.
89 Augusta Webster, *Portraits*, London, 1870, 23–34, 24, 29, 28.
90 Ibid., 31.
91 'A Castaway', *Portraits*, 35–62.
92 Amy Levy, 'Magdalen', *A Minor Poet, and Other Verses*, London, 1884, 65–8.
93 Augusta Webster, 'Medea, in Athens', *Portraits*, 1–13; Amy Levy, 'Medea', *A Minor Poet*, 35ff.
94 Amy Levy, 'Xantippe', *Xantippe and Other Verse*, Cambridge, 1881, 1–13.

95 'On a Torso of Cupid', *The Poetical Works of Mathilde Blind*, Arthur Symons, ed., London, 1900, 365–6.
96 *The Heather on Fire*, ibid., 129, 130–1 (the grandmother's death).
97 Ibid., 124.
98 'Motherhood', *Poetical Works*, 201.

PART III ANOTHER CULTURE? ANOTHER POETICS?

Introduction: The 1860s and after – aesthetics, language, power and high finance

1 Walter Pater, *The Renaissance: Studies in Art and Poetry* (1873), Kenneth Clark, ed., Harmondsworth, 1961, 'Winckelmann', 206–7. This edition makes available the text of the revised second edition of 1877 and the 'Conclusion' of the first edition omitted in 1877.
2 Walter Pater, *Appreciations: with an Essay on Style* (1889), 3rd edn, London, 1895, 13.
3 Ibid., 27–8.
4 Arthur Symons, *The Symbolist Movement in Literature* (1899), 2nd edn, London, 1908, 8–9.
5 T. S. Eliot, 'Swinburne as critic', *The Sacred Wood: Essays on Poetry and Criticism*, London, 1920, 15–22. Swinburne is unable to understand 'Sensuous thought' (20).
6 Pater is far less certain of the borders of selfhood than Hallam: the force that decays the eye rusts iron (*Renaissance*, 220): the self is a tissue or network of permeable material relations. Marshall McLuhan's influential essay on Hallam's affinity with fin-de-siècle writing requires some modification. See 'Tennyson's picturesque poetry', *Critical Essays on the Poetry of Tennyson*, John Killham, ed., London, 1960, 67–85.
7 Pater quotes Hegel in the Winckelmann essay (*Renaissance*, 209) and uses his aesthetic categories. In *Appreciations* the Kantian H. L. Mansel is his model: see 18.
8 *Appreciations*, 35: 'the absolute correspondence of the term to its import'.
9 H. M. Hyndman, *Commercial Crises of the Nineteenth Century*, London, 1892, 'The crisis of 1866', 89–98.
10 Robert Buchanan, 'The Fleshly School of poetry', *Contemporary Review*, 1871, in *The Victorian Poet: Poetics and Persona*, Joseph Bristow, ed., London, 1987, 142. The occasion was a review of D. G. Rossetti's poems, which Buchanan associated with the radical 'Grotesque' (143).
11 Ibid., 144.
12 D. G. Rossetti: ibid., 149. Rossetti replied to Buchanan in the *Athenaeum*, 1871.
13 Swinburne: Bristow, *The Victorian Poet*, 157. Swinburne defended his work in *Notes on Poems and Reviews*, London, 1866.
14 Walter Bagehot's essay appeared in the *National Review*, III (October 1858), 342–79. It was collected in *Literary Studies*, 2 vols, London, 1879. It has also been re-edited in *The Collected Works of Walter Bagehot*, Norman St John Stevas, ed., 8 vols, London, 1965–74, I, 433–76. Matthew Arnold's essay on Shelley was published in *The Nineteenth Century*, January 1888, and incorporated into *Essays in Criticism, Second Series*, London, 1895, 204–52.
15 *Edward Fitzgerald: Selected Works*, Joanna Richardson, ed., London, 1962, 225–73.
16 See above, Part II, p. 341.
17 Pater, *Renaissance*, 'Preface', 31. *Appreciations*, 14.

18 Pater, *Renaissance*, 129.

19 Ibid., 108, 109, 123, 122.

20 Ibid., 224.

21 Ibid., 222.

22 H. L. Mansel, *Metaphysics or the Philosophy of Consciousness Phenomenal and Real*, Edinburgh, 1860, 53.

23 Ibid., 58, 45.

24 Ibid., 87, 175.

25 Ibid., 34.

26 Ibid., 187–8.

27 *The Annotated Alice: Alice's Adventures in Wonderland and Through the Looking-Glass* (1865, 1871), Martin Gardner, ed., rev. edn, Harmondsworth, 1970, 98–9.

28 Ibid., 270.

29 Ibid., 269.

30 Mansel, *Metaphysics*, 189–90.

31 Hyndman, *Commercial Crises*, 93–4.

32 *Essays and Reviews*, Benjamin Jowett, ed., London, 1860. See 'On the interpretation of Scripture', 390–8. Rowland Williams used the geological analogy in his essay on Bunsen; as in geological process, the idea that 'causes still in operation' (50) determined experience had widened the idea of Revelation (51).

33 Charles Darwin, *The Origin of Species by means of Natural Selection* (1859), J. W. Burrow, ed., Harmondsworth, 1968. Darwin's chapter on 'Natural selection' (130–72) best illustrates the way in which his thought destabilised the accepted terminology of family, society and polity.

34 Max Müller, *Lectures on the Science of Language*, 2nd rev. edn, London, 1862, 70. Language is a system which cannot be altered by decree or action. It is in this sense 'independent of history' and laws can be formulated about it, abstract and permanent.

35 Ibid., 37, 73: language is outside the 'caprice' of man.

36 Ibid., 48.

37 Ibid., 385.

38 Ibid., 52.

39 Ibid., 66.

40 Darwin, *Origin of Species*, 415.

41 Müller, *Lectures*, 213.

42 Ibid., 72.

43 Ibid., 284.

44 Ibid., 65.

45 *The Journals and Papers of Gerard Manley Hopkins*, Humphrey House and Graham Story, eds, London and New York, 1959, 11. As an example, Hopkins' commentary of 1863 distinguishes a root 'Fli' and related forms, meaning 'to touch or strike lightly'.

46 Herbert Spencer's *Principles of Sociology* (1876–96) and *The Study of Sociology* (1876) emphasise the division of labour and the complexity of function in social organisation on analogy with organisms, rather than the element of struggle.

47 J. S. Mill, *Considerations on Representative Government* (1861), *John Stuart Mill: Three Essays*, Richard Wolheim, ed., London, 1975, 248. In the same year Matthew Arnold's discussion of democracy formed the Introduction to *Popular Education in France*. See *The Complete Works of Matthew Arnold*, R. H. Super, ed., 11 vols, Ann Arbor, 1960–73, II, 3–32.

48 Edward Eyre was governor of Jamaica from 1864 to 1866 and suppressed a Black revolt so ferociously that over 400 were executed. Torture and beatings

were common reprisals. He was indicted for murder in 1868 after a parliamentary campaign by Mill and, among others, T. H. Huxley and Herbert Spencer.
49 Friedrich Engels published *The Origin of the Family, Private Property and the State* in German in 1884.
50 'I ought to have begun by an exposition of the Phenomenology'. *The George Eliot Letters*, Gordon S. Haight, ed., 9 vols, London and New Haven, 1954–78, IX, 11. Letter of 6 February 1871 to Charles Edward Appleton.
51 George Eliot, *Middlemarch* (1872), W. J. Harvey, ed., Harmondsworth, 1965, chapter 11. George Eliot here grasps that Hegel's dialectic depends on the struggle for recognition.
52 Quoted by Martha Vicinus, *The Industrial Muse: A Study of Nineteenth-Century British Working-Class Literature*, London, 1974, 267.
53 Ibid., 272–3.
54 Ibid., 265, 317–18.
55 Ibid., 277.
56 J. B. Leno, *Female Labour: Tracts for Rich and Poor*, 1, London, 1863, 3. Throughout Leno argues that women workers depress wages, and gives as one of his examples Emily Faithful's introduction of women into the printing industry (6).
57 Joseph Skipsey, *Selected Poems*, Basil Bunting, ed., Sunderland, 1976, 22.
58 Ibid., 31 (stanza 19).

13 Swinburne: agonistic republican – the poetry of sensation as democratic critique

1 Quoted by Philip Henderson, *Swinburne, The Portrait of a Poet*, London, 1974, 148.
2 *The Swinburne Letters*, Cecil Y. Lang, ed., 6 vols, New Haven, 1960, III, 232. Letter of 12 December 1876 to Theodore Watts. Swinburne describes the despatches from Jamaica as like extracts 'from the very worst chapters of *Justine*' (231).
3 Quotations from Hopkins' poetry are from *The Poems of Gerard Manley Hopkins*, W. H. Gardner and N. H. Mackenzie, eds, 4th rev. edn, London, 1967. Hopkins, *The Wreck of the Deutschland*, stanza 8: 'My name is a consuming', Althaea says. She means the name of mother, which forces her into contradictory ties of loyalty. Algernon Charles Swinburne, *Atalanta in Calydon: A Tragedy* (1865), new edn, London, 1894, 81.
4 Algernon Charles Swinburne, 'Dolores', *Poems and Ballads* (1860), new edn, London, 1893, 190; *Atalanta*, 47.
5 Roland Barthes, *Sade Fourier Loyola* (1971), trans. Richard Miller, London, 1977.
6 Harold Bloom, 'Freud's concepts of defence and the poetic will', *The Literary Freud: Mechanisms of Defense and the Poetic Will*, Joseph H. Smith, ed., New Haven, 1980, 1–28.
7 Swinburne, *Poems and Ballads*, 'Dolores', 183; 'Laus Veneris', 20.
8 'The Poems of Dantë Gabriel Rossetti', *Essays and Studies* (1866), *The Complete Works of Algernon Charles Swinburne*, Edmund Gosse and T. J. Wise, eds, 20 vols, London 1925–7, XV (*Prose Works*, V), 15, 13. *Les Fleurs du Mal* (1862), Edmund Gosse, ed., London, 1913, 14.
9 *Les Fleurs du Mal*, 12, 13.
10 Ibid., 4.
11 Jacques Derrida, 'From a restricted to a general economy', *Writing and Difference*, trans. Alan Bass, London, 1978, 251–77.
12 Lang, *The Swinburne Letters*, I, 125.

NOTES

13 *Atalanta, Poems and Ballads*, 47.

14 Simone de Beauvoir, 'Must we burn Sade?', Introduction, *The Marquis de Sade: The 120 Days of Sodom and Other Writings*, Austryn Wainhouse and Richard Seaver, ed. and trans., 2 vols, New York, 1967, I, 3–64: 45.

15 *Atalanta, Poems and Ballads*, 15, 31.

16 Ibid., 90.

17 Ibid., 77.

18 Ibid., 73.

19 Ibid., 79.

20 Ibid., 3.

21 Ibid., 4.

22 Ibid., 72.

23 Ibid., 80, 81.

24 Ibid., 43, 49.

25 Ibid., 14.

26 *Les Fleurs du Mal*, 12, 5, 6.

27 *Victorian Prose and Poetry*, Harold Bloom and Lionel Trilling, eds, Oxford, 1973, 710–15: 711 (144–9). See also *Decadence and the 1890s*, Stratford-upon-Avon Studies, 17, Ian Fletcher, ed., Stratford-upon-Avon, 1979.

28 Bloom and Trilling, *Victorian Prose and Poetry*, 717–18.

29 Ibid., 720–71: 721 (49–52).

30 'Laus Veneris', *Poems and Ballads*, 26, 22.

31 'Hermaphroditus', *Poems and Ballads*, 90.

14 Hopkins: agonistic reactionary – the Grotesque as conservative form

1 *The Journals and Papers of Gerard Manley Hopkins*, Humphrey House and Graham Story, eds, London and New York, 1959, 127.

2 For a discussion of Pater and Hopkins see John Robinson, *In Extremity: A Study of Gerard Manley Hopkins*, London, 1978, 24–33. For a discussion of Green, see W. David Shaw, *The Lucid Veil: Poetic Truth in the Victorian Age*, London, 1987, 101–4.

3 *Journals and Papers*, 120.

4 Ibid., 122.

5 *The Letters of Gerard Manley Hopkins to Robert Bridges*, Claude Colleer Abbott, ed., London and New York, 1935, 79 (letter of 22 April 1879).

6 *Journals and Papers*, 27. Entry for 30 June 1864.

7 T. H. Green, 'Introduction to Hume's "Treatise of Human Nature" ', *Works*, R. L. Nettleship, ed., 3 vols, London, 1885, I, 200, 201.

8 Ibid., 252: 'But no combination of ideas can yield a relation which remains the same while the ideas change, and changes while they remain the same'.

9 Ibid., 264, 277.

10 Ibid., 274, 281.

11 Ibid., 151.

12 Ibid., 299.

13 Quotations from Hopkins's poetry are from *The Poems of Gerard Manley Hopkins*, W. H. Gardner and N. H. Mackenzie, eds, 4th rev. edn, London, 1967.

14 *Journals and Papers*, 122.

15 Ibid., 126.

16 Of a word-series '*Grind, gride, gird, grit, groat, grate, greet*', Hopkins writes (1863) that all derive from an original meaning 'strike': 'I believe these words to be onomatopoetic', *Journals and Papers*, 5.

17 Ibid., 125.

18 Ibid., 11.

19 Ibid., 21.

20 *Letters of Hopkins to Bridges*, 50 (13 May 1878): he emphasised that the new is 'not really odd'. Criticism of the unusual is 'barbarous' because it is unable to accommodate to innovation. He speaks of his 'distinctiveness' (66: 15 February 1879).

21 *Journals and Papers*, 125.

22 Ibid.

23 Flagellation was a part of both men's lives. Hopkins used the scourge and chains after entering the priesthood. See R. B. Martin, *Gerard Manley Hopkins: A Very Private Life*, London, 1991, 195–6. Interestingly, Hopkins took Swinburne's poetry to Mannesa where began the arduous initiation into Jesuit discipline, but was not allowed to read it. Ibid., 192.

24 I have discussed the effects of Hopkins' increasing sense of isolation in chapter 1 of my *Language as Living Form in Nineteenth Century Poetry*, Brighton, 1982.

25 *The Works of John Ruskin*, E. T. Cook and Alexander Wedderburn, eds, 39 vols, London, 1903–12, III, 11, 178, 181.

26 Paul De Man, 'The rhetoric of temporality', *Interpretation Theory and Practice*, Charles S. Singleton, ed., Baltimore, 1969, 173–209: 194–7. This important early essay posits modernity in terms of the Baudelairean fall, a literal physical fall or tripping up which brings with it an ironised world in which consciousness is aware of its estrangement from the world, and in which the unity of subject and object is mocked and deconstructed.

27 For Hopkins's response to William Barnes see James Milroy, *The Language of Gerard Manley Hopkins*, London, 1977, 76–9.

28 Heidegger's attack on technology and his understanding of the atomisation of modern physics propelled him towards an atavistic account of poetry as a consolidation of organic experience which confirmed the archaic social bonds of home and nation. The same anxieties about modernity led him to think of poetic language in terms of unique, unmediated 'thingness'. Discussions of both Heidegger and Hopkins in terms of fascist aesthetics are problematic because the work of both yields reactionary and radical interpretations, but the affinity is marked. See Martin Heidegger, *Poetry, Language, Thought* (1971), trans. Albert Hofstadter, New York, 1975, 112, 166–8.

29 *Letters of Hopkins to Bridges*, 27–8 (letter of 2 August 1871).

15 Meredith and others: Hard, gem-like dissidence

1 Jack Lindsay, *George Meredith: His Life and Work*, London, 1956, 30–1, 42.

2 *The Poems of George Meredith*, Phyllis B. Bartlett, ed., 2 vols, New Haven, 1978, I, xxx.

3 Ibid., 273.

4 See, for Hardy's assessment, Lindsay, *George Meredith*, 332. *Odes in contribution to the Song of French History*, comprising 'The Revolution', 'Napoleon' and 'Alsace-Lorraine', were published in 1898.

5 In his important essay, which is both a history of post-Romantic–pre-modern culture and a rhetorical analysis, Paul De Man writes that irony and allegory interplay with one another in a typically post-Romantic way, just as they deconstruct 'mystified forms of language (such as Symbolic or mimetic representation)'. Meredith's understanding of the linguistic construction of the world has an affinity with the 'negative' deconstructive moment De Man associates

with Baudelaire and the later nineteenth century. 'The rhetoric of temporality', *Interpretation Theory and Practice*, Charles S. Singleton, ed., Baltimore, 1969, 173–209, 207.

6 *Westminster Review*, LXVII (N.S., II) (1857), 602–20: 608.

7 'Essay on the idea of comedy and of the uses of the comic spirit' (1877), *The Works of George Meredith* (Memorial Edn), 27 vols, London, 1910, XXIII, 3–55: 32, 26, 47, 3, 48, 36.

8 'Essay on comedy', 30. 'We lose a large audience among our cultivated middle class that we should expect to support Comedy' (15). See also 41 on the 'National disposition' for morality and sentiment.

9 Ibid., 46.

10 Ibid., 47.

11 Ibid., 5.

12 Ibid., 14.

13 Ibid., 51.

14 Ibid., 17.

15 Ibid., 3.

16 Ibid., 15.

17 Ibid., 17.

18 Ibid., 35.

19 'Tendencies of religious thought in England 1688–1750', *Essays and Reviews*, Benjamin Jowett, ed., London, 1860. Mark Pattison argued that the history of the Church of England since the Restoration was 'the failure of a prudential system of ethics as a restraining force' (320).

20 'Essay on comedy', 19.

21 *Modern Love*, Bartlett, *Poems of Meredith*, 15–45. This edition can be usefully supplemented by *Modern Love*, Stephen Regan, ed., Peterborough, 1988.

22 In the comparison between French and German comedy, for instance: 'Essay on comedy', 53–4.

23 *The Angel in the House*, *The Poems of Coventry Patmore*, Frederick Page, ed., London, 1949, 61–337.

24 Patricia M. Ball, 'Odes of bereavement', *The Heart's Events: The Victorian Poetry of Relationships*, London, 1976, 58–84.

25 'Jenny', *The Poetical Works of D. G. Rossetti*, William M. Rossetti, ed., new one-vol. edn, London, 1891, 83–94.

26 Patmore's three prose works (*Principle in Art*, London, 1889, *Religio Poetae*, London, 1893, and *The Rod, the Root and the Flower*, London, 1895) develop a sacramental account of the indivisibility of the body and soul, by implication the essence of the Word and poetic language. They are analogies or forms of the divine, as 'the sheath is the likeness of the sword', a characteristically phallic metaphor (*The Rod, the Root and the Flower*, 8). Patmore transcendentalises what earlier Pre-Raphaelites sought to demystify.

27 Walter Pater, 'Dante Gabriel Rossetti' (1883), *Appreciations: with an Essay on Style* (1889), 3rd edn, London, 1895, 213–27, 220.

28 Ibid., 221.

29 Linda Dowling has made a study of the crisis in accounts of language in the late-nineteenth century, arguing that Romantic philology and linguistics fundamentally destabilised the Victorian assumption of the historical continuity of English and the dominance and cultural hegemony of the English language. See *Language and Decadence in the Victorian Fin de Siècle*, Princeton, 1986.

16 James Thomson: atheist, blasphemer and anarchist – the Grotesque sublime

1 *Shelley, a Poem*: with other Writings relating to Shelley, by the late James Thomson ('B.V.'): to which is added an Essay on the Poems of William Blake, Chiswick, 1884, 1–13. Thomson used the initials 'B.V.' (Bysshe, Vanolis), to denote his admiration for Shelley and 'Novalis', the German poet, Hardenberg.
2 'Shelley's Religious Opinions' (1860), *Shelley*, 30.
3 Ibid., 29.
4 Charles Bradlaugh, *A Plea for Atheism*, London, 1877, 13.
5 *Shelley*, 10.
6 Alfred Austen, *Lyrical Poems*, London and New York, 1891, 43–5, 44.
7 Charles Bradlaugh, *The Land, the People, and the Coming Struggle* (1872), 3rd edn, London, 1877, 4–8. Like *A Plea for Atheism*, Bradlaugh published this essay as a pamphlet through the Freethought Publishing Company.
8 Arthur O'Shaughnessy, 'A Discord', *An Epic of Women and Other Poems*, London, 1870, 174.
9 W. E. Henley, 'Suicide', 'In Hospital', 24, *A Book of Verses*, London, 1888. John Davidson, 'Thirty Bob a Week', *Victorian Prose and Poetry*, Lionel Trilling and Harold Bloom, eds, Oxford, 1973, 715–17.
10 O'Shaughnessy, 'Ode', *Music and Moonlight*, London, 1874, 1–5.
11 James Thomson, *The City of Dreadful Night and Other Poems*, London, 1880, I. 6.
12 'A Lady of Sorrow' (1862), *Essays and Phantasies*, London, 1881, 1–50: 3.
13 *The City of Dreadful Night*, I. 3–4.
14 Bradlaugh, *A Plea for Atheism*, 6.
15 'A Lady of Sorrow', 5.
16 Annie Besant, *The Law of Population: Its Consequences and Its Bearing upon Human Conduct and Morals*, London, 1877, 20.
17 Bradlaugh, *A Plea for Atheism*, 20.
18 Bradlaugh, *A Plea for Atheism*, 5. Because there is nothing outside the material universe, substance may decay and change, but not disappear, i.e. the world never was created out of nothing.
19 Bradlaugh, *A Plea for Atheism*, 11.
20 Ibid.
21 *The City of Dreadful Night*, XVI. 42.
22 'A Lady of Sorrow', 26.
23 Bradlaugh, *A Plea for Atheism*, 13.
24 Ibid., 8.
25 Ibid., 16.
26 'A Lady of Sorrow', 16–17.
27 Bartram Dobell, *The Laureate of Pessimism*, A Sketch of the Life and Character of James Thomson ('B.V.'), London, 1910.
28 Ibid., 19–20, 22: George Eliot asked Thomson to celebrate 'the sublimity of the social order, and the courage of resistance to all that would dissolve it.'
29 James Thomson, *Satires and Profanities*, G. W. Foote, ed., London, 1884, viii.
30 'A Commission of Enquiry on Royalty', *Satires*, 172.
31 'The Swinburne Controversy', ibid., 99.
32 'The Devil in the Church of England', ibid., 16.
33 'Christmas Eve in the Upper Circles', ibid., 54, 55.
34 'A Word on Blasphemy', ibid., 69.
35 'Vane's Story', *Vane's Story, Weddah and Om-El-Bonain, and Other Poems*, London, 1881, 3. *Weddah* appeared first in 1871.

36 'Vane's Story', 17.
37 Ibid., 41.
38 James Thomson, *A Voice from the Nile and Other Poems*, Bartram Dobell, ed., London, 1884, 2, 5.
39 'A Voice from the Nile', 2.

POSTSCRIPT

1 'Clive' (9), in *Robert Browning: The Poems*, John Pettigrew and Thomas J. Collins, eds, 2 vols, Harmondsworth, 1981, II, 618–27. For *The Ring and the Book* see Isobel Armstrong, 'The problem of representation in *The Ring and the Book*: politics, aesthetics, language', *Browning e Venezia*, Sergio Perosa, ed., Florence, 1991, 205–32.

2 W. B. Yeats, 'The Irish National Literary Society', *Selected Criticism*, A. Norman Jeffares, ed., London, 1964, 17–21: 18.

3 W. B. Yeats, *The Poems*, Daniel Albright, ed., London, 1990, 60.

4 I use 'aura' in Walter Benjamin's sense as the uniqueness of high art prior to the age of technology and mass reproduction: 'The work of art in an age of mechanical reproduction', *Illuminations*, Hannah Arendt, ed., New York, 1968, 217–51.

5 Rudyard Kipling, *Barrack-Room Ballads and Other Verses*, London, 1892, 66–9: 68.

6 *The Poems of Alice Meynell* (complete edn), London, 1923, 3–4.

7 See M. van. Wyk Smith, *Drummer Hodge. The Poetry of the Anglo-Boer War (1899–1902)*, Oxford, 1978, 137. Edward Carpenter, *Towards Democracy*, London and Manchester, 1883. A. H. Miles edited *The Poets and the People*, in 1905, an anthology which indicates the fate of radical writing. It includes work by Chartist poets, Hood, Elizabeth and Robert Browning: the latter part of the century, however, is represented by lampoons – that is to say, polemical poetry tending to agitprop rather than meditative or analytical writing. Carpenter's Whitmanesque poem is an exception in the later period. Robert Brough's 'My Lord Tomnoddy' (25–6) and H. S. Salt (biographer of Thomson), who contributed 'A Song of the Respectables' (26–7) – 'We realise the need/Of more and more coercion for the masses' (26) – are typical late-century pieces.

8 Thomas Hardy, *The Dynasts: An Epic-Drama*, *The Poetical Works of Thomas Hardy*, 2 vols, vol. II, London, 1923, Part III, I. iv. 342.

9 Ibid., Part II, III. i. 206–10; Part III, I. ix. 354.

10 Ibid., Part III, I. i. 329: Napoleon has India as an ultimate goal for which the European war is a mere instrument.

11 Ibid., Part III, VII. vii. 505.

12 Ibid., Part III, After Scene, 524: 'Who knows if all the Spectacle be true/Or an illusion of the gods the Will,/To wit, some hocus-pocus to fulfil?'

13 Ibid., Part III, VII. iv. 496.

14 *Monthly Repository*, N.S., VIII (1834), 131.

15 Ibid., 137–8.

INDEX